A Bibliography of American Naval History

WITHDRAWN

A BIBLIOGRAPHY OF
AMERICAN NAVAL HISTORY

COMPILED BY PAOLO E. COLETTA

NAVAL INSTITUTE PRESS
Annapolis, Maryland

Library of Congress Cataloging in Publication Data

Coletta, Paolo Enrico, 1916-
  A bibliography of American naval history.
  Includes indexes.
  1. United States--History, Naval--Bibliography.
2. United States. Navy--Bibliography. I. Title.
Z1249.N3C64   [E182]   016.973   ˙ 80-24864
ISBN 0-87021-105-6

Printed in the United States of America

CONTENTS

EXPLANATORY NOTES

An interesting and important subject, American naval history should not be studied or portrayed in a vacuum. Hence, in addition to strictly naval matters, attention is given herein, where necessary and appropriate, to diplomatic, maritime, Marine Corps, military, aviation, geographical, political, economic, social, intellectual, scientific, technological, organizational, administrative, and personal history, and to the U.S. Coast Guard when it operated as part of the U.S. Navy.

This working bibliography encompasses the published writings that teaching experience shows are relevant and should be among the holdings of the average university library. Titles included are those published as of 31 December 1979.

By chapter, titles are listed in the following order: books, documents, dissertations and theses, articles in periodicals or essays in books, transcripts of oral interviews, and fiction. Items not identified as theses are dissertations. All works are in English. In the interest of brevity the names of translators, professional titles, and military grades have been omitted and the names of many publishing houses have been shortened.

Arabic numerals in the author and subject indices are the consecutive numbers that precede the titles in the text, and those that are shown at the top of each page indicate the titles shown on that page.

Library of Congress call numbers for books have been provided wherever possible. In cases where no such number is available, every effort has been made to provide the name of a repository that holds the material.

Asterisks denote works on the U.S. Marine Corps.

vii

ACKNOWLEDGMENTS

I am indebted to a number of persons for their valuable aid. John W. Reynolds, Senior Cataloger, Nimitz Library, U.S. Naval Academy, made available the National Union Catalog. Henry C. Long, Government Documents and Reference Librarian in the same library, looked up call numbers and annotated documents. Mrs. Patty M. Maddocks, Director, Library and Photographic Services, U.S. Naval Institute, put her library at my disposal. The following provided judicious comments on chapters as indicated: 1) Mary Veronica Amoss, Senior Manuscript Editor, U.S. Naval Institute; 2) A.J.R. Russell-Wood, History Department, Johns Hopkins University; 3) and 4) Craig L. Symonds, History Department, U.S. Naval Academy; 5) K. Jack Bauer, History Department, Rensselaer Polytechnic Institute; 6) Neville Kirk, Professor Emeritus, History Department, U.S. Naval Academy; 8) and 9), Ronald Spector, Office of Chief of Military History; 10) Hanson W. Baldwin, military historian; 11) David F. Trask, Historian, State Department; 12) Gerald E. Wheeler, Dean, School of Social Sciences, San Jose State University; 13), 14), and 15), Robert W. Love, History Department, U.S. Naval Academy; 16), 17), and 18), Philip A. Crowl, Strategy Department, U.S. Naval War College; 19) and 20), Norman A. Graebner, History Department, University of Virginia; 21) Rear Admiral John R. Wadleigh, USN (Ret.); 22) Rear Admiral Ernest M. Eller, USN (Ret.). Aid throughout the project on form and content was provided by Frank Uhlig, Senior Editor, U.S. Naval Institute; help with oral history programs was furnished by John T. Mason, Jr., Director, Oral History Programs, U.S. Naval Institute; and Wilson L. Helfin, Department of English, U.S. Naval Academy, steered me through American naval historical fiction.

PERTINENT PERIODICALS

The best current American periodicals that deal with naval matters are *All Hands*, *American Neptune*, *Armed Forces Journal*, *American Society of Naval Engineers Journal*, *Deep-Sea Research*, *Direction*, *Naval Aviation News*, *Naval War College Review*, *Sea Power* (the outlet of the Navy League known from 1958 to 1971 as *Navy*, and from 1949-1958 as *Now Hear This*); *Navy Times*, *Shipmate* (organ of the U.S. Naval Academy Alumni Association), and U.S. Naval Institute *Proceedings*. Items devoted to naval subjects have appeared in *American Heritage*, *American Historical Review*, *American History Illustrated*, *American Review of Reviews* (1890-1937), *Atlantic Civil War History*, *Civil War History Illustrated*, *Diplomatic History*, *Civil War Times Illustrated Forum* (to 1940), *Galaxy* (1860-1877), *Harper's*, *Hispanic-American Historical Review*, *Iron Age*, *Journal of American History* (follow-on to the *Mississippi Valley Historical Review*), *Journal of American Studies* (British), *Journal of Modern History*, *Journal of Southern History*, *Life*, *Literary Digest* (to the mid-1930s), *Newsweek*, *Niles Weekly Register* (1811-1849), *Pacific Affairs*, *Popular Science*, *Prologue*, *Ramparts*, *South Atlantic Quarterly*, *Scientific American*, *Strategic Review*, *United States Air Service* (1915-1956), *William and Mary Quarterly*, and *Yale Review*.

Data relevant particularly to organizational changes in the defense establishment may be found in *Air University Review* (follow-on to the *Air University Quarterly Review*), *American Political Science Review*, *Armed Forces Management*, *Congressional Digest*, *Current History*, *Political Administration Review*, *Political Science Quarterly*, and *Review of Politics*.

Air Force matters are discussed primarily in *Air Force Magazine*, *Aviation Weekly and Space Technology*, and *Air University Review*. British opinion is available in *British History Illustrated*, *Contemporary Review* (which has incorporated *Fortnightly Review*), *English Historical Review*, *Historian*, *Historical Journal*, *History Today*, *Journal of British Studies*, *Journal of Naval Science*, *Mariner's Mirror*, *Nautical Magazine*, *Political Quarterly*, *Royal Air Force Quarterly*, *Royal United Service Institution Journal*, and *United Service Magazine* (1829-1920); European opinion in

East Europe, Encounter, and *European Studies Review;* Soviet opinion in *Russian Review, Soviet Military Review,* and *Soviet Naval Digest.* For diplomatic matters, *see* especially *Department of State Bulletin, Department of State Newsletter, Diplomatic History, Foreign Affairs,* and *Foreign Service Journal.* Material of broad international scope is to be found in *American Journal of International Law, Conflict Studies, Current, Current History, Daedalus, Defense and Foreign Affairs Digest, Defense Management Journal, International Conciliation, International Defense Review, International Journal, International Organization, International Security, International Security Review, International Studies, Journal of African History, Journal of Conflict Resolution, Journal of Contemporary History, Journal of Intra-American Studies and World Affairs, Journal of Politics, Middle East Journal, NATO's Fifteen Nations, NATO Review, Ocean Development and International Law, Survey of International Affairs* (annual), *Survival, United Nations Monthly Chronicle, World Affairs,* and *World Politics.*

Three publications are devoted to Marine Corps matters: the popularly-written *Leatherneck,* the more scholarly *Marine Corps Gazette,* and the newsletter of the Marine Corps History and Museums Division, *Fortitudine. Perspectives in Defense Management,* issued by the Industrial College of the Armed Forces (now merged into the National Defense University), has appeared irregularly since February 1967.

Sources of information about China include *China News Analysis* (Hong Kong), *China Quarterly* (London), *China Report* (Delhi, India), and *Free China Review.* For information on Japan, there is *Contemporary Japan;* on Canada, *Crowsnest: The Royal Canadian Navy's Magazine.*

Specialized information abounds: *Electrical Engineering, Electrical World, Electronic Warfare, Electronics, Electronics and Power, Engineer, Engineering, Environmental Science and Technology, Marine Engineer, Flying, Journal of Marine Research, Journal of Physical Oceanography, Journal of Political and Military Sociology, Journal of Spacecraft and Rockets, Journal of Aero-Nautical Services, Marine Biology, Marine Ecology, Mechanical Engineering, Naval Engineers Journal, Navy Civil Engineer, Nuclear Technology, Ocean Industry, Operational Research Quarterly, Planetary and Space Science, Polar Record, Transactions of the Society of Naval Architects and Marine Engineers,* and *Surface Warfare.*

FRUITFUL BROWSING

Browsing can be made more fruitful if one pays attention to the Library of Congress classification system for naval science, which is as follows:

Naval History, *see* D-F
Naval science (General)

V	720-743	Naval life, manners, and customs
	750-995	War vessels: Construction armament, etc.
	990-995	Fleet ballistic missile systems
.VA		Navies: Organization, description, facilities, etc., including the naval situation and policy of individual countries
VB		Naval administration
VC		Naval maintenance
VD		Naval seamen
VE		Marines
VF		Naval Ordnance
VG		Minor services of navies, including communications, bands, air service, medical service, public relations, social work, recreation
VK		Navigation. Merchant marine
	588-597	Marine hydrography. Hydrographic surveying
	600-794	Tide and current tables
	798-997	Pilot guides; sailing directions
	1000-1249	Lighthouse service
	1250-1299	Shipwrecks and fires
	1300-1491	Saving of life and property
	1500-1661	Pilots and pilotage
VM		Naval architecture. Shipbuilding, Marine engineering
	975-989	Diving

ABBREVIATIONS

AAHSJ	*American Aviation Historical Society Journal*
Acad.	Academy
AEI	American Enterprise Institute
AF	*Air Force Magazine*
AFB	Air Force Base
AFJ	*Armed Forces Journal*
AFS	*Armed Forces and Society*
AH	*American Heritage*
AHI	*American History Illustrated*
AHR	*American Historical Review*
AJIL	*American Journal of International Law*
AM	*American Mercury*
Am.	American
AN	*American Neptune*
ANL	*Army & Navy Life*
Annals	*Annals of the American Society of Political & Social Science*
APSR	*American Political Science Review*
ARR	*American Review of Reviews*
ASNEJ	*American Society of Naval Engineers Journal*
AUQR	*Air University Quarterly Review*
AUR	*Air University Review*
AWST	*Aviation Week & Space Technology*
BAS	*Bulletin of the Atomic Scientists*
Bull.	Bulletin
CH	*Current History*
Chap.	Chapter
CNO	Chief of Naval Operations
Coauth.	Co-author
Comp.	Compiler
CRS	Congressional Reference Service
CWH	*Civil War History*
CWHI	*Civil War History Illustrated*
CWTI	*Civil War Times Illustrated*

Dept.	Department
DH	*Diplomatic History*
Div.	Division
DMJ	*Defense Management Journal*
DOD	Department of Defense
ed.	editor/edition
enl.	enlarged
FA	*Foreign Affairs*
FP	*Foreign Policy*
FSJ	*Foreign Service Journal*
GCNY	Garden City, N.Y.
GPO	Government Printing Office
GSA	General Services Administration
HAHR	*Hispanic American Historical Review*
Hist.	History/historical
HMSO	Her (His) Majesty's Stationery Office
HQ	Headquarters
HUP	Harvard University Press
IA	*International Affairs*
ICAF	Industrial College of the Armed Forces
IHR	*International History Review*
Inf. Jour.	*Infantry Journal*
IS	*International Security*
ISQ	*International Studies Quarterly*
ISR	*International Security Review*
ISS	Institute for Strategic Studies
IST	*International Studies*
JAH	*Journal of American History*
JAS	*Journal of American Studies*
JBS	*Journal of British Studies*
JCR	*Journal of Conflict Resolution*
JMH	*Journal of Modern History*
JNH	*Journal of Negro History*
Jour.	*Journal*
JSH	*Journal of Southern History*
LC	Library of Congress
LD	*Literary Digest*
Lib.	Library
LRS	Library Reference Service
LSUP	Louisiana State University Press
MA	*Military Affairs*
MCG	*Marine Corps Gazette*
MHM	*Maryland Historical*
MHS	Massachusetts Historical Society
MHSP	*Massachusetts Historical Society Proceedings*
MM	*Mariner's Mirror*
MR	*Military Review*
MVHR	*Mississippi Valley Historical Review*
NA	National Archives
NAN	*Naval Aviation News*

NAR	*North American Review*
NARG	National Archives Reference Group
NARS	National Archives and Reference Service
NASA	National Aviation and Space Administration
Nat. Geog.	*National Geographic Magazine*
ND	*National Defense*
NEJ	*Naval Engineers Journal*
NIP	Naval Institute Press
NSIC	National Strategy Information Center
NWCR	*Naval War College Review*
NYPL	New York Public Library
OAFH	Office of Air Force History
OCMH	Office of Chief of Military History
P.	Press
Phila.	Philadelphia
PHR	*Pacific Historical Review*
PMBH	*Pennsylvania Magazine of History and Biography*
Pop. Sci.	*Popular Science*
PSQ	*Political Science Quarterly*
pt.	part
Pub.	Publisher/Publication
PUP	Princeton University Press
Q.	Quarterly
rev.	revised
RP	*Review of Politics*
rpt.	reprint
RUSIJ	*Royal United Service Institution Journal*
S	*Survival*
SA	*Scientific American*
SAC	Strategic Air Command
SAQ	*South Atlantic Quarterly*
SEP	*Saturday Evening Post*
Soc.	Society
SR	*Strategic Review*
S&T	*Strategy & Tactics*
SUNY	State University of New York
SW	*Surface Warfare*
T&C	*Technology and Culture*
TSONAME	*Transactions of the Society of Naval Architects and Marine Engineers*
U.	University
UNCP	University of North Carolina Press
UP	University Press
USA	U.S. Army
USAF	U.S. Air Force
USMC	U.S. Marine Corps
USN	U.S. Navy
USNA	U.S. Naval Academy
USNI	U.S. Naval Institute
USNIP	U.S. Naval Institute *Proceedings*

V. or Vol.	Volume
VMHB	*Virginia Magazine of History and Biography*
WA	*World Affairs*
Wash.	Washington, D.C.
WI	*Warship International*
WP	*World Politics*
WW	*World's Work*
YUP	Yale University Press

A Bibliography of American Naval History

SELECTED BIBLIOGRAPHIC AIDS AND REFERENCE WORKS
A. General; B. Ships and Aircraft; C. Chronologies; D. Naval Terms;
E. Maps and Battle Diagrams; F. Personal Histories; G. Pictorial
Histories; H. Transcripts of Oral Interviews; I. Fiction.

A. GENERAL

BOOKS

1. TL788 .5U5

   Aeronautics and Space Report for the President: [Year] Activities. Wash.: GPO, [Year].

2. Periodical

   Air University Index to Military Periodicals. Maxwell AFB, Ala.: AU Lib., Vol. 1- , 1949- .

3. REF Z6834 H5A4

   Albion, Robert G. *Naval and Maritime History: An Annotated Bibliography,* 4th ed., rev. and expanded. Mystic, Conn.: Munson Institute of American Maritime Hist., 1972.

4.

   Allard, Dean C., Martha L. Crawley, and Mary W. Edmison, comps. and eds. *U.S. Naval History Sources in the United States.* Wash: Dept. of the Navy, Naval Hist. Div., 1979. By state, lists repositories and their manuscript, archival, and special holdings of papers of military and civilian individuals, business firms, and Congressional committee chairmen.

5. Z6835 .U5U44

   Allard, Dean C., and Betty Bern, comps. *United States Naval History: Sources in the Washington Area and Suggested Research Subjects,* 3d ed., rev. Wash.: Dept. of the Navy, Naval Hist. Div., 1970.

6. Periodical

   America: History and Life—A Guide to Periodical Literature. Santa Barbara, Calif.: ABC-Clio P., Vol. 1- , 1964- .

7. Z6834 .S9A5

   Anderson, Frank J. *Submarines, Submariners, Submarining: A Checklist of Submarine Books in the English Language, Principally of the Twentieth Century.* Hamden, Conn.: Shoe String, 1963. Cites about 650 titles.

8. Z6005   Arctic Institute of North America. *Arctic*
    .P7A7   *Bibliography*, 12 vols. Wash.: GPO, 1953-
                  1965.

9. REF   Bayliss, Gwyn M. *Bibliographical Guide to*
    Z6027   *the Two World Wars: An Annotated Survey of*
    .E8B39   *English-Language Reference Materials.*
                  N.Y.: Bowker, 1977.

10. CD3047   Beers, Henry P. *Guide to the Archives of*
    .B4   *the Government of the Confederate States*
                  of America. Wash.: GPO, 1968. For the
                  Navy Dept., *see* pp. 337-87.

11. Z6465   Bemis, Samuel F., and Grace G. Griffin,
    .U5B4   eds. *Guide to the Diplomatic History of*
                  the United States, 1775-1921. Wash: GPO,
                  1921. As yet the basic guide. An updated
                  version is expected from other hands.

12. Z1002   *The Bibliographic Index: A Cumulative Bib-*
    .B594   *liography of Bibliographies.* N.Y.: H.W.
                  Wilson, 1938- . Quarterly.

13. Z6834   *Bivins, Harold A., comp. *An Annotated Bib-*
    .A6B5   *liography of Naval Gunfire Support.* Wash.:
                  USMC, HQ, Hist. Div., 1971. Ten pages.

14. Z3319   Blanchard, Carroll H., Jr. *Korean War Bib-*
    .K6B5   *liography and Maps of Korea.* Albany, N.Y.:
                  Korean Conflict Research Foundation, 1964.

15. VG90   Blattman, Walter C., ed. *Air Operations in*
    .U62   *Naval Warfare: Reading Supplement.* Annapo-
                  lis, Md.: USNI, 1957.

16. REF   Bloomberg, Marty, and Hans H. Weber. *World*
    Z6207   *War II and Its Origins: A Select Annotated*
    .W8B58   *Bibliography of Books in English.* Little-
                  ton, Colo.: Libraries Unlimited, 1975.

17. E208   Boatner, Mark M. III. *Encyclopedia of the*
    .B68   *American Revolution.* N.Y.: McKay, 1966.

18. E468   _____. *The Civil War Dictionary.* N.Y.:
    .B7   McKay, 1959.

19. REF   Bolander, Louis, comp. *Bibliography of Na-*
    Z6834   *val Literature in the United States Naval*
    .B6U5   *Academy Library.* Annapolis, Md.: USNA,
             1929. Includes 4,200 items dealing with
             naval history and biography, but not with
             strategy, tactics, ordnance, seamanship,
             or navigation.

20. VA573   Breyer, Siegfried. *Guide to the Soviet Na-*
    .B715   *vy.* Annapolis, Md.: USNI, 1970, 1977.

21. U27   Brodie, Bernard, and Fawn Brodie. *From*
    .B76   *Crossbow to H-Bomb.* N.Y.: Dell, 1962. The
             story of research in ordnance and antisub-
             marine warfare since antiquity.

22. E182   Bryant, Samuel W. *The Sea and the States:*
    .B92   *A Maritime History of the American People.*
             N.Y.: Crowell, 1947, 1970.

23. Xerox   Bryce, Barbara A. *An Annotated Literature*
    "AD273660" *Survey of Submarines, Torpedoes, Anti-*
    in LC   *Submarine Warfare, Undersea Weapon Systems*
             and Oceanography: 1941 to January 1962.
             Los Angeles: Autonetics, 9 Mar. 1962.

24. Z3014   Bryson, Thomas A. *United States/Middle East*
    .R44B79 *Diplomatic Relations, 1784-1978: An Anno-*
             tated Bibliography. Metuchen, N.J.: Scare-
             crow, 1979.

25. Peri-   *Bulletin of Bibliography.* Boston: Boston
    odical   Book Co.; Faxon. Vol. 1- ; 1897- .

26. Z6464   Burns, Richard D. *Arms Control and Disarma-*
    .D6B87   *ment: A Bibliography.* Santa Barbara,
             Calif.: Clio, 1977.

27. Z7401   Caldwell, Lynton K., ed. *Science, Technol-*
    .I55   *ogy, and Public Policy: A Selected and*
             Annotated Bibliography, 2 vols. Blooming-
             ton: Indiana U., Dept. of Government, 1969.

28. REF   Callendar, Geoffrey A.R. *Bibliography of*
    Z6835   *Naval History.* London: Historical Assoc.,
    .G7C2   1924.

29. VA58   Clark, Joseph J., and Dwight H. Barnes.
    .C55   *Sea Power and Its Meaning,* rev. ed. N.Y.:
             Watts, 1968.

3

30. UG   Collier, Basil. *A History of Air Power.*
    630.C56   N.Y.: Macmillan, 1974.
    1974b

31. Z6201   Coulter, Edith M., and Melanie Gersten-
    .A1C8   feld. *Historical Bibliographies: A Sys-*
               tematic and Annotated Guide. Berkeley,
               Calif.: U. of Calif. P., 1935. By country.

32. Z6724   Craig, Hardin, Jr., comp. *A Bibliography*
    .D5C7   *of Encyclopedias and Dictionaries Dealing*
               with Military, Naval, and Maritime Af-
               fairs, 1557-1963, 4th ed. Houston:
               Fondren Lib., Rice U., 1970.

33. REF   Crandall, Marjorie L. *Confederate Imprints:*
    A1242   *A Check List....* Boston: Boston Antheneum,
    .5.C7   1955.

34. Z6725   Cresswell, Mary, and Carl Berger, comps.
    .U5C73   *United States Air Force History.* Wash.:
               OAFH, 1971.

35. REF   _____. and Samuel D. Miller, comps.
    A6725   *An Aerospace Bibliography.* Wash.: OAFH,
    .U5M54   1978.

36. Z1245   Cronon, E. David, and Theodore D. Rosenof.
    .C70   *The Second World War and the Atomic Age,*
               1970-1973. Northbrook, Ill.: AHM, 1975.
               A Goldentree bibliography.

37. VB230   Deacon, Richard. *The Silent War: A History*
    .D4   *of Western Naval Intelligence.* N.Y.: Hippo-
               crene, 1978.

38. REF   Dexter, Byron, ed. *The Foreign Affairs 50-*
    Z6461   *Year Bibliography...1920-1970.* N.Y.:
    .F62   Bowker, 1972.

39. Z5064   Dickson, Katherine M., comp. *History of*
    .A8D5   *Aeronautics and Astronautics: A Prelimi-*
               nary Bibliography. Wash.: NASA, Hist. Div.,
               1968.

40. REF   *Dictionary of American Naval Fighting*
    VA61   *Ships*, 6 vols. - . Wash.: Dept. of the Na-
    .A53   vy. Naval Hist. Div., 1959- . Contains
               much more than ship biographies.

4

41. Micro Peri-odicals — *Dissertation Abstracts International.* Ann Arbor, Mich.: U. Microfilms, 1969- . v.1 -, 1938.

42. REF 6725 .U5D6 — *Dollen, Charles. *Bibliography of the United States Marine Corps.* N.Y.: Scarecrow, 1963.

43. REF UA23 .U55 — Dornan, James E., Jr. *The U.S. War Machine: An Encyclopedia of American Military Equipment and Strategy.* N.Y.: Crown, 1978.

44. UG497 .U6D8 — Duncan, Robert C. *America's Use of Sea Mines.* White Oak, Md.: U.S. Naval Ordnance Laboratory, 1962. From 1780.

45. D25 .A2D8 — Dupuy, R. Ernest, and N. Trevor Dupuy. *The Encyclopedia of Military History from 3,500 B.C. to the Present.* N.Y.: Harper & Row, 1970.

46. D25 .E35 — Eggenberger, David. *A Dictionary of Battles.* N.Y.: Crowell, 1967.

47. Z6835 .U5E4 — Ellinger, Werner B., and Herbert Rosinski, comps. *Sea Power in the Pacific, 1936-1941; Selected Bibliography of Books, Periodical Articles, and Maps from the End of the London Naval Conference to the Beginning of the War in the Pacific.* Princeton: PUP, 1942. 80 pp.

48. Z6834 .S9J35 — Ellis, William A., comp. *"Torpedoes: A List of References to Material in the New York Public Library"* in NYPL, Bull. of the NYPL 21 (1917): 657-726. Useful for World War I.

49. E182 .E54 — Emmons, George F. *The Navy of the United States, from the Commencement, 1775 to 1853, with a Brief History of Each Vessel's Service....* Wash.: Gideon, 1853.

50. AE5 E333 1975 — *Encyclopedia Americana,* 30 vols. N.Y.: Americana Corp., 1975.

51. AE5 .E363 — *Encyclopedia Britannica.* Various publishers and dates. At this writing, the 30-volume set issued in 1974 is the latest.

52. Peri-
    odical
    Engineering Index. Chicago: Assoc. of En-
gineering Societies; Engineering Index,
Inc., Vol. 1- ; 1884- .

53. REF
    Z6208
    .W8E57
    Enser, A.G.S. *A Subject Bibliography of
the Second World War: Books in English,
1937-1974.* Boulder, Colo.: Westview, 1977.

54. Z5064
    .P64E8
    Estep, Raymond. *An Aerospace Bibliography.*
Maxwell AFB, Ala.: Air U., 1962. Covers
years 1957-1961.

55. D410
    .N44
    Facts on File. News Dictionary. N.Y.:
Facts on File, 1941- . Digest of international affairs.

56. Z6207
    .E8F2
    Falls, Cyril. *War Books: A Critical Guide.*
London: Peter Davies, 1930. World War I.

57. REF
    Z1236
    .F77
    Freidel, Frank, and others. *Harvard Guide
to American History,* rev. ed., 2 vols.
Cambridge: HUP, 1974.

58. REF
    V27
    .F73
    Frere-Cook, Gervis, and Kenneth Mackesy.
The Guiness History of Sea Warfare. En-
field, Middlesex: Guiness Superlatives,
1975. Short, concise articles on topics
ranging from oars and spears to nuclear
power.

59. REF
    Z7207
    .W85C394
    Funk, Arthur L., comp. *The Second World
War: A Bibliography.* Gainesville, Fla.:
American Committee on the History of the
Second World War, 1975.

60. Z5063
    .N56
    1971
    Gamble, William B., comp. *History of Aero-
nautics: A Selected List of References to
Materials in the New York Public Library.*
N.Y.: NYPL, 1971.

61. D619
    .G49
    Genthe, Charles V. *American War Narratives
1917-1918: A Study and Bibliography.* N.Y.:
D. Lewis, 1969.

62. DA500
    .G5
    Gipson, Lawrence H. *A Bibliographical Guide
to the History of the British Empire, 1748-
1776.* Vol. 14 of *The British Empire Before
the American Revolution.* N.Y.: Knopf, 1958.

63. Z1361   Greenwood, John. *American Defense Policy*
    .D4G73   *Since 1945: A Preliminary Bibliography.*
                 Lawrence: UP of Kansas, 1973.

64. REF   Gregory, Nathaniel. *Department of Defense*
    A1249   *Organization: Selected References, 1944-*
    .E9G74   *1974.* Wash.: LC, CRS, 1974.

65. LC   Griffin, Appleton P.C., comp. *List of*
                 Works Relating to the French Alliance in
                 the American Revolution. Wash.: GPO, 1907.

66. Z1241   Haferkorn, Henry E. *The War with Mexico,*
    .H21   *1846-1848: A Selected Bibliography....*
                 Wash.: Washington Barracks, 1914; rpt.,
                 Documentary Publications, 1970.

67. REF   Hanniball, August. *Aircraft, Engines, and*
    Z5063   *Airmen: A Selective Review of the Periodi-*
    .A2H34   *cal Literature, 1930-1969.* Metuchen, N.J.:
                 Scarecrow, 1972.

68. REF   Harbeck, Charles T. *A Contribution to the*
    Z6835   *Bibliography of the History of the United*
    .U5H2   *States Navy.* Cambridge, Mass.: Riverside
                 P., 1906, 1970.

69. D25   Harbottle, Thomas B. *Dictionary of Battles,*
    .A2H2   rev. and updated by George Bruce. N.Y.:
                 Stein & Day, 1971.

70. A1242.5   Harwell, Richard B. *The Confederate Hun-*
    .H314   *dred: A Bibliophilic Selection of Confed-*
                 erate Books. Urbana, Ill.: Beta Phi Mu,
                 1964.

71. REF   _____. *More Confederate Imprints.* Rich-
    A1242   mond: Virginia State Lib., 1957. *See*
    .5.H33   Crandall, Marjorie L.

72. JF1525   Haswell, Chetwynd J.D. *Spies & Spymasters:*
    .I6H37   *A Concise History of Intelligence.* London:
                 Thames & Hudson, 1977.

73. UG630   Heflin, Woodford A., ed. *The United States*
    .U637   *Air Force Dictionary.* Maxwell, Ala.: Air
                 UP, 1956.

74. U19   Heinl, Robert D. *Dictionary of Military and*
    .H4   *Naval Quotations.* Annapolis, Md.: USNI,
                 1966.

75. REF   Higham, Robin D., ed. *A Guide to the*
     Z1249   *Sources of United States Military History.*
     .M5G83   Hamden, Conn.: Archon Books, 1975.

76. REF   _____. ed. *Official Histories: Essays*
     Z6724   *and Bibliographies from Around the World.*
     .H6H5   Manhattan: Kansas State U. Lib., 1970.

77. Z6834   _____. *An Introduction to Maritime,*
     .H5H5   *Naval, and Aeronautical History.* Chapel
                   Hill: UNC Lib., 1960. 48 pp.

78. Z6207   *Hilliard, Jack B., comp. *An Annotated*
     .E8H58   *Bibliography of the United States Marine*
                   Corps in the First World War. Wash.: USMC,
                   HQ, Hist. Div., 1967.

79. Z1361   *_____, and Harold A. Bivins, comps. *An*
     .D4H5   *Annotated Reading List of United States*
                   Marine Corps History. Wash.: USMC, HQ,
                   Hist. Div., 1971.

80. Z7401   Hines, Theodore D., ed. *McGraw-Hill Bibli-*
     .M23   *ography of Science and Technology....*N.Y.:
                   McGraw-Hill, 1966.

81. VK555   Hobbs, Richard R. *Marine Navigation,* 2
     .H67   vols. Annapolis, Md.: NIP, 1974. v. 1.
                   Piloting. v. 2. Celestial and Electronic.

82. GC19   Idyll, Clarence P., ed. *Exploring the Ocean*
     .E95   *World: A History of Oceanography.* N.Y.:
                   Crowell, 1969.

83. Z6835   *Johnstone, John H., comp. *An Annotated*
     .U5M3   *Bibliography of United States Marines in*
     No. 5   *Guerrilla-Type Actions,* rev. Wash.: USMC,
                   HQ, Hist. Div., 1962.

84. REF   Jones, David R., ed. *Military-Naval Ency-*
     UA770   *clopedia of Russia and the Soviet Union.*
     .M55   Gulf Breeze, Fla.: Academic International
                   P., vol. 1, 1978. About 50 vols. pro-
                   jected.

85. REF   Keegan, John, and others, eds. *The Rand*
     D740   *McNally Encyclopedia of World War II.*
     .R36   Chicago: Rand McNally, 1977.

8

86. Z6004
    .P6L34
Lewis, Charles L. *Book of the Sea: An Introduction to Nautical Literature.* Annapolis, Md.: USNI, 1943.

87. REF
    VA55
    .U43
List of Logbooks of U.S. Navy Ships, Stations, and Miscellaneous Units, 1801-1947. Wash.: NA, 1978.

88. U24
    .L93
Luttwak, Edward. *A Dictionary of Modern War.* London: Penguin, 1971.

89. Z1238
    .L92
Lynch, Barbara A., comp. *The War at Sea. France and the American Revolution: A Bibliography.* Wash.: Dept. of the Navy, Naval Hist. Div., 1976.

90. VE23
    .M25
McEwen, William A., and A.H. Lewis. *Encyclopedia of Nautical Knowledge.* Cambridge, Mass.: Cornell Maritime P., 1953.

91. REF
    Z6835
    .G7M2
Manwaring, George E. *A Bibliography of British Naval History.* London: Conway Maritime P., 1929, 1970.

92. PZ1
    .M3815
    AM
Mason, Francis van Wyck, ed. *American Men at Arms.* Boston: Little, Brown, 1964. Collection of American fiction about World War I, World War II, and the Korean War.

93. Z6207
    .E8T85
Mayer, Sydney L. *The Two World Wars: Selective Bibliography.* N.Y.: Pergamon, 1964.

94. REF
    Z1361
    .R4T7
Meyer, Michael C., comp. and ed. *Supplement to a Bibliography of United States-Latin American Relations Since 1910.* Lincoln: U. of Nebraska P., 1979. *See* Trask, David F.

95. REF
    Z6725
    .U5M54
Miller, Samuel D., comp. *An Aerospace Bibliography.* Wash.: OAFH, 1978. Updates the work of Cresswell and Berger.

96. Z6725
    .U5M67
*Moran, John B. *Creating a Legend: The Complete Record of Writing About the United States Marine Corps.* Chicago: Moran/Andrews, 1973. Lists more than 1,100 books relating to various segments of Marine Corps history. 681 pp.

9

97. E174.5   Morris, Richard G., ed. *Encyclopedia of*
     .M847   *American History.* N.Y.: Harper, 1976.

98. CD3047   Munden, Kenneth W., and Henry P. Beers.
     .M8   *Guide to Federal Archives Relating to the*
               Civil War. Wash.: NA, GSA, NARS, 1962.

99. Z68.34   National Research Council. Committee on
     .S9N3   Undersea Warfare. *An Annotated Bibliog-*
               raphy of Submarine Technical Literature,
               1557 to 1953. Wash.: 1954.

100. REF   NYPL. *Subject Catalogue of the World War*
     6207   *II Collections,* 3 vols. Boston: G.K. Hall,
     .W8N48   1977.

101. REF   _____. *Subject Catalog of the World War*
     Z6207   *I Collection,* 4 vols. Boston: G.K. Hall &
     .E8N48   Co., 1961.

102. Z6835   *O'Quinlivan, Michael, and James S. San-
     .U5M3   telli, comps. *An Annotated Bibliography*
     No. 6   *of the United States Marine Corps in the*
               Korean War, rev. Wash.: USMC, HQ, Hist.
               Div., 1970.

103. Z6725   * _____, and Jack B. Hilliard, comps. *An*
     .U507   *Annotated Bibliography of the United States*
               Marine Corps in the Second World War.
               Wash.: USMC, HQ, Hist. Div., 1965.

104. Z6835   * _____, comp. *An Annotated Bibliography*
     .U5M3   *of the United States Marines in the Boxer*
               Rebellion. Wash.: USMC, HQ, Hist. Div.,
               1961.

105. Z6835   * _____. comp. *An Annotated Bibliography*
     .U5M3   *of United States Marines in the Civil War.*
     No. 2   Wash.: USMC, HQ, Hist. Div., 1963.

106. D740   Parrish, Thomas, ed. *The Simon and Schuster*
     .S57   *Encyclopedia of World War II.* N.Y.: Simon
               & Schuster, 1978.

107. D27   Parsons, Iaian, ed. *The Encyclopedia of*
     .E6   *Sea Warfare: From the First Ironclads to*
               The Present Day. London: Spring Books,
               1975. Popular, illustrated.

108. REF   Patterson, Andrew, Jr., and Robert A.
     Z6834   Winters, eds. *Historical Bibliography of*
     .M5P3   *Sea Mine Warfare.* Wash.: National Academy
     of Sciences, 1977.

109. REF   *Poole's Index to Periodical Literature,*
     AI3   6 vols., rpt., Gloucester, Mass.: Peter
     .P723   Smith. For the years 1802-1906.

110. Peri-   Public Affairs Information Service: *An-*
     odical   *nual Cumulated Bulletin.* N.Y.: PAIS, Vol.
     1- ; 1924- .

111. REF   *Reader's Guide to Periodical Literature.*
     N.Y.: H.W. Wilson, 1900- .

112. J81   Richardson, James D., comp. *A Compilation*
     .B96   *of the Messages and Papers of the Presi-*
     dents, 1789-1897, 10 vols. Wash.: Bureau
     of National Literature and Art, 1902.
     Supplements.

113. Micro   *Russell, William H. *Bibliography of Am-*
     Z6724   *phibious Warfare As Developed by the U.S.*
     .A5R87   *Marine Corps.* Annapolis, Md.: USNA, Nimitz
     Lib., c. 1951.

114. Micro   *_____. *Bibliography of Naval Literature*
     Z6834   *in the U.S. Naval Academy Library.* Annap-
     .B6U5   olis, Md.: USNA, Nimitz Lib., c 1951.

115. Micro   *_____. *Bibliography of Amphibious War-*
     Z6724   *fare as Developed by U.S. Marine Corps.*
     A5R87   Micro 1975. Also appears as Item I in
     Micro reel No. 2 in *Gallipoli Studies at*
     U.S. Marine Corps Schools, Quantico,
     1932- . D568.3.G35. Five reels.

116. Z6724   *Santelli, James S., comp. *An Annotated*
     .A38S35   *Bibliography of the United States Marine*
     Corps' Concept of Close Air Support.
     Wash.: USMC, HQ, Hist. Div., 1968.

117. Z6834   Schultz, Charles R. *Bibliography of Mari-*
     .H5B5   *time and Naval History Periodical Articles*
     Published during 1970. Mystic, Conn.:
     Marine Hist. Assoc., 1971.

118. D27   *Sea Warfare: The Encyclopedia of Sea War-*
     .E6   *fare.* N.Y.: Crowell, 1975.

119. REF
Z6207
.E853

Shaffer, Ronald. *The United States in World War I: A Selected Bibliography*. Santa Barbara, Calif.: ABC-Clio, 1978.

120. D771
.S55

Showell, Jak P.M. *The German Navy in World War Two: An Illustrated Reference Guide to the Kreigsmarine, 1920-1945*. Annapolis, Md.: NIP, 1979.

121. Z1238
.S45

Shy, John, comp. *The American Revolution*. Northbrook, Ill.: AHM, 1973. Goldentree Bibliography.

122. REF
HJ7469
.S58

Sivard, Ruth L. *World Military and Social Expenditures, 1977*. Leesburg, Va., WMSE Publications, 1978.

123. REF
Z1238
.S58

Smith, Dwight L., ed. *Era of the American Revolution: A Bibliography*. Santa Barbara, Calif.: ABC-Clio, 1975.

124. REF
Z1238
.S58

_____, and Terry A. Simmerman, eds. *Era of the American Revolution: A Bibliography*. Santa Barbara, Calif.: ABC-Clio, 1975.

125. REF
Z6207
.E8S45

Smith, Myron J., Jr. *World War I in the Air: A Bibliography and Chronology*. Metuchen, N.J.: Scarecrow, 1977.

126. Z6207
.W8S56

_____. *Air War Bibliography, 1939-1945: English Language Sources*, 4 vols. Metuchen, N.J.: Scarecrow, 1977-1978.

127. REF
Z6207
.W8S57

_____. *World War II at Sea: A Bibliography on Sources in English*, 3 vols. Metuchen, N.J.: Scarecrow, 1976.

128. REF
Z6835
.U5S6

_____. *The American Navy: A Bibliography*, 5 vols. Metuchen, N.J.: Scarecrow, 1973-1975.

129. Z6835
.U5S6
v. 1.

_____. *Navies in the American Revolution*. Metuchen, N.J.: Scarecrow, 1973.

130. Z6207
.W8S72

Spier, Henry O., ed. *World War II in Our Magazines and Books: September 1939 to September 1945*. N.Y.: Stuyvesant, 1945.

131. Z1245   Stapleton, Margaret L. *The Truman and*
     .S7   *Eisenhower Years, 1945-1960: A Selective*
                  Bibliography. Metuchen, N.J.: Scarecrow,
                  1973.

132. Z1244   Stewart, William J. *The Era of Franklin*
     .S73   *D. Roosevelt: A Selected Bibliography of*
                  Periodicals and Dissertation Literature,
                  1945-1971. N.Y.: GSA, NARS, F.D. Roose-
                  velt Lib., 1974.

133. V25   *To Use the Sea: Readings in Seapower and*
     .T59   *Maritime Affairs.* Annapolis, Md.: NIP,
                  1973; Suppl. 1975, V25.T6; 2nd ed., 1977,
                  V25.T59.

134. REF   Trask, David F., Michael C. Meyer, and
     A1361   Roger R. Trask. *A Bibliography of United*
     .R4T7   *States-Latin American Relations Since*
                  1810.... Lincoln: U. of Nebraska P., 1968.

135. Z6835   *Tyson Carolyn A., and Roland P. Gill. *An*
     .U5T9   *Annotated Bibliography of Marines in the*
                  American Revolution. Wash.: USMC, HQ, Hist.
                  Div., 1972. 72 pp.

136. REF   U.S. Bureau of the Census. *Historical Sta-*
     HA202   *tistics of the United States: Colonial*
     .A385   *Times to* [year]. Wash.: GPO, year.

137. UA24   *United States Military Posture for FY19 /*
     .A57   *19* . Wash.: GPO, year.

138. Micro   U.S. NARS *Area File of the Naval Records*
     VB255   *Collection, NARG 45.*
     .2.A7
     No. 625

139. Z5060   U.S. NASA. *Aerospace Bibliography,* 5th ed.
     A2A32   Wash.: GPO, 1970.

140. Z1236   U.S. National Historical Publications Com-
     .L331   mission. *Writings on American History.* In
                  or supplement to *Annual Report* of the
                  American Historical Assoc.

141. REF   U.S. Navy. Naval Operations Office. *U.S.*
     Z6835   *Naval History, Naval Biography, Naval*
     .U5U45   *Strategy and Tactics--Bibliography.* Wash.:
                  GPO, 1959.

142. REF   *U.S. Naval History: A Bibliography*. Wash.:
6825   Naval Hist. Div., 6th ed., 1972. 800 cita-
.U5U45   tions of official and secondary sources.
1972

143. Z3308   Ward, Robert E., and Frank J. Shulman,
.A5W35   comps. and eds. *The Allied Occupation of Japan, 1945-1952: An Annotated Bibliography of Western-language Material*. Chicago: Am. Lib. Assoc., 1974.

144. D27   Warner, Oliver, and others. *The Encyclopedia of Sea Warfare from the First Ironclads to the Present Day*. N.Y.: Crowell, 1975.
.E6

145. REF   Winchell, Constance M. *Guide to Reference Books*, 8th ed. Chicago: Am. Lib. Assoc., 1967.
Z1035
.W79

146. REF   Winsor, Justin. *Readers Handbook of the American Revolution*. Boston: Houghton Mifflin, 1880. Still valuable for the earlier, especially military, literature.
Z1238
.W78

147. Z1236   *Writings on American History: A Subject Index of Articles*, 1962. Millwood, N.Y.: Kraus-Thompson, 1974.
.L331

148. VA456   Young, John, comp. *A Dictionary of Ships of the Royal Navy of the Second World War*. Cambridge: Stephens, 1975. Over 2,000 ships.
.Y68

149. Z6839   Young, Lucien, comp. *Catalogue of Works by American Naval Authors*. Wash.: U.S. Navy Dept. Bureau of Navigation, 1888.
.U5Y7

150. REF   Ziegler, Janet, comp. *World War II: Books in English, 1945-1965*. Stanford: Hoover Institution P., 1971.
6207
.W8Z5

DOCUMENTS

151.   *American State Papers, 1789-1838*. [Naval Affairs in Serials 020-038.] Readex Microprint.

152.   *Annual DOD Bibliography of Logistic Studies and Related Documents*. Fort Lee, Va.: Army Logistics Management Center, 1966- .

153.   *Catalogue of the Public Documents of the
                              Congress, and of all Departments of
                              the Government of the United States for
                              the Period from 1893-1940.* Wash.: GPO,
                              year.

154. REF   *Checklist of United States Public Docu-
      Z1223   ments, 1787-1909.* Wash.: GPO, 1911.
      .A113

155.   *Cumulative Index to Publications of the
                              United States Congress.* Wash.: Congres-
                              sional Information Service, 1900- .

156. LC2:2   Gephart, Ronald M., comp. *Revolutionary
      Am3   America, 1763-1789: A Bibliography.* Wash.:
                              LC, 1971.

157. D743   O'Neill, James E., and Robert W. Krauskopf.
      .42.C66   *World War II: An Account of Its Documents.*
      1971   Wash.: Howard UP, 1976.

158. D301.5/5   Paszek, Lawrence J. *United States Air Force
      H62   History: A Guide to Documentary Sources.*
                              Wash.: OAFH, 1973.

159. J33   U.S. Congress. *American State Papers.
                              Documents, Legislative and Executive, of
                              the Congress of the United States.* Wash.:
                              Gales and Seaton, 1832-1861, 38 vols.
                              (Class VI. Naval Affairs, 4 vols.)
                              Vol. 1, Mar. 3, 1789-Mar. 5, 1825.
                              Vol. 2, May 13, 1824-Jan. 5, 1827.
                              Vol. 3, Jan. 12, 1827-Mar. 1, 1841.
                              Vol. 4, Mar. 1, 1831-June 15, 1836.

160. REF   *U.S. Defense Documentation Center. *ADCC
      Z6724   Bibliography of Amphibious Operations,* 4
      .A6U5   vols. Cameron Station, Alexandria, Va.,
                              DCC. 652 citations of materials acquired
                              from Mar. 1944 through July 1968. Vols.
                              3 & 4 are Conf. and Secret, respectively.
                              Vol. 2 includes Military Tactics and
                              Strategy; Logistics, Air Support; Person-
                              nel Training, Amphibious Vehicles. Vol.
                              1, 1969, has the same arrangements as Vol.
                              2.

161. Z7911   Gibbs, Katye M., and Elizabeth H. Halls, comps.
    .A1U58   *Bibliography of Bibliographies: A Report Bibli-*
             ography. Arlington, Va.: U.S. DOD Defense Sup-
             ply Agency, Defense Documentation Center, Armed
             Services Technical Information Agency, 1962.
             Supplements.

162. Z6005   U.S., DOD *Arctic Bibliography.* Vol. 1- ; 1953- .
    .P7A72   Wash.: GPO.

163. UA23   U.S. DOD. *Functions of the Armed Forces and*
    .U49   *Joint Chiefs of Staff,* rev. ed. Wash.: DOD,
             1953.

164. JX233   U.S. Department of State. *Papers Relating to*
    .A3   *the Foreign Relations of the United States.*
             Wash.: Dept. of State, 1861- .

165. REF   U.S. GPO. *Monthly Catalog of U.S. Public Docu-*
             ments. Wash.: GPO, 1930- .

166. Z1361   U.S. LC, Div. of Bibliography. *Selected List*
    .UD4U75 *of Recent References on American National De-*
             fense. Wash.: LC, 16 June 1936.

167. U15   U.S., LC, Technical Information Div. *The Polar*
    .U645   *Bibliography.* Wash.: LC, 1956.

168. Z881   U.S., LC. *European Imprints for the War Years*
    .A1U4   *Received in the Library of Congress and other*
             Federal Libraries, 3 parts. Wash.: LC, 1946.
             Part 1: Italian imprints. Part 2. French im-
             prints. Part 3. German imprints.

                    DISSERTATIONS AND THESES

169. Micro   *Dissertation Abstracts International.* Ann Arbor,
    Peri-   Mich.: U. Microfilms, 1969- .
    odical

170. Z6201   Kuehl, Warren F., ed. *Dissertations in History:*
    .K8   *An Index to Dissertations Completed in History*
             Departments of United States and Canadian
             Universities, 1873-1960. Lexington: U. of Ken-
             tucky P., 1965.

171. Z6946   Xerox University Microfilms. *Comprehensive Dis-*
    .S47   *sertation Index, 1861-1972: History.* Ann Arbor,
             Mich.: Xerox U. Microfilms, 1973.

ARTICLES

172.   "Bibliography of Space Literature," AF 41 (Mar.
            1958):168-74.

173.   Brodie, Bernard. "Some Notes on the Evolution
            of Air Doctrine," WP 7 (Apr. 1955):349-70.

174.   Brody, Richard A. "Deterrence Strategies: An
            Annotated Bibliography," JCR 4 (Dec. 1960):
            444-57.

175.   Cappon, Lester J. "The Collection of World War
            I Materials in the States," AHR 48 (July 1943):
            733-45.

176.   Cole, Wayne S. "American Entry into World War
            II: A Historiographical Appraisal," MVHR 43
            (Mar. 1957):595-617.

177.   Guggisberg, Hans R. "The Uses of the European
            Past in American Historiography," JAS 41 (July
            1970):1-18.

178.   Hasdorff, James C. "Sources in Aerospace His-
            tory: The USAF Oral History Collection,"
            Aerospace Historian 23 (Summer/June 1976):
            103-04.

179.   Hecht, J. Jean. "The Reign of George III in
            Recent Historiography: A Bibliographical Essay,"
            Bull. NYPL 70 (1966):279-304.

180.   Hosmer, Helen R., comp. "Submarines in Peri-
            odical Literature, 1911-1917," *The Franklin
            Institute Journal* 184 (1917):251-306.
            Annotated.

181.   Kirk, Neville T. "Sentinel for a Century: The
            Proceedings, the Navy, and the Nation, 1873-
            1973," USNIP 99 (Oct. 1973):96-115.

182.   Lundeberg, Philip D. "German Naval Literature
            of World War II: A Bibliographical Survey,"
            USNIP 82 (Jan. 1956):95-105.

183.   Merrill, James M. "Successors of Mahan: A Sur-
            vey of Writing on American Naval History, 1914-
            1960," MVHR 50 (Mar. 1964):79-99.

184.   Morton, Louis. "Pearl Harbor in Perspective: A Bibliographic Survey," USNIP 81 (Apr. 1955): 461-68.

185.   Ney, Virgil. "Guerrilla Warfare: Annotated Bibliography," MR 41 (Nov. 1961):97-112.

186.   "Notable Naval Books of the Year," USNIP, 1950- , Vol. 76- .

187.   Park, Hong-Kyu. "The Korean War Revisited: A Survey of Historical Writings," WA 137 (Spring 1975):336-44.

188.   Smith, Daniel M. "National Interest and American Intervention, 1917: An Historiographical Appraisal," JAH 52 (June 1965):5-24.

189.   Sunderman, James F. "A Missile and Space Bibliography," AF 45 (Apr. 1962):175-83.

190.   Watson, Richard L., Jr. "Woodrow Wilson and His Interpreters, 1947-1957," MVHR 44 (Sept. 1957): 376-91.

191.   Werrell, Kenneth P. "The USAAF over Europe and Its Foes: A Selected, Subjective, and Critical Bibliography," *Aerospace Historian* 16 (Winter 1978):231-33, 236-43.

B. SHIPS AND AIRCRAFT

BOOKS

192. V858   Alden, John D. *The Fleet Submarine in the U.S.*
      .A43   *Navy: A Design and Construction History*. Annapolis, Md.: NIP, 1979.

193. VA484   Archibald, E.H.H. *The Metal Fighting Ship*.
      .A66   N.Y.: Arco, 1971.

194. Va454   _____. *The Wooden Fighting Ship*. N.Y.: Arco,
      .A67   1968. British Royal Navy.

195. V858   Barnes, Robert H. *United States Submarines*, 3d
      .B29   ed. New Haven: H.F. Morse, 1946.

196. VA61   Bauer, K. Jack. *Ships of the Navy, 1775-1969*.
      .B37   Troy, N.Y.: Rensselaer Polytechnic Institute, 1970. Vol. 1. *Combat Vessels*.

197. V765   Breyer, Siegfried. *Battleships and Battle*
     .B6813   *Cruisers, 1905-1970*. GCNY: Doubleday, 1973.

198. V874   Castillo, Edmund L. *Flat-tops: The Story of*
     .C38   *Aircraft Carriers*. N.Y.: Random House, 1969.

199. V799   *Conway's All the World's Fighting Ships, 1860-*
     .C66   *1905*. Annapolis, Md.: NIP, 1979.

200. VA500   Couhat, Jean L., ed. *Combat Fleets of the*
     .L313   *World: Their Ships, Aircraft, and Armament*.
              Annapolis, Md.: NIP. A biennial since 1976/77.

201. V767   Dulin, Robert O., Jr., and William H. Garzke,
     .D78   Jr. *Battleships: United States Battleships in*
              World War II. Annapolis, Md.: NIP, 1976.

202. VA61   Fahey, James C. *The Ships and Aircraft of the*
     .S47   *United States Fleet*. Various editors and pub-
              lishers, 1939- .

203. D580   Fitzsimons, Bernard, ed. *Warships and Sea Bat-*
     .W9   *tles of World War I*. N.Y.: Beekman House, 1973.

204. V825   Hodges, Peter, and Norman Friedman. *Destroyer*
     .H6   *Weapons of World War 2*. Annapolis, Md.: NIP,
              1979.

205. D436   Hornsey, Pat, ed. *Ships at War*. London: New
     .S54   English Lib., 1978. Naval history and battles,
              20th century.

206. V750   Hough, Richard. *Man o'War: The Fighting Ship in*
     .H645   *History*. N.Y.: Scribner, 1979. The story of 15
              famous fighting ships, including 5 American.

207. REF   Ireland, Bernard. *Warships of the World: Major*
     V767   *Classes*. N.Y.: Scribner, 1976.
     .I73

208. V825   _____. *Warships of the World: Escort Vessels*.
     .I73   N.Y.: Scribner, 1979. Ships displacing between
              1,000 and 5,000 tons.

209. VA40   Jane, Frederick T. *Jane's Fighting Ships*.
     .F523   Various publishers, 1898- .

210. TL501   *Jane's All the World's Aircraft*. London: Sampson
     .J3   Low, Marston, 1909- . An annual.

19

211. E182   Leeming, Joseph. *The Book of American Fighting*
     .L45   *Ships*. N.Y.: Harper, 1939.

212. VA70   Lemmon, Sue, and E.D. Wichels. *Sidewheelers to*
     .M3L45   *Nuclear Power: A Pictorial Essay Covering 123*
                   Years at the Mare Island Naval Shipyard. Annap-
                   olis, Md.: Leeward Pubs., 1977.

213. V858   Lenton, Henry T. *American Submarines: Navies of*
     .L45   *of the Second War*. GCNY: Doubleday, 1973.

214. V874   Melhorn, Charles M. *Two-Block Fox: The Rise of*
     .3.M44   *the Aircraft Carrier, 1911-1929*. Annapolis,
                   Md.: NIP, 1974.

215. VM22   Millar, John F. *American Ships of the Colonial*
     .M54   *and Revolutionary Periods*. N.Y.: Norton, 1978.

216. V874   Pawlowski, Gareth L. *Flat-Tops and Fledglings:*
     .3.P38   *A History of American Aircraft Carriers*. N.Y.:
                   Castle Books, 1971.

217. VA61   Polmar, Norman, ed. *The Ships and Aircraft of*
     .S47   *the U.S. Fleet*, 11th ed. Annapolis, Md.: NIP,
                   1978.

218. V765   Preston, Antony, ed. *Warships*. Annapolis, Md.:
     .W362   NIP, Vol. 10 , 1977- .

219. V859   _____. *U-Boats*. London: Arms and Armour P.,
     .G3P73   1978.

220. V767   _____. *Battleships of World War I: An Il-*
     .P24   *lustrated Encyclopedia of the Battleships of*
                   All Nations, 1914-1918. Harrisburg, Pa.:
                   Stackpole, 1972.

221. VM18   Rossell, Howey E. *Types of Naval Ships*. N.Y.:
     .R8   The Society of Naval Architects and Marine En-
                   gineers, 1945.

222. V799   Sandler, Stanley L. *The Emergence of the Modern*
     .S26   *Capital Ship, 1860-1870*. Newark: U. of Delaware
                   P., 1979.

223. V825   Schofield, William G. *Destroyers, 60 Years*.
     .3.S3   N.Y.: Rand McNally, 1962.

224. VA58   Silverstone, Paul H. *U.S. Warship of World War*
     .S58   *II*. GCNY: Doubleday, 1966.

225. V895   Skiera, Joseph A. *Aircraft Carriers in Peace*
     .S58   *and War*. N.Y.: Watts, 1965.

226. V765   Thornton, J.M. *Warships, 1860-1970*. N.Y.:
     .T43   Arco, 1973.

227. TL755   Toland, John. *Ships in the Sky: The Story of*
     .T6   *the Great Dirigibles*. N.Y.: Holt, 1957, 1972.

228. VA61   U.S. Bureau of Construction and Repair *and*
     .A3   U.S. Bureau of Ships. *Ships' Data, U.S. Naval*
             Vessels. Wash.: GPO, 1911-1949. Later volumes
             are classified.

229. V10   *Weyer's Warships of the World*. Annapolis, Md.:
     .W47   USNI, 1967- .

230. V825   Yates, Brock W. *Destroyers and Destroyermen:*
     .3.Y3   *The Story of Our "Tin Can" Navy*. N.Y.: Harper,
             1959.

ARTICLES

231.   Beers, Henry P. "Bibliography of Publications
             Containing Lists or other Data Pertaining to
             United States Naval Vessel," *Bull. of Bibli-*
             ography, pt. 1, 18 (May-Aug. 1945):160-63; pt.
             2, 18 (Sept.-Dec. 1945):182-84.

232.   Cross, Richard F., III. "Essex: More than a
             Ship: More than a Class," USNIP 101 (Sept.
             1975):58-69.

233.   Paist, Paul H. "Monitors: Ships that Changed
             War," USNIP 87 (June 1961):76-89. Pictorial.

234.   Smart, Larry R. "Evolution of the Torpedo Boat."
             MA 23 (Summer 1959):97-101.

C. CHRONOLOGIES

BOOKS

235. E463   American Heritage. *American Heritage Civil War*
     .3.A7   *Chronology, with Notes on the Leading Partici-*
             pants. N.Y.: American Heritage, 1960. Supple-
             ment available.

236. D790   Carter, Kit C., and Robert Mueller, comps. *The
      .C29   Army Air Forces in World War II: Combat Chro-
                  nology, 1941-1945*. Wash.: OAFH, 1973.

237. REF   Cooney, David. *Chronology of the U.S. Navy,
      E182   1776-1975*. N.Y.: Watts, 1975.
      .C73

238. TL521   Emme, Eugene M. *Aeronautics and Astronautics:
      .A54283   An American Chronology of Science and Technol-
                  ogy in the Exploration of Space, 1915-1960*.
                  Wash.: NASA, 1961.

239. REF   Gurney, Gene. *Chronology of World Aviation*.
      TL515   N.Y.: Watts, 1965. Both civil and military
      G83   aviation.

240. REF   Haws, Duncan. *Ships and the Sea: A Chronolog-
      Oversize   ical Review*. N.Y.: Crowell, 1975.
      VM15
      .H33

241. V23   *Miller, William M., and John H. Johnstone,
      .U546   comps. *A Chronology of the United States Marine
                  Corps*, 4 vols. Wash.: USMC, HQ, Hist. Div.,
                  1970.

242. D522   Mudd, Thomas B.R. *The Yanks are Coming: A Chro-
      .5.M8   nological and Documentary Review of World War
                  I*. N.Y.: Vantage, 1958.

243. V53   *Naval and Maritime Chronology, 1961-1971*.
      .N38   Annapolis, Md.: NIP, 1973. From ten years of
                  the *Naval Review*.

244. E182   Neeser, Robert W. *Statistical and Chronological
      .N38   History of the United States Navy, 1775-1909*,
                  2 vols. N.Y.: Macmillan, 1909; rpt., N.Y.: B.
                  Franklin, 1970. Vol. 1 contains the most ex-
                  tensive naval bibliography published in America
                  prior to that of Myron Smith, *q.v.*, author
                  index.

245. VM615   Preble, George H. *A Chronological History of
      .P92   the Origin and Development of Steam Navigation,
                  1543-1882*. Phila.: Hamersly, 1883, 1896.

246. D770   Rohwer, Jurgen, and G. Hummelchen. *Chronology
      .R5913   of the War at Sea, 1939-1945*, 2 vols. London:
                  Allan, 1972-1974.

247. REF   Smith, Myron, Jr. *Air War Chronology, 1939-1945,*
      D785   2 vols. Metuchen, N.J.: Scarecrow, 1977.
      .S55

248. UG633   U.S. Dept. of the Air Force. *A Chronology of*
      .A3764   *American Aviation Events from 1903 Through 1964.*
      210-1-1   Wash.: OAFH, 1965. 85 pp.

249. UG633   *A Chronology of American Aviation Events: His-*
      A3764   *torical Data.* Wash.: U.S. Dept. of the Air
               Force, 1955.

250. D743   U.S. Dept. of the Navy. *United States Naval*
      .5.U63   *Chronology, World War II.* Wash.: Navy Dept.:
               Naval Hist. Div., 1955.

251. E591   U.S. Navy Dept. *Civil War Naval Chronology,*
      .U568   *1861-1865.* Wash.: U.S. Navy Dept., Naval Hist.
               Div., 1961-1966.

252. V23   *USMC. A Chronology of the U.S. Marine Corps,* 4
      .U546   vols. Wash.: USMC, HQ, 1965-1970. V. 1, 1775-
               1934; V. 2, 1935-1946; V. 3, 1947-1964; V. 4,
               1965-1969.

253. V10   U.S. Naval Institute *Proceedings.* The May
               issue, entitled *Naval Review.* Annual since
               1962.

254. Doc   U.S. Office of Naval Operations. *United States*
      D202.2.:Av *Naval Aviation, 1910-1970,* 2d ed. Prepared at
      5/2/910-   the Direction of the Deputy CNO (Air) and the
      70   Commander, Naval Air Systems Command. Wash.:
               GPO, 1970.

255. D769   Williams, Mary H., comp. *Chronology, 1941-1945.*
      .A533   Wash.: OCMH, 1960.
      v.8
      pt. 5

DISSERTATIONS AND THESES

256. D773   Richard, Dorothy E. "The U.S. Navy in World War
      .R5   II: A Chronology," 2 vols. Thesis, Georgetown
               U., 1949.

ARTICLES

257.   *"All Hands Chronology, 1941-1945." All Hands,*
               No. 690 (July 1974):50-59.

258.   "Chronology of World War II," CH, NS 8 (June 1945):492-96.

259.   *Jenkins, James C. "Chronology of Outstanding Events of the American Marines," MCG 24 (1940): 15, 81-90.

260.   *"Korean Chronology," *Leatherneck* 34 (Nov. 1951):28-29. Brief chronology of Korean operations, 25 June 1950-30 June 1951.

D. NAVAL TERMS

BOOKS

261. V23 .B75   Bradford, Gershom. *A Glossary of Sea Terms.* London: Cassell, 1954.

262. U19 .H4   Heinl, Robert D. *Dictionary of Military and Naval Quotations.* Annapolis, Md.: NIP, 1966.

263. GC9 .H85   Hunt, Lee M., and D.G. Groves, eds. *A Glossary of Ocean Science and Undersea Technology Terms....* Arlington, Va.: Compass Publications, 1965.

264. VA23 .086   Kemp, Peter. *The Oxford Companion to Ships and the Sea.* London: Oxford UP, 1976.

265. V23 .L4   Layton, Cyril W.T. *Dictionary of Nautical Words and Terms.* Glasgow: Brown, Son, and Ferguson, 1955.

266. V23 .N6   Noel, John V., and Edward L. Beach, eds. *Naval Terms Dictionary*, 4th ed. Annapolis, Md.: NIP, 1978.

267. REF V23 .J36   Palmer, Joseph, comp. *Jane's Dictionary of Naval Terms.* London: Macdonald and Jane's, 1975.

268. V23 .B32   Villiers, Alan J., and Basil W. Bathe. *The Visual Encyclopedia of Nautical Terms Under Sail.* N.Y.: Crown, 1978.

269. V23 .W43   Wedertz, Bill, comp. and ed. *Dictionary of Naval Abbreviations*, 2nd ed. Annapolis, Md.: NIP, 1977.

BOOKS

270. REF
     G1037
     .B35

Banks, Arthur. Commentary by Alan Palmer. *A Military Atlas of the First World War*. N.Y.: Taplinger, 1975.

271. D743.3
     .B7

Brown, Ernest F. *The War in Maps: An Atlas of the New York Times Maps*. N.Y.: Oxford UP, 1946.

272. G1201
     .S3A8

Cappon, Lester J., and others. *Atlas of Early American History: The Revolutionary Era, 1760-1790*. Princeton: PUP, 1975.

273. F230
     .C322

Carrington, Henry B. *Battles of the American Revolution: Battle Maps and Charts of the American Revolution*, new ed. N.Y.: New York Times, 1968.

274. D431
     .C58

Cook, Chris, and John Stevenson. *The Atlas of Modern Warfare*. N.Y.: Putnam, 1978.

275. G1201
     .S5U6

Davis, George B., Leslie J. Perry, and Joseph W. Kirkley. Compiled by Captain Calvin D. Cowles. *The Official Military Atlas of the Civil War*. N.Y.: Arno/Crown Book, 1978.

276. U102
     .U52

Dept. of Military Art and Engineering. *Summaries of Selected Military Campaigns*. West Point, N.Y.: U.S. Military Academy, 1953.

277. G1201
     .S5U58

Esposito, Vincent J. *The West Point Atlas of the Civil War*. N.Y.: Praeger, 1962.

278. REF
     G1201
     .S1U5

_____, and others, eds. *The West Point Atlas of American Wars, 1689-1953*, 2 vols. N.Y.: Praeger, 1959.

279. REF
     Z1201
     .S1G5

Gilbert, Martin. *American History Atlas*. N.Y.: Macmillan, 1968.

280. GA405
     .5.H37

Harley, John B., and others. *Mapping the American Revolutionary War*. Chicago: U. of Chicago P., 1978.

281. D743
     .3H6

Horrabin, James F. *An Atlas-History of the Second World War*, 10 vols. N.Y.: T. Nelson, 1940-1946.

282. G1210   Marshall, Douglas W., and Howard H. Peckham.
     .S3M25   *Campaigns of the American Revolution: An Atlas
                of MSS Maps.* Ann Arbor: U. of Michigan P.,
                1976.

283. REF   Martin, Gilbert. *First World War Atlas.* N.Y.:
     G1037.G5   Macmillan, 1973.

284. REF   Nebenzahl, Kenneth. *Atlas of the American Revo-
     G1201   lution.* Chicago: Rand McNally, 1974.
     .S3N4

285. D27   Pemsel, Helmut. *A History of War at Sea.* Annap-
     .P4713   olis, Md.: NIP, 1978.

286. D743   Stamp, Thomas D., and Vincent J. Esposito, eds.
     .U465   *A Military History of World War II: Atlas.* West
                Point, N.Y.: The Academy, 1953.

287. D743.3   Stembridge, Jasper H. *The Oxford War Atlas,* 4
     .S8   vols. N.Y.: Oxford UP, 1941-1946.

288. REF   Young, Peter, ed. *Atlas of the Second World War.*
     G1038   N.Y.: Putnam, 1973.
     .Y6

F. PERSONAL HISTORIES

BOOKS

289. REF   *Appleton's Cyclopedia of American Biography.*
     E176   N.Y.: Appleton, 1887.
     .A65

290. E353   Bailey, Isaac, comp. *American Naval Biography.*
     .B16   Providence, R.I.: Isaac Bailey, 1815. Covers
                naval biography, War of 1812, and Washington
                Irving.

291. VE23   *Blakeney, Jane. *Heroes, U.S. Marine Corps, 1861-
     .B56   1955.* Wash.: Guthrie, 1957.

292. E208   Boatner, Mark M. *Cassell's Biographical Dic-
     .B58   tionary of the War of Independence.* London:
                Cassell, 1973.

293.   Borsodi, Marion S., comp. *Fleet Admiral Chester
                William Nimitz, USN: A Selected Bibliography
                from the Collection of the Nimitz Lib.* Annap-
                olis, Md.: USNA, Nimitz Lib., 1973.

294. D736   Chamberlain, Thomas H. *The Generals and the*
     .C48   *Admirals*, 2 vols. N.Y.: Devin-Adair, 1945.

295. REF   *Current Biography*. N.Y.: H.H. Wilson Co.,
     CT100   1940- .
     .C8

296. REF   *Dictionary of American Biography*. N.Y.:
     E176   Scribner, 1928- .
     .D56

297. U52   Dunleavy, T.M., ed. *Generals of the Army and*
     .G4   *the Air Force and Admirals of the Navy*. Wash.:
             Dunleavy Pub. Co., 1954.

298. REF   Hamersly, Lewis R. *Biographical Sketches of*
     E181   *Distinguished Officers of the Army and Navy*.
     .H18   N.Y.: Hamersly, 1905.

299. V11   *_____. *List of Officers of the Navy and of*
     .U7C2   *the Marine Corps from 1775 to 1900*.... N.Y.:
             Hamersly, 1901.

300. D110   Hough, Richard A. *The Great Admirals*. N.Y.:
     .H68   Morrow, 1977. Biographical sketches of 21
     1977   generals and admirals. *See* particularly de
             Grasse, Raeder, Yamamoto, Nimitz, Spruance, and
             Halsey.

301. REF   Keegan, John, and Catherine Bradley, eds. *Who*
     D737   *Was Who in World War II*. N.Y.: Crowell, 1978.
     .W56

302. E182   *Lewis, Charles L. *Famous American Marines*.
     .L56   Boston: Page, 1950.

303. REF   Mason, David. *Who's Who in World War II*. Boston:
     D736   Little, Brown, 1978.
     .M33
     1978

304. REF   *National Cyclopedia of American Biography*.
     E176   N.Y.: James T. White, 1937- .
     .N29

305. Z5301   O'Neill, Edward H. *Biography by Americans, 1658-*
     .O58   *1936: A Subject Bibliography*. Phil.: U. of Pa.
             P., 1939.

306. REF   Reynolds, Clark G., *Famous American Admirals*.
    V62   N.Y.: Van Nostrand Reinhold, 1978. Biographi-
    .R48   cal sketches of some 200 flag officers educated
            at the U.S. Naval Academy, with photographs.

307. E182   *Schuon, Karl, ed. *U.S. Marine Corps Biographical
    .S39   Dictionary*. N.Y.: Watts, 1963.

308. REF   _____. *U.S. Navy Biographical Dictionary*.
    E1982   N.Y.: Watts, 1965.
    .S45

309. REF   Tunney, Christopher. *Biographical Dictionary of
    D736   World War II*. N.Y.: St. Martin, 1972.
    .T78

310. JK1010 U.S. Congress. *Biographical Dictionary of the
    .A5   American Congress, 1774-* . Wash.: GPO, various
            dates.

311. REF   U.S. Naval Academy Alumni Association. *Register
    V415   of Alumni, 1845-* . Annapolis, Md.: USNA Alumni
    .H5   Assoc., year.

312. REF   *Who Was Who in American History: The Military*.
    U52   Chicago: Marquis, 1975.
    .W48

G. PICTORIAL HISTORIES

BOOKS

313. E746   Alden, John D. *The American Steel Navy...*
    .A6   [1883-1908]. Annapolis, Md.: NIP, 1972.

314. E188   American Heritage. *The French and Indian Wars*.
    .A504   N.Y.: AH, 1962.

315. E468   _____. *The American Heritage Picture History
    .7.A6   of the Civil War*. N.Y.: AH, 1960.

316. D773   *Battle Stations! Your Navy in Action: A Photo-
    .B36   graphic Epic of the Naval Operations of World
            War II....* N.Y.: H. Wise, 1946.

317. E468   Blay, John S. *The Civil War: A Pictorial Pro-
    .7.B5   file*. N.Y.: Crowell, 1958.

318. REF   Bonds, Ray, ed. *The Vietnam War: The Illustrated
    U42   History of the Conflict in Southeast Asia*. N.Y.:
    .E53   Crown, 1979.

28

319. VG93   *Caidin, Martin. *Golden Wings: A Pictorial His-*
     .C23   *tory of the United States Navy and Marine Corps
               in the Air.* N.Y.: Random House, 1960.

320. VM15   Casson, L. *Illustrated History of Ships and
     .C34   Boats.* GCNY: Doubleday, 1965.

321. D745   *Collier's Photographic History of World War
     .2.C64   II.* N.Y.: Collier's, 1946. Also published
               as *The Picture History of World War II, 1939-
               1945*, by Grosset and Dunlap, 1960.

322. D527.C7   *Collier's Photographic History of the European
     1916   War....* N.Y.: Collier, 1916.

323. VE23   *Crane, John deM. C. *The United States Marines*:
     .C77   *A Pictorial History of the Marines.* Baton Rouge,
               La.: Army and Navy Pub. Co., 1952. 73 pp. In-
               cludes a summary of engagements from 1950-1952.

324. DS918   *Duncan, David D. *This is War! A Photo-
     .D8   Narrative in Three Parts.* N.Y.: Harper, 1951.
               Photographic essay by a *Life* photographer
               covering Marine actions from the Pusan Perim-
               eter through the Hungnam evacuation.

325. E715   *Harper's Pictorial History of The War with
     .H27   Spain.* N.Y.: Harper, 1899.

326. D769   Hatlem, John C., Kenneth E. Hunter, and Mar-
     .A533   garet E. Tackley, comps. *The War Against
     v. 5   Germany and Italy: Mediterranean and Adjacent
     pt. 2   Areas.* Wash.: OCMH, 1951.

327. D767.99 *Henri, Raymond. *Iwo Jima: Springboard to Final
     .I9H4   Victory.* N.Y.: U.S. Camera, 1945.

328. V210   Horton, Edward. *The Illustrated History of the
     .H64   Submarine.* London: Sidgwick & Jackson, 1974.

329. D769   Hunter, Kenneth E. *The War Against Germany:
     .A533   Europe and Adjacent Areas.* Wash.: OCMH, 1951.
     v. 5
     pt. 2

330 D769   _____, and Margaret E. Tackley, comps. *The
     .A533   War Against Japan.* Wash.: OCMH, 1952.
     v. 5
     pt. 3

331. D790 Jensen, Oliver. *Carrier War*. N.Y.: Simon &
     .J4   Schuster, 1945.

332. E468 Johnson, Rossier. *Campfires and Battlefields:*
     .7.J64 *A Pictorial Narrative of the Civil War.* N.Y.:
            Blue and Grey P., 1958.

333. VG93 Knott, Richard C. *The American Flying Boat: An*
     .K596 *Illustrated History.* Annapolis, Md.: NIP, 1979.
            1912- .

334. VG93 *Larkins, William T. *U.S. Marine Aircraft, 1914-*
     .L3   *1959.* Concord, Calif.: Aviation History Publi-
            cations, 1959. Photographs, with brief descrip-
            tive and historical data.

335. D743 *Life Goes to War: A Picture History of World*
     .2.L483 *War II.* Boston: Little, Brown, 1977.

336. E354 Lossing, Benson J. *Pictorial Field-Book of the*
     .L87   *War of 1812.* N.Y.: Harper, 1868.

337. E468 _____. *Pictorial History of the Civil War in*
     .L88   *the United States of America,* 3 vols. Phila.:
            Childs, 1866-1868.

338. E208
     .L882 _____. *The Pictorial Field-Book of the Revo-*
            lution, 2 vols. NY.: Harper, 1850; rpt., Reprint
            Co., 1969.

339. D743 Martin, Ralph G. *World War II: A Photographic*
     .2.M29 *Record of the War in the Pacific from Pearl*
            Harbor to V-J Day. Greenwich, Conn.: Fawcett
            Pubs., 1965.

340. D732 _____, and Richard Harrity. *World War II: A*
     .2.M28 *Photographic Record of the War in Europe from*
            D-Day to V-E Day. Greenwich, Conn.: Gold Medal
            Books, 1962.

341. E468 Miller, Francis T., and Robert S. Lanier, eds.
     .7.M64 *The Photographic History of the Civil War,* 10
            vols. N.Y.: Review of Reviews, 1911; rpt.,
            N.Y.: Yoseloff, 1957.

342. D811 Miller, Max. *The Far Shore: With Official U.S.*
     .M523 *Navy and Coast Guard Photographs.* N.Y.:
            Whittlesey House, 1945.

343. E468   Moat, Louis S., ed. *Frank Leslie's Illustrated*
    .7.M87   *History of the Civil War.* N.Y.: Mrs. F. Leslie,
    1895.

344. DS557   Moeser, Robert D. *U.S. Navy: Vietnam.* Annapolis,
    .A61M58   Md.: USNI, 1969.

345. VE23   *Montross, Lynn. *The United States Marines: A*
    .M6   *Pictorial History.* N.Y.: Rinehart, 1959.

346. VM453   Nelson, Stewart B. *Oceanographic Ships, Fore and*
    .N44   *Aft.* Wash.: GPO, 1971.

347. V874   Polmar, Norman. *Aircraft Carriers: A Graphic*
    .P6   *History of Carrier Aviation and Its Influence*
    on World Events. GCNY: Doubleday, 1969.

348. E182   Potter, Elmer B. *The Naval Academy Illustrated*
    .P78   *History of the United States Navy.* N.Y.:
    Crowell, 1971.

349. V47   Preston, Antony. *The Navies of the American*
    .P73   *Revolution.* London: Cooper, 1975.

350. V767   _____. *Battleships of World War I....* Harris-
    .P74   burg, Pa.: Stackpole, 1972.

351. V859   _____. *U-Boats.* London: Arms and Armour P.,
    .G3P73   1978.

352. VC303   Rankin, Robert H. *Uniforms of the Sea Services:*
    .R3   *A Pictorial History.* Annapolis, Md.: USNI, 1962.

353. E468   Robertson, James I. *The Concise Illustrated His-*
    .R72   *tory of the Civil War.* Harrisburg, Pa.: Stack-
    pole, 1971.

354. E182   Roscoe, Theodore, and Fred Freeman. *Picture His-*
    .R84   *tory of the U.S. Navy, from the Old Navy to the*
    New, 1776-1897. N.Y.: Scribner, 1956.

355. D589   Russell, James C., and William E. Moore. *The*
    .U6R8   *United States Navy in the World War: Official*
    Pictures.... Wash.: Pictorial Bureau, 1921.

356. D527   Stallings, Laurence, ed. *The First World War:*
    .S73   *A Photographic History.* N.Y.: Simon & Schuster,
    1933.

357. D767
.U51

*Steichen, Edward, comp. *U.S. Navy War Photo-graphs, Pearl Harbor to Tokyo Harbor: A Collec-tion of Official U.S. Navy, Marine Corps, and Coast Guard Photographs*. N.Y.: U.S. Camera, (1964?).

358. E596
.S8

Stern, Philip V. *Confederate Navy: A Pictorial History*. GCNY: Doubleday, 1962.

359. D743
.2.S8

Sulzberger, Cyrus L., and the Editors of Ameri-can Heritage. *The American Heritage Picture History of World War II*. N.Y.: American Heri-tage, 1966.

360. UG93
.S92

Swanborough, Frederick G., and Peter M. Bowers. *United States Navy Aircraft Since 1911*. N.Y.: Funk & Wagnalls, 1968; 2d ed., Annapolis, Md.: NIP, 1976.

361. D522
.T3

Taylor, Alan J.P. *Illustrated History of the First World War*. N.Y.: Putnam, 1964.

362. D522
.T4

Terraine, John. *The Great War, 1914-1948: A Pictorial History*. London: Hutchinson, 1965.

363. E468
.7W45

Werstein, Irving. *1861-1865: Adventures of the Civil War told with Pictures*. N.Y.: Cooper Square Pub., 1969.

364. E715
.W39

_____. *1898: The Spanish-American War told with Pictures*. N.Y.: Cooper Square Pub., 1966.

365. D522
.W54

_____. *1914-1918: World War I told with Pictures*, 2nd ed. N.Y.: Cooper Square Pub., 1966.

ARTICLES

366.

*Bradshaw, Harvey D. "Marine Corps Aviation: Cunnington to Cu Lai," USNIP 92 (Nov. 1966): 106-23.

367

Duddy, Frank E., Jr. "Cruisers in the U.S. Navy," USNIP 78 (Mar. 1952):304-17.

368.

Ellis, Richard W. "Battleships of the United States Navy," USNIP 89 (Feb. 1963):94-114.

369.

Miller, Richard T. "Sixty Years of Destroyers: A Study of Evolution," USNIP 88 (Nov. 1962): 93-111.

370.   Paist, Paul H. "Monitors--Ships that Changed
            War," USNIP 87 (June 1961):76-89.

371.   "Photographic Milestones of the Naval War, by
            the U.S. Navy," USNIP 71 (Dec. 1945):1405-13.

372.   Rankin, Robert H. "Goodbye to the Gas Bags,"
            USNIP 87 (Oct. 1961):91-108.

H. TRANSCRIPTS OF ORAL INTERVIEWS

373. Z6835   Frank, Benis M., comp. *Marine Corps Oral History*
     .U5F72 *Collection Catalog*. Wash.: USMC, HQ, Hist. and
             Museums Div., 1975, 1979.

374.   Mason, Elizabeth B., and Louis M. Starr, eds.
            The Oral History Collection of Columbia Uni-
            versity. N.Y.: The Columbia University Oral
            History Research Office, 1973, 1979.

375.   U.S. Naval Institute Oral History Program.
            Annapolis, Md.: U.S. Institute.

In addition, the other military services and the presidential
libraries have their own programs.

I. FICTION

376. PS374   Dickinson, A.T., Jr. *American Historical Fic-*
     .H5D5   *tion*, 3d ed. Metuchen, N.J.: Scarecrow, 1971.

377. Z5917   Knight, Francis. *The Sea Story*. N.Y.: Macmillan,
     .S4K5   1958.

378. Z6004   Lewis, Charles L. *Book of the Sea: An Introduc-*
     .P6L34 *tion to Nautical Literature*. Annapolis, Md.:
             USNI, 1943.

379. REF   McGarry, Daniel D., and Sarah H. White. *World*
     Z5917   *Historical Fiction Guide*.... Metuchen, N.J.:
     .H6M3   Scarecrow, 1973.

380. PR1111 Parkinson, Cyril N. *Portsmouth Point: The Navy*
     .N4P3   *in Fiction, 1793-1815*. London: Hodder &
             Stoughton, 1948.

381. Z5917   Smith, Myron J., Jr., and Robert C. Weller.
     .S4S64 *Sea Fiction Guide*. Metuchen, N.J.: Scarecrow,
             1976.

382. REF   Wright, Lyle H. *American Fiction, 1774-1850.*
     Z1231   San Marino, Calif.: Huntington Lib., 1939.
     .F4W9

THE EUROPEAN HERITAGE

While they were subjects of Great Britain, colonists in North America derived much of their income from shipbuilding, seaborne trade, and fisheries. However, because the defense of these and other interests was largely a British burden, they learned to sail rather than to fight ships. For almost 175 years, the only kind of war at sea in which the colonists engaged was privateering. Consequently, while some of the works cited herein deal with the British warship they fought after 4 July 1776, most of them concern the development of the sailing ship. In addition, attention is paid to the French and Spanish colonies in America. Last, note is made of the divergence of interests between colonies and the mother country that eventually led to revolution and war.

This chapter is divided into: A. Seaborne Weapon Systems and Tactics; B. Colonial Expansion and Competition; and C. Revolution Against Mercantilism.

A. SEABORNE WEAPON SYSTEMS AND TACTICS

BOOKS

383. D27
      .A4

Albert, Marvin H. *Broadsides and Boarders*. N.Y.: Appleton, 1957. Fighting under sail.

384. VM15
      .A6

Anderson, Romola, and R.C. Anderson. *The Sailing Ship: Six Thousand Years of History*, new ed. N.Y.: Norton, 1963.

385. VA454
      .A67

Archibald, Edward H.H. *The Wooden Fighting Ship in the Royal Navy, A.D. 897-1860*. London: Blandford, 1968.

386. DA450
      .B4

Belloc, Hilaire. *James II*. Phila.: Lippincott, 1928. As the Duke of York, James greatly influenced the tactics of naval warfare.

387. VM307
      .B6

Bloomster, Edgar L. *Sailing and Small Craft Down the Ages*, rev. ed. Annapolis, Md.: USNI, 1969.

388. D57
      .C25

Cambridge Ancient History, 12 vols. Cambridge, England: UP, 1924-1939.

389. UF565
      .E9C5

Cipolla, Carlo M. *Guns, Sails, and Empires*. N.Y.: Random House, 1966.

390. HC240   Clapham, J.H., and Eileen Power, eds. *The Cam-*
      .C3   *bridge Economic History of Europe from the De-*
              cline of the Roman Empire, 6 vols. Cambridge,
              England: UP, 1941.

391. VM15   Clowes, Geoffrey S.L. *Sailing Ships: Their His-*
      .C68   *tory and Development*, 2nd ed., 2 parts. Part I.
              Historical Notes. London: HMSO, 1932.

392. UF520   Comprato, F.C. *Age of Great Guns: Cannon Kings*
      .C7   *and Cannoners Who Forged the Firepower of*
              Artillery. Harrisburg, Pa.: Stackpole, 1965.
              Good for the period after Napoleon.

393. V169   Creswell, John. *British Admirals of the Eigh-*
      .C7   *teenth Century: Tactics in Battle*. Hamden,
              Conn.: Shoe String P., 1972.

394. U39   _____. *Generals and Admirals: The Story of*
      .C74   *Amphibious Command*. London: Longmans, 1952.

395. REF   Cucari, Attilio. *Sailing Ships*. Chicago: Rand
      VM15   McNally, 1978.
      .C8613

396. F1035.5 Downey, Fairfax B. *Louisbourg: Key to a Conti-*
      .L8D6   *nent*. Englewood Cliffs, N.J.: Prentice-Hall,
              1965.

397. VM23   Goldenberg, Joseph A. *Shipbuilding in Colonial*
      .G64   *America*. Charlottlesville: UP of Virginia, 1976.

398. DA88   Graham, Gerald S. *The Politics of Naval Suprem-*
      .G7   *acy: Studies in British Maritime Ascendancy*.
              Cambridge, England: UP, 1965.

399. V765   Hovgaard, William. *Modern History of Warships*.
      .H6   London: E. & F. Spon, 1920.

400. E105   _____. *Voyages of the Norseman to America*.
      .H89   N.Y.: 1914; rpt. Kraus, 1979.

401. VK23   Laing, Alexander. *The American Heritage History*
      .L29   *of Seafaring America*. Annapolis, Md.: NIP,
              1974.

402. VF57   Lewis, Michael. *Armada Guns: A Comparative*
      .L4   *Study of English and Spanish Armaments*. London:
              Allen & Unwin, 1961.

403. VA454   _____. *The Navy of Britain: A Historical*
     .L595   *Portrait*. London: Allen & Unwin, 1948.

404. VB315   _____. *England's Sea-Officers: The Story of*
     .G7L4   *the Naval Profession*. London: Allen & Unwin,
                   1939.

405. V750   Macintyre, Donald G., and Basil W. Bathe. *Man-*
     .M32   *of-War: A History of the Combat Vessel*. N.Y.:
                   McGraw-Hill, 1969.

406. D27   Mahan, Alfred T. *The Influence of Sea Power upon*
     .M21   *History, 1660-1783*. Boston: Little, Brown, 1890.

407. VA454   Marcus, Geoffrey J. *A Naval History of England*,
     .M32   3 vols. London: Longmans, Green, 1961. Vol. 1.
                   The Formative Centuries.

408. C550   May, William E., and P.G.W. Annis. *Swords for*
     .G74   *Sea Service*, 2 vols. London: HMSO, 1970.

409. VM25   Morrison, John H. *History of New York Ship*
     .N5M8   *Yards*. N.Y.: William F. Sametz, 1909; rpt.,
                   Pt. Washington, N.Y.: J.J. Friedman, 1970.

410. VM16   Morrison, John S., and R.T. Williams. *Greek*
     .M67   *Oared Ships, 900-322 B.C.* London: Cambridge
                   UP, 1968.

411. VF15   Padfield, Peter. *Guns at Sea*. N.Y.: St. Martin,
     .P33   1974.

412. V765   _____. *The Battleship Era*. N.Y.: McKay, 1972.
     .P33   Since the 1500s.

413. DA86   Penn, Christopher D. *The Navy Under the Early*
     .P37   *Stuarts*. London: Hogg, 1920.

414. PR3618   Pollard, Richard. *Pepys: A Biography*. N.Y.:
     .P205   Holt, Rinehart and Winston, 1974.

415. U800   Pope, Dudley. *Guns: From the Invention of Gun-*
     .P6   *powder to the Twentieth Century*. N.Y.:
                   Delacorte, 1965.

416. V27   Robertson, Frederick L. *The Evolution of Naval*
     .R59   *Armament*. London: H.T. Storey, 1968.

417. V167   Robison, Samuel S. *A History of Naval Tactics*
     .R6   *from 1530 to 1930*. Annapolis, Md.: USNI, 1942.

418. V210   Roland, Alex. *Underwater Warfare in the Age of*
     .R64   *Sail*. Bloomington: Indiana UP, 1977.

419. HF3025 Shepherd, James F., and Gary M. Walton. *Ship-*
     .S717   *ping, Maritime Trade, and the Economic Develop-*
             ment of Colonial North America. Cambridge:
             Cambridge UP, 1972.

420. V103   Southworth, John V. *War at Sea*, 3 vols. N.Y.:
     .S64   Twayne, 1968-1972.

421. VM365   Sueter, Murray F. *The Evolution of the Submarine*
     .S8   *Boat, Mine, and Torpedo from the Sixteenth Cen-*
             tury to the Present Time. Portsmouth, England:
             J. Griffin & Co., 1907. A classic.

422. V61   Warner, Oliver. *Command at Sea: Fighting Ad-*
     .W37   *mirals from Hawke to Nimitz*. N.Y.: St. Martin,
             1976.

423. D27   _____. *Great Sea Battles*. N.Y.: Macmillan,
     .W35   1963. Especially good for tactics.

424. DA77   Waters, David W. *Notes on the Convoy System of*
     .W36   *Naval Warfare, Thirteenth to the Twentieth Cen-*
             turies. Ottowa: E. Cloutier, 1957.

425. DA87.1 Whipple, Addison B.C. *Fighting Sail*. Alexandria,
     .N4W55 Va.: Time-Life Books, 1978.

426. D25   Whitehouse, Arthur "Arch" G.J. *Amphibious Opera-*
     .5.W45   *tions*. GCNY: Doubleday, 1963.

427. VA454   Wilcox, Leslie A. *Mr. Pepys' Navy*. South
     .W88   Brunswick, N.J.: A.S. Barnes, 1968.

ARTICLES

428.   Chard, Donald G. "The Impact of French Priva-
             teering on New England, 1689-1713," AN 35
             (July 1975):153-65.

429. U39   Ropp, Theodore. "Continental Doctrines of Sea
     .E2   Power," Edward M. Earle, ed. *Makers of Modern*
             Strategy: Military Thought from Machiavelli to
             Hitler. Princeton: PUP, 1943, pp. 446-56. Use
             of cruiser warfare by continental powers
             against sea powers while defeating the enemy
             on land.

430.   Sheehan, J.M. "Samuel Pepys, Naval Administrator Extraordinary," USNIP 74 (July 1948):865-75.

431.   Syrett, David. "The Methodology of British Amphibious Operations during the Seven Years' and American Wars," MM 58 (Aug. 1972):269-80.

B. COLONIAL EXPANSION AND COMPETITION

BOOKS

432. HF3025   Beer, George L. *The Commercial Policy of*
     .B43   *England Toward the American Colonies*. N.Y.: Columbia UP, 1893.

433. E178   Bourne, Edward G. *Spain in America, 1450-1580*.
     .A54   N.Y.: Harper, 1905.

434. DP538   Boxer, Charles R. *Portuguese Seaborne Empire,*
     .B68   *1415-1825*. N.Y.: Knopf, 1969.

435. JV2511   _____. *The Dutch Seaborne Empire, 1600-1800*.
     .D67   N.Y.: Knopf, 1965.

436. DA483   Brown, Peter D. *William Pitt, Earl of Chat-*
     .P6B76   *ham*.... Boston: Allen & Unwin, 1978.

437. HB91   Buck, Philip. *The Politics of Mercantilism*.
     .B8   N.Y.: Holt, 1942.

438. DA30   *Cambridge History of the British Empire*, 8
     .C3   vols. Cambridge, England: UP, 1929- . Vol. 1 is an excellent study of the Anglo-French colonial struggle.

439. E178   Carse, Robert. *The Seafarers: A History of*
     .C3   *Maritime America, 1620-1820*. N.Y.: Harper, 1964.

440. HC275   Cole, Charles W. *French Mercantilism, 1683-*
     .C64   *1700*. N.Y.: Octagon, 1943, 1965.

441. HB105   _____. *Colbert and a Century of French Mer-*
     .C6C6   *cantilism*, 2 vols. Columbia UP, 1939; rpt., Hamden, Conn.: Archon Books, 1964. -

442. DA87   Corbett, Julian S. *England in the Seven Years'*
     .C7   *War*, 2 vols. London: Longmans, 1907. The standard British authority.

443. DP583   Diffle, Bailey, and George D. Winius. *Founda-*
     .D53   *tions of the Portuguese Empire, 1415-1580.*
              Minneapolis: U. of Minn. P., 1977.

444. E199   Donaldson, Gordon. *Battle for a Continent:*
     .D66   *Quebec, 1759.* GCNY: Doubleday, 1973.

445. E199   Duffy, James. *Shipwreck and Empire: Being an*
     .D66   *Account of Portuguese Maritime Disasters in a*
              Century of Decline. Cambridge: HUP, 1955.

446. E199   Furneaux, Rupert. *The Seven Years' War.* London:
     .F98   Hart-Davis MacGibbon, 1973.

447. E45   Graham, Gerald S. *Empire of the North Atlantic:*
     .G7   *The Maritime Struggle for North America.* Toron-
              to: U. of Toronto P., 1950. Three centuries of
              colonial expansion and competition.

448. GC63   Guberlet, Muriel L. *Explorers of the Sea: Famous*
     .G8   *Oceanographic Expeditions.* N.Y.: Ronald P.,
              1964.

449. VM15   Jobe, Joseph, ed. *The Great Age of Sail.* Annap-
     .J613   olis, Md.: NIP, 1971. From the Age of Dis-
              covery.

450. UA15   Katcher, Philip R.N. *Armies of the American*
     .K36   *Wars, 1753-1815.* N.Y.: Hastings House, 1975.

451. JV1011   Knorr, Klaus E. *British Colonial Theories*
     .K6   *1570-1850.* Chicago: U. of Chicago P., 1941.

452. E199   Kopperman, Paul E. *Braddock at the Monongahela.*
     .K77   Pittsburgh: U. of Pittsburgh P., 1976.

453. DS33   Lach, Donald F. *Asia in the Making of Europe,*
     .1.L3   2 vols. Chicago: U. of Chicago P., 1965.

454. F1410   Lang, James. *Conquest and Commerce: Spain and*
     .L29   *England in the Americas.* N.Y.: Academic P.,
              1975.

455. E188   Lawson, Don. *The Colonial Wars: Prelude to the*
     .L37   *American Revolution... 1689-1763.* N.Y.:
              Abelard-Schuman, 1972.

456. V210   MacIntyre, Donald G.F.W. *Fighting Under the Sea.*
     .M23   N.Y.: Norton, 1966. Underwater warfare from
              1578 through World War II, in popular style.

457. HF3505   Minchinton, W.E., ed. *The Growth of English*
     .4.M48   *Overseas Trade in the Seventeenth and Eigh-*
               teenth Centuries. London: Methuen, 1969.

458. E121   Morison, Samuel E. *The European Discovery of*
     .M60   *America: The Southern Voyages, A.D. 1492-1616.*
               N.Y.: Oxford UP, 1974.

459. E101   _____. *The European Discovery of America:*
     .M85   *The Northern Voyages, A.D. 500-1600.* N.Y.:
               Oxford UP, 1971.

460. G80   Nowell, Charles E. *The Great Discoveries and*
     .N6   *the First Colonial Empires.* Ithaca: Cornell
               UP, 1954.

461. JX5261   Pares, R. *Colonial Blockade and Neutral Rights,*
     .G7P3   *1739-1763.* Oxford: Clarendon P., 1938.

462. F1621   _____. *War and Trade in the West Indies,*
     .P32   *1739-1763.* Oxford: Clarendon P., 1938.

463. F1030   Parkman, Francis. *Montcalm and Wolfe: France*
     .P25   *and England in North America,* 2 vols. Boston:
               Little, Brown, 1899.

464. JV165   Parry, John H. *Trade and Dominion: The European*
     .P35   *Overseas Empires in the Eighteenth Century.*
               N.Y.: Praeger, 1971.

465. F1410   _____. *The Spanish Seaborne Empire.* London:
     .P63   Hutchinson, 1966.

466. JV61   _____. *Europe and a Wider World,* *1415-1715.*
     .P3   London: Hutchinson, 1949.

467. G95   Penrose, Boies. *Travel and Discovery in the*
     .P45   *Renaissance, 1420-1620.* Cambridge: HUP, 1952.

468. D279   Powley, Edward B. *The Naval Side of King Wil-*
     .5.P69   *liam's War.* Hamden, Conn.: Shoe String P.,
               1974.

469. DA87   Richmond, Herbert. *The Navy in the War of 1739-*
     .R5   *1748,* 3 vols. Cambridge: UP, 1920.

470. E18   Savelle, Max. *Empires to Nations: Expansion in*
     .S33   *America, 1713-1824.* Minneapolis: U. of Minne-
               sota P., 1974.

471. DA483   Sherrard, Owen A. *Lord Chatham: Pitt and the*
     .P6S53   *Seven Years' War.* London: Bodley Head, 1955.

472. JV1016   Steele, I.K. *Politics of Colonial Policy: Board*
     .S73   *of Trade in Colonial Administration, 1696-1720.*
               Oxford: Clarendon P., 1968.

473. HC125   Stein, Stanley, and Barbara H. Stein. *The Colo-*
     .S76   *nial Heritage of Latin America....* N.Y.: Oxford
               UP, 1970.

474. HC45   Wallerstein, Immanuel M. *The Modern World-*
     .W35   *System: Capitalist Agriculture and the Origins*
               of the European World-Economy in the Sixteenth
               Century. N.Y.: Academic P., 1974.

475. DA86   Woodrooffe, Thomas. *Vantage at Sea: England's*
     .W62   *Emergence as an Oceanic Power.* N.Y.: St. Martin,
               1958.

476. G95   Wright, Louis B. *Gold, Glory, and the Gospel:*
     .W73   *The Adventurous Lives and Times of the Renais-*
               sance Explorers. N.Y.: Academic P., 1970.

477. F1030   Wrong, George M. *The Rise and Fall of New*
     .W95   *France*, 2 vols. N.Y.: Macmillan, 1928.

DISSERTATIONS AND THESES

478.   Day, Ronnie M. "Neptune's Forge: The Evolution
               of the Royal Navy under the Early Tudors, 1485-
               1547," Texas Christian U., 1971.

479.   Peterson, Charles W. "English and Danish Naval
               Strategy in the Seventeenth Century," U. of
               Maine, 1975.

480.   Pollitt, Roland L. "The Elizabethan Navy Board:
               A Study in Administrative Evolution," North-
               western U., 1968.

ARTICLES

481.   Hess, Andrew C. "The Evolution of the Ottoman
               Seaborne Empire in the Age of Oceanic Discover-
               ies, 1453-1525," AHR 75 (Dec. 1970):1892-1919.

482.   Kleber, Louis C. "Britain and France in North
               America." *History Today* 34 (Dec. 1974):819-36.

483.   Lane, Frederic C. "Venetian Shipping during the Commercial Revolution," AHR 38 (Jan. 1933): 219-39.

484.   Riker, Thad W. "The Politics Behind Braddock's Expedition," AHR 13 (July 1908):742-52.

485.   Scammel, G.V. "Manning the English Merchant Service in the Sixteenth Century," MM 56 (May 1970):131-54.

486.   Scott, H.M. "The Importance of Bourbon Naval Reconstruction to the Strategy of Choiseul after the Seven Years' War," IHR 1 (Jan. 1979): 17-35.

487.   Thompson, I.A.A. "Spanish Armada Guns," MM 62 (May 1976):355-71.

488.   Washington, George. "The Braddock Campaign," AHI 5 (Nov. 1970):4-13.

C. REVOLUTION AGAINST MERCANTILISM

BOOKS

489. VA454   Albion, Robert G. *Forests and Sea Power*. Cam-
      .A6   bridge: HUP, 1926.

490. JV1016   Basye, Arthur H. *The Lords Commissioners of
      .B3   Trade and Plantations, 1748-1782*. New Haven: YUP, 1925.

491. JK128   Becker, Carl L. *The Declaration of Independence: A Study in the History of Political Ideas*. N.Y.:
      .B4   Knopf, 1942.

492. HD9515   Bining, Arthur C. *British Regulation of the Colonial Iron Industry*. Phila.: U. of Pa. P.,
      .B5   1933.

493. DA16   Bolton, Geoffrey C. *Britain's Legacy Overseas*.
      .B6   N.Y.: Oxford UP, 1973.

494. E322   Bowen, Catherine D. *John Adams and the American
      .B68   Revolution*. Boston: Little, Brown, 1950.

495. HC508   Brock, Leslie V. *The Currency of the American Colonies, 1700-1764: A Study in Colonial Finance
      .B7   and Imperial Relations*. N.Y.: Arno P., 1975.

43

496. HB91 Buck, Philip N. *The Continental Congress.*
     .B8   N.Y.: Octagon Books, 1964.

497. F82   Chapin, Howard M. *Rhode Island Privateers in*
     .C483 *King George's War, 1739-1748.* Providence: R.I.
           Hist. Soc., 1926.

498. E210 Christie, Ian R., and Benjamin W. Labaree. *Em-*
     .C54 *pire or Independence, 1760-1776: A British-*
           American Dialogue on the Coming of the American
           Revolution. N.Y.: Norton, 1976.

499. E215 Dickerson, Oliver M. *The Navigation Acts and*
     .1.D53 *the American Revolution.* Phila.: U. of Pa. P.,
           1951.

500. E83.67 Ellis, George W., and John E. Morris. *King*
     .E47 *Philip's War....* N.Y.: Grafton P., 1906.

501. E241 Flood, Charles B. *Rise and Fight Again: Peri-*
     .03F56 *lous Times Along the Road to Independence.*
           N.Y.: Dodd, Mead, 1976.

502. HE587 Harper, Lawrence A. *The English Navigation Laws.*
     .G7H3 N.Y.: Columbia UP, 1939.

503. JV1016 Henretta, James A. *Salutary Neglect: Colonial*
     .H45 *Administration under the Duke of Newcastle.*
           Princeton: PUP, 1972.

504. DA512 Hoffman, Ross J.S. *The Marquis. A Study of Lord*
     .R6H63 *Rockingham, 1730-1782.* N.Y.: Fordham UP, 1973.

505. E210 Knollenberg, Bernhard. *Origin of the American*
     .K65 *Revolution, 1759-1766.* N.Y.: Macmillan, 1960.

506. JK54 Labaree, Leonard W. *Royal Government in America.*
     .L3   New Haven: YUP, 1930.

507. E332 Malone, Dumas. *Jefferson the Virginian.* Boston:
     .M25 Little, Brown, 1948.

508. HD9769 Malone, Joseph J. *Pine Trees and Politics: The*
     .N33U65 *Naval Stores and Forest Policy in Colonial New*
           England, 1691-1775. Seattle: U. of Washington
           P., 1964.

509. E302.6 Miller, John C. *Sam Adams: Pioneer in Propagan-*
     .A2M56 *da.* Standford: Stanford UP, 1936, 1960.

510. E210   _____. *Origins of the American Revolution.*
     .M5   Boston: Little, Brown, 1943.

511. HF3505   Minchinton, W.F., ed. *The Growth of English*
     .4.M48   *Overseas Trade in the Seventeenth and Eighteenth*
                Centuries. London: Methuen, 1969.

512. E208   Mitchell, Broadus. *The Price of Independence: A*
     .M55   *Realistic View of the American Revolution.* N.Y.:
                Oxford UP, 1974.

513. E210   Mullett, Charles F. *Colonial Claims to Home Rule*
     .M95   *(1764-1775): An Essay on Imperial Politics.* Co-
                lumbia: U. of Missouri, 1927.

514. E195   Olson, Alison G., and Richard M. Brown, eds.
     .A55   *Anglo-American Political Relations, 1675-1775.*
                New Brunswick, N.J.: Rutgers UP, 1970.

515. JK31   Rossiter, Clinton L. *Seedtime of the Republic.*
     .R6   N.Y.: Harcourt Brace, 1953.

516. KF361   Russell, Elmer B. *The Review of American Colo-*
     R88   *nial Legislation by the King in Council.* N.Y.:
     1976   c. 1915; rpt., Octagon Books, 1976.

517. HF3025   Schlesinger, Arthur M., Sr. *The Colonial Mer-*
     .S3   *chants and the American Revolution, 1773-1776.*
                N.Y.: Ungar, 1918, 1957.

518. E210   Stout, Neil R. *The Perfect Crisis: The Begin-*
     .S85   *nings of the Revolutionary War.* Washington
                Square, N.Y.: New York UP, 1976.

519. E179.5   Turner, Frederick J. *The Frontier in American*
     .T95   *History.* N.Y.: Holt, 1920.

520. E216   Ubbelohde, Carl. *The Vice-Admiralty Courts and*
     .U22   *the American Revolution.* Chapel Hill: UNCP,
                1960.

521. E302.6   Van Doren, Carl C. *Benjamin Franklin.* N.Y.:
     .F8V32   Viking, 1938.

522. DA505   Watson, John S. *The Reign of George III, 1760-*
     .W38   *1815. Oxford History of England,* v. 12. Oxford:
                Clarendon P., 1960.

523. E215   Weslager, Clinton A. *The Stamp Act Congress.*
     .2.W47   Newark: U. of Delaware P., 1976.

DISSERTATIONS AND THESES

524.   Bullion, John L. "Honor, Trade and Empire: Grevenille's Treasury and 'The American Question,' 1763-1975," U. of Texas, 1977.

ARTICLES

525.   Bell, Herbert C. "The West India Trade before the American Revolution," AHR 22 (Jan. 1917): 272-87.

526.   Hall, Hubert. "Chatham's Colonial Policy," AHR 5 (July 1900):659-75.

527.   Savelle, Max. "The Appearance of an American Attitude toward External Affairs, 1750-1775," AHR 52 (July 1947):655-66.

528.   Williams, Justin. "English Mercantilism and Carolina Naval Stores, 1705-1776," JSH 1 (May 1935):169-85.

FICTION

529.   PS3501   Allen, Hervey. *Anthony Adverse*. N.Y.: Rinehart,
      .L5A58   1933. Travel adventure, 18th century.

530.   P23   Ford, Charles. *Death Sails with Magellan*. N.Y.:
      .F75   Random House, 1937.
      De

531.   PR6011   Forester, Cecil S. *Admiral Hornblower in the*
      .O56A34   *West Indies*. Boston: Little, Brown, 1958. One of the many interesting books in the Hornblower series.

532.   PS3525   Mason, Francis van Wyck. *Manila Galleon*. Boston:
      .A822   Little, Brown, 1961. Circumnavigation of the
      M35   globe, 1740-1744, by Commodore George Anson.

533.   PS3527   Nordhoff, Charles B. *Mutiny on the Bounty*. Bos-
      .O437   ton: Little, Brown, 1932. Mutiny caused by
      M88   harsh discipline.

534.   PS3535   Roberts, Kenneth L. *Oliver Wiswell*. GCNY:
      .O176   Doubleday, 1940. The American Revolution from
      .O45   the Tory viewpoint.

535. PS3535   _____. *Northwest Passage*. GCNY: Doubleday,
     .0176   1937.
     .N67

536. PS3535   _____. *Rabble in Arms*. GCNY: Doubleday,
     .0176   1933.
     .R32

537. PS643   Tyler, Royall. *The Algerian Captive*.... Warpole,
     .A5   N.H.: D. Carlisle, 1797. The horrors of a slave
                ship's voyage.

3

THE WAR OF THE AMERICAN REVOLUTION

BOOKS

538. E322   Adams, John. *The Diary and Autobiography of*
     A3   *John Adams.* Ed. by L.H. Butterfield. Cambridge:
             Belknap Press of HUP, 1961.

539. E182   Albion, Robert G., and Jennie B. Pope. *Sea*
     .A33   *Lanes in Wartime: The American Experience, 1775-*
             1945, 2nd ed., enl. Hamden, Conn.: Archon
             Books, 1969.

540. E208   Alden, John R. *A History of the American Revolu-*
     .A38   *tion.* N.Y.: Knopf, 1969.

541. F213   _____. *The South in the Revolution, 1763-*
     A4   *1789.* Vol. 3 of *The History of the South.*
             Baton Rouge: LSUP, 1957. A standard work on
             this theater.

542. E208   _____. *The American Revolution, 1775-1783.*
     .A35   N.Y.: Harper, 1954.

543. E271   Allen, Gardner W. *A Naval History of the Ameri-*
     .A42   *can Revolution,* 2 vols. Boston: Houghton
             Mifflin, 1913; rpt., Russell, 1962, and Corner
             House, 1970.

544. V858   Anderson, Frank. *Beginning of Modern Submarine*
     .A72   *Warfare Under Captain Lieutenant David Bushnell.*
     1881a   Hamden, Conn.: Anchor Books, 1966. Reproduc-
             tion of rare 1881 pamphlet.

545. E267   Anderson, Troyer S. *The Command of the Howe*
     .A34   *Brothers During the American Revolution.* N.Y.:
             Oxford UP, 1936, 1972.

546. E265   Balch, Thomas.*The French in America During the*
     .B17   *War of Independence of the United States, 1777-*
             1783, 2 vols. Phila.: Porter & Coates, 1891-
             1895.

547. PZ7   Barnes, James. *With the Flag in the Channel.*
     B262   N.Y.: Appleton, 1902. Life of Gustavus
             Conyngham.

548. E353.1   _____. *Commodore Bainbridge: From the Gunroom*
      .B2B2   *to the Quarterdeck*. N.Y.: Appleton, 1897.
                     Covers years 1774-1823.

549. HJ6621   Barrow, Thomas C. *Trade and Empire: the British*
      .B3   *Customs Service in Colonial America, 1660-1775*.
                     Cambridge: HUP, 1967.

550. V162   Baylis, John, and others. *Continental Strategy:*
      .C66   *Theories and Policies*. N.Y.: Holmes & Meier,
                     1975.

551. DA85   Beatson, Robert. *Naval and Military Memoirs of*
      .B3   *Great Britain, from 1727 to 1783*, 6 vols. Lon-
                     don: Longman, Hurst..., 1804.

552. E271   Beattie, Donald W., and J. Richard Collins.
      .B4   *Washington's New England Fleet: Beverly's Role*
                     in Its Origins, 1775-1777. Salem, Mass.: New-
                     comb & Gauss, 1969.

553. E183.7   Bemis, Samuel F. *The Diplomacy of the American*
      .B48   *Revolution*. N.Y.: Appleton-Century, 1935; rpt.,
      v.1   Peter Smith, 1957.

554. E207   Benz, Francis E. *Commodore Barry: Navy Hero*.
      .B2B45   N.Y.: Dodd, Mead, 1950.

555. E267   Billias, George A., ed. *George Washington's*
      .B56   *Opponents: British Generals and Admirals of the*
                     American Revolution. N.Y.: Morrow, 1969. Essays
                     on 12 British leaders.

556. E231   Bird, Harrison. *Attack on Quebec: The American*
      .B5   *Invasion of Canada, 1775*. N.Y.: Oxford UP, 1968.

557. E162   _____. *Navies in the Mountains: The Battles*
      .B5   *on the Waters of Lake Champlain and Lake George*,
                     1609-1814. N.Y.: Oxford UP, 1962.

558. E267   Bowler, R. Arthur. *Logistics in the Failure of*
      .B8   *the British Army in America, 1775-1783*. Prince-
                     ton: PUP, 1975.

559. DA506   Brooke, John. *King George III*. N.Y.: McGraw-
      .A2B75   Hill, 1972.

560. DA483   Brown, Gerald S. *The American Secretary: The*
      .S2B7   *Colonial Policy of Lord George Germain, 1775-*
                     1778. Ann Arbor: U. of Michigan P., 1963.

561. E277   Brown, Wallace. *The Good Americans: The Loyal-*
     .B8   *ists in the American Revolution.* N.Y.: Morrow,
             1969.

562. DA501   Browning, Reed. *The Duke of Newcastle.* New
     .N5B76 Haven: YUP, 1975.

563. E182   Bryant, Samuel W. *The Sea and the States: A*
     .B92   *Maritime History of the American People.* N.Y.:
             Crowell, 1947, 1967.   Includes naval as well as
             maritime history.

564. DC146   Buckman, Peter. *Lafayette: A Biography.* N.Y.:
     .L2B78 Padding P., 1977.

565. E308   Burnett, Edmund C. *The Continental Congress.*
     .B98   N.Y.: Macmillan, 1941.

566. E277   Calhoon, Robert M. *The Loyalists in Revolution-*
     .C24   *ary America.* N.Y.: Harcourt Brace Jovanovich,
             1973.

567. DC52   Caron, Max. *Admiral De Grasse: One of the Great*
     .G8C33 *Forgotten Men.* Boston: Four Seas, 1924.

568. E230   Carrington, Henry B. *Battles of the American*
     .C32   *Revolution, 1775-1781.* N.Y.: Barnes, 1876; rpt.,
             Arno, 1968.

569. VA58   Carrison, Daniel J. *The United States Navy.*
     .C3   N.Y.: Praeger, 1968.

570. VA144   Chapelle, Howard I. *The Search for Speed Under*
     .C28   *Sail, 1700-1855.* N.Y.: Norton, 1967.

571. VA56   _____. *The American Sailing Navy.* N.Y.:
     .C5   Norton, 1949.

572. E237   Chidsey, Donald B. *Victory at Yorktown.* N.Y.:
     .C47   Crown, 1962.

573. E182   _____. *The American Privateers.* N.Y.: Dodd,
     .C5   Mead, 1962.

574. E182   Clark, Thomas. *Naval History of the United*
     .C60   *States, from the Commencement of the Revolu-*
             tionary War to the Present Time, 2 vols., 2d
             ed. Phila.: M. Carey, 1814.   The first attempt
             to write a history of the American Navy, Clark's
             book is virtually a primary source work for the
             Revolutionary era.

575. E207   Clark, William B. *Gallant John Barry, 1745-*
     .B2C5   *1803.* N.Y.: Macmillan, 1938.

576. E207   _____. *Captain Dauntless: The Story of*
     .B48C6 *Nicholas Biddle of the Continental Navy.*
             Baton Rouge: LSUP, 1949.

577. E207   _____. *The First* Saratoga: *Being the Saga of*
     .Y6C5   *John Young and His Sloop-of-War.* Baton Rouge:
             LSUP, 1953.

578. E302.6 _____. *Ben Franklin's Privateers: A Naval*
     .F8C55 *Epic of the American Revolution.* Baton Rouge:
             LSUP, 1956.

579. E207   _____. *Lambert Wickes: Sea Raider and Diplo-*
     .W63C7 *mat.* New Haven: YUP, 1932.

580. E271   _____. *George Washington's Navy.* Baton
     .C57   Rouge: LSUP, 1960.

581. DA70   Clowes, William L. *The Royal Navy,* 7 vols.
     .C68   London: Sampson Low, Marston, 1897-1903, 1966.

582. E230   Coakley, Robert W., and Stetson Conn. *The War*
     .C62   *of the American Revolution.* Wash.: GPO, 1975.

583. E231   Codman, John. *Arnold's Expedition to Quebec.*
     .C671   N.Y.: Macmillan, 1902.

584. E271   Coggins, Jack. *Ships and Seamen of the American*
     C.63   *Revolution: Vessels, Crews, Weapons, Gear, Nav-*
             al Tactics, and Actions of the War for Indepen-
             dence. Harrisburg, Pa.: Stackpole Books, 1969.

585. E182   Cooper, James F. *Lives of Distinguished Ameri-*
     .C85   *can Naval Officers,* 2 vols. Phila.: Carey and
             Hart, 1846. Includes lengthy biographies of
             Jones and Dale.

586. E241   Davis, Burke. *The Campaign That Won America:*
     .Y6D28 *The Story of Yorktown.* N.Y.: Dial, 1970

587. E210   Donoughue, Bernard. *British Politics and the*
     .D6   *American Revolution: The Path to War, 1773-*
             1775. N.Y.: St. Martin, 1965.

588. E265   Dull, Jonathan. *The French Navy and American*
     .C85   *Independence: A Study of Arms and Diplomacy,*
             1774-1787. Princeton: PUP, 1975.

589. UG497   Duncan, Robert C. *America's Use of Sea Mines.*
     .U6DS   White Oak, Md.: U.S. Naval Ordnance Laboratory,
                1962. From the American Revolution to date of
                publication.

590. E269   Dupuy, R. Ernest, Gay Hammerman, and Grace P.
     .F67D86   Hayes. *The American Revolution: A Global War.*
                N.Y.: McKay, 1977.

591. E271   Dupuy, Trevor N., and Grace P. Hayes. *The Mili-
     .D85   tary History of Revolutionary War Naval Bat-
                tles.* N.Y.: Watts, 1970.

592. E241   Eckenrode, Hamilton J. *The Story of the Campaign
     .Y6E32   and Siege of Yorktown.* Wash.: GPO, 1931.

593. H31.56   Edler, Fredrich. *The Dutch Republic and the
     ser. 29   American Revolution.* Baltimore: Johns Hopkins
     Wc.2   P., 1911.

594. E230   Evans, R.E. *The War of American Independence.*
     .E92   N.Y.: Cambridge UP, 1976.

595. E182   Ferguson, Eugene S., *Truxtun of the* Constella-
     .T7F43   tion: *The Life of Commodore Thomas Truxtun,
                U.S. Navy, 1755-1822.* Baltimore: Johns Hopkins
                P., 1956.

596. E207   Field, Edward. *Esek Hopkins, Commander-in-Chief
     .H7F4   of the Continental Navy During the American
                Revolution, 1775-1778.* Providence: Preston &
                Rounds, 1898.

597. DS63.2   Field, James A. *Americans and the Mediterranean
     .U5F47   World, 1776-1882.* Princeton: PUP, 1969.

598. E207   Fink, Leo G. *Barry or Jones, "Father of the
     .B2F5   United States Navy": Historical Reconnaissance.*
                Phila.: Jefferies and Manz, 1962. Leans toward
                Barry.

599. E241   Fleming, Thomas. *Beat the Last Drum: The Siege
     .Y6F55   of Yorktown.* N.Y.: St. Martin, 1963.

600. E312.2   Flexner, James T. *George Washington in the
     F69   American Revolution, 1775-1783.* Boston: Little,
                Brown, 1968.

601. E312.2   _____. *George Washington: The Forge of Ex-
     F6   perience, 1732-1775.* Boston: Little, Brown,
                1968.

602. E241
     .03F56

Flood, Charles B. *Rise and Fight Again: Perilous Times Along the Road to Independence*. N.Y.: Dodd, Mead, 1976.

603. E353.1
     .B26F7

Footner, Hulbert. *Sailor of Fortune: The Life and Adventures of Commodore Barney, U.S.N.* N.Y.: Harper, 1940.

604. E127
     .F67

Foss, M. *Undreamed Shores: England's Wasted Empire in America*. N.Y.: Scribner, 1974.

605. E271
     .F68

Fowler, William M., Jr. *Rebels Under Sail: The American Navy during the Revolution*. N.Y.: Scribner, 1976. The best single-volume study.

606. E312
     .F82

Freeman, Douglas S. *George Washington: A Biography*, 7 vols. N.Y.: Scribner, 1948-1957. Most pertinent are vols. 4 & 5.

607. E208
     .F73

French, Allen. *The First Year of the American Revolution*. Boston: Houghton Mifflin, 1934, 1961, 1968. Heavily downgrades King George III and his ministers.

608. E182
     .F81

Frost, Holloway H. *We Build a Navy*. Annapolis, Md.: USNI, 1929.

609. E233
     .F9

Furneaux, Rupert. *Saratoga: The Decisive Battle*. N.Y.: Stein & Day, 1971.

610. VB57
     .G36

Gardiner, Leslie. *The British Admiralty*. Annapolis, Md.: USNI, 1968. An administrative history of the Royal Navy including the period overseen by the Earl of Sandwich.

611. E207
     .G5

Gipson, Laurence H. *The Coming of the Revolution, 1763-1775*. N.Y.: Harper, 1954. Chronologically, the volume ahead of Alden's study.

612. DA67.1
     .B8G58

Glover, Michael. *General Burgoyne in Canada and America: Scapegoat for a System*. London: Gordon & Cremonesi, 1976.

613. VM23
     .G64

Goldenberg, Joseph A. *Shipbuilding in Colonial America*. Published for the Mariners Museum, Newport News, Va.: by the UP of Virginia, Charlottesville, 1976.

614. FD202
     .G67

Gordon, Maurice. *Naval and Maritime Medicine During the American Revolution*. Ventnor, N.J.: Ventnor Publishers, 1978.

615. E182
.H93G7
Grant, Bruce. *Isaac Hull, Captain of* Old Ironsides. Chicago: Pellegrini & Cudahy, 1947.

616. E271
.M27
Greenwood, Isaac J. *Captain John Manley: Second-in-Rank in the United States Navy, 1776-1783.* Boston: Goodspeed, 1915; rpt., 1970.

617. E172
.A60
Griffin, Martin I.J. *Commodore John Barry: The Father of the American Navy: The Record of His Services for our Country.* Phila.: The Author, 1902, 1903.

618. E208
.G83
Griffith, Samuel B., II. *In Defense of the Public Liberty: Britain, America, and the Struggle for Independence: From 1760 to the Surrender at Yorktown in 1781.* GCNY: Doubleday, 1976.

619. E267
.G86
Gruber, Ira D. *The Howe Brothers and the American Revolution.* N.Y.: Atheneum, 1972.

620. E207
.B2G92
Gurn, Joseph. *Commodore John Barry: Father of the American Navy.* N.Y.: P.J. Kennedy, 1933.

621. VA56
.G8
Guthridge, Leonard F., and Jay D. Smith. *The Commodores: The United States Navy in the Age of Sail.* N.Y.: Harper, 1969.

622. E183.8
.M8H3
Hall, Luella A. *The United States and Morocco, 1776-1956.* Metuchen, N.J.: Scarecrow, 1971.

623. E182
.H212
Hammersly, Sydney E. *The Lake Champlain Naval Battles of 1776-1814.* Hudson-Champlain, 1959, 350th Anniversary Edition. Waterford, N.Y.: 1959.

624. E353.1
.B2H3
Harris, Thomas. *The Life and Services of William Bainbridge, U.S.N.* Phila.: Carey, Lea, & Blanchard, 1837.

625. JV1016
.H45
Henretta, James A. *Salutary Neglect: Colonial Administration under the Duke of Newcastle.* Princeton: PUP, 1972.

626. E210
.H63
Higginbotham, Don. *The War of American Independence: Military Attitudes, Policies, and Practice, 1763-1789.* N.Y.: Macmillan, 1971.

627. E204
.R4
_____, ed. *Reconsiderations on the Revolutionary War: Selected Essays.* Westport, Conn.: Greenwood, 1978.

628. Micro   Hough, Franklin B., ed. *The Siege of Savannah*
    973.3   *by the Combined American and French Forces*
    Am3   *under the Command of Gen. Lincoln and the Count*
    366-6   *D'Estaing in the Autumn of 1779.* Albany, N.Y.:
               1779.

629. E271   Howard, James L. *Seth Harding, Mariner: A Naval*
    .H72   *Picture of the Revolution.* New Haven: YUP, 1930.

630. V210   Hoyt, Edwin P. *From the Turtle to the Nautilus:*
    .H66   *The Story of Submarines.* Boston: Little, Brown,
               1963.

631. E271   Jackson, John W. *The Pennsylvania Navy, 1775-*
    .J26   *1781: The Defense of the Delaware.* New Bruns-
               wick, N.J.: Rutgers UP, 1974.

632. E271   James, William M. *The British Navy in Adversity:*
    .J28   *A Study of the War of American Independence.*
               London: Longmans, Green, 1926, rpt., Russell &
               Russell, 1970. Includes administration as well
               as operations.

633. E209   Jameson, John F. *The American Revolution Con-*
    .J33   *sidered as a Social Movement.* Princeton: PUP,
               1926; rpt., P. Smith, 1950.

634. DA47.1   Jarrett, Derek. *The Begetters of Revolution:*
    .J36   *England's Involvement with France, 1759-1789.*
               Totowa, N.J.: Rowman & Littlefield, 1973.

635. E195   Jensen, Merrill. *The Founding of a Nation: A*
    .J4   *History of the American Revolution, 1763-1776.*
               N.Y.: Oxford UP, 1968.

636. JK131   _____. *The Articles of Confederation: An*
    .J4   *Interpretation of the Social and Constitutional*
               History of the American Revolution, 1774-1781.
               Madison: U. of Wisconsin P., 1940.

637. E241   Johnston, Henry P. *The Yorktown Campaign and*
    .Y657   *the Surrender of Cornwallis, 1781.* N.Y.: Harper,
               1881.

638. E195   Kammen, Michael G. *A Rope of Sand: The Colonial*
    .K28   *Agents, British Politics, and the American Rev-*
               olution. Ithaca: Cornell UP, 1968.

639. E265   Kennett, Lee. *The French Forces in America,*
     .K37   *1780-1783.* Westport, Conn.: Greenwood, 1977.
             Especially good on how the French provided
             their logistic support.

640. HJ6645 King, Irving H. *George Washington's Coast Guard.*
     .K5   Annapolis, Md.: NIP, 1978.

641. E210   Knollenberg, Bernhard. *Origin of the American*
     .K65   *Revolution, 1759-1766.* N.Y.: Macmillan, 1960.

642. E312   Knox, Dudley W. *The Naval Genius of George*
     .23.K67 *Washington.* Boston: Houghton Mifflin, 1932.

643. E215.7 Labaree, Benjamin W. *The Boston Tea Party.* N.Y.:
     .L3   Oxford UP, 1964.

644. E241   Landers, Howard L. *The Virginia Campaign and*
     .Y6U38   *the Blockade and Siege of Yorktown 1781.* Wash.:
             U.S. Army War College, 1931.

645. F2178   Langley, Lester D. *Struggle for the American*
     .U6L36   *Mediterranean: United States-European Rivalry*
             in the Gulf-Caribbean, 1774-1904. Athens: U.
             of Georgia P., 1976.

646. E271   Larrabee, Harold A. *Decision at the Chesapeake.*
     .L3   N.Y.: Potter, 1964.

647. E241   Lawrence, Alexander A. *Storm over Savannah: The*
     .S26L3   *Story of Count D'Estaing and the Siege of the*
             Town in 1779, rev. ed. Athens: U. of Georgia P.,
             1968. The operation failed.

648. E265   Lewis, Charles L. *Admiral De Grasse and Ameri-*
     .L45   *can Independence.* Annapolis, Md.: USNI, 1945.

649. VA454   Lewis, Michael A. *The History of the British*
     .L59   *Navy.* Fairlawn, N.J.: Essential Books, 1954.

650. E207   Lorenz, Lincoln. *John Paul Jones: Fighter for*
     .J7L8   *Freedom and Glory.* Annapolis, Md.: USNI, 1943;
             rpt., Kraus, 1969.

651. F90   Loughrey, Mary E. *France and Rhode Island,*
     .F7L6   *1686-1800.* N.Y.: King's Crown P., 1944.

652. VA65   Lundeberg, Philip K. *The Continental Gunboat*
     .P544L8 Philadelphia *and the Northern Campaign of 1776.*
             Wash.: Smithsonian Institution P., 1966.

56

653. V856.5   _____. *Samuel Colt's Submarine Battery*.
     .U6L86   Wash.: Smithsonian Institution P., 1974.

654. E271   McCusker, John J. Alfred: *The First Continental*
     .M17   *Flagship. 1775-1778*. Wash.: Smithsonian Insti-
                   tution P., 1973.

655. E207   Mackenzie, Alexander S. *Life of Paul Jones*, 2
     .J7M14   vols. Boston: Hilliard, Gray, 1841.

656. E208   Mackesy, Piers. *The War for America, 1775-1783*.
     .M14   Cambridge: HUP, 1964.

657. E207   Maclay, Edgar S. *Moses Brown: Captain, USN*.
     .B87M16   N.Y.: Baker & Taylor, 1904.

658. E182   _____. *A History of American Privateers*.
     .M16   N.Y.: Appleton, 1899, 1967.

659. D295   Madariaga, Isabel de. *Britain, Russia, and the*
     .M23   *Armed Neutrality of 1780*. New Haven: YUP, 1962.

660. E271   Mahan, Alfred T. *The Major Operations of the*
     .M22   *Navies in the War of American Independence*.
                   Boston: Little, Brown, 1913; rpt., Greenwood,
                   1969.

661. E210   Maier, Pauline. *From Resistance to Revolution:*
     .M27   *Colonial Radicals and the Development of Ameri-*
                   can Opposition to Britain, 1765-1776. N.Y.:
                   Knopf, 1972.

662. E332   Malone, Dumas. *Jefferson and His Time*. Boston:
     .M25   Little, Brown, 1948-1974. Vol. 2 of *Jefferson*
     v.2   *and the Rights of Man* (1951).

663. HD9769   Malone, Joseph J. *Pine Trees and Politics: The*
     .N33U65   *Naval Stores and Forest Policy in Colonial New*
                   England, 1691-1775. Seattle: U. of Washington
                   P., 1964.

664. DC145   Manceron, Claude. *The Wind from America: Nec-*
     .M3513   *ker's Defeat and Victory at Yorktown, 1778-*
     1977   *1782*. N.Y.: Knopf, 1978.
     v.2

665. VA454   Marcus, Godfrey J. *Heart of Oak: A Survey of*
     .M319   *British Sea Power in the Georgian Era*. N.Y.:
                   Oxford UP, 1975. Covers the years 1750-1815.

57

666. F99   Middlebrook, Louis F. *History of Maritime Con-*
     .M63   *necticut During the American Revolution, 1775-*
              1783, 2 vols. Salem, Mass.: Essex Institute,
              1925.

667. E210   Miller, John C. *Origins of the American Revolu-*
     .M5   *tion*. Boston: Little, Brown, 1943.

668. E271   Miller, Nathan. *Sea of Glory: The Continental*
     .M52   *Navy Fights for Independence, 1775-1783*. N.Y.:
              McKay, 1974. Journalistic and sometimes care-
              less with facts.

669. E320   Mintz, Max M. *Gouverneur Morris and the Ameri-*
     .6.M7M5 *can Revolution*. Norman: U. of Oklahoma P., 1970.

670. E208   Mitchell, Broadus. *The Price of Independence:*
     .M55   *A Realistic View of the American Revolution*.
              N.Y.: Oxford UP, 1974.

671. E302.6   _____. *Alexander Hamilton: The Revolutionary*
     .H2M62   *Years*. N.Y.: Crowell, 1970.

672. E230   Mitchell, Joseph B. *Decisive Battles of the*
     .M5   *American Revolution*. N.Y.: Putnam, 1962.

673. E303   Montross, Lynn. *The Reluctant Rebels: The Story*
     .M82   *of the Continental Congress, 1774-1789*. N.Y.:
              Harper, 1970.

674. E271   Morgan, William J. *Captains to the Northward:*
     .M67   *The New England Captains in the Continental Na-*
              vy. Barre, Mass.: Barre Gazette, 1959.

675. E207   Morison, Samuel E. *John Paul Jones: A Sailor's*
     .J7M6   *Biography*. Boston: Little, Brown, 1959. The
              best of more than 30 biographies.

676. HE745   Morris, James H. *Our Maritime Heritage: Mari-*
     .M72   *time Developments and Their Impact on American*
              Life. Wash.: UP of America, 1979.

677. E269   Nell, William C. *Services of Colored Americans*
     .N3N45   *in the Wars of 1776 and 1812*. Boston: R.W.
              Wallcot, 1852.

678. U815   Neumann, George C. *The History of Weapons of*
     .N4   *the American Revolution*. N.Y.: Bonanza Books,
              1967.

58

679. E303   Nevins, Allan. *The American States During and*
     .N52   *After the Revolution, 1775-1789.* N.Y.: Macmil-
               lan, 1924.

680. E233   Nickerson, Hoffman. *The Turning Point of the*
     .N63   *Revolution: Or Burgoyne in America.* Boston:
               Houghton Mifflin, 1928. Still the classic
               study of the battles and tactics of Burgoyne's
               campaign.

681. E353.1   Paine, Ralph D. *Joshua Barney: A Forgotten Hero*
     .B26P2   *of Blue Water.* N.Y.: Century, 1924.

682. PS3531   _____. *Privateers of '76.* Phila.: Penn Pub.,
     .A275   1923.
     P75

683. E230   Palmer, Dave R. *The Way of the Fox: American*
     .P24   *Strategy in the War for America, 1775-1783.*
               Westport, Conn.: Greenwood, 1975.

684. E233   Pancake, John S. *1777: The Year of the Hangman.*
     .P27   University: U. of Alabama P., 1977. Battle
               of Saratoga.

685. E271   Paullin, Charles O. *The Navy of the American*
     .P298   *Revolution: Its Administration, Its Policy and*
               Its Achievements. Chicago: Burrows Bros., 1906;
               rpt., N.Y.: Haskell House, 1971.

686. E265   Perkins, James B. *France in the American Revo-*
     .P44   *lution.* Boston: Houghton Mifflin, 1911; rpt.,
               B. Franklin, 1970; Corner House, 1970.

687. V47   Preston, A., D. Lyon, and J.H. Batchelor, eds.
     .P73   *Navies of the American Revolution.* Englewood
               Cliffs, N.J.: Prentice-Hall, 1975.

688. E269   Quarles, Benjamin. *The Negro in the American*
     .N3Q3   *Revolution.* Chapel Hill: UNCP, 1961.

689. E265   Rice, Howard O., ed. *The American Campaigns of*
     .R64   *Rochambeau's Army....* Princeton: PUP, 1971.

690. DA510   Ritcheson, C.R. *British Politics and the Ameri-*
     .R5   *can Revolution.* Norman: U. of Oklahoma P., 1954.

691. E203   Ryan, Dennis P., ed. *A Salute to Courage: The* .S15   *American Revolution as Seen through Wartime Writings of Officers of the Continental Army and Navy.* N.Y.: Columbia UP, 1979.

692. HF3025   Schlesinger, Arthur M., Sr. *The Colonial Mer-* .S3   *chants and the American Revolution.* N.Y.: Columbia UP, 1918.

693. E230   Selby, John. *The Road to Yorktown.* N.Y.: St. .S44   Martin, 1976.

694. E271   Shea, John D.G., ed. *The Operations of the* .061   *French Fleet Under the Count De Grasse in 1781-1782.* N.Y.: 1864; rpt., Da Capo, 1971.

695. E207   Sheppard, John H. *The Life of Samuel Tucker,* .T8S7   *Commodore in the American Revolution.* Boston: A. Mudge & Son, 1868.

696. E230   Shy, John. *A People Numerous and Armed: Reflec-* .P43   *tions on the Military Struggle for American Independence.* N.Y.: Oxford UP, 1976.

697. E210   _____. *Toward Lexington: The Role of the* .S5   *British Army in the Coming of the Revolution.* Princeton: PUP, 1965.

698. E208   Smelser, Marshall. *The Winning of Independence:* .S64   *A Story of America's War for Independence.* Totowa, N.J.: Roman & Littlefield, 1972.

699. E271   *Smith, Charles R. *Marines in the American Revo-* .S46   *lution, 1775-1783.* Wash.: USMC, HQ, Hist. and Museums Div., 1975.

700. E208   Smith, Page. *A New Age Now Begins: A People's* .S67   *History of the American Revolution,* 2 vols. N.Y.: McGraw-Hill, 1976.

701. E233   Smith, Samuel S. *Fight for the Delaware, 1777.* .S63   Monmouth Beach, N.J.: Philip Freneau P., 1970.

702. F280   Stewart, Robert A. *The History of Virginia's* .S84   *Navy of the Revolution.* Richmond: Mitchell & Hotchkiss, 1934.

703. E271   Still, William N., Jr. *North Carolina's Revolu-* .S76   *tionary Navy.* Zebulon, N.C.: Theo. Davis Sons, 1976.

704. E249
    .S86

Stinchcombe, William C. *The American Revolution and the French Alliance*. Syracuse: Syracuse UP, 1969.

705. VA55
    .S83

Stivers, Reuben E. *Privateers and Volunteers: The Men and Women of Our Reserve Naval Forces, 1776-1866*. Annapolis, Md.: NIP, 1975. Attempts to build a privateering heritage for today's naval reserve.

706. E216
    .S76

Stout, Neil R. *The Royal Navy in America, 1760-1775: A Study of the Enforcement of British Colonial Policy in the Era of the American Revolution*. Annapolis, Md.: NIP, 1973.

707. HE564
    .E3G79

Syrett, David. *Shipping and the American War, 1775-1783: A Study of British Transport Organization*. London: Athlone, 1970.

708. E237
    .T47

Thayer, Theodore. *Yorktown: Campaign of Strategic Options*. Phila.: Lippincott, 1975.

709. E207
    .C9T48

_____. *Nathanael Green: Strategist of the Revolution*. N.Y.: Twayne, 1960. George Washington's ablest subordinate.

710. E271
    .T6

Tornquist, Karl G. *The Naval Campaigns of Count de Grasse during the American Revolution, 1781-1783*. Phila.: Swedish Colonial Soc., 1942.

711. E263
    .W5A53

Toth, Charles W., ed. *The American Revolution and the West Indies*. Port Washington, N.Y.: Kennikat P., 1975.

712. E207
    .L2T65

Tower, Charlemagne. *The Marquis de la Lafayette in the American Revolution....* 2 vols. Phila.: Lippincott, 1895.

713. E237
    .T7

Treacy, N.F. *Prelude to Yorktown: The Southern Campaigns of Nathanael Greene, 1780-1781*. Chapel Hill: UNCP, 1963.

714. E207
    .T13T7

Tuckerman, Henry T. *The Life of Silas Talbot, a Commodore in the Navy of the United States*. N.Y.: J.C. Riker, 1850.

715. E216
    .U22

Ubbelode, Carl. *The Vice-Admiralty Courts and the American Revolution*. Chapel Hill: UNCP, 1960.

716. E241 Uhlendorf, Bernard A., ed. *The Siege of Charles-*
.C4U5 *ton....* 1938; rpt., N.Y.: New York Times, 1968.
Narratives of Hessian Officers.

717. DA483 Valentine, Allen. *Lord George Germain*. Oxford:
.S2U2 Clarendon P., 1962.

718. E208 Van Alstyne, Richard W. *Empire and Independence:*
.V28 *The International History of the American Revo-*
lution. N.Y.: Wiley, 1965.

719. E302 Ver Steeg, Clarence. *Robert Morris: Revolution-*
.M8V4 *ary Financier*. Phila.: U. of Pa. P., 1954.

720. E207 Wagner, Fredrick. *Submarine Fighter of the*
.B92W3 *American Revolution: The Story of David Bush-*
nell. N.Y.: Dodd, Mead, 1963.

721. E271 Walsh, John E. *Night on Fire: The First Com-*
.W2 *plete Account of John Paul Jones' Greatest*
Battle. N.Y.: McGraw Hill, 1978.

722. E230 Ward, Christopher. *War of the American Revolu-*
.W34 *tion*, 2 vols. N.Y.: Macmillan, 1952.

723. E210 Wickwire, Franklin B. *British Subministers and*
.W5 *Colonial America, 1763-1783*. Princeton: PUP,
1966.

724. E267 _____, and Mary. *Cornwallis: An Adventure*.
.W48 Boston: Houghton Mifflin, 1976.

725. DA67 Willcox, William B. *Portrait of a General: Sir*
.1.C55W5 *Henry Clinton in the War of Independence*. N.Y.:
Knopf, 1964. Great detail on his relations
with the Royal Navy; their co-operation and mutual dissatisfaction.

726. E277 Wright, Esmond, ed. *Red, White, and True Blue:*
.R3 *The Loyalists in the Revolution*. N.Y.: AMS
Press, 1976.

727. E209 _____, ed. *Causes and Consequences of the*
.W75 *American Revolution*. Chicago: Quadrangle Books,
1966. Readings.

728. DA70   Barnes, G.R., and H.J. Owen, eds. *The Private*
     .A1   *Papers of John, Earl Sandwich, First Lord of*
     v.69   *the Admiralty, 1771-1782.* London: Naval Records
             Soc., 1932.

729. E271   Barnes, John S., ed. *Fanning's Narrative: Being*
     .F22   *the Memoirs of Nathaniel Fanning, an Officer of*
             the Revolutionary Navy, 1778-1783. N.Y.: Naval
             Hist. Soc., 1912; rpt., Arno, 1969.

730. E271   _____, ed. *The Log of the* Serapis--Alliance--
     .B27   Ariel, *Under the Command of John Paul Jones.*
             N.Y.: Naval Hist. Soc., 1911.

731. E237   Chapwick, French E., ed. *The Graves Papers and*
     .C43   *Others Documents Relating to the Naval Opera-*
             tions of the Yorktown Campaign July to October
             1781. N.Y.: Naval Hist. Soc., 1916.

732. E271   Clark William B., and William J. Morgan, eds.
     .U583   *Naval Documents of the American Revolution,* 7
             vols.- . Wash.: GPO, 1964- .

733. E203   Davies, Kenneth G., ed. *Documents of the Ameri-*
     .G68   *can Revolution, 1770-1783,* 21 vols. Irish
             Academic P., Ltd., c/o Totowa, N.J.: Biblio
             Distribution Center, 1979. Records of the Brit-
             ish Colonial Office.

734. E271   Hopkins, Esek. *The Correspondence of Esek Hop-*
     .H662   *kins, Commander-in-Chief of the United States*
             Navy ... in the Library of the Rhode Island
             Historical Society. Ed. by Alverda S. Beck.
             Providence: Rhode Island Hist. Soc., 1933.

735. E353   Hull, Isaac. *Commodore Hull: Papers of Isaac*
     .1.H8H8 *Hull, Commodore, United States Navy.* Ed. by
             Gardner W. Allen. Boston: Atheneum, 1929.

736. E271   *Letter Books and Order Book of George, Lord*
     R76   *Rodney, Admiral of the White Squadron, 1780-*
             1782, 2 vols. Charlottesville: U. of Virginia
             P., 1932.

737. E271   Neeser, Robert W., ed. *Letters and Papers Relat-*
     .C77   *ing to the Cruises of Gustavus Conyngham, a*
             Captain of the Continental Navy, 1777-1779.
             N.Y.: Naval Hist. Soc., 1915; rpt., Kennikat,
             1970.

738. DA70 _____, ed. *Dispatches of Molyneux Shuldham,*
     .A1   *1717?-1798.* N.Y.: Naval Hist. Soc., 1913.
     v.64

739. E271 Paullin, Charles O. *Out Letters of the Contin-*
     .U56 *tal Marine Committee and Board of Admiralty,*
           2 vols. N.Y.: Naval Hist. Soc., 1914.

740. E231 Roberts, Kenneth L., comp. *March to Quebec,* 4th
     .R63 ed. N.Y.: Doubleday, Doran, 1938. Journals of
           the members of Arnold's expedition. Annotated.

741. E203 Stevens, Benjamin F., comp. *B.F. Stevens's Fac-*
     .S84 *similies of Manuscripts in European Archives*
           Relating to America, 1773-1783. London: Malby
           & Sons, 1889-1895; rpt., Mellifont, 1970.

742. Micro U.S. NARG 45. Naval Records Collection of the
     VB255 Office of Naval Records and Library. *Area File*
     .2.A7 *of the Naval Records Collection,* 1775-1910.
           Letters to and from Washington and personnel on
           the various "distant stations."

743.   U.S. Continental Congress. *Journals of the Con-*
          tinental Congress, 1774-1789, 34 vols. Wash.:
          GPO, 1904-1937.

744. E249 Wharton, Francis, ed. *The Revolutionary Diplo-*
     .U583 *matic Correspondence of the United States,* 6
           vols. Wash.: GPO, 1886.

                    DISSERTATIONS AND THESES

745.   Begnaud, Allen E. "British Operations in the
          Caribbean and the American Revolution," Tulane
          U., 1967.

746.   Breen, K.C. "The [British] Navy and the Yorktown
          Campaign, 1781," U. of London, 1966.

747.   Bulger, William T. "The British Expedition to
          Charleston, 1779-1780," U. of Michigan, 1957.

748.   Morse, Sidney G. "New England Privateering in
          the American Revolution," Harvard U., 1941.

749. VB23 Powers, Stephen T. "The Decline and Extinction
     .S7   of American Naval Power, 1781-1787," Notre Dame
           U., 1965.

750.   Wickwire, Mary B. "Lord Sandwich and the King's
         Ships: British Naval Administration, 1771-1782,"
         Yale U., 1963.

751.   Nelson, Dennis D. "The Integration of the Negro
         into the United States Navy, 1776-1947." M.A.
         Thesis, Howard U., 1937.

ARTICLES

752.   Adams, Randolph G. "A View of Cornwallis's Sur-
         render at Yorktown," AHR 37 (Oct. 1931):25-49.

753.   Alden, John R. "Why the March to Concord?" AHR
         69 (Apr. 1944):446-54.

754.   Barritt, M.K. "The Navy and the Clyde in the
         American War, 1777-1783," MM 55 (Jan. 1969):
         33-42.

755.   Barton, John A. "The Battle of Valcour Island,
         1776: Benedict Arnold's Defence," *History Today*
         9 (Dec. 1959):791-99.

756.   Baugh, Barney. "History of Naval Mine Warfare:
         Kegs, Cabbages, and Acoustics," *All Hands* No.
         481, 1957.

757.   Bellico, Russell. "The Great Penobscot Blun-
         der," AHI 13 (Dec. 1978):4-9, 44-48.

758.   Biddle, Edward. "Captain Nicholas Biddle, 1750-
         1778," USNIP 43 (Sept. 1917):1993-2003.

759.   "The Birth of a Navy," USNIP 101 (Oct. 1975):
         18-65.

760.   Boatner, Mark M., III. "The Negro in the Revo-
         lution," AHI 4 (Aug. 1969):36-44.

761.   Bolander, Louis H. "Arnold's Retreat from Val-
         cour Island," USNIP 55 (Dec. 1929):1060-62.

762.   _____. "A Forgotten Hero of the Revolution,"
         USNIP 22 (Apr. 1928):119-28. Lambert Wickes.

763.   Brewington, Marion V. "American Naval Guns,
         1775-1785," AN 3 (Jan. 1943):11-18; 3 (Apr.
         1943):148-58.

764. _____. "The Design of Our First Frigates,"
      AN 8 (Jan. 1948):11-25.

765. _____. "The Battle of Delaware Bay, 1782,"
      USNIP 65 (Feb. 1939):231-40.

766. Broomfield, F.H. "Lord Sandwich at the Admiral-
      ty Board: Politics and the British Navy, 1771-
      1778," MM 51 (Feb. 1965):7-18.

767. Brown, Wallace. "The American Colonies and the
      West Indies," AHI 9 (May 1974):12-23.

768. _____. "Negroes and the American Revolution,"
      History Today 14 (Aug. 1964):556-63.

769. Calkins, Carlos G. "The American Navy and the
      Opinions of One of its Founders, John Adams,
      1735-1826," USNIP 37 (June 1911):453-83.

770. Carleton, William R. "New England Masts and the
      King's Navy," *New England Q.* 12 (March 1939):
      4-18.

771. Carr, James A. "Sea Power in the Revolution,"
      National Defense, Sept.-Oct. 1976, pp. 123-28.

772. Chadwick, French E. "Sea Power: The Decisive
      Factor in Our Struggle for Independence," *An-
      nual Report of the Amer. Hist. Assoc.*, 1915,
      pp. 171-89.

773. Chapelle, Howard I. "The Design of the American
      Frigates of the Revolution and Joshua Hum-
      phreys," AN 9 (July 1949):161-68.

774. Clark, William B. "American Naval Policy, 1775-
      1776," AN 1 (Jan. 1941):26-41.

775. *Colby, Chester M. "The United States Marines in
      the Penobscot Bay Expedition," MCG 3 (Dec.
      1918):281-92.

776. Coletta, Paolo E. "Naval Mine Warfare," *Navy*
      (U.S.) 2 (Nov. 1959):16-24.

777. _____. "Naval Mine Warfare," USNIP 85 (Nov.
      1959):82-126. Pictorial.

778. "The Concise History of the American Revolu-
      tion," AHI 7 (Apr. 1972): entire issue.

779.   Corwin, Edward S. "The French Objective in the American Revolution," AHR 21 (Oct. 1915):33-61.

780.   Cross, F.E. "The Father of the American Navy," USNIP 53 (Dec. 1927):1296-97. Contends the title belongs to no one person.

781.   Cullen, Joseph P. "The Concise Illustrated History of the American Revolution," AHI 6 (Apr. 1972):1-65.

782.   _____. "John Paul Jones: A Personality Profile," AHI 1 (Apr. 1966):12-19.

783.   Daveluy, R. "A Study of Naval Strategy: Part Five, The War of American Independence," USNIP 36 (June 1910):391-428.

784.   Dearden, Paul F. "The Siege of Newport: Inauspicious Dawn of Alliance," *Rhode Island Hist.* 29 (Jan.-Feb. 1970):17-35. Franco-American efforts to drive the British from Newport during the American Revolution.

785.   Detweiler, Robert. "Why the British Lost the War: the American Revolution in Modern Perspective," MCG 59 (July 1976):18-24.

786.   Dow, H.E. "Captain John Manley of the Continental Navy," USNIP 52 (Aug. 1926):1554-61.

787.   Dowdell, Vincent J. "Captain Mugford and the Powder Ship," USNIP 82 (Dec. 1956):1358-59. On the capture of the British transport *Hope* by Mugford's schooner *Franklin* and the American's battle to the death on April 6, 1776.

788.   *Dunn, Lucius C. "The U.S. Navy's First Seagoing Marine Officer," USNIP 75 (Aug. 1949):919-23.

789.   Eller, Ernest M. "Sea Power in the American Revolution," USNIP 62 (June 1936):777-89.

790.   _____. "From Across the Sea," USNIP 59 (Oct. 1933):1457-62. French aid in the American war for independence.

791.   Evans, Edward J. "Time on Target: 177 Years," MCG 37 (Feb. 1954):36-39. Marine artillery, 1775-1945.

792.   *Fagan, Louis S. "Samuel Nicholas, First Officer of American Marines," MCG 18 (Nov. 1933):4-15.

793.   Fowler, William. "Disaster in Penobscot Bay," NWCR 31 (Winter 1978):75-80.

794.   Fremantle, E. "Seapower and the American War of Independence," RUSIJ 52 (Aug. 1917):471-505.

795.   Frost, Holloway H. "Our Heritage from John Paul Jones," USNIP 44 (Oct. 1918):2275-2332.

796.   Frothingham, Thomas G. "The Sequence that Led to Yorktown," USNIP 57 (Oct. 1931):1326-30.

797.   Gilligan, Arthur E. "The Battle of Valcour Island," USNIP 92 (Oct. 1967):157-60.

798.   Goodrich, Caspar F. "The Sailor in the Revolution," USNIP 23, No. 3 (1897):469-94.

799.   _____. "Howe and D'Estaing: A Study in Coast Defense," USNIP 22, No. 3 (1896):577-86.

800.   Greathouse, Ronald H. "The Battle of Valcour Bay: A Victorious Defeat," MCG 42 (Nov. 1958): 16-18.

801.   Guttridge, George H. "Lord George Germain in Office, 1775-1782," AHR 33 (Oct. 1927):23-43.

802.   Haggerty, J.J. "The Influence of British Naval Power upon the American Colonies," Army Q. 87 (Apr. 1964):43-52.

803.   Hall, Hubert. "Chatham's Colonial Policy," AHR 5 (July 1900):659-75.

804.   Handlin, Oscar. "Independence at Yorktown: Chance or Destiny?" Atlantic Monthly 194 (Dec. 1954):27-32.

805.   Hanks, Carlos U. "A Cruise for Gunpowder," USNIP 65 (Mar. 1939):324-27. New Providence raid.

806.   Hayes, Frederic H. "John Adams and American Sea Power," AN 25 (Jan. 1965):34-45. A discussion of his Revolutionary service on the Congressional Marine Committee.

807.   *Heinl, Robert D. "The U.S. Marine Corps: Author
        of Modern Amphibious War," USNIP 73 (Nov. 1947):
        1310-23.

808.   Hooper, Edwin. "Over the Span of 200 Years:
        Technology and the United States Navy," *Naval
        Engineers Jour.* 88 (Aug. 1976):24-36.

809.   Hubbard, Timothy W. "The Battle of Valcour
        Island: Benedict Arnold as Hero," *Am. Her.* 17
        (Oct. 1966):8-11, 87-91.

810.   Humphreys, Henry H. "Who Built the First United
        States Navy?" JAH 10 (Jan. 1916):49-89.

811.   Jameson, J. Franklin. "St. Eustatius in the
        American Revolution," AHR 8 (July 1903):683-708.

812.   Johnson, Leland R. "First Salvo at Yorktown:
        Sword, Shovel, and Compass," *Mil. Eng.* 68 (May-
        June 1976):175-79.

813.   Keller, Allan. "The [American] Revolution at
        Sea," AHI 8 (July 1973):4-11.

814.   _____. "Valcour Island," AHI 7 (July 1972):
        26-33.

815.   Knox, Dudley W. "Navies in the American Revolu-
        tion: The Influence of Sea Power on Military
        Operations," *Army Ordnance* (15 (Jan.-Feb. 1935):
        213-16.

816.   _____. "D'Estaing's Fleet Revealed," USNIP
        61 (Feb. 1935):153-68. Historical account with
        six illustrations.

817.   Larrabee, Harold A. "A Near Thing at Yorktown,"
        Am. Her. 12 (Oct. 1961):56-64, 69-73. Naval
        battle of the Virginia Capes.

818.   Lemisch, Jesse. "Jack Tar in the Streets: Mer-
        chant Seamen in the Politics of Revolutionary
        America." *William and Mary Q.*, 3rd Series, 25
        (July 1968):371-407.

819.   Leslie, William R. "The *Gaspee* Affair: A Study
        of its Constitutional Significance," MVHR 39
        (Sept. 1952):233-56.

820.   Lint, Gregg L. "John Adams on the Drafting of
        the Treaty Plan of 1776," *Dip. Hist.* 2 (Summer
        1978):313-20.

821.   *McClellan, Edwin N. "American Marines in the
        Revolution," USNIP 49 (June 1923):957-63.

822.   _____. "The Navy at the Battles of Trenton
        and Princeton," USNIP 49 (Nov. 1923):1848-55.

823.   McLaughlin, Patrick. "The American Revolution
        in Maps," *Am. Archivist* 37 (Jan. 1974):43-54.

824.   McCusker, John J., Jr. "The American Invasion
        of Nassau in the Bahamas," AN 25 (July 1965):
        189-217.

825.   Mackesy, Piers. "British Strategy in the War of
        American Independence," *Yale Rev.* 52 (Summer
        1963):539-57. Includes naval strategy.

826.   Mahan, Alfred T. "John Paul Jones in the Revolu-
        tion," *Scribner's Mag.* 24 (July-Aug. 1898):22-
        36, 204-19. Still one of the best essays.

827.   _____. "Major Operations of the Royal Navy,
        1762-1783," in William L. Clowes, *The Royal
        Navy...*, 7 vols. Boston: Little, Brown, 1893,
        3:353-68.

828.   Majet, Horace S. "The Navy's Forgotten Hero,"
        USNIP 63 (March 1937):347-54. Abraham Whipple.

829.   Malo, Henri. "American Privateers at Dunkerque,"
        USNIP 37 (Sept. 1911):933-93.

830.   Martin, Asa E. "American Privateers and the
        West India Trade, 1776-1777," AHR 39 (July
        1934):100-06.

831.   Maurer, Maurer. "Coppered Bottoms for the Royal
        Navy: A Factor in the Maritime War of 1778-
        1783," MA 14 (Apr. 1950):57-61.

832.   Miles, A.H. "Naval Views of the Yorktown Cam-
        paign," USNIP 57 (Oct. 1931):1303-12.

833.   _____. "Sea Power and the Yorktown Campaign,"
        USNIP 53 (Nov. 1927):1169-84.

834.   Moran, Charles. "D'Estaing: An Early Exponent
           of Amphibious Warfare," MA 9 (Winter 1945):
           314-32.

835.   Morgan, William J. "Privateering in America's
           War for Independence, 1775-1783," AN 36 (Apr.
           1976):79-87.

836.   _____. "The Pivot Upon Which Everything
           Turned: French Naval Superiority That Insured
           Victory at Yorktown," *The Iron Worker* 22
           (Spring 1958):1-9. Reprinted under title of
           "Seapower Turns the Tide: 1781," in *All Hands*,
           Dec. 1959, pp. 59-63.

837.   _____. "The Stormy Career of Captain McNeill,
           Continental Navy," MA 16 (Fall 1952):119-22.

838.   Morse, Sidney G. "State or Continental Priva-
           teers?" AHR 52 (Oct. 1946):68-73.

839.   Mullett, Charles F. "English Imperial Thinking,
           1764-1783," PSQ 45 (Dec. 1930):548-79.

840.   Norris, Walter B. "Who is the Father of the
           American Navy?" CH 27 (Dec. 1927):354-60.
           Concludes it is "useless to try to make one man
           'Father of the American Navy,' or one ship the
           First American Warship."

841.   Northrup, Everett H. "Burgoyne's Invasion,
           1777," *Bull. of Bibliography*. pt. 2, 16 (May-
           Aug. 1939):175-77; pt. 2, 16 (Sept.-Dec. 1939):
           197-99; pt. 3, 17 (Jan.-Apr. 1940):12-13.

842.   Paullin, Charles O. "When Was Our Navy Founded?"
           USNIP 36 (Mar. 1910):255-61.

843.   _____. The Conditions of Continental Naval
           Service," USNIP 32 (Mar. 1906):585-95.

844.   _____. "The Administration of the Massachu-
           setts and Virginia Navies of the American Revo-
           lution," USNIP 37 (Mar. 1906):131-64.

845.   _____. "The Administration of the Continental
           Navy of the American Revolution," USNIP 31
           (Sept. 1905):625-75.

846.   _____. "Classes of Operations of the Continental Navy of the American Revolution," USNIP 21 (May 1905):153-64.

847.   Perry, James M. "Disaster on the Delaware," USNIP 88 (Jan. 1962):84-91. Defeat of the Pennsylvania galleys by the British en route to take Forts Mifflin and Mercer in 1777.

848.   Rathbun, Frank H. "Rathbun's Raid on Nassau," USNIP 96 (Nov. 1970):40-47.

849.   Rothbottam, W.B. "Robert Fulton's Turtle Boat," USNIP 62 (Dec. 1936):1746-49.

850.   Sanders, Harry. "The First American Submarine," USNIP 62 (Dec. 1936):1743-45. The *Turtle*.

851.   Shafroth, John F. "The Strategy of the Yorktown Campaign, 1781," USNIP 57 (June 1931):721-36.

852.   Shaw, Henry I. "Penobscot Assault--1779," MA 17 (Summer 1953):83-94. The best article on the subject to date.

853.   Smith, David B. "The Capture of the WASHINGTON," MM 20 (Oct. 1934):420-25. In 1775.

854.   Spencer, Frank. "Lord Sandwich, Russian Masts, and American Independence," MM 44 (Apr. 1958):116-27.

855.   Stephenson, Orlando W. "The Supply of Gunpowder in 1776," AHR 30 (Jan. 1925):271-81.

856.   *Stevens, Harold R. "Samuel Nicholas: Innkeeper: Marine," MCG 11 (Nov. 1953):12-15.

857.   Syrett, David. "The Fleet That Failed," USNIP 101 (Oct. 1975):66-67. The Royal Navy during the War of the American Revolution.

858.   Thom, De Courcy W. "Captain Lambert Wickes, C.N.: A Maryland Forerunner of Commodore John Paul Jones, C.N.," *Maryland Hist.* 27 (Spring 1932):1-17.

859.   Thomson, David W. "David Bushnell and the First American Submarine," USNIP 68 (Feb.1962):176-86.

860.   Usher, Roland Q. "Royal Navy Impressment during the American Revolution," MVHR 37 (Mar. 1951): 673-88.

861.   Van Ryne, Claude H. "French Aid before the Alliance of 1778," AHR 31 (Oct. 1925):20-40.

862.   _____. "Influences Which Determined the French Government to Make the Treaty with America, 1778," AHR 21 (Apr. 1916):528-41.

863.   Warner, Oliver. "The Action off Flamborough Head," AH 14 (Apr. 1963):42-49, 105. J.P. Jones in the *Bonhomme Richard* vs HMS *Serapis*, 1779.

864.   Weed, Richmond. "Battle of the Virginia Capes, 1781," USNIP 66 (Apr. 1940):524-32.

865.   Willcox, William B. "British [Naval] Strategy in America, 1778," JMH 19 (June 1947):97-121.

866.   _____. "Rhode Island in British Strategy, 1780-1781," JMH 17 (Dec. 1945):304-31.

867.   _____. "The British Road to Yorktown: A Study in Divided Command," AHR 52 (Oct. 1946): 1-35.

868.   York, Neil L. "Clandestine Aid and the American Revolutionary War Effort: A Re-examination," MA 43 (Feb. 1979):26-30.

FICTION

869. PZ3   Chambers, Robert W. *The Reckoning*. London:
     .C355 Constable, 1905. Battle of Yorktown.
     Re

870. PS1297 Churchill, Winston [the American]. *Richard
     .R52   Carvel*, 2 vols. N.Y.: Macmillan, 1899. A Maryland sailor who serves under John Paul Jones during the Revolution.

871. PS643   Cooper, James F. *The Red Rover: A Tale*.
     .A5   Phila.: Carey, Lea & Carey, 1828. A pirate turns patriot during the War of the American Revolution.

872. PS1412
.A1
         _____. *The Pilot: A Tale of the Sea*. N.Y.: Charles Wiley, 1824. John Paul Jones in British waters during the American Revolution.

873. P23
.J4433
Se
    Jennings, John E. *The Sea Eagles: A Story of the American Navy During the Revolution....* GCNY: Doubleday, 1950. Mainly Joshua Barney.

874. PS3525
.A822
G8
    Mason, F. Van Wyck. *Guns for the Rebellion*. GCNY: Doubleday, 1977.

875. PS3525
.A822
T58
    _____. *Rivers of Glory*. N.Y.: Grosset & Dunlap, 1942.

876. PS3525
.A822
S83
    _____. *Stars of the Sea*. N.Y.: Grosset & Dunlap, 1940.

877. PS3525
.A822
.T57
    _____. *Three Harbours*. N.Y.: Grosset & Dunlap, 1938.

878. P24
.P27
Su 3
    Partington, Norman. *The Sunshine Patriot: A Novel of the American War of Independence*. N.Y.: St. Martin, 1975. Arnold at Valcour Island.

879. PZ7
.R336
GO
    Reynolds, John M. *The Guns of Yorktown*. N.Y.: Appleton, 1932.

880. PZ3
.R48C1
    Ripley, Clements. *Clear for Action: A Novel about John Paul Jones*. N.Y.: Appleton-Century, 1940.

881. PS3535
.O176
C36
    Roberts, Kenneth. *Captain Cautious: A Chronicle of Arundel*. GCNY: Doubleday, Doran, 1934.

882. PS3535
.O176
O45
    _____. *Oliver Wiswell*. GCNY: Doubleday, 1940. The American Revolution from a Loyalist's point of view.

883. PS3535
.O176
A78
    _____. *Arundel....* N.Y.: Doubleday, 1933, 1956. Arnold's expedition against Quebec, winter of 1775.

884. PS3535   _____. *Northwest Passage*. GCNY: Doubleday,
     .0176   1937.
     N67

885. PS3535   _____. *Rabble in Arms*. GCNY: Doubleday,
     .0176   1933.
     R32

4

A CHIP ON THE EUROPEAN WAR TABLE, 1783-1815

BOOKS

886. E302
     .A24

Adams, Henry. *The War of 1812*. Ed. H.A. DeWeerd. Wash.: Inf. Jour., 1944.

887. E322
     .A3

Adams, John. *Diary and Autobiography*. Ed. L.H. Butterfield. Cambridge: Belknap Press of HUP, 1961.

888. F2161
     .A48

Allen, Gardner. *Our Navy and the West Indies Pirates*. Salem, Mass.: Essex Institute, 1929.

889. E323
     .A42

_____. *Our Naval War with France*. Boston: Houghton Mifflin, 1909.

890 E335
     .A42

_____. *Our Navy and the Barbary Corsairs*. Boston: Houghton Mifflin, 1905.

891. E183.8
     .G7A47

Allen, Harry C. *Great Britain and the United States: A History of Anglo-American Relations*. N.Y.: St. Martin, 1955, 1969. Useful for the period from 1789 to the end of the War of 1812.

892. E353.1
     .D29A25

Anthony, Irvin. *Decatur*. N.Y.: Scribner, 1931.

893. E1838
     .A6B3

Barnby, H.G. *The Prisoners of Algiers: An Account of the Forgotten American-Algerian, 1785-1797*. Totowa, N.J.: Rowman & Littlefield, 1966.

894. E353
     .1B2.B2

Barnes, James. *Commodore Bainbridge: From the Gunroom to the Quarterdeck*. N.Y.: Appleton, 1897.

895. E360
     .B26

_____. *Naval Actions of the War of 1812*. N.Y.: Harper, 1896.

896. E182
     .B28

Barrow, Clayton R., J., comp. and ed. *America Spreads Her Sails: U.S. Seapower in the Nineteenth Century*. Annapolis, Md.: NIP, 1973.

897. V799
     .B3

Baxter, James P. *The Introduction of the Ironclad Warship*. Cambridge, Mass.: HUP, 1933.

898. D354   Beirne, Francis R. *The War of 1812*. N.Y.:
      .B44   Dutton, 1949.

899. E162   Bird, Harrison. *Navies in the Mountains: The*
      .B5   *Battles on Water of Lake Champlain and Lake*
                George, 1609-1814. N.Y.: Oxford UP, 1962.

900. E310   _____. *War for the West, 1790-1813*. N.Y.:
      .B57   Oxford UP, 1971.

901. E183.8   Bowman, Albert H. *The Struggle for Neutrality:*
      .F8B5   *Franco-American Diplomacy During the Federalist*
                Era. Knoxville: U. of Tennessee P., 1974.

902. DE80   Bradford, Ernie D.S. *Mediterranean: Portrait of*
      .B7   *a Sea*. N.Y.: Harcourt Brace Jovanovich, 1971.

903. F1623   Bradlee, Francis B. *Piracy in the West Indies*
      .B81   *and Its Suppression*. Salem, Mass.: Essex Insti-
                tute, 1923; rpt., Lib. Editions, 1970.

904. E342   Brant, Irving. *The Fourth President: A Life of*
      .B72   *James Madison*. Indianapolis: Bobbs-Merrill,
                1970.

905. E321   Brown, Ralph A. *The Presidency of John Adams*.
      .B84   Lawrence: UP of Kansas, 1975.

906. E357   Brown, Roger H. *The Republic in Peril: 1812*.
      .B86   N.Y.: Columbia UP, 1964.

907. E356   Brown, Wilburt S. *The Amphibious Campaign for*
      .N5B73   *West Florida and Louisiana, 1814-1815*. Uni-
                versity: U. of Alabama P., 1969.

908. E360.6   Byron, Gilbert. *The War of 1812 on Chesapeake*
      .S575   *Bay*. Baltimore: Maryland Hist. Soc., 1964.

909. E356   Carter, Samuel, III. *Blaze of Glory: The Fight*
      .N5C37   *for New Orleans, 1814-1815*. N.Y.: St. Martin,
                1971.

910. VA56   Chapelle, Howard I. *The American Sailing Navy*.
      .C5   N.Y.: Norton, 1949.

911. E335   Chidsey, Donald B. *The Wars in Barbary: Arab*
      .C48   *Piracy and the Birth of the United States Navy*.
                N.Y.: Crown, 1971.

912. E302.6
.P5C55

Clarfield, Gerald H. *Timothy Pickering and American Diplomacy, 1795-1800*. Columbia: U. of Missouri P., 1969.

913. E182
.C85

Cooper, James F. *Lives of Distinguished American Naval Officers*, 2 vols. in 1. Phila.: Carey & Hart, 1846. Vol. 1: Bainbridge, Somers, Shaw, Shubrick, Preble. Vol. 2: Jones, Woolsey, Perry, Dale.

914. E182
.C785

_____. *History of the Navy of the United States of America*, 2d ed., 2 vols. Phila.: Lea & Blanchard, 1840. An excellent account of battles by a former naval person. Supported Elliott vs O.H. Perry on Battle of Lake Erie.

915. E360
.C78

Cranwell, John, and William B. Crane. *Men of Marque: A History of Private Armed Vessels out of Baltimore During the War of 1812*. N.Y.: Norton, 1940.

916. HF3105
.C75

Crosby, Alfred W., Jr. *America, Russia, Hemp, and Napoleon: American Trade with Russia and the Baltic, 1783-1812*. Columbus: Ohio State UP, 1965.

917. DT201
.C8

Currey, Edward H. *Sea Wolves of the Mediterranean*. N.Y.: Frederick A. Stokes, 1929. The Barbary Corsairs.

918. E353.1
.B2D3

Dearborn, Henry A. *The Life of William Bainbridge, Esq. of the United States Navy*. Princeton: PUP, 1931.

919. E323
.D4

DeConde, Alexander. *The Quasi War: The Politics and Diplomacy of the Undeclared War with France, 1797-1801*. N.Y.: Scribner, 1966.

920. E311
.D4

_____. *Entangling Alliance: Politics and Diplomacy under George Washington*. Durham: Duke UP, 1958.

921. VM140
.F9D5

Dickinson, Henry W. *Robert Fulton: Engineer and Artist*. London: Lane, 1913.

922. E353.1
.P4D54

Dillon, Richard. *We Have Met the Enemy: Oliver Hazard Perry, Wilderness Commodore*. N.Y.: McGraw-Hill, 1978.

923. VA65   Donovan, Frank. *The Odyssey of the* Essex. N.Y.:
     .E781D6   McKay, 1969. The exploits of the noted frigate,
                Captain David Porter commanding, in the southern
                oceans during the War of 1812.

924. E182   _____. *The Tall Frigates*. N.Y.: Dodd, Mead,
     .D6   1962. Battles afloat during the War of 1812.

925. DE96   Earle, Peter. *Corsairs of Malta and Barbary*.
     .E27   Annapolis, Md.: USNI, 1970.

926. VB23   Eckert, Edward K. *The Navy Department in the
     .E34   War of 1812*. Gainesville: U. of Florida P.,
                1973.

927. E182   Ferguson, Eugene S. *Truxtun of the* Constella-
     .T7F43   tion. Baltimore: Johns Hopkins P., 1956.

928. DS632   Field, James A. *America and the Mediterranean
     .U5F47   World 1776-1882*. Princeton: PUP, 1969.

929. D383   Fisher, John O.H.F. *1815: An End and a Begin-
     .F5   ning*. N.Y.: Harper & Row, 1963.

930. E312   Flexner, James T. *George Washington: Anguish
     .29.F26   and Farewell, 1793-1799*. Boston: Little, Brown,
                1972.

931. E312   _____. *George Washington and the New Nation*,
     .29.F55   *1783-1793*. Boston: Little, Brown, 1970.

932. E360   Forester, Cecil S. *The Age of Fighting Sail: The
     .F69   Story of the Naval War of 1812*. GCNY: Double-
                day, 1956.

933. E182   Frost, Holloway. *We Build a Navy*. Annapolis,
     .F81   Md.: USNI, 1929.

934. DT194   Gallagher, Charles F. *The United States and
     .G15   North Africa: Morocco, Algeria, and Tunisia*.
                Cambridge, Mass.: HUP, 1963.

935. VB57   Gardiner, Leslie. *The British Admiralty*. Annap-
     .G36   olis, Md.: USNI, 1968. Some of its decisions
                and designs greatly influenced U.S. naval re-
                sponses between 1789 and 1860.

936. HE752   Garitee, Jerome R. *The Republic's Private Navy:
     .M3G37   The American Privateering Business as Practiced
                by Baltimore During the War of 1812*. Middletown,
                Conn.: Wesleyan UP, 1977.

937. E355
     .7.G5
Gilpin, Alec R. *The War of 1812 in the Old Northwest*. East Lansing: Michigan State UP, 1958.

938. E353
     .L4G5
Gleaves, Albert. *James Lawrence, Captain, U.S. Navy: Commander of the* Chesapeake. N.Y.: Putnam, 1904.

939. E182
     .G62
Goldsborough, Charles W. *United States Naval Chronicle*. Wash.: J. Wilson, 1824. Originally conceived as a periodical, but only one volume was ever printed. The author, an employee of the Navy Department for years, has here gathered an infinite amount of important--if sometimes misleading--early naval data.

940. E182
     .H93G7
Grant, Bruce. *Isaac Hull: Captain of* Old Ironsides. Chicago: Pellegrini & Cudahy, 1947.

941. VA56
     .G8
Guttridge, Leonard F., and Jay D. Smith. *The Commodores*. N.Y.: Harper & Row, 1969. Barbary Wars.

942. E353.1
     .B26B2
Harris, Thomas. *Life and Services of William Bainbridge*. Boston: Gray C. Bowen, 1832.

943. E183.8
     .F8H5
Hill, Peter. *William Vans Murray, Federalist Diplomat: The Shaping of Peace with France*. Syracuse: Syracuse UP, 1971.

944. E353.1
     .P4H6
Hoyt, Edwin P. *The Tragic Commodore: The Story of Oliver Hazard Perry*. N.Y.: Abelard-Schuman, 1966.

945. E335
     .I75
Irwin, Ray W. *The Diplomatic Relations of the United States with the Barbary Powers, 1776-1816*. Chapel Hill: UNCP, 1931; rpt., N.Y.: Russell & Russell, 1970.

946. E354
     .J3
Jacobs, James R., and Glenn Tucker. *The War of 1812: A Compact History*. N.Y.: Hawthorn, 1969.

947. VA65
     .C758J4
Jennings, John E. *Tattered Ensign: The Story of America's Most Famous Fighting Frigate, U.S.S.* Constitution. N.Y.: Crowell, 1966.

948. E182
     .J54
Johnson, Robert E. *The Far China Station: The U.S. Navy in Asiatic Waters, 1800-1890*. Annapolis, Md.: NIP, 1979.

80

949. E183.8 Jones, Wilbur D. *The American Problem in Brit-*
     .G7J66 *ish Diplomacy.* Athens: U. of Georgia P., 1974.

950. UC483 Katcher, Philip R.N. *The American War, 1812-*
     .K37 *1814.* N.Y.: Hippocrene, 1974. 40 pp.

951. E182 Knipe, Emilie B., and Alden A. Knipe. *The*
     .K72 *Story of Old Ironsides: The Cradle of the U.S.*
           Navy. N.Y.: Tudor, 1935.

952. E354 Lawson, Don. *The War of 1812: America's Second*
     .L8 *War for Independence.* N.Y.: Abelard-Schuman,
          1966.

953. E353.1 Lewis, Charles L. *The Romantic Decatur.* Phila.:
     .D29L5 U. of Pa. P., 1937.

954. E354 Lloyd, Alan. *The Scorching of Washington: The*
     .L55 *War of 1812.* Wash.: Robert B. Luce, 1974.

955. E353.1 Long, David G. *Nothing Too Daring: A Biography*
     .P7L6 *of Commodore David Porter, 1780-1843.* Annapolis,
            Md.: USNI, 1970.

956. E354 Lord, Walter. *The Dawn's Early Light.* N.Y.:
     .L85 Norton, 1972.

957. E353.1 Lyman, Olin L. *Commodore Oliver Hazard Perry*
     .P4L9 *and the War on the Lakes.* N.Y.: Amsterdam, 1905.

958. E182 McKee, Christopher. *Edward Preble: A Naval Biog-*
     .P88M32 *raphy, 1761-1807.* Annapolis, Md.: NIP, 1972.

959. E353 Mackenzie, Alexander S. *Life of Stephen Decatur:*
     .1D29M2 *A Commodore in the Navy of the United States.*
             Boston: Little, Brown, 1846.

960. E353.1 _____. *Life of Commodore Oliver Hazard Perry.*
     .P4Mi4a N.Y.: Harper, 1840.

961. E354 Mahan, Alfred T. *Sea Power in Its Relation to*
     .M212 *the War of 1812,* 2 vols. Boston: Little, Brown,
            1905; rpt., Greenwood, 1968, Haskell, 1970.

962. E355 Mahon, John K. *The War of 1812.* Gainesville: U.
     .M33 of Florida P., 1972.

963. E332 Malone, Dumas. *Jefferson the President: Second*
     .M25 *Term, 1805-1809.* Boston: Little, Brown, 1974.
     v. 5

964. E332   _____. *Jefferson the President: First Term,*
     .M25   *1801-1805.* Boston: Little, Brown, 1970.
     v. 4

965. E322   _____. *Jefferson and the Ordeal of Liberty.*
     .M25   Boston: Little, Brown, 1962.
     V. 3

966. E353   Mills, James C. *Oliver Hazard Perry and the*
     .1.P4M6   *Battle of Lake Erie.* Detroit: Phelps, 1913.

967. VM140   Morgan, John S. *Robert Fulton.* N.Y.: Mason/
     .F9M67   Charter, 1977.

968. E353   Morris, Charles. *The Autobiography of Commodore*
     .1.M8M8   *Charles Morris, USN....* Boston: Williams, 1880.

969. E355   Muller, Charles G. *The Darkest Day: 1814: The*
     .6.M8   *Washington-Baltimore Campaign.* Phila.: Lippin-
                 cott, 1963.

970. E360   Munro, Wilfred H. *The Most Successful American*
     .M96   *Privateer: An Episode of the War of 1812.*
                 Worcester, Mass.: The Society, 1913.

971. UA646   Myers, Kenneth A. *North Atlantic Security: The*
     .3.M93   *Forgotten Flank?* Beverly Hills, Calif.: Sage,
                 1979.

972. E182   Nash, Howard P. *The Forgotten Wars: The Role of*
     .N218   *the U.S. Navy in the Quasi-War with France and*
                 the Barbary Wars, 1798-1805. N.Y.: A.S. Barnes,
                 1968.

973. E269   Nell, William C. *Services of Colored Americans*
     .N3N45   *in the Wars of 1776 & 1812.* N.Y.: AMS Press,
                 1976. Reprint of 24 articles dated 1851.

974. E353.1   Nicolay, Helen. *Decatur of the Old Navy.* N.Y.:
     .D29N5   Appleton-Century, 1942.

975. E173   Paine, Ralph D. *The Fight for a Free Sea: A*
     .C55   *Chronicle of The War of 1812.* New Haven: YUP,
     v.7   1920.

976. VM365   Parsons, William B. *Robert Fulton and the Sub-*
     .P3   *marine.* N.Y.: Columbia UP, 1922; rpt., AMS P.,
                 1967.

977. DS518   Paullin, Charles O. *American Voyages to the*
     .8.P38   *Orient, 1690-1865*.... Annapolis, Md.: NIP,
                1971. Collection of articles from the U.S.
                Naval Institute *Proceedings*.

978. E353.1   _____. *Commodore John Rodgers, Captain,*
     .R7P28   *Commodore, and Senior Officer of the American*
                Navy, 1773-1838: A Biography. Cleveland: Clark,
                1910.

979. E183.8   Perkins, Bradford. *The First Rapprochement:*
     .G7P4   *England and the United States, 1795-1805*.
                Berkeley: U. of California P., 1967.

980. E357   _____. *Prologue to War: England and the*
     .P66   *United States 1805-1812*. Berkeley: U. of Cali-
                fornia P., 1961.

981. Q115   Ponko, Vincent. *Ships, Seas, and Scientists:*
     .P66   *U.S. Naval Exploration and Discovery in the*
                Nineteenth Century. Annapolis, Md.: NIP, 1974.

982. E360   Poolman, Kenneth. *Guns Off Cape Ann: The Story*
     .P6   *of the* Shannon *and the* Chesapeake. Chicago:
                Rand McNally, 1962.

983. E182   Pratt, Fletcher. *Preble's Boys: Commodore Preble*
     .P88P7   *and the Birth of American Sea Power*. N.Y.:
                Sloane, 1950.

984. E357   Pratt, Julius W. *Expansionists of 1812*. N.Y.:
     .P9   Macmillan, 1925.

985. E360   Pullen, Hugh F. *The* Shannon *and the* Chesapeake.
     .C5P8   Toronto: McClelland & Stewart, 1970.

986. UA830   Rajendra, Singh K. *The Indian Ocean: Big Power*
     .R75   *Presence and Local Response*. Columbia, Mo.:
                South Asia Books, 1978.

987. E355   Reilly, Robin. *The British at the Gates: The*
     .R42   *New Orleans Campaign in the War of 1812*. N.Y.:
                Putnam, 1974.

988. E313   Ritcheson, Charles R. *Aftermath of the Revolu-*
     .R5   *tion: British Policy toward the United States,*
                1783-1795. Dallas: Southern Methodist UP, 1969.

989. E360   Roosevelt, Theodore. *The Naval War of 1812*.
     .R86   N.Y.: Putnam, 1882; rpt. of 3d ed. by Haskell,
                1968.

990. E338   Rutland, Robert A. *Madison's Alternatives: The*
     .R88   *Jeffersonian Republicans and the Coming of War,*
          1805-1812. Phila.: Lippincott, 1975.

991. JX5297 Savage, Carleton, ed. *The Policy of the United*
     .S3   *States Toward Maritime Commerce in War,* 2 vols.
          Wash.: GPO, 1934-1936, 1969.

992. E336.5 Sears, Louis M. *Jefferson and the Embargo.*
     .S42   Durham: Duke UP, 1927; rpt., N.Y.: Octagon
          Books, 1966.

993. E182   Smelser, Marshall. *The Congress Founds the Na-*
     .S57   *vy, 1787-1798.* Notre Dame: U. of Notre Dame P.,
          1959.

994. E182   Soley, James R. *The Boys of 1812 and Other Na-*
     .S68   *val Heroes.* Boston: Estes & Lauriat, 1887.

995. E182   Sprout, Harold and Margaret. *The Rise of Ameri-*
     .S78   *can Naval Power, 1776-1918.* Princeton: PUP,
          1939; rpt., NIP, 1980. A classic pronavy
          history of U.S. naval policy-making.

996.   Symonds, Craig L. *Navalists and Antinavalists:*
          The Naval Policy Debate in the United States,
          1785-1827. Newark: U. of Delaware P., 1980.
          A reinterpretation of the Sprout book listed
          above.

997. E357   Taylor, George R. *The War of 1812: Past Justi-*
     .T35   *fications and Present Interpretations.* Boston:
          Heath, 1963.

998. E335   Tucker, Glenn. *Dawn Like Thunder: The Barbary*
     .T8   *Wars and the Birth of the U.S. Navy.* Indianap-
          olis: Bobbs-Merrill, 1963. A popular account.

999. E354   _____. *Poltroons and Patriots: A Popular*
     .T8   *Account of the War of 1812,* 2 vols. Indianap-
          olis: Bobbs-Merrill, 1954.

1000. E358   Updyke, Frank A. *The Diplomacy of the War of*
     .U66   *1812.* Baltimore: Johns Hopkins UP, 1915, 1969.

1001. E302.6 Walters, Raymond, Jr. *Albert Gallatin: Jeffer-*
     .G16W3 *sonian Financier and Diplomat.* N.Y.: Macmillan,
          1957.

1002. E335   Watson, Paul B. *The Tragic Career of Commodore*
      .B256   *James Barron, U.S.N.* N.Y.: Coward-McCann, 1942.

1003. E353   Wheeler, Richard. *In Pirate Waters*, N.Y.:
      .1.P7W5 Crowell, 1969. David Porter and pirate sup-
              pression, 1825.

1004. E183.7 White, Patrick C.T. *The Critical Years: Ameri-*
      .W65   *can Foreign Policy, 1793-1823.* N.Y.: Wiley,
              1970.

1005. E354   _____. *A Nation on Trial: America and the*
      .W5   *War of 1812.* N.Y.: Wiley, 1965.

1006. F1058   Zaslow, Morris, and Wesley B. Turner, eds. *The*
      .Z3   *Defended Border: Upper Canada and the War of*
              1812. Toronto: Macmillan of Canada, 1964.

DOCUMENTS

1007. G477   Porter, David. *Journal of a Cruise Made to the*
      .P84   *Pacific Ocean, by Captain David Porter, in the*
              United States Frigate Essex, *in the Years 1812,*
              1813, and 1814, 2 vols. N.Y.: Wiley & Halstead,
              1815; rpt., Gregg, 1970.

1008. Micro   U.S. NARG 45. Navy Department. *Letters Sent by*
      VB255   *the Secretary of the Navy to Officers, 1798-*
      .1.U6   *1871.*

1009. Micro   U.S. NARG 330. Navy Department. *Abstracts of*
      V11   *Service Records of Naval Officers 1798-1893.*
      .U8U10 RG24. Records of the Bureau of Naval Personnel,
      9 vols. No. 330.

1010. Micro   U.S. NA. M124. Navy Department. *Miscellaneous*
      VB255   *Letters Received by the Secretary of the Navy,*
      .L.M5   *1801-1884.* 647 reels.

1011. Micro   U.S. NA. Micro No. 148. Navy Department. *Let-*
      VB255   *ters Received by the Secretary of the Navy from*
      .1.04   *Officers Below the Rank of Commander 1802-1866.*
              RG45. 518 reels.

1012. Micro   U.S. NA. Micro Series 125. Navy Department.
              Letters Received by the Secretary of the Navy
              (Captain's Letters, 1805-1885.) 407 reels.

1013. Micro   U.S. NARG 45. Naval Records Collection of the
      VB255.1   Office of Naval Records and Library. *Letters*
      .U6   *Sent by the Secretary of the Navy to Officers,*
                   1798-1871.

1014. Micro V   U.S. NARG 45. Naval Records Collection of the
      VB255.1   Office of Naval Records and Library. *Letters*
      M3   *Received by the Secretary of the Navy from Com-*
                   manders 1804-1886.

1015. E323   U.S. Office of Naval Records and Library. *Na-*
      .U75   *val Documents Related to the Quasi-War between*
                   the United States and France: Naval Operations
                   from February 1797 to December 1801, 7 vols.
                   Ed. Dudley W. Knox.

1016. E335   U.S. Office of Naval Records and Library. *Na-*
      .A35   *val Documents Related to the United States Wars*
                   with the Barbary Powers: Naval Operations in-
                   cluding Diplomatic Background from 1785 through
                   1807, 6 vols. Ed. Dudley W. Knox. Wash.: GPO,
                   1939-1944.

DISSERTATIONS AND THESES

1017.   Anderson, William G. "John Adams and the Crea-
                   tion of the American Navy," SUNY-Stony Brook,
                   1975.

1018.   Eckert, Edward K. "William Jones and the Role
                   of the Secretary of the Navy in the War of
                   1812," U. of Florida, 1969.

1019.   Harmon, Judd S. "Suppress and Protect: The
                   United States Navy, the African Slave Trade,
                   and Maritime Commerce, 1794-1862," College of
                   William and Mary, 1977.

1020.   Kimball, Jeffrey P. "Strategy on the Northern
                   Frontier, 1814," Louisiana State U., 1969.

1021.   Richmond, Arthur A., III. "The United States
                   in the Armed Neutrality of 1800," Yale U.,
                   1951.

1022. E338   Shoemaker, Raymond L. "Diplomacy from the
      .S484   Quarterdeck: The U.S. Navy in the Caribbean,
                   1815-1830," Indiana U., 1976.

1023.   Stillson, Albert C. "The Development and Maintenance of the Naval Establishment," Columbia U., 1959.

ARTICLES

1024.   Aimone, Alan C. "The Cruise of the U.S. Sloop *Hornet* in 1815," MM 61 (Nov. 1975):377-84.

1025.   Ainsworth, W.L. "An Amphibious Operation that Failed: The Battle of New Orleans," USNIP 71 (1945):193-201.

1026.   Albion, Robert G. "The First Days of the Navy Department," MA 21 (Spring 1848):1-11.

1027.   Anderson, William G. "John Adams, the Navy, and the Quasi-War with France," AN 30 (Apr. 1970: 117-23.

1028. E356   Bancroft, George. "A History of the Battle of
      .E6B2   Lake Erie," in Oliver Dyer. *Life and Writings of Bancroft*. N.Y.: R. Bonner's Sons, 1891, pp. 129-99.

1029.   Barley, Frederick. "A British Sailor Looks at the United States Navy of the Early Nineteenth Century," AN 21 (Jan. 1961):57-69.

1030.   Barry, James P. "The Battle of Lake Erie," AHI 2 (July 1967):4-11.

1031.   Bauer, K. Jack. "Naval Shipbuilding Programs, 1794-1860," MA 29 (Spring 1965):29-40.

1032.   Beach, Edward L., Sr. "The Court-Martial of Commodore David Porter, U.S.N.," USNIP 33 (Dec. 1907):1391-1403.

1033.   Bemis, Samuel F. "The United States and the Abortive Armed Neutrality of 1794," AHR 24 (Oct. 1918):26-47.

1034.   Bolander, Louis H. "The Introduction of Shells and Shell-guns in the USN," MM 17 (Apr. 1931): 10-512.

1035.   Brown, Kenneth L. "Mr. Madison's Secretary of the Navy," USNIP 72 (Aug. 1947):967-75.

1036. Calderhead, William L. "Naval Innovation in Crisis: War in the Chesapeake, 1813," AN 36 (July 1976):206-11.

1037. _____. "U.S.S. *Constellation* in the War of 1812: An Accidental Fleet-in-Being," MA 40 (Apr. 1976):79-83.

1038. Carr, James A. "The Battle of New Orleans and the Treaty of Ghent," *Dip. Hist.* 3 (Summer 1979):273-82.

1039. _____. "John Adams and the Barbary Problem: The Myth and the Record," AN 26 (Oct. 1966): 231-57.

1040. Carter, Edward C., II. "Mathew Carey: Advocate of American Naval Power, 1785-1814," AN 26 (July 1966):177-88.

1041. Castel, Albert. "The Battle for New Orleans." AHI 4 (Aug. 1969):19-34.

1042. Chadwick, French E. "The American Navy, 1775-1815," MSH *Proceedings* 46 (1913):191-208.

1043. Cooke, Mary L., and Charles L. Lewis. "An American Naval Officer in the Mediterranean, 1802-1807," USNIP 67 (Nov. 1941):1533-39.

1044. Davis, George E. "Robert Smith and the Navy," MHM 14 (Dec. 1919):305-22.

1045. Davis, Milton S. "The Capture of Washington," USNIP 53 (June 1937):839-50.

1046. DeConde, Alexander. "The Quasi-War," AHI 12 (Apr. 1977):4-9, 44-48.

1047. Dierdorff, Ross A. "Captain James Lawrence," USNIP 84 (Jan. 1958):114.

1048. Duke, Marvin L. "The Navy Founds A Nation," USNIP 96 (Sept. 1970):59-61.

1049. Dye, Ira. "Seafarers of 1812: A Profile," *Prologue* 5 (Spring 1973):3-14.

1050. Eckert, Edward K. "Early Reform in the Navy Department," AN 32 (Oct. 1973):246-57.

1051. _____. "William Jones: Mr. Madison's Secretary of the Navy," PMHB 9 (Apr. 1972):167-82.

1052. Egan, Clifford L. "Origins of the War of 1812: Three Decades of Historical Writing," MA 38 (Apr. 1974):72-75.

1053. Ferguson, Eugene S. "Mr. Jefferson's Dry Docks," AN 11 (Apr. 1951):108-14.

1054. Fisher, Charles R. "The Great Guns of the Navy, 1797-1843," AN 75 (Oct. 1976):267-95.

1055. Goodman, Warren H. "The Origins of the War of 1812: A Survey of Changing Interpretations," MVHR 28 (Sept. 1941):171-86.

1056. Goodrich, Caspar F. "Our Navy and the West Indian Pirates: A Documentary History," USNIP 62 (1916):1171-92, 1461-83, 1923-39; 63 (1917):83-98, 313-24, 483-96, 683-98, 973-84, 1197-1206, 1449-61, 1727-38, 2023-35.

1057. Gurley, Ralph G. "The U.S.S. *Fulton* the First," USNIP 61 (Mar. 1935):337-52.

1058. Hayes, Frederic H. "John Adams and American Seapower," AN 15 (Jan. 1965):35-45.

1059. Headley, Joel T. "The Battle on the Lakes," *Harper's New Monthly Magazine*, 20 (July 1853): 208-13.

1060. Hislam, Percival A. "The Beginnings of the United States Navy," ANL 9 (Dec. 1906):623-31.

1061. Hobbs, Richard R. "Congreve War Rockets, 1800-1825," USNIP 94 (Mar. 1968):80-88.

1062. Howland, Felix. "The Blockade of Tripoli, 1801-1802," USNIP 63 (Dec. 1937):1702-04.

1063. _____. "Eaton's Declaration of the Blockade of Tripoli, 1801," USNIP 58 (Aug. 1932):1186-90.

1064. Hyneman, Charles S. "Neutrality During the European Wars of 1792-1815," AJIL 24 (Apr. 1930):279-309.

1065. Jahncke, Ernest L. "The Battle of New Orleans," USNIP 57 (Mar. 1931):293-98.

1066.   Jones, Robert F. "The Naval Thought and Policy of Benjamin Stoddert, First Secretary of the Navy, 1798-1801," AN 24 (Jan. 1964):61-69.

1067.   Kaplan, Lawrence S. "France and the War of 1812," JAG 57 (June 1970):36-47.

1068.   Keller, Allan. "The Battle of Lake Champlain," AHI 12 (Jan. 1978):4-9.

1069.   Langley, Harold D. "The Negro in the Navy and Merchant Marine, 1798-1860," JNH 52 (July 1967): 273-86.

1070.   McClellan, Edwin N. "The Navy at the Battle of New Orleans," USNIP 50 (Dec. 1924):2041-60.

1071.   McKee, Linda. *"Constitution* vs. *Guerriere,"* USNIP 88 (Aug. 1962):72-79.

1072.   McLeod, Julia. "Jefferson and the Navy: A Defense," *Huntington Lib. Q.* 8 (Feb. 1945):153-84. An important, groundbreaking article.

1073.   Mahan, Alfred T. "Commodore Macdonough at Plattsburg," NAR 200 (Aug. 1914):203-21.

1074.   _____. "The Negotiations at Ghent in 1814," AHR 11 (Oct. 1905):68-87.

1075.   Norton, Paul F. "Jefferson's Plan for Mothballing the Frigates," USNIP 82 (May 1956):736-41.

1076.   Oliver, F.L. "Commodore Oliver Hazard Perry of Newport, Rhode Island," USNIP 80 (July 1954): 777-83.

1077.   Owsley, Frank L., Jr. "The Role of the South in the British Grand Strategy in the War of 1812," *Tenn. Hist. Q.* 31 (Spring 1972):22-38.

1078.   Parks, E. Taylor. "Robert Fulton and Submarine Warfare," MA 26 (Fall 1961):177-82.

1079.   Paullin, Charles O. "The Services of Commodore John Rodgers in the War of 1812," USNIP 35 (June 1909):473-511.

1080.   _____. "The Services of Commodore John Rodgers in Our Wars with the Barbary Corsairs," USNIP 34 (Dec. 1908):1141-88.

1081. _____. "Naval Administration Under Secretaries of the Navy Smith, Hamilton, and Jones, 1801-1814," USNIP 32 (Dec. 1906):1289-1328.

1082. Perry, Percival. "The Naval-Stores Industry in the Old South, 1790-1860," JSH 34 (Nov. 1968): 509-26.

1083. Post, Waldron K. "The Case of Captain [James] Lawrence," USNIP 62 (July 1936):969-74.

1084. Purcell, Hugh D. "Don't Give Up the Ship," USNIP 91 (May 1965):82-94.

1085. Robison, S.S. "Commodore Thomas Truxtun, U.S. Navy," USNIP 68 (April 1932):541-54.

1086. Roosevelt, Franklin D. "Our First Frigates: Some Unpublished Facts About Their Construction." TSONAME 22 (1914):139-55.

1087. Roosevelt, Theodore. "The War with the United States, 1812-1815," in William L. Clowes, *The Royal Navy....*, 7 vols. London: S. Low, Marston, 1901, 6:1-180.

1088. Scheina, Robert L. "Benjamin Stoddert, Politics, and the Navy," AN 35 (Jan. 1976):54-68.

1089. Smelser, Marshall. "The Passing of the Naval Act of 1794," MA 22 (Spring 1958):1-12.

1090. Smith, Geoffrey S. "The Navy Before Darwinism: Science, Exploration, and Diplomacy in Antebellum America," *Am.Q.* 28 (Spring 1976):41-55.

1091. Smith, Jay D. "Commodore James Barron: Guilty as Charged?" USNIP 93 (Nov. 1967):79-85.

1092. Sokol, Anthony E. "The Barbary Corsairs: a Lesson in Appeasement and International Cooperation," USNIP 75 (July 1949):797-803.

1093. Soley, James R. "The Naval Campaign of 1812," USNIP 7 (Oct. 20, 1881):297-324.

1094. _____. "Operations of the American Squadron Under Commodore Edward Preble in 1803-04," USNIP 5 (Jan. 9, 1879):51-98.

1095.   Steel, Anthony. "Impressment in the Monroe-Pinkney Negotiations, 1806-1807," AHR 57 (Jan. 1952):352-69.

1096.   Strauss, W. Patrick. "Captain David Porter: Pioneer Pacific Strategist," USNIP 93 (Feb. 1967):158-60.

1097.   Symonds, Craig. "The Antinavalists: The Opponents of Naval Expansion in the Early National Period," AN 39 (Jan. 1979):22-28.

1098.   _____. "The American Naval Expedition to Penobscot, 1779," NWCR 24 (Apr. 1972):64-71.

1099.   Thomson, David W. "Robert Fulton's 'Torpedo System' in the War of 1812," USNIP 72 (Sept. 1946):1207-17.

1100.   Tyler, David B. "Fulton's Steam Frigate," AN 6 (Apr. 1946):253-74.

1101.   Washburn, Harold C. "The Battle of Lake Champlain," USNIP 40 (Sept.-Oct. 1914):1365-86.

1102.   Westcott, Allan. "Commodore Jesse D. Elliott: A Stormy Petrel of the Navy," USNIP 54 (Sept. 1928):773-78.

1103.   Wilkinson, Dave. "Victory at Fayal," AHI 13 (Nov. 1978):10-19. War of 1812.

1104.   Wilson, H.W. "The War of 1812-1815," in *Cambridge Modern History*, 7: 335-48.

1105.   Wood, Daniel W. "The All-Volunteer Force in 1798," USNIP 105 (June 1979):45-48.

1106.   Woolsey, L.H. "Early Cases on the Doctrine of Continuous Voyage," AJIL 4 (Oct. 1910):823-47.

1107.   Wright, C.Q. "The Tripoli Monument," USNIP 48 (Nov. 1922):1931-41.

FICTION

1108. PZ7   Dean, Leon W. *Guns Over Champlain*. N.Y.:
     .D345Gu   Rinehart, 1946.

1109. PZ3   Harper, Robert S. *Trumpet in the Wilderness*.
      .H234   N.Y.: Mill, 1940. O.H. Perry on Lake Erie.
      Tr

1110. PZ4   Hepburn, Andrew. *Letter of Marque*. Boston:
      .H527   Little, Brown, 1959. Privateering during the
      Le   War of 1812.

1111. PS3515   Hergesheimer, Joseph. *Java Head*. N.Y.: Knopf,
      .E628J38   1918. Recreates New England in the heyday of
                 the old sailing ships.

1112. PZ3   Jennings, John E. *The Tall Ships*. N.Y.: McGraw-
      .J4433   Hill, 1958. War of 1812.
      Tal

1113. PS3525   Mason, F. Van Wyck. *Guns for the Rebellion*.
      .A822   GCNY: Doubleday, 1977.

1114. PS3525   _____. *Wild Horizon*. Boston: Little, Brown,
      .A822   1966.

1115. PS3525   _____. *Eagle in the Sky*. Phila.: Lippincott,
      .A822   1948.
      E34

1116. PS3525   _____. *Rivers of Glory*. N.Y.: Grosset & Dun-
      .A822   lap, 1942.
      R58

1117. PS3525   _____. *Stars on the Sea*. N.Y.: Grosset &
      .A822   Dunlap, 1940.
      S83

1118. PS3525   _____. *Three Harbours*. N.Y.: Grosset & Dun-
      .A822   lap, 1938.
      T57

1119. PS2384   Melville, Herman. *Billy Budd: Foretopman*. N.Y.:
      .B54F71   various publishers, 1891- . A sailor strikes
                 an officer during the mutinies of 1797.

1120. PZ7   Muller, Charles G. *Hero of Champlain*. N.Y.:
      M915   Stein & Day, 1961. Thomas Macdonough.
      He

1121. PS3535   Roberts, Kenneth L. *Lydia Bailey*. GCNY:
      .0176   Doubleday, 1947. Includes the War with Tripoli.
      L83

1122. PS3535   _____. *The Lively Lady*.... GCNY: Doubleday,
      .0176   Doran, 1931. War of 1812.
      L58

1123. PZ7   Swanson, Neil H. *The Star-Spangled Banner*....
      .8972St   N.Y.: Holt, 1958. Baltimore besieged, War of
                1812.

5

THE U.S. NAVY AT PEACE AND WAR, 1815-1861

BOOKS

1124. PS2528   Aderman, Ralph M., ed. *The Letters of James*
       .A45   *Kirke Paulding*. Madison: U. of Wisconsin P.,
                 1962.

1125. E467.1   Alden, Carroll S. *George Hamilton Perkins, Com-*
       .P4A35   *modore, U.S.N.: His Life and Letters*. Boston:
                 Houghton Mifflin, 1914. Covers the years
                 1836-1899.

1126. E182   _____. *Lawrence Kearny, Sailor Diplomat*.
       .K25   Princeton: PUP, 1936.

1127. F2161   Allen, Gardner W. *Our Navy and the West Indies*
       .A48   *Pirates*. Salem, Mass.: Essex Institute, 1929.

1128. V63   *Autobiography of Rear Admiral Charles Wilkes*,
       .W5A3   *USN, 1798-1877*. Eds. William J. Morgan and
                 others. Wash.: Naval Hist. Center, 1979.

1129. F861   Bancroft, Hubert H. *History of California*, 7
       .B19   vols. San Francisco: The History Co., 1884-
                 1890. Vol. 5 deals with the conquest of Cali-
                 fornia by the United States.

1130. E182   Barrow, Clayton R., Jr., comp. and ed. *America*
       .B28   *Spreads Her Sails: U.S. Seapower in the Nine-*
                 teenth Century. Annapolis, Md.: NIP, 1973.

1131. E182   Barrows, Edward M. *The Great Commodore: The*
       .P454   *Exploits of Matthew Calbraith Perry*. Indianap-
                 olis: Bobbs-Merrill, 1935. Use with care.

1132. E404   Bauer, K. Jack. *The Mexican War, 1846-1848*.
       .B37   N.Y.: Macmillan, 1974.

1133. E410   _____. *Surfboats and Horse Marines: U.S.*
       .B38   *Naval Operations in the Mexican War, 1846-1848*.
                 Annapolis, Md.: USNI, 1969.

1134. V799   Baxter, James P. *Introduction of the Ironclad*
       .B3   *Warship*. Cambridge, Mass.: HUP, 1933.

1135. E403   Bayard, Samuel J. *The Life of Commodore Robert*
       .1.S8B3   *F. Stockton*. N.Y.: Derby and Jackson, 1856.

1136. VA55   Bennett, Frank M. *The Steam Navy of the United*
      .B48   *States: A History of the Growth of the Steam*
                 Vessel of War in the United States Navy, and of
                 the Naval Engineer Corps. Pittsburgh: W.T.
                 Nicholson, 1896.

1137. E340   Bixby, William. *The Forgotten Voyage of Charles*
      .W6B5   *Wilkes.* N.Y.: McKay, 1966.

1138. E415.9   Bohner, Charles H. *John Pendleton Kennedy: Gen-*
      .K35B6   *tleman from Baltimore.* Baltimore: Johns Hopkins
                 UP, 1961.

1139. E83   Buker, George E. *Swamp Sailors: Riverine Warfare*
      .835.B8   *in the Everglades.* Gainesville: U. Presses of
                 Florida, 1975.

1140. GC30   Caskie, Jaquelin A. *Life and Letters of Matthew*
      .M4C3   *Fontaine Maury.* Richmond, Va.: Richmond P.,
                 1928.

1141. VM23   Chapelle, Howard I. *The Baltimore Clipper: Its*
      .C5   *Origin and Development.* Salem, Mass.: Marine
                 Research Soc., 1930, 1972.

1142. VK19   Clark, Arthur H. *The Clipper Ship Era....* N.Y.:
      .C55   Putnam, 1910.

1143. E410   Conner, Philip S.P. *The Home Squadron Under*
      .C75   *Commodore Conner in the War with Mexico.* Phila.:
                 Privately printed, 1896.

1144. E404   Connor, Seymour, and Odie B. Faulk. *North America*
      .C8   *Divided: The Mexican War, 1846-1848.* N.Y.: Ox-
                 ford UP, 1971.

1145. G662   Corner, George W. *Doctor Kane of the Arctic*
      .K36C67   *Seas.* Phila.: Temple UP, 1972.

1146. E410   Downey, Joseph T. Ed. by Howard Lamar. *The*
      .D65   *Cruise of the* Portsmouth, *1845-1847: A Sailor's*
                 View of the Naval Conquest of California. New
                 Haven: YUP, 1963.

1147. E411   Dubois, William E.B. *The Suppression of the*
      .D81   *African Slave Trade to the United States of*
                 America, 1638-1870. 1898; rpt., N.Y.: Russell
                 & Russell, 1965.

1148. E404   Dufour, Charles L. *The Mexican War: A Compact*
      .D87   *History, 1846-1848.* N.Y.: Hawthorn, 1968.

1149. HF3120 Dulles, Foster R. *The Old China Trade.* Boston:
      .D8   Houghton Mifflin, 1930; rpt., AMS, 1970.

1150. SH381   _____. *Lowered Boats: A Chronicle of Ameri-*
      .D8   *can Whaling.* N.Y.: Harcourt Brace, 1933.

1151. E467.1 DuPont, Henry A. *Rear Admiral Samuel Francis*
      .D9D89 *DuPont, United States Navy: A Biography.* N.Y.:
              National Am. Soc., 1926.

1152. E591   DuPont, Samuel F. *Official Despatches and Let-*
      .D93   *ters.... 1846, 1848, 1861, 1863.* Wilmington,
              Del.: Ferris Bros., 1883.

1153. DU29   Falk, Edwin R. *From Perry to Pearl Harbor: The*
      .F3   *Struggle for Supremacy in the Pacific.* GCNY:
              Doubleday, Doran, 1943.

1154. DS757   Fay, Peter W. *The Opium War, 1840-1842....*
      .5.F39 Chapel Hill: UNCP, 1975. Detailed day-by-day
              account.

1155. DS63.2 Field, James A. *Americans and the Mediterranean*
      .U5F47 *World, 1776-1882.* Princeton: PUP, 1969.

1156. E661.7 Grenville, John A.S., and George B. Young. *Pol-*
      .G7   *itics, Strategy, and American Diplomacy: Studies*
              in Foreign Policy, 1873-1917. New Haven: Yale
              UP, 1966.

1157. E183.8 Griffin, Charles C. *The United States and the*
      .S7G72 *Disruption of the Spanish Empire, 1810-1822....*
              N.Y.: Columbia UP, 1937.

1158. E182   Griffis, William E. *Matthew Calbraith Perry:*
      .P46   *A Typical American Naval Officer.* Boston: Cup-
              ples & Hurd, 1887. In no way comparable to
              the biography by S.E. Morison.

1159. VA56   Guttridge, Leonard F., and Jay D. Smith. *The*
      .G8   *Commodores.* N.Y.: Harper & Row, 1969. Person-
              alities who served on the Board of Navy Com-
              missioners.

1160. E340   Hall, Claude H. *Abel Parker Upshur: Conserva-*
      .U6H3   *tive Virginian, 1790-1844.* Madison: State Hist.
              Soc. of Wisconsin, 1964.

1161. GC30   Hawthorne, Hildegarde. *Matthew Fontaine Maury:*
      .M4H3   *Trail Maker of the Seas.* N.Y.: Longmans, Green,
                1943.

1162. E340   Henderson, Daniel M. *The Hidden Coasts: A Biog-*
      .W6H4   *raphy of Admiral Charles Wilkes.* N.Y.: Sloane,
                1953; rpt., Greenwood, 1970.

1163. PS2528   Herold, Amos L. *James Kirke Paulding: Versatile*
      .H4   *American.* N.Y.: Columbia UP, 1926, 1970.

1164. E382   James, Marquis. *Andrew Jackson: Portrait of a*
      .J27   *President.* Indianapolis: Bobbs-Merrill, 1937.

1165. Q11   Johnson, Daniel N. *The Journals of Daniel Noble*
      .S7   *Johnson, 1822-1863, United States Navy.* Ed.
                Mondel L. Peterson. Wash.: Smithsonian Insti-
                tute, 1950. Cruise of the *Delaware* to Brazil,
                1841-1842.

1166. E182   Johnson, Robert E. *Rear Admiral John Rodgers,*
      .R68J6   *1812-1882.* Annapolis, Md.: USNI, 1967.

1167. E182   _____. *Thence Round Cape Horn: The Story of*
      .J58   *United States Naval Forces on Pacific Station,*
                1818-1923. Annapolis, Md.: USNI, 1963.

1168. VB23   Langley, Harold D. *Social Reform in the United*
      .L3   *States Navy, 1798-1862.* Urbana: U. of Illinois
                P., 1967.

1169. E405   Lawson, Don. *The United States in the Mexican*
      .L38   *War.* N.Y.: Abelard-Schuman, 1976.

1170. GC30   Lewis, Charles L. *Matthew Fontaine Maury: The*
      .M4L4   *Pathfinder of the Seas.* Annapolis, Md.: USNI,
                1927.

1171. E353   Long, David F. *Nothing Too Daring: A Biography*
      .1.P7L6   *of Commodore David Porter, 1780-1843.* Annapolis,
                Md., USNI, 1970.

1172. DS107   Lynch, William G. *Narrative of the United States*
      .L98   *Expedition to the River Jordan and the Dead Sea,*
                6th ed. Phila.: Lea & Blanchard, 1849.

1173. E182   Meade, Rebecca P. *Life of Hiram Paulding, Rear*
      .P32   *Admiral, U.S.N.* N.Y.: Baker & Taylor, 1910.

1174. V63   Meissner, Mme. Sophie (Radford) de. *Old Naval*
       R3M4   *Days: Sketches from the Life of Rear Admiral*
                William Radford, U.S.N. N.Y.: Holt, 1920.

1175. V63   Morgan, William J., and others, eds. *Autobiog-*
       .W5A3   *raphy of Rear Admiral Charles Wilkes, USN,*
                1798-1877. Wash.: GPO, 1979.

1176. E182   Morison, Samuel E. *"Old Bruin": Commodore*
       .P466   *Matthew C. Perry, 1794-1858.* Boston: Little,
                Brown, 1967.

1177. JX1407   Paullin, Charles O. *Diplomatic Negotiations of*
       .P3   *American Naval Officers, 1778-1883.* Baltimore:
                Johns Hopkins P., 1912.

1178. E353.1   _____. *Commodore John Rodgers: Captain, Com-*
       .R7P28   *modore, and Senior Officer of the American Na-*
                vy, 1773-1838: A Biography. Cleveland: Clark,
                1910.

1179. DS809   Perry, Matthew C. *Narrative of the Expedition*
       .P45   *of an American Squadron to the China Seas and*
                Japan, Performed in the Years 1852, 1853, and
                1854, Under the Command of Commodore M.C. Perry
                United States Navy, 3 vols. Ed. Francis L.
                Hawks. N.Y.: Appleton, 1857; rpt., Arno, 1968.

1180. DS881   Preble, George H. *The Opening of Japan: A Diary*
       .8.P7   *of Discovery in the Far East, 1853-1856. From*
                the Original Manuscript in the Massachusetts
                Historical Society. Ed. Boleslaw Szczesniak.
                Norman: U. of Oklahoma P., 1962.

1181. E404   Ripley, Roswell S. *The War with Mexico.* N.Y.:
       .R59   Harper, 1949.

1182. F1232   Rives, George L. *The United States and Mexico,*
       .R62   2 vols. N.Y.: Scribner, 1913.

1183. E182   Sands, Benjamin F. *From Reefer to Rear Admiral:*
       .S21   *Reminiscences of Nearly Half a Century of Na-*
                val Life, 1827-1874. N.Y.: F.A. Stokes, 1899.

1184. E183.8   Schmitt, Karl M. *Mexico and the United States,*
       .M6S35   *1821-1973.* N.Y.: Wiley, 1974.

1185. E415.9   Sears, Louis M. *John Slidell.* Durham: Duke UP,
       .S58S4   1925.

1186. DS755   Selby, John M. *The Paper Dragon: An Account of*
       .S4   *the China Wars, 1840-1900.* N.Y.: Praeger, 1968.

1187. E404   Semmes, Raphael. *Service Afloat and Ashore Dur-*
       .S47   *ing the Mexican War.* Cincinnati: W.H. Moore,
                 1851.

1188. E338   Shoemaker, Raymond L. *Diplomacy from the Quar-*
       .S484   *terdeck: The U.S. Navy in the Caribbean, 1815-*
                 1830. Bloomington: Indiana UP, 1976.

1189. E404   Singletary, Otis A. *The Mexican War.* Chicago:
       .S5   U. of Chicago P., 1960.

1190. Z675   Skallerup, Harry K. *Books Afloat and Ashore: A*
       .N3554   *History of Books, Libraries, and Reading Among*
                 Seamen during the Age of Sail. Hamden, Conn.:
                 Shoe String, 1974.

1191. E404   Smith, Justin H. *The War With Mexico*, 2 vols.
       .S66   N.Y.: Macmillan, 1919; rpt., Gloucester, Mass.:
                 P. Smith, 1963.

1192. H31.J6   Soulsby, Hugh G. *The Right of Search and the*
       Ser. 51   *Slave Trade in Anglo-American Relations, 1814-*
       No.2   *1862.* Baltimore: Johns Hopkins P., 1933.

1193. Q115   Stanton, William. *The Great United States Ex-*
       .S74   *ploring Expedition of 1838-1842.* Berkeley:
                 U. of California P., 1975. Very critical of
                 Wilkes.

1194. V83   Stevens, William O. *An Affair of Honor: The*
       .B34S7   *Biography of Commodore James Barron.* Chesa-
                 peake, Va.: Norfolk County Hist. Soc., 1969.

1195. E353.1   Turnbull, Archibald D. *Commodore David Porter,*
       .P7T95   *1780-1843.* N.Y.: Century, 1929.

1196. Q11   Tyler, David B. *The Wilkes Expedition: The*
       .P612   *First United States Exploring Expedition, 1838-*
       v.73   *1842.* Phila.: Am. Philosophical Soc., 1968.

1197. DS881   Walworth, Arthur. *Black Ships Off Japan: The*
       .8.W3   *Story of Commodore Perry's Expedition.* N.Y.:
                 Knopf, 1946; rpt., Shoe String, 1966.

1198. GC30   Wayland, John W. *The Pathfinder of the Seas:*
       .M4W3   *The Life of Matthew Fontaine Maury.* Richmond,
                 Va.: Garrett and Massie, 1930.

1199. E404 Weems, John E. *To Conquer a Peace: The War*
      .W35 *Between the United States and Mexico.* GCNY:
            Doubleday, 1974.

1200. E353.1 Wheeler, Richard. *In Pirate Waters.* N.Y.:
      .P7W5   Crowell, 1969. History of the Brazil Squadron.

1201. E473 White, William C., and Ruth (Morris) White.
      .2.W6 *Yankee from Sweden: The Dream and Reality in*
             the Days of John Ericsson. N.Y.: Holt, 1960.

1202. Wilkes, Charles. *See* Autobiography of, above.

1203. GC30 Williams, Frances L. *Matthew Fontaine Maury:*
      .M4W5 *Scientist of the Sea.* New Brunswick, N.J.:
             Rutgers UP, 1963.

DOCUMENTS

1204. Schwartz, William L. "Commodore Perry at
       Okinawa: From the Unpublished Diary of a
       British Missionary," AHR 51 (Jan. 1946):
       262-76.

1205. U.S. Congress. House. *Reports and Despatches*
       Exhibiting the Operations of U.S. Naval
       Forces During the War with Mexico. H. Exec.
       Doc. No. 1, pp. 1006-1237, 30th Cong., 2d
       Sess. Wash.: Wendell & Van Benthuysen, 1848.

1206. U.S. Congress. House. *Mexican War Corres-*
       pondence. H. Exec. Doc. No. 60, 30th Cong.,
       1st Sess. Wash.: Wendell & Van Benthuysen,
       1848.

1207. JX233 U.S. Department of State. *Papers Relating to*
      A3   *the Foreign Relations of the United States.*
      (year) Wash.: Dept. of State, 1861- .

1208. Micro   U.S. NARG 45. *Letters Sent by the Secretary of*
      VB255   *the Navy to the Chiefs of Navy Bureaus 1842-*
      .1.U75 *1886.*

1209. Micro   U.S. NARG 45. Naval Records Collection of the
      VB255.1   Office of Naval Records and Library. *Letters*
      .C48   *Received by the Secretary of the Navy from*
                Chiefs of Navy Bureaus 1842-1885. 87 vols. on
                33 reels.

| 1210. | Micro
V415
.L1A4 | U.S. NARG 405. U.S. Naval Academy. *Letters Received by the Superintendent of the U.S. Naval Academy, 1845-1887.* 11 reels. |

DISSERTATIONS AND THESES

1211. Betts, John L. "The United States Navy in the Mexican War," U. of Chicago, 1954.

1212. Micro E182 .J78 Bradley, Udolpho T. "The Contentious Commodore: Thomas ap Catesby Jones of the Old Navy, 1788-1858," Cornell U., 1933.

1213. Henson, Curtis T. "The United States Navy and China, 1839-1861," Tulane U., 1965.

1214. Manno, Francis J. "History of United States Naval Operations, 1846-1848: With Particular Emphasis on the War with Mexico," Georgetown U., 1954.

1215. Pitt, M.R. "Great Britain and Belligerent Maritime Rights from the Declaration of Paris, 1856, to the Declaration of London, 1909," U. of London, 1964.

1216. Towle, Edward L. "Science, Commerce, and the Navy on the Seafaring Frontier (1842-1869): The Role of Lieutenant M.F. Maury and the U.S. Naval Hydrographic Office in Naval Exploration, Commercial Expansion, and Oceanography Before the Civil War," U. of Rochester, 1966.

ARTICLES

1217. Allin, Lawrence C. "The Dignity of Discipline As Conceived by Secretary of the Navy Abel P. Upshur," *Shipmate* 41 (Apr. 1978):16-18; rpt. from NWCR 22 (June 1970):85-91.

1218. G525 .B255 Baldwin, Hanson. "Mutiny on the Brig *Somers:* 1842," in his *Sea Fights and Shipwrecks.* GCNY: Hanover House, 1955, pp. 183-206.

1219. Barbour, Violet. "Privateers and Pirates of the West Indies," AHR 16 (Apr. 1911):529-66.

1220. Bauer, K. Jack. "The Veracruz Expedition of 1847," MA 20 (Fall 1956):162-69.

1221. Ben-Arieh, Yehoshua. "William G. Lynch's Expedition to the Dead Sea, 1847-1848," *Prologue* 5 (Spring 1973):15-21.

1222.   Bluff, Harry [Matthew F. Maury], "On Reorganiz-
          ing the Navy," *Southern Literary Messenger*
          (1841).

1223.   Bolander, Louis H. "The Introduction of Shells,
          and Shell Guns in the United States Navy,"
          MM 17 (Apr. 1931):105-12.

1224.   Bradley, Udolpho T. "Commodore Rodgers and the
          Bureau System of Naval Administration," USNIP
          57 (Mar. 1931):307-16.

1225.   Brant, Irving. "Madison and the War of 1812,"
          VMHB 74 (Jan. 1966):51-67.

1226.   Brooke, George M., Jr. "The Vest Pocket War of
          Commodore Jones," PHR 31 (Aug. 1962):217-33.
          Jones's taking of Monterey in 1842.

1227.   _____. "The Role of the United States Navy
          in the Suppression of the African Slave Trade,"
          AN 31 (Jan. 1961):28-41.

1228.   Brown, F.C. "The U.S. Asiatic Fleet," *Military
          Jour.*, Sept. 1978, pp. 7-11.

1229.   Brown, F.M. "A Half Century of Frustration: A
          Study of the Failure of Naval Academy Legisla-
          tion Between 1800 and 1845," USNIP 80 (June
          1954):631-35.

1230.   Bryan, George S. "The Wilkes Exploring Expedi-
          tion," USNIP 65 (Oct. 1939):1452-64.

1231.   Buell, Thomas B. "Saga of Drydock One," USNIP
          96 (July 1970):60-67. Use of drydock No. 1,
          at Norfolk, since 1825.

1232.   Coletta, Paolo E. "Oceanography: Maury to
          Mohole," USNIP 86 (Apr. 1960):98+.

1233.   Daniel, Robert L. "American Influences in the
          Near East Before 1861," *Am. Q.* 16 (Spring 1964):
          72-84.

1234.   Doenhoff, Richard A. von. "Biddle, Perry, and
          Japan," USNIP 92 (Nov. 1966):78-87.

1235.   Dyson, George W. "Charles H. Haswell and the
          Steam Navy," USNIP 61 (Feb. 1939):225-30.

1236.   Earle, Ralph. "John Adolphus Dahlgren," USNIP
            51 (Mar. 1925):424-36.

1237.   Egan, Clifford L. "The Origins of the War of
            1812: Three Decades of Historical Writing,"
            MA 38 (Apr. 1974):72-79.

1238.   Farley, M. Fosler. "Josiah Tattnall: American
            Sea Dog," *Hist. Today* 29 (Mar. 1979):163-71.

1239.   Giffin, Donald W. "The American Navy at Work on
            the Brazil Station, 1827-1860," AN 19 (Oct.
            1959):239-56.

1240.   Gleaves, Albert. "The [Lt. Edwin J.] DeHaven
            Arctic Expedition: A Forgotten Page in American
            Naval History," USNIP 54 (July 1928):579-91.

1241.   Gurley, Ralph L. The U.S.S. *Fulton the First,*"
            USNIP 61 (Mar. 1935):322-28.

1242.   Hall, Claude H. "Abel Parker Upshur: An Eastern
            Shoreman Reforms the United States Navy [1841-
            1844]," *Va. Cavalcade*, Spring 1974, pp. 29-37.

1243.   Hanks, Robert J. "Commodore Lawrence Kearny:
            The Diplomatic Seaman," USNIP 96 (Nov. 1970):
            70-72.

1244.   Harmon, Judd S. "Marriage of Convenience: The
            United States Navy in Africa, 1820-1843," AN
            32 (Oct. 1972):264-74.

1245.   Hill, Jim D. "Charles Wilkes: Turbulent Scholar
            of the Old Navy," USNIP 57 (July 1931):867-87.

1246.   Holbrook, Francis X. "The Navy's Cross: William
            Walker," MA 49 (Dec. 1975):197-202.

1247.   Hooper, Edwin B. "Developing Naval Concepts:
            The Early Years," *Defense Management Jour.* 12
            (July 1976):19-24. Board of Navy Commissioners.

1248.   Horan, Leo F.S. "Flogging in the U.S. Navy: Un-
            familiar Facts Regarding its Origin and Aboli-
            tion [in 1850]," USNIP 76 (Sept. 1950):968-75.

1249.   Hunt, Livingston. "The Attempted Mutiny on the
            U.S. Brig *Somers*," USNIP 51 (Nov. 1925):2062-99.

1250.   Janes, Henry L. "The *Black Warrior* Affair,"
         AHR 12 (Jan. 1907):280-98. Imposition of
         Spain's navigation laws upon American trade
         with Cuba, 1854.

1251.   *Jenkins, James C. "Brigadier General Archibald
         Henderson, USMC," MCG 25 (June 1941):18, 50-54.

1252.   Jones, Oakah L. "The Pacific Squadron and the
         Conquest of California, 1846-1847," *Jour. of
         the West*. 5 (Apr. 1966):187-202.

1253.   Kendall, David W. "The Navy in the Orient in
         1842," USNIP 68 (May 1942):645-50. Lawrence
         Kearny's activities.

1254.   Klapp, Orrin E. "Matthew Fontaine Maury, Naval
         Scientist," USNIP 71 (Nov. 1945):1315-25.

1255.   Krafft, Herman F. "The Navy and Flogging,"
         USNIP 55 (Mar. 1929):270-73.

1256.   _____. "Commodore John Downes, from His Of-
         ficial Correspondence," USNIP 54 (Jan. 1928):
         36-48.

1257.   Krout, Mary H. "Rear Admiral Charles Wilkes and
         His Exploits," USNIP 50 (Mar. 1924):405-16.

1258.   _____. "Perry's Expedition to Japan," USNIP
         47 (Feb. 1921):215-29.

1259.   Kublin, Hyman. "Commodore Perry and the Bonin
         Islands," USNIP 78 (Mar. 1952):282-91.

1260.   *Lanier, William D. "The Halls of Montezuma,"
         USNIP 67 (Oct. 1941):1385-98. Operations of
         the USMC in Mexico.

1261.   Littlehales, George W. "William Chauvenet and
         the United States Naval Academy," USNIP 31
         (Sept. 1905):605-12.

1262.   Livermore, Seward W. "American Naval-Base Policy
         in the Far East, 1850-1914," PHR 13 (June 1944):
         113-35.

1263.   Luce, Stephen B. "Commodore James Biddle's
         Visit to Japan in 1846," USNIP 31 (Sept. 1905):
         556-63.

1264. Maclay, Edgar S. "The Chastisement of the Qualla Battooans," *Harper's* 88 (May 1894): 858-70.

1265. MacMaster, Richard K. "United States Navy and African Exploration," *Mid-America* 46 (July 1964):187-203.

1266. Merrill, James M. "The Asiatic Squadron 1835-1907," AN 29 (Apr. 1969):106-17.

1267. Mitchell, Donald W. "Abel Upshur: Forgotten Prophet of the Old Navy," USNIP 75 (Nov. 1949): 1366-75.

1268. *Montross, Lynn. "War with the Seminoles," *Leatherneck* 43 (Nov. 1960):40-43. An account of Marine actions against Seminole Indians in Florida, 1835-1842.

1269. Morris, Charles. "Autobiography of Commodore C. Morris, USN," USNIP 6, No. 12 (1880):111-219.

1270. Morris, H.H. "The USS *Somers* Affair," AHI 9 (Aug. 1974):24-31.

1271. Morsberger, Robert E. "The Wilkes Expedition, 1838-1842," AHI 7 (June 1972):4-10.

1272. F596 O'Connor, Raymond G. "The Navy and the Fron-
        .M53   tier," *The American Military on the Frontier:
        1976   Proceedings of the Seventh Military History
               Symposium*, 30 September-1 October 1976. Ed.
               James P. Tate. Wash.: GPO, 1978.

1273. Orth, Michael. "The Stevens Battery," USNIP 92 (June 1966):92-99.

1274. Paullin, Charles O. "Naval Administration, 1842-1861," USNIP 33 (Dec. 1907):1435-77.

1275. _____. "Naval Administration Under the Navy Commissioners, 1816-1842," USNIP 33 (June 1907): 597-642.

1276. Ray, Thomas W. "The Bureaus Go On Forever," USNIP 94 (Jan. 1968):50-63. Covers the years 1842 to 1966.

1277.   Reynolds, Clark G. "The Great Experiment: Hunter's Horizontal Wheel," AN 24 (June 1964):5-24.

1278.   *Smith, Cornelius C., Jr. "Our First Amphibious Assault," MR 38 (Feb. 1959):18-28. Vera Cruz during the Mexican War.

1279.   Smith, Geoffrey S. "The Navy before Darwinism: Science, Exploration, and Diplomacy in Antebellum America," *Am. Q.* 28 (Spring 1976):41-55.

1280.   Taggart, Robert. "The Early Development of the Screw Propeller," *Am. Soc. of Naval Engineers Jour.* 71 (May 1959):259-76.

1281.   Thom, J.C. "The American Navy and the Dead Sea," USNIP 52 (Sept. 1926):1689-1700. The Lynch expedition.

1282.   Tiernay, John A. "William Chauvenet: Father of the Naval Academy," *Shipmate* 32 (Sept.-Oct. 1969):6-11.

1283.   Workman, Gilbert. "A Forgotten Firebrand," USNIP 94 (Sept. 1968):79-87. Catesby Jones.

FICTION

1284.   PS643   Averill, Charles E. *The Secret Service Ship:*
       .A5   *Or, The Fall of San Juan d'Ulloa. A Thrilling Tale of the Mexican War.* Boston: F. Gleason, 1848.

1285.   P21   Ballou, Maturin M. *The Sea Witch...: A Story*
       N93   *of the Slave Coast.* N.Y.: Samuel French, 1855?
       No. 91   On the African antislave ship patrol in the 1850s.

1286.   PZ3   Bellah, James W. *The Journal of Colonel de*
       .B4158   *Tancey.* Phila.: Chilton, 1967. The U.S. Navy
       Jo   thwarts filibusterer William Walker in Central America.

1287.   P27   Bishop, Farnaham. *The Black Bloodhound.* Boston:
       .525   Little, Brown, 1927. Excitement in West Indian
       B1   waters in the 1840s.

1288.   PZ7   Brady, Cyrus T. *On the Old "Kearsarge": A Story*
       B729   *of the Civil War.* N.Y.: Scribner, 1919. Battle
       On   between the *Alabama* and the *Kearsarge*.

1289. PR6003   Bullen, Frank T. *The Cruise of the Cachalot....*
      U23C78   N.Y.: Appleton, 1899. A whaling ship in the
                South Seas.

1290. PS3553   Carlisle, Henry. *Voyage to the First of Decem-*
      A72U69   *ber.* N.Y.: Putnam, 1972. The mutiny in the
                U.S.S. *Somers.*

1291. PZ3   Chidsey, Donald B. *Stronghold.* GCNY: Doubleday,
      .C4346   1948. Impressment, War of 1812.
      St

1292. PR6005   Conrad, Joseph. *Lord Jim.* N.Y.: Macmillan, 1899.
      .04L67   Psychological analysis of a seaman presumed to
                be a coward.

1293. G540   Dana, Richard H., Jr. *Two Years Before the*
      .D2   *Mast....* N.Y.: Houghton, 1840. Autobiographi-
                cal reporting on merchant-ship voyages around
                the Horn from New England to California.

1294. PS3513   Gerson, Noel B., pseud. *Clear for Action.* GCNY:
      .E8679   Doubleday, 1970. David G. Farragut.
      C55

1295. E599   Hunt, Cornelius E. *The* Shenandoah: *or the Last*
      .S5H9   *Confederate Cruiser.* N.Y.: Carleton, 1967.

1296. PS2384   Melville, Herman. *Moby-Dick, Or: the White*
      .M6F75   *Whale.* N.Y.: Harper, 1851. Whale hunt with
                philosophical comments on human life and fate.

1297. PS2719   Robertson, Morgan. *Sinful Peck: A Novel.* N.Y.:
      .R38S55   Harper, 1908. Covers the years 1861-1915.

1298. PZ3   *Slaughter, Frank G. *Fort Everglades.* GCNY:
      S63165   Doubleday, 1951. Navymen and marines in the
                Seminole War.

1299. PS3537   Street, James H. *By Valour and Arms.* GCNY:
      .T8278   Dial, 1944. The Confederate ironclad *Arkansas*
                on the Mississippi during the Civil War.

6

NAVAL POWER AND THE AMERICAN CIVIL WAR, 1861-1865

BOOKS

1300. E591
       .A13
Abbot, Willis J. *Blue Jackets of '61: A History of the Navy in the War of Secession.* N.Y.: Dodd, Mead, 1886. Journalistic but solid.

1301. E469
       .A25
Adams, Ephraim D. *Great Britain and the American Civil War,* 2 vols. London: Longmans, 1925. Why Britain favored first the South, then the North.

1302. E470
       .A2
Adams, Michael C.C. *Our Masters the Rebels: A Speculation on Union Military Failure in the East, 1861-1865.* Cambridge, Mass.: HUP, 1978.

1303. DA74
       .A3
Adams, William H.D. *Farragut and Other Great Commanders: A Series of Naval Biographies.* N.Y.: Routledge, [18??].

1304. V903
       .A6
American Iron and Steel Association. *History of the Manufacture of Armor Plate for the United States Navy.* Phila.: The Association, 1899. Includes the Civil War period.

1305. E182
       .A51
       v. 2
Ammen, Daniel. *The Navy in the Civil War: The Atlantic Coast.* N.Y.: Scribner, 1883. For the other 2 vols. in this series *see* Mahan, Alfred T., and Soley, James R.

1306. E591
       .A51
Anderson, Bern. *By Sea and by River: The Naval History of the Civil War.* N.Y.: Knopf, 1962.

1307. E467
       .1F23B2
Barnes, James. *David G. Farragut.* Boston: Small, Maynard, 1899. Not as good as Lewis, Charles L.

1308. E468
       .B33
Bassler, Roy P. *A Short History of the American Civil War.* N.Y.: Basic Books, 1967.

1309. V799
       .B3
Baxter, James P. *The Introduction of the Ironclad Warship.* Cambridge, Mass.: HUP, 1933. Chs. 12-14 relate to the Civil War.

1310. VA65
       .C136B4
Bearss, Edwin C. *Hardluck Ironclad: The Sinking and Salvage of the* Cairo...*Including A History of the Western Flotilla of Which She Was a Part.* Baton Rouge: LSUP, 1966.

1311. VA55   Bennett, Frank M. *The* Monitor *and the Navy Un-*
      .B47   *der Steam.* Boston: Houghton Mifflin, 1900.

1312.   _____. *The Steam Navy of the United States.*
              Pittsburgh: Warren, 1896.

1313. JX5261 Bernath, Stuart L. *Squall Across the Atlantic:*
      .U6B46 *American Civil War Prize Cases and Diplomacy.*
              Berkeley: U. of California P., 1970. Brilliant
              exposition of diplomacy and law.

1314. E469   Bigelow, John. *France and the Confederate Navy,*
      .B7   *1862-1868: An International Episode.* N.Y.:
              Harper, 1888; rpt., Berman, 1968. France built
              ships and rams destined for the Confederacy but
              decided against letting them leave France.

1315. E183.8 Blumenthal, Henry. *France and the United States:*
      .F8B4   *Their Diplomatic Relations, 1789-1914.* Chapel
              Hill: UNCP, 1970.

1316. E183   Bourne, Kenneth. *Britain and the Balance of*
      .G7B68 *Power in North America, 1815-1908.* London:
              Longmans, 1967.

1317. E467.1 Boykin, Edward C. *Ghost Ship of the Confederacy:*
      .S47B72 *The Story of the* Alabama *and Her Captain, Raphael*
              Semmes. N.Y.: Funk and Wagnalls, 1957.

1318. E467.1 _____. *Sea Devil of the Confederacy: The*
      .M35B6 *Story of the* Florida *and Her Captain, John*
              Newland Maggitt. N.Y.: Funk and Wagnalls, 1959.

1319. E591   Boynton, Charles B. *History of the Navy during*
      .B79   *the Rebellion,* 2 vols. N.Y.: Appleton, 1867-
              1868; Ann Arbor, Michi.: U. Microfilms Inter-
              national, 1976. Especially good on naval
              ordnance.

1320. E470   Bradford, Larned, ed. *Battles and Leaders of*
      .B344   *the Civil War.* N.Y.: Appleton-Century-Crofts,
              1956.

1321. E600   Bradlee, Francis B.C. *Blockade Running During*
      .B82   *the Civil War and the Effect of Land and Water*
              Transportation on the Confederacy. Salem,
              Mass.: Essex Institute, 1925.

1322. V25   Brodie, Bernard. *Sea Power in the Machine Age,*
      .B7   2d ed. Princeton: PUP, 1943.

1323. E491   Bruce, Robert. *Lincoln and the Tools of War*.
      .B7   Indianapolis: Bobbs-Merrill, 1956.

1324. E488   Bulloch, James D. *The Secret Service of the*
      .B93   *Confederate States in Europe or How the Con-*
      1959   *federate Cruisers Were Equipped*, 2 vols. N.Y.:
                1883; rpt., N.Y.: T. Yoseloff, 1959.

1325. E470.65   Burton, E. Milby. *The Siege of Charleston*,
      .B87   *1861, 1865*. Columbia: U of SC P., 1970

1326. E487   Callahan, James M. *Diplomatic History of the*
      .C14   *Southern Confederacy*. Baltimore: Johns Hopkins
                P., 1901.

1327. VF23   Canfield, Eugene B. *Civil War Ordnance*. Wash.:
      .C29   GPO, 1969. Twenty pages crammed with statisti-
                cal data, plus photographs.

1328. VF23.5   _____. *Notes on Naval Ordnance of the Ameri-*
      .C3   *can Civil War*. Wash.: American Ordnance Assoc.,
                1960.

1329. E183.8   Carroll, Daniel B. *Henri Mercier and the Ameri-*
      .F8C25   *can Civil War*. Princeton: PUP, 1971. How the
                Union tried to prevent European aid to the Con-
                federacy is revealed in this study of the
                French ambassador to the United States from
                1860 to 1863.

1330. E600   Carse, Robert. *Blockade: The Civil War at Sea*.
      .C3   N.Y.: Rinehart, 1958.

1331. E469   Case, Lynn M., and Warren F. Spencer. *The*
      .C32   *United States and France: Civil War Diplomacy*.
                Phila.: U. of Pa. P., 1970.

1332. E468   Catton, Bruce. *The Civil War*. N.Y.: American
      .C293   Heritage, 1971.

1333. E468   _____. *The Centennial History of the Civil*
      .C29   *War*, 3 vols. GCNY: Doubleday, 1961-1965.

1334. T40   Church, William C. *The Life of John Ericcson*,
      .E8C6   2 vols. N.Y.: Scribner, 1890.

1335. E600   Cochran, Hamilton. *Blockade Runners of the Con-*
      .C6   *federacy*. Indianapolis: Bobbs-Merrill, 1958.

1336. VC23.   Coggins, Jack. *Arms and Equipment of the Civil*
     .C6   *War*. GCNY: Doubleday, 1962.

1337. E464   Commager, Henry, S., ed. *The Blue and the Gray:*
     .C6   *The Story of the Civil War as Told by Partici-*
              pants, 2 vols. Indianapolis: Bobbs-Merrill,
              1950.

1338. E470   Congdon, Don, ed. *Combat: The Civil War*. N.Y.:
     .C8   Delacorte, 1967.

1339. E487   Coulter, Ellis M. *The Confederate States of*
     .C83   *America, 1861-1865*. Baton Rouge: LSUP, 1950.

1340. E591   Crandall, Warren D., and Isaac D. Newell. *His-*
     .C89   *tory of the Ram Fleet and the Mississippi*
              Marine Brigade, 2 vols. in 1. St. Louis:
              Buschart Brothers, 1907. The basic account.

1341. E469   Crook, David P. *The North, the South, and the*
     .C76   *Powers 1861-65; American Diplomacy During the*
              Civil War. N.Y.: Wiley, 1974.

1342. E475   Cunningham, Edward C. *The Port Hudson Campaign,*
     .42C8   *1862-1863*. Baton Rouge: LSUP, 1963.

1343. E467.1   Dahlgren, Madeleine V. *Memoirs of John A.*
     .D13D2   *Dahlgren, Rear Admiral United States Navy, by*
              His Widow. Boston: J.R. Osgood, 1882. Biog-
              raphy of the Union's oustanding ordnance expert.

1344. E473   Daly, Robert W. *How the* Merrimac *Won: The Stra-*
     .2.D3   *tegic Story of the C.S.S.* Virginia. N.Y.:
              Crowell, 1957.

1345. E467.1   Davis, Charles H., Jr. *Life of Charles Henry*
     .D24D2   *Davis, Rear Admiral, 1807-1877*. Boston:
              Houghton Mifflin, 1899.

1346. E473   Davis, William C. *Duel Between the First Iron-*
     .2.D36   *clads*. GCNY: Doubleday, 1975.

1347. E470   Deaderick, Barron. *Strategy in the Civil War*.
     .D4   Harrisburg, Pa.: Military Service Pub. Co.,
              1946.

1348. E596   Delaney, Norman C. *John McIntosh Kell of the*
     .K292K44   *Raider* Alabama. University: U. of Alabama P.,
              1973. Kell was executive officer of the
              Sumter and of the *Alabama*.

1349. HD9519
.T7D4

Dew, Charles B. *Ironmaker to the Confederacy: Joseph R. Anderson and the Tredegar Iron Works*. New Haven: YUP, 1966.

1350. E468
.D65

Donald, David, ed. *Why the North Won the Civil War*. Baton Rouge: LSUP, 1960. Five essays.

1351. E591
.D6

Donovan, Frank. *Ironclads of the Civil War*. N.Y.: American Heritage, 1964.

1352. TA140
.E2D6

Dorsey, Florence L. *Road to the Sea: The Story of James B. Eads and the Mississippi River*. N.Y.: Rinehart, 1947. Eads built many of the Union's river gunboats.

1353. E467.1
.A2D8

Duberman, Martin B. *Charles Francis Adams, 1807-1886*. Boston: Houghton Mifflin, 1961. The Union minister who successfully supported Union aims in London.

1354. E467.1
.D9D89

DuPont, Henry A. *Rear Admiral Samuel Francis DuPont, United States Navy: a Biography*. N.Y.: National Americana Soc., 1926.

1355. E591
.D93

DuPont, Samuel F. *Official Dispatches and Letters...1846-1848, 1861-1863*. Wilmington, Del.: Ferris Bros., 1883.

1356. E596
.M3D8

Durkin, Joseph T. *Stephen R. Mallory: Confederate Navy Chief*. Chapel Hill: UNCP, 1954.

1357. E599
.A3E22

Edge, Frank M. *The* Alabama *and the* Kearsarge. Phila.: King & Baird, 1868.

1358. E182
.B925

Eliot, George F. *Daring Sea Warrior: Franklin Buchanan*. N.Y.: Messner, 1962. Buchanan "went South" and fought valiantly at Norfolk and at Mobile Bay.

1359. E467.1
.W77E4

Ellicott, John M. *The Life of John Ancrum Winslow, Rear Admiral, USN, Who Commanded the U.S. Steamer "Kearsarge" in Her Action with the Confederate Cruiser "Alabama."* N.Y.: Putnam, 1902.

1360. E182
.E92

Evans, Robley D. *A Sailor's Log*. N.Y.: D. Appleton, 1901. As a midshipman, Evans engaged in the Fort Fisher operation and was wounded in both knees.

1361. HJ6645   Evans, Stephen H. *The United States Coast*
      .E8   *Guard, 1790-1915*. Annapolis, Md.: USNI, 1963.

1362. E182   Falk, Edwin A. *Fighting Bob Evans*. N.Y.:
      .E934   Cape & Smith, 1931.

1363. E467   Farragut, Loyall. *The Life and Letters of Ad-*
      .F23F2   *miral Farragut, First Admiral of the United*
                States Navy. N.Y.: D. Appleton, 1879. Lewis,
                Charles L., is better.

1364. E469   Ferris, Norman. *The* Trent *Affair: A Diplomatic*
      .F387   *Crisis*. Knoxville: U. of Tennessee P., 1977.

1365. E470.8   Fiske, John. *The Mississippi Valley in the*
      .F54   *Civil War*. Boston: Houghton Mifflin, 1900.

1366. E468   Foote, Shelby. *The Civil War: A Narrative*,
      .F7   3 vols. N.Y.: Random House, 1958-1974.

1367. E591   Gosnell, Harpur A. *Guns on the Western Waters:*
      .G67   *The Story of the River Gunboats in the Civil*
                War. Baton Rouge: LSUP, 1949.

1368. E182   Hall, Asaph. *Biographical Memoir of John*
      .R68H3   *Rodgers, 1812-1882*. Wash.: Judd and Detweiller,
                1906.

1369. E591   Hayes, John D., ed. *Samuel Francis DuPont: A*
      .D9   *Selection from His War Letters*, 3 vols. Ithaca:
                Cornell U. P., 1969. Particularly pertinent
                is correspondence concerning the operation at
                Charleston, S.C.

1370. E467   Headley, Joel T. *Farragut and Our Naval Com-*
      .H43   *manders*. N.Y.: E.B. Treat, 1867.

1371. E471   Heyward, DuBose, and Ravanel S. Herbert. *Fort*
      .1.H49   *Sumter: 1861-1865*. N.Y.: Farrar & Rinehart,
                1938.

1372. E182   *Hicks, Norman W. *A Brief History of the United*
      .M28   *States Marine Corps in the Civil War*. Wash.:
                USMC, HQ, Hist. Div., 1961, 1964.

1373. E467   Hill, Jim D. *Sea Dogs of the Sixties: Farragut*
      .H65   *and Seven Contemporaries*. Minneapolis: U. of
                Minnesota P., 1935. The other seven are James
                D. Bulloch, Charles Wilkes, John Wilkinson,
                John Rodgers II, Charles W. Read, John A.
                Winslow, and James I. Waddell.

1374. E473   Hoehling, Adolph A. *Thunder At Hampton Roads*.
      2.H57   Englewood Cliffs, N.J.: Prentice-Hall, 1976.
              The *Monitor* vs. the *Merrimac*.

1375. E467.1 Holzman, Robert S. *Stormy Ben Butler*. N.Y.:
      .B87H6 Macmillan, 1954. Butler engaged in several
              combined operations but was superseded by
              General Terry for the Fort Fisher campaign.

1376. E467.1 Hoppin, James M. *The Life of Andrew Hull Foote*,
      .F68H7 *Rear Admiral*, *USN*. N.Y.: Harper, 1874. Saga
              of an expert in riverine warfare.

1377. E599   Horn, Stanley F. *Gallant Rebel: The Fabulous*
      .S5H6   *Cruise of the C.S.S.* Shenandoah. New Bruns-
              wick, N.J.: Rutgers UP, 1947.

1378. E600   Horner, Dave. *The Blockade-Runners: True Tales*
      .H67   *of Running the Yankee Blockade of the Confed-*
              erate Coast. N.Y.: Dodd, Mead, 1968.

1379. E470   Hubbell, John T., ed. *Battles Lost and Won:*
      .B35   *Essays on Civil War History.* Westport, Conn.:
              Greenwood, 1976.

1380. E599   Hunt, Cornelius E. *The* Shenandoah: *or the Last*
      .S5H9   *Confederate Cruiser.* N.Y.: Carleton, 1867.

1381. E469.8 Jenkins, Brian A. *Britain and the War for the*
      .J46   *Union.* Montreal: McGill-Queens UP, 1974.

1382. E476.33 Johnson, Ludwell H. *Red River Campaign: Poli-*
      .J6   *tics and Cotton in the Civil War.* Baltimore:
              Johns Hopkins P., 1958.

1383. E470   Johnson, Robert U., and C.C. Buell, eds. *Bat-*
      .B33   *tles and Leaders of the Civil War*, 4 vols.
              N.Y.: Century, 1887-1888.

1384. E469   Jones, Donaldson, and Edwin J. Pratt. *Europe*
      .8.J75 *and the American Civil War.* N.Y.: Octagon,
              1931, 1969.

1385. E420.65 Jones, Samuel. *The Siege of Charleston and the*
      .J77   *Operations on the South Atlantic Coast in the*
              War Among the States. N.Y.: Neale, 1911.

1386. E591   Jones, Virgil C. *The Civil War at Sea*, 3 vols.
      .J6   N.Y.: Holt, Rinehart, & Winston, 1960-1962.

1387. E183   Jones, Wilbur D. *The American Problem in Brit-*
      .G7J66   *ish Diplomacy, 1841-1861.* Athens: UP of Georgia,
                1974.

1388. E595   Keeler, William F. *Aboard the USS* Monitor,
      .M7K4   *1862: The Letters of Acting Paymaster William*
                Frederick Keeler, U.S. Navy. Ed. Robert W.
                Daly. Annapolis, Md.: USNI, 1964.

1389. E468   Lawson, Don. *The United States in the Civil War.*
      .L39   N.Y.: Abelard-Schuman, 1977.

1390. HJ254   Lester, Richard I. *Confederate Finance and Pur-*
      .L47   *chasing in Great Britain.* Charlottesville: UP
                of Virginia, 1975.

1391. UF523   Lewis, Berkeley R. *Notes on Ammunition of the*
      .L43   *American Civil War.* Wash.: American Ordnance
                Assoc., 1959.

1392. E467.1 Lewis, Charles L. *David Glasgow Farragut: Our*
      .F23L48 *First Admiral.* Annapolis, Md.: USNI, 1943.

1393. E182   _____. *Admiral Franklin Buchanan: Fearless*
      .B93   *Man of Action.* Baltimore: The Norman Remington
                Co., 1929.

1394. E461.1 Lewis, Paul, pseud. *Yankee Admiral: A Biography*
      .P78G4   *of David Dixon Porter.* N.Y.: McKay, 1968.

1395. V799   MacBride, Robert. *Civil War Ironclads: The Dawn*
      .M3   *of Naval Armor.* Phila.: Chilton Books, 1962.

1396. E467   Macartney, Clarence E. *Mr. Lincoln's Admirals.*
      .M116   N.Y.: Funk & Wagnalls, 1956.

1397. E473   McCordock, Robert S. *The Yankee Cheese Box.*
      .2.M24   Phila.: Dorrance, 1938. The USS *Monitor.*

1398. E591   Mahan, Alfred T. *The Navy in the Civil War:*
      .M32   *The Gulf and Inland Waters.* N.Y.: Scribner,
      v.3   1883. For the other 2 vols. in this series
                see Ammen, Daniel, and Soley, James R.

1399. E467.1 _____. *Admiral Farragut.* N.Y.: Appleton,
      .F23M2   1892.

1400. E467.1 Martin, Christopher, pseud. *Damn the Torpedoes:*
      .F23H6   *The Story of America's First Admiral, David*
                Glasgow Farragut. N.Y.: Abelard-Schuman, 1970.

1401. E470   Matloff, Maurice. *The Civil War: A Concise*
       .C55   *Military History of the War Between the States,*
                 1861-1865. N.Y.: McKay, 1978.

1402. E182   Meade, Rebecca P. *Life of Hiram Paulding, Rear-*
       .P32   *Admiral U.S.N.* N.Y.: Baker and Taylor, 1910.
                 Aged and slow, Paulding proved ineffective in
                 saving Norfolk for the Union.

1403. E596   Melton, Maurice. *The Confederate Ironclads.*
       .M48   South Brunswick, N.J.: T. Yoseloff, 1968.

1404. E596   Merli, Frank J. *Great Britain and the Confed-*
       .M5   *erate Navy, 1864-1865.* Bloomington: U. of
                 Indiana P., 1970.

1405. E591   Merrill, James M. *The Rebel Shore: The Story of*
       .M48   *Union Sea Power in the Civil War.* Boston:
                 Little, Brown, 1957.

1406. E470   _____. *Battle Flags South: The Story of the*
       .8.M46   *Civil War Navies on Western Waters.* Rutherford,
                 N.J.: Fairleigh Dickinson UP, 1970.

1407. E591   Milligan, John D. *Gunboats Down the Mississippi.*
       .M55   Annapolis, Md., USNI, 1965.

1408. E470   Mitchell, Joseph B. *Decisive Battles of the*
       .M69   *Civil War.* N.Y.: Putnam, 1955.

1409. E599   Morgan, Murray. *Dixie Raider: The Saga of the*
       .S5M7   *C.S.S.* Shenandoah. N.Y.: Dutton, 1948.

1410. E415.7   Nevins, Allan. *The Emergence of Lincoln*, 2
       .N38   vols. N.Y.: Scribner, 1950.

1411. E415   _____. *The Ordeal of the Union*, 2 vols.
       .7.N4   N.Y.: Scribner, 1947.

1412. E468   Newman, Ralph G., and E.B. Long. *The Civil War*
       .N44   *Digest.* N.Y.: Grosset and Dunlap, 1960.

1413. E467.1   Niven, John. *Gideon Welles: Lincoln's Secretary*
       .W46N5   *of the Navy.* N.Y.: Oxford UP, 1973. A biography
                 that deals fully with Welles's Civil War years.

1414. E488   Owsley, Frank L. Ed. Harriet Owsley, 2nd ed.
       .O85   *King Cotton Diplomacy.* Chicago: U. of Chicago
       1959   P., 1959. Still the best discussion on this
                 subject.

1415. V820 Owsley, Frank L., Jr. *The C.S.S.* Florida: *Her*
.09 *Building and Operations.* Phila.: U. of Pa. P.,
1965.

1416. E179.5 Paolino, Ernest N. *The Foundations of American*
.P29 *Empire: William Henry Seward and U.S. Foreign*
Policy [1861-1869]. Ithaca: Cornell UP, 1973.
Seward originally sought to dominate Lincoln,
then served him well in subordination.

1417. E468 Parish, Peter J. *The American Civil War.* N.Y.:
.P27 Holmes & Meier, 1975.

1418. E476.85 Parker, Foxhall A. *The Battle of Mobile Bay and*
.P24 *the Capture of Forts Powell, Gaines, and Morgan.*
Boston: Williams, 1878.

1419. E596 Perry, Milton F. *Infernal Machines: The Story*
.P4 *of Confederate Submarine and Mine Warfare.*
Baton Rouge: LSUP, 1965.

1420. E591 Porter, David D. *The Naval History of the Civil*
.P84 *War.* N.Y.: Sherman, 1886. The author occasion-
ally gave himself more credit than he merited.

1421. E601 _____. *Incidents and Anecdotes of the Civil*
.P74 *War.* N.Y.: Appleton, 1885.

1422. E591 Pratt, Fletcher. *Civil War on Western Waters.*
.P87 N.Y.: Holt, 1956. Popularly written.

1423. E473 _____. *The* Monitor *and the* Merrimac. N.Y.:
.2.P7 Random House, 1951.

1424. E540 Quarles, Benjamin. *The Negro in the Civil War.*
.N3Q3 Boston: Little, Brown, 1953.

1425. E457 Randall, James G. *Lincoln the President*, 4
.R2 vols. N.Y.: Dodd, Mead, 1945-1955.

1426. E470 Reed, Rowena. *Combined Operations in the Civil*
.R33 *War.* Annapolis, Md.: NIP, 1978.

1427. E468 Rhodes, James F. *History of the Civil War,*
.R47 *1861-1865.* N.Y.: Macmillan, 1917.

1428. UF23 Ripley, Warren. *Artillery and Ammunition of the*
.R56 *Civil War.* N.Y.: Van Nostrand Reinhold, 1970.

1429. E596
      .R65
Robinson, William M. *The Confederate Privateers.*
New Haven: YUP, 1928.

1430. E467.1
      .C98R6
Roske, Ralph J., and Charles Van Doren. *Lincoln's Commando: The Biography of Commander William B. Cushing, USN.* N.Y.: Harper, 1957.

1431. JX5297
      .S3
Savage, Carlton. *Policy of the United States Toward Maritime Commerce in War*, 2 vols.
Wash.: GPO, 1934-1936.

1432. E596
      .S31
Scharf, J. Thomas. *History of the Confederate States Navy*....N.Y.: Rogers and Isherwood, 1887; rpt., Books for Libraries, 1969. The seminal work on the subject.

1433. E415.9
      .S58S4
Sears, Louis M. *John Slidell.* Durham: Duke UP, 1925. Confederate diplomat involved in the *"Trent* affair" as well as other matters.

1434. E182
      .S47
Selfridge, Thomas O. *Memoirs of Thomas O. Selfridge, Jr., Rear Admiral, U.S.N.* N.Y.: Putnam, 1924. Of the Academy class of 1854, Selfridge served in the Civil War and in the 1870-1871 conducted a survey of the Isthmus of Darien.

1435. E599
      .A3S64
Semmes, Raphael. *Memoirs of Service Afloat During the War Between the States.* N.Y.: Rogers & Isherwood, 1887. The leading privateer captain.

1436. V63
      .I8S5
Sloan, Edward W. *Benjamin Franklin Isherwood, Naval Engineer: The Years as Engineer-in-Chief.* Annapolis, Md.: USNI, 1965.

1437. E467.1
      .P78S6
Soley, James R. *Admiral [David D.] Porter.* N.Y.: D. Appleton, 1903.

1438. E591
      .N32
      v.1
_____. *The Navy in the Civil War: The Blockade and the Cruisers.* N.Y.: Scribner, 1883. For the other 2 vols in this series *see* Ammes, Daniel, and Mahan, Alfred T.

1439. E182
      .S74
Spears, John R. *History of the United States Navy from Its Origin to the Present Day, 1775-1897*, 5 vols. N.Y.: Scribner, 1897-1899.

1440. E182   Sprout, Harold, and Margaret Sprout. *The Rise*
       .S78   *of American Sea Power, 1776-1918*. Princeton:
                 PUP, 1939; rpt., Annapolis, Md.: NIP, 1980.

1441. VM23   Still, William N. *Confederate Shipbuilding*.
       .5.S8   Athens: U. of Georgia P., 1969.

1442. E596   _____. *Iron Afloat: The Story of the Confed-*
       .S84   *erate Armorclads*. Nashville: Vanderbilt UP,
                 1971.

1443. VA55   Stivers, Reuben E. *Privateers and Volunteers:*
       .S83   *The Men and Women of Our Naval Reserve Force,*
                 1766-1866. Annapolis, Md.: NIP, 1975.

1444. E599   Summersell, C.G. *The Cruise of the C.S.S.*
       .S8S8   *Sumter.* Tuscaloosa, Ala.: Confederate Pub. Co.,
                 1965.

1445. E471   Swanberg, W.A. *First Blood: The Story of Fort*
       .IS9   *Sumter*. N.Y.: Scribner, 1957. An excellent,
                 almost minute-by-minute, account.

1446. E600   Symonds, Craig L., ed. *Charleston Blockade: The*
       .M37   *Journals of John B. Marchand, U.S. Navy, 1861-*
                 1862. Newport: Naval War College, 1976.

1447. E487   Thomas, Emory M. *The Confederate Nation, 1861-*
       .T483   *1865*. N.Y.: Harper & Row, 1979. Various re-
                 viewers challenge the assertion that the Con-
                 federacy was ever a "nation."

1448.   Thomas, Frances. *The Career of Rear Admiral*
                 John G. Walker. Boston: Priv. print., 1959.
                 Walker served well throughout the Civil War,
                 left the service for several years, and re-
                 turned to it in 1881.

1449. E545   Thompson, Samuel B. *Confederate Purchasing*
       .T47   *Operations Abroad*. Chapel Hill: UNCP, 1935.

1450. E491   Turner, George E. *Victory Rode the Rails: The*
       .T95   *Strategic Place of Railroads in the Civil*
                 War. Indianapolis: Bobbs-Merrill, 1953.

1451. E591   Vail, Israel E. *Three Years on the Blockade:*
       .V12   *A Naval Experience*. N.Y.: Abbey P., 1902.

1452. E415   Van Deusen, Glyndon G. *William Henry Seward*.
       .9S4V3   N.Y.: Oxford UP, 1967. For this chapter,
                 interest centers upon his service as Secretary
                 of State during the Civil War.

1453. E600   Vandiver, Frank E. *Confederate Blockade Running*
       .V3   *Through Bermuda, 1861-1865*. Austin: U. of Texas
                 P., 1947. Good story by a competent historian.

1454. E469   Villers, Brougham C.W.H. *Anglo-American Rela-*
       .S53   *tions, 1861-1865*. N.Y.: Scribner, 1920. Pri-
                 marily devoted to the question of neutral
                 rights.

1455. E599   Waddell, James I. *C.S.S.* Shenandoah: *The Memoirs*
       .S5W3   *of Lieutenant Commanding James I. Waddell*. Ed.
                 James D. Horan. N.Y.: Crown, 1960.

1456. E591   Walke, Henry. *Naval Scenes and Reminiscences of*
       .W17   *the Civil War....1861...1863....* N.Y.: Reed,
                 1877. Mostly about the operations of river
                 gunboats by an artist who was also a naval
                 officer.

1457. F349   Walker, Peter E. *Vicksburg: A People at War*,
       .V6W3   *1860-1865*. Chapel Hill: UNCP, 1960.

1458. E600   Watson, William. *Adventures of a Blockade Run-*
       .W34   *ner*.... London: Fisher Unwin, 1892.

1459. E470   Webb, Alexander S. *The Peninsula: McClellan's*
       .C17   *Campaign of 1962*. N.Y.: Scribner, 1882. In-
       v.3   terest centers upon the naval support provided
                 McClellan.

1460. E468   Welles, Gideon. *The Diary of Gideon Welles*,
       .W444   *Secretary of the Navy under Lincoln and*
                 Johnson, 3 vols. Ed. Howard K. Beale. N.Y.:
                 Norton, 1960. Comments on numerous men and
                 measures by a truly literate and perceptive
                 man.

1461. VA393   Wells, Tom H. *The Confederate Navy: A Study in*
       .W44   *Organization*. University: U. of Alabama P.,
                 1971. Well-organized narrative.

1462. E468   Werstein, Irving. *1861-1865: The Adventure of*
       .7.W45   *the Civil War*. N.Y.: Cooper Square Pub., 1964,
                 1969. Journalistic.

1463. E467.1   West, Richard S. *Lincoln's Scapegoat General:*
      .B87W43   *A Life of Benjamin F. Butler, 1818-1893*. Bos-
                ton: Houghton Mifflin, 1965. Includes Butler's
                part in the combined operations of the Civil
                War.

1464. E591   _____. *Mr. Lincoln's Navy*. N.Y.: Longmans,
      .W44   1957.

1465. E467.1   _____. *Gideon Welles: Lincoln's Navy Depart-*
      .W46W4   *ment*. Indianapolis: Bobbs-Merrill, 1943.

1466. E467.1   _____. *The Second Admiral: A Life of David*
      .P78W4   *Dixon Porter*. N.Y.: Coward-McCann, 1937.

1467. T40   White, Ruth (Morris). *Yankee from Sweden; the*
      .E8W5   *Dream and Reality in the Days of John Ericsson*.
                N.Y.: Holt, 1960.

1468. D362   Wilson, Herbert W. *Ironclads in Action: a*
      .W74   *Sketch of Naval Warfare from 1855 to 1898, with*
                Some Account of the Development of the Battle-
                ship in England, 2 vols. Boston: Little, Brown,
                1896. By a perceptive and capable historian.

1469. E473.2   Worden, John L., S. Dana Greene, and H. Ashton
      .W92   Ramsay. *The* Monitor *and the* Merrimac. N.Y.:
                Harper, 1912. By men who served in the *Monitor*.

DOCUMENTS

1470. E591   Fox, Gustavus V. *Confidential Correspondence*
      .F79   *of Gustavus V. Fox, Assistant Secretary of the*
                Navy, 1861-1865, 2 vols. Ed. by Robert M.
                Thompson and Richard Wainwright. N.Y.: Naval
                Hist. Soc., 1918-1919. Shows how Fox acted
                as a chief of naval operations for Welles.

1471. E591   *Official Records of the Union and Confederate*
                Navies in the War of the Rebellion. Series I,
                27 vols.; Series, II, 4 vols. Ed. Dudley W.
                Knox. Wash.: GPO, 1894-1927.

DISSERTATIONS AND THESES

1472.   Allen, John M., Jr. "Corporate Values Invade
                the Navy: The Growth of Modern American Sea
                Power, 1861-1882," Syracuse U., 1976.

1473. V1   Allin, Lawrence C. "The United States Naval
      .U75A6 Institute: Intellectual Forum of the New Navy,
              1873-1899," U. of Maine, 1976. Published by
              Manhattan, Kans.: *Military Affairs/Aerospace
              Historian*, 1978.

1474.   Evans, Elliott A.P. "Napoleon III and the Ameri-
              can Civil War," Stanford U., 1940.

1475.   Ferris, Norman B. "Tempestuous Mission, 1861-
              1862: The Early Diplomatic Career of Charles
              Francis Adams," Emory U., 1962.

1476.   Gradner, Audrey. "Henry Walke, 1809-1896, Ro-
              mantic Painter and Naval Hero," George Washing-
              ton U., 1971.

1477.   Jeffries, William W. "The Civil War Career
              of Charles Wilkes," Vanderbilt U., 1941.

1478.   Merrill, James M. "Naval Operations along the
              South Atlantic Coast, 1861-1865," U. of Cali-
              fornia at Los Angeles, 1954.

1479. VB23   Polser, Aubrey H., J. "The Administration of
      .5P65   the United States Navy, 1861-1865," U. of
              Nebraska, 1975.

1480.   Sullivan, William. "Gustavus Vasa Fox and Naval
              Administration, 1861-1866," Catholic U., 1977.

ARTICLES

1481.   Abbott, John S.C. "Opening the Mississippi,"
              Harper's 32 (Aug. 1866):296-309.

1482.   _____. "Military Adventures Beyond the
              Mississippi," *Harper's* 30 (Apr. 1865):575-92.
              Actions on the Western Rivers.

1483.   _____. "Siege and Capture of Port Hudson,"
              Harper's 30 (Mar. 1865):425-39.

1484.   Abbott, Martin. "The First Shot at Fort Sumter,"
              CWH 2 (Mar. 1957):41-46.

1485.   "A Concise Illustrated History of the Civil
              War," AHI 6 (May 1971):entire issue.

1486.   Adams, William T. "Guns for the Navy," *Ordnance*
              45 (Jan.-Feb.1961):508-11.

1487.   Alden, Carroll S. "Stephen Bleecker Luce, U.S.N.," USNIP 39 (June 1913):761-79.

1488.   Ambrose, Stephen E., and others. "Struggle for Vicksburg: The Battles and Siege that Decided the Civil War." CWTI 6 (July 1967):1-66.

1489.   _____. "Fort Donelson: A 'Disastrous' Blow to the South," CWTI 5 (June 1966):4-13, 42-49.

1490.   Anderson, Bern. "The Naval Strategy of the Civil War," MA 26 (Spring 1962):11-21.

1491.   Anderson, Stuart. "1861: Blockade vs. Closing the Confederate Ports," MA 41 (Dec. 1977):190-94.

1492.   Aptheker, Herbert. "The Negro in the Union Navy," JNH 32 (Apr. 1947):169-200.

1493.   Arnault, Charles C. "The Employment of Torpedoes in Steam Launches Against Men-of-War," USNIP 6 (Jan. 31, 1880):79-98. Diary of torpedo employment from the destruction of the *Housatonic*, Feb. 17, 1864, through the Russo-Turkish War of 1877.

1494.   Barbet, Paul. "Naval Encounter between the *Kearsarge* and *Alabama* Fought in Sight of Cherbourg, France, on June 19, 1864," USNIP 52 (Aug. 1926):1681-86.

1495.   Barnes, James. "Rear Admiral John G. Walker," ARR 16 (Sept. 1897):298-302.

1496.   Basoco, Richard W., William E. Geoghegan, and Frank J. Merli, eds. "A British View of the Union Navy, 1864; a Report Addressed to Her Majesty's Minister at Washington," AN 27 (Jan. 1967):30-45.

1497.   Baxter, James P., III. "The British Government and Neutral Rights, 1861-1865," AHR 34 (Oct. 1928):9-29.

1498.   Bearss, Edwin C. "The Ironclads at Fort Donelson: The Ironclads Sail for the Cumberland (Part I)," *Register of the Kentucky Hist. Soc.* (Jan. 1976):1-9; "The Confederates Prepare for the Ironclads (Part II)," ibid. (Apr. 1976):73-84; and "The Ironclads Fail (Part III)," ibid. (July 1976):167-91.

1499.   _____. "The Union Raid Down the Mississippi and Up the Yazoo, August 16-27, 1862," MA 27 (Fall 1962):108-19.

1500.   _____, and Warren E. Graham. "How Porter's Flotilla Ran the Gauntlet Past Vicksburg," CWTI 1 (Dec. 1962):38-48.

1501.   _____, and Howard P. Nash. "Fort Henry," CWTI 4 (Nov. 1965):9-15.

1502.   Beaudoin, Frederic J. "Union Victory: Manpower, Management of Resources, or Generalship?" NWCR 25 (Mar.-Apr. 1973):36-40.

1503.   Beers, Henry P. "The Bureau of Navigation, 1862-1942," Am. Archivist 6 (Oct. 1943):212-52.

1504.   Beloff, Max. "Great Britain and the American Civil War." History 37 (Feb. 1952):40-48.

1505.   Bennett, Frank M. "The Albemarle in Albermarle Sound," United Service, NS, 11 (May 1893):438-57.

1506.   Bernath, Stuart W. "British Neutrality and the Civil War Prize Cases," CWH 15 (Dec. 1969): 320-31.

1507.   _____. "Squall Across the Atlantic: The Peterhoff Episode," JSH 34 (Aug. 1968):381-401.

1508.   Blair, Carvell H. "Submarines of the Confederate Navy," USNIP 78 (Oct. 1952):1114-21.

1509.   Blair, C.H.M. "An Historical Ketch of the Confederate Navy," United Service 41 (May 1903): 1155-83.

1510.   Bolander, Louis H. "The Alligator, First Federal Submarine of the Civil War," USNIP 54 (June 1938):845-54.

1511.   Brent, Robert. "Mahan: Mariner or Misfit?" USNIP 92 (Apr. 1966):92-103.

1512.   Buhl, Lance C. "Mariners and Machines: Resistance to Technological Change in the American Navy, 1865-69," JAH 51 (Dec. 1974):703-27.

1513.   Canfield, Eugene B. "Porter's Mortar Schooners,"
         CWTI 6 (Oct. 1967):28-36.

1514.   Colvocoresses, George M. "Admiral Porter,"
         USNIP 34 (Mar. 1908):309-14.

1515.   Cushing, William B. "War Experiences of William
         B. Cushing as Told by Himself," USNIP 38 (Sept.
         1912):940-91.

1516.   *Daly, Robert W. "Burnside's Amphibious Divi-
         sion," MCG 35 (Dec. 1951):30-38.

1517.   Damaree, Albert L. "Our Navy's Worst Headache:
         The Merrimack," USNIP 88 (Mar. 1962):66-84.

1518.   Davidson, Hunter. "Torpedoes in Our War,"
         USNIP 24 (June 1898):349-54.

1519.   Davis, William C. "First Clash of the Iron-
         clads," AH 10 (Nov. 1975):38-48.

1520.   Dillon, John F. "The Role of Riverine Warfare
         in the Civil War," NWCR 25 (Mar.-Apr. 1973):
         58-78.

1521.   Dohrman, Horatio G. "Old Man River, 1863,"
         USNIP 60 (June 1934):809-16.

1522.   Dyer, Brainerd. "Confederate Naval and Priva-
         teering Activities in the Pacific," PHR 3
         (Dec. 1934):433-43.

1523.   Dyson, George W. "Benjamin Franklin Isherwood,"
         USNIP 67 (Aug. 1941):1139-46.

1524.   Earle, Ralph. "John Adolphus Dahlgren," USNIP
         51 (Mar. 1925):424-36.

1525.   Eller, Ernest M., and Dudley W. Knox. "Seapower:
         Decisive Influence of the Civil War," Navy 4
         (Jan.-Feb. 1961):17-20, 25-30.

1526.   Foote, Shelby. "DuPont Storms Charleston," AH
         11 (June 1963):28-34, 89-92.

1527.   Gilbert, Benjamin F. "The Confederate Raider
         Shenandoah: the Elusive Destroyer in the Pacif-
         ic and Arctic," Jour. of the West 14 (Apr.
         1965):169-82.

1528. Golder, F. A. "The Russian Fleet and the Civil War," AHR 20 (July 1915):801-12.

1529. Goldsborough, Louis M. "Narrative of Rear Admiral Goldsborough, U.S. Navy," USNIP 59 (July 1933):1023-31.

1530. Goodrich, Casper F. "Farragut," USNIP 49 (Dec. 1923):1961-86.

1531. Greene, S. Dana. "The *Monitor* at Sea and in Battle," USNIP 49 (Nov. 1923):1839-49.

1532. Hagerman, George. "Confederate Submarines," USNIP 103 (Sept. 1977):74-75.

1533. Hanford, Franklin. "How I Entered the Navy; Including a Personal Interview with Abraham Lincoln." Edited by S.W. Jackson. USNIP 91 (June 1965):75-87. Life at the Newport-based USNA.

1534. Hanks, Carlos C. "The Last Confederate Raid," USNIP 67 (Jan. 1941):21-32.

1535. Hanna, Kathryn A. "Incidents of the Confederate Blockade," JSH 5 (May 1945):214-29.

1536. Hayes, John D. "Captain Fox: He is the Navy Department," USNIP 91 (Nov. 1965):64-71.

1537. _____. "Sea Power in the Civil War," USNIP 88 (Nov. 1961):60-69.

1538. *_____. "The Marine Corps in the American Civil War," *Shipmate* 23 (Nov. 1960):2-4. Emphasizes organizational problems and the philosophy of employment of the U.S. Marine Corps and other amphibious forces in the Civil War.

1539. Heffernan, John B. "The Blockade of the Southern Confederacy; 1861-1865," *Smithsonian Jour. of Hist.* 2 (Winter 1967-1968):23-44.

1540. Hendren, Paul. "The Confederate Blockade Runners," USNIP 59 (Apr. 1933):506-12.

1541. Henig, Gerald S. "Admiral Samuel F. DuPont, the Navy Department, and the Attack on Charleston, April 1863," NWCR 30 (Feb. 1979):68-77.

1542.   Hoogenboom, Ari. "Gustavus Fox and the Relief of Fort Sumter," CWH 9 (Dec. 1963):383-98.

1543.   Johnson, Ludwell H. "Contraband Trade During the Last Year of the Civil War," MVHR 49 (Mar. 1963):635-52.

1544.   Johnson, Robert E. "Investment by Sea: The Civil War Blockade," AN 32 (Jan. 1972):45-57.

1545.   Jones, Robert H. "Anglo-American Relations, 1861-1865: Reconsidered," Mid-America 45 (Jan. 1963):36-49.

1546.   Jones, Virgil C. "Mr. Lincoln's Blockade," CWTI 10 (Dec. 1971):10-24.

1547.   _____. "How the South Created a Navy," CWTI 8 (July 1969):4-9, 42-48.

1548.   _____. "The Mighty Ram Albemarle," CWTI 1 (June 1962):6-11, 43-45.

1549.   Kaplan, Hyman R. "The U.S. Coast Guard and the Civil War," USNIP 86 (Aug. 1960):40-50.

1550.   Kellar, A.L. "Confederate Submarines and P.T. Boats," All Hands 470 (Apr. 1956):59-63.

1551.   _____. "Confederate Submarines," VMHB 61 (July 1953):293-303.

1552.   Kennett, Lee. "The Strange Career of the Stonewall," USNIP 94 (Feb. 1968):74-85.

1553.   Key, Hobart. "Star of the West," Shipmate 42 (May 1979):26.

1554.   *King, Joseph E. "The Fort Fisher Campaigns, 1864-1865," USNIP 77 (Aug. 1951):842-55. General account with emphasis on the operations of the "naval brigade" composed of Marines and sailors.

1555.   Kirk, Neville T. "The Father of American Naval Engineering," USNIP 81 (May 1955):486-89. Benjamin Isherwood.

1556.   Knox, Dudley W. "River Navies of the Civil War," MA 18 (Spring 1954):29-32.

1557.   Kreen, David F. "Russell's Decision to Retain the Laird Rams," CWH 22 (June 1976):158-63.

1558.   Krout, Mary H. "Rear Admiral Charles Wilkes and His Exploits," USNIP 50 (Mar., July 1924): 405-16, 1131-33.

1559.   Leary, William M., Jr. "*Alabama* Versus *Kearsarge:* A Diplomatic View," AN 29 (July 1969):167-73.

1560.   Lester, Richard R. "The Procurement of Confederate Blockade Runners and other Vessels in Great Britain during the American Civil War," MM 61 (Aug. 1975):255-70.

1561.   Lockwood, H.C. "The Capture of Fort Fisher," *Atlantic* 27 (May-June 1871):622-36, 684-90.

1562.   Long, John S. "The Gosport Affair, 1861," JSH 23 (May 1957):155-72. The Union's loss of the Norfolk navy yard.

1563.   Luraghi, Raimondo. "The Confederate Raider *Alabama*: A Journal by Its Boarding Officer," *Georgia Hist. Q.* 1 (Winter 1977):347-63.

1564.   *Luvaas, Jay. "The Fall of Fort Fisher," CWTI 3 (Aug. 1964):5-9, 31-35.

1565.   *McClellan, Edwin N. "The Capture of Fort Fisher," MCG 5 (Mar. 1920):59-80. An account emphasizing the operations of the U.S. Marines, interspered with quotations from various official reports.

1566.   *_____. "The Capture of New Orleans," MCG 5 (Dec. 1920):360-69. U.S. Marines in the New Orleans operation, Apr. 1862, with many quotations from contemporary sources.

1567.   MacCord, Charles W. "Ericsson and His *Monitor*," NAR 149 (Oct. 1889):460-71.

1568.   Magruder, P.H. "The U.S. Naval Academy and Annapolis During the Civil War, 1861-1865," USNIP 72 (Apr. 1946):69-73.

1569.   Maynard, Douglas H. "Plotting the Escape of the *Alabama*," JSH 20 (May 1954):197-209.

1570.   _____. "Union Efforts to Prevent the Escape of the *Alabama*," MVHR 41 (June 1954):41-60.

1571.   Melvin, Philip. "Stephen Russell Mallory: Southern Naval Statesman," JSH 10 (May 1944): 137-60.

1572.   Merli, Frank J., and Thomas W. Green. "Great Britain and the Confederate Navy 1861-1865," *Hist. Today* 14 (Oct. 1964):687-95.

1573.   Merrill, James M. "Strategy Makers in the Union Navy Department, 1861-65," *Mid-America* 44 (Jan. 1962):19-32.

1574.   _____. "Notes on the Yankee Blockade of the South Atlantic Seaboard 1861-1865," CWH 4 (Dec. 1958):387-97.

1575.   Miller, John, Jr. "The Execution of Union Strategy," *Army Information Digest* 16 (Aug. 1961):22-44.

1576.   Milligan, John D. "Charles Ellet, Naval Architect: A Study in Nineteenth Century Professionalism," AN 31 (Jan. 1971):52-72.

1577.   Moore, Ross H. "The Vicksburg Campaign of 1863," *Jour. of Miss. Hist.* 1 (June 1939): 151-68.

1578.   Morgan, James M. "The Confederate Cruiser *Florida*," USNIP 42 (Sept.-Oct. 1916):1581-88.

1579.   Oliver, Frederick L. "The Officers of the *Monitor* and *Merrimack*," *Shipmate* 26 (Aug. 1963):6-7.

1580.   O'Neill, Charles. "Engagement Between the *Cumberland* and *Merrimack*," USNIP 48 (June 1922):863-93.

1581.   Owsley, Frank L. "America and the Freedom of the Seas, 1861-1865," in Avery Craven, ed., *Essays in Honor of William E. Dodd, by His Former Students at the University of Chicago.* Chicago: U. of Chicago P., 1935, pp. 194-256.

1582.   Parker, Foxhall A. "The *Monitor* and *Merrimac*," USNIP 1 (1874):155-62.

1583.   Parks, W.M. "Building a Warship in the Southern
         Confederacy," USNIP 49 (Aug. 1923):1299-1307.

1584.   Paullin, Charles O. "President Lincoln and the
         Navy," AHR 14 (Jan. 1909):284-303.

1585.   Powells, James M. "The *Hunley* Sinks the
         Housatonic," *Navy* 8 (Jan. 1965):23-25.

1586.   Pratt, Julius W. "Naval Operations on the Vir-
         ginia Rivers in the Civil War," USNIP 45 (Feb.
         1919):185-95.

1587.   Pullar, Walter S. "Abe Lincoln's Brown Water
         Navy," NWCR 21 (Apr. 1969):71-88.

1588.   Ramsdell, Charles W. "Lincoln and Fort Sumter,"
         JSH 3 (Aug. 1937):259-88.

1589.   Roberts, John C., and Richard H. Webber. "Gun-
         boats in the River War, 1861-1865," USNIP 91
         (Mar. 1965):83-100.

1590.   Robinson, William M., Jr. "Drewry's Bluff: Na-
         val Defense of Richmond," CWH 7 (June 1961):
         167-75.

1591.   Rochester, Harry A. "'Albermarle' Cushing: The
         Civil War Exploits of an Alumnus of 1861,"
         Shipmate 41 (Oct. 1978):23-25.

1592.   Rutledge, Archibald. "Abraham Lincoln Fights
         the Battle of Fort Sumter," SAQ 34 (Oct. 1935):
         368-83.

1593.   Smith, Alan C. "The *Monitor-Merrimac* Legend,"
         USNIP 46 (Mar. 1940):385-89.

1594.   Snow, Elliot. "The Metamorphosis of the
         Merrimac," USNIP 57 (Nov. 1931):1518-21.

1595.   Squires, J. Duane. "Aeronautics in the Civil
         War," AHR 42 (July 1937):652-69.

1596.   Stampp, Kenneth M. "Lincoln and the Strategy
         of Defense in the Crisis of 1861," JSH 11
         (Aug. 1945):297-323.

1597.   Stevenson, Charles S. "Abraham Lincoln and the
         Russian Fleet Myth," MR 50 (Aug. 1970):35-37.

1598.   Steward, Charles W. "William Barker Cushing,"
         USNIP 38 (Aug.-Sept. 1912):425-91, 913-39.

1599.   Still, William N., Jr. "Technology Afloat,"
         CWTI 14 (Nov. 1975):4-9, 40-47.

1600.   _____. "Facilities for the Construction of
         War Vessels in the Confederacy," JSH 31 (Aug.
         1965):285-304.

1601.   _____. "Confederate Naval Strategy: the
         Ironclad," JSH 27 (Aug. 1961):330-43.

1602.   Swartz, Oretha D. "Franklin Buchanan: a Study
         in Divided Loyalties," USNIP 88 (Dec. 1962):
         61-71.

1603.   Thom, J.C. "Unity of Command in the Civil War,"
         USNIP 58 (Mar. 1932):371-74.

1604.   Thomas, Mary E. "The CSS *Tallahassee*: A Factor
         in Anglo-American Relations, 1864-1866," CWH
         21 (June 1975):148-59.

1605.   Tyson, Carl P. "Highway of War: Red River Cam-
         paign, 1864," *Red River Valley Hist. Rev.*,
         Summer 1978, pp. 28-51.

1606.   Von Kolnitz, Harry. "The Confederate Submarine,"
         USNIP 43 (Oct. 1937):1453-57.

1607.   Webber, Richard, and John C. Roberts. "James
         B. Eads: Master Builder," *Navy* 8 (Mar. 1965):
         23-25.

1608.   Werner, Herman O. "The Fall of New Orleans,
         1862," USNIP 88 (Apr. 1962):78-86.

1609.   West, Richard S., Jr. "Lincoln's Hand in Naval
         Matters," CWH 4 (June 1958):175-83.

1610.   _____. "Admiral Farragut and General Butler,"
         USNIP 82 (June 1956):634-43.

1611.   Williams, Harold. "Yankee Whaling Fleets Raided
         by Confederate Cruisers: the Story of the Bark
         Jerah Swift, Captain Thomas W. Williams," AN
         27 (Oct. 1967):263-67.

1612.   Wilson, Herbert W. "Naval Operations of the
               Civil War (1861-1865)," in *The Cambridge Modern
               History*, 14 vols. N.Y.: Macmillan, 1906,
               7:549-68.

1613.   Woodward, D. "Launching the Confederate Navy,"
               Hist. Today 12 (Mar. 1962):206-12.

1614.   Yates, R.W., ed. "From Wooden Walls to Dread-
               noughts in a Lifetime, [1862-1912]," MM 48
               (Nov. 1962):291-303.

FICTION

1615. PZ3   Branch, Houston, and Frank Waters. *Diamond Head*.
       .B73633   N.Y.: Farrar, 1948. The C.S.S. *Shenandoah* in
       Di   the Civil War.

1616. PS1474   Cupples, George. *Adventures of a Naval Lieu-
       .C6G74   tenant: or, The Green Hand*. N.Y.: Dutton, 1904.

1617. PZ7   Eggleston, George C. *The Bale Marked X: A
       .E30B   Blockade Running Adventure*. Boston: Lothrop,
                 1902.

1618. PS3523   Mason, Francis van Wyck. *Blue Hurricane*.
       .A822   Phila.: Lippincott, 1954. Captain Henry Walke
                 and the U.S. gunboat *Carondelet*. Mason has
                 also written 4 novels about the American Revo-
                 lution and 3 about the Civil War.

7

THE POST-CIVIL WAR DENOUEMENT AND THE
RISE OF THE NEW NAVY, 1865-1898

BOOKS

1619. E746
.A6

Alden, John D. *The American Steel Navy*. Annapolis, Md.: NIP, 1972.

1620. V799
.B3

Baxter, James P. *The Introduction of the Ironclad Warship*. Cambridge, Mass.: HUP, 1933.

1621. VA55
.B48

Bennett, Frank M. *The Steam Navy of the United States: A History of the Growth of the Steam Vessel of War in the U.S. Navy, and of the Naval Engineer Corps*. Pittsburgh: W.T. Nicholson, 1896.

1622. V767
.B78

Bowles, Francis T. *Ships of War*. N.Y.: A.J. Johnson, 1885. Rpt. of an article in *Johnson's Universal Encyclopedia*.

1623. V25
.B7

Brodie, Bernard. *Sea Power in the Machine Age*. Princeton: PUP, 1941.

1624. VM25
.N4B76

Brown, Alexander C. *The Good Ships of Newport News*. Cambridge, Md.: Tidewater Pub., 1976.

1625. VM140
.C8B8

Buell, Augustus C. *The Memoirs of Charles H. Cramp*. Phila.: Lippincott, 1906.

1626. V63
.F57C64

Coletta, Paolo E. *Admiral Bradley A. Fiske and the American Navy*. Lawrence: Regents P. of Kansas, 1979.

1627. E664
.T72C66

Cooling, Benjamin F. *Benjamin Franklin Tracy: Father of the Modern American Fighting Navy*. Hamden, Conn.: Shoe String, 1973.

1628. G662
.K36C67

Corner, George W. *Doctor Kane of the Arctic Seas*. Phila.: Temple UP, 1972.

1629. VB230
.D67

Dorwart, Jeffery M. *The Office of Naval Intelligence: The Birth of America's First Intelligence Agency 1865-1918*. Annapolis, Md.: NIP, 1979.

1630. V63
.E85A3

Evans, Holden A. *One Man's Fight for a Better Navy*. N.Y.: Dodd, Mead, 1940.

1631.   E182   Evans, Robley D. *A Sailor's Log: Recollections*
        .E92   *of Forty Years of Naval Life.* N.Y.: Appleton,
                   1901.

1632.   E182   Falk, Edwin A. *Fighting Bob Evans.* N.Y.: Cape
        .E934   and Smith, 1931.

1633.   E182   Fiske, Bradley A. *From Midshipman to Rear-*
        .F54   *Admiral.* N.Y.: Century, 1919. Memoirs of a
                   progressive in administration and a great naval
                   inventor.

1634.   E182   Gleaves, Albert. *Life and Letters of Rear-*
        .L92   *Admiral Stephen B. Luce, U.S. Navy: Founder of*
                   the Naval War College. N.Y.: Putnam, 1925.

1635.   E182   Hagan, Kenneth J. *American Gunboat Diplomacy*
        .H5   *and the Old Navy, 1877-1899.* Westport, Conn.:
                   Greenwood, 1973.

1636.   Q11   Hammett, Hugh B. *Hilary Abner Herbert: A*
        P612   *Southerner Returns to the Union.* Phila.:
        v.110   American Philosophical Soc., 1976.

1637.   E182   Herrick, Walter R. *The American Naval Revolu-*
        .H46   *tion.* Baton Rouge: LSUP, 1967.

1638.   E664   Hirsch, Mark D. *William C. Whitney: Modern*
        .W613H5   *Warwick.* N.Y.: Dodd, Mead, 1948.

1639.   E664   Hunt, Thomas. *The Life of William H. Hunt.*
        .H947H9   Brattleboro, Ver.: E.L. Hildreth, 1922.

1640.   VB313   Karsten, Peter. *The Naval Aristocracy: The*
        .K36   *Golden Age of Annapolis and the Emergence of*
                   Modern American Navalism. N.Y.: Free Press,
                   1972.

1641.   E661   LaFeber, Walter. *The New Empire: An Interpre-*
        .7.L21   *tation of American Expansion, 1860-1898.*
                   Ithaca: Cornell UP, 1963. An important, if
                   controversial, work.

1642.   QC16   Livingston, Dorothy M. *The Master of Light:*
        .M56L58   *A Biography of Albert A. Michelson.* N.Y.:
                   Scribner, 1973.

1643.   E727   Long, John D. *The New American Navy,* 2 vols.
        .L84   N.Y.: Outlook Co., 1903. Long was Secretary
                   of the Navy from 1897 to 1902.

1644. E182 Morison, Elting E. *The War of Ideas: The United*
      .M68 *States Navy, 1870-1890.* Colorado Springs, Col.;
            USAF Academy, 1969. A lecture that distills
            the essence of his work on William S. Sims.

1645. VM140 Morris, Richard K. *John P. Holland, 1841-1914:*
      .H6M57 *Inventor of the Modern Submarine.* Annapolis,
             Md.: NIP, 1966.

1646. E697 Nevins, Allan. *Grover Cleveland: A Study in*
      .N465 *Courage.* N.Y.: Dodd, Mead, 1931.

1647. E467.1 Niven, John. *Gideon Welles: Lincoln's Secretary*
      .W46N5 *of the Navy.* N.Y.: Oxford UP, 1973. The best
              extant biography of Welles.

1648. E692 Reeves, Thomas C. *Gentleman Boss: The Life of*
      .R43 *Chester Alan Arthur.* N.Y.: Knopf, 1975. A
            machine politician who, as president, author-
            ized the beginnings of the New Navy.

1649. E664 Richardson, Leon B. *William E. Chandler: Re-*
      .C38R5 *publican.* N.Y.: Dodd, Mead, 1940. A hack
             politician, perhaps, but during his tour as
             Secretary of the Navy he approved the founding
             of the Office of Naval Intelligence and the
             Naval War College.

1650. V63 Schroeder, Seaton. *A Half Century of Naval*
      .S4A3 *Service.* N.Y.: D. Appleton, 1923.

1651. E182 Seager, Robert, II. *Alfred Thayer Mahan: The*
      .M242 *Man and His Letters.* Annapolis, Md.: NIP, 1977.
            The best extant biography of Mahan.

1652. V63 Sloan, Edward W. *Benjamin Franklin Isherwood,*
      .I8S5 *Naval Engineer: The Years as Engineer-in-Chief,*
            1861-1869. Annapolis, Md.: NIP, 1975.

1653. Spector, Ronald. *Professors of War: The Naval*
       War College and the Development of the Profes-
       sion. Newport: Naval War College P., 1977.

1654. _____. *Professors of War: The Naval War*
       College and the Modern American Navy. New
       Haven: Yale UP, 1967.

1655. E182 Sprout, Harold and Margaret Sprout. *The Rise*
      .S78 *of American Naval Power, 1776-1938.* Prince-
            ton: PUP, 1939; rpt., Annapolis, Md.: NIP, 1980.

1656. Micro   *Strategic Planning in the U.S. Navy: Its*
             Evolution and Execution, 1891-1945. Wilming-
             ton, Del.: Scholarly Resources, 6 reels.

1657. VM140   Swann, Leonard A. *John Roach, Maritime Entre-*
      .R6S9   *preneur: The Years as Naval Constructor, 1882-*
             1886. Annapolis, Md.: NIP, 1965. Roach built
             the first four ships of the New Navy.

1658. E467.1 West, Richard S. *The Second Admiral: A Life*
      .P78W4 *of David Dixon Porter, 1813-1891.* N.Y.:
             Coward-McCann, 1937.

1659. E183   Young, Marilyn B. *The Rhetoric of Empire:*
      .8.C5Y63 *American China Policy, 1895-1901.* Cambridge:
             HUP, 1968.

1660. VA58   Zogbaum, Rufus F. *"All Hands": Pictures of*
      .Z85   *Life in the United States Navy.* N.Y.: Harper,
             1897.

1661. E746   _____. *From Sail to* Saratoga: *A Naval Auto-*
      .Z6A3   *Biography.* Rome, Italy: n.d.

DOCUMENTS

1662. G700   DeLong, George W. *The Voyage of the* Jeannette:
      1879   *The Ship and Ice Journals of George W. Delong,*
      .A32   *Lieutenant-Commander U.S.N., and Commander of*
             the Polar Expedition, 1879-1881, 2 vols. Bos-
             ton: Houghton Mifflin, 1883.

1663. E182   Seager, Robert II, and Doris D. Maguire, eds.
      .M24   *The Letters and Papers of Alfred Thayer Mahan,*
             3 vols. Annapolis, Md.: NIP, 1975.

1664. Micro   U.S. NARG 45. Naval Records Collection of the
      VB155.4 Office of Naval Records and Library. *Letters*
      .S7E9   *Received by the Secretary of the Navy from*
             Commanding Officers of the European Squadron
             1865-1885.

1665. Micro   U.S. NARG 45. Naval Records Collection of the
      VB255   Office of Naval Records and Library. *Letters*
      .1.U56 *to Flag Officers Commanding Squadrons, Vessels*
             and Stations Sent by the Secretary of Navy
             1867-1886. 4 reels. Wash.: 1947.

137

1666. Micro   U.S. NARG 45. Naval Records Collection of the
      VB255.1 Office of Naval Records and Library. *Letters*
      .U58   *to Naval Academy, Commanding Officers, and*
               Other Officers, Sent by the Secretary of the
               Navy 1869-1884.

DISSERTATIONS AND THESES

1667.   Allen, John M., Jr. "Corporate Values Invade
         the Navy: The Growth of Modern American Sea
         Power, 1861-1882," Syracuse U., 1976.

1668.   Allin, Lawrence C. "The U.S. Naval Institute:
         Intellectual Forum of the New Navy, 1873-1889,"
         U. of Maine, 1976.

1669.   Buhl, Lance C. "The Smooth Water Navy: Ameri-
         can Policy and Politics, 1865-1876," 2 vols.
         Harvard U., 1968.

1670. E182   Chadbourne, Charles C. "Sailors and Diplomats:
      .C413   U.S. Naval Operations in China, 1865-1877," U.
             of Washington, 1976.

1671.   Sexton, Donald J. "Forging the Sword: Congress
         and the American Naval Renaissance, 1880-
         1890," U. of Tennessee, 1976.

1672.   Allard, Dean C. "The Influence of the U.S. Navy
         upon the American Steel Industry, 1880-1900,"
         M.A. thesis, Georgetown U., 1959.

1673.   Green, James R. "The First Sixty Years of the
         Office of Naval Intelligence," M.A. thesis,
         American U., 1963.

ARTICLES

1674.   Allin, Lawrence C. "The First Cubic War: The
         Virginius Affair," AN 38 (Oct. 1978): 233-48.

1675.   *Bauer, K. Jack. "The Korean Expedition of
         1871," USNIP 74 (Feb. 1948):197-203. A sum-
         mary of the military aspects of the first en-
         gagement between Korean forces and U.S. Marines
         in June 1871.

1676.   Benjamin, Park. "The Nerves of the Warship,"
         Harper's 92 (Mar. 1896):631-36. Bradley A.
         Fiske's internal communications systems.

1677.   Bennett, Frank M. "Honorably Mentioned for 1894: Naval Reform," USNIP 27, No. 70 (1894): 251-92.

1678.   Buhl, Lance C. "Mariners and Machines: Resistance to Technological Change in the American Navy, 1865-1869," JAH 59 (Dec. 1974):703-27. The best short exposition on the 1865-1873 period.

1679.   Chandler, L.H. "Is Amalgamation a Failure?" USNIP 31 (Dec. 1905):823-44. The line officer and engineer.

1680.   Coletta, Paolo E. "French Ensor Chadwick: The First American Naval Attaché," AN 39 (June 1979):126-41.

1681.   Cooling, Benjamin F. "The Formative Years of the Naval-Industrial Complex: Their Meaning for Studies of Institutions Today," NWCR 27 (Mar.-Apr. 1975):53-62.

1682.   Ellicott, John M. "The Passing of the Cadet Engineers," USNIP 64 (Aug. 1938):1123-34. The USNA would educate midshipmen to be both line officers and engineers after the end of the cadet program.

1683.   Greene, Fred. "The Military View of American National Policy, 1904-1940," AHR 66 (Jan. 1961):354-77.

1684.   Gurley, Ralph R. "The *Wampanoag*," USNIP 63 (Dec. 1937):1732-36. The fast sail-steamer laid up by Adm. D.D. Porter because she burned coal.

1685.   Holbrook, Francis S., and John Nikol. "The Chilean Crisis of 1891-1892," AN 38 (Oct. 1978): 291-300.

1686.   Kennon, John W. "U.S.S. *Vesuvius*," USNIP 80 (Feb. 1954):183-90. An experiment with "dynamite guns" in which the propellant was compressed air.

1687.   Luce, Stephen B. "Naval Administration," USNIP 14 (June 1888):561-88. An early plug for a naval general staff.

1688.   Parker, Foxhall. "Our Fleet Maneuvers in the
            Bay of Florida," USNIP 1 (Dec. 10, 1874):163-
            76. Reveals many inadequacies.

1689.   Reisinger, W.W. "Torpedoes," USNIP 14, No. 3
            (1888):483-538.

1690.   "Report of the Policy Board," USNIP 16, No. 53
            (1890):201-77.

1691.   Russell, Kay. "Stephen Bleecker Luce and the
            Naval War College," NWCR 30 (Apr.-May 1979):
            20-41.

1692.   Sandler, Stanley. "A Navy in Decay: Some Stra-
            tegic Technological Results of Disarmament,
            1865-1869," MA 35 (Dec. 1971):138-42.

1693.   Schratz, Paul. "Mahan: Philosopher of Sea
            Power," *Shipmate* 41 (Dec. 1978):3, 18.

1694.   Seager, Robert II. "Ten Years Before Mahan,"
            MVHR 40 (Dec. 1953):491-512.

1695. U39   Sprout, Margaret T. "Mahan: Evangelist of Sea
       .E2   Power," Edward M. Earle, ed. *Makers of Modern
            Strategy: Military Thought from Machiavelli to
            Hitler.* Princeton: PUP, 1943, pp. 415-45.

1696.   Wadleigh, John R. "The Best Was Yet to Be,"
            USNIP 99 (Nov. 1973):56-70. The sad state of
            the U.S. Navy in 1873.

1697.   Zogbaum, Rufus I. "With Uncle Sam's Blue Jack-
            ets Afloat," *Scribner's Mag.* 7 (Sept. 1890):
            267-83. Life in the *Chicago*.

                        FICTION

1698. G700 Ellsberg, Edward. *Hell on Ice: The Saga of the
       .1897 Jeannette.* N.Y.: Dodd, Mead, 1938. Arctic ex-
       .E4   ploration.

8

THE SPANISH-AMERICAN WAR, THE PHILIPPINE
INSURRECTION, AND THE BOXER REBELLION

BOOKS

1699. E715   Alger, Russell A. *The Spanish-American War.*
       .A39   N.Y.: Harper, 1901.

1700. E715   *American-Spanish War: A History by the War*
       .A51   *Leaders.* Norwich, Conn.: Charles C. Haskell and
                Son, 1899.

1701. E723   Benton, Elbert J. *International Law and Diplo-*
       .B47   *macy of the Spanish-American War.* Baltimore:
                Johns Hopkins P., 1908. Most erudite.

1702. E182   Braisted, William R. *The U.S. Navy in the Pa-*
       .B73   *cific, 1897-1909.* Austin: U. of Texas P., 1958.
                A serious, scholarly study.

1703. E169.1   Burns, Edward McN. *The American Idea of Mission.*
       .B943   New Brunswick, N.J.: Rutgers UP, 1957.

1704. E183.8   Chadwick, French E. *The Relations of the United*
       .S7C4   *States and Spain: Diplomacy.* N.Y.: Scribner,
                1909. Spanish-American diplomatic relations
                from 1492 to 1909.

1705. E715   _____. *The Relations of the United States*
       .C43   *and Spain: The Spanish-American War*, 2 vols.
                N.Y.: Scribner, 1911. Still the best diploma-
                tic account.

1706. E744   Challener, Richard. *Admirals, Generals, and*
       .C42   *American Foreign Policy, 1898-1914.* Princeton:
                PUP, 1973. A thorough account but in some
                respects already outdated.

1707. E182   Clark, Charles E. *My Fifty Years in the Navy.*
       .C57   Boston: Little, Brown, 1917.

1708. DS771   Clements, Paul H. *The Boxer Rebellion: A Po-*
       .C6   *litical and Diplomatic Review.* N.Y.: Columbia
                UP, 1915; rpt., AMSP., 1967.

1709.   Coletta, Paolo E. *French Ensor Chadwick:*
                Scholarly Warrior. Wash.: UP of America, 1980.

1710. _____. *Bowman Hendry McCalla: A Fighting Sailor*. Wash.: UP of America, 1979.

1711. V63   _____. *Admiral Bradley A. Fiske and the*
      .F57C64 *American Navy*. Lawrence: Regents P. of Kansas, 1979.

1712. E664   _____. *William Jennings Bryan I: 1860-1908*.
      .B87C55 Lincoln: U. of Nebraska P., 1964.

1713. E725.3   Cosmas, Graham A. *An Army for Empire: The*
      .C6   *United States Army in the Spanish-American War*.
               Columbia: U. of Missouri P., 1971. The best account of Army participation in the war.

1714.   Daggett, A.S. *America in the China Relief Expedition*. Kansas City: Hudson-Kimberly Pub. Co., 1903.

1715. E664   Dennett, Tyler. *John Hay: From Poetry to Politics*. N.Y.: Dodd, Mead, 1933.
      .H41D3

1716. JX1415   Dennis, Alfred L.P. *Adventures in Diplomacy,*
      .D4   *1896-1906*. N.Y.: Dutton, 1928; rpt., N.Y.: Johnson Reprint Corp., 1969.

1717. E714.6   Dewey, George. *Autobiography of George Dewey:*
      .D51D52   *Admiral of the Navy*. N.Y.: Scribner, 1913; rpt. AMS, 1970, and Scholarly P., 1971. Ghosted.

1718. DS771   Duiker, William J. *Cultures in Collision: The*
      .D84   *Boxer Rebellion*. San Rafael, Calif.: Presidio, 1978.

1719. DS668   Elliott, Charles B. *The Philippines to the End*
      .E4   *of the Military Regime: America Overseas*. Indianapolis: Bobbs-Merrill, 1916.

1720. E182   Evans, Robley D. *A Sailor's Log: Recollections*
      .E92   *of Forty Years of Naval Life*. N.Y.: Appleton, 1901.

1721. E182   Fiske, Bradley A. *From Midshipman to Rear Admiral*. N.Y.: Century, 1919.
      .F54

1722. DS679   _____. *Wartime in Manila*. Boston: Gorham,
      .F5   1913. Eye-witness account.

1723. DS685   Forbes, William C. *The Philippine Islands*,
      .F6   2 vols. Boston: Houghton Mifflin, 1928.

1724. E715   Freidel, Frank B. *The Splendid Little War*. Bos-
      .F7   ton: Little, Brown, 1958.

1725. DS679   Gates, John B. *Schoolbooks and Krags: The U.S.
      .G38   Army in the Philippines 1898-1902*. Westport,
              Conn.: Greenwood, 1973.

1726. E727   Goode, William A.M. *With Sampson Through the
      .G64   War*. N.Y.: Doubleday & McClure, 1899. A Brit-
              ish correspondent's account. Very favorable
              to Sampson.

1727. E727   Graham, George E. *Schley and Santiago*. Chicago:
      .G73   Conkey, 1902. Favors Schley over Sampson.

1728. E661.7 Grenville, John A.S., and George B. Young.
      .G7   *Politics, Strategy, and American Diplomacy*.
              New Haven: YUP, 1966.

1729. E757   Harbaugh, William H. *Power and Responsibility:
      .H28   The Life and Times of Theodore Roosevelt*. N.Y.:
              Farrar, Straus & Cudahy, 1961.

1730. E183.8 Healy, David F. *The United States in Cuba, 1898-
      .C9H4   1902: Generals, Politicians, and the Search for
              Policy*. Madison: U. of Wisconsin P., 1963.

1731. E727   Hobson, Richmond P. *The Sinking of the* Merrimac.
      .H68   N.Y.: Century, 1899. Exciting narrative.

1732. E715   King, W. Nephew. *The Story of the War of 1898
      .K54   and the Revolt in the Philippines*. N.Y.: Peter
              Fenelon Collier and Son, 1901.

1733. E711.6 Leech, Margaret. *In the Days of McKinley*. N.Y.:
      .L4   Harper, 1959. Superbly written, with stress
              on Mrs. McKinley.

1734. E715   *Leslie's Official History of the Spanish Ameri-
      .L63   can War*.... Wash.: Leslie's Weekly, 1899.

1735. E169.1 Linderman, Gerald F. *The Mirror of War: American
      .L5435   Society and the Spanish-American War*. Ann Arbor,
              Mich.: U. of Michigan P., 1974. An interesting,
              unusual approach. Sometimes badly reviewed;
              nevertheless shows how Americans channeled the
              tensions, fears, and antagonisms of a domestic
              presidential campaign into a crusade for Cuban
              freedom that resulted in war.

1736. E715 Lodge, Henry C. *The War with Spain*. N.Y.: Har-
      .L82   per, 1899.

1737. E727 Long, John D. *The New American Navy*, 2 vols.
      .L84   N.Y.: Outlook Co., 1903.

1738. E664 Long, Margaret, ed. *The Journal of John D.
      .L84A3 Long*. Rindge, N.H.: R. Smith, 1956.

1739. E182 Maclay, Edgar S. *Life and Adventures of "Jack"
      .P54   Philip, Rear Admiral United States Navy*. N.Y.:
             The Illustrated Navy, 1903.

1740. E182 _____. *A History of the United States Navy
      .M21   from 1775 to 1901*, new and enl. ed., 3 vols.
             N.Y.: D. Appleton, 1901. Contains criticisms
             of Schley that led to his requesting a court of
             inquiry.

1741. E727 Mahan, Alfred T. *Lessons of the War with Spain
      .M21   and Other Articles*. Boston: Little, Brown,
             1899; rpt., Books for Libraries, 1970.

1742. D664 Mayo, L.S., ed. *America of Yesterday, as Re-
      .L84L8 flected in the Journal of John Davis Long*.
             Boston: Atlantic Monthly P., 1923.

1743. E715 Millis, Walter *The Martial Spirit: A Study Of
      .M76   Our War with Spain*. Boston: Houghton Mifflin,
             1931. Pokes gentle fun at the United States.

1744. E711.6 Morgan, H. Wayne. *William McKinley and His
      .M7   America*. Syracuse: Syracuse UP, 1963. Best
              extant biography.

1745. E715 _____. *America's Road to Empire: The War
      .M85   with Spain and Overseas Expansion*. N.Y.: Wiley,
             1965. Much of this is contained in the work
             above.

1746. Micro *Naval Contingency War Plans [1890-1941]*.
             Wilmington, Del.: Scholarly Resources, 1979.

1747. DS771 O'Connor, Richard. *The Spirit Soldiers: A His-
      .O28   torical Narrative of the Boxer Rebellion*.
             N.Y.: Putnam, 1973.

1748. E727 Parker, James. *Rear-Admirals Schley, Sampson,
      .P25   and Cervera*. N.Y.: McNeal, 1910.

1749. E713 Pratt, Julius W. *Expansionists of 1898*. Balti-
   .P895 more: Johns Hopkins P., 1936. Path-breaking
       study.

1750. E7216 Rickover, Hyman G. *How the Battleship* Maine *Was*
   .R5   *Destroyed*. Wash.: Naval Hist. Div., 1976.

1751. E717.7 Sargent, Nathan, comp. *Admiral Dewey and the*
   .S3   *Manila Campaign*. Wash.: Naval Hist. Foundation,
       1947.

1752. E182 Schley, Winfield S. *Forty-five Years Under the*
   .S34 *Flag*. N.Y.: Appleton, 1904. His apologia.

1753. V63   Schroeder, Seaton. *A Half Century of Naval Ser-*
   .S4A3 *vice*. N.Y.: Appleton, 1923.

1754. E727 Spears, John R. *Our Navy in the War with Spain*.
   .S739 N.Y.: Scribner, 1898.

1755. E714.6 Spector, Ronald. *Admiral of the New Empire: The*
   .D51568 *Life and Career of George Dewey*. Baton Rouge:
       LSUP, 1974. The best biography to date.

1756. PN4874 Swanberg, W.A. *Citizen Hearst: A Biography of*
   .H4S83 *William Randolph Hearst*. N.Y.: Scribner, 1961.

1757. H31   Tan, Chester C. *The Boxer Catastrophe*. N.Y.:
   .C7   Columbia UP, 1955; rpt., N.Y.: Octagon Books,
       1967.

1758. E721 Weems, John E. *The Fate of the* Maine. N.Y.:
   .6W.4 Holt, 1958. Good reading but of no scholarly
       value.

1759. E714.5 West, Richard S. *Admirals of American Empire:*
   .W4   *The Combined Story of George Dewey, Alfred*
       Thayer Mahan, Winfield Scott Schley. and William
       Thomas Sampson. Indianapolis: Bobbs-Merrill,
       1948.

1760. DS685 Williams, Daniel R. *The United States and the*
   .W5   *Philippines*. GCNY: Doubleday, Page, 1924.

1761. E727 Wilson, Herbert W. *The Downfall of Spain: Naval*
   .W74 *History of the Spanish-American War*. Boston:
       Little, Brown, 1900; rpt., B. Franklin, 1971.
       The best naval account.

1762. US682 Wolff, Leon. *Little Brown Brother*....GCNY:
   .A1W6 Doubleday, 1961. Popularly written. Sympa-
       thetic to the Filipino.

1763. DS685   Worcester, Dean C., and Ralston Hayden. *The*
     .W8   *Philippines: Past and Present*, 2 vols. N.Y.:
                Macmillan, 1914. Worcester had served as
                governor-general of the Philippines.

DOCUMENTS

1764. Micro   U.S. NARS. NARG 45. *Naval War Board, Letters*
     E727   *and Telegrams Sent April 29 to Aug. 24, 1898.*
     .U5   1 reel.

1765.   U.S. Navy Department. Bureau of Navigation.
                Appendix to the Report of the Chief of the
                Bureau of Navigation. Wash.: GPO, 1899. Rec-
                ords of operations and correspondence during
                the Spanish-American War.

1766. E727   U.S. Navy Department. *Record of Proceedings of*
     .S315   *a Court of Inquiry in the Case of Rear-Admiral*
                Winfield S. Schley..., 2 vols. Wash.: GPO,
                1902.

1767.   U.S. War Department. Adjutant General's Office.
                Correspondence Relating to the War with Spain
                and Conditions Growing Out of Same, Including
                the Insurrection in the Philippines and the
                China Relief Expedition, 2 vols. Wash.: GPO,
                1902.

DISSERTATIONS AND THESES

1768.   Damiani, Brian P. "Advocates of Empire: William
                McKinley, the Senate and American Expansion,
                1898-1899," U. of Delaware, 1978.

ARTICLES

1769.   Agnew, James C. "Coalition War: Relieving the
                Peking Legations, 1900." MR 56 (Oct. 1976):
                58-69.

1770.   Bailey, Thomas A. "Dewey and the Germans at
                Manila Bay," AHR 45 (Oct. 1939):59-81.

1771.   Beach, Edward L., Sr. "Manila Bay in 1898,"
                USNIP 46 (Apr. 1920):587-602.

1772.   Capehart, E.E. "The Mine Defense of Santiago
                Harbor," USNIP 24 (Dec. 1898):585-604.

1773.   Coletta, Paolo E. "Bowman H. McCalla at Guantánamo Bay," *Shipmate* 41 (June 1978): 25-28.

1774.   _____. "McKinley, the Peace Negotiations, and the Acquisition of the Philippines," PHR 30 (Nov. 1961):341-50.

1775.   _____. "Bryan, McKinley, and the Treaty of Paris," PHR 26 (May 1957):131-46.

1776.   Davidson, W.C. "Operations in North China," USNIP 26 (Dec. 1900):637-46.

1777.   Ellicott, John M. "The Naval Battle of Manila," USNIP 26 (Sept. 1900):489-514.

1778.   _____. "Effect of Gun-Fire, Battle of Manila Bay," USNIP 25 (June 1899):323-34.

1779.   A Friend of the Navy. "Some Neglected Naval Lessons of the Spanish War," NAR 174 (Mar. 1902): 338-47.

1780.   Halle, Louis J. "Civil-Military Relations: Historical Case Studies. III, 1898: The United States in the Pacific," MA 20 (Summer 1956): 76-80.

1781.   *Heinl, Robert D. "Hell in China," MCG 43 (Nov. 1959):55-68. A thorough account of Marine participation in the Boxer Rebellion, 1900-1901.

1782. E743   Hofstadter, Richard. "Cuba, the Philippines,
      .H632   and Manifest Destiny," *The Paranoid Style in American Politics and Other Essays*. N.Y.: Knopf, 1965.

1783.   Hunt, Michael. "The Forgotten Occupation: Peking, 1900-1901," PHR 48 (Nov. 1979):501-30.

1784.   *McCawley, Charles L. "The Guantánamo Campaign of 1898," MCG 5 (Sep. 1916):221-42. An excellent account from firsthand experience of the four-month Cuban tour of the 1st Marine Batallion in 1898.

1785.   McCormick, Thomas. "Insular Imperialism and
            the Open Door: The China Market and the Spanish-
            American War," PHR 32 (May 1963):155-69.

1786.   McCutcheon, John T., and Thomas A. Bailey. The
            Battle of Manila Bay," USNIP 66 (June 1940):
            843-53.   The British did not interfere between
            the U.S. and German ships; Germany was the
            aggressor in Manila Bay.

1787.   May, Glenn A. "Filipino Resistance to American
            Occupation: Batangas, 1899-1902," PHR 48 (Nov.
            1979):531-56.

1788.   *Myers, John T. "Military Operations and De-
            fenses of the Siege of Peking," USNIP 28 (Sept.
            1902):541-51.

1789.   *Niblack, Albert P. "Operations of the Navy
            and Marine Corps in the Philippine Archipelago,
            1898-1902," USNIP 30 (Dec. 1904):745-73.

1790.   Owen, Norman G. "Winding Down the War in Albay
            [Philippines], 1900-1903," PHR 48 (Nov. 1979):
            557-90.

1791.   Perez, Louis A. "Cuba Between Empires, 1898-
            1899," PHR 48 (Nov. 1979):473-500.

1792.   Pratt, Julius W. "The 'Large Policy of 1898,'"
            MVHR 19 (Sept. 1932):219-42.

1793.   *Russell, William H. "The Genesis of FMF Doc-
            trine: 1879-1899," MCG 35 (Apr. 1951):52-59,
            (May 1951):49-53, and (July 1951):52-59.

1794.   Smith, Oliver P. "We Will Do Our Best," USNIP
            54 (Nov. 1928):979-92.

1795.   Spector, Ronald. "Who Planned the Attack on
            Manila Bay?" *Mid America*, Apr. 1971, pp.94-102.

1796.   *Taussig, Joseph K. "Experiences During the
            Boxer Rebellion," USNIP 53 (Apr. 1927):403-20.

9

THE U.S. NAVY COMES OF AGE, 1898-1914

BOOKS

1797. E757   Beale, Howard K. *Theodore Roosevelt and the*
      .B4   *Rise of America to World Power.* Baltimore:
              Johns Hopkins P., 1956. A masterful study.

1798. E183   Braisted, William R. *The United States Navy in*
      .B732   *the Pacific, 1909-1922.* Austin: U. of Texas
              P., 1971. This volume and the subsequent one
              preempt the field.

1799. E182   _____. *The United States Navy in the Pacific,*
      .B73   *1897-1909.* Austin: U. of Texas P., 1958.

1800. V25   Brodie, Bernard. *Sea Power in the Machine Age,*
      .B7   2d ed. Princeton: PUP, 1943.
      1943

1801. F1418   Callcott, Wilfrid H. *The Caribbean Policy of*
      .C22   *the United States, 1890-1920.* Baltimore: Johns
              Hopkins P., 1942. Still the best study for
              the period it covers.

1802. TC724   Cameron, Ian, pseud. *The Impossible Dream: The*
      .P38   *Building of the Panama Canal.* N.Y.: Morrow,
              1972.

1803. E183   Campbell, Charles S. *Anglo-American Understand-*
      .8G7   *ing, 1898-1903.* Baltimore: Johns Hopkins P.,
              1957.

1804. E746   Carter, Samuel III. *The Incredible Great White*
      .C33   *Fleet.* N.Y.: Crowell-Collier, 1971.

1805. E744   Challener, Richard D. *Admirals, Generals, and*
      .C42   *American Foreign Policy 1898-1914.* Princeton:
              PUP, 1973.

1806. E173   Clinard, Outten J. *Japan's Influence on Ameri-*
      .C15   *can Naval Power, 1897-1917.* Berkeley: U. of
              California P., 1947. Tends to overstress the
              influence.

1807. E744   Collier, Basil. *"The Lion and the Eagle": Brit-*
      .C64   *ish and Anglo-American Strategy, 1900-1950.*
              N.Y.: Putnam, 1972.

1808. E182 .C74 Coontz, Robert E. *From the Mississippi to the Sea*. Phila.: Dorrance, 1930. A member of the class of 1885, Coontz served as CNO and as Commander in Chief of the U.S. Fleet.

1809. VG93 .C72 Craven, Thomas T. *History of Aviation in the United States Navy: From its Beginning Until the Spring of 1920*. Wash.: Naval Hist. Div., 1977. The author served as director of naval aviation.

1810. E766 .D29 Cronon, E. David, ed. *The Cabinet Diaries of Josephus Daniels, 1913-1921*. Lincoln: U. of Nebraska P., 1963. Extremely valuable even if the years 1914 and 1916 are missing.

1811. E182 .W138 Cummings, Damon. *Richard Wainwright and the United States Fleet*. Wash.: Navy Dept., 1962. An example of what poor writing can do to a good subject.

1812. UA23 .D29 Davis, Vincent. *The Admirals Lobby*. Chapel Hill: UNCP, 1967.

1813. E664 .H41D3 Dennett, Tyler. *John Hay*. N.Y.: Dodd, Mead, 1933. As Secretary of State, Hay was involved in the Alaskan and Venezuelan boundary controversies, negotiations with Britain over an isthmian canal, the Boxers, and Far Eastern affairs, for which he devised the Open Door policy.

1814. E183.8 .J3E8 Esthus, Raymond A. *Theodore Roosevelt and Japan*. Seattle: U. of Washington P., 1966. The best study of the subject to date.

1815. E182 .E91 Evans, Robley D. *A Sailor's Log....* N.Y.: D. Appleton, 1901. A member of the Academy class of 1864, Evans saw action in the assault on Fort Fisher during the Civil War and in the Spanish-American War. Later, in his *Admiral's Log*, (No. 1816), he brought the story through his tour as Commander in Chief of the Great White Fleet on the first leg of its around-the-world cruise.

1816. E182 .E172 _____. *An Admiral's Log*. N.Y.: D. Appleton, 1910.

1817. E182   Falk, Edwin R. *Fighting Bob Evans*. N.Y.: Cape
     .E934   and Smith, 1931. Good reading even if somewhat
        idolatrous.

1818. E182   Fiske, Bradley A. *From Midshipman to Rear Ad-*
     .F54   *miral*. N.Y.: Century, 1919. Life of one of
        the navy's greatest inventors and critics.

1819. D5518   Griswold, A. Whitney. *The Far Eastern Policy*
     .8G75   *of the United States*. N.Y.: Harcourt Brace,
        1938. Superbly written account.

1820. E757   Harbaugh, William H. *Power and Responsibility:*
     .H28   *The Life and Times of Theodore Roosevelt*. N.Y.:
        Farrar, Straus and Cudahy, 1961. The best
        extant full biography.

1821. VB263   Harrod, Frederick S. *Manning the New Navy: The*
     .H37   *Development of a Modern Naval Enlisted Force,*
        1899-1940. Westport, Conn.: Greenwood, 1977.
        Excellent--and only--account of the subject.

1822. E182   Hart, Robert A. *The Great White Fleet: Its*
     .H27   *Voyage Around the World 1907-1909*. Boston:
        Little, Brown, 1965. Perhaps too heavy on
        the public-relations objectives of the journey.

1823. TL540   Hatch, Alden. *Glenn Curtiss: Pioneer of Naval*
     .C9H3   *Aviation*. N.Y.: Messner, 1942.

1824. E183.8   Healy, David F. *Gunboat Diplomacy in the Wilson*
     .H2H42   *Era: The U.S. Navy in Haiti, 1915-1916*. Madison:
        U. of Wisconsin P., 1976.

1825. E183.8   Heindel, Richard H. *The American Impact on*
     .G7H5   *Great Britain, 1898-1914: A Study of the United*
        States in World History. Phila.: U. of Pa. P.,
        1940.

1826. E756   Hill, Howard C. *Roosevelt and the Caribbean*.
     .H65   Chicago: U. of Chicago P., 1927.

1827. G635   Hobbs, William H. *Peary*. N.Y.: Macmillan, 1936.
     .P4H6

1828. Q141   Hovgaard, William. *Biographical Memoir of David*
     .N22   *Watson Taylor, 1864-1940*. Wash.: National Acad.
        of Sciences, 1941. 18 pp.

1829. E664   Howe, Mark A. De Wolfe. *George von Lengerke*
       .M573H5   *Meyer: His Life and Public Services*. N.Y.:
                      Dodd, Mead, 1919. Meyer was a businessman,
                      diplomat, postmaster general under T. Roose-
                      velt, and secretary of the navy under Taft.

1830. TA140   Hughes, Thomas P. *Elmer A. Sperry: Inventor*
       .S68H79   *and Engineer*. Baltimore: Johns Hopkins P.,
                      1971. Beautifully written account showing
                      good understanding of science and technology.

1831. UG633   Hurley, Alfred F. *Billy Mitchell: Crusader for*
       .M45H8   *Air Power*. N.Y.: Watts, 1964; Bloomington:
                      Indiana UP, 1975.

1832. E183   Iriye, Akira. *Pacific Estrangement: Japanese*
       .8J3I74   *and American Expansion, 1897-1911*. Cambridge,
                      Mass.: HUP, 1972.

1833. VG93   *Johnson, Edward D. Ed. by Graham A. Cosmas.
       .J63   *Marine Corps Aviation: The Early Years, 1912-*
                      1940. Wash.: USMC, HQ, Hist. and Museums Div.,
                      1977. Also available GPO.

1834. DA89   Jordan, Gerald, ed. *Naval Warfare in the Twen-*
       .N38   *tieth Century: Essays in Honour of Arthur*
                      Marder. N.Y.: Crane & Russak, 1977.

1835. F2178   Langley, Lester D. *Struggle for the American*
       .U6L36   *Mediterranean: United States-European Rivalry*
                      in the Gulf-Caribbean, 1776-1904. Athens: U.
                      of Georgia P., 1976. Perforce a general sum-
                      mary.

1836. E727   Long, John D. *The New American Navy*, 2 vols.
       .L84   N.Y.: Outlook Co., 1903. Especially good on
                      men and events while he was secretary of the
                      navy, 1897-1902.

1837. VA55   Mahan, Alfred T. *From Sail to Steam: Recollec-*
       .M2   *tions of a Naval Life*. N.Y.: Harper, 1907.
                      Ponderous. Better is Puleston, William D.,
                      q.v. Best is Seager, Robert, *q.v.*

1838. DA88   Marder, Arthur. *The Anatomy of British Sea*
       .M3   *Power: A History of British Naval Policy in*
                      the Pre-dreadnought Era, 1880-1905. N.Y.:
                      Knopf, 1940.

1839. VA52   Morison, Elting E. *Naval Administration 1915-*
      .A1U52   *1940*. Wash.: Navy Dept., 1945 (?). Good com-
                pilation especially of naval legislative his-
                tory.

1840. E748   _____. *Admiral Sims and the Modern American*
      .S52M6   *Navy*. Boston: Houghton Mifflin, 1942. Pertinent
                here are his early tours following graduation
                with the class of 1880, his service as naval
                attaché, his reporting on discrepancies in
                ships, his tour as inspector of target practice
                and aide to President Roosevelt, his command of
                the Atlantic destroyer flotilla, his swinging
                about the hook during the intervention in Mexi-
                co in 1914, his tour as Commander, U.S. Naval
                Forces in European waters, and as president of
                the Naval War College.

1841. VM140   Morris, Richard K. *John P. Holland, 1841-1914:*
      .H6M57   *Inventor of the Modern Submarine*. Annapolis,
                Md.: USNI, 1966.

1842. E756   Mowry, George E. *The Era of Theodore Roosevelt,*
      .M85   *1900-1912*. N.Y.: Harper, 1958. As yet the best
                account of the subject.

1843. VA58   Neeser, Robert W. *Our Many-Sided Navy*. New
      .N54   Haven: YUP, 1914.

1844. E183   Neu, Charles E. *An Uncertain Friendship:*
      .8J3N37   *Theodore Roosevelt and Japan 1906-1909*. Cam-
                bridge, Mass.: HUP, 1967. Compare with Esthus,
                Raymond A.

1845. E664   Nevins, Allan. *Henry White: Thirty Years of*
      .W594   *American Diplomacy*. N.Y.: Harper, 1930. Mas-
      N52   terful account by a good journalist who became
                a superb historian.

1846. E182   O'Gara, Gordon C. *Theodore Roosevelt and the*
      .O34   *Rise of the Modern Navy*. Princeton: PUP, 1943.
                Still the best account of this subject.

1847. E183.8   Perkins, Bradford. *The Great Rapprochement:*
      .G7P42   *England and the United States, 1895-1914*.
                N.Y.: Atheneum, 1968.

1848. E757   Pringle, Henry F. *Theodore Roosevelt: A Biog-*
      .P96   *raphy*. N.Y.: Harcourt Brace, 1931. Entertain-
                ing account if one agrees with the author that
                Roosevelt's mental age was six years. Harbaugh,
                William, *q.v.*, is much better balanced.

1849. E182   Puleston, William D. *Mahan: The Life and Work*
      .M256   *of Captain Alfred Thayer Mahan*. New Haven:
               YUP, 1939.

1850. F1234   Quirk, Robert E. *An Affair of Honor: Woodrow*
      .Q62   *Wilson and the Occupation of Veracruz*. Lexing-
               ton: U. of Kentucky P., 1962. Excellent
               account.

1851. VA49   Rappaport, Armin. *The Navy League of the United*
      .N4R3   *States*. Detroit, Mich.: Wayne State UP, 1962.
               The only work on the subject. Well written
               and well balanced.

1852. TL540   Roseberry, Cecil R. *Glenn Curtiss: Pioneer of*
      .C9R67   *Flight*. GCNY: Doubleday, 1972.

1853. DS683.5 Sawyer, Frederick L. *Sons of Gunboats*. Annap-
      P3S3   olis, Md.: USNI, 1953. Gunboat activities
               during the Philippine Insurrection.

1854. VG93   Shanahan, William O. *Procurement of Naval Air-*
      .S4   *craft 1907-1909*. Wash.: Deputy CNO, (Air),
               1946.

1855. U21.2   Simpson, B. Mitchell, ed. *War, Strategy, and*
      .W38   *Maritime Power*. New Brunswick, N.J.: Rutgers
               UP, 1977. Nineteen essays on very diverse
               subjects. Most important are Reitzel's sum-
               mary of Mahan, Ambrose's comments on naval
               strategy of the two world wars, and Hatten-
               dorf's examination of the impact of technology
               on the pre-World War I U.S. Navy.

1856. E714.6 Spector, Ronald. *Admiral of the New Empire:*
      .D51568 *The Life and Career of George Dewey*. Baton
               Rouge: LSUP, 1974. The best biography to
               date.

1857. E182   Sprout, Harold, and Margaret Sprout. *The Rise*
      .S78   *of American Naval Power, 1776-1918*. Princeton:
               PUP, 1939; rpt., Annapolis, Md.: NIP, 1980.

1858. V63   Stirling, Yates. *Sea Duty: The Memoirs of a*
      .S75   *Fighting Admiral*. N.Y.: Putnam, 1939. Stirling
      A3   was one of the progressive officers of his
               period who, like Fiske and Sims, wanted a
               naval general staff.

1859. F1234   Sweetman, Jack., *The Landing at Veracruz....*
      .S95   Annapolis, Md.: USNI, 1968.

1860. H31
.C7
No. 583

Tan, Chester C. *The Boxer Catastrophe*. N.Y.:
Columbia UP, 1953; rpt., Octagon, 1967.

1861. VG93
.A79

U.S. Navy Department. Office of Naval Operations. *United States Naval Aviation, 1910-1960*.
Wash.: Navy Dept., 1960.

1862. TL540
.L3V3

Vaeth, Joseph G. *Langley: Man of Science and
Flight*. N.Y.: Ronald, 1966. Langley's aero-
dynamic theories were correct but his gear
failed to function.

1863. V63
.E44V36

Van Deurs, George. *Anchors in the Sky: Spuds
Ellyson, The First Naval Aviator*. San Rafael,
Calif.: Presidio, 1979.

1864. VG93
.V3

_____. *Wings for the Fleet: A Narrative of
Naval Aviation's Early Development*. Annapolis,
Md.: USNI, 1966.

1865. VA93
.A79
1971

Van Fleet, Clarke, Lee Pearson, and Adrien O.
Van Wyen. *United States Naval Aviation, 1910-
1970*. Wash.: GPO, 1971.

1866. E182
.W55

Wiley, Henry A. *An Admiral from Texas*. GCNY:
Doubleday, Doran, 1934. A graduate of the
class of 1888, Wiley tells of his naval experiences ending with his tour as Commander
in Chief of the U.S. Fleet in 1929.

1867. VE23
.W5

*Wise, Frederic M. *A Marine Tells It to You*.
N.Y.: Sears, 1929. Reminiscences of 27 years
of service.

DOCUMENTS

1868.

U.S. Navy Department. *Record of Proceedings of
a Court of Inquiry in the Case of Rear-Admiral
Winfield S. Schley, U.S. Navy, Convened at the
Navy-Yard, Washington, D.C., September 12,
1901*, 2 vols. Wash.: GPO, 1902.

DISSERTATIONS AND THESES

1869.

Anderson, Stuart L. "Race and Rapprochement:
Anglo-Saxonism and Anglo-American Relations,
1895-1904," Claremont Graduate School, 1978.

1870.

Collins, George W. "United States-Moroccan
Relations, 1904-12," U. of Colorado, 1965.

1871.   Coogan, John W. "The End of Neutrality: The United States, Britain, and Neutral Rights, 1899-1915," Yale U., 1976.

1872.   Costello, Daniel J. "Planning for War: A History of the General Board of the Navy, 1900-1914," Fletcher School of Diplomacy, 1958. An excellent study.

1873.   Fritz, David L. "The Philippine Question: American Civil/Military Policy in the Philippines, 1898-1905," U. of Texas, Austin, 1977.

1874.   Hourihan, William J. "Roosevelt and the Sultans: The United States Navy in the Mediterranean, 1904," U. of Mass., 1975. Ann Arbor, Mich.: U. Microfilms, 1975.

1875.   Livermore, Seward W. "American Naval Development, 1898-1914: With Special Reference to Foreign Affairs," Harvard U., 1944.

1876.   Olsen, Frederick. "The Navy and the White Man's Burden: Naval Administration of Samoa," Washington U. of St. Louis, 1976.

1877.   Schaller, Michael. "The United States and China, 1938-1945," U. of Michigan, 1974. Published under title of *The United States and China in the Twentieth Century* by Oxford UP, 1979.

1878. U420   Spector, Ronald. "Professors of War: The Naval
       .L1   War College and the Modern American Navy,"
       S64   Yale U., 1967.

1879.   Stillson, Albert C. "The Development and Maintenance of the American Naval Establishment, 1901-1909," Columbia U., 1959.

1880. E664   Wiegand, Wayne A. "Patrician in the Progressive
      .M573   Era: A Biography of George von Lengerke Meyer,"
      W54   Carbondale: Southern Illinois U., 1974.

ARTICLES

1881.   *Allen, Lindsley S. "Uncle Joe," *Leatherneck* 32 (Jan. 1949):13-15, 53-54. The story of Major General Joseph H. Pendleton with emphasis on Marine operations in Nicaragua in 1912 and in the Dominican Republic in 1916.

1882.   Armstrong, William J. "Aircraft Go to Sea: a
            Brief History of Aviation in the U.S. Navy,"
            Aerospace Historian 25 (Summer 78):79-91.

1883.   Ashbrook, Lincoln. "The United States Navy and
            the Rise of the Doctrine of Air Power," MA 15
            (Fall 1951):145-56.

1884.   *Asprey, Robert B. "Waller," MCG 45 (May 1961):
            36-41; (June 1961):44-48. Littleton Waller
            Tazewell Waller.

1885.   Avalone, E.M. "Submarine Development Prior to
            World War I," ASNE *Journal* (now: *Naval Engineers
            Journal*) 72 (May 1960):278-83.

1886.   Baecker, Thomas. "The Arms of the *Ypiranga:* The
            German Side," *Americas* 30 (July 1973):1-11. The
            story of the German merchantman whose arrival in
            Mexico with a cargo of arms helped trigger the
            American landing at and seizure of Veracruz in
            1914.

1887.   Bowers, Gay L. "The Energetic Sperrys," *Aero-
            space Historian* 14 (Summer 1967):93-102.

1888.   Braisted, William R. "The United States Navy's
            Dilemma in the Pacific, 1906-1909," PHR 26
            (Aug. 1957):235-44.

1889.   _____. "The Philippine Naval Base Problem,
            1898-1909," MVHR 41 (June 1954):21-40.

1890.   *Coffey, R.B. "A Brief History of the Interven-
            tion in Haiti," USNIP 48 (Aug. 1922):1325-44.
            An account of the United States' intervention
            in Haiti, 1915-1934, with emphasis on Marine
            activities in restoring order and maintaining
            peace within the country.

1891.   Coletta, Paolo E. "The Perils of Invention:
            Bradley A. Fiske and the Torpedo Plane," AN
            37 (June 1977):111-27.

1892.   Curry, Roy W. "Woodrow Wilson and Philippine
            Policy," MVHR 41 (Dec. 1954):435-52.

1893.   De Novo, John A. "Petroleum in the United
            States Navy before World War I," MVHR 41
            (Mar. 1954):641-56.

1894.   Duncan, Donald B., and H.M. Dater. "Administrative History of U.S. Naval Aviation," *Air Affairs: An International Q.* 1 (Summer 1947): 526-39.

1895.   Emmott, Norman W. "Airborne Torpedoes," USNIP 103 (Aug. 1977):46-54.

1896.   Featherston, Fran H. "A History and a Heritage," USNIP 94 (Feb. 1968):33-45. The development of USN aviation since 1910, especially of the Air Engineer Duty Only officers.

1897.   Grenville, John A.S. "Diplomacy and War Plans in the United States, 1890-1917," *Trans. of the Royal Hist. Soc.*, 5th Series (London) 11: (1961):1-21.

1898.   _____. "Great Britain and the Isthmian Canal, 1898-1901," AHR 61 (Oct. 1955):48-69.

1899.   *Harrington, Samuel M. "The Strategy and Tactics of Small Wars," MCG 6 (Dec. 1921):474-91; 7 (Mar. 1922):83-92. An excellent analysis of lessons learned in small-war tactics and techniques from Indian Wars through Mexico, Haiti, Nicaragua, and Santo Domingo.

1900.   Hattendorf, John. "Technology and Strategy: A Study in the Professional Thought of the U.S. Navy, 1900-1916," NWCR 24 (Nov. 1971):25-48.

1901.   Heffron, Paul T. "Secretary Moody and Naval Administrative Reform: 1902-1904," AN 29 (Jan. 1969):30-53.

1902.   Hood, John. Prize Essay, "Naval Administration and Organization," USNIP 27 (Mar. 1901):1-27.

1903.   Hourihan, William J. "The Best Ambassador: Rear Admiral Cotton and the Cruise of the European Squadron, 1903," NWCR 32 (June-July 1979): 63-72.

1904.   _____. "Marlinspike Diplomacy: The Navy in the Mediterranean, 1904," USNIP 104 (Jan. 1979): 42-51.

1905.   Johnson, Arthur M. "Theodore Roosevelt and the Navy," USNIP 84 (Oct. 1958):76-82.

1906.   Little, William M. "The Strategic Naval War
            Game or Chart Maneuvers," USNIP 38 (Dec. 1912):
            1213-34.

1907.   Livermore, Seward W. "American Naval Base
            Policy in the Far East, 1850-1914," PHR 13
            (June 1944):113-35.

1908.   _____. "The American Navy as a Factor in
            World Politics, 1903-1913," AHR 42 (July 1958):
            863-79.

1909.   _____. "Battleship Diplomacy in South
            America, 1905-1925," JMH 16 (March 1944):31-48.

1910.   Luce, Stephen B. "Naval Administration," USNIP
            28 (Dec. 1902):839-50.

1911.   _____. "Naval Administration, III," USNIP
            29 (Sept. 1903):809-22.

1912.   Mahan, A.T. "The U.S. Navy Department," *Scrib-
            ner's Mag.* 33 (May 1903):566-77.

1913.   Meadows, Martin. "Eugene Hale [US senator from
            Maine, 1881-1911] and the American Navy," AN
            22 (July 1962):187-93.

1914.   Morton, Louis. "Interservice Co-operation and
            Politico Military Collaboration, 1900-1938,"
            in Harry L. Coles, ed., *Problems in Civilian
            Control of the Military.* Columbus: Ohio State
            UP, 1961, pp. 131-60.

1915.   Paullin, Charles O. "The American Navy in the
            Orient in Recent Years," USNIP 37 (Dec. 1911):
            1137-75, and 38 (Mar. 1912):87-115.

1916.   Radford, G.S. "Organization: An Essay of Funda-
            mental Principles, with Special Reference to
            the Navy," USNIP 39 (Dec. 1913):1683-1718.

1917.   Taussig, Joseph K. "Experiences during the
            Boxer Rebllion," USNIP 53 (Apr. 1927):403-20.

1918.   Taylor, Henry C. "Memorandum on General Staff
            for the U.S. Navy," USNIP 26 (Sept. 1900):
            441-48.

1919. Tomblin, Barbara B. "The United States Navy and the Philippine Insurrection," AN 35 (July 1975):183-96.

1920. Turk, Richard W. "The United States Navy and the 'Taking' of Panama," MA 38 (Oct. 1974): 92-96.

1921. Vagts, Alfred. "Hopes and Fears of an American-German War, 1870-1915," PSQ 54 (Dec. 1939): 514-35 and 55 (Mar. 1940):53-76.

1922. Warner, Edward. "Douhet, Mitchell, Seversky: Theories of Air Warfare," Edward M. Earle, ed. *Makers of Modern Strategy: Military Thought from Machiavelli to Hitler*. Princeton: PUP, 1943, pp. 485-503.

1923. Welborn, Mary C. "Naval Contributions to Aeronautical Science, 1908-1913," USNIP 74 (Aug. 1948):991-97.

1924. Wise, James E., Jr. "The Dawn of ASW," USNIP 90 (Feb. 1964):92-105. Pictorial.

1925. Woodhouse, Henry, "U.S. Naval Aeronautic Policies, 1904-1942," USNIP 78 (Feb. 1942):161-75.

1926. Zahm, A.F. "A National Aeronautical Laboratory," NAR 198 (Aug. 1913):178-87.

10

NAVAL POWER AND WORLD WAR I:
EUROPE, 1914-1917

Although the United States did not become a participant until 6 April 1917, the war in Europe affected almost every aspect of American life. Particularly important were the long debates over preparedness, the kind of navy that should be built, and violations of neutrality by both belligerent camps. The works listed in this chapter will be helpful to those who wish to study the European phase of the war and its impact upon the United States.

BOOKS

1927. D521   Aston, George G. *The Great War of 1914-1918.*
      .A76   London: Butterworth, 1930.

1928. DA88.1 *_____. Memoirs of a Marine: An Amphibiog-
      .A7A3   raphy.* London: Murray, 1919.

1929. D581   Auten, Harold. *Q Boat Adventures: The Exploits
      .A8   of the Famous Mystery Ships.* London: Jenkins,
             1919.

1930. D580   Bacon, Reginald H.S., *Naval Battles of the
      .B4   First World War.* N.Y.: Scribner, 1968.

1931. D582   _____. *The Battle of Jutland.* London:
      .J8B53 Batsford, 1964.

1932. DA89.1 _____. *Life of Lord Fisher of Kilverstone,*
      .F5B3   2 vols. N.Y.: Doubleday, 1929.

1933. D582   _____. *The Jutland Scandal,* 4th ed. London:.
      .J8B34 Hutchinson, 1925.

1934. D581   _____. *The Dover Patrol, 1915-1917,* 2 vols.
      .B2   N.Y.: George H. Doran, 1919.

1935. D592   Bailey, Thomas A., and Paul B. Ryan. *The
      .L8N34 Lusitania Disaster: An Episode in Modern War-
             fare and Diplomacy.* N.Y.: Free P., 1975.

1936. E767   Baker, Ray S. *Woodrow Wilson: Life and Letters,*
      .B16   8 vols. GCNY: Doubleday, Page, 1927-1939.

1937. G21   Baldwin, Hanson W. *World War I: An Outline His-
      .B24   tory.* N.Y.: Harper & Row, 1962.

1938. D619
    .B37
Bass, Herbert J., ed. *America's Entry into World War I: Submarines, Sentiment, or Security.* N.Y.: Holt, Rinehart & Winston, 1964.

1939. D580
    .B4
Bennett, Geoffrey M. *Naval Battles of the First World War.* N.Y.: Scribner, 1969.

1940. D582
    .F2B4
_____. *Coronel and the Falklands.* N.Y.: Macmillan, 1962.

1941. D619
    .B56
Birnbaum, Karl E. *Peace Moves and U-Boat Warfare: A Study of Imperial Germany's Policy toward the United States, April 18, 1916-January 9, 1917.* Hamden, Conn.: Archon Books, 1970.

1942. E767
    .B64
Blum, John M. *Woodrow Wilson and the Politics of Morality.* Boston: Little, Brown, 1956.

1943. D568
    .3.B87
Bush, Eric W. *Gallipoli.* N.Y.: St. Martin, 1975. By a participant.

1944. D522
    .A52
By the Editors of American Heritage. Narrative by S.L.A. Marshall. *The American Heritage History of World War I.* N.Y.: American Heritage, 1964.

1945. D593
    .C25
Campbell, Gordon. *My Mystery Ships.* London: Hodder & Stoughton, 1928.

1946. E744
    .C42
Challener, Richard D. *Admirals, Generals and American Foreign Policy 1898-1914.* Princetón: PUP, 1973.

1947. DA89.1
    B4C5
Chalmers, William S. *Life and Letters of David, Earl Beatty.* London: Hodder & Stoughton, 1951.

1948. D580
    .C57
    1934a
Chatterton, Edward K. *Danger Zone: The Story of the Queenstown Command.* Boston: Little, Brown, 1934.

1949. D568
    .3.C53
_____. *Dardanelles Dilemma: The Story of the Naval Operations.* London: Rich & Cowan, 1935.

1950. D521
    .C5
Churchill, Winston. *The World Crisis,* 4 vols. N.Y.: Scribner, 1927-1930.

1951. D546   Clark, Alan. *The Donkeys*. N.Y.: Morrow, 1962.
       .C6   Sequentially, follows Barbara Tuchman, *The Guns of August*. The *N.Y. Times* called it "The Case against the British High Command of World War I." Involved are John French and Douglas Haig, for the year 1915.

1952. UG700   Clark, Ronald W. *The Role of the Bomber*. N.Y.:
       .C58   Crowell, 1977. An assessment of the impact of the manned bomber as a strategic weapon system from World War I to the present. Pictorial, 166 pp.

1953. D521   Congdon, Don, ed. *Combat: World War I*. N.Y.:
       .C584   Delacorte, 1964.

1954. D635   Consett, Montague W.W.P. *The Triumph of Unarmed*
       .C57   *Forces 1914-1918*.... London: Williams & Norgate, 1923.

1955. D580   Corbett, Julian S., and Henry Newbolt. *History*
       .C75   *of the Great War, Based on Official Documents*, 5 vols. London: Longmans, 1920-1931.

1956. V856   Cowie, John S. *Mines, Minelayers, and Minelay-*
       .C68   *ing*. N.Y.: Oxford UP, 1949. Covers the two world wars.

1957. D521   Cruttwell, Charles R.M.F. *A History of the Great*
       .C7   *War*. Oxford: Clarendon P., 1934.

1958. E766   Daniels, Josephus. *The Wilson Era: Years of*
       .D3   *Peace, 1910-1917*. Chapel Hill: UNCP, 1944.

1959. D619   Devlin, Patrick. *Too Proud to Fight: Woodrow*
       .D49   *Wilson's Neutrality*. N.Y.: Oxford UP, 1975.

1960. V210   Domville-Fife, Charles W. *Submarines, Mines,*
       .D6   *and Torpedoes in the War*. London: Hodder & Stoughton, 1914.

1961. UG630   Douhet, Giulio. *The Command of the Air*, 2d ed.,
       .D62   1927; rpt., N.Y.: Coward-McCann, 1942. Douhet was the Italian who provided the earliest justification for strategic air bombardment.

1962. D521   Esposito, Vincent J., ed. *A Concise History of*
       .E49   *World War I*. N.Y.: Praeger, 1964.

1963. D621   Farrar, Marjorie M. *Conflict and Compromise:*
       .F8F37   *The Strategy, Politics, and Diplomacy of the*
                French Blockade, 1914-1918. The Hague: Martinus
                Nijhoff, 1974.

1964. D581   Fayle, C. Ernest. *Seaborne Trade,* 3 vols. Lon-
       .F3   don: J. Murray, 1920-1924.

1965. D619   Finnegan, John P. *Against the Specter of a*
       .F45   *Dragon: The Camapign for American Military Pre-*
                paredness, 1914-1917. Westport, Conn.: Green-
                wood, 1974.

1966. DA89.1 Fisher, Admiral of the Fleet Lord. *Memories and*
       .F5A5   *Records,* 2 vols. London: Hodder & Stoughton,
                1919. The most interesting part of this book
                is the defense of the "Baltic project," which
                was the real cause of his objection to the
                Dardanelles adventure.

1967. E807   Freidel, Frank B. *Franklin D. Roosevelt,* 4
       .F74   vols. Boston: Little, Brown, 1952- . Vol. 3.
                The Triumph, 1956.

1968. D580   Frothingham, Thomas G. *The Naval History of the*
       .F75   *World War,* 3 vols. Cambridge, Mass.: HUP, 1924-
                1926.

1969. D570   _____. *The American Reinforcement in the World*
       .F7   *War.* GCNY: Doubleday, Page, 1927.

1970. D591   Gibson, Richard H., and Maurice Prendergast.
       .G5   *The German Submarine War, 1914-1918.* London:
                Constable, 1931; rpt. R.R. Smith, 1941. The
                most comprehensive English source on U-boat
                operations in World War I.

1971. D580   Gill, Charles C. *Naval Power in the War (1914-*
       .G5   *1918).* N.Y.: George H. Doran, 1918.

1972. DK265   Graf, H. *The Russian Navy in War and Revolution*
       .G65   *from 1914 up to 1918.* N.Y.: Kolands, 1923.

1973. VB230   Grant, Robert M. *U-Boats Intelligence, 1914-*
       .G7   *1918.* Hamden, Conn.: Archon Books, 1969.

1974. V210   _____. *U-Boats Destroyed: The Effect of Anti-*
       .G7   *Submarine Warfare, 1914-1918.* London: Putnam,
                1964.

1975. D593   Gray, Edwyn. *The Underwater War: Submarines*
      .G7   *1914-1918*. N.Y.: Scribner's, 1971. British
               submarine service.

1976. D593   _____. *A Damned Un-English Weapon: The*
      .G7   *Story of British Submarine Warfare, 1914-1918*.
               London: Seeley Service, 1971.

1977. D591   _____. *The Killing Time: The U-boat War*
      .G68   *1914-1918*. N.Y.: Scribner, 1972.

1978. DA566.9 Gretton, Peter. *Former Naval Person: Winston*
      .C5G74   *Churchill and the Royal Navy*. London: Cassell,
               1968.

1979. V163   Groos, Otto. *Lessons of Naval Warfare in the*
      .G713   *Light of the World War*. Newport: Naval War
               College, 1936.

1980. D581   _____. *War in the North Sea*. Newport: Naval
      .G882   War College, 1931.

1981. D580   Guichard, Louis. *The Naval Blockade, 1914-1918*.
      .G98   N.Y.: Appleton-Century-Crofts, 1930.

1982. D546   Guinn, Paul. *British Strategy and Politics,*
      .G5   *1914 to 1918*. Oxford: Clarendon P., 1965.

1983. D568   Hamilton, Ian S.M. *Gallipoli Diary*, 2 vols.
      .3.H25   N.Y.: George H. Doran, 1920. Sir Ian commanded
               the British army at Gallipoli.

1984. HC56   Hardach, Gerd. *The First World War*. Berkeley:
      .H27   U. of California P., 1977.

1985. D521   Hayes, Grace P. *World War I: A Compact History*.
      .H353   N.Y.: Hawthorn, 1965.

1986. D568   Higgins, Trumbull. *Winston Churchill and the*
      .3.H5   *Dardanelles: A Dialogue in Ends and Means*.
               N.Y.: Macmillan, 1963.

1987. D971   Hodgkinson, Harry. *The Adriatic Sea*. London:
      .H6   Cape, 1955.

1988. D580   Hoehling, Adolph R., and Mary Hoehling. *The*
      .H6   *Great War at Sea: A History of Naval Action*
               1914-1918. N.Y.: Crowell, 1965.

1989. DA89.1 Hough, Richard A. *Admiral of the Fleet: The*
      .F5H6   *Life of John Fisher.* N.Y.: Macmillan, 1970.

1990. D582   Hoyt, Edwin P. *Swan of the East: The Life and*
      .E6H662 *Death of the German Cruiser* Emden *in World War*
              I. N.Y.: Macmillan, 1968.

1991. D581   Hurd, Archibald S. *The Merchant Navy*, 3 vols.
      .H855   London: Longmans, Green, 1921-1929.

1992. UG633 Hurley, Alfred F. *Billy Mitchell: Crusader for*
      .M45H8 *Air Power.* Bloomington: Indiana UP, 1975.

1993. D598   Jellicoe, John R. *The Submarine Peril: The*
      .J4   *Admiralty Policy in 1917.* London: Cassell,
              1934.

1994. D581   _____. *The Crisis of the Naval War.* London:
      .J36   Cassell, 1920.

1995. D581   _____. *The Grand Fleet 1914-1916.* N.Y.:
      .J4   George H. Doran, 1919.

1996. D400   Kerr, Mark. *Land, Sea, and Air.* London: Long-
      .K4A3   mans, 1927. Humorous autobiography of a Brit-
              ish admiral who at one time commanded the Greek
              Navy; then the British squadron in the Adriatic
              in 1916; and "fathered" the Royal Air Force in
              1918.

1997. D581   Keyes, Roger J.B. *The Naval Memoirs of Admiral*
      .K382   *of the Fleet Sir Roger Keyes: Scapa Flow to*
              Dover Straits. N.Y.: Dutton, 1935.

1998. D592   Koenig, Paul. *Voyage of the* Deutschland: *The*
      .D4A5   *First Merchant Submarine.* N.Y.: Hearst's In-
              ternational Lib., 1916.

1999. D532   Kopp, George. *Two Lone Ships:* Goeben *and*
      .G7K63 Breslau. London: Hutchinson, 1931.

2000. D570.8 Lyddon, William G. *British War Mission to the*
      .M6B52 *United States, 1914-1918.* N.Y.: Oxford UP, 1938.

2001. D570   *McClellan, Edwin N. *The U.S. Marine Corps in*
      .45A5   *the World War.* Wash.: GPO, 1920, 1968.

2002. A454   Marder, Arthur J. *From the* Dreadnought *to*
      .M35   *Scapa Flow: The Royal Navy in the Fisher Era.*
               N.Y.: Oxford UP, 1961-1970. 1. *The Road to War*
               1904-1914 (1961); 2. *The War Years to the Eve*
               of Jutland, 1914-1916 (1965); 3. *Jutland and*
               After, May 1916-Dec. 1916 (2nd ed., 1978); 4.
               1917: Year of Crisis (1970); 5. *Victory and*
               Aftermath, Jan. 1918-June 1919 (1970).

2003. D521   Maurice, Frederick. *Lessons of Allied Coopera-*
      .M46   *tion: Naval, Military, and Air, 1914-1918.*
               N.Y.: Oxford UP, 1942.

2004. D595   Moffat, Alexander W. *Maverick Navy.* Middletown,
      .A45M63 Conn.: Wesleyan UP, 1976.

2005. UG625   Momyer, William W., ed. *Air Power in Three Wars.*
      .M65   Wash.: Dept. of the AF, 1978.

2006. D580   Newbolt, Henry J. *A Naval History of the War.*
      .N4   London: Hodder & Stoughton, 1920.

2007. D590   _____. *Submarine and Anti-Submarine.* London:
      .N45   Longmans, 1918.

2008. V65.T94 Patterson, A. Temple. *Tyrwhitt of the Harwich*
      P37   *Force: The Life of Admiral of the Fleet Sir*
               Reginald Tyrwhitt. London: Macdonald & Jane's,
               1973.

2009. DA89.1 _____. *Jellicoe: A Biography.* London: Mac-
      .J4P3   millan, 1969.

2010. D582   Pitt, Barrie. *Revenge at Sea: Coronel and Falk-*
      .F2P55   *lands.* N.Y.: Stein & Day, 1964.

2011. UG735   Powers, Barry D. *Strategy without Slide-Rule:*
      .G7P68   *British Air Strategy, 1914-1938.* N.Y.: Holmes
               & Meier, 1976. Origins of British air strategy
               to the end of World War II.

2012. V214   Price, Alfred. *Aircraft versus Submarine: The*
      .P68   *Evolution of Antisubmarine Aircraft, 1912 to*
               1972. Annapolis, Md.: NIP, 1973.

2013. D771   Roskill, Stephen. *Churchill and the Admirals.*
      .R67   London: Collins, 1977.

2014. DA566.9   _____. *Hankey: Man of Secrets*, 3 vols. N.Y.:
.H286R6   St. Martin, 1971.

2015. D566   Sanders, Liman von. *Five Years in Turkey*.
.L53   Annapolis, Md.: USNI, 1927.

2016. DK265.35   Saul, Norman E. *Sailors in Revolt: The Russian*
.B3S28   *Baltic Fleet in 1917*. Lawrence: Regents P. of
    Kansas, 1978.

2017. UG630   Saundby, Robert. *Air Bombardment: The Story of*
.S26   *Its Development*. N.Y.: Harper, 1961.

2018. D581   Scheer, Reinhard. *Germany's High Sea Fleet in*
.S25   *the World War*. London: Cassell, 1920.

2019. V163   Schurman, Donald M. *The Education of a Navy:*
.S3   *British Naval Strategic Thought, 1867-1914*.
    London: Cassell, 1965.

2020. DA88   Scott, Percy. *Fifty Years in the Royal Navy*.
.1.S3   N.Y.: George H. Doran, 1919.

2021. D581   Siney, Marion C. *The Allied Blockade of Germany,*
.S5   *1914-1916*. Ann Arbor, Mich.: U. of Michigan
    P., 1957.

2022. E173   Smith, Daniel M. *Robert Lansing and American*
.C15   *Neutrality, 1914-1917*. Berkeley: U. of Califor-
    nia P., 1958.

2023. D619   Smith, Gaddis. *Britain's Clandestine Submarines,*
.S59   *1914-1915*. New Haven; YUP, 1964.

2024. VA473   Sokol, Anthony E. *The Imperial and Royal Austro-*
.S63   *Hungarian Navy*. Annapolis, Md.: USNI, 1968.

2025. D522   Taylor, A.J.P. *Illustrated History of the First*
.T3   *World War*. N.Y.: Putnam, 1964.

2026. D570   Thomason, John S. *Fix Bayonets!* N.Y.: Scribner,
.348   1926. Probably the best American book on the
5thT5   War, and one of the best books of any national-
    ity on the War.

2027. DD231   Tirpitz, Alfred von. *My Memoirs*, 2 vols. N.Y.:
.T5A5   Dodd, Mead, 1919.

2028. D530   Tuchman, Barbara. *The Guns of August*. N.Y.:
.T8   Macmillan, 1962.

2029.   D606   *The U.S. Air Service in World War I*, 2 vols.
        .U54   Vol. 1. *The Final Report and A Tactical History*;
               Vol.2. *Early Concepts of Military Aviation.*
               Wash.: GPO, 1978.

2030.   DA47.2   Woodward, Ernest L. *Great Britain and the German*
        .W6   *Navy.* Oxford: Clarendon P., 1935.

2031.   D546   Woodward, Llewellyn. *Great Britain and the War*
        .W6   *of 1914-1918.* London: Methuen, 1967.

2032.   D521   Wren, Jack. *The Great Battles of World War I.*
        .W73   N.Y.: Grosset & Dunlap, 1971.

2033.   D786   Wykeham, Peter. *Fighter Command: A Study of Air*
        .W9   *Defence, 1914-1960.* London: Putnam, 1960.

DOCUMENTS

2034.   Admiralty Naval Staff. *Merchant Shipping Losses.*
                London: HMSO, 1919.

2035.   _____. *Report of the Committee Appointed to*
                Investigate the Attacks Delivered on the Enemy
                Defense of the Dardanelles Straits. London:
                HMSO, 1919.

2036.   _____. *War Instructions for British Merchant*
                Ships. London: HMSO, 1917.

2037.   U.S. Navy Dept. Bureau of Yards and Docks.
                Activities of the Bureau of Yards and Docks,
                Navy Department, in the World War, 1917-1918.
                Wash.: GPO, 1921.

DISSERTATIONS AND THESES

2038.   Bentinck-Smith, J. "The Forcing Period: A Study
                of the American Merchant Marine, 1914-1917,"
                Radcliffe, 1958.

2039.   Burk, Kathleen M. "British War Missions to the
                United States, 1914-1918," Oxford U., England,
                1977.

2040.   Chrisman, Herman H. "Naval Operations in the
                Mediterranean during the World War, 1914-1918,"
                Standford U., 1931.

2041.   Coady, J.W. "F.D.R.'s Early Washington Years,
                1913-1920," St. John's U., 1968.

2042.   Easterling, Verlin R. "Great Britain's Peril and the Convoy Controversy: A Study of the Intended Effects of Unrestricted U-Boat Warfare and the Convoy System as a Counter-Measure, World War I," Colorado U., 1951.

2043.   Farrar, Marjorie M. "French Blockade Policy, 1914-1918," Stanford U., 1968; Ann Arbor, Mich.: Xerox U. Microfilms, 1975.

2044.   Lever, A.W. "The British Empire and the German Colonies, 1914-1919," U. of Wisconsin, 1963.

ARTICLES

2045. G525   Baldwin, Hanson. "Admiral Death: The Battle of
       .B255   Jutland, 1916," in his *Sea Fights and Shipwrecks*. GCNY: Hanover House, 1955, pp. 267-86.

2046.   Buchanan, Russell. "Theodore Roosevelt and American Neutrality, 1914-1917," AHR 43 (July 1938):775-90.

2047.   Cronan, W.P. "The Greatest Need of the United States Navy: Proper Organization for the Successful Conduct of War," USNIP 42 (Jul.-Aug. 1916):1137-70.

2048.   Edit. "England's Proposal to Germany for a Naval Holiday," *Independent* 76 (Oct. 30, 1913): 190.

2049.   English, J.A. "The Trafalgar Syndrome: Jutland and the Indecisiveness of Modern Naval Warfare," NWCR 32 (May-June 1979):60-77.

2050.   Faculty of the Naval War College. "Soviet Strategic Thinking, 1917-1962: Some History Reexamined," NWCR (Feb. 1972):24-34.

2051.   Fry, M.G. "The Imperial War Cabinet, the United States, and the Freedom of the Seas," RUSIJ 110 (Nov. 1965):353-62.

2052.   Herwig, Holger H., and David F. Trask. "The Failure of Imperial Germany's Undersea Offensive against World Shipping, February 1917-October 1918," *Historian* 33 (Aug. 1971): 611-36.

2053.   Knox, Dudley W. "The Role of Doctrine in Naval Warfare," USNIP 41 (Mar.-Apr. 1915):325-66.

2054.   Lingelbach, William E. "Belgian Neutrality: Its Origin and Interpretation," AHR 39 (Oct. 1933): 48-72.

2055.   Lundeberg, Philip D. "Undersea Warfare and Allied Strategy in World War I. Part I. To 1916," *Smithsonian Jour. of Hist.* 1 (Autumn 1966): 1-30; Part II. 1916-1918, ibid. 1 (Winter 1966): 49-72.

2056.   Marder, Arthur J. "Winston Churchill as First Lord of the Admiralty," USNIP 79 (Jan. 1953): 18-27.

2057.   "Mr. Churchill's Failure to Stop Naval Rivalry," LD 47 (Nov. 15, 1913):936-37.

2058.   Romer, Jeffrey A. "The German High Seas Fleet: A Reappraisal," USNIP 104 (Jan. 1978):56-61.

2059.   *Rothenberg, Gunther E. "From Gallipoli to Guadalcanal: The Development of U.S. Marine Corps Amphibious Assault Doctrine, 1915-1942," *Records of the Second International Colloquy in Military History, Stockholm, 12-15 August 1973.* Brussels, 1975, pp. 115-22.

2060.   Ruge, Friedrich. "German Naval Strategy Across Two Wars," USNIP 81 (Feb. 1955):153-66.

2061.   Seymour, Charles. "American Neutrality: The Experience of 1914-1917," FA 14 (Oct. 1935): 26-36.

2062.   Van der Veer, Norman R. "Mining Operations in the War," USNIP 45 (Nov. 1919):1857-65.

FICTION

2063. PZ3   Bell, John J. *Little Grey Ships*. London: Mur-
       .B413   ray, 1916. Small Craft, World War I.
       Li

2064.   Remarque, Erich Maria. *All Quiet on the Western Front.* Boston: Little, Brown, 1929.

11

THE U.S. NAVY IN WORLD WAR I, 1917-1919

BOOKS

2065. E182
.A33
Albion, Robert G., and Jennie B. Pope. *Sea Lanes in Wartime: The American Experience, 1775-1945*. N.Y.: Norton, 1942: 2d ed. Hamden, Conn.: Archon, 1968.

2066. D545
.B4A8
*Asprey, Robert B. *At Belleau Wood*. N.Y.: Putnam, 1965. An account of the Marines' most familiar battle in World War I.

2067. D522
.A52
Editors of American Heritage. Narrative by S.L.A. Marshall. *The American Heritage History of World War I*. N.Y.: American Heritage, 1964.

2068. D619
.B25
Bailey, Thomas A. *The United States and the Neutrals, 1917-1918*. Baltimore: Johns Hopkins P., 1942.

2069. E767
.B16
Baker, Ray S. *Woodrow Wilson: Life and Letters*, 8 vols. GCNY: Doubleday, Doran, 1927-1939.

2070. VA52
.A24
No. 5
Beers, Henry P. *U.S. Naval Forces in Northern Russia (Archangel and Murmansk), 1918-1919*. Wash.: U.S. Navy Dept., 1943.

2071. D590
.B4
Belknap, Reginald R. *The Yankee Mining Squadron: Or Laying the North Sea Mine Barrage*. Annapolis, Md.: USNI, 1920.

2072. DK265
.4.B67
Bradley, John. *Allied Intervention in Russia, 1917-1920*. N.Y.: Basic Books, 1968.

2073. D570.9
.C28
*Catlin, Albertus W., with the Collaboration of Walter A. Dyer. *"With the Help of God and a Few Marines."* GCNY: Doubleday, Page, 1919. An important memoir of the U.S. Marines on the Western Front.

2074.
Chambers, Hilary R. *U.S. Submarine Chasers in the Mediterranean, Adriatic, and the Attack on Durazzo*. N.Y.: Knickerbocker P., 1920. Available NC State Library, Raleigh.

2075. D591
.C6
Clark, William B. *When the U-Boats Came to America*. Boston: Little, Brown, 1929.

2076. HC106   Clarkson, Grosvenor. *Industrial America in the*
      .2.C67   *World War: The Strategy Behind the Lines.* Bos-
               ton: Houghton Mifflin, 1923.

2077. VC553   Clephane, Lewis P. *History of the Naval Over-*
      .C6   *seas Transport Service in World War I.* Wash.:
               Naval Hist. Div., 1969.

2078. D619   Cohen, Warren I., ed. *Intervention, 1917: Why*
      .C63   *America Fought.* Lexington, Mass.: Heath, 1966.

2079. E664   Coletta, Paolo E. *William Jennings Bryan: Pro-*
      .B87C55 *gressive Politician and Moral Statesman, 1909-*
               1915. Lincoln: U. of Nebraska P., 1969.

2080. D589   Connolly, James B. *The U-Boat Hunters.* N.Y.:
      .U6C7   Scribner, 1918.

2081. E766   Cronon, E. David, ed. *The Cabinet Diaries of*
      .D29   *Josephus Daniels, 1913-1921.* Lincoln: U. of
               Nebraska P., 1963.

2082. D570   Crowell, Benedict, and Robert F. Wilson. *The*
      .75C7   *Armies of Industry,* 5 vols. New Haven: YUP,
               1921.

2083. HC106   Cuff, Robert D. *The War Industries Board; Busi-*
      .2.C8   *ness-Government Relations during World War I.*
               Baltimore: Johns Hopkins P., 1973.

2084. E766   Daniels, Josephus. *The Wilson Era: Years of*
      .D33   *War and After, 1917-1923.* Chapel Hill: UNCP,
               1946.

2085.   _____. *The Cabinet Diaries of Josephus*
               Daniels, 1913-1921. Lincoln: U. of Nebraska
               P., 1963. *See* Cronon, E. David.

2086.   *The Development of the Heavy Bomber, 1918-1944.*
               USAF Hist. Div., Research Studies Institute,
               AU, 1951. USAF Hist. Studies No. 6.

2087.   *The Development of Air Doctrine in the Army*
               Air Arm, 1917-1941. USAF Hist. Div., Research
               Studies Institute, AU, 1955. USAF Hist.
               Studies No. 89.

2088. D619   Finnegan, John P. *Against the Specter of a*
      .F45   *Dragon: The Campaign for American Military Pre-*
               paredness, 1914-1917. Westport, Conn.: Green-
               wood, 1974.

2089. E182
      .F54

Fiske, Bradley A. *From Midshipman to Rear-Admiral*. N.Y.: Century, 1919.

2090. E183.8
      .G7F68

Fowler, Wilfred B. *British-American Relations, 1917-1918; The Role of Sir William Wiseman*. Princeton: PUP, 1969.

2091. D570
      .F7

Frothingham, Thomas G. *The American Reinforcement in the World War*. GCNY: Doubleday, Page, 1927.

2092. D580
      .F75

_____. *The Naval History of the World War*, 3 vols. Cambridge, Mass.: HUP, 1924-1926.

2093. D591
      .G5

Gibson, R.H., and Maurice Prendergast. *The German Submarine War, 1914-1918*. N.Y.: Richard R. Smith, 1931.

2094. D570
      .72.G6

Gleaves, Albert. *A History of the Transport Service: Adventures and Experiences of United States Transports and Cruisers in World War II*. N.Y.: Doran, 1921.

2095. V210
      .G7

Grant, Robert M. *U-Boats Destroyed: The Effect of Anti-submarine Warfare, 1914-1918*. London: Putnam, 1964.

2096. VG93
      .U53

Grimes, J. *Aviation in the Fleet Exercises, 1911-1935*. Wash.: Office of CNO, 1943.

2097. VA390
      .H26A3

Hancock, Joy B. *Lady in the Navy: A Personal Reminiscence*. Annapolis, Md.: NIP, 1972.

2098. E664
      .P15H4

Hendrick, Burton J. *The Life and Letters of Walter H. Page*, 3 vols. GCNY: Doubleday, Page, 1922-1925.

2099. D580
      .H6

Hoehling, Adolph A. *The Great War at Sea: A History of Naval Action 1914-1918*. N.Y.: Crowell, 1965.

2100. UG633
      .H6

Holley, Irving M., Jr. *Ideas and Weapons: Exploitation of the Aerial Weapon by the United States During World War I. A Study in the Relationship of Technological Advance, Military Doctrine, and the Development of Weapons*. New Haven: YUP, 1953.

2101. D664
      .H7

House, Edward M., and Harris Seymour, eds. *What Really Happened at Paris*. N.Y.: Scribner, 1921.

2102. D606   Hudson, James J. *Hostile Skies: A Combat History*
      .H8   *of the American Air Service in World War I.*
             Syracuse UP, 1968.

2103. TA140 Hughes, Thomas P. *Elmer Sperry: Inventor and*
      .S68H79 *Engineer.* Baltimore: Johns Hopkins P., 1971.

2104. D508   Hunter, Francis T. *Beatty, Jellicoe, Sims and*
      .H8   *Rodman.*... N.Y.: Doubleday, 1919.

2105. UG633 Hurley, Alfred F. *Billy Mitchell: Crusader for*
      .M45H8 *Air Power.* Bloomington: Indiana UP, 1975.

2106. VM23   Hurley, Edward N. *The Bridge to France.* Phila.:
      .H8   Lippincott, 1927.

2107. D589   Husband, Joseph. *On the Coast of France: The*
      .U6H8   *Story of the United States Naval Forces in*
             French Waters. Chicago: McClure, 1919.

2108. D589   _____. *A Year in the Navy.* Boston: Houghton
      .U6H85 Mifflin, 1919.

2109. D591   James, Henry J. *German Subs in Yankee Waters:*
      .J3   *First World War.* N.Y.: Gotham House, 1940.

2110. DA89   Jordan, Gerald, ed. *Naval Warfare in the Twen-*
      .N38   *tieth Century.* N.Y.: Crane & Russak, 1977.

2111. D589   Kauffman, Reginald W. *Our Navy at Work: The*
      .U6K3   *Yankee Fleet in French Waters.* Indianapolis:
             Bobbs-Merrill, 1918.

2112. D589   Kittredge, Tracy. *Naval Lessons of the Great*
      .U6K6   *War.*... GCNY: Doubleday, Page, 1921. Support
             for Sims against "the establishment" for his
             part in World War I.

2113. D589   Leighton, John L. *SIMSADUS, London: The Ameri-*
      .U6L4   *can Navy in Europe.* N.Y.: Holt, 1920. Written
             by a Naval Reserve officer who served at HQ.
             Gives an appreciative description of the work
             done by the Navy and the Force Commander, W.S.
             Sims.

2114. E182   *Lejeune, John A. *The Reminiscences of a Marine.*
      .L53   Phila.: Dorrance, 1930; rpt., Quantico, Va.,
             1979.

2115.   Link, Arthur S. *Woodrow Wilson: Revolution, War,*
                and Peace. Arlington Heights, Ill.: AHM, 1979.

2116. E767   _____. *Wilson: Campaigns for Progressivism*
       .L65   *and Peace, 1916-1917.* Princeton: PUP, 1965.
       v.5

2117. E767   _____. *Wilson: Confusions and Crises, 1915-*
       .L65   *1916.* Princeton: PUP, 1964.
       v.4

2118. E767   _____. *Wilson: The Struggle for Neutrality,*
       .L65   *1914-1915.* Princeton: PUP, 1960.
       v.3

2119. E766   _____. *Woodrow Wilson and the Progressive*
       .L5   *Era, 1910-1917.* N.Y.: Harper, 1954.

2120. E780   Livermore, Seward W. *Politics Is Adjourned:*
       .L5   *Woodrow Wilson and the War Congress, 1916-*
                 1918. Seattle: U. of Washington P., 1968.
                 Deals particularly with congressional opposi-
                 tion to the Wilson administration's conduct of
                 the war.

2121. D570   *McClellan, Edwin N. *The United States Marine*
       .45.A5   *Corps in the World War.* Wash.: GPO, 1920, 1968.

2122. E183.8   Maddox, Robert J. *The Unknown War with Russia:*
       .R9M246   *Wilson's Siberian Intervention.* San Raphael,
                 Calif.: Presidio, 1977.

2123. D570.8   Martin, Franklin H. *Digest of the Proceedings*
       .C7M3   *of the Council of National Defense During the*
                 World War. Wash.: GPO, 1934.

2124. HE745   Mattox, W.C. *Building the Emergency Fleet.*
       .M43   Cleveland: Penton Pub. Co., 1920; rpt. N.Y.:
                 Lib. Editions, 1970.

2125. D606   Maurer, Maurer, ed. *The U.S. Air Service in*
       .U54   *World War I.* Vol. 2, *Early Concepts of Mili-*
                 tary Aviation. Wash.: OAFH, 1978.

2126. D642   Maurice, Frederick B. *The Armistice of 1918.*
       .M36   N.Y.: Oxford UP, 1943.

2127. D521   _____. *Lessons of Allied Cooperation: Naval*
       .M46   *Military, and Air, 1914-1918.* London: Oxford
                 UP, 1942.

2128. D619   May, Ernest. *The World War and American Isola-*
       .M383   *tion, 1914-1917.* Cambridge, Mass.: HUP, 1959.

2129. D589   Millholland, Ray. *The Splinter Fleet of the*
       .U6M5   *Otranto Barrage.* N.Y.: Bobbs-Merrill, 1936.
                Exciting adventures of an American subchaser
                in World War I, including the attack on Durazzo.

2130. D619   Millis, Walter. *Road to War: America, 1914-1917.*
       .M47   Boston: Houghton Mifflin, 1935.

2131. D606   Mitchell, William. *Memoirs of World War I: "From*
       .M5   *Start to Finish of our Greatest War."* N.Y.:
                Random House, 1960.

2132. UG633   _____. *Winged Defense: The Development and*
       .M43   *Possibilities of Modern Air Power--Economic and*
                Military. N.Y.: Putnam, 1925.

2133. D595   Moffatt, Alexander W. *Maverick Navy.* Middle-
       .A45M63 town, Conn.: Wesleyan UP, 1976. Antisubmarine
                warfare in World War I.

2134. E748   Morison, Elting E. *Admiral Sims and the Modern*
       .S52M6   *American Navy.* Boston: Houghton Mifflin 1942.
                By an excellent historian and son-in-law of
                Sims.

2135. D619   Morrissey, Alice M. *The American Defense of*
       .M64   *Neutral Rights, 1914-1917.* Cambridge, Mass.:
                HUP, 1939.

2136. D570   Naval Aviation War Book Committee. *Flying Of-*
       .65N3   *ficers of the U.S.N.* Wash.: Naval Aviation War
                Book Committee, 1919.

2137. D580   Newbolt, Henry J. *A Naval History of the War,*
       .N4   *1914-1918.* London: Hodder & Stoughton, 1920.

2138. D589   *The Northern Barrage, Mine Force United States*
       .U6N6   *Atlantic Fleet, the North Sea, 1918.* Ed. by
                All Hands. Annapolis, Md., USNI, 1919.

2139. D590   Nutting, William W. *The Cinderellas of the*
       .N8   *Fleet.* Jersey City, N.J.: The Standard Motor
                Construction Co., 1920. Submarine chasers.

2140. D606   Paine, Ralph D. *The First Yale Unit: A Story*
       .P3   *of Naval Aviation, 1916-1919,* 2 vols. Cambridge,
                Mass.: Riverside P., 1925.

2141. D589   _____. *The Fighting Fleets*.... Boston:
      .U6P3   Houghton Mifflin, 1918.

2142. D589   Perry, Lawrence. *Our Navy in the War*. Vol. 4 of
      .U6P4   *America in the War*. N.Y.: Scribner, 1918.

2143. D590   Roebling Manufacturing. *Wire-Roping the German
      .R8   Submarine*.... Trenton, N.J.: John A. Roebling's
               Sons, 1920.

2144. D581   Ruge, Friedrich. *Scapa Flow, 1919: The End of
      .R813   the German Fleet*. London: Allan, 1973.

2145. VA52   Scott, Lloyd N. *Naval Consulting Board of U.S.
      .A89S4   Navy Department*. Wash.: GPO, 1920.

2146. D521   Simonds, Frank H. *History of the World War*, 5
      .S56   vols. N.Y.: Doubleday, Page, 1917-1920.

2147. E768   Smith, Daniel M. *Robert Lansing and American
      .L32S58 Neutrality, 1914-1917*. Berkeley: U. of Cali-
               fornia P., 1958.

2148. E767   Smith, Gene. *When the Cheering Stopped: The
      .S65   Last Years of Woodrow Wilson*. N.Y.: Morrow,
               1964.

2149. UA15   Spaulding, Oliver L., and John W. Wright. *The
      .S74   Second Division American Expeditionary Force
               in France 1917-1919*. N.Y.: Hillsman P., 1937.
               Tries to be fair to the Army and the Marine
               halves of the division.

2150. TL540   Studer, Clara. *Sky Storming Yankee: The Life of
      .C9S8   Glenn Curtiss*. N.Y.: Stackpole, 1937. Excellent
               reading.

2151. D619   Tansill, Charles C. *America Goes to War*. Boston:
      .T32   Little, Brown, 1938. A revisionist account.

2152. V394   Taylor, Albert H. *The First Twenty-Five Years
      .B4T3   of the Naval Research Laboratory*. Wash.: Navy
               Dept., 1948.

2153. E182   *Thomas, Lowell. *Old Gimlet Eye: The Adventures
      .B975   of Smedley D. Butler*. N.Y.: Farrar & Rinehart,
               1933.

2154. D591   _____. *Raiders of the Deep*. GCNY: Doubleday,
      .T5   Doran, 1928.

2155. E182   Tolley, Kemp. *Yangtze Patrol: The U.S. Navy in*
      .T8   *China.* Annapolis, Md.: NIP, 1971.

2156. D611   Trask, David F. *Captains and Cabinets: Anglo-*
      .T73   *American Naval Relations, 1917-1918.* Columbia:
              U. of Missouri P., 1972.

2157. D544   _____. *The United States in the Supreme War*
      .T7   *Council: American War Aims and Inter-Allied*
              Strategy, 1917-1918. Middletown, Conn.: Wesleyan
              UP, 1961.

2158. D511   Tuchman, Barbara. *The Zimmermann Telegram.* N.Y.:
      .T77   Viking, 1958.

2159. UD480   Tugwell, Maurice. *Airborne to Battle: A History*
      .T84   *of Airborne Warfare, 1918-1971.* London: Kimber,
              1971.

2160. VG93   Van Wyen, Adrian O. *Naval Aviation in World War*
      .A79   *I.* Wash.: GPO, 1971.

2161. D589   Wilson, Henry B. *An Account of the Operations*
      .U6W7   *of the American Navy in France during the War*
              with Germany. N.P., 1919?

2162. VG90   Woodhouse, Henry, ed. *Text Book of Naval Aero-*
      .W6   *nautics.* N.Y.: Century, 1917.

2163. D651   Yates, Louis A.R. *United States and French Se-*
      .F643   *curity 1917-1921: a Study in American Diplomat-*
              ic History. N.Y.: Twayne, 1957.

DOCUMENTS

2164. VA52   [Morison, Elting E.] *Naval Administration: Se-*
      .A1U52 *lected Documents on Navy Department Organiza-*
              tion, 1915-1940. Wash.: Office of CNO, 1945.

2165.   U.S. Navy Department, Bureau of Engineering.
              History of the Bureau of Engineering, Navy
              Department, during the World War. Wash.: GPO,
              1922.

2166. VF23   U.S. Navy Department, Bureau of Ordnance. *Navy*
      .A6   *Ordnance Activities, World War 1917-1918.* Wash.:
      1918   GPO, 1920.

2167. VM23   U.S. Navy Department. Bureau of Yards and Docks.
      .A53   *Activities of the Bureau of Yards and Docks...*
              in the World War, 1917-1918. Wash.: GPO, 1921.

2168.   U.S. Navy Department, Office of Naval Intelli-
              gence, Historical Section. *The American Plan-*
              ning Section, London. Wash.: GPO, 1923.

2169. D589   U.S. Navy Department, Office of Naval Records.
      .U5A4   *The North Sea Mine Barrage and Other Mining*
      No. 2   *Activities.* Wash.: GPO, 1920.

2170. D589   U.S. Department of the Navy, Office of Naval
      .U5A4   Records. *German Submarine Activities on the*
      No. 1   *Atlantic Coast of the United States and Canada.*
              Wash.: GPO, 1920.

                   DISSERTATIONS AND THESES

2171.   Baldwin, Fred D. "The American Enlisted Man in
              World War I," Princeton U., 1964; Ann Arbor,
              Mich.: U. Microfilms, 1965.

2172.   DeWeerd, Harvey. "Production Lag in the American
              Ordnance Program, 1917-1918," Michigan U., 1937.

2173.   Hunter, Charles H. "Anglo-American Relations
              during the Period of American Belligerency,
              1917-1918," Stanford U., 1935.

2174.   Klatchko, Mary. "Anglo-American Naval Competi-
              tion, 1918-1922," Columbia U., 1962.

2175. HF1455   Safford, Jeffrey J. "The United States Merchant
      .S25   Marine and American Commercial Expansion, 1860-
              1920," Rutgers U., 1968.

2176.   Schilling, Warner R. "Admirals and Foreign Pol-
              icy," Yale U., 1953.

                          ARTICLES

2177.   Alden, Carroll S. "American Submarine Operations
              in the War," USNIP 46 (June 1920):811-50, and
              46 (July 1920):1013-48.

2178.   Andrews, Hal. "Fifty Years of Naval Aircraft,"
              (11 parts), *Naval Aviation News*, Feb.-Dec.
              1961.

2179.   "Armed Merchantmen as Submarine Prey," LD 52
            (Feb. 26, 1916):490-91.

2180.   Bartlett, H.T. "Mission of Aircraft with the
            Fleet," USNIP 45 (May 1919):729-42.

2181.   Beers, Henry. "The Development of the Office of
            Chief of Naval Operations," MA 10 (Spring 1946):
            40-68; 10 (Fall 1946):10-38; 11 (Summer, 1947):
            88-99; and 11 (Winter 1947):229-37.

2182.   Belknap, Reginald R. "The Yankee Mining Squad-
            ron, or Laying the North Sea Mine Barrage,"
            USNIP 45 (Dec. 1919):1973-2012; 46 (Jan. 1920):
            5-32; and 46 (Feb. 1920):197-230.

2183.   _____. "The North Sea Mine Barrage," *Nat.
            Geog.* 35 (Feb. 1919):85-110.

2184.   Benjamin, Park. "Fiske Torpedoplane," *Indepen-
            dent* 90 (May 12, 1917):281-82.

2185.   Birdsall, Paul. "Neutrality and Economic Pres-
            sures, 1914-1917," *Science & Society* 3 (Spring
            1939):217-28.

2186.   Brown, Charles R. "The Development of Fleet
            Aviation During the World War," USNIP 64 (Sept.
            1938):1297-1303.

2187.   Carlisle, Rodney. "Black-Owned Shipping Before
            Marcus Garvey," AN 35 (July 1975):197-206.

2188.   Carney, Robert B. "The Capture of the U-58,"
            USNIP 60 (Oct. 1934):1401-04.

2189.   Carter, A.F. "The Functions of the Office of
            Naval Operations," USNIP 46 (Feb. 1920):169-
            76.

2190.   Cate, James L. "Development of United States
            Air Doctrine, 1917-1941," AUQR 1 (Winter 1947):
            11-22.

2191.   Catlin, George L. "Paravanes," USNIP 45 (July
            1919):1134-57.

2192.   Churchill, Winston L.S. "Naval Organization:
            American and British," *Atlantic* 120 (Aug.
            1917):277-84.

2193.   Cianflone, Frank A. "The Eagle Boats of World
            War I," USNIP 99 (June 1973):76-80.

2194.   Claudy, Carl H. "Preparing the Navy Ashore: War
            Work of the Bureau of Yards and Docks," SA 117
            (Dec. 1, 1917):416-17.

2195.   Cope, Harley F. "U.S. Submarines in the War
            Zone," USNIP 56 (Aug. 1930):711-16.

2196.   Craven, Thomas T. "Naval Aviation," USNIP 46
            (Feb. 1920):181-92.

2197.   Davis, Noel. "The Removal of the North Sea Mine
            Barrage," Nat. Geog. 37 (Feb. 1920):103-33.

2198.   Dyer, George P. "The Navy Supply Department in
            War Time," USNIP 46 (Mar. 1920):379-92.

2199.   Edwards, Walter A. "The United States Naval Air
            Force in Action, 1917-1918," USNIP 48 (Nov.
            1922):1863-82.

2200.   *Emmons, Robert M. "Marine Combat Squadrons in
            World War I," MCG 62 (Nov. 1978):78-81.

2201.   Field, Richard S. "Spalato, 1919," USNIP 51
            (May 1925):775-789.

2202.   Fifield, Russell H. "Disposal of the Carolines,
            Marshalls, and Marianas at the Paris Peace Con-
            ference," AHR 51 (Apr. 1946):472-79.

2203.   "Freighting 2,000,000 Men," ARR 58 (Nov. 1918):
            458-59.

2204.   Frothingham, Thomas G. "The Strategy of the
            World War and the Lessons of the Effort of the
            United States," USNIP 47 (May 1921):669-83.

2205.   Furer, Julius A. "The 110-Foot Submarine Chasers
            and Eagle Boats," USNIP 45 (May 1919):743-52.

2206.   Gosnell, H.A. "World War Losses of the U.S.
            Navy," USNIP 63 (May 1937):630-34.

2207.   Grant, Robert M. "Aircraft Against U-Boats,"
            USNIP 65 (June 1939):824-28.

2208.   "The Gyro-compass in the Navy," SA 112
         (2-13-15):153. Sperry gear in 20 BBs, 1 ar-
         mored cruiser, and 15 SS + training men to
         handle.

2209.   Hale, Frederick A. "Fritz Fischer and the His-
         toriography of World War One," *Hist. Teacher*,
         Feb. 1976, 258-79.

2210.   Hinkamp, Clarence N. "Pipe Sweepers," USNIP 46
         (Sept. 1920):1477-84. Postwar mine-clearing.

2211.   Hovenstein, E. Jay, Jr. "Lessons of World War
         I," *Annals* 238 (Mar. 1945):180-87.

2212.   Hunsaker, Jerome C. "How American Ingenuity
         Designed the NC Boats," *Automotive Industries*
         41 (July 10, 24, 1919):68-72, 120-23, 172-76.

2213.   Kevles, Daniel J. "Federal Legislation for En-
         gineering Experiment Stations: The Episode of
         World War I," T&C 12 (Apr. 1971):182-89.

2214.   Koistinen, Paul A.C. "The 'Industrial-Military
         Complex' in Historical Perspective: World War
         I," *Bus. Hist. Rev.* 41 (Winter 1967):378-403.

2215.   Lundeberg, Philip K. "Undersea Warfare and Al-
         lied Strategy in World War I: Part 1. to 1916,"
         Smithsonian Jour. of Hist. 1 (Autumn 1966):1-
         30; "Part 2. 1916-1918," ibid. (Winter 1966):
         49-72.

2216.   _____. "The German Naval Critique of the
         U-boat Campaign, 1915-1918," MA 27 (Spring
         1963):105-18.

2217.   McDowell, C.S. "Naval Research," USNIP 45
         (June 1919):895-918.

2218.   Merrill, James M. "Submarine Scare, 1918," MA
         17 (Winter 1953):181-90.

2219.   "The Monitor to the Front," *Nation* 105 (Sept.
         13, 1917):284-85.

2220.   "The Navy Repudiates Admiral Mahan," WW 38
         (Oct. 1919):569-71.

2221.   "Plans for a Big American Navy," LD 51 (Oct. 16, 1919):826-27.

2222.   "The President's Preparedness Tour," *Independent* 85 (Feb. 14, 1916):216-17.

2223.   Raquet, Edward C. "United States Submarine Chasers at Gibraltar, November 1918," USNIP 62 (Dec. 1936):1703-11.

2224.   Rigler, Frank V. "The Naval Railway Battery: An Outstanding Example of Versatility and Innovation," *Shipmate* 40 (Nov. 1977):33-35.

2225.   Schilling, Warner R. "Civil-Naval Politics in World War I," WP 7 (July 1955):572-91. In the absence of the equivalent of a national security council, the Navy drafted its own plans for foreign-policy contingencies.

2226.   "Ships Armed by Presidential Proclamation," CH 6, pt. 1 (Apr. 1917):55-57.

2227.   *Shulimson, Jack. "The First to Fight: Marine Corps Expansion, 1914-1918," *Prologue* 8 (Spring 1976):5-16.

2228.   Sims, William S. "How We Nearly Lost the War," WW 53 (Mar. 1927):474-85.

2229.   Smith, Dean. "The Zimmermann Telegram, 1917," AHI 13 (June 1978):28-37.

2230.   Smith, J. Russell. "Building Ships to Beat the Submarines," ARR 56 (Oct. 1917):393-96.

2231.   Taussig, Joseph K. "Destroyer Experiences during the Great War," USNIP 48 (Dec. 1922):2015-40; 49 (Jan.-Mar. 1923):36-69, 221-48, 383-408.

2232.   *Thomason, John W., Jr. "The Marine Brigade," USNIP 54 (Nov. 1918):963-68.

2233.   Trask, David F. "Woodrow Wilson and World War I," Warren F. Kimball, ed. *American Diplomacy in the Twentieth Century*. St. Louis: Forum, 1980, No. 2.

2234.   "The U-Boats off Our Coasts," SA 119 (Aug. 24, 1918):146.

2235. Van Alstyne, Richard W. "The Policy of the United States Regarding the Declaration of London at the Outbreak of the Great War," JMH 7 (Dec. 1935):435-47.

2236. Van Deurs, George. "The AJAX and Her Fliers: Naval Aviation in the Pacific Fleet [to 1925]," *Shipmate* 41 (Dec. 1978):19-21.

2237. Wheeler, William J. "Reminiscences of World War Convoy Work," USNIP 55 (May 1929):385-92.

2238. *"When the Marines Went to France, 1917-1918," USNIP 93 (Nov. 1967):86-100. Pictorial.

2239. Williams, Henry. "The Naval Controversy between the Line and the Staff Corps," NAR 208 (Nov. 1918):736-44.

2240. _____. "Preparing the Navy Yards for War," USNIP 43 (Mar. 1917):463-72.

2241. Wise, James E., Jr. "U-Boats Off Our Coasts," USNIP 91 (Oct. 1965):84-101.

2242. Woodhouse, Henry. "The Torpedoplane: A New Weapon Which Promises to Revolutionize Naval Tactics," USNIP 45 (May 1919):743-52.

2243. _____. "The Aircraft's Part in Beating the U-Boat," USNIP 44 (Dec. 1918):2727-39.

FICTION

2244. D590 Buranelli, Prosper. *Maggie of the Suicide*
       .B8   *Fleet*.... GCNY: Doubleday, 1930. USN in World War I.

12

NAVAL DISARMAMENT AND REARMAMENT 1918-1941

2245. D770   Abbazia, Patrick. *Mr. Roosevelt's Navy: The*
      .A23   *Private War of the U.S. Atlantic Fleet, 1939-*
               1942. Annapolis, Md.: NIP, 1975.

2246. V210   Acworth, Bernard. *Life in a Submarine.* London:
      .A25   Tuck, 1941. Story of a submarine commander who
               helped develop ASDIC.

2247. VA454   _____. *Britain in Danger: An Examination of*
      .A18   *Our New Navy.* London: Eyre & Spottiswoode, 1937.

2248. VA454   _____. *The Navy and the Next War: A Vindica-*
      .A22   *tion of Sea Power.* London: Eyre & Spottiswoode,
               1934.

2249. VA454   _____. *The Navies of Today and Tomorrow: A*
      .A2   *Study of the Naval Crisis from Within.* London:
               Eyre & Spottiswoode, 1930.

2250. D755   Adams, Henry H. *Years of Deadly Peril: The Com-*
      .A3   *ing of the War 1939-1941.* N.Y.: McKay, 1969.

2251. E774   Adler, Selig. *The Isolationist Impulse: Its*
      .A26   *Twentieth Century Reaction.* N.Y.: Abelard-
               Schuman, 1957.

2252. JV308   Albertini, Rudolf von. *Decolonization: The Ad-*
      .A6513   *ministration and Future of the Colonies, 1919-*
               1960.

2253. E746   Arpee, Edward. *From Frigates to Flat-Tops.* Lake
      .M6A7   Forest, Ill.: Priv. print., 1953. Life of
               William A. Moffett.

2254. VG93   Arthur, Reginald W. *Contact: Careers of U.S.*
      .A93   *Naval Aviators.* N.Y.: Timely Pub., 1972.

2255. D741   Aster, Sidney. *1939: The Making of the Second*
      .A75   *World War.* N.Y.: Simon & Schuster, 1973.

2256. V163   Bacon, Reginald H.S., and Francis E. McMurtrie.
      .B2   *Modern Naval Strategy.* Brooklyn, N.Y.: Chemi-
               cal Pub. Co., 1941.

2257. DT387.8 Baer, George W. *The Coming of the Italian-*
      .B333   *Ethiopian War.* Cambridge, Mass.: HUP, 1967.

2258. D755   Baldwin, Hanson W. *The Crucial Years, 1939-1941:*
      .B27   *The World at War: From the Beginning through*
                Pearl Harbor. N.Y.: Harper and Row, 1976.

2259. VA48   Beard, Charles A. *The Navy: Defense or Portent?*
      .B45   N.Y.: Harper, 1932. Critical of the U.S.N.

2260. CB5   _____, ed. *Toward Civilization.* N.Y.: Long-
      .B38   mans, Green, 1930. Essays expressing deep
                postwar pessimism.

2261. D755.1   Beaufré, André. *The Fall of France.* London:
      .B3813   Cassell, 1967.

2262. VA52   Beers, Henry P. *U.S. Naval Detachment in Turkish*
      .A24   *Waters, 1919-1924.* Wash.: U.S. Navy Dept., 1943.
      No. 2   29 pp.

2263. DK63   Beloff, Max. *The Foreign Policy of Soviet Rus-*
      .B4   *sia, 1929-41,* 2 vols. N.Y.: Oxford UP, 1947-
                1949. A superb account.

2264. D643   Birdsall, Paul. *Versailles Twenty Years After.*
      .A7B5   N.Y.: Reynal & Hitchcock, 1941. Changes in two
                decades that scrapped the terms of the Treaty
                of Versailles.

2265. DS784   Borg, Dorothy. *The United States and the Far*
      .B65   *Eastern Crisis of 1933-1938: From the Manchurian*
                Incident Through the Initial Stage of the Unde-
                clared Sino-Japanese War. Cambridge, Mass.: HUP,
                1964.

2266. E746   Bowen, Harold G. *Ships, Machinery and Mossbacks:*
      .B6   *The Autobiography of a Naval Engineer.* Prince-
                ton: PUP, 1954.

2267. E785   Buckley, Thomas H. *The United States and the*
      .B8   *Washington Conference, 1921-1922.* Knoxville:
                U. of Tennessee P., 1970. The best study thus
                far.

2268. JX1974   Buell, Raymond L. *The Washington Conference.*
      .5.B82   N.Y.: Appleton, 1922. By a reporter who at-
                tended the conference.

2269. UG633   Burlingame, Roger. *General Billy Mitchell:*
      .M45B8   *Champion of Air Defense.* N.Y.: McGraw-Hill,
                1952. Not quite as good as Alfred Hurley's
                study, for which see No. 1831.

2270. E802   Burner, David. *Herbert Hoover: A Public Life*.
      .B87   N.Y.: Knopf, 1979.

2271. E807   Burns, James McG. [F.D.] *Roosevelt: The Lion*
      .B835   *and the Fox*. N.Y.: Harcourt Brace, 1956.
              Probably the best single-volume biography.

2272. G850   Byrd, Richard E. *Discovery: The Story of the*
      1933   *Second Byrd Antarctic Expedition*. N.Y.: Putnam,
              1935; rpt., Gale, 1971.

2273. V58   Bywater, Hector C. *Navies and Nations: A Review*
      .B8   *of Naval Developments Since the Great War*. Bos-
              ton: Houghton Mifflin, 1927.

2274. VA50   _____. *Sea-Power in the Pacific: A Study of the*
      .B87   *American-Japanese Naval Problem*, 2nd ed. Boston:
              Houghton Mifflin, 1934; rpt. of 1921 ed. by
              Arno, 1970.

2275. DD120   Carr, Edward H. *German-Soviet Relations Between*
      .R8C3   *the Two World Wars, 1919-1939*. Baltimore: Johns
              Hopkins P., 1951.

2276. JX1974 Chaput, Rolland Q. *Disarmament in British For-*
      .C45   *eign Policy*. London: Allen & Unwin, 1935.

2277. DA88.1 Chatfield, Alfred E.M. *It Might Happen Again:*
      .C5A3   *The Navy and Defence*, 2 vols. London: Heinemann,
              1947. Vol. 1 deals with the Washington Con-
              ference; vol. 2 with the period 1922-1939.

2278. JX1961 Chatfield, Charles. *For Peace and Justice:*
      .U6C5   *Pacifism in America, 1914-1941*. Knoxville:
              U. of Tennessee P., 1971.

2279. E182   Coontz, Robert E. *From Mississippi to the Sea*.
      .C74   Phila.: Dorrance, 1930. Covers years 1885-
              1925, including his term as CNO.

2280. E806   Dallek, Robert *Franklin D. Roosevelt and Ameri-*
      .D33   *can Foreign Policy, 1932-1945*. N.Y.: Oxford
              UP, 1979.

2281. E766   Daniels, Josephus. *The Wilson Era: Years of*
      .D33   *War and After, 1917-1923*. Chapel Hill: UNCP,
              1946. Among other things, contains the
              author's version of how civilian supremacy
              was maintained during World War I.

2282. UG633   Davis, Burke. *The Billy Mitchell Affair*. N.Y.:
      .M45D3   Random House, 1967.

2283. E807   Davis, Kenneth S. *FDR: The Beckoning of Destiny,
      .D36   1882-1928. A History*. N.Y.: Putnam, 1971.

2284. UG638   *The Development of Air Doctrine in the Army Air
      .U53   Arm, 1917-1941*. USAF Air U., Research Studies
               Institute, Hist. Div., 1955.

2285. JX1974   Dingman, Roger. *Power in the Pacific: The Ori-
      .D465   gins of Naval Arms Limitation, 1914-1922*.
               Chicago: U. of Chicago P., 1976. An excellent
               multiarchival study.

2286. DS77   Dorn, Frank. *The Sino-Japanese War, 1937-1941:
      .55.D67 From Marco Polo Bridge to Pearl Harbor*. N.Y.:
               Macmillan, 1974.

2287. UA23   Eliot, George F. *The Ramparts We Watch: A Study
      .E43   of the Problems of American National Defense*.
               N.Y.: Reynal & Hitchcock, 1938.

2288. E784   Ellis, L. Ethan. *Republican Foreign Policy
      .E4   1921-1933*. New Brunswick, N.J.: Rutgers UP,
               1968.

2289. E791   _____. *Frank D. Kellogg and American Foreign
      .E5   Relations, 1925-1929*. New Brunswick. N.J.: Rut-
               gers UP, 1961.

2290. E801   Emerson, E. *Hoover and His Times*. Saxton, Pa.:
      .E75   Brandywine Books, 1932.

2291. JX1974   Falk, Richard A., and Richard J. Barnet, eds.
      .B27   *Security in Disarmament*. Princeton: PUP, 1965.

2292. E801   Ferrell, Robert H. *American Diplomacy in the
      .F4   Great Depression: Hoover-Stimson Foreign Policy,
               1929-1933*. New Haven: YUP, 1957.

2293. E807   Freidel, Frank B. *Franklin D. Roosevelt*, 4 vols.
      .F74   Boston: Little, Brown, 1952- . Vol. 4. *Launch-
               ing the New Deal*, 1973.

2294. D751   Friedländer, Saul. *Prelude to Downfall: Hitler
      .F713   and the United States, 1939-1941*. N.Y.: Knopf,
               1967.

189

2295. E183.8   Fry, Michael C. *Illusions of Security: North*
       .G7F7   *Atlantic Diplomacy, 1918-1922.* Toronto: U. of
                     Toronto P., 1972.

2296. F1938   *Fuller, Stephen M., and Graham A. Cosmas.
       .45.F84   *Marines in the Dominican Republic, 1916-1924.*
                     Wash.: USMC, HQ, Hist. and Museums Div., 1974.

2297. VB57   Gardiner, Leslie. *The British Admiralty.*
       .G36   Annapolis: USNI, 1968.

2298. E664   Garraty, John A. *Henry Cabot Lodge: A Biography.*
       .L7G3   N.Y.: Knopf, 1953.

2299. VG93   Grimes, J. *Aviation in the Fleet Exercises,*
       .U53   *1911-1935.* Wash.: Office of the CNO, 1943.

2300. DS518   Griswold, Alfred W. *The Far Eastern Policy of*
       .8.G75   *the United States.* N.Y.: Harcourt Brace, 1938.
                     A now outdated classic.

2301. L532   Harriman, Florence J. (Hurst). *Mission to the*
       .H3   *North.* Phila.: Lippincott, 1941. Reminiscences
                     of the U.S. Ambassador to Norway, 1937-1941,
                     including the *City of Flint* episode in 1939.

2302. E182   Harris, Brayton. *The Age of the Battleship,*
       .H25   *1890-1922.* N.Y.: Watts, 1965.

2303. E183.8   Herzog, James H. *Closing the Open Door: Ameri-*
       .J3H47   *can-Japanese Negotiations, 1936-1941.* Annapolis,
                     Md.: NIP, 1973.

2304. HD9698   Hewlett, Richard G., and Oscar E. Anderson. *A*
       .U52H48   *History of the United States Atomic Energy*
                     Commission. Vol. 1: *The New World, 1939-1946.*
                     Phila.: Pa. State UP, 1962.

2305. E784   Hicks, John D. *Republican Ascendancy, 1921-*
       .H5   *1933.* N.Y.: Harper, 1960.

2306. DA89   Hinsley, Francis H. *Command of the Sea: The*
       .H5   *Naval Side of British History from 1919 to*
                     the End of the Second World War. London:
                     Christophers, 1950.

2307. JX1974   Hoag, Charles L. *Preface to Preparedness: The*
       .5.H6   *Washington Conference and Public Opinion.* Wash:
                     American Council on Public Affairs, 1941.

2308. E802   Hoover, Herbert. *The Memoirs of Herbert Hoover:*
      .H7   *The Cabinet and the Presidency*, 3 vols. N.Y.:
              Macmillan, 1951-1952.

2309. TL650   Horton, Edward. *The Age of the Airship*. Chicago:
      .H65   Regnery, 1973.
      1973b

2310. D644   House, Edward M., and Harris Seymour, eds. *What*
      .H7   *Really Happened at Paris: The Story of the Peace*
              Conference, 1918-1919. N.Y.: Scribner, 1921.
              Essays by key participants.

2311. DA70   Howarth, David A. *Sovereign of the Seas: The*
      .H73   *Story of Britain and the Sea* [*to World War II*].
              N.Y.: Atheneum, 1974.

2312. G875   Huxley, Elspeth. *Scott of the Antarctic*. N.Y.:
      .S35E88 Atheneum, rpt. ed., 1978.

2313. DS518   Iriye, Akira. *After Imperialism: The Search for*
      .I75   *a New Order in the Far East, 1921-1931*. Cam-
              bridge, Mass.: HUP, 1965.

2314. DS888   Kasai, Jiuji G. *The United States and Japan in*
      .5K355   *the Pacific* [in the 1930s].... 1935; rpt.,
              N.Y.: Arno, 1970. The Japanese viewpoint.

2315. DK63   Kennan, George F. *Soviet Foreign Policy 1917-*
      .K4   *1941*. Princeton, N.J.: Van Nostrand, 1960. By
              a career foreign service officer who served in
              Moscow.

2316. E806   Kenney, William. *The Crucial Years, 1940-1945*.
      .K43   N.Y.: McFadden, 1962.

2317. E182   King, Ernest J., and Walter M. Whitehill. *Fleet*
      .K53   *Admiral King: A Naval Record*. N.Y.: Norton,
              1952. Superseded by Buell, Thomas B., 1980.

2318. JX1974 Knox, Dudley W. *The Eclipse of American Sea*
      .5.K6   *Power*. N.Y.: Am. Army and Navy Jour., 1922.
              Knox's conclusions on the effects of the Wash-
              ington Naval Conference.

2319. D753   Lash, Joseph P. *Roosevelt and Churchill 1939-*
      .L27   *1941*. N.Y.: Norton, 1976.

2320. D769   Leahy, William D. *I Was There: The Personal*
.L4   *Story of the Chief of Staff to Presidents*
Roosevelt and Truman. N.Y.: McGraw-Hill, 1950.
Stops with the end of World War II.

2321. DS518.4 Lee, Bradford A. *Britain and the Sino-Japanese*
.L43   *War, 1937-1939.* Standford: Stanford UP, 1973.

2322. E183.8   Leffler, Melvyn P. *The Elusive Quest: America's*
.F8L43   *Pursuit of European Stability and French Secu-*
rity, 1919-1933. Chapel Hill: UNCP, 1978.

2323. DS849   Lensen, George A. *The Russian Push Toward Japan.*
.R7L39   N.Y.: Octagon Books, 1959.

2324. DS777   Lu, David J. *From the Marco Polo Bridge to Pearl*
.53L8   *Harbor: Japan's Entry into World War II.* Wash.:
Public Affairs P., 1961.

2325. E284   McCoy, Donald R. *Coming of Age: The United*
.M32   *States during the 1920s and 1930s.* Baltimore:
Penguin, 1973.

2326. E792   _____. *Calvin Coolidge: The Quiet President.*
.M117   N.Y.: Macmillan, 1967. Some coverage of naval
affairs 1923-1929.

2327. E748   McFarland, Keith D. *Secretary of War Harry H.*
.W79M32 *Woodring and the Problems of Readiness, Rearma-*
ment, and Neutrality, 1936-1940. Lawrence: U.
of Kansas P., 1975.

2328. D443   Mackintosh, John. *The Paths that Led to War,*
.M246   *1919-1939.* London: Blackie, 1940.

2329. RD89   Marder, Arthur J. *Portrait of an Admiral: The*
.A.R5A3 *Life and Papers of Sir Herbert Richmond.* London: Cape, 1952.

2330. D644   Marks, Sally. *The Illusion of Peace: Inter-*
.M37   *national Relations in Europe, 1918-1933.* N.Y.:
St. Martin, 1976.

2331. DA47.2   Middlemas, Robert K. *The Strategy of Appease-*
.M53   *ment: The British Government and Germany, 1937-*
1939. Chicago: Quadrangle Books, 1972.

2332. VA50   Moore, Frederick. *America's Naval Challenge.*
.M6   Saxton, Pa.: Brandywine Books, 1929.

2333. DD240   Morgan, John H. *Assize of Arms: The Disarmament*
      .M62   *of Germany and Her Rearmament [1919-1939]*. Lon-
               don: Methuen, 1946.

2334. E748   Morison, Elting E. *Turmoil and Tradition: A*
      .S883M6   *Study of the Life and Times of Henry L. Stim-*
               son. Boston: Houghton Mifflin, 1960.

2335. DA578   Mowat, Charles L. *Britain Between the Wars,*
      .M67   *1918-1940*. Chicago: U. of Chicago P., 1955.

2336. E806   Nixon, Edgar B. *Franklin D. Roosevelt and For-*
      .R7427   *eign Affairs*, 3 vols. Cambridge, Mass.: Belknap
               Press of HUP, 1969.

2337. JX1974   O'Connor, Raymond G. *Perilous Equilibrium: The*
      .L6   *United States and the London Naval Conference*
               of 1930. Lawrence: U. of Kansas P., 1962.

2338. D753   Offner, Arnold A., ed. *America and the Origins*
      .O37   *of World War II, 1933-1941*. Boston: Houghton
               Mifflin, 1971.

2339. JX5361   Orvik, N. *The Decline of Neutrality 1914-1941:*
      .O3   *With Special Reference to the United States*
               and the Northern Neutrals, 2d ed. Oslo: Tatum,
               1933; rpt., London: 1971.

2340. TK6575   Page, Robert M. *The Origin of Radar*. GCNY:
      .P3   Anchor Books, 1962.

2341. D742   Pelz, Stephen. *Race to Pearl Harbor*. Cambridge,
      .J3P44   Mass.: HUP, 1974. Excellent multiarchival
               study.

2342. E183.8   Perry, Hamilton D. *The* Panay *Incident: Prelude*
      .J3   *to Pearl Harbor*. N.Y.: Macmillan, 1969.

2343. JX1807   Pollen, Arthur J.H. *Disarmament in Its Relation*
      .A8   *to the Naval Policy and the Naval Building Pro-*
      No.161   *gram of the U.S.* N.Y.: Am. Assoc. for Intl.
               Conciliation, 1921.

2344. DU647   Pomeroy, Earl S. *Pacific Outpost: American*
      .P6   *Strategy in Guam & Micronesia*. Stanford:
               Stanford UP, 1951. Goes up to 1939.

2345. DA586   Pratt, Lawrence R. *East of Malta, West of Suez:*
      .P67   *Britain's Mediterranean Crisis 1936-1939*.
               Cambridge: UP, 1975.

2346. E183.8   Preston, Richard A. *The Defence of the Unde-*
      .C2P73   *fended Border: Planning for War in North*
                America, 1867-1939. Montreal: McGill-Queens
                UP, 1977.

2347. KF8745   Pusey, Merlo J. *Charles Evans Hughes*, 2 vols.
      .H8P8   N.Y.: Macmillan, 1951.

2348. V25   Richmond, Herbert W. *Sea Power in the Modern*
      .R5   *World.* N.Y.: Reynal & Hitchcock, 1934. Rpt.
                1973. Considered heretical in its time, the
                author's work opposed the concepts of fleet
                concentration stressed by Mahan and of giant
                battleships, and sponsored joint commands
                among ground, sea, and air forces.

2349. DD256   Robertson, Esmonde M. *Hitler's Prewar Policy*
      .5.R54   *and Military Plans, 1937-1939.* London: Long-
                mans, 1963.

2350. E801   Robinson, Edgar E., and Vaughn D. Bornet.
      .R57   *Herbert Hoover: President of the United States.*
                Stanford, Calif.: Hoover Institute P., 1975.

2351. DU29   Roosevelt, Nicholas. *The Restless Pacific.*
      .R6   N.Y.: Scribner, 1928.

2352. D436   Roskill, Stephen. *Naval Policy Between the*
      .R68   *Wars.* Vol. 1. *The Period of Anglo-American*
                Antagonism, 1919-1929. N.Y.: Walker, 1968.

2353. D436   _____. *Naval Policy Between the Wars.* Vol.
      .R68   2. *The Period of Reluctant Rearmament, 1930-*
                1939. Annapolis, Md.: NIP, 1976.

2354. D810   Rowe, Albert P. *One Story of Radar.* Cambridge:
      .R33R6   Cambridge UP, 1948.

2355. D581   Ruge, Friedrich. *Scapa Flow, 1919.* Annapolis,
      .R8   Md.: NIP, 1975.

2356. E183.8   Schaller, Michael. *The U.S. Crusade in China,*
      .C5S325   *1938-1945.* N.Y.: Columbia UP, 1979.

2357. Micro   *Naval Preparedness Reports: "Are We Ready*
                Studies, 1931-1941." Wilmington, Del.:
                Scholarly Resources, 1979. Annual Reports
                of the CNO and CINC of the U.S. Pacific Fleet.

2358. UA647 Shay, Robert P., Jr. *British Rearmament in the*
       .S37   *Thirties: Politics and Profits.* Princeton:
              PUP, 1977.

2359. UG630 Sherman. W.C. *Air Warfare.* N.Y.: Ronald, 1926.
       .S5

2360. TL721 Smith, Richard K. *First Across: The U.S. Navy's*
       .N3S65 *Transatlantic Flight of 1919.* Annapolis, Md.:
              NIP, 1973.

2361. TL659 _____. *The Airships* Akron and Macon: *Flying*
       .A456 *Aircraft Carriers of the United States Navy.*
              Annapolis, Md.: USNI, 1965.

2362. E182   Sprout, Harold, and Margaret Sprout. *Toward a*
       .S79   *New Order of Sea Power, 1918-1922.* Princeton:
              PUP, 1940; rpt., Greenwood, 1969. The post-
              war naval settlement and the Washington Naval
              Disarmament Conference.

2363. V415   Stirling, Yates. *How to be a Naval Officer.*
       .Q1S73 N.Y.: McBride, 1940.

2364. V63   _____. *Sea Duty: The Memoirs of a Fighting*
       .S75A3 *Admiral.* N.Y.: Putnam, 1939. Early advocate
              of a naval general staff and persistent cru-
              sader for naval preparedness.

2365. JX1974 Sullivan, Mark. *The Great Adventure at Washing-*
       .5.S8 *ton: The Story of the Conference.* GCNY: Double-
              day, Page, 1922. Report on the Washington Naval
              Disarmament Conference by a well-known reporter-
              historian.

2366. JX1974 Tate, Merze. *The United States and Armaments.*
       .T32   Cambridge, Mass.: HUP, 1948.

2367. V394   Taylor, Albert H. *The First Twenty-five Years*
       .B4T3 *of the Naval Research Laboratory.* Wash.: Navy
              Dept., 1948. The years 1923-1945.

2368. UG626.2 Thomas, Lowell, and Edward Jablonski. *Doolittle:*
       .D66T46 *a Biography.* GCNY: Doubleday, 1976. Compare
              with Glines, Carroll V., *q.v.*

2369. DS783 Thorne, Christopher G. *The Limits of Foreign*
       .7T48 *Policy: The West, the League, and the Far*
              Eastern Crisis of 1931-1933. N.Y.: Putnam,
              1972.

2370. D645   Tillman, Seth P. *Anglo-American Relations at*
       .T5   *the Paris Peace Conference of 1919.* Princeton:
                PUP, 1961.

2371. E182   Tolley, Kemp. *Yangtze Patrol: The U.S. Navy in*
       .T8   *China.* Annapolis, Md.: NIP, 1971.

2372. D742   Trefousse, Hans. *Germany and American Neutral-*
       .U5T66   *ity, 1939-1941.* N.Y.: Octagon Books, 1951.

2373. VG93   Turnbull, Archibald D., and Clifford L. Lord.
       .T8   *History of United States Naval Aviation.* New
                Haven: YUP, 1949.

2374. E785   Vinson, John C. *The Parchment Peace: The United*
       .J58   *States Senate and the Washington Conference,*
                1921-1922. Athens: U. of Georgia P., 1955.

2375. E746   Wheeler, Gerald E. *Prelude to Pearl Harbor:*
       .W5   *The United States Navy and the Far East, 1921-*
                1931. Columbia: U. of Missouri P., 1963.

2376. V63.P7   _____. *Admiral William Veazie Pratt, U.S.*
       .W45   *Navy: A Sailor's Life.* Wash.: Department of
                the Navy, Naval Hist. Div., 1974. Pratt held
                every major billet in the U.S. Navy, then wrote
                on current naval affairs.

2377. E792   White, William A. *A Puritan in Babylon: The*
       .W577   *Story of Calvin Coolidge.* N.Y.: Macmillan, 1938.

2378. JX1974   Williams, Benjamin H. *The United States and Dis-*
       .W57   *armament.* N.Y.: Whittlesey House, 1931.

2379. VG93   Wilson, Eugene E. *Slipstream: The Autobiography*
       .W47   *of an Air Craftsman.* N.Y.: Whittlesey House,
                1950.

2380. DA471   Woodward, Ernest L. *Great Britain and the Ger-*
       .2.W6   *man Navy.* Oxford: Clarendon P., 1935.

2381. DC369   Young, Robert J. *In Command of France: French*
       .Y68   *Foreign Policy and Military Planning, 1933-*
                1940. Cambridge, Mass.: HUP, 1978. Disappoint-
                ing because narrowly based.

2382.   [U.S.] Congress. Joint Select Committee. *Hearings on the Pearl Harbor Attack*, 39 vols. Wash.: GPO, 1946, 1972. An important source out of which much speculation and criticism have grown.

2383.   [U.S.] Congress. Joint Select Committee. *Hearings on the Pearl Harbor Attack. Report.* Wash.: GPO, 1946. Sen. Doc. 244, 79th Cong., 2nd sess., 1946. Includes preceding events as well as the actual Japanese strike.

2384. D589   U.S. Congress. Senate. Naval Affairs Committee.
        U5A5   *Naval Investigation.* Wash.: GPO, 1921. 2 vols. The Sims-Daniels dispute over civilian vs. military control of the Navy Department.

2385.   *[U.S.] Marine Corps. Marine Corps Schools. *Tentative Manual of Landing Operations.* Quantico, Va., 1934. The doctrinal foundation for all Marine activity in this area.

2386. VA52   [Morison, Elting E.] *Naval Administration: Selected Documents on Navy Department Organization, 1915-1940.* Wash.: Navy Dept., 1945 (?). A superb collection of legislative history.
        .A1U52

2387.   [U.S.] President. Aircraft Board. *The President's Aircraft Board Hearings*, 4 vols. Wash.: GPO, 1925.

2388.   U.S. State Department. *The Right to Protect Citizens in Foreign Countries by Landing Forces.* Wash.: GPO, 1934.

2389.   U.S. Congress. *Hearings before the Select Committee of Inquiry into Operations of the United States Air Services, House of Representatives, 68th Cong., 2d Sess., on Matters Relating to the Operations of the United States Air Services*, 6 vols. Wash.: GPO, 1925.

197

2390. Alch, Mark L. "Germany's Naval Resurgence: British Appeasement and the Anglo-German Naval Agreement of 1935," U. of California, Los Angeles, 1977.

2391. Allen, Scott. "A Comparison of the Washington Naval Arms Limitation Treaty of 1922 and the SALT Agreements of 1972," U. of Hawaii, 1976.

2392. Andrade, Ernest. "United States Naval Policy in the Disarmament Era, 1921-1937," Michigan State U., 1966.

2393. Belote, James H. "The Development of German Naval Policy, 1933-1939," U. of California, 1954.

2394. Brune, Lester H. "The Foundations of American Air Power Doctrine-Aviation and National Defense, 1919-1933: A Study of the Relationship between Force Weapons, Power Concepts, and Foreign Policy," Rochester U., 1959.

2395. Buzanski, Peter M. "Admiral Mark L. Bristol and Turkish-American Relations, 1919-1922," U. of California, Berkeley, 1960.

2396. DS777 Cole, David B. "The United States in China, .47.C65 1925-1928," Auburn U., 1978.

2397. Doyle, Michael K. "The U.S. Navy: Strategy, Defense, and Foreign Policy, 1932-1941," U. of Washington, 1977.

2398. Fagan, George V. "Anglo-American Naval Relations, 1927-1937," U. of Pennsylvania, 1954.

2399. Klatchko, Mary. "Anglo-American Naval Competition, 1918-1922," Columbia U., 1962.

2400. Lincoln, Ashworth. "The United States Navy and Air Power: A History of Naval Aviation, 1920-1934," U. of California, Berkeley, 1946.

2401. VM23 Muir, Malcolm, Jr. "The Capital Ship Program .M85 in the U.S. Navy, 1934-1945," Ohio State U., 1976.

2402.   Newton, Christina. "Anglo-American Tensions and Bureaucratic Relations 1927-1930. U. of Illinois, 1975.

2403.   O'Connor, Raymond G. "The United States and the London Naval Conference of 1930," Stanford U., 1957.

2404.   Perett, William G. "French Naval Policy and Foreign Affairs, 1930-1939," Stanford U., 1977.

2405.   Shaw, Roger. "The London Naval Conference of 1930: A Study in Naval and Political Relations among the Western Powers," Fordham U., 1946.

2406.   Snowbarger, Willis. "The Development of Pearl Harbor," U. of California, Berkeley, 1950.

2407. UG633 .T35   Tate, James P. "The Army and its Air Corps: A Study of the Evolution of Army Policy towards Aviation, 1919-1941," Indiana U., 1976; Ann Arbor: U. Microfilms International, 1978.

2408. VA50 .T83   Tuleja, Thaddeus V. "U.S. Naval Policy in the Pacific, 1930-1941," Fordham U., 1961.

2409.   Wilson, John R.M. "Herbert Hoover and the Armed Forces: A Study of Presidential Attitudes and Policy," Northwestern U., 1971.

2410.   Winkler, Fred H. "The United States and the World Disarmament Conference, 1926-1935: A Study of the Formulation of Foreign Policy," New York U., 1957.

ARTICLES

2411.   Adamson, Gordon, and Douglas Van Patten. "Motor Torpedo Boats, a Technical Study," USNIP 66 (July 1940):977-96.

2412.   "Aircraft Carriers in a Fleet Action," USNIP 52 (Nov. 1926):2329-35.

2413.   Akers, George W. "The Groundwork for Today's Naval Reserve," USNIP 65 (Apr. 1939):494-500.

2414.   Alden, Carroll S. "The Changing Naval Academy: A Retrospect of Twenty-five Years," USNIP 55 (June 1929):495-501.

2415.   "American Military and Naval Aeronautics,"
         Aviation 28 (Mar. 22, 1930):597-99.

2416.   Anderson, Walter S. "Guns Allowed Aircraft Car-
         riers: A Paradox," USNIP 53 (May 1927):539-43.

2417.   _____. "Submarines and the Disarmament Con-
         ference," USNIP 53 (Jan. 1927):50-69.

2418.   Andrade, Ernest, Jr. "Submarine Policy in the
         United States Navy, 1919-1941," MA 35 (Apr.
         1971):50-56.

2419.   _____. "The Ship That Never Was: The Flying-
         Deck Cruiser," MA 32 (Dec. 1968):132-40.

2420.   *Ansel, Walter C. "Naval Gunfire in Support of a
         Landing," MCG 17 (May 1932):23-26.

2421.   Ashbrook, Allan W. "Naval Mines," USNIP 49 (Feb.
         1923):303-12.

2422.   *Asprey, Robert B. "John A. Lejeune: True Sol-
         dier," MCG 46 (Apr. 1962):34-41.

2423.   Bagby, Oliver W. "Naval Mining and Naval Mines,"
         USNIP 51 (Dec. 1925):2244-57.

2424.   Baker, Wilder D. "Submarine Capabilities and
         Limitations," USNIP 51 (Aug. 1925):1398-1407.

2425.   Baldwin, Hanson W. "America Rearms," FA 16 (Apr.
         1938):430-44.

2426.   Beers, Henry P. "U.S. Naval Detachment in Tur-
         kish Waters, 1919-1924," Administrative Refer-
         ence Service Report, no 2. Wash.: Administra-
         tive Office, Dept. of the Navy, 1943. Details
         on the appointment and duties of Rear Admiral
         Mark L. Bristol as U.S. representative to
         Constantinople and of the operations of the
         naval forces under his command.

2427.   Berg, Meredith W. "Admiral William H. Standley
         and the Second London Naval Treaty," *Historian*
         33 (Feb. 1971):215-36.

2428.   Bird, Keith W. "The Origins and Role of German
         Naval History in the Inter-War Period 1918-
         1939," NWCR 32 (A-May 1979):42-58.

2429.   Bliss, Tasker H. "What Is Disarmament?" FA 4
        (Apr. 1926):353-68.

2430.   Bowen, Frank C. "Minelaying," *The Navy* (British)
        31 (Apr. 1926):99-100.

2431.   "Brig. General Mitchell's Startling Testimony:
        Claims Aircraft can Render Big Naval Battleships
        Obsolete," *Aviation* 10 (Feb. 7, 1921):164-67.

2432.   *Broadbent, Ernest W. "The Fleet and the
        Marines," USNIP 57 (Mar. 1931):369-72.

2433.   Brownson, Howard G. "Sea Power and World Peace,"
        USNIP 63 (Dec. 1937):1689-1701.

2434.   Brune, Lester H. "United States Sea Power, Air
        Power, and War Plans, 1919-1939," in David H.
        White, ed. *Proceedings of the Conference on War
        and Diplomacy*. Charleston, S.C.: The Citadel,
        1976, pp. 37-43.

2435.   _____. "Foreign Policy and the Air Power Dis-
        pute, 1919-1932," *Historian* 23 (Aug. 1961):449-
        64.

2436.   Burns, Richard D. "Regulating Submarine Warfare,
        1921-1941: A Case Study in Arms Control and
        Limited War," MA 35 (Apr. 1971):56-62.

2437.   Burrough, Edmund W. "Submarine Sizes," USNIP 52
        (Dec. 1927):1292-94.

2438.   Bywater, Hector C. "Battleship vs. Plane Still
        a Naval Puzzle," USNIP 54 (Aug. 1928):710-12.

2439.   _____. "The Battleship and Its Uses," USNIP
        52 (Mar. 1926):407-26.

2440.   Carroll, John. "American Isolationism in the
        1920s," Warren F. Kimball, ed. *American Diplo-
        macy in the Twentieth Century*. St. Louis, Forum,
        1980, No. 3.

2441.   Chamberlain, William H. "Naval Bases in the
        Pacific," FA 15 (Apr. 1937):484-94.

2442.   _____. "Aims of the Japanese Army and Navy,"
        FA 15 (Oct. 1936):112-23.

2443.   Chaplin, Philip A. "The Reincarnation of the
         Four-Stackers," USNIP 86 (Mar. 1960):95-103.
         Pictorial.

2444.   "Comparison of the U.S. and Japanese Navies,"
         SA 164 (March 1941):148-49.

2445.   Cook, Charles O. "The Strange Case of Rainbow-
         5," USNIP 104 (Aug. 1978):67-73.

2446.   Cook, Merlyn G. "The Proposal for an Indepen-
         dent Air Service," USNIP 51 (Feb. 1925):215-32.

2447.   Coontz, Robert E. "The Material Condition of
         the U.S. Fleet," Aviation 16 (May 26, 1924):
         571.

2448.   _____. "The Navy," USNIP 49 (May 1923):
         747-58.

2449.   Corey, Herbert. "America's Need of Sea Power,"
         CH 41 (Dec. 1934):264-72.

2450.   *Cosmas, Graham A. "The Formative Years of
         Marine Corps Aviation, 1912-1937," Aerospace
         Historian 24 (Summer 1977):82-93.

2451.   Cox, Ormond L. "The Problem of the Naval De-
         sign Engineer as Affected by the Limitation
         of Armament Treaty," USNIP 54 (Oct. 1928):
         875-78.

2452.   Craig, Paul M. "Lexington and Saratoga, the
         Beginning," USNIP 95 (Dec. 1969):85-92.

2453.   Craven, Thomas T. "Naval Aviation and a United
         Air Service," Flying 10 (Apr. 1921):96-100.

2454.   Cummings, Damon E. "'Aviation' or 'Naval Avia-
         tion': Which?" USNIP 46 (Feb. 1920):177-80.

2455.   Davis, John W. "Anglo-American Relations and
         Sea Power," FA 7 (Apr. 1929):345-55.

2456.   Davis, Norman H. "The New Naval Agreement," FA
         14 (July 1936):578-83.

2457.   "The Development of the NC Seaplanes," Aviation
         6 (June 1, 1919):468-74.

2458.   Dulles, Allen W. "The Threat of Anglo-American Naval Rivalry," FA 7 (Jan. 1929):173-82.

2459.   _____. "Some Misconceptions About Disarmament," FA 5 (Apr. 1927):413-24.

2460.   *Dyer, George C. "Naval Amphibious Landmarks," USNIP 92 (Aug. 1966):51-60. Development of amphibious warfare between World War I and World War II.

2461.   Earle, Edward M. "The Navy's Influence on Our Foreign Relations," CH 23 (Feb. 1926):648-55.

2462.   Eberle, Edward W. "A Few Reflections on Our Navy and Its Needs," USNIP 50 (Sept. 1924): 1399-1407.

2463.   Eliot, George F. "Against a Separate Air Force: The Record," FA 20 (Oct. 1941):30-48.

2464.   Elliott, Charles F. "The Genesis of the Modern U.S. Navy," USNIP 92 (Mar. 1966):62-69. Starts with 1934.

2465.   Fagan, George V. "Franklin D. Roosevelt and Naval Limitation," USNIP 81 (Apr. 1955):411-18.

2466.   Fallodon, Viscount Grey of. "Freedom of the Seas," FA 8 (Apr. 1930):325-35.

2467.   Géraud, André. "France and the Anglo-German Naval Treaty," FA 14 (Oct. 1935):51-61.

2468.   Gibbs, Norman. "The Naval Conferences of the Interwar Years: A Study in Anglo-American Relations," NWCR 30 (Summer 1977):50-63.

2469.   Greene, Fred. "The Military View of American National Policy, 1904-1940," AHR 66 (Jan. 1961):354-77.

2470.   Grow, Harold B. "Bombing Tests on the *Virginia* and *New Jersey*." USNIP 49 (Dec. 1923):1987-96.

2471.   Hayes, John D. "Admiral Joseph Mason Reeves, U.S.N. (1872-1946)," NWCR 23 (Nov. 1970):48-57 and 24 (Jan. 1972):50-64.

2472. _____. "Joseph Mason Reeves '94 (1872-1948)," *Shipmate* 25 (May 1962):10-11.

2473. *Hittle, James D. "20th Century Amphibious Warfare," MCG 38 (Jan 1954):14-21.

2474. Hone, Thomas C. "The Effectiveness of the Washington Treaty Navy," NWCR 32 (Nov.-Dec. 1979): 35-59.

2475. "Mr. Hoover and Naval Disarmament," *New Republic* 57 (Nov. 28, 1928):31-32.

2476. Hudson, George E. "Soviet Naval Doctrine Under Lenin and Stalin," *Soviet Studies* 28 (Jan. 1976):42-65.

2477. Iyenaga, T. "How Japan Views the Arms Conference," CH 14 (Apr. 1922):22-25.

2478. Johnson, Alfred W. "The Proposal for a United Air Service," USNIP 50 (Aug 1924):1422-42.

2479. Johnson, William S. "Naval Diplomacy and the Failure of Balanced Security in the Far East, 1921-1935," NWCR 24 (Feb. 1972):67-88.

2480. [U.S.] Joint Army and Navy Board. "Report of the Joint Army and Navy Board on Bombing and Ordnance Tests," USNIP 47 (Oct. 1921):1641-47.

2481. Jones, Hilary P. "A Just Man Armed Keepeth His House in Order," USNIP 49 (May 1923):759-66.

2482. Kennedy, H.A.S. "Flight to Hawaii," *Outlook* 141 (Sept. 16, 1925):77-78.

2483. Kelin, Ira. "Whitehall, Washington, and the Anglo-Japanese Alliance," PHR 41 (Nov. 1972): 460-83.

2484. Knapp, Harry S. "The Limitation of Armament at the Conference of Washington," *Proceedings of the American Society of International Law, 1922.* Wash.: 1922. The Navy's objections to the limitations.

2485. Knox, Dudley W. "The London Treaty and American Naval Policy," USNIP 57 (Aug. 1931):1079-88.

2486.   _____. "Trade," USNIP 53 (Nov. 1927):1207-10.

2487.   _____. "A Defense of United States Naval
Policy," CH 22 (June 1925):339-44.

2488.   _____. "Our 'Stake' in Sea Power," USNIP
53 (Oct. 1926):1087-89.

2489.   Koistinen, Paul A.C. "The 'Industrial-Military
Complex' in Historical Perspective: The Inter-
war Years," JAH 56 (Mar. 1970):819-39.

2490.   "The Launch of the United States Airplane Carrier *Saratoga*," USNIP 52 (Nov. 1926):2319-25.

2491.   *Lejeune, John A. "The Marines Corps, 1926,"
USNIP 52 (Oct. 1926):1961-69.

2492.   Lincoln, Ashbrook. "The United States Navy and
the Rise of the Doctrine of Air Power," MA 15
(Fall 1951):145-56.

2493.   McDowell, Clyde S. "Naval Research," USNIP 45
(June 1919):895-908.

2494.   McHugh, F.D. "Our Third-rate Navy Could not
Fight Japan," SA 148 (May 1933):268-71.

2495.   Macintyre, Donald. "Shipborne Radar," USNIP
93 (Sept. 1967):70-84.

2496.   Magdeburger, E.C. "The Diesel Engine in the
United States Navy, 1898-1948," ASNEJ 61 (Feb.
1949):45-93.

2497.   Matloff, Maurice. "Pre-War Military Plans and
Preparations, 1939-1941," USNIP 79 (July 1953):
741-48.

2498.   Mitchell, William. "Aircraft Dominate Seacraft,"
SEP 197 (Jan. 24, 1925):22-23.

2499.   _____. "Air Power vs. Sea Power," ARR 63
(Mar. 1921):273-77.

2500.   _____. "Aviation over the Water," ARR 62
(Oct. 1920):391-98.

2501.   Moffett, William A. "Air Service *versus* Air
         Force," *Forum* 74 (Feb. 1926):179-85. The
         Navy's objections to Mitchell's demand for
         a united air service.

2502.   _____. "Aviation Progress in America," CH
         17 (Feb. 1922):775-82. Moffett's answer to
         Mitchell.

2503.   *Montross, Lynn. "The Mystery of Pete Ellis,"
         MCG 33 (July 1954):30-33.

2504.   Moran, Charles. "From Greenland's Icy Moun-
         tains," USNIP 66 (Sept. 1940):1261-68.

2505.   Morton, Louis. "Interservice Co-operation and
         Political-Military Collaboration, 1900-1938"
         in Harry L. Coles, ed. *Total War and Cold War:*
         Problems in Civilian Control of the Military.
         Columbus: Ohio State UP, 1962, pp. 131-60.

2506.   "The Navy Repudiates Admiral Mahan," WW 38
         (Oct. 1919):569-71.

2507.   Nelson, Frederick J. "Guam, Our Western Out-
         post," USNIP 66 (Jan. 1940):83-88.

2508.   "The New Menace to Sea Power: Bombing and
         Ordnance Tests, June-July 1921," USNIP 47
         (Sept. 1921):1451-61, 1826, 1828-29.

2509.   *"1917-1937," *Leatherneck* 40 (Nov. 1957):16-31.

2510.   Nomura, Kichisaburo. "Japan's Demand for Naval
         Equality," FA 13 (Jan. 1935):196-203.

2511.   O'Brien, T.J. "The Navy's Part in Modern Aero-
         logical Development," USNIP 61 (Mar. 1935):
         385-99.

2512.   O'Connor, Raymond G. "The 'Yardstick' and
         Naval Disarmament in the 1920s," MVHR 45
         (Dec. 1958):441-63.

2513.   Offner, Arnold A. "Appeasement Revisited: The
         United States, Great Britain, and Germany,
         1933-1940," JAH 64 (Sept. 1977):373-93.

2514.   Oglesby, Joseph E. "First Landing at the [South]
         Pole," USNIP 83 (Nov. 1957):1188-95.

2515.   Okumiya, Masatake. "How the *Panay* was Sunk,"
            USNIP 79 (June 1953):587-96.

2516.   Padelford, Norman J. "An Atlantic Naval Policy
            for the United States," USNIP 66 (Sept. 1940):
            1297-1308.

2517.   "The PN-9, No. 1, on the West Coast-Hawaiian
            Flight," *Aviation* 19 (Sept. 14-21, 1925):315-
            17, 350-52.

2518.   Paxson, F.L. "The Naval Air Station at Alameda,
            1916-1940: A Case Study in the Aptitude of
            Democracy for Defense," PHR 13 (Sept. 1944):
            235-50.

2519.   Pollen, Arthur J.H. "The Submarine," FA 25
            (July 1927):553-66. Suggests abandoning the
            torpedo.

2520.   Pratt, William V. "Pending Naval Questions,"
            FA 13 (Apr. 1935):409-19.

2521.   _____. "Naval Policy and Its Relation to
            World Politics," USNIP 49 (July 1923):1073-84.

2522.   _____. "The Case for the Naval Treaty,"
            CH 18 (Apr. 1923):1-5.

2523.   _____. "Some Considerations Affecting Naval
            Policy," USNIP 48 (Oct. 1922):1845-62.

2524.   _____. "Naval Policy and the Naval Treaty,"
            NAR 215 (May 1922):590-99.

2525.   Provenzo, Eugene F., Jr. "Thomas W. Benoist:
            Early Pioneer of St. Louis Aviator (1874-1917),"
            Bull. of the Missouri Hist. Soc., Jan. 1976,
            pp. 91-104.

2526.   Puleston, William D. "A Reexamination of Mahan's
            Concept of Seapower," USNIP 66 (Sept. 1940):
            1229-36.

2527.   Pye, William S. "Joint Army and Navy Opera-
            tions," USNIP 50 (Dec. 1924):1963-76; 51 (Jan.
            1925):1-14. Comment on pp. 223-45, 386-99,
            589-99, 975-1000.

2528.   Quinlan, Robert J. "The United States Fleet:
            Diplomacy, Strategy, and the Allocation of
            Ships, 1940-1941," in Harold Stein, ed.,
            *American Civil-Military Decisions: A Book of
            Case Studies.* University: U. of Alabama P.,
            1963, pp. 153-201.

2529.   Ramsey, C. DeWitt. "The Development of Aviation
            in the Fleet," USNIP 49 (Sept. 1923):1395-1417.

2530.   Ransom, Harry H. "The Battleship Meets the
            Airplane," MA 23 (Spring 1959):21-27.

2531.   Ranson, M.A. "Little Gray Ships," USNIP 62
            (Sept. 1936):1280-94. Mine craft.

2532.   Read, Conyers. "Recent United States and Brit-
            ish Government Publication on the London Naval
            Conference of 1930," AHR 54 (Jan. 1949):307-14.

2533.   *Reber, John J. "Pete Ellis: Amphibious Warfare
            Prophet," USNIP 103 (Oct. 1977):53-64.

2534.   "Report of Lampert Aircraft Committee," USNIP
            52 (Jan. 1926):221-25.

2535.   "Report of President's Aircraft Board," USNIP
            52 (Jan. 1926):196-220.

2536.   "Report of National Advisory Committee for
            Aeronautics, 1925," USNIP 52 (Mar. 1926):579-
            89.

2537.   Richards, David K.K. "The Beginnings of Pearl
            Harbor, July 1909 to December 7, 1941," USNIP
            70 (May 1944):536-45.

2538.   Richmond, Herbert. "Naval Problems of 1935,"
            FA 13 (Oct. 1934):45-58.

2539.   _____. "Immediate Problems of Naval Reduc-
            tion," FA 9 (Apr. 1931):371-88.

2540.   Roosevelt, F.D. "Shall We Trust Japan?" *Asia*
            23 (July 1923):475-78, 526-29.

2541.   Roosevelt, Henry L. "The United States Navy
            and Its Functions," USNIP 62 (Oct. 1936):
            1383-90.

2542.   Roosevelt, Theodore, Assistant Secretary of the
          Navy. "Maintenance of the Treaty Navy," USNIP 49
          (May 1923):739-46.

2543.   Rosendahl, Charles E. "The Loss of the *Akron*,"
          USNIP 60 (July 1934):921-33.

2544.   *Rowell, Ross E. "Aircraft in Bush Warfare," MCG
          14 (Sept. 1929):180-203. A detailed treatise
          on Marine aviation in Nicaragua.

2545.   Scammell, J.M. "The Industrial College of the
          Armed Forces: Twenty Years of Army-Navy Co-
          operation," USNIP 73 (Mar. 1947):295-301.
          Covers the years 1927-1947.

2546.   Schornstheimer, Graser. "America's Present
          Naval Organization," CH 19 (Oct. 1923):131-34.

2547.   _____. "The Case Against the Naval Treaty,"
          CH 18 (June 1923):401-06.

2548.   _____. "Our Navy Unready for War," CH 17
          (Dec. 1922):624-31.

2549.   _____. "Japan's Naval Mastery of the Sea,"
          CH 16 (Aug. 1922):744-52.

2550.   _____. "Facts About Naval Disarmament," CH
          15 (Oct. 1921):41-46.

2551.   Shotwell, James T. "Sea Power and the Far East,"
          Ch 41 (Mar. 1935):660-66.

2552.   Sims, William S. "Status of the American Navy,"
          CH 16 (May 1922):185-94.

2553.   Spencer, Ivor D. "U.S. Naval Air Bases from
          1914-1939," USNIP 75 (Nov. 1949):1242-55.

2554.   Stevens, William O. "Scrapping Mahan," *Yale
          Rev.* NS 12 (Apr. 1923):528-42. The apparent
          result of the Washington Naval Treaty.

2555.   Stirling, Yates. "Bureaucracy Rules the Navy:
          The Absence of a General Staff Seriously Im-
          perils the Value of Our Naval Forces," CH 51
          (Mar. 1940):30-32.

2556.   Tolley, Kemp. "Admiral-Ambassador Standley,"
            Shipmate 40 (Sept. 1977):27-29.

2557.   Turnbull, Archibald D. "The United States as
            a Second-class Naval Power," CH 19 (Aug. 1924):
            969-83.

2558.   *Upshur, William P. "The United States Marine
            Corps Reserve," USNIP 65 (Mar. 1939):437-93.

2559.   Utley, Jonathan G. "Conflicting Policies over
            the Sino-Japanese War: State, War, and Navy,
            1937-1941," in David H. White, ed. *Proceedings
            of the Conference on War and Diplomacy.*
            Charleston, S.C.: The Citadel, 1976, pp. 154-61.

2560.   Van Meter, Robert H., Jr. "The Washington Con-
            ference of 1921-22: A New Look," PHR 56 (Nov.
            1977): 603-24.

2561.   Wallin, Homer N. "Permissible Building Programs
            Under the London Naval Treaty," USNIP 56 (Dec.
            1930):1074-79.

2562.   Warner, Edward P. "An Air Policy for the United
            States," USNIP 51 (May 1925):722-36.

2563.   Wheeler, Gerald E. "William Veazie Pratt:
            Silhouette of an Admiral," NWCR 21 (May 1969):
            36-61.

2564.   _____. "National Policy Planning Between the
            World Wars: Conflict Between Ends and Means,"
            NWCR 21 (Feb. 1969):54-69.

2565.   _____. "The United States Navy in the Pa-
            cific, 1919-1941," WA 30 (Oct. 1959):199-225.

2566.   _____. "The United States Navy and the
            Japanese 'Enemy'," MA 21 (Summer 1957):61-74.

2567.   Widersheim, William A., III. "Factors in the
            Growth of the Reichmarine, 1919-1939," USNIP
            74 (Mar. 1948):316-25.

2568.   Wilds, Thomas. "How Japan Fortified the Man-
            dated Islands," USNIP 81 (Apr. 1955):401-07.

2569.   Wilkinson, Ford L., Jr. "The United States
Navy Post-graduate School, 1909-1948," *Scientific Monthly* 66 (Mar. 1948):183-94.

2570.   Woodhouse, Henry. "U.S. Naval Aeronautic Policies, 1904-1942," USNIP 68 (Dec. 1924):161-75.

FICTION

2571. P27
.E477

Ellsberg, Edward. *Submerged: A Novel*. London: Hurst & Blackett, 1934. U.S. submarines 1919-1941.

2572. PS3509
.L57P5

_____. *Pig Boats*. N.Y.: Dodd, Mead, 1931. U.S. submarines.

2573. PS3563
.A3155
S3

McKenna, Richard. *The Sand Pebbles: A Novel*. N.Y.: Harper, 1963. An American gunboat in China during the 1920s.

2574. PZ3
.W8605
Yan

Woodrooffe, Thomas. *Yangtze Skipper*. N.Y.: Sheridan House, 1937. A British gunboat on river patrol, China, in 1920s. More sympathetic to China than *Sand Pebbles*.

13

THE COMING OF WORLD WAR II

BOOKS

2575. D770   Abbazia, Patrick. *Mr. Roosevelt's Navy: The*
      .A238   *Private War of the U.S. Atlantic Fleet, 1939-*
                  1942. Annapolis, Md.: NIP, 1975.

2576. D755   Adams, Henry H. *Years of Deadly Peril: The Com-*
      .A3   *ing of the War, 1939-1941.* N.Y.: McKay, 1969.

2577. D741   Adamthwaite, Anthony P. *The Making of the Second*
      .A34   *World War.* Reading, Mass.: Allen and Unwin,
                  1977.

2578. DC396   _____. *France and the Coming of the Second*
      .A46   *World War, 1936-1939.* London: Frank Cass, 1977.

2579. E744   Adler, Selig. *The Isolationist Impulse: Its*
      .A26   *Twentieth Century Reaction.* N.Y.: Abelard-
                  Schuman, 1957.

2580. D511   Aster, Sidney. *1939: The Making of the Second*
      .A77   *World War.* N.Y.: Simon and Schuster, 1973.

2581. D773   Bailey, Thomas, and Paul B. Ryan. *Hitler vs.*
      .B28   *Roosevelt: The Undeclared Naval War.* N.Y.:
                  Macmillan, 1979.

2582. D763   Balchen, Bernt, and others. *War Below Zero: The*
      .5.B3   *Battle for Greenland.* Boston: Houghton Mifflin,
                  1944.

2583. D756   Baldwin, Hanson W. *The Crucial Years, 1939-*
      .B27   *1941: The World at War.* N.Y.: Harper & Row,
                  1976.

2584. DG568   Barclay, Glen. *The Rise and Fall of the New*
      .5B37   *Roman Empire: Italy's Bid for World Power,*
                  1890-1943. N.Y.: St. Martin, 1973.

2585. E806   Beard, Charles A. *President Roosevelt and the*
      .B434   *Coming of the War, 1941: A Study in Appearances*
                  and Realities. 1948; rpt., Hamden, Conn.:
                  Archon Books, 1968. An anti-Roosevelt work
                  that provoked a lengthy reply by Basil Raunch,
                  q.v.

2586. D643   Birdsall, Paul. *Versailles Twenty Years After*.
       .A7B5   N.Y.: Reynal and Hitchcock, 1941.

2587. DS518   Bisson, Thomas A. *American Policy in the Far*
       .8.B5   *East, 1931-1940*. N.Y.: Institute of Pacific
                 Relations, 1940.

2588. HJ257   Blum, John, ed. *From the Morgenthau Diaries:*
       .B6   *Years of Urgency, 1938-1941*. Houghton Miffin,
                 1965.

2589. DS784   Borg, Dorothy. *The United States and the Far*
       .B65   *Eastern Crisis of 1933-1938*. Cambridge: HUP,
                 1964.

2590. E183.8   _____, and Shumpei Okamoto, Eds. *Pearl*
       .K3B67   *Harbor As History: Japanese-American Relations*,
                 1931-1941. N.Y.: Columbia UP, 1973.

2591. D743   Butler, James R.M. *Grand Strategy: September*
       .B83   *1939 to June 1941*. Vol. 2 of James R.M. Butler,
                 ed., *Grand Strategy: History of the Second*
                 World War. United Kingdom Military Series.
                 London: HMSO, 1957-1972.

2592. DS890   Butow, Robert J.C. *Tojo and the Coming of the*
       .T57B8   *War*. Princeton: PUP, 1961.

2593. VA50   Bywater, Hector C. *Sea-Power in the Pacific: A*
       .B87   *Study of the American-Japanese Naval Problem*,
                 new ed. N.Y.: Houghton Mifflin, 1934. Outdated
                 but contains a suggestive outline for a Japa-
                 nese-American war in the Pacific.

2594. D743   Churchill, Winston. *The Second World War*, 6
       .C47   vols. Boston: Houghton Mifflin, 1948-1953.
                 Vol. 1. *The Gathering Storm*, 1948.

2595. DD247   Compton, James V. *The Swastika and the Eagle*.
       .H5C58   Boston: Houghton Mifflin, 1967. America's un-
                 declared war in the Atlantic.

2596. D753.2   Dawson, Raymond H. *The Decision to Aid Russia*,
       .R9D3   *1941: Foreign Policy and Domestic Politics*.
                 Chapel Hill: UNCP, 1959.

2597. DU29   Denlinger, Sutherland, and Charles B. Gary.
       .D4   *War in the Pacific: A Study of Navies, Peoples*,
                 and Battle Problems. N.Y.: McBride, 1936. In-
                 teresting speculation.

2598. E806   Divine, Robert A. *The Illusion of Neutrality*.
      .D58   Chicago: U. of Chicago P., 1962.

2599. E806   Drummond, Donald F. *The Passing of American
      .D7   Neutrality, 1937-1941*. Ann Arbor, Mich.: U.
                of Michigan P., 1951.

2600. UA23   Eliot, George F. *The Ramparts We Watch: Study
      .E43   of the Problems of American National Defense*.
                N.Y.: Reynal & Hitchcock, 1938.

2601. D741   Elson, Robert T. *Prelude to War*. N.Y.: Time-
      .E43   Life Books, 1976.

2602. JX1428   Esthus, Raymond A. *From Enmity to Alliance:
      .A75E8   U.S.-Australian Relations, 1931-1941*. Seattle:
                U. of Washington P., 1964.

2603. E806   Fehrenbach, T.R. *F.D.R.'s Undeclared War, 1939-
      .F33   1941*. N.Y.: McKay, 1967.

2604. D753   Feis, Herbert. *The Road to Pearl Harbor: The
      .F4   Coming of the War Between the United States
                and Japan*. Princeton: PUP, 1950.

2605. D751   Friedländer, Saul. *Prelude to Downfall: Hitler
      .F713   and the United States, 1939-1941*. N.Y.: Knopf,
                1967.

2606. D743   Gibbs, N.H. *Grand Strategy, to September 1939*.
      .B83   Vol. 1 of James R.M. Butler, ed. *Grand Strat-
                egy: History of the Second World War*. United
                Kingdom Series. London: HMSO, 1957, 1957-1972.
                Rearmament policy.

2607. D753.2   Goodhart, Philip. *Fifty Ships that Saved the
      .G7G6   World: The Foundation of the Anglo-American
                Alliance*. GCNY: Doubleday, 1965. Destroyers-
                bases deal.

2608. DS849   Grew, Joseph C. *Ten Years in Japan*. N.Y.: Simon
      .U6G7   and Schuster, 1944.

2609. E183.8   Herzog, James H. *Closing the Open Door: Ameri-
      .J3H47   can-Japanese Diplomatic Negotiations, 1936-
                1941*. Annapolis, Md.: NIP, 1973.

2610. E806   Hoehling, Adolph A. *America's Road to War:
      .H59   1939-1941*. N.Y.: Abelard-Schuman, 1970.

2611. D741   Hoffman, Ross J.S., and C. Grove Haines. *The*
       H3   *Origins and Background of the Second World War.*
               N.Y.: Oxford UP, 1943.

2612. E748   Hull, Cordell. *The Memoirs of Cordell Hull*, 2
       .H93A3   vols. N.Y.: Macmillan, 1948.

2613. Micro.   *Joint Staff Conversations.* Wilmington, Del.:
               Scholarly Resources, 1979.   Pre-World War II.

2614. E744   Jonas, Manfred. *Isolationism in America, 1935-*
       .J667   *1951.* Ithaca: Cornell UP, 1966.

2615. E748.K   Kennan, George F. *Memoirs, 1925-1950.* Boston:
       374A3   Little, Brown, 1967.

2616. D753   Kimball, Warren F. *The Most Unsordid Act: Lend-*
       .K5   *Lease, 1939-1941.* Baltimore: Johns Hopkins UP,
               1969.

2617. E806   Kinsella, William E., Jr. *Leadership in Isola-*
       .K56   *tion: FDR and the Origins of the Second World*
               War. Cambridge, Mass.: Schenkman, 1978.

2618. MS   Kittredge, Tracy B. "United States-British
               Naval Cooperation, 1940-1945," MS. Washington:
               Naval Hist. Center.

2619. E183.8   Koginos, Manny. *The* Panay *Incident: Prelude to*
       .J3K56   *War.* Lafayette, Ind.: Purdue U. Studies, 1967.

2620. D744   Langer, William L., and S. Everett Gleason. *The*
       .L3   *Challenge to Isolation, 1937-1940.* N.Y.: Har-
               per, 1953.

2621. D748   _____. *The Undeclared War, 1940-1941.* N.Y.:
       .L3   Harper, 1953.

2622. D750   Leutze, James R. *Bargaining for Supremacy:*
       .L47   *Anglo-American Naval Collaboration, 1937-1941.*
               Chapel Hill: UNCP, 1977.

2623. D655   Lukacs, John. *The Last European War, September*
       .L84   *1939-December 1941.* GCNY: Doubleday, 1976.

2624. D443   Mackintosh, John. *The Paths That Led to War:*
       .M246   *Europe, 1919-1939.* London: Blackie, 1940; rpt.,
               Kennikat, 1970.

2625. E748
.S883
.M6

Morison, Elting E. *Turmoil and Tradition: A Study of the Life and Times of Henry L. Stimson.* Boston: Houghton Mifflin, 1960.

2626. D741
.M65

Mosley, Leonard. *On Borrowed Time: How World War II Began.* N.Y.: Random House, 1969.

2627. E744
.M87

Murphy, Robert D. *Diplomat Among Warriors.* GCNY: Doubleday, 1964.

2628. E183.8
.G7N49

Nicholas, Herbert. *Britain and the U.S.A.* Baltimore: Johns Hopkins P., 1963. Covers the years 1938 to 1961.

2929. E744
.O43

Offner, Arnold A. *The Origins of the Second World War: American Foreign Policy and World Politics, 1917-1941.* N.Y.: Praeger, 1975.

2930. E183.7
B46

Pratt, Julius. *Cordell Hull,* 2 vols. N.Y.: Cooper Square Pub., 1964.

2631. V767
.F74

Preston, Adrian, ed. *General Staff and Diplomacy before the Second World War.* Totowa, N.J.: Rowman and Littlefield, 1978.

2632. E807
.R3

Rauch, Basil. *Roosevelt: From Munich to Pearl Harbor.* N.Y.: Creative Age P., 1950.

2633. D741
.R62

Robertson, Esmonde M., ed. *The Origins of the Second World War: Historical Interpretations.* London: Macmillan, 1971.

2634. D742
.J3S38

Schroeder, Paul W. *The Axis Alliance and Japanese-American Relations, 1941.* Ithaca: Cornell UP, 1948.

2635. DA47.9
.C6S5

Shai, Aron. *The Origins of the War in the East: Britain, China, and Japan 1937-1939.* London: Croom Helm, 1976.

2636. E807
.S45

Sherwood, Robert E. *Roosevelt and Hopkins.* N.Y.: Harper, 1948.

2637. DC335
.S47

Shirer, William L. *The Collapse of the Third Republic: An Inquiry into the Fall of France in 1940.* N.Y.: Simon & Schuster, 1969.

2638. E806
.T8

Tansill, Charles C. *Back Door to War: The Roosevelt Foreign Policy, 1933-1941.* Chicago: Henry Regnery, 1952. Revisionist.

2639. D742 Trefouse, Hans L. *Germany and American Neutrality, 1939-1941*. N.Y.: Bookman, 1951.
.U5T66

2640. E744 Welles, Sumner. *Time for Decision*. N.Y.: Harper, 1944.
.W52

2641. E746 Wheeler, Gerald E. *Prelude to Pearl Harbor: The United States Navy and the Far East, 1921-1931*. Columbia: U. of Missouri P., 1963.
.W5

2642. D734 Wilson, Theodore A. *The First Summit: Roosevelt and Churchill at Placentia Bay, 1941*. Boston: Houghton Mifflin, 1969.
.A8W5

DISSERTATIONS AND THESES

2643. Ferrell, Henry C., Jr. "Claude Swanson of Virginia," U. of Virginia, 1964.

2644. Hunt, John J. "The United States Occupation of Iceland, 1941-1946," Georgetown U., 1966. A solid and comprehensive work.

2645. Mark, Steven M. "An American Interventionist: Frank Knox and United States Foreign Relations," U. of Maryland, 1977.

ARTICLES

2646. "Breach with the Axis Widened by the Nazi Sinking of the *Robin Moor*," *Newsweek* 17 (June 23, 1941):13-16.

2647. Bywater, Hector C. "Britain on the Seas," FA 16 (Jan. 1938):210-21.

2648. Cole, Wayne S. "Franklin D. Roosevelt and the Isolationists, 1932-1945," in David H. White, ed. *Proceedings of the Conference on War and Diplomacy*. Charleston, S.C.: The Citadel, 1976, pp. 1-11.

2649. Deac, Wilfred P. "America's Undeclared Naval War," USNIP 87 (Oct. 1961):70-79.

2650. Dulles, Allen W. "Cash and Carry Neutrality: The Pittman Act," FA 18 (Jan. 1940):179-95.

2651. Greenberg, Daniel S. "U.S. Destroyers for British Bases: Fifty Old Ships Go to War," USNIP 88 (Nov. 1962):70-83.

2652.   Grenfell, Russell. "Mediterranean Strategy after the Franco Victory," FA 18 (July 1937):732-39.

2653.   Herwig, Holger. "Prelude to Weltblitzkrieg: Germany's Naval Policy toward the United States of America, 1939-1941," JMH 43 (Dec. 1971): 649-68.

2654.   Herzog, James H. "Influence of the United States Navy in the Embargo of Oil to Japan, 1940-1941," PHR 35 (Aug. 1966):317-28.

2655.   Jones, Manfred. "Roosevelt, Churchill and America's Entrance into World War II," in David H. White, ed. *Proceedings of the Conference on War and Diplomacy*. Charleston, S.C.: The Citadel, 1976, pp. 81-87.

2656.   Kay, Howard N. "The Fifty Old Maids Come Through," USNIP 76 (Sept. 1950):976-79.

2657.   Langenberg, William H. "Destroyers for Naval Bases: Highlights of an Unprecedented Trade," NWCR 22 (Sept. 1970):80-92.

2658.   Leutze, James R. "Technology and Bargaining in Anglo-American Naval Relations: 1938-1946," USNIP 103 (June 1977):50-61.

2659.   Matloff, Maurice. "Prewar Military Plans and Preparations, 1939-1941," USNIP 79 (July 1953): 741-48.

2660.   Maurer, Maurer. "A Delicate Mission: Aerial Reconnaissance of Japanese Islands before World War II," MA 26 (Summer 1962):66-75.

2661.   Nomura, Kichisaburo. "Stepping Stones to War," USNIP 77 (Sept. 1951):927-31.

2662.   Pratt, Lawrence. "The Anglo-American Naval Conversations on the Far East of January 1938," IA 47 (Oct. 1971):745-63.

2663. E744 Quinlan, Robert J. "The United States Fleet:
       .S845 Diplomacy, Strategy and the Allocation of Ships, (1940-1941)," in Harold Stein, ed., *American Civil-Military Decisions: A Book of Case Studies*. Birmingham: U. of Ala. P., 1963, pp. 153-202.

2664.   Roosevelt, Franklin D. "The Shooting Has Started: Navy Day Address, October 27, 1941," *Vital Speeches* 8 (Nov. 15, 1941):66-68.

2665.   _____. "Sinking of the *Robin Moor:* Message to Congress, June 20, 1941," *Vital Speeches* 7 (July 1, 1941):546.

2666.   Schaller, Michael. "American Strategy in China, 1939-1941: The Origins of Clandestine Air Warfare," *Am.Q.* 28 (Spring 1976):3-19.

2667.   Swanson, Harlan J. "The *Panay* Incident: Prelude to Pearl Harbor," USNIP 93 (Dec. 1967):26-37.

2668.   Vogel, Bertram. "Diplomatic Prelude to Pearl Harbor," USNIP 75 (Apr. 1949):415-21. A chronological review from the sinking of the *Panay* to the attack on Pearl Harbor.

2669.   Walter, John C. "Exploding a Myth: F.D.R. and the Politics of U.S. Naval Expansion During the New Deal," *Shipmate* 41 (Oct. 1978):15-18.

2670.   Watson, Mark S. "First Vigorous Steps in Rearming, 1938-39," MA 12 (Summer 1948):65-78.

2671.   Weigley, Russell F. "The Crossing of the Rhine: American Strategic Thought to World War II," *Armed Forces and Society* 5 (Winter 1979):302-20.

2672.   Wheeler, Gerald E. "The Road to War: The United States and Japan, 1931-1941," Warren F. Kimball, ed. *American Diplomacy in the Twentieth Century.* St. Louis: Forum, 1980, no. 4.

FICTION

2673. PS3513 Goodrich, Marcus. *Delilah.* N.Y.: Farrar & Rine-
   .05352D4 hart, 1941. A destroyer hunts U-boats during the neutrality period of World War II.

14

WORLD WAR II IN EUROPEAN WATERS,
September 1939-December 1941

GENERAL

Most of the works in this section deal with the opening actions of the belligerents, in which the Allies hunted U-boats and
German surface-ship raiders, tried to prevent Hitler's conquest
of Norway and France and, with Italy's help after May 1943, to
prohibit the cutting of the British lifeline in the Mediterranean.
Some of these actions, however, provoked reactions from neutral
nations, especially from the United States, causing the latter to
seek allies and belatedly to prepare for war. An understanding
of the worldwide strategic situation at the time of the Japanese
attack on Pearl Harbor is considered essential to an understanding
of the decisions the United States had to make once it entered the
war. Many titles included in this chapter nevertheless go beyond
the period covered, some carrying the story to the end of the war,
and are therefore useful for all chapters dealing with the war.
Special attention is given to the U-boat campaign in Chapter
15, section D, The Battle of the Atlantic.

BOOKS

2674. D770   Abbazia, Patrick. *Mr. Roosevelt's Navy: The*
       .A238   *Private War of the U.S. Atlantic Fleet, 1939-*
                   1942. Annapolis, Md.: NIP, 1975.

2675. D759   Agar, Herbert. *The Darkest Year: Britain Alone*,
       .A13   *June 1940-June 1941.* London: Bodley Head, 1972.

2676. D761.9   Aghion, Raoul. *Fighting French.* N.Y.: Holt,
       .F7A64   1943.

2677. D771   Ansel, Walter C. *Hitler Confronts England.*
       .A746   Durham: Duke UP, 1960.

2678. D766   _____. *Hitler and the Middle Sea.* Durham:
       .A65   Duke UP, 1972. Battle for the Mediterranean.

2679. VA58   Armitage, Merle. *The United States Navy.* N.Y.:
       .A67   Longmans, Green, 1940. The status of the U.S.
                   Navy at the beginning of World War II.

2680. D779.F7   Auphan, Paul, and Jacques Mordal. *The French*
       .A823   *Navy in World War II.* Annapolis, Md.: USNI,
                   1957; rpt. Greenwood, 1976.

2681. D786   Bader, Douglas. *Fight for the Sky*. London:
        .B2   Sidgwick & Jackson, 1973. British air opera-
                    tions, World War II.

2682. D763   Badoglio, Pietro. *Italy in the Second World War:*
        .I8B27   *Memories and Documents*. London: Oxford UP, 1948.

2683. V857   Bagnasco, Erminio. *Submarines of World War II*.
        .B3313   Annapolis, Md.: NIP, 1977.

2684. D743   Baldwin, Hanson W. *Battles Lost and Won: Great*
        .B34   *Campaigns of World War II*. N.Y.: Harper & Row,
                    1966.

2685. D756.5   Barker, Arthur J. *Dunkirk: The Great Escape*.
        .D8B37   N.Y.: McKay, 1977.

2686. D755.1   Beaufre, André. *1940: The Fall of France*. Lon-
        .B3813   don: Cassell, 1967.

2687. D810   Beesly, Patrick. *Very Special Intelligence: The*
        .S7B4   *Story of the Admiralty's Operational Intelli-*
                    gence Centre, 1939-1945. London: Hamilton, 1977.

2688. D763   Beith, John H., pseud. *Malta Epic*. N.Y.: Apple-
        .M3B4   ton-Century, 1943.

2689. D771   Bekker, Cajus D., pseud. *The German Navy, 1939-*
        .B38814   *1945*. N.Y.: Dial, 1974.

2690. D771   _____. *Hitler's Naval War*. GCNY: Doubleday,
        .B38813   1974.

2691. D771   _____. *Defeat at Sea: The Struggle and Even-*
        .B383   *tual Destruction of the German Navy, 1939-1945*.
                    N.Y.: Holt, 1955. Episodic, but excellent on
                    such things as "Negros" [one-man torpedo] and
                    "Beavers" [midget submarines].

2692. D770   Belot, Raymond de. *The Struggle for the Mediter-*
        .B453   *ranean, 1939-1945*. Princeton: PUP, 1951.

2693. D770   Bennett, Geoffrey. *Naval Battles of World War*
        .B456   *II*. N.Y.: McKay, 1975.

2694. D772   _____. *Battle of the River Plate*. Annapolis,
        .G7C45   Md.: NIP, 1972. Brief account.

2695. D772   Berthold, Will. *The Sinking of the* Bismarck.
        .B5B84   London: Longmans, Green, 1958. A German
                    account.

2696. D766.8 Bingham, James K.W., and Werner Haupt. *The*
.H3413 *North African Campaign, 1940-1943.* London:
MacDonald, 1969.

2697. D756.5 Bishop, Edward. *The Battle of Britain.* London:
.B7B5 Allen & Unwin, 1960.

2698. D775 Borghese, Iunio V. *Sea Devils.* London: Melrose,
B613 1955. Italian "human torpedoes" in World War
II.

2699. D772 Bradford, Ernle D.S. *The Mighty* Hood. London:
.H6B7 Hodder & Stoughton, 1959.

2700. D775 Bragadin, Marc' Antonio. *The Italian Navy in*
.B683 *World War II.* Annapolis, Md.: USNI, 1957.

2701. D790 Brereton, Lewis H. *The Brereton Diaries: The*
.B67 *War in the Air in the Pacific, in the Middle*
East and in Europe, 3 October 1941-8 May 1945.
N.Y.: Morrow, 1946.

2702. DA566.9 Broad, Lewis. *Winston Churchill: A Biography,*
.C5B69 3 vols. N.Y.: Hawthorn, 1958-1963.

2703. D780 Brou, Willy C. *Combat Beneath the Sea.* N.Y.:
.B713 Crowell, 1957. Midget submarines of World
War II.

2704. D772 Brown, David. Tirpitz: *Floating Fortress.*
.T5B75 Annapolis, Md.: NIP, 1977.

2705. D770 _____. *Carrier Operations in World War II.*
.B75 Vol. 1: *The Royal Navy*; rev. ed. London: Allan,
1974.

2706. D743 Bryant, Arthur. *Triumph in the War: A History*
.B73 *of the War Years Based on the Diaries of Field-*
Marshal Lord Alanbrook, Chief of the Imperial
Staff. GCNY: Doubleday, 1959.

2707. D766 Buckley, Christopher. *Greece and Crete, 1941.*
.3.B8 London: HMSO, 1952.

2708. Busch, Harald. *U-boats at War.* London: Putnam,
1955. Useful for the period of America's undeclared naval war with Nazi Germany.

2709. D743 Calvocoressi, Peter, and Guy Wint. *Total War:*
.C24 *The Story of World War II.* N.Y.: Pantheon, 1972.

2710. D763   Cameron, Ian, pseud. *Red Duster, White Ensign:*
      .M3   *The True Story of Malta and the Malta Convoys.*
                London: White Lion, 1960.

2711.   Cant, Gilbert. *The War at Sea.* N.Y.: John Day,
                1942.

2712. D770   _____. *The War at Sea: with Photographs and*
      .C3   *Battle Diagrams.* N.Y.: Stein & Day, 1942. From
                Sept. 1939 through Pearl Harbor.

2713. D756   Carse, Robert. *Dunkirk, 1940: A History.* Engle-
      .5.D8C37 wood Cliffs, N.J.: Prentice-Hall, 1970.

2714. D761   Chapman, Guy. *Why France Collapsed.* London:
      .C485   Cassell, 1968.

2715. D765.5   Chatterton, Edward K. *The Epic of Dunkirk.* Lon-
      .D8C5   don: Hurst & Blackett, 1940.

2716. D781   _____. *Commerce Raiders.* London: Hurst &
      .C49   Blackett, 1948. Brief account of German
                raiders.

2717. D743   Churchill, Winston. *The Second World War*, 6
      .C47   vols. Boston: Houghton Mifflin, 1948-1953.
                Vol. 1. *The Gathering Storm*, and Vol. 2. *Their*
                Finest Hour.

2718. D766.7   Clark, Alan. *The Fall of Crete.* London: Blond,
      C7C5   1962.

2719. Q143   Clark, Ronald W. *Tizard.* Cambridge: MIT, 1965.
      .T5C6

2720. D787   Collier, Basil. *The Battle of Britain.* N.Y.:
      .C6   Macmillan, 1962.

2721. D756.5   Collier, Richard. *The Sands of Dunkirk.* N.Y.:
      .D8C6   Dutton, 1961.

2722. D743   Commager, Henry S., ed. *History of the Second*
      .C55   *World War.* Boston: Little, Brown, 1945.

2723. D770   Creswell, John. *Sea Warfare, 1939-1945.* N.Y.:
      .C7   Longmans, 1950.

2724. DA89.1   Cunningham, Andrew B. *A Sailor's Odyssey.* N.Y.:
      .C8A3   Dutton, 1951.

2725. D756.5   Deighton, Len. *Fighter: The True Story of the*
      .B7D4   *Battle of Britain*. N.Y.: Knopf, 1978.

2726. DC373   De Montmorency, Alec. *The Enigma of Admiral*
      .D35D4   *Darlan*. N.Y.: Dutton, 1943.

2727. D763   Derry, T.K. *The Campaign in Norway*. London:
      .N6D47   HMSO, 1952.

2728. D763   Dickens, Peter. *Narvik: Battles in the Fjords*.
      .N6D52   Annapolis, Md.: NIP, 1974.

2729. D771   _____. *Night Action: MTB Flotilla at War*.
      .D44   Annapolis, Md.: NIP, 1974. 1942-43 along the
                Western Wall.

2730. UF767   Dornberger, Walter. *V-2*. N.Y.: Viking, 1954.
      .D655

2731. D810   Eggleston, Wilfrid. *Scientists at War*. London:
      .S2E4   Oxford UP, 1951.

2732. U162   Farago, Ladislas, ed. *The Axis Grand Strategy:*
      .F36   *Blueprints for Total War*. N.Y.: Farrar & Rine-
                hart, 1942.

2733. D786   Fleming, Peter. *Operation Sea Lion: The Pro-*
      .F56   *jected Invasion of England in 1940. An Account*
                of the German Preparation and the British
                Counter-Measures. N.Y.: Simon & Schuster, 1957.

2734. D757.5   Forty, George. *Afrika Korps at War*, 2 vols.
      .G4F67   N.Y.: Scribner, 1978. Vol. 1. *The Road to*
                Alexandria; Vol. 2. *The Long Road Back*.

2735. D763   Gerárd, Francis. *Malta Magnificent*. N.Y.:
      .M3G4   Whittlesey House, 1943.

2736. D800   Gordon, David L., and Royden Dangerfield. *The*
      .G6   *Hidden Weapon: The Story of Economic Warfare*.
                N.Y.: Harper, 1947.

2737. D770   Great Britain. Admiralty. *Fueher Conferences*
      .G42   *on Naval Affairs, 1939-1945*, 7 vols. London:
                Admiralty, 1947; Micro. Wash.: U. Publications
                of America, 1978.

2738. VA454   Grenfell, Russell. *Sea Power*. London: Cape,
      .G68   1940.

2739. D783   Grider, George. *Warfish*. Boston: Little, Brown,
      .G7   1958. World War II naval operations.

2740. D743   Gwyer, J.M.A., and James R.M. Butler. *Grand*
      .B83   *Strategy: Part 1. From 2 June 1941 to August*
             1942. James R.M. Butler, ed. *Grand Strategy:*
             History of the Second World War. United King-
             dom Military Series. London: HMSO, 1957-1972.
             Vol. 3.

2741. D800   Hall, Hessel D. *North American Supply*. London:
      .H3   HSMO, 1955.

2742. D761   Hartcup, Guy. *Code Name Mulberry: The Planning,*
      .H37   *Building, and Operation of the Normandy Har-*
             bours. N.Y.: Hippocrene, 1977.

2743. UF535 _____. *The Challenge of War: Britain's Sci-*
      .G7H36 *entific and Engineering Contributions to World*
             War Two. N.Y.: Taplinger, 1970.

2744. D779   Heckstall-Smith, Anthony. *The Fleet that Faced*
      .F7H4 *Both Ways*. London: Blond, 1963. The Vichy
             fleet.

2745. D744   Higgins, Trumbull. *Winston Churchill and the*
      .H5   *Second Front, 1940-1943*. N.Y.: Oxford UP, 1957.

2746. D770   Hinsley, Francis H. *Hitler's Strategy: The*
      .H5   *Naval Evidence*. Cambridge: UP, 1951.

2747. DA89   _____. *Command of the Sea: The Naval Side*
      .H5   *of British History from 1918 to the End of the*
             Second World War. London: Christophers, 1950.

2748. UF525 Hogg, Ian V. *German Secret Weapons of World*
      .G3H6 *War II*. N.Y.: Arco, 1970. 70 pp.

2749. D766   Howard, Michael. *The Mediterranean Strategy in*
      .H6   *the Second World War*. N.Y.: Praeger, 1968.

2750. D743   _____. *Grand Strategy: August 1942 to Sep-*
      .B83   *tember 1943*. James R.M. Butler, ed. *Grand*
             Strategy: History of the Second World War.
             United Kingdom Military series, London: HMSO,
             1957-1972. Vol. 4.

2751. D771   Humble, Richard. *Hitler's High Seas Fleet*.
      .H77   N.Y.: Ballantine, 1971.

2752. D757   Irving, David J.C. *Hitler's War*. N.Y.: Viking,
      .I69   1977.

2753. D779
.R9
I813

Isakov, Ovan S. *The Red Fleet in the Second World War*. London: Hutchinson, 1947.

2754. D766
.82.J27

Jackson, William G.F. *The Battle for North Africa*. N.Y.: Mason/Charter, 1976.

2755. D763
.I8J25

_____. *Battle For Italy*. London: Batsford, 1967.

2756. D771
.J27

James, William M. *The British Navies in the Second World War*. London: Longmans, Green, 1946.

2757. D810
.C88J66

Jones, Reginald. *The Wizard War: British Scientific Intelligence, 1939-1945*. N.Y.: Coward, McCann & Geoghegan, 1978.

2758. D772
.S35K45

Kemp, Peter. *Escape of the* Scharnhorst *and* Gneisenau. Annapolis, Md.: NIP, 1975.

2759. D771
.K38
1957a

_____. *Key to Victory: The Triumph of British Sea Power in World War II*. Boston: Little Brown, 1957.

2760. D772
.B5K46

Kennedy, Ludovic. *Pursuit: The Chase and Sinking of the Battleship* Bismarck. N.Y.: Viking, 1974. The best account to date.

2761. DA65
.K4

Keyes, Admiral of the Fleet Lord. *Amphibious Warfare and Combined Operations*. Cambridge: UP, 1943.

2762. D779
.N4K72

Kroese, A. *The Dutch Navy at War*. London: Allen & Unwin, 1945.

2763. D756.5
.D5L4

Leasor, James. *Green Beach*. N.Y.: Morrow, 1975. World War II commando raid to seize German radar stations.

2764. VA503
.L4513

LeMasson, Henri. *The French Navy*, 2 vols. London: Macdonald, 1969.

2765. DS810
.S7L43

Lewin, Ronald. *Ultra Goes to War*. N.Y.: McGraw-Hill, 1979.

2766. DA566
.9.C5L46

_____. *Churchill as War Lord*. N.Y.: Stein & Day, 1973.

2767. D743
.L514

Liddell-Hart, Basil H. *History of the Second World War*. N.Y.: Putnam, 1970.

2768. D763   Maass, Walter B. *The Netherlands at War, 1940-*
       .N4M3   *1945*. London: Abelard-Schuman, 1970.

2769. DA89.1   Macintyre, Donald G.F.W. *Fighting Admiral: The*
       .86M3   *Life and Battles of Admiral of the Fleet Sir*
                     James Somerville. London: Evans, 1961.

2770. D766.99   Marder, Arthur. *Operation "Menace": The Dakar*
       .S4M37   *Expedition and the Dudley North Affair*. London:
                     Oxford UP, 1976.

2771. D784   Mars, Alastair. *British Submarines at War,*
       .G7M26   *1939-1945*. London: Kimber, 1971; Annapolis,
                     Md.: NIP, 1971.

2772. D810   Masterman, John C. *The Double-Cross System in*
       .S7M28   *the War of 1939 to 1945*. New Haven: YUP, 1972.
                     The care and cure of double agents.

2773. D770   Masters, Davis. *Epics of Salvage*. Boston:
       .M3   Little, Brown, 1954.

2774. D800   Medlicott, William N. *The Economic Blockade.*
       .M4   *History of the Second World War*, 2 vols. United
                     Kingdom Series. London: HMSO, 1952-1959.

2775. D787   Middleton, Drew. *The Sky Suspended: The Battle*
       .M5   *of Britain*. London: Secker & Warburg, 1960.

2776. D772   Mohr, Ulrich. Atlantis: *The Story of a German*
       .A74M58   *Surface Raider*. London: Laurie, 1955.

2777. D810   Montagu, Ewen. *Beyond Top Secret Ultra*. N.Y.:
       .C88M66   Coward, McCann & Geoghegan, 1978.

2778. D763   Moulton, James L. *A Study of Warfare in Three*
       .N6M68   *Dimensions: The Norwegian Campaign of 1940*.
                     Athens: Ohio UP, 1968.

2779. D771   Muggenthaler, August K. *German Raiders of World*
       .M83   *War II*. Englewood Cliffs, N.J.: Prentice-Hall,
                     1977.

2780. D786   Newton, Don, and A. Cecil Hampshire. *Taranto*.
       .N49   London: Kimber, 1959.

2781. D772   Ogden, Michael. *The Battle of North Cape*. Lon-
       .S3504   don: Kimber, 1962. Sinking of the *Scharnhorst*.

2782. DC396   Osgood, Samuel M., comp. *The Fall of France,*
      .08   *1940: Causes, and Responsibilities.* Boston:
                     Heath, 1966.

2783. V65.C85   Pack, S.W.C. *Cunningham the Commander.* Lon-
      .P3   don: Batsford, 1974.

2784. D766.7   _____. *The Battle of Crete.* Annapolis, Md.:
      .C7P24   NIP, 1973.

2785. D27   _____. *Sea Power in the Mediterranean.* Lon-
      .P2   don: Barker, 1971.

2786. D775.5   _____. *The Battle of Matapan.* N.Y.: Mac-
      .M3P3   millan, 1961.

2787. D772   Peillard, Léonce. *U-boats to the Rescue: The*
      .L23   *Laconia Incident.* London: Cape, 1963. After
                     U-boats rescued survivors of the *Laconia,*
                     Dönitz forbade submarines from rescuing sur-
                     vivors.

2788. D772   _____. *Sink the* Tirpitz. N.Y.: Putnam,
      .T5P413   1968.

2789. D766.82   Pendar, Kenneth W. *Adventure in Diplomacy:*
      .P4   *Our French Dilemma.* N.Y.: Dodd, Mead, 1945.
                     Anglo-American relations with Darlan and then
                     de Gaulle.

2790. D763   Perowne, Stewart H. *The Siege Within the Walls:*
      .M3P4   *Malta, 1940-1943.* London: Hodder and Stoughton,
                     1970.

2791. D802   Petrow, Richard. *The Bitter Years: The Inva-*
      .D4P45   *sion and Occupation of Denmark and Norway,*
                     April 1940-May 1945. N.Y.: Morrow, 1974.

2792. D771   Potter, John D. *Fiasco: The Breakout of the*
      .P64   *German Battleships.* N.Y.: Stein & Day, 1970.
                     Scharnhorst and *Gneisenau* and the cruiser
                     Prinz Eugen in World War II.

2793. DA89   Pound, Reginald. *Evans of the Broke: A*
      .1.M6P6   *Biography of Admiral Lord Mountevans.* N.Y.:
                     Oxford UP, 1963. Destroyers in World War I.

2794. DD231.R17   Raeder, Erich. *My Life: Grand Admiral Erich*
      A313   *Raeder.* Annapolis, Md.: USNI, 1960.

2795. DD231   _____. *Struggle for the Sea*. London: Kimber,
      .R17   1959.
      A3132

2796. D811.5   Reynolds, Quentin. *Dress Rehearsal: The Story
      R38   of Dieppe*. N.Y.: Random House, 1943.

2797. D775   Ritchie, Lewis A.C. *East of Malta, West of
      .G7   Suez: The Official Admiralty Account of the
             Mediterranean Fleet, 1939-1943*. Boston: Little,
             Brown, 1944.

2798. D771   Roskill, Stephen W. *The War at Sea, 1939-1945*,
      .R69   3 vols. London: HMSO, 1954-1956. Vol.1. The
             Defensive; Vol. 2. The Period of Balance; Vol.
             3. The Offensive.

2799. D756.5   Ruge, Friedrich. *Rommel in Normandy: Reminis-
      .N6R813   cences by Friedrich Ruge*. San Rafael, Calif.:
             Presidio, 1979.

2800. D779   _____. *The Soviets as Naval Opponents 1941-
      .R9R84   1945*. Annapolis, Md.: NIP, 1979.

2801. D770   _____. *Der Seekrieg: The German Navy's Story*,
      .R833   *1939-1945*. Annapolis, Md.: USNI, 1957.

2802. D770   Schofield, Brian B. *Operation Neptune*. Annapo-
      .S38   lis, Md.: NIP, 1974.

2803. D786   _____. *The Attack on Taranto*. Annapolis,
      .S365   Md.: NIP, 1973.

2804. D772   _____. *Loss of the* Bismarck. Annapolis, Md.:
      .B5S36   NIP, 1972. A brief account.

2805. HE823   _____, and L.F. Martyn. *The Rescue Ships*.
      .S3   Edinburgh: Blackwood, 1968.

2806. D779   Schull, Joseph. *The Far Distant Ships. An Of-
      .C2S27   ficial Account of Canadian Naval Operations in
             the Second World War*. Ottawa: Edmund Cloutier,
             King's Printer, 1952.

2807. D775.5   Seth, Ronald. *Two Fleets Surprised: The Story
      .M3S4   of the Battle of Cape Matapan*. London: Bles,
             1960.

2808. D772 Shirer, William L. *The Sinking of the* Bismarck.
   .B5S5 N.Y.: Random House, 1962. A fairly brief account by the famous reporter on Hitler's Reich.

2809. D771 Showell, Jak M. *The German Navy in World War*
   .S55 *II.* Annapolis, Md.: NIP, 1979.

2810. V859 _____. *U-Boats under the Swastika: An Introduction to German Submarines, 1939-1945.* London: Ian Allan, 1974.
   .G3S5

2811. Q127 Simon, Leslie E. *German Research in World War*
   .G3S5 *II.* N.Y.: Wiley, 1947.

2812. DA585 Slessor, John C. *The Central Blue: Recollections and Reflections.* London: Cassell, 1956. Commander in chief, Coastal Command, in World War II.
   .S58A3

2813. D763 Smith, Peter, and Edwin Walker. *The Battles of the Malta Striking Forces.* Annapolis, Md.: NIP, 1974.
   .M3S58

2814. D771 Smith, Peter C. *The Great Ships Pass: British Battleships at War 1939-1945.* Annapolis, Md.: NIP, 1978.
   .S6

2815. D748 Snell, John L. *Illusion and Necessity: The Diplomacy of Global War.* Boston: Houghton Mifflin, 1963.
   .S57

2816. D810 Stevenson, William. *A Man Called Intrepid: The Secret War.* N.Y.: Harcourt Brace Jovanovich, 1976.
   .S8S85

2817. D766.7 Stewart, I.McD.G. *The Struggle for Crete....* London: Oxford UP, 1966.
   .C7S734

2818. D766.82 Strawson, John. *The Battle for North Africa.* N.Y.: Scribner, 1969.
   .S68

2819. D766.7 Thomas, David A. *Nazi Victory: Crete 1941.* N.Y.: Stein & Day, 1942.
   .C7T46

2820. D756.5 Townsend, Peter. *Duel of Eagles.* London: Weidenfeld & Nicolson, 1970. Battle of Britain.
   .B7T69

2821. D771 Tuleja, Thaddeus V. *Twilight of the Sea Gods.* N.Y.: Norton, 1958. The men, ships, and battles of the German Navy in World War II.
   .T74

2822. D756.5   Turnbull, Patrick. *Dunkirk: Anatomy of Dis-*
      .D8T87   *aster*. N.Y.: Holmes & Meier, 1978.

2823. D771   Turner, John L. *Service Most Silent: The Navy's*
      .T8   *Fight Against Enemy Mines*. London: Harrap,
                1955. Heavy on World War II.

2824. D771   Von der Porten, Edward P. *The German Navy in*
      .V65   *World War II*. N.Y.: Ballantine, 1969. An
                excellent account.

2825. DA87.1   Warner, Oliver. *Admiral of the Fleet, Cunning-*
      .C8W3   *ham of Hyndhope: the Battle for the Mediter-*
                ranean. Columbus: Ohio State UP, 1967.

2826. D784   Warren, Charles E.T. *Midget Raiders: The War-*
      .G7W3   *time Story of Human Torpedoes and Midget Sub-*
                marines. N.Y.: Sloane, 1954.

2827. D772   Watts, Anthony J. *Loss of the* Scharnhorst.
      .S35W3   Annapolis, Md.: USNI, 1970. A brief but de-
                tailed account.

2828. D780   Werner, Herbert. *Iron Coffins: A Personal Ac-*
      .W45   *count of the German U-boat Battles of World*
                War II. N.Y.: Holt, 1969.

2829. D811   Weygand, M., and J. Weygand. *The Role of*
      .W443   *General Weygand*. London: Eyre & Spottiswoode,
                1948.

2830. D771   Wheatley, Roland. *Operation Sea Lion*. Oxford:
      .W38   Clarendon P., 1958.

2831. D810   Wilhelm, Maria. *The Man Who Watched the Rising*
      .S8Z39   *Sun: The Story of Admiral Ellis M. Zacharias*.
                N.Y.: Watts, 1967.

2832. D770   Wilkinson, Burke. *By Sea and By Stealth*. N.Y.:
      .W5   Coward-McCann, 1956. Naval operations, World
                War II.

2833. D743   Wilmot, Chester. *The Struggle for Europe*
      .W53   *[1939-1945]*. London: Collins, 1952.

2834. D756   Wilt, Alan F. *The Atlantic Wall: Hitler's De-*
      .W58   *fenses in the West, 1941-1944*. Ames: Iowa
                State UP, 1975.

2835. D810   Winterbotham, Frederick W. *The Ultra Secret*.
      .C88W46   London: Weidenfeld & Nicolson, 1974.

2836. D771   Winton, J., pseud., ed. *The War at Sea, 1939-*
      .W42   *1945: The British Navy in World War II*. Lon-
              don: Hutchinson, 1967.

2837. D771   Woodward, David. *The Secret Raiders: The Story*
      .W58   *of the Operations of the German Armed Merchant*
              Raiders in the Second World War. London: Kim-
              ber, 1955. Involved were the *Atlantis*, *Orion*,
              Widder, *Thor*, *Pinguin*, *Komet*, and *Kormoran*.

2838. Q143   Zuckerman, Solly. *From Apes to Warlords*. N.Y.:
      .Z8Z8   Harper & Row, 1978. Bombing analysis World
              War II.

DOCUMENTS

2839.   Stafford, David A.T. "Ultra: and the British
              Official Histories: A Documentary Note," MA
              42 (2-78):29-31.

DISSERTATIONS AND THESES

2840. E748   Holmes, James H. "Admiral Leahy in France,"
      .L4H65 George Washington U., 1974.

2841. D753   LeBeau, John J. "Civilian Military-Political
      .L4   Leadership in Wartime: Roosevelt, the Military,
              and the Second Front Decision," U. of Massa-
              chusetts, 1977.

ARTICLES

2842.   Ambrose, Stephen E. "Applied Strategy of World
              War II," NWCR 22 (May 1970):62-70.

2843   _____. "Grand Strategy of World War II,"
              NWCR 22 (Apr. 1970):62-70.

2844.   Anderson, Bern. "The U.S. Navy's Attitude on
              Convoys," USNIP 83 (July 1957):782-83.

2845.   Armstrong, Hamilton F. "The Downfall of
              France," FA 19 (Oct. 1940):55-144.

2846.   Ashley, L.R.N. "The Royal Air Force and Sea
              Mining in World War II," AUQR 14 (Summer 1963):
              38-48.

2847.   Assmann, K. "The Invasion of Norway," MR 32
              (Feb. 1953):92-106.

2848.   Auphan, Paul. "The French Navy Enters World
                  War II," USNIP 82 (1956):592-601.

2849. G525   Baldwin, Hanson. "Sea Raider: The Life and
       .B255   Death of the *Admiral Graf Spee*, 1939," in his
                  Sea Fights and Shipwrecks. GCNY: Hanover House,
                  1955, pp. 207-221.

2850.   _____. "The Grand Strategy of the War," *New
                  York Times Mag*. (Feb. 23, 1941):13-15.

2851.   Belot, Raymond de. "The French Fleet in Being
                  [After the fall of France in 1940]," USNIP 79
                  (Oct. 1951):1056-67.

2852.   Bowling, R.A. "Escort-of-Convoy Still the Only
                  Way," USNIP 95 (Dec. 1969):46-56. Points out
                  errors made in the early days of the war.

2853.   Bragadin, M.A. "Mediterranean Convoys in World
                  War II," USNIP 76 (Feb. 1950):143-57.

2854.   Cooke, Henry D. "The Atlantic Convoys," USNIP
                  76 (Aug. 1950):862-69.

2855.   Cope, Harley. "--and Sank Same," USNIP 72 (July
                  1946):953-61. Aircraft vs U-boats.

2856.   Deutsch, Harold C. "The Influence of Ultra in
                  WWII," *Paramaters* 8 (Dec. 1978):2-15.

2857.   Durand de la Penne, Luigi. "The Italian Attack
                  on the Alexandria Naval Base," USNIP 82 (Feb.
                  1956):125-35.

2858.   Eastman, James N., Jr. "The Development of Big
                  Bombers," *Aerospace Historian* 25 (Winter 1978):
                  211-19.

2859.   Fairchild, Byron. "The Decision to Land United
                  States Forces in Iceland, 1941," in Kent R.
                  Greenfield, ed., *Command Decisions*. Wash.:
                  OCMH, 1960, pp. 73-97.

2860.   "Fiasco at Dakar," *Time* 36 (Oct. 7, 1940):32+

2861.   Fioravanzo, Guiseppe. "Italian Strategy in the
                  Mediterranean, 1940-1943," USNIP 84 (Sept.
                  1958):65-72.

2862.   _____. "The Japanese Military [Naval] Mis-
               sion to Italy in 1941," USNIP 81 (Jan. 1955):
               24-31.

2863.   Gerhard, T., and F. Bidingmair. "Exploits and
               End of the Battleship *Bismarck*," USNIP 84
               (July 1958):77-87.

2864.   Gullett, William M. "Malta: Focal Point of
               Mediterranean Control," USNIP 67 (Jan. 1941):
               15-20.

2865.   Hampshire, A. Cecil. "Triumph at Taranto,"
               USNIP 75 (Mar. 1959):71-79.

2866.   Kauffman, D.L. "German Naval Strategy in World
               War II," USNIP 80 (Jan. 1954):1-12.

2867.   Koch, Karl W., Jr. "The Luftwaffe and Malta: A
               Case of 'Hercules' Chained," *Aerospace His-
               torian* 23 (Summer 1976):94-100.

2868.   Langdon, Robert M. "Live Men Do Tell Tales,"
               USNIP 78 (Jan. 1952):17-22. Tales of U-boat
               actions.

2869.   Meckel, Hans. "Radar and the U-Boat," USNIP
               90 (Aug. 1964):123.

2870.   Melton, George E. "The Foreign Policy of Ad-
               miral Jean Darlan," in David H. White, ed.
               *Proceedings of the Conference on War and
               Diplomacy*. Charleston, S.C.: The Citadel,
               1976, pp. 102-07.

2871.   Morton, Louis. "Germany First: The Basic Con-
               cept of Allied Strategy in World War II," in
               Kent R. Greenfield, ed. *Command Decisions*.
               Wash.: OCMH, 1960, pp. 11-48.

2872.   O'Connell, Jerome A. "Radar and the U-Boat,"
               USNIP 89 (Sept. 1963):53-65.

2873.   Pattee, Richard S. "The Cruise of the German
               Raider *Atlantis*," USNIP 75 (Dec. 1949):1322-33.

2874.   Peter, Karl-Hinrich. "The Sinking of the
               Scharnhorst," USNIP 82 (Jan. 1956):48-53.

2875.   Puleston, W.D. "Strategy with a One-Ocean Navy," *Atlantic* 166 (Dec. 1940):707-12.

2876.   Reinicke, H.J. "German Surface Force Strategy in World War II," USNIP 83 (Feb. 1957):181-87.

2877.   _____. "The German Side of the Channel Dash," USNIP 81 (June 1955):637-46.

2878.   Robinson, Walton L. "Naval Actions, 1939-1941," USNIP 68 (Aug. 1942):1125-33.

2879.   Rogers, Lindsay. "National Defense: Plan or Patchwork?" FA 19 (Oct. 1940):1-11.

2880.   Ruge, Friedrich. "German Mine Sweepers in World War II," USNIP 78 (Sept. 1952):994-1003.

2881.   Sas, Anthony. "Military Campaigns: Strategy in the Mediterranean," MR 46 (Oct. 1966):3-7.

2882.   Saunders, Malcolm G. "Hitler's Admirals," RUSIJ 104 (Aug. 1959):320-30.

2883.   Schreiner, Charles W. "The Dieppe Raid--Its Origins, Aims, and Results," NWCR 25 (May-June 1973):83-98.

2884.   Seagren, Leonard W. "The Last Fuehrer [Dönitz]," USNIP 80 (May 1954):522-37.

2885.   Spilman, C.H. "Three Years of Warfare at Sea," USNIP 68 (Dec. 1942):1704-09.

2886.   _____. "What of the British Fleet if Britain Falls?" *Reader's Digest* 39 (Aug. 1941):1-5.

2887.   Zimmerman, John L. "Force in Readiness," USNIP 83 (Feb. 1957):165-71. The American occupation of Iceland.

FICTION

2888. D772 Forester, Cecil S. *The Last Nine Days of the*
   .B5F67 Bismarck. Boston: Little, Brown, 1959.

15

THE U.S. NAVY IN WORLD WAR II:
ATLANTIC THEATER

Because of the large number of works on the U.S. Navy and World War II in the Atlantic, titles are listed under the following categories: A. General; B. Northern Europe; C. The Mediterranean; D. Battle of the Atlantic.

A. GENERAL

BOOKS

2889. D755   Adams, Henry H. *1942: The Year That Doomed the*
       .4A4   *Axis.* N.Y.: McKay, 1967.

2890. D755   _____. *Years to Victory.* N.Y.: McKay, 1973.
       A6A3

2891. D755   _____. *Years of Expectation: Guadalcanal to*
       .5A3   *Normandy.* N.Y.: McKay, 1973.

2892. V825.3   Alden, John D. *Flush Decks and Four Pipes.*
       .A7   Annapolis, Md.: USNI, 1965.

2893. E836   Ambrose, Stephen E. *The Supreme Commander: The*
       .A83   *War Years of General Dwight D. Eisenhower.*
                  GCNY: Doubleday, 1970.

2894. D755   _____. *Eisenhower and Berlin, 1945: The De-*
       .7.A45   *cision to Halt at the Elbe.* N.Y.: Norton, 1967.

2895. D771   Ansel, Walter C. *Hitler Confronts England.*
       .A746   Durham: Duke UP, 1960.

2896. D815   Armstrong, Anne. *Unconditional Surrender: The*
       .A7   *Impact of the Casablanca Policy upon World War*
                  II. New Brunswick, N.J.: Rutgers UP, 1961.

2897. D743   Baldwin, Hanson W. *Battles Lost and Won: Great*
       .B34   *Campaigns of World War II.* N.Y.: Harper & Row,
                  1966.

2898. D773   Ballantine, Duncan S. *U.S. Naval Logistics in*
       .B34   *the Second World War.* Princeton: PUP, 1947.

2899. D750   Barker, Elisabeth. *British Policy in Southeast*
       .B37   *Europe in the Second World War.* N.Y.: Barnes
                  and Noble, 1976.

2900. Q127   Baxter, James P. *Scientists Against Time*. Bos-
       .U6B3   ton: Little, Brown, 1948.

2901. D810   Beesly, Patrick. *Very Special Intelligence:*
       .C88B43 *The Story of the Admiralty's Operational In-*
                telligence Centre, 1939-1945. GCNY: Doubleday,
                1978.

2902. D748   Beitzell, Robert. *The Uneasy Alliance: America,*
       .B35   *Britain, and Russia, 1941-1943*. Totowa, N.J.:
                Rowman & Littlefield, 1972.

2903. D770   Bennett, Geoffrey M. *Naval Battles of World*
       .B456   *War II*. London: Batsford, 1975.

2904. VG87   Berry, Erick, pseud. *Underwater Warriors: The*
       .B35   *Story of the American Frogmen [in World War*
                II]. N.Y.: McKay, 1967.

2905. VG87   Best, Herbert. *The Webfoot Warriors: The Story*
       B4   *of UDT, the U.S. Navy's Underwater Demolition*
                Team. N.Y.: John Day, 1962.

2906. JH257   Blum, John M. *From the Morgenthau Diaries:*
       .B6   *Years of War, 1941-1945*. Boston: Houghton
                Mifflin, 1967.

2907. D795   Bowman, Waldo G. *American Military Engineering*
       .U6B6   *in Europe, from Normandy to the Rhine....* N.Y.:
                McGraw-Hill, 1946.

2908. D756   Bradley, Omar N. *A Soldier's Story*. N.Y.: Holt,
       .B7   1951.

2909. D775   Bragadin, Marc' A. *The Italian Navy in World*
       .B683   *War II*. Annapolis, Md.: USNI, 1957.

2910. D790   Brereton, Lewis H. *The Brereton Diaries: The*
       .B67   *War in the Air in the Pacific, Middle East*
                and Europe, 3 Oct. 1941-8 May 1945. N.Y.:
                Morrow, 1946.

2911. D731   Brookhouser, Frank, ed. *This Was Your War: An*
       .B73   *Anthology of Great Writings from World War II*.
                GCNY: Doubleday, 1960.

2912. D810   Buchanan, Albert R. *Black Americans in World*
       .N4B82   *War II*. Santa Barbara, Calif.: Clio Books,
                1977.

2913. D769   _____. *The United States and World War II*,
      .B8   2 vols. N.Y.: Harper & Row, 1964.

2914. D790   _____. *The Navy's Air War: A Mission Com-*
      .A5   *pleted*. By the Aviation Hist. Unit, OP-519B,
                DCNO (Air). N.Y.: Harper, 1946.

2915. D773   Bunker, John G. *Liberty Ships: The Ugly Duck-*
      .B83   *lings of World War II*. Annapolis, Md.: NIP,
                1972.

2916. D774   Burns, Eugene. *Then There Was One: The U.S.S.*
      .E5B8   Enterprise *and the First Year of the War*. N.Y.:
                Harcourt Brace, 1944.

2917. D810   Carse, Robert. *The Long Haul: The United States*
      .T8C25   *Merchant Service in World War II*. N.Y.: Norton,
                1965.

2918. D773   _____. *Lifeline: The Ships and Men of Our*
      .C29   *Merchant Marine at War*. N.Y.: Morrow, 1943.

2919. D773   Carter, Worrall R., and Elmer E. Duvall. *Ships,*
      .C33   *Salvage and Sinews of War: The Story of Fleet*
                Logistics Afloat in Atlantic and Mediterranean
                Waters during World War II. Wash.: GPO, 1954.

2920. D756.5   Chatterton, Edward K. *The Epic of Dunkirk*.
      .D8C5   London: Hurst & Blackett, 1940.

2921. D73   Churchill, Winston. *The Second World War*. Vol.
      .C47   3, *The Grand Alliance* (1950); Vol. 4, *The Hinge*
                of Fate (1950); Vol. 5, *Closing the Ring* (1951).

2922. UA23   Condit, Kenneth W. *The History of the Joint*
                Chiefs of Staff and National Policy. Wash.:
                JCS, Joint Secretariat, Hist. Div., 1978.

2923. D769   Conn, Stetson, and others. *Guarding the United*
      .A533   *States and Its Outposts*. Wash.: OCMH, 1964.
      v. 12   Areas in the Western Hemisphere.
      pt. 2

2924. VC263   Connery, Robert H. *The Navy and the Industrial*
      .C65   *Mobilization in World War II*. Princeton: PUP,
                1951.

2925. V200   Cranwell, John P. *The Destiny of Sea Power and*
      .C7   *Its Influence on Land Power and Air Power*.
                N.Y.: Norton, 1942.

2926. VM455   Crump, Irving. *Our Tanker Fleet*. N.Y.: Dodd,
      .C7   Mead, 1952.

2927. D769   Davis, Kenneth S. *Experience of War: The
      .D3   United States in World War II*. GCNY: Double-
                 day, 1965.

2928. D753.2   Dawson, Raymond H. *The Decision to Aid Russia,
      .R9D3   1941*. Chapel Hill: UNCP, 1959.

2929. D781   Dönitz, Karl. *Memoirs: Ten Years and Twenty
      .D613   Days*. London: Weidenfeld & Nicolson, 1959.

2930. TL540   DuPre, Flint O. *Hap Arnold: Architect of
      .A69D86   American Air Power*. N.Y.: Macmillan, 1972.

2931. D743   Dupuy, Trevor N. *The Military History of World
      .7.D8   War II*, 19 vols. N.Y.: Watts, 1967. Particu-
                 larly pertinent are vols. 4. *The Naval War in
                 the West: Raiders*; 5. *The Naval War in the
                 West: Wolf Packs*; 11. *The Naval War in the
                 Pacific: The Rising Sun of Nippon*; 12. *The
                 Naval War in the Pacific: On to Tokyo*; and
                 19. *A Chronological Survey of World War II*.

2932. D769   Dziuban, Stanley W. *Military Relations between
      .A533   the United States and Canada, 1939-1945*. Wash.:
      v. 8   OCMH, 1959.
      pt. 4

2933. D743   Ehrman, John. *Grand Strategy: From August 1943
      .B83   to September 1944*. James R.M. Butler, ed.
                 *Grand Strategy: History of the Second World
                 War*. United Kingdom Military Series, 6 vols.
                 London: HMSO, 1957-1972. Vol. 5.

2934. D743   Eisenhower, Dwight D. *Crusade in Europe*. GCNY:
      .E35   Doubleday, 1948.

2935. D770   Elliott, Peter. *Allied Escort Ships in World
      .E58   War II*. London: Macdonald & Janes, 1977.

2936. V825.3   _____. *American Destroyer Escorts of World
      .E44   War II*. London: Almark, 1974.

2937. D780   Fane, Francis D. *The Naked Warriors*. N.Y.:
      .F3   Appleton, 1956. Navy frogmen in World War II.

2938. VM23   Fischer, Gerald J. *A Statistical Summary of*
      .F5   *Shipbuilding Under the U.S. Maritime Commission*
              During World War II. Wash.: GPO, 1949.

2939. D769   Gavin, James M. *Airborne Warfare*. Wash.: Inf.
      .345.G3 Jour., 1947.

2940. UG1242 Green, William *Famous Fights of the Second*
      .F5G70 *World War*, 2 vols. N.Y.: Hanover House, 1957-
              62. Excellent on the history and characteris-
              tics of all U.S. fighter aircraft during World
              War II.

2941. D754   Hayes, Carleton J.H. *Wartime Mission in Spain*
      .S7H3   *1942-1945*. N.Y.: Macmillan, 1945.

2942. V825   Hodges, Peter, and Norman Friedman. *Destroyer*
      .H6   *Weapons of World War 2*. Annapolis, Md.: NIP,
              1979. American and British.

2943. UF525   Hogg, Ian V. *German Secret Weapons of World*
      .G3H6   *War II*. N.Y.: Arco, 1970.

2944. D777   Hough, Richard A. *Death of the Battleship*.
      .H65   N.Y.: Macmillan, 1963. Examines the question
              of why three great sea powers of World War I
              and World War II continued to base their
              strategy on the doomed battleship.

2945. D743   Howard, Michael. *Grand Strategy: August 1942*
      .B83   *to September 1943*. James R.M. Butler, ed.
              History of the Second World War. United King-
              dom Military Series. London: HMSO, 1957-1972.
              Vol. 4.

2946. D769   Huie, William B. *Can Do: The Story of the*
      .55H8   *Seabees*. N.Y.: Dutton, 1945.

2947. D749   Huston, James A. *Out of the Blue: U.S. Army*
      .345.H87 *Airborne Operations in World War II*. Lafayette,
              Ind.: Purdue UP, 1972.

2948. D773   Ingraham, Reginald. *First Fleet: The Story of*
      .I55   *the U.S. Coast Guard at War*. Indianapolis:
              Bobbs-Merrill, 1944.

2949. QC773   Irving, David J.C. *The German Atomic Bomb*.
      .A1I69 N.Y.: Simon & Schuster, 1967.

2950. D779   Isakov, Ivan S. *The Red Fleet in the Second*
      .R19   *World War*. London: Hutchinson, 1947.
      I813

2951. OC782 Junetka, James W. *"City of Fire": Los Alamos*
      .8.U6L *and the Birth of the Atomic Age, 1943-1945.*
      674   Englewood Cliffs, N.J.: Prentice-Hall, 1978.

2952. D810   Keil, Sally V. *Those Wonderful Women in Their*
      .W7K43 *Flying Machines: The Unknown Heroines of World*
             War II. N.Y.: Rawson, Wade, 1979.

2953. D829   Kimball, Warren F. *Swords or Ploughshares? The*
      .G3K53 *Morgenthau Plan for Defeated Nazi Germany,*
             1943-1946. Phila.: Lippincott, 1976.

2954. D775   King, Ernest J. *Navy at War, 1941-1945: Offi-*
      .A5   *cial Report to the Secretary of the Navy....*
      1944   Wash.: Navy Dept., 1946.

2955. E182   King, Ernest J., and Walter M. Whitehill.
      .K53   *Fleet Admiral King: A Naval Record*. N.Y.:
             Norton, 1952.

2956. VM23   Lane, Frederic C. *Ships for Victory: A History*
      .L23   *of Shipbuilding Under the U.S. Maritime Com-*
             mission in World War II. Baltimore: Johns
             Hopkins P., 1951.

2957. D753   Langer, William L. *Our Vichy Gamble*. N.Y.:
      .L25   Norton, 1947.

2958. D769   Leahy, William D. *I Was There*. N.Y.: McGraw-
      .L4   Hill, 1950.

2959. D750   Leutze, James W. *Bargaining for Supremacy:*
      .L47   *Anglo-American Naval Collaboration, 1937-1941.*
             Chapel Hill: UNCP, 1977. The compelling story
             of the struggle for leadership between the U.S.
             and G.B. during the crucial period that pre-
             ceded America's entry into World War II.

2960. D743   Liddell Hart, Basil H. *History of the Second*
      .L514 *World War*. London: Cassell, 1970.

2961. D753   Louis, Robert W.R. *Imperialism at Bay: The*
      .L67   *United States and the Decolonization of the*
             British Empire, 1941-1945. N.Y.: Oxford UP,
             1977.

2962. D785   MacDonald, Charles B. *Airborne*. N.Y.: Ballan-
      .M26   tine, 1970.

2963. D756   _____. *The Mighty Endeavor: American Armed
      .M27   Forces in the European Theater in World War II*.
              N.Y.: Oxford UP, 1969.

2964. E748   McFarland, Keith D. *Harry H. Woodring*. Law-
      .W79M32 rence: UP of Kansas, 1975.

2965. D771   Macintyre, Donald. *The Naval War Against Hit-
      .M276   ler*. N.Y.: Scribner, 1971.

2966. D771   Martienssen, Anthony. *Hitler and His Admirals*.
      .M3   London: Secker & Warburg, 1948.

2967. D769   Matloff, Maurice. *Strategic Planning for Coali-
      .A533   tion Warfare, 1943-1944*. Wash.: OCMH, 1953.
      v. 4

2968. D769   _____, and Edwin M. Snell. *Strategic Plan-
      .A533   ning for Coalition Warfare, 1941-1942*. Wash.:
      v. 2   OCMH, 1953.

2969. D773   Mercey, Arch A., and Lee Groves, eds. *Sea,
      .M4   Surf, and Hell: The U.S. Coast Guard in World
              War II*. N.Y.: Prentice-Hall, 1945.

2970. E813   Millis, Walter, ed. *The Forrestal Diaries*.
      .F6   N.Y.: Viking, 1951.

2971. D766   Montgomery of Alamein, Bernard L. *El Alamein
      .82.M57 to the River Sangro, Normandy to the Baltic*,
              2 vols. in 1. N.Y.: St. Martin, 1974.

2972. D773   Morison, Samuel E. *The Two Ocean War: A Short
      .M62   History of the United States Navy in the
              Second World War*. Boston: Little, Brown, 1963.
              A distillation from his 15-volume study of the
              same subject.

2973. D743   _____. *Strategy and Compromise*. Boston:
      .M74   Little, Brown, 1958. Lectures.

2974. D769   Morton, Louis. *Strategy and Command: The First
      .A533   Two Years*. Wash.: OCMH, 1962.
      v. 2
      pt. 15

2975. D756   Mosley, Leonard. *Battle of Britain: World War*
      .5.B7M67   *II.* Alexandria, Va.: Time-Life Books, 1962.

2976. D816   O'Connor, Raymond G. *Diplomacy for Victory:*
      .024   *FDR and Unconditional Surrender.* N.Y.: Norton,
                  1971.

2977. E745   Pogue, Forrest. *George C. Marshall: Ordeal and*
      .M37P6   *Hope, 1939-1942.* N.Y.: Viking, 1966.

2978. E745   _____. *George C. Marshall: Organizer of Vic-*
      .M37P6   *tory, 1943-1945.* N.Y.: Viking, 1973.

2979. D769   _____. *The Supreme Command: U.S. Army in*
      .A533   *World War Two.* Wash.: GPO, 1954
      v. 3.

2980. D772   Powell, Michael. *Death in the South Atlantic:*
      .G7P63   *The Last Voyage of the* Graf Spee. N.Y.: Rine-
                  hart, 1957.

2981. D773   Roscoe, Theodore. *United States Destroyer Op-*
      .R6   *erations in World War II.* Annapolis, Md.: USNI,
                  1953.

2982. D783   _____. *United States Submarine Operations*
      .R6   *in World War II.* Annapolis, Md.: USNI, 1949.

2983. D771   Roskill, Stephen W. *The War at Sea,* 3 vols.
      .R68   in 4. London: HMSO, 1954-1961.

2984. VF23   Rowland, Buford, and William B. Boyd. *U.S.*
      .A62   *Navy Bureau of Ordnance in World War II.* Wash.:
                  GPO, 1953.

2985. D770   Ruge, Friedrich. *Der Seekrieg: The German*
      .R833   *Navy's Story, 1939-1945.* Annapolis, Md.: USNI,
                  1957.

2986. CD373   Schoenbrun, David. *The Three Lives of Charles*
      .G3S36   *de Gaulle.* N.Y.: Atheneum, 1965.

2987. DA566.9   Schoenfeld, Maxwell P. *The War Ministry of*
      .C5S36   *Winston Churchill.* Totowa, N.J.: Rowman and
                  Littlefield, 1972.

2988. D770   Schofield, Brian B. *Operation Neptune.* Annapo-
      .S38   lis, Md.: NIP, 1974. The naval side of Opera-
                  tion Overlord.

2989. VA454   _____. *British Sea Power: Naval Policy in*
      .S27   *the Twentieth Century.* London: Batsford, 1967.

2990. D773   Schofield, William G. *Eastward the Convoys.*
      .S4   Chicago: Rand McNally, 1965.

2991. VA23   Sherry, Michael S. *Preparing for the Next War:*
      .S47   *American Plans for Postwar Defense, 1941-1945.*
               New Haven: YUP, 1977.

2992. D810   Silvera, J.D. *The Negro in World War II.* Baton
      .N4S5   Rouge: 1946; rpt. N.Y.: Arco, 1969.

2993. DA585   Slessor, John C. *The Central Blue: Recollec-*
      .S58A3   *tions and Reflections.* London: Cassell, 1956.
               Air operations, World War II.

2994. D753   Smith, Gaddis. *American Diplomacy During the*
      .S54   *Second World War, 1941-1945.* N.Y.: Wiley, 1965.

2995. D773   Smith, S.E. *The United States Navy in World War*
      .S6   *II.* N.Y.: Morrow, 1966. A huge, excellent
               collection of short readings.

2996. D734   Snell, John L. *The Meaning of Yalta.* Baton
      .C7   Rouge: LSUP, 1956, 1965.

2997. D748   _____. *Illusions and Necessity: The Diplo-*
      .S57   *macy of Global War, 1939-1945.* Boston: Houghton
               Mifflin, 1963.

2998. DD247   Speer, Albert. *Inside the Third Reich....* N.Y.:
      .S63A313 Macmillan, 1970.

2999. D753   Steele, Richard W. *Roosevelt, Marshall, and the*
      .S73   *First Offensive: The Politics of Strategy Mak-*
               ing, 1941-1942. Baltimore: Johns Hopkins P.,
               1969.

3000. Q180   Stewart, Irvin. *Organizing Scientific Research*
      .U5S8   *for War: The Administrative History of the Of-*
               fice of Scientific Research and Development.
               Boston: Little, Brown, 1948.

3001. D748   Stoler, Mark A. *The Politics of the Second*
      .S76   *Front: American Military Planning and Diplomacy*
               in Coalition Warfare, 1941-1943. Westport,
               Conn.: Greenwood, 1977.

3002. DA69.3   Tedder, Arthur. *With Prejudice*. Boston: Little,
      .T35A3   Brown, 1966. Reminiscences of a British
                airmen.

3003. D767   Tillman, Barrett. *Hellcat: The F6F in World
      .T54   War II*. Annapolis, Md.: NIP, 1979.

3004. D767   _____. *The Dauntless Dive Bomber of World
      .T54   War II*. Annapolis, Md.: NIP, 1976.

3005. D755   Toland, John. *The Last 100 Days* [of Hitler's
      .7.T6   Reich]. N.Y.; Random House, 1965.

3006. DD247   Trevor-Roper, Hugh R. *The Last Days of Hitler*.
      .H5T7   London: Macmillan, 1956.

3007. D771   Tuleja, Thaddeus V. *Twilight of the Sea Gods*.
      .T74   N.Y.: Norton, 1958. The men, ships, and bat-
                tles of the German Navy in World War II.

3008. UA24   U.S. Joint Chiefs of Staff. *A Concise History
      .A675U45 of the Organization of the Joint Chiefs of
                Staff, 1942-1978*. Wash.: Hist. Div., Joint
                Secretariat, JCS, 1979. 58 pp.

3009. V214   Waddington, C.H. *OR in World War II: Opera-
      .W3   tional Research Against the U-boat*. London:
                Elek, 1973.

3010. HC106   Walton, Francis. *The Miracle of World War II:
      .4.W296   How American Industry Made Victory Possible*.
                N.Y.: Macmillan, 1956.

3011. UG633   Warren, John C. *Airborne Operations in World
      .A37784   War II: European Theater*. USAF Hist. Div.,
                Research Studies Institute, AU, 1956.

3012. D769   Watson, Mark. *Chief of Staff: Prewar Plans
      .A533   and Preparations*. Wash.: OCMH, 1950.
      v. 4

3013. D770   Weichold, Eberhard. *German Surface Ships:
      .W452   Policy and Operations in World War II*. Wash.:
                ONI, 1946. By a vice-admiral of the former
                German Navy.

3014. D773   Willoughby, Malcolm F. *The U.S. Coast Guard
      .W48   in World War II*. Annapolis, Md.: USNI, 1957.

3015. D743   Wilmot, Chester. *The Struggle for Europe* [1939-
     .W53   1945]. London: Collins, 1952.

3016. D810   Winterbotham, F.W. *The Ultra Secret*. N.Y.:
     .C88W56 Harper, 1975. British unscrambling of German
                 codes.

3017. D771   Winton, John, pseud. *Air Power at Sea, 1939-*
     .W42   *1945*. N.Y.: Crowell, 1976.

3018. Q143   Zuckerman, Solly. *From Apes to Warlords*. N.Y.:
     .Z8Z8   Harper & Row, 1978. Bombing analysis, World
                 War II.

DOCUMENTS

3019. D769   Buchanan, A. Russell. *The United States and*
     .B82   *World War II: Military and Diplomatic Docu-*
                 ments. Columbia: U. of South Carolina P., 1972.
                 Also a Harper Torchbook. Especially useful
                 for its technological slant.

3020. JX233   U.S. Department of State. *The Conferences at*
     .A31   *Cairo and Teheran, 1943*, 6 vols. Wash.: GPO,
                 1961. Includes Conferences at Washington,
                 1941-1942; at Washington and Quebec, 1942-
                 1943; at Quebec, 1944; and at Berlin (Potsdam),
                 1945.

3021. D785   U.S. Strategic Bombing Survey. *Overall Report*
     .U6   *(European War), September 30, 1945*. Wash.:
                 USSBS, 1945.

3022. D735   U.S. Department of State. *The Axis in Defeat:*
     .U6A53 *A Collection of Documents of American Policy*
                 toward Germany and Japan. Wash.: Department
                 of State, 1945.

3023.   U.S. Navy Department. Bureau of Ships. *Adminis-*
                 trative History, First Narrative, 4 vols.
                 Wash.: Bureau of Ships, 1954.

3024. D785   *U.S. Strategic Bombing Survey*. Wash.: USSBS,
                 1945-1947.

DISSERTATIONS AND THESES

3025.   Holmes, James H. "Admiral [William D.] Leahy
                 in Vichy France, 1940-1942," George Washington
                 U., 1974.

3026. D829 Knox, Robert S. "High Level Planning in the
      .G3K58 United States Regarding Germany, 1941-1946,"
              Georgetown U., 1949.

ARTICLES

3027. Allen, Jerome L. "Leaves from a Greenland
       Diary," USNIP 68 (Feb. 1942):201-08. By a
       witness during the early days of American
       occupation.

3028. Baldwin, Hanson W. "America at War: December
       1942-May 1943," FA 21 (July 1943):606-17.

3029. _____. "America at War: The First Year,"
       USNIP 69 (Mar. 1943):425-32.

3030. _____. "America at War: The First Year,"
       FA 21 (Jan. 1943):197-210.

3031. Balfour, Michael. "The Origin of the Formula:
       Unconditional Surrender in World War II,"
       Armed Forces and Society 5 (Winter 1979):281-
       301.

3032. Black, Henry. "Hopes, Fears, and Premonitions:
       The French Navy, 1940-1942," *South. Q.* 8 (Apr.
       1970):47-71. American and British maneuvering
       to keep the French fleet out of German hands.

3033. Brooks, Russell. "The Unknown Darlan," USNIP
       81 (Aug. 1955):879-92.

3034. "The Bureau of Ships," USNIP 75 (July 1949):
       813-21.

3035. Coakley, Robert W. "The Persian Corridor as a
       Route for Aid to the U.S.S.R. (1942)," in Kent
       R. Greenfield, ed., *Command Decisions*. Wash.:
       OCMH, 1960, pp. 154-81.

3036. Cope, Harley F. "Play Ball, Navy," USNIP 69
       (Oct. 1943):1311-18. U.S. naval operations in
       North Africa.

3037. Cowie, John S. "The Role of the U.S. Navy in
       Mine Warfare," USNIP 91 (Jan. 1965):52-63.

3038. *Croizat, Victor J. "The Marines' Amphibian,"
       MCG 37 (June 1953):40-49. The Amtrack.

3039.   Dater, Henry M. "The Development of the Escort
            Carrier," MA 12 (Summer 1948):79-90. Covers
            both Britain and the U.S.

3040.   Davis, Henry F.D. "Building Major Combatant Ships
            in World War II," USNIP 73 (May 1947):565-79.

3041.   _____. "Building U.S. Submarines in World
            War II," USNIP 72 (July 1946):933-39.

3042.   Eckelmeyer, Edward H., Jr. "The Story of the
            Self-Sealing [Aircraft] Tank," USNIP 72 (Feb.
            1946):205-19.

3043.   Eliot, George F. "Against a Separate Air Force:
            The Record," FA 20 (Oct. 1941):30-48.

3044.   Elting, John R. "World War II," Ency. Am.,
            1979, 29:364-533.

3045.   Etzold, Thomas H. "Why America Fought Germany
            in World War II," Warren F. Kimball, ed. Ameri-
            can Diplomacy in the Twentieth Century. St.
            Louis: Forum, 1980. No. 5.

3046.   Furer, Julius A. "Naval Research and Develop-
            ment in World War II," Jour. of the Am. Soc.
            of Naval Engineers, 62 (Feb. 1950):21-53.

3047.   Glennon, A.N. "The Weapon That Came Too Late,"
            USNIP 86 (Mar. 1961):85-93. The German type
            XXI U-boat.

3048.   Gray, James S. "Development of Naval Night
            Fighters in World War II," USNIP 74 (July
            1948):847-51.

3049.   Halsey, Ashley, Jr., "The CVL's Success Story,"
            USNIP 72 (Apr. 1946):523-31.

3050.   *Heinl, Robert D. "Naval Gunfire: Scourge of the
            Beaches," USNIP 71 (Nov. 1945):1309-13.

3051.   *_____. "Naval Gunfire Support in Landings,"
            MCG 29 (Sept. 1945):40-43.

3052.   Herring, George C., Jr. "Lend-Lease to Russia
            and the Origins of the Cold War, 1944-1945,"
            JAG 56 (June 1959):93-114.

3053. Hessler, William H. "The Carrier Task Force in World War II," USNIP 71 (Nov. 1945):1271-81.

3054. Hill, Perry C. "Love Charley Item," USNIP 71 (June 1945):675-79. Development of the LCI.

3055. Ide, John M. "Sonar: Secret Weapon of the Sea," USNIP 73 (Apr. 1947):439-43.

3056. Loeb, Leonard B. "Naval Research in Peace and War," USNIP 71 (Oct. 1945):1169-91.

3057. Leoning, Grover. "Ships over the Sea: Possibilities and Limitations of Air Transport in War," FA 20 (Apr. 1942):489-502. By an aviation pioneer.

3058. *McMillian, Ira E. "The Development of Naval Gunfire Support of Amphibious Operations," USNIP 74 (Jan. 1948):1-15.

3059. U27 Matloff, Maurice. "American Leadership in World
      .M48 War II," *Proceedings of the Fourth Military History Symposium, U.S. Air Force Academy, 1970.* Colorado Springs, Colo.: USAF Academy, 1973.

3060. May, Ernest R. "The United States, the Soviet Union, and the Far Eastern War," PHR 24 (May 1955):153-74. Supports the thesis that military necessity was responsible for Roosevelt's decision to bring Russia into the Pacific War.

3061. Milkman, Raymond H. "Operations Research in World War II," USNIP 94 (May 1968):78-83.

3062. Mitchell, Donald W. "Building a Seven Seas Navy," USNIP 71 (May 1945):507-13.

3063. Moran, E.M. "The Patrol Plane Controversy," USNIP 69 (July 1943):939-48.

3064. Mosely, Philip E. "Iceland and Greenland: An American Problem," FA 18 (July 1940):742-46.

3065. Muir, Malcolm, Jr. "Misuse of the Fast Battleship in World War II," USNIP 105 (Feb. 1979): 57-62.

3066. Pell, Claiborne, "The Coast Guard in the War," USNIP 67 (Dec. 1942):1744-46.

3067. Percival, Franklin G. "Wanted: A New Naval
       Development Policy," USNIP 69 (May 1943):
       655-66.

3068. Pogue, Forrest. "SHAEF: A Retrospect on Coali-
       tion Command," JMH 23 (Dec. 1951):329-35.

3069. Pratt, Fletcher. "The Torpedoes that Failed,"
       Atlantic 186 (July 1950):25-30.

3070. *Ramsey, Logan C. "The Aero-Amphibious Phase of
       the Present War," USNIP 69 (May 1943):695-701.

3071. Roop, Wendell P. "Technological Warfare," USNIP
       70 (Sept. 1944):1095-1106.

3072. *Sendall, W.R. "The Sea Flank Was Open: Lost
       Opportunities of Amphibious Warfare," MR 32
       (Mar. 1953):107-09. Openings he saw along the
       Dutch coast and elsewhere along the northern
       stretch of Hitler's West Wall.

3073. Steele, Richard W. "Political Aspects of
       American Military Planning, 1941-1942," MA
       35 (Apr. 1971):68-74.

3074. Steinhardt, Jacinto. "The Role of Operations
       Research in the Navy," USNIP 72 (May 1946):
       649-55.

3075. Stoler, Mark A. "The 'Second Front' and Ameri-
       can Fear of Soviet Expansion, 1941-1943," MA
       39 (Oct. 1975):136-41.

3076. Sumrall, Robert F. "Ship Camouflage (WWII):
       Deceptive Art," USNIP 11 (Jan. 1973):67-81,
       90-92.

3077. Uhlig, Frank R., Jr. "The New Battle Cruisers,"
       USNIP 75 (Jan. 1949):33-37. The *Alaska* class.

3078. Weller, Donald M. "Salvo-Splash! The Develop-
       ment of Naval Gunfire Support in World War
       II," USNIP 80 (Aug. 1954):839-49, (Sept. 1954):
       1011-21.

3079. *Willoughby, Malcolm F. "The Beach Pounders,"
       USNIP 83 (Aug. 1957):818-27. The part men of
       the Coast Guard played in amphibious landings.

3080.　　　　　　　Woodhouse, Henry. "U.S. Naval Aeronautic Poli-
　　　　　　　　　cies, 1904-42," USNIP 68 (Feb. 1942):161-75.

3081.　　　　　　　Wright. E.A. "The Bureau of Ships: A Study in
　　　　　　　　　Organization," *Jour. of the Am. Soc. of Naval
　　　　　　　　　Engineers* 71 (May 1959):315-27.

B. NORTHERN EUROPE

BOOKS

3082.　D756.5　　Army Times, Editor of. *D-day: The Greatest In-
　　　.W6D3　　　vasion.* N.Y.: Putnam, 1968.

3083.　D771　　　Berenbrok, Hans D., pseud. *Hitler's Naval War.*
　　　.B38813　　GCNY: Doubleday, 1974.

3084.　D756　　　Botting, Douglas. *The Second Front.* Alexandria,
　　　.5.N6B6　　Va.: Time-Life Books, 1978.

3085.　D774　　　Burns, Eugene. *Then There Was One: The U.S.S.
　　　.E5.B8　　　Enterprise and the First Year of the War.* N.Y.:
　　　　　　　　　Harcourt Brace, 1944.

3086.　D810　　　Cave Brown, Anthony. *Bodyguard of Lies.* N.Y.:
　　　.S7C36　　　Harper & Row, 1975.　D-day deception of Hitler.

3087.　D763　　　*Clifford, Kenneth J., ed. *The United States
　　　.I2U5　　　Marines in Iceland, 1941-1942.* Wash.: USMC, HQ,
　　　　　　　　　Hist. Div. 1970.　22 pp.

3088.　PR6053　　Cox, Richard H.F., ed. *Operation Sealion.* San
　　　.096906　　Rafael, Calif.: Presidio, 1977.

3089.　DA566　　Dreyer, Frederick C. *The Sea Heritage: A Study
　　　.5.D7　　　of Maritime Warfare.* London: Museum P., 1955.
　　　　　　　　　Assessment of ASW, World War II.

3090.　D770　　　Edwards, Kenneth. *Operation Neptune.* London:
　　　.E4　　　　Collins, 1946.　The naval side of Operation
　　　　　　　　　Overlord.

3091.　D756.5　　Eisenhower Foundation. *D-Day: The Normandy In-
　　　.N6D35　　vasion in Retrospect.* Lawrence: UP of Kansas,
　　　　　　　　　1971.

3092.　D756　　　Ellis, Lionel F., and others. *Victory in the
　　　.E39　　　West: The Battle of Normandy.* Vol. 1 of *His-
　　　　　　　　　tory of the Second World War.* London: HMSO,
　　　　　　　　　1962.

3093. D761   Ellsberg, Edward. *The Far Shore*. N.Y.: Dodd,
      .E35   Mead, 1960.

3094. E7451   Farago, Ladislas. *Patton: Ordeal and Triumph*.
      .P3F3   N.Y.: Obolensky, 1964.

3095. D786   Fleming, Peter. *Operation Sea Lion: The Pro-
      .F56   jected Invasion of England in 1940: An Account
                of the German Preparations and the British
                Counter-Measures*. N.Y.: Simon & Schuster, 1957.

3096. VB23   Furer, Julius A. *Administration of the Navy
      .F8   Department in World War II*. Wash.: GPO, 1959.

3097. D772   Gallagher, Thomas. *The X-Craft Raid*. N.Y.:
      .T5G33   Harcourt Brace Jovanovich, 1971. British
                midget submarines that put the *Tirpitz* out
                of action.

3098. D769   Gavin, James M. *On to Berlin: Battles of an
      .346/82d Airborne Commander*. N.Y.: Viking, 1978.
      .G38

3099. D790   Hansell, Haywood S., Jr. *The Air Plan that De-
      .H26   feated Hitler*. Atlanta: The author, 1972. Air
                Plans Division AWPD-1.

3100. D761   Hartcup, Guy. *Code Name Mulberry: The Planning,
      .H37   Building, and Operation of the Normandy Har-
                bours*. N.Y.: Hippocrene, 1977.

3101. D756   Howarth, David A. *D-Day: The Sixth of June,
      .H67   1944*. N.Y.: McGraw-Hill, 1959.

3102. D756   Ingersoll, Ralph. *Top Secret*. N.Y.: Harcourt
      .I5   Brace, 1946. Planning for Operation Overlord.

3103. Micro   *Intelligence Reports on the War in the Atlantic
                1942-1945*. Wilmington, Del.: Michael Glazier,
                1979.

3104. D785   Jackson, Robert. *Storm from the Skies: The
      .J33   Strategic Bombing Offensive, 1943-1945*. Lon-
                don: Barker, 1974.

3105. E836   Lyon, Peter. *Eisenhower: Portrait of the Hero*.
      .L96   Boston: Little, Brown, 1974.

3106. D756.5   Marshall, Samuel L.A. *Night Drop: The American
      .M6M3   Airborne Invasion of Normandy*. Boston: Atlan-
                tic Monthly P., 1962.

252

3107. D756   Michie, Allan A. *The Invasion of Europe: The*
      .M48   *Story Behind D-Day*. N.Y.: Dodd, Mead, 1964.

3108. D756   Montgomery, Field Marshal. *Normandy to the*
      .M58   *Baltic*. Germany: British Army of the Rhine,
               1946.

3109. DA69.3   _____. *Memoirs*. Cleveland: World, 1958.
      .M56A3

3110. D756   Morgan, Frederick. *Overture to Overlord*. GCNY:
      .M64   Doubleday, 1950. The planning for the cross-
               Channel invasion of the continent of Europe.

3111. D770   Norman, Albert. *Operation Overlord*, *Design*
      .N6   *and Reality: The Allied Invasion of Western*
               Europe. Harrisburg, Pa.: Military Service
               Pub. Co., 1952.

3112. E835   Parmet, Herbert S. *Eisenhower and the Ameri-*
      .P3   *can Crusades*. N.Y.: Macmillan, 1972.

3113. D761   Perrault, Gilles. *The Secret of D-Day*. Boston:
      .P393   Little, Brown, 1957.

3114. D774   Randall, Lewis V. *Bridgehead to Victory: Plans*
      .R2   *for the Invasion of Europe*. GCNY: Doubleday,
               Doran, 1943. Manpower, air, and naval power
               needed for assaulting various points on the
               European continent.

3115. D771   Robertson, Terence. *Channel Dash: The Drama of*
      .R57   *Twenty-four Hours*. N.Y.: Dutton, 1958. The run
               of the *Gneisenau*, *Scharnhorst*, and *Prinz Eugen*
               from French to Norwegian ports.

3116. D762   Robichon, Jacques. *The Second D-Day*. N.Y.:
      .P7R63   Walker, 1962. Invasion of the South of France.

3117. D756   Ryan, Cornelius. *The Longest Day: June 6, 1944*.
      .5N6R9   N.Y.: Simon & Schuster, 1959.

3118. D761   Stanford, Alfred. *Force Mulberry: The Planning*
      .S66   *and Installation of the Artificial Harbor Off*
               U.S. Normandy Beaches in World War II. N.Y.:
               Morrow, 1951.

3119.   Tregaskis, Richard W. *Invasion Diary*. N.Y.:
               Random House, 1944. One of many diaries, the
               last of which deals with Vietnam.

3120.   Ziemke, Earl F. *The German Northern Theatre of Operations 1940-1945*. Department of Army Pamphlet, no. 201271. Wash.: GPO, 1959.

DOCUMENTS

3121.   U.S. Navy Department. *Building the Navy's Bases in World War II: History of the Bureau of Yards and Docks and Civil Engineer Corps, 1940-1946*. 2 vols. Wash.: GPO, 1947.

3122.   U.S. Office of Scientific Research and Development, War Department and Navy Department. *U.S. Rocket Ordnance: Development and Use in World War II*. Wash.: GPO, 1946.

3123.   D785
       .U63   U.S. Strategic Bombing Survey. *Overall Report (European War), Sept. 30, 1945*. Wash.: USSBS, 1945.

3124.   U.S. War Department, Historical Division. *Omaha Beachhead, 6 June-13 June 1944*. Wash.: GPO, 1945.

ARTICLES

3125.   "Artificial Harbors Floated to France," USNIP 70 (Nov. 1944):1417-19.

3126.   Assmann, K. "Normandy, 1944," MR 34 (Feb. 1955):86-93.

3127.   Baldwin, Hanson W. "Amphibious Aspects of the Normandy Invasion," MCG 28 (Dec. 1944):34.

3128.   Clagett, John H. "Admiral H. Kent Hewitt, U.S. Navy. Part II. High Command," NWCR 28 (Fall 1975):60-86.

3129.   Cowie, John S. "British Mines and the Channel Dash," USNIP 84 (Apr. 1958):39-47.

3130.   Elsey, George M. "Naval Aspects of Normandy in Retrospect," in The Eisenhower Foundation, eds. *D-Day: The Normandy Invasion in Retrospect*. Lawrence: U. of Kansas P., 1971, pp. 170-97.

3131.   Karig, Walter. "One More River [the Rhine] to Cross," USNIP 71 (Oct. 1945):1193-1201.

3132.   _____, and C.L. Freeland. "Rhinos and Mul-
                         berries," USNIP 71 (Dec. 1945):1415-25.

3133.   Leighton, Richard M. "OVERLORD Revisited: An
                         Interpretation of American Strategy in the
                         European War, 1942-1944," AHR 48 (July 1963):
                         919-37.

3134.   _____. "Overlord versus the Mediterranean
                         at the Cairo-Tehran Conferences," in Kent R.
                         Greenfield, ed. *Command Decisions*. Wash.:
                         OCMH, 1960, pp. 255-86.

3135.   Lutes, Leroy. "Supply, World War II: for Eisen-
                         hower's First Crusade," *Antiaircraft Journ.* 95
                         (Nov.-Dec. 1952):4-8.

3136.   Moore, Rufus J. "Operation Pluto," USNIP 80
                         (May 1954):647-53. The acronym PLUTO stood
                         for Pipe Lines Under the Ocean, in this case
                         under the English Channel in 1944.

3137.   "Operation Neptune," USNIP 80 (June 1954):
                         672-85.

3138.   Pogue, Forrest C. "The Decision to Halt at
                         the Elbe," in Kent R. Greenfield, ed. *Command
                         Decisions*. Wash.: OCMH, 1960, pp. 479-92.

3139.   Wilkinson, Burke. "A *Tirpitz* Tale," USNIP 80
                         (Apr. 1954):374-83.

C. THE MEDITERRANEAN

BOOKS

3140. D766   Ansel, Walter C. *Hitler and the Middle Sea*.
       .A65   Durham: Duke UP, 1972.

3141. D770   Belot, Raymond de. *The Struggle for the Medi-
       .B453   terranean, 1939-1945*. Princeton: PUP, 1951.

3142. D756   Bliven, Bruce. *From Casablanca to Berlin: The
       .B55   War in North Africa and Europe, 1942-1945*.
                       N.Y.: Random House, 1965.

3143. D763   Blumenson, Martin. *Anzio: The Gamble that
       .I82   Failed*. Phila.: Lippincott, 1963.
       A55

3144. D744   *Burton, Earl. *By Sea and By Land: The Story Of*
       .B87   *Our Amphibious Forces*. N.Y.: Whittlesey House,
                      1944. Illustrated with photographs of the
                      landings in Sicily.

3145. D766   Clark, Mark W. *Calculated Risk*. N.Y.: Harper,
       .82.C5   1950. Politics of the North African invasion.

3146. D766.3   Crisp, R. *The Gods were Neutral: A Story of the*
       .C7   *Greek Campaign, 1941*. Totowa, N.J.: Rowman &
                      Littlefield, 1975.

3147. DA89.1   Cunningham of Hyndhope, Admiral of the Fleet,
       .C843   Viscount. *A Sailor's Odyssey*. London: Hutchin-
                      son, 1951.

3148. DC373   de Montmorency, Alec. *The Enigma of Admiral*
       .D35D4   *Darlan*. N.Y.: Dutton, 1943.

3149. D766.82   Ellsberg, Edward. *No Banners, No Bugles*. N.Y.:
       .E58   Dodd, Mead, 1949. War in North Africa:
                      Salvage.

3150. D776.82   Funk, Arthur L. *The Politics of Torch: The Al-*
       .F86   *lied Landings and the Algiers "Putsch," 1942*.
                      Lawrence: UP of Kansas, 1974.

3151. D786   Guedalla, Philip. *Middle East, 1940-1942: A*
       .G8   *Study in Air Power*. London: Hodder & Stoughton,
                      1944.

3152. D769   Howe, George F. *Northwest Africa: Seizing the*
       .A533   *Initiative in the West*. Wash.: OCMH, 1957.
       v. 11
       pt. 1

3153. U55   Irving, David J.C. *The Trail of the Fox: The*
       .R6178   *Search for the True Field Marshal Rommel*. N.Y.:
                      Dutton, 1977.

3154. D763.I82   Jackson, William G.F. *The Battle for Italy*.
       .R626   London: Batsford, 1967.

3155. DG498   Kogan, Norman. *Italy and the Allies*. Cambridge,
       .K6   Mass.: HUP, 1956.

3156. D766   Macintyre, Donald. *The Battle for the Mediter-*
       .M2   *ranean*. London: Batsford, 1964.

3157. D773　　　　Morison, Samuel E. *History of United States*
　　　　.M6　　　　*Naval Operations in World War II*. Boston:
　　　　　　　　　Houghton Mifflin, 1947-1962. Vol. 2. *Opera-*
　　　　　　　　　tions in North African Waters, Oct. 1942-June
　　　　　　　　　1943 (1947); Vol. 9. *Sicily, Salerno, Anzio,*
　　　　　　　　　Jan. 1943-June 1944 (1954).

3158. D744　　　　Murphy, Robert D. *Diplomat Among Warriors.*
　　　　.M87　　　　GCNY: Doubleday, 1964.

3159. D776　　　　Pack, S.W.C. *The Battle for North Africa*. N.Y.:
　　　　.82J27　　　Mason/Charter, 1976.

3160. D763　　　　Pond, Hugh. *Salerno*. Boston: Little, Brown,
　　　　.I8P65　　　1961.

3161. D786　　　　Schofield, Brian B. *The Attack on Taranto.*
　　　　.S365　　　　Annapolis, Md.: NIP, 1973.

3162. D763　　　　Smith, Peter C. *Battles of the Malta Striking*
　　　　.M3S58　　　*Forces*. Annapolis, Md.: NIP, 1974.

3163. D766　　　　_____, and Edwin Walker. *War in the Aegean.*
　　　　.S6　　　　　London: Kimber, 1974.

3164. D769　　　　Smyth, Howard M., and Albert N. Garland. *Sicily*
　　　　.A533　　　　*and the Surrender of Italy*. Wash.: OMCH, 1965.
　　　　v. 11
　　　　pt. 2

3165. D763　　　　Vaughan-Thomas, Wynford. *Anzio*. N.Y.: Holt,
　　　　.I82A63　　　1961.

3166. DG572　　　　Villari, Luigi. *The Liberation of Italy, 1943-*
　　　　.U53　　　　*1947*. London: Holborn, 1959.

3167. D763　　　　Wallace, Robert. *The Italian Campaign*. Alexan-
　　　　.I8W33　　　dria, Va.: Time-Life Books, 1978.

3168. DA8a.1　　　Warner, Oliver. *Admiral of the Fleet Cunningham*
　　　　.C8W3　　　　*of Hyndhope: The Battle for the Mediterranean.*
　　　　　　　　　Athens: Ohio UP, 1967.

3169. UG633　　　Warren, John C. *Airborne Missions in the Medi-*
　　　　.A37784　　*terranean, 1942-1945*. Wash.: USAF, Hist. Div.,
　　　　No. 97　　　1955.

257

3170. D754   Weber, Frank. *The Evasive Neutral: Germany,*
      .T8W42   *Britain, and the Quest for a Turkish Alliance*
               in the Second World War. Columbia: U. of
               Missouri P., 1979.

3171. D763   Werstein, Irving. *The Battle of Salerno.* N.Y.:
      .I82S25 Crowell, 1965.

DISSERTATIONS AND THESES

3172.   Simpson, Benjamin M., III. The [American] Navy
               and United States-French Relations, 1942-1944,"
               Fletcher School of Law and Diplomacy, 1968.

ARTICLES

3173.   Blumenson, Martin. "General Lucas at Anzio,"
               in Kent R. Greenfield, ed. *Command Decisions.*
               Wash.: OCMH, 1960, pp. 323-50.

3174.   Brooks, Russel M. "Casablanca: The French Side
               of the French," USNIP 77 (Sept. 1951):909-25.

3175.   Clagett, John H. "Admiral H. Kent Hewitt, U.S.
               Navy. Part II: High Command," NWCR 28 (Fall,
               1975):60-86.

3176.   Devers, Jacob L. "Operation Dragoon: The Inva-
               sion of Southern France," MA 10 (Summer 1946):
               3-41.

3177.   Feis, Herbert. "Oil for Spain: A Critical
               Episode of the War," FA 26 (Jan. 1948):377-99.

3178.   Funk, Arthur L. "Eisenhower, Giraud, and the
               Command of 'Torch,'" MA 35 (Oct. 1971):103-08.

3179.   Hewitt, Henry K. "Executing Operation Anvil-
               Dragoon," USNIP 80 (Aug. 1954):896-925.

3180.   _____. "Planning Operation Anvil-Dragoon,"
               USNIP 80 (July 1954):731-45.

3181.   _____. "The Allied Navies at Salerno: 'Op-
               eration Avalanche,' September 1943," USNIP 79
               (Sept. 1953):958-76.

3182.   . "Naval Aspects of the Sicilian Campaign: U.S. Naval Operations in the Northwestern African-Mediterranean Theater, March-August 1943," USNIP 79 (July 1953):704-23.

3183.   Lowry, F.J. "The Naval Side of Anzio," USNIP 80 (Jan. 1954):22-31.

3184.   Matloff, Maurice. "The ANVIL Decision: Crossroads of Strategy," in Kent R. Greenfield, ed. *Command Decisions*. Wash.: OCMH, 1960, pp. 383-400.

3185.   . "Was the Invasion of Southern France a Blunder?" USNIP 84 (July 1958):35-45.

3186.   Meyer, Leo J. "The Decision to Invade North Africa (TORCH)," in Kent R. Greenfield, ed. *Command Decisions*. Wash.: OCMH, 1960, pp. 173-98.

3187.   North, John. "Lessons of the North African Campaign," MA 8 (Fall 1944):161-68.

3188.   Richards, Guy, and John L. Zimmerman. "America's African Beachhead," USNIP 74 (Nov. 1948): 1386-95.

3189.   Richmond, Herbert W. "Seapower and the Italian Surrender," USNIP 70 (Feb. 1944):137-41.

3190.   "The Surrender of the Italian Fleet," *Engineer* 176 (July 17, 1943):712-13.

3191.   U.S. War Department, Hist. Div. *Anzio Beachhead*, 22 January-25 May 1944. Wash.: GPO, 1947.

D. BATTLE OF THE ATLANTIC

BOOKS

3192. D772   Brennecke, Hans J. *The* Tirpitz: *The Drama of*
      .T5B7   *the "Lone Queen of the North."* London: Hale, 1963.

3193. D772   . *The Battleship* Scheer. London: Kimber, 1956.
      .A2K713

3194. D771   Broome, John E. *Convoy Is to Scatter*. Totowa,
     .B653   N.J.: Rowman & Littlefield, 1972.

3195. D781   Chatterton, Edward K. *Commerce Raiders*. Lon-
     .C49   don: Hurst & Blackett, 1943.

3196. D590   _____. *Fighting the U-boats*. London: Hurst
     .C49   & Blackett, 1942.

3197. D773   Coale, Griffith B. *North Atlantic Patrol*. N.Y.:
     .C6   Farrar & Rinehart, 1942.

3198. D783   Farago, Ladislas. *The Tenth Fleet*. N.Y.: Oblen-
     .F3   sky, 1962. Admiral King's "think tank" on
               killing U-boats.

3199. D772   Frere-Cook, Gervis. *The Attacks on the* Tirpitz.
     .T5F7   Annapolis, Md.: NIP, 1973. It took four years
               and attacks by aircraft, midget submarines, and
               big bombs, the "Dambusters," to obliterate the
               ship.

3200. D782   Gallery, Daniel V. *Twenty Million Tons Under*
     .U18G3   *the Sea*. Chicago: Regnery, 1956.

3201. D773   Gibson, Charles D. *The Ordeal of Convoy NY*
     .G53   *119*.... N.Y.: South Street Seaport Museum,
               1973.

3202. D780   [Great Britain] Admiralty. *The Battle of the*
     .G72   *Atlantic: The Official Account of the Fight*
               Against the U-boats, 1939-1945. London: HSMO,
               1946.

3203. D773   Grenfell, Russell. *The* Bismarck *Episode*. N.Y.:
     .B5GV   Macmillan, 1949.

3204. D770   Gretton, Peter. *Crisis Convoy*. Annapolis, MD.:
     .G74   NIP, 1975. Readings about 6 escorts vs. 20
               U-boats.

3205. D781   Hoyt, Edwin P. *U-boats Offshore: When Hitler*
     .H69   *Struck America*. N.Y.: Stein & Day, 1978.

3206. D770   Hughes, Terry, and John Costello. *The Battle*
     .H83   *of the Atlantic*. N.Y.: Dial, 1977. 400
               photographs.

3207. D773   Karig, Walter. *Battle Report*, 7 vols. N.Y.:
     .K3   various publishers. Vol. 2. *The Atlantic War*.
               (Farrar, 1946.)

3208. D771   Knox, Collie. *Atlantic Battle*. London:
      .K56   Methuen, 1941.

3209. D772   Krancke, Theodor, and H.J. Brennecke. *Pocket*
      .A2K73 *Battleship: The Story of the* Admiral Scheer.
               N.Y.: Norton, 1958.

3210. VM365   Lent, Henry B. *Submariner: The Story of Basic*
      .L4   *Training at the Navy's Famed Submarine School*.
               N.Y.: Macmillan, 1962.

3211. V210   Lewis, David D. *The Fight for the Sea: The*
      .L4   *Past, Present and Future of Submarine Warfare*
               in the Atlantic. Cleveland: World, 1961.

3212. D784   Mars, Alastair. *British Submarines at War:*
      .G7M26 *1939-1945*. Annapolis, Md.: NIP, 1971.

3213. D770   Middlebrook, Martin. *Convoy*. N.Y.: Morrow,
      .M5   1977.

3214. D773   Morison, Samuel E. *History of United States*
      .M6   *Naval Operations in World War Two*. Boston:
               Houghton Mifflin, 1947-1962. Vol. 1. *The Battle*
               of the Atlantic, Sept. 1939-May 1943 (1947);
               Vol. 10. *The Atlantic Battle Won. May 1943-*
               May 1945 (1956).

3215. D771   Pope, Dudley. *'73 North: The Battle of the*
      .P6   *Barents Sea*. London: Weidenfeld & Nicolson,
               1958.

3216. D770   Rohwer, Jurgen. *The Critical Convoy Battles*
      .R59313 *of March, 1943*. Annapolis, Md.: NIP, 1977.
               By a German in a position in radio intelligence
               similar to Beesly's in Britain.

3217. D773   Roscoe, Theodore. *United States Submarine Op-*
      .R6   *erations in World War II*. Annapolis, Md.:
               USNI, 1948.

3218. D743   Salomon, Henry. *Victory at Sea*. GCNY: Double-
      .2.S28 day, 1959. From the NBC TV series.

3219. D773   Schofield, Brian B. *Eastward the Convoys*.
      .S4   Chicago: Rand McNally, 1965.

3220. D770   Seth, Ronald. *The Fiercest Battle: The Story*
      .S43   *of North Atlantic Convoy ONS 5, 22nd April-*
               7th May 1942. N.Y.: Norton, 1961.

3221.   Turner, Leonard C.F., and others. *War in the Southern Oceans*. N.Y.: Oxford UP, 1961. Available U. of Chicago.

3222.   D771   Woodward, David. *The Secret Raiders: The Story of the Armed Merchant Raiders in the Second World War*. N.Y.: Norton, 1965.
       .W58

3223.   D772   _____. *The* Tirpitz *and the Battle for the* North Atlantic. N.Y.: Norton, 1954.
       .T5W6

DISSERTATIONS AND THESES

3224.   Lundeberg, Philip K. "American Anti-Submarine Operations in the Atlantic, May 1943-May 1945," Harvard U., 1954.

ARTICLES

3225.   Assman, Kurt. "Why U-Boat Warfare Failed in World War II," FA 28 (July 1959):659-70.

3226.   Dater, Henry M. "Tactical Uses of Air Power in World War II: The Navy Experience," MA 14 (Winter 1950):192-200.

3227.   _____. "Development of the Escort Carrier," MA 12 (Summer 1948):79-90.

3228.   Eliot, George F. "The Submarine War," FA 21 (Apr. 1943):385-400.

3229.   Huston, James A. "Tactical Uses of Air Power in World War II: The Army Experience," MA 14 (Winter 1950):166-85.

3230.   Maycock, Thomas J. "Tactical Uses of Air Power in World War II: Notes on the Development of AAF Tactical Doctrine," MA 14 (Winter 1950): 186-91.

3231.   Norton, Douglas M. "The Open Secret: The U.S. Navy in the Battle of the Atlantic April-December 1941," NWCR 26 (Jan.-Feb. 1974): 63-73.

3232.   Stokesbury, James L. "1943: Invasion of Italy,"
                         AHI 12 (Dec. 1977):26-36.

FICTION

3233. PZ3   Carse, Robert. *The Beckoning Waters*. N.Y.:
      .C2383   Scribner, 1953. U.S. merchant marine in World
      Be   War II.

16

WORLD WAR II IN THE PACIFIC. PART I: FROM PEARL HARBOR TO GUADALCANAL

The titles herein are divided into: A. General; B. Pearl Harbor; C. Wake, Guam, and Loss of the Southern Resources Area; D. Early Allied Carrier Raids and the Battle of the Coral Sea; E. Battle of Midway; F. The Aleutians.

A. GENERAL

BOOKS

3234. D777 .A613

Albas, Andrieu D'. *Death of a Navy: The Fleets of the Mikado in the Second World War, 1941-1945.* London: Hale, 1957.

3235. D769.37 .3d.A8

*Aurthur, Robert R., and Kenneth Cohlmia. *The Third Marine Division in World War II.* Wash.: Inf. Jour. P., 1948.

3236. D767 .B38

Bateson, Charles. *The War with Japan.* East Lansing, Mich.: Michigan State UP, 1968.

3237. D773 .B4

Bell, Frederick J. *Condition Red: Destroyer Action in the South Pacific.* N.Y.: Longmans, 1943.

3238. D754 .A8B44

Bell, Roger J. *Unequal Allies: Australian-American Relations and the Pacific War.* Melbourne: Melbourne UP, 1977.

3239. E746 .C3B55

*Blankfort, Michael. *The Big Yankee: the Life of Carlson of the Raiders.* Boston: Little, Brown, 1947. A biography of Brigadier General Evans F. Carlson, USMC, with emphasis on his part in organizing and leading the 2d Marine Raider Battalion in World War II. Included are the experiences of Carlson as a guerrilla with the Chinese, from whom he learned much of value later incorporated into the methods of his raider battalion.

3240. D767 .B55

Bliven, Bruce. *From Pearl Harbor to Okinawa: The War in the Pacific, 1941-1945.* N.Y.: Random House, 1960.

3241. D770 .B75

Brown, David. *Carrier Operations in World War II*: Vol. 2: *The Pacific Navies, December 1941-February 1943.* London: Allan, 1974.

3242. D763 .S5B7

*Brown, John M. *The All Hands: An Amphibious Venture.* N.Y.: McGraw-Hill, 1943.

3243. V63   Buell, Thomas B. *The Quiet Warrior: A Biography*
       .S68B3   *of Admiral Raymond A. Spruance*. Boston:
                   Little, Brown, 1974.

3244. U313   Bywater, Hector C. *The Great Pacific War: A*
       .B8   *History of the American-Japanese Campaign of*
                   1931-33. London: Constable, 1925. Prediction
                   of the Pearl Harbor disaster and war in 1941.

3245. D769.537   Carter, Worrall R. *Beans, Bullets and Black*
       10th. C3   *Oil: The Story of Fleet Logistics Afloat in*
                   the Pacific During World War II. Wash.: GPO,
                   1953.

3246. D769.376   *Cass, Beven G. *History of the Sixth Marine*
       th.A5   *Division*. Wash.: Inf. Jour. P., 1948.

3247. E745   Chennault, Claire L. *Way of a Fighter: The*
       .C35A3   *Memoirs of Claire Lee Channault*. N.Y.: Putnam,
                   1949.

3248. E746   Clark, Joseph, and Clark G. Reynolds. *Carrier*
       .C55A3   *Admiral*. N.Y.: McKay, 1967. An autobiography
                   of Admiral Clark.

3249. D767   Coffey, Thomas M. *Imperial Tragedy: Japan in*
       .2.C6   *World War II, The First Days and the Last*.
                   N.Y.: World, 1970.

3250. D767   Collier, Basil. *The War in the Far East, 1941-*
       .C58   *1945: A Military History*. N.Y.: Morrow, 1969.

3251. VE23   *Condit, Kenneth W., and Edwin T. Turnbladh.
       .25 4th   *Hold High the Torch: A History of the 4th*
       .A53   *Marines*. Wash.: USMC, HQ, Hist. Div., 1960.
                   Bataan to Okinawa.

3252. D767   *Congdon, Don, ed. *Combat: The War with Japan*.
       .C63   N.Y.: Dell, 1962.

3253. D769.37   *Conner, Howard M. *The Spearhead: The World War*
       5th.C6   *II History of the 5th Marine Division*. Wash.:
                   Inf. Jour. P., 1950. Iwo Jima.

3254. VE23   *Crump, Irving. *Our Marines*.... N.Y.: Dodd,
       .C78   Mead, 1944.

3255. D767.99   Cunningham, Winfield S., with Lydel Sims.
       .W3C8   *Wake Island Command*. Boston: Little, Brown,
                   1961; N.Y.: Popular Books, 1962.

3256.　D790
.D37

*DeChant, John A. *Devilbirds: The Story of United States Marine Corps Aviation in World War II*. N.Y.: Harper, 1947.

3257.　D777
.D8

Dull, Paul S. *A Battle History of the Imperial Japanese Navy, 1941-1945*. Annapolis, Md.: NIP, 1977.

3258.　E183.8
.C5F4

Feis, Herbert. *The China Tangle: The American Effort in China from Pearl Harbor to the Marshall Mission*. Princeton: PUP, 1953.

3259.　D767
.F6

Forrestel, Emmet P. *Admiral Raymond A. Spruance, USN: A Study in Command*. Wash.: GPO, 1966. Buell, Thomas B., is better.

3260.　E746
.H3F72

Frank, Benis. *Halsey*. N.Y.: Ballantine, 1974.

3261.　VE23
.253d.F7

*＿＿＿＿, ed. *A Brief History of the Third Marines*. Wash.: USMC, HQ, Hist. Div., 1968. 47 pp.

3262.　DJ132
.F7

Franks, Horace G. *Holland Afloat*. London: Netherlands Pub. Co., 1942. World War II naval operations.

3263.　D767
.G3

Gallagher, O'Dowd. *Action in the East*. GCNY: Doubleday, 1942. Early World War II in Southeast Asia.

3264.　E746
.H3A3

Halsey, William F., and J. Bryan III. *Admiral Halsey's Story*. N.Y.: McGraw-Hill, 1947.

3265.　D784
.J3H3

Hashimoto, Mochitsura. *Sunk: The Story of the Japanese Submarine Fleet, 1941-1945*. N.Y.: Holt, 1954. Includes sinking of the USS *Indianapolis* by the *I-58*.

3266.

Holmes, W.J. *Double-Edged Secrets: U.S. Naval Intelligence Operations in the Pacific During World War II*. Annapolis, Md.: NIP, 1979.

3267.　D769
.369.H6

*Hough, Frank O. *The Island War: The United States Marine Corps in the Pacific*. Phila.: Lippincott, 1947.

3268.　D762.2
.I313

Ienaga, Saburo. *The Pacific War: World War II and the Japanese, 1931-1945*. N.Y.: Pantheon, 1978.

3269. D769   *Isely, Jeter A., and Philip A. Crowl. *The*
      .25I7   *Pacific War: World War II and the Japanese,*
               1931-1945. Princeton: PUP, 1951.

3270. E745   James, Dorris C. *The Years of MacArthur*. Bos-
      .M353   ton: Houghton Mifflin, 1970.

3271. D969.37 *Johnson, Richard W. *Follow Me! The Story of*
      2d.J65   *the Second Marine Division in World War II*.
                N.Y.: Random House, 1948.

3272. D742   Johnston, George H. *Pacific Partners*. London:
      .A8J6   Golancz, 1944. The U.S. and Australia in
                World War II.

3273. E746   Jordan, Ralph B. *Born to Fight: The Life of*
      .H3J6   *Admiral Halsey*. Phila.: David McKay, 1946.

3274. D767   Leckie, Robert. *Challenge for the Pacific:*
      .98L4   *Guadalcanal, the Turning Point of the War*.
                GCNY: Doubleday, 1965.

3275. D767   *_____. *Strong Men Armed: The United States*
      .L38   *Marines Against Japan*. N.Y.: Random House,
                1962.

3276. D811   *_____. *Helmet for My Pillow*. N.Y.: Random
      .L3547   House, 1957. Personal narratives. Good intro-
                duction to the Marine Corps.

3277. E182   *Lewis, Charles Lee. *Famous American Marines:*
      .L56   *an Account of the Corps: The Exploits of Of-*
                ficers and Men on Land, by Air and Sea, from
                the Decks of the Bon Homme Richard *to the*
                Summit of Mount Suribachi. Boston: Page, 1950.
                Short biographies of Marine Generals A.A.
                Vandegrift, Holland M. Smith, and Roy Stanley
                Geiger, all of whom figured prominently in
                World War II.

3278. D774   Lundstrom, John B. *The First South Pacific*
      .C63L86   *Campaign: Pacific Fleet Strategy, December*
                1941-June 1942. Annapolis, Md.: NIP, 1976.

3279. D769.37 *McMillan, George. *The Old Breed: A History of*
      1stM3   *the First Marine Division in World War II*.
                Wash.: Inf. Jour. P., 1949.

3280. D769.37
.A2&5

*_____, and others. *Uncommon Valor: Marine Divisions in Action*. Wash. Inf. Jour., 1946. Short history of each of the six Marine divisions.

3281. E745
.M3M3

Manchester, William. *American Caesar: Douglas MacArthur 1880-1964*. N.Y.: Little, Brown, 1978. Ineffective when stops following James, Dorris C., *q.v.*

3282. V63
.H34M7

Merrill, James M. *A Sailor's Admiral: A Biography of William F. Halsey*. N.Y.: Crowell, 1976.

3283. D769
.64M5

Miles, Milton E. *A Different Kind of War: The Little-Known Story of the Combined Guerrilla Forces Created in China by the U.S. Navy and the Chinese During World War II*. GCNY: Doubleday, 1967.

3284. E183.8
.J3N39

Neumann, William L. *America Encounters Japan: From Perry to MacArthur*. Baltimore: Johns Hopkins P., 1963.

3285. D777
.J3

O'Connor, Raymond G., ed. *The Japanese Navy in World War II*. Annapolis, Md.: USNI, 1969. Japanese naval and air officials tell their side of the story.

3286. V63
.N55P67

Potter, E.B. *Nimitz*. Annapolis, Md.: NIP, 1976.

3287. DS890
.Y25P6

Potter, John D. *Yamamoto: The Man Who Menaced America*. N.Y.: Viking, 1965.

3288. D769.47
4th.P7

*Proehl, Carl W. *The Fourth Marine Division in World War II*. Wash.: Inf. Jour. P., 1946.

3289. VA845
.P8

Puleston, William D. *The Armed Forces of the Pacific: A Comparison of the Military and Naval Power of the United States and Japan*. New Haven: YUP, 1941. Outdated but useful for naval policies, organization, and strategy.

3290. V63.R53
.A33

Richardson, James O. *On the Treadmill to Pearl Harbor: The Memoirs of James O. Richardson, USN (Ret.) as told to Vice Admiral George C. Dyer, USN (Ret.)*. Wash.: Naval Hist. Div., 1973.

3291. D792   Sakai, Saburo, with Martin Caiden and Fred
      .J3S3   Saito. *Samurai!* N.Y.: Dutton, 1957. Japanese
               aviation in World War II, including the
               kamikazes.

3292. DS777.53 Schaller, Michael. *The U.S. Crusade in China,*
      .S39   *1938-1945.* N.Y.: Columbia UP, 1979.

3293. Micro   *Operational and Administrative Histories*
               ["Battle Experience Reports"], *Pacific, 1941-*
               1945. Wilmington, Del.: Scholarly Resources,
               1979.

3294. DS777   Scott, Robert L. *Flying Tiger: Chennault of*
      .53.S38 *China.* GCNY: Doubleday, 1959.

3295. D790   *Sherrod, Robert. *History of Marine Corps Avia-*
      .S495   *tion in World War II.* Wash.: Combat Forces P.,
               1952.

3296. VE23.25   *Smith, Charles R. *A Brief History of the 12th*
      12th.S65 *Marines.* Wash.: GPO, 1972. 84 pp.

3297.   Thomas, Davis A. *Japan's War at Sea: Pearl*
               Harbor to the Coral Sea. London: Andrew
               Deutsch, 1978. The role of Japan's aircraft
               carriers.

3298. VE23   *Updegraph, C.L., Jr. *Special Marine Corps*
      .U67   *Units of World War II.* Wash.: USMC, HQ, Hist.
               Div., 1972.

DOCUMENTS

3299. Micro   *The MAGIC Documents: Summaries and Transcripts*
               of the Top Secret Diplomatic Communications of
               Japan, 1938-1945. Publications of America,
               1980. 14 reels.

3300. D742   U.S. Department of Defense. *The "MAGIC" Back-*
      .U5U53   *ground of Pearl Harbor,* 5 vols. Wash.: Depart-
               ment of Defense, 1978. Available at GPO.

3301.   U.S. Army. *History of Technical Intelligence:*
               South West and Western Pacific Areas, 1942-
               1945, 2 vols. Tokyo: U.S. Army, Technical
               Intelligence Center, 1955.

3302.   U.S. Army. Japan HQ. *Borneo Operations, 1945-*
               1945. Tokyo: OCMH, 1957.

DISSERTATIONS AND THESES

3303. D750   Klein, David H. "Anglo-American Diplomacy and
        .K56   the Pacific War: The Politics of Confronta-
                  tion," U. of Pa., 1977.

ARTICLES

3304.   Ainsworth, Walden L. "Japanese 'Long Lance'
                  Torpedoes," USNIP 84 (June 1958):106-07.

3305.   "American and Allied Strategy in the Far East,"
                  MR 29 (Nov.-Dec. 1949):22-41. Brief but com-
                  prehensive.

3306.   Brodie, Bernard. "The Naval Strategy of the
                  Pacific War," *Inf. Jour.* 57 (Aug. 1945):34-39.

3307.   *Chapin, John C. "History of the 4th Marine
                  Division," *Leatherneck* 29 (Apr. 1946):20-21+.

3308.   Cook, Charles O., Jr. "The Pacific Command
                  Divided: The Most Unexplicable Decision,"
                  USNIP 104 (Sept. 1978):55-61.

3309.   *Creswell, John. "Amphibious Commands in the
                  Pacific, 1942-45." In his *Generals and Ad-
                  mirals: the Story of Amphibious Command*. Lon-
                  don: Longmans, Green, 1952. pp. 172-188.
                  notes. A brief account of the development
                  of command relationships between the Marine
                  and naval commanders in the Pacific theater
                  during World War II.

3310.   Falk, Stanley L. "Japanese Strategy in World
                  War II," MR 62 (June 1962):70-81.

3311.   Fane, Francis D. "The Naked Warriors," USNIP
                  82 (Sept. 1956):913-22. UDTs in the Pacific,
                  World War II.

3312.   Field, James A., Jr. "Admiral Yamamoto,"
                  USNIP 75 (Oct. 1949):1105-13.

3313.   Harrington, Daniel F. "A Careless Hope: Ameri-
                  can Air Power and Japan, 1941," PHR 48 (May
                  48 (May 1979):217-38.

3314.   *Hart, Thomas C. "Amphibious War Against Japan,"
                  USNIP 69 (Feb. 1943):267-72.

3315.   Horie, Y. "The Failure of the Japanese Convoy Escort," USNIP 82 (Oct. 1956):1072-81.

3316.   Ingram, M.D. "The United States Navy in Japan, 1945-1950," USNIP 78 (Apr. 1952):378-88.

3317. U39   Kiralfy, Alexander. "Japanese Naval Strategy,"
       .E2   Edward M. Earle, ed. *Makers of Modern Strategy: Military Thought from Machivaelli to Hitler*. Princeton: PUP, 1943, pp. 457-84.

3318.   Livermore, Seward. "American Strategic Diplomacy in the South Pacific," PHR 12 (Mar. 1943): 42-49.

3319.   Meigs, John F. "Japanese Sea Power," USNIP 70 (Feb. 1944):121-29.

3320.   Miles, Milton E. "U.S. Naval Group, China," USNIP 72 (July 1945):921-31.

3321.   Morton, Louis. "Command in the Pacific, 1941-1945," MR 41 (Dec. 1961):76-88.

3322.   Ohmae, Toshikazu, and Roger Pineau. "Japanese Naval Aviation," USNIP 98 (Jan. 1972):68-78.

3323.   Possony, Stefan T. "Japanese Naval Strategy," USNIP 70 (May 1944):515-24.

3324.   Potter, Elmer B. "Chester William Nimitz, 1885-1966," USNIP 92 (July 1966):31-55.

3325.   Ramsay, DeWitt C. "America's Prime Weapon: Carrier-Based Aviation," *Aviation* 43 (June 1944):108-11.

3326.   *Simmons, Edwin H. "The United States Marine Corps, 1941-1943," MCG 58 (Aug. 1974):39-46.

3327.   Spagnola, James A. "Never Forgotten," USNIP 75 (May 1949):590-91. Nimitz.

3328.   Stanford, Peter M. "The Battle Fleet and World Air Power," USNIP 69 (Dec. 1943):1533-39.

3329.   Stove, G.W. "The Queen's Navy at War: Operations of the Royal Netherlands Navy in the Southwest Pacific During the Invasion of the Philippines, Malacca, and the East Indies," USNIP 76 (March 1950):288-301.

3330.   Weddle, Robert S. "Texas to Tokyo Bay: Admiral Chester W. Nimitz," AHI 10 (Aug. 1975):4-9.

3331.   Wellings, Joseph H. "Captain 'Bull' Halsey: An Example of Command Leadership," *Shipmate* 41 (Sept. 1978):29-30.

B. PEARL HARBOR

BOOKS

3332. D767.92   Bartlett, Bruce M. *Cover-up: The Politics of* .B343   *Pearl Harbor, 1941-1946.* New Rochelle, N.Y.: Arlington House, 1978.

3333. E183.8   Borg, Dorothy, and Shumpei Okamoto. *Pearl Har-* .J3B67   *bor as History: Japanese-American Relations 1931-1941.* N.Y.: Columbia UP, 1973.

3334. D742   Farago, Ladislas. *The Broken Seal: The Story* .U5F3   *of "Operation Magic" and the Pearl Harbor Disaster.* N.Y.: Random House, 1967.

3335. D753   Feis, Herbert. *The Road to Pearl Harbor.* .F4   Princeton: PUP, 1950.

3336. D767   Hoehling, Adolph R. *The Week Before Pearl* .92.H6   *Harbor.* N.Y.: Norton, 1963.

3337. D769   *Hough, Frank O., Verle E. Ludwig, and Henry .369   I. Shaw. *Pearl Harbor to Guadalcanal.* Wash.: USMC, HQ, Hist. Div., 1958.

3338. D773   Karig, Walter, and Welbourne Kelley. *Battle* .K3   *Report: Pearl Harbor to Coral Sea.* Vol. 1. N.Y.: Farrar and Rinehart, 1944.

3339. D767   Kimmel, Husband E. *Admiral Kimmel's Story.* .92.K54   Chicago: Regnery, 1955.

3340. D767   Lord, Walter. *Day of Infamy.* N.Y.: Holt, .92L6   1957. The attack on Pearl Harbor.

3341. D748   Millis, Walter. *This Is Pearl! The United* .M5   *States and Japan--1941.* N.Y.: Morrow, 1947.

3342. D767   Morgenstern, George. *Pearl Harbor: The Story* .92.M6   *of the Secret War.* N.Y.: Devin-Adair, 1947.

3343. D742   Pelz, Stephen E. *Race to Pearl Harbor: The*
        .J3P44   *Failure of the Second Naval Conference and*
                    the Onset of World War II. Cambridge, Mass.:
                    HUP, 1974.

3344. E806   Tansill, Charles D. *Backdoor to War.* Chicago:
        .T3   Regnery, 1952.

3345. D769   Theobald, Robert A. *The Final Secret of Pearl*
        .92.T5   *Harbor: The Washington Contribution to the*
                    Japanese Attack. N.Y.: Devin-Adair, 1954.

3346. D767   Trefouse, Hans, ed. *What Happened at Pearl*
        .92T7   *Harbor.* N.Y.: Twayne, 1958.

3347. D810   Van Der Rhoer, Edward J. *Deadly Magic: A*
        .C88V36   *Personal Account of Communications Intelli-*
                    gence in World War II in the Pacific. N.Y.:
                    Scribner, 1978.

3348. D767.92   Willin, Homer N. *Pearl Harbor: Why, How, Fleet*
        .W3   *Salvage and Final Appraisal.* Wash.: Naval
                    Hist. Div., 1968.

3349. D810   Wilhelm, Maria. *The Man Who Watched the Rising*
        .S8Z39   *Sun: The Story of Admiral Ellis M. Zacharias.*
                    N.Y.: Watts, 1967.

3350. D767   Wohlstetter, Barbara. *Pearl Harbor: Warning*
        .92W6   *and Decision.* Stanford: Stanford UP, 1962.

DOCUMENTS

3351. Micro   *Intercepted Japanese Messages (Operation*
                    "Magic"), 1938-1945. Wilmington, Del.:
                    Michael Glazier, 1979.

3352. Doc   U.S. Congress, Joint Committee on the Investi-
        Y4   gation of the Pearl Harbor Attack. *Pearl Harbor*
        .P31:P31 *Attack: Hearings...,* 39 vols. Wash.: GPO, 1946.

DISSERTATIONS AND THESES

3353.   Godson, Susan H. "The Development of Amphibious
                    Warfare in World War II as Reflected in the
                    Campaigns of John Lesslie Hall, Jr., USN,"
                    American U., 1979; Ann Arbor, Mich.: University
                    Microfilms International, 1979.

3354.   Iles, William P. "In Quest of Blame: Inquiries
            Conducted 1941-1946 into America's Involvement
            in the Pacific War," U. of Iowa, 1978.

                         ARTICLES

3355.   Adams, Frederick C. "The Road, to Pearl Harbor:
            A Reexamination of American Far Eastern Policy,
            July 1937-December 1938," JAH 58 (June 1971):
            73-92.

3356.   Burtness, Paul S., and Warren U. Ober. "Re-
            search Methodology: The Problem of the Pearl
            Harbor Intelligence Reports," MA 25 (Fall
            1961):132-46.

3357.   Cope, Harley F. "Climb Mount Niitaka!" USNIP
            72 (Dec. 1946):1515-19. Japanese directive
            to attack Pearl Harbor.

3358.   Cranwell, John P. "Did the Japanese Win at
            Pearl Harbor?" USNIP 70 (June 1944):661-67.
            The Japanese erred in not hitting logistic
            facilities at Pearl.

3359.   Dupuy, Trevor N. "Who Blundered at Pearl Har-
            bor?" AH 13 (Feb. 1962):64-81.

3360.   Esthus, Raymond. "President Roosevelt's Commit-
            ment to Britain to Intervene in a Pacific War,"
            MVHR 50 (June 1963):28-38.

3361.   Eyre, James K., Jr. "The Background to Japanese
            Naval Treachery in the Pacific," USNIP 70 (July
            1944):874-84.

3362.   Feis, Herbert. "War Came to Pearl Harbor: Sus-
            picions Considered," Yale Rev. 45 (Spring
            1946):378-90.

3363.   Ferrell, Robert H. "Pearl Harbor and the Re-
            visionists," Historian 17 (Spring 1955):215-33.

3364.   Field, James A., Jr. "Admiral Yamamoto," USNIP
            75 (Oct. 1949):1105-13.

3365.   Higgins, Trumbull. "Japanese Strategy in
            1941," USNIP 82 (Dec. 1956):1330-31.

3366.   _____. "East Wind Rain," USNIP 81 (Nov. 1955):1198-1205. Japanese diplomatic code words about the attack on Pearl Harbor.

3367.   Howard, Michael. "Military Intelligence and Surprise Attack: The 'Lessons' of Pearl Harbor," WP 15 (July 1963):701-11.

3368. D445   Leonard, Thomas M. "The 'Magic' Messages and
       .C68   Pearl Harbor Revisited," in David H. White,
       1976   ed. *Proceedings of the Conference on War and Diplomacy*. Charleston, S.C.: The Citadel, 1976, pp. 95-101.

3369.   Melosi, Martin V. "National Security Misused: The Aftermath of Pearl Harbor," *Prologue* 9 (Summer 1977):75-90.

3370.   Morton, Louis. "Japan's Decision for War," in Kent R. Greenfield, ed. *Command Decisions*. Wash.: OCMH, 1960, pp. 99-124.

3371.   _____. "War Plan *Orange*," WP 11 (Jan. 1959):221-50.

3372.   _____. "Pearl Harbor in Perspective," USNIP 81 (Apr. 1955):461-68.

3373.   _____. "The Japanese Decision for War," USNIP 80 (Dec. 1954):1324-35.

3374.   Ramsey, Logan C. "The 'Ifs' of Pearl Harbor," USNIP 76 (Apr. 1950):365-71.

3375.   Richards, David K. "The Beginning of Pearl Harbor, July 1909 to December 7, 1941," USNIP 70 (May 1944):536-45.

3376.   Sokol, Anthony E. "Why Pearl Harbor?" USNIP 71 (Apr. 1945):401-09.

3377.   Taussig, Joseph K., Jr. "I Remember Pearl Harbor," USNIP 98 (Jan. 1972):18-24.

3378.   Vogel, Bertram. "Diplomatic Prelude to Pearl Harbor," USNIP 75 (Apr. 1949):414-21.

3379.   Ward, Robert E. "The Inside Story of the [Japa-
              nese] Pearl Harbor Plan," USNIP 77 (Dec. 1951):
              1270-83.

              C. WAKE, GUAM, AND LOSS OF THE
                 SOUTHERN RESOURCES AREA

                          BOOKS

3380. D777   Ash, Bernard. *Someone Had Blundered: The Story
      .A8   of the* Repulse *and the* Prince of Wales. GCNY:
              Doubleday, 1961.

3381. D767.55 Attiwill, Kenneth. *Fortress: The Story of the
      .A87   Siege and Fall of Singapore.* GCNY: Doubleday,
              1960.

3382. D767   Belote, James H., and William M. Belote. *Cor-
      .4.B4   regidor: The Saga of a Fortress.* N.Y.: Harper,
              1967.

3383. D777   Bennett, Geoffrey M. *The Loss of the* Prince of
      .B37   Wales *and* Repulse. Annapolis, Md.: NIP, 1973.

3384. D767   Caffrey, Kate. *Out in the Midday Sun, Singa-
      .55C33 pore, 1941-1945: The End of an Empire.* N.Y.:
              Stein & Day, 1973.

3385. D773   Casey, Robert J. *Torpedo Junction: With the
      .C35   Pacific Fleet from Pearl Harbor to Midway.*
              Indianapolis: Bobbs-Merrill, 1942. Reporter's
              account, based on his diary.

3386. D767   Conroy, Robert. *The Battle of Bataan: Ameri-
      .4.C6   ca's Greatest Defeat.* N.Y.: Macmillan, 1969.

3387. D767   *Cunningham, Winfield S. *Wake Island Command.*
      .99   Boston: Little, Brown, 1961. Contradicts
      .W3C8   much of Devereux, below, on command relation-
              ships.

3388. D767.99 *Devereux, James P.S. *The Story of Wake Island.*
      .W3D4   Phila.: Lippincott, 1947.

3389. D767   Falk, Stanley L. *Seventy Days to Singapore.*
      .5F34   N.Y.: Putnam, 1975. Includes an account of
              the sinking of the *Prince of Wales* and *Repulse.*

3390. D770   Grenfell, Russell. *Main Fleet to Singapore.*
      .G73   N.Y.: Macmillan, 1952.

3391. D767.99   *Heinl, Robert D. *The Defense of Wake*. Wash.:
      .W3U5   USMC, HQ, Hist. Div., 1947.

3392. DS598   Leasor, James. *Singapore: The Battle That
      .S7L38   Changed the World*. GCNY: Doubleday, 1968.

3393. D811   Morrill, John H., and Pete Martin. *South From
      .M64   Corregidor*. N.Y.: Simon & Schuster, 1943.

3394. D769   Morton, Louis. *The Fall of the Philippines*.
      .A533   Wash.: OCMH, 1963. Contains an excellent
      v. 2   bibliography.
      pt. 1

3395. D774   Oosten, F.C. van. *The Battle of the Java Sea*.
      .J3056   Annapolis, Md.: NIP, 1976.

3396. D767.99   *Schultz, Duane P. *Wake Island: The Heroic
      .W5S37   Gallant Fight*. N.Y.: St. Martin, 1978.

3397. D774   Thomas, David A. *Battle of the Java Sea*. N.Y.:
      .J3T5   Stein & Day, 1968.

3398. D767.4   Underbrink, Robert L. *Destination Corregidor*.
      .U53   Annapolis, Md.: NIP, 1971.

3399. E745   Wainwright, Jonathan M. *General Wainwright's
      .W3   Story*. Ed. Robert Considine. GCNY: Doubleday,
                   Doran, 1946.

3400. D767   Walker, Allan S. *The Island Campaigns*. Can-
      .8.W3   berra: Australian War Memorial, 1957. Austra-
                   lia in World World II.

3401. D881   White, William L. *They Were Expendable*. Lon-
      .W45   don: Hamilton, 1942. Fall of the Philippines.
                   Story by 4 officers of MTBs.

ARTICLES

3402.   Baldwin, Hanson W. "The Fall of Corregidor,"
                 AH 17 (Aug. 1966):16-23.

3403. G525   _____. "Saga of a Stout Ship: The *Houston*,
      .B255   1942," in his *Sea Fights and Shipwrecks*. GCNY:
                 Hanover House, 1955, pp. 76-91.

3404.   *Burroughs, J.R. "The Siege of Wake Island," AH
                 10 (June 1959):65-76.

3405.   Cook, Charles O., Jr. "The Strange Case of
          Rainbow-5," USNIP 104 (8-78):67-73.

3406.   Eyre, James K., Jr. "Java Sea: A Memorable
          Naval Battle," USNIP 69 (Apr. 1943):516-23.

3407.   Mack, William R. "The Battle of the Java Sea,"
          USNIP 69 (Aug. 1943):1052-60.

3408.   Mountbatten, Admiral the Viscount, of Burma.
          "The Strategy of the Southeast Asia Campaign,"
          RUSIJ 91 (Nov. 1946):479-83.

3409.   Parker, Thomas C. "The Epic of Corregidor-
          Bataan, December 24, 1941-May 6, 1942," USNIP
          69 (Jan. 1943):9-22.

3410.   Pratt, Fletcher. "Americans in Battle--No. 1:
          Campaign in the Java Sea," *Harper's* 185 (Nov.
          1942):561-74.

3411.   *Votaw, Homer C. "Wake Island," USNIP 67 (Jan.
          1941):52-55.

D. EARLY ALLIED CARRIER RAIDS AND THE
BATTLE OF THE CORAL SEA

BOOKS

3412. D774   Bates, Richard W. *The Battle of the Coral*
       .S318B38   *Sea*....Springfield, Va.: National Technical
                   Information Service, 1947.

3413. D790   Glines, Carroll V. *Doolittle's Tokyo Raiders.*
       .G55   Princeton, N.J.: Van Nostrand, 1964.

3414. D774   Hoehling, Adolph A. *The* Lexington *Goes Down.*
       .L4H6   Englewood Cliffs, N.J.: Prentice-Hall, 1971.

3415. D774   Hoyt, Edwin P. *Blue Skies and Blood: The*
       .C63G69   *Battle of the Coral Sea.* N.Y.: Eriksson, 1975.

3416. D774   Johnston, Stanley. *Queen of the Flat-tops: The*
       .L4J6   *U.S.S.* Lexington *and the Coral Sea Battle.*
                   N.Y.: Dutton, 1942; N.Y.: Bantam, 1979.

3417. D790   Merrill, James M. *Target Tokyo: The Halsey-*
       .M46   *Doolittle Raid.* Chicago: Rand McNally, 1964.

3418. D774   Millot, Bernard. *The Battle of the Coral Sea*.
      .C63   Annapolis, Md.: NIP, 1974.
      .M5413

3419. TL540   Reynolds, Quentin. *The Amazing Mr. Doolittle*.
      .D62R4   N.Y.: Appleton-Century-Crofts, 1953.

3420. D773   Sherman, Frederick C. *Combat Command: The*
      .S52   *American Aircraft Carriers in the Pacific War*.
               N.Y.: Dutton, 1950.

3421. D774   Stafford, Edward P. *The Big E*. N.Y.: Random
      .E5S7   House, 1962. Battle history of the *Enterprise*,
               CV-6.

3422.   U.S. Navy Department. Office of Chief of Naval
              Operations. *U.S. Naval Aviation in the Pacific*.
              Wash.: GPO, 1947.

ARTICLES

3423.   "The First Carrier Battle," *All Hands*, No. 533
              (June 1961):27-31. Battle of the Coral Sea.

3424.   Critchfield, John S. "The Halsey-Doolittle
              Tokyo Raid," *Sea Power* 14 (Dec. 1971):25-29.

3425.   Pratt, Fletcher. "Americans in Battle--No. 3:
              Campaign in the Coral Sea," *Harper's* 186 (Mar.
              1943):356-68.

E. BATTLE OF MIDWAY

BOOKS

3426. D774   Barker, A.J. *Midway: The Turning Point*. N.Y.:
      .M5B37   Ballantine, 1971.

3427. D774   Castillo, Edmund L. *Midway: Battle for the*
      .M5C3   *Pacific*. N.Y.: Random House, 1968.

3428. D767   Coale, Griffith B. *Victory at Midway*. N.Y.:
      .94.C6   Farrar & Rinehart, 1944.

3429. D774   Frank, Patrick H.H., and Joseph D. Harrington.
      .M5F7   *Rendezvous at Midway: U.S.S.* Yorktown *and the*
               Japanese Carrier Fleet. N.Y.: Stein & Day,
               1967.

3430. D774   Fuchida, Mitsuo, and Masatake Okumiya. *Midway:*
      .M5F814   *The Battle That Doomed Japan.* Annapolis, Md.:
                USNI, 1955.

3431. D774   Lord, Walter. *Incredible Victory.* N.Y.: Harper
      .M5L6   & Row, 1967.

3432. D774   Smith, Chester L. *Midway, 4 June 1942.* London:
      .M5S6   Regency, 1962.

3433. D774   Smith, William W. *Midway: Turning Point of the*
      .M5S63   *Pacific.* N.Y.: Crowell, 1966.

3434. D774   Tuleja, Thaddeus V. *Climax at Midway.* N.Y.:
      .M5T8   Norton, 1960.

3435. D774   U.S. Office of Naval Intelligence. *The Japanese*
      .M5A5   *Story of the Battle of Midway.* Wash.: GPO,
                1947.

DISSERTATIONS AND THESES

3436.   Prange, Gordon W. "The Battle of Midway: A
               Study in Command," U. of Maryland, 1971.

ARTICLES

3437.   Byrd, Martha H. "Six Minutes to Victory: Mid-
               way," AHI 10 (May 1975):32-48.

3438.   *D'Andrea, Thomas M. "Marines at Midway," MCG
               48 (Nov. 1964):27-31.

3439.   "The Full Story of Midway," USNIP 68 (Sept.
               1942):1317-21+, 1347-54, 1515-17.

3440.   Fuchida, Mitsuo, and Masatake Okumiya. "Five
               Fateful Minutes at Midway," USNIP 81 (June
               1955):660-65.

3441.   Morison, Samuel E. "Six Minutes that Changed
               the World," AH 14 (Feb. 1963):5-56, 102-03.

3442.   Tanabe, Yahachi, with Joseph D. Harrington. "I
               Sank the *Yorktown* at Midway," USNIP 89 (May
               1963):58-65.

3443.   Wadleigh, John R. "Memories of Midway, Thirty
               Years Ago," *Shipmate* 35 (June 1972):3-8. The
               author served in the *Yorktown.*

F. THE ALEUTIANS

BOOKS

3444. D769.87 Ford, Corey. *Short Cut to Tokyo: The Battle*
.A4F6 *for the Aleutians.* N.Y.: Scribner, 1943.

3445. D769.87 Garfield, Brian W. *The Thousand-Mile War:*
.A4G4 *World War II in Alaska.* GCNY: Doubleday, 1969.

3446. D769.87 Handleman, Howard. *Bridge to Victory: The*
.A4H3 *Story of the Reconquest of the Aleutian*
Islands. N.Y.: Random House, 1943.

3447. UA23 Potter, Jean C. *Alaska Under Arms.* N.Y.:
.P6 Macmillan, 1942.

ARTICLES

3448. Chikaya, Masatake. "The Mysterious Withdrawal
from Kiska," USNIP 84 (Feb. 1958):31-47. Ex-
planation by a Japanese.

3449. Eyre, James K., Jr. "Alaska and the Aleutians:
Cockpit of the North Pacific," USNIP 69 (Oct.
1943):1287-97.

3450. Karig, Walter, and Eric Purdon. "The Koman-
dorskis: A Little Known Victory," USNIP 72
(Nov. 1946):1411-15.

3451. McCandless, Bruce. "The Battle of the Pips,"
USNIP 84 (Feb. 1958):40-56. Off Kiska, July
25-26, 1943.

3452. Pratt, Fletcher. "Campaign without Glory: The
Navy in the Aleutians, 1942-1943," *Harper's*
189 (Nov. 1944):558-69.

3453. Stokesbury, James. "Battle of Attu," AHI 14
(Apr. 1979):30-38.

17

WORLD WAR II IN THE PACIFIC.
PART II: THE CAMPAIGN AGAINST RABAUL

BOOKS

3454. D774
.C63B38
Bates, Richard W. *The Battle of Savo Island...*, 2 pts. Springfield, Va.: National Technical Information Service, 1950.

3455. D767
.B47
Belote, James H., and William M. Belote. *Titans of the Seas: The Development and Operations of American Carrier Task Forces during World War II*. N.Y.: Harper & Row, 1975. Ends abruptly at the Battle of the Philippine Sea.

3456. D790
.B473
Birdsall, Steve. *Flying Buccaneers: The Illustrated Story of Kenney's Fifth Air Force*. GCNY: Doubleday, 1977.

3457. D790
.B63
*Boyington, Gregory. *Baa Baa Black Sheep*. N.Y.: Putnam, 1958. Autobiography of a Marine ace and Medal of Honor winner encompassing his service with Marine Fighter Squadron VMF-222 (the "Black Sheep") in the Solomons and as a prisoner of war.

3458. D770
.B25
Brown, David. *Carrier Operations in World War II: The Pacific Navies*. London: Ian Allan, 1974.

3459. D769.372
9th.A5
*Burrus, Luther D., ed. *The Ninth Marines: A Brief History of the Ninth Marine Regiment*. Wash.: Inf. Jour. P., 1946. Bougainville, Guam, Iwo Jima.

3460. D769
.A533
v.2
pt.5
Cannon, M. Hamlin. *Leyte: The Return to the Philippines*. Wash.: OCMH, 1954.

3461. D773
.C27
Cant, Gilbert. *America's Navy in World War II*. N.Y.: John Day, 1943.

3462. D767
.98.C3
Cave, Hugh B. *Long Were the Nights: The Saga of PT Squadron "X" in the Solomons*. N.Y.: Dodd, Mead, 1943.

3463. D767.98 *Coggins, Jack. *The Campaign for Guadalcanal*.
       .C58   GCNY: Doubleday, 1972.

3464. D767   Cook, Charles. *The Battle of Cape Esperance:*
       .98.C6   *Encounter at Guadalcanal*. N.Y.: Crowell,
                  1968.

3465. D790   Davis, Burke. *Get Yamamoto*. N.Y.: Random
       .D34   House, 1969.

3466. E746   * _____ . *Marine: The Life of Lt. Gen. Lewis B.*
       .88D3   *(Chesty) Puller, U.S.M.C. (Ret.)*. Boston:
                  Little, Brown, 1962. Guadalcanal, New Britain,
                  Peleliu, Korea.

3467. D767   *Dyer, George C. *The Amphibians Came to Conquer:*
       .D9   *The Story of Admiral Richmond Kelly Turner*, 2
                  vols. Wash.: Dept. of the Navy, 1971.

3468. D810   Feldt, Eric A. *The Coast Watchers*. N.Y.: Bal-
       .S7F4   lantine, 1959. World War II Secret Service,
                  Australia.

3469. D767   *Foster, John T. *Guadalcanal General: The Story*
       .98.F6   *of A.A. Vandegrift, U.S.M.C.* N.Y.: Morrow,
                  1966.

3470. E746   Frank, Benis. *Halsey*. N.Y.: Ballantine, 1974.
       .H3F72

3471. D767   Graham, Burton. *None Shall Survive: The Graphic*
       .95.G7   *Story of the Annihilation of the Japanese Ar-*
                  mada in the Bismarck Sea Battle. Sydney: F.H.
                  Johnston, 1944.

3472. D774   Griffin, Alexander R. *A Ship to Remember: The*
       .H6G7   *Saga of the* Hornet. N.Y.: Howell, Soskin, 1943.
                  Sinking of the *Hornet* in Battle of the Santa
                  Cruz Islands, Oct. 26, 1942.

3473. D767   *Griffith, Samuel B. *The Battle for Guadalcanal*.
       .98.G7   Phila.: Lippincott, 1963.

3474. E746   Halsey, William F., and J. Bryan III. *Admiral*
       .H3A3   *Halsey's Story*. N.Y.: McGraw-Hill, 1947.

3475. D767   *Hannah, Dick. *Tarawa: The Toughest Battle in*
       .917   *Marine Corps History*. N.Y.: Duell, Sloan &
                  Pearce, 1944. Chronological collection of a
                  combat correspondent's accounts accompanying
                  a photographic survey of the battle.

3476. D767.99 *Hough, Frank O., and John A. Crown. *The Cam-*
      .N4U52   *paign on New Britain*. Wash.: USMC, HQ, Hist.
                Div., 1952.

3477. D790   Howard, Clive, and others. *One Damned Island
      .H7   After Another*. Chapel Hill: UNCP, 1946. The
                Seventh Air Force from Pearl Harbor to the end
                of the war.

3478. D767   Hoyt, Edwin P. *How They Won the War in the
      .H65   Pacific: Nimitz and His Admirals*. N.Y.: Wey-
                bright and Talley, 1970.

3479. V864   _____. *The Glorious Flattops*. Boston:
      .H6   Little, Brown, 1965.

3480. D749   Huston, James A. *Out of the Blue: U.S. Army
      .345   Airborne Operations in World War II*. West
      .H87   Lafayette, Ind.: Purdue UP, 1972.

3481. D769.52 Jones, Ken. *Destroyer Squadron 23: The Combat
      .D456   Exploits of Arleigh Burke's Gallant Force*.
                Phila.: Chilton, 1959.

3482. E182   _____, and Hubert Kelly. *Admiral Arleigh
      .B96J6   [31 knot] Burke: The Story of a Fighting
                Sailor*. Phila.: Chilton, 1962.

3483. D773   *Karig, Walter. *Battle Report: Pacific War*,
      .K3   *Middle Phase*, Vol. 3. N.Y.: Rinehart, 1946.

3484. D811   Kenney, George C. *General Kenney Reports*. N.Y.:
      .K42   Duell, Sloan & Pearce, 1959. Kenney commanded
                the Army air forces that supported MacArthur in
                the New Guinea campaign.

3485. D773   King, Ernest J. *U.S. Navy at War, 1941-1945:
      .A5   Official Reports to the Secretary of the Navy
      1945   by Fleet Admiral Ernest J. King, USN*. Wash.:
                Navy Dept., 1946.

3486. D767   *Leckie, Robert. *Challenge for the Pacific:
      .98.L4   Guadalcanal, the Turning Point of the War*.
                GCNY: Doubleday, 1965.

3487. D767.9   Lord, Walter. *Lonely Vigil: Coastwatchers of
      .L67   the Solomons*. N.Y.: Viking, 1977.

3488. D769.99 *Marshall, Samuel L.A. *Island Victory: The Bat-*
.M3M3 *tle of Kwajalein Atoll*. Wash.: Inf. Jour.,
1944.

3489. D767 *Merillat, Herbert L. *The Island: A History of*
.98.M4 *the First Marine Division on Guadalcanal*,
August 7-December 9, 1942. Boston: Houghton
Mifflin, 1944.

3490. V63 Merrill, James M. *A Sailor's Admiral: A Biog-*
.H34 *raphy of William F. Halsey*. N.Y.: Crowell,
M47 1976.

3491. D769 Miller, John, Jr. *CARTWHEEL: The Reduction of*
.A533 *Rabaul*. Wash.: OCMH, 1959.
v.2

3492. D769 * _____ . *Guadalcanal, the First Offensive--*
.A533 *United States Army in World War II--The War in*
v.2 *the Pacific*. Wash.: OCMH, 1949. A detailed
pt.3 account of the entire Guadalcanal campaign
with emphasis on Army participation. Includes
Army staff lists.

3493. D767 Miller, Thomas G. *The Cactus Air Force*. N.Y.:
.98.M5 Harper & Row, 1969. "Cactus" was the code word
for the island of Guadalcanal.

3494. D769 Milner, Samuel. *Victory in Papua*. Wash.: OCMH,
.A533 1957.
v.2
pt.7

3495. D773 Morison, Samuel E. *History of United States*
.M6 *Naval Operations in World War II*, 15 vols.
Boston: Little, Brown, 1947-1962. Vol. 7.
Aleutians, Gilberts, and Marshalls, June 1942-
April 1944.

3496. D773 _____ . *History of United States Naval Opera-*
.M6 *tions in World War II*. 15 vols. Boston: Little,
Brown, 1947-1962. Vol. 7. *New Guinea and the*
Marianas, March 1944-Aug. 1944. (1953).

3497. E746 Murphy, Francis X. *Fighting Admiral: The Story*
.C27M87 *of Dan Callaghan*. N.Y.: Vantage, 1952.

3498. D774 Newcomb, Richard F. *Savo: The Incredible Naval*
.S318N4 *Debacle off Guadalcanal*. N.Y.: Holt, Rinehart
& Winston, 1961.

3499. VA65   Newell, Gordon R., and Allan E. Smith. *MIGHTY*
      .M685N7   *MO. The U.S.S.* Missouri: *A Biography of the*
                 Last Battleship. Seattle: Superior Pub. Co.,
                 1969.

3500. D767   *Pratt, Fletcher. *The Marine's War: An Account*
      .P7   *of the Struggle for the Pacific from both*
                 American and Japanese Sources. N.Y.: W. Sloane
                 Associates, 1948.

3501. D769   _____. *Night Work: The Story of Task Force*
      .5339th   *39.* N.Y.: Holt, 1946. Admiral "Tip" Merrill
      .P7   and the Battle of Empress Augusta Bay.

3502. D773   _____. *Fleet Against Japan.* N.Y.: Harper,
      .P68   1946.

3503. D767   *Rentz, John N. *Marines in the Central Solomons.*
      .98U53   Wash.: USMC, HQ, Hist. Div., 1952.

3504. D767.98   * _____. *Bougainville and the Northern Solo-*
      .U5   *mons.* Wash.: USMC, HQ, Hist. Div., 1948.
      1948

3505. D767   Robinson, Pat. *The Fight for New Guinea: Gen-*
      .95.R6   *eral MacArthur's First Offensive.* N.Y.: Random
                 House, 1943.

3506. D767.99   *Shaw, Henry L., and others. *The Isolation of*
      .045U52   *Rabaul.* Wash.: USMC, HQ, Hist. Div., 1963.

3507. D767   *Sherrod, Robert. *On to the Westward: War in*
      .S55   *the Central Pacific.* N.Y.: Duell, Sloan &
                 Pearce, 1945. The landings and battles on
                 Tarawa, Saipan, Iwo Jima, and Okinawa.

3508. D769   Smith, Robert R. *The Approach to the Philip-*
      .A5B3   *pines.* Wash.: OCMH, 1953.

3509. E842   Tregaskis, Richard. *John F. Kennedy and PT-109.*
      .K4T7   N.Y.: Random House, 1962.

3510. D767   * _____. *Guadalcanal Diary.* N.Y.: Random
      .98.T7   House, 1943.

3511. Doc   U.S. Navy Department. Naval History Division.
      N 1.2:   *United States Submarine Losses, World War II.*
      Sul   Wash.: GPO, 1963.

3512. D767.99   U.S. Strategic Bombing Survey. *The Allied Cam-*
      .N4U5   *paign Against Rabaul.* Wash.: USSBS, 1946.

3513. D767   Vader, John. *New Guinea: The Tide Is Stemmed.*
      .95V3   N.Y.: Ballantine, 1971.

3514. E746   *Vandegrift, Alexander A. *Once a Marine: The*
      .V3   *Memoirs of General A.A. Vandegrift, USMC.* N.Y.:
               Norton, 1964.

3515. D767   *Werstein, Irving. *Guadalcanal.* N.Y.: Crowell,
      .98.W4   1963.

3516. D767   *Willard, Warren W. *The Leathernecks Come*
      .98.W5   *Through.* N.Y.: Revell, 1944. Solomons and
               Gilberts.

3517. U53   *Willock, Roger. *Unaccustomed to Fear: A Biog-*
      .G4W5   *raphy of the Late General Roy S. Geiger, USMC.*
               Princeton: PUP, 1968.

3518. D767   *Wilson, Earl J., and others. *Betio Beachhead:*
      .917.W5   *U.S. Marines' Own Story of the Battle of*
               Tarawa. N.Y.: Putnam, 1945. Combat corres-
               pondent's account of the 2d Marine Division
               in the struggle for Tarawa.

3519. D767   *Wolfert, Ira. *The Battle for the Solomons.* Bos-
      .98.W6   ton: Houghton Mifflin, 1943.

3520. D767   *Zimmerman, John L. *The Guadalcanal Campaign:*
      .98.u5   *August 1942-February 1943.* Wash.: USMC, HQ,
               Hist. Div., 1949.

ARTICLES

3521.   Baldwin, Hanson W. "America at War: The End of
               the Second Year," FA 22 (Jan. 1944):209-24.

3522.   Barbey, Daniel E. "MacArthur's Navy," USNIP
               95 (Sept. 1969):88-99. Pictorial.

3523.   Bartlett, Donald. "Vice Admiral Chuichi Hara:
               Unforgettable Foe," USNIP 96 (Oct. 1970):51-
               56.

3524.   "The Battle of Vella Gulf," *All Hands*, No.
               586 (Nov. 1965):56-60.

3525.   Bell, Charles. "Shootout at Savo," AHI 9 (Jan. 1975):28-38.

3526.   Birdsall, Steve. "Target Rabaul!" AF 58 (Sept. 1975):108-13.

3527.   *Bowser, Alpha L., Jr. "End Run in the Solomons," MCG 31 (Nov. 1947):24-32.

3528.   Brodie, Bernard. "The Naval Strategy of the Pacific War," Inf. Jour. 56 (Aug. 1945):34-39.

3529.   Conolly, Richard L. "The Strategy of the War in the Pacific," 19th Century 146 (Aug. 1949): 67-79.

3530.   "Cruisers in Action," Engineering 154 (Oct. 16, 1942):311-312. Loss of American cruisers in Battle of Savo Island.

3531.   Eyre, James K., Jr. "Shattering the Myth of Japanese Invincibility," USNIP 71 (Aug. 1945): 977-87.

3532.   Falk, Stanley L. "The Ambush of Admiral Yamamoto," Navy 6 (Apr. 1963):32-34.

3533.   Fukudome, Shigeru. "The Hawaiian Operation," USNIP 81 (Dec. 1955):939-52. A Japanese view of the attack on Pearl Harbor.

3534.   Graybar, Lloyd J. "Admiral King's Toughest Battle," NWCR 32 (Feb. 1979):38-47. Battle of Guadalcanal.

3535.   *Isby, David C. "Island War: The United States Amphibious Offensive Against Imperial Japan, 1942 to 1945," S&T, September-October 1975, pp. 21-36.

3536.   Karig, Walter, and Eric Purdon. "The Battle of Empress Augusta Bay," USNIP 72 (Dec. 1946): 1569-75.

3537.   "King of the Cans: Arleigh A. Burke," Time 44 (July 17, 1944):55.

3538.   Kiralfy, Alexander. "Why Japan's Fleet Avoids Action," FA 22 (Oct. 1943):45-58.

3539.   McKiernan, Patrick L. "Tarawa: The Tide that
            Failed," USNIP 28 (Feb. 1962):38-49.

3540.   Miller, John, Jr. "MacArthur and the Admiral-
            ties," in Kent R. Greenfield, ed. *Command De-
            cisions*. Wash.: OCMH, (1959), pp. 287-302.

3541.   *Moore, Robert W. "Round About Grim Tarawa,"
            Nat. Geog. 87 (Feb. 1945):137-66.

3542.   Morton, Louis. "Japanese Policy and Strategy
            in Mid-War," USNIP 85 (Feb. 1959):52-64.

3543.   Ohmae, Tosohikazu. "The Battle of Savo Island,"
            USNIP 83 (Dec. 1957):1263-78.

3544.   Pratt, Fletcher. "The Loss of the *Wasp*," USNIP
            72 (July 1946):909-15.

3545.   _____. "Nimitz and His Admirals," *Harper's*
            190 (Feb. 1945):209-17.

3546.   Reynolds, Clark G. "'Sara' in the East," USNIP
            87 (Dec. 1961):74-83.

3547.   *Shaw, Henry I. "Jungle and Coral: Bougainville
            and Tarawa," *Shipmate* 41 (Nov. 1978):19-20.

3548.   Shaw, James C. "The Rise and Ruin of Rabaul,"
            USNIP 77 (June 1951):624-29.

3549.   _____. "Papua: A Lesson in Sea Power," USNIP
            76 (Nov. 1950):1204-11.

3550.   _____. "*Jarvis* (DD-393): The Destroyer That
            Vanished," USNIP 76 (Feb. 1950):118-27. The
            Battle of Savo Island.

3551.   Sherman, V.A. "The Battle of Vella Gulf," USNIP
            71 (Jan. 1945):61-69.

3552.   Smedberg, William R., III. "A September After-
            noon: The Sinking of the USS WASP," *Shipmate*
            41 (Sept. 1978):21-22.

3553.   *Smith, Julian C. "Tarawa," USNIP 79 (Nov.
            1953):163-73.

3554.   *Tanaka, Raizo. "Japan's Losing Struggle for
              Guadalcanal," ed. Roger Pineau. USNIP 82 (Aug.
              1956):687-99. 814-31.

                           FICTION

3555. PS3552   Beach, Edward L., Jr. *Dust on the Sea*. N.Y.:
       .E12D8   Holt, 1972. Submarine wolfpacks against
                 Japan--by one who was there.

3556. PZ4   _____. *Run Silent, Run Deep*. N.Y.: Holt,
       .B36SRu   1955.

3557. PS3569   Stephens, Edward. *Blow Negative!* GCNY: Double-
       .T385   day, 1962. Battle within the Navy for and
       B53   against a nuclear-powered submarine.

3558. PS3545   Wouk, Herman W. *War and Remembrance*. Boston:
       .O98W3   Little, Brown, 1978.

3559. PS3545   _____. *The Winds of War: A Novel*. Boston:
       .O98W55   Little, Brown, 1971.

3560. PS3545   _____. *The Caine Mutiny: A Novel of World
       .O98C29   War II*. GCNY: Doubleday, 1951.

18

WORLD WAR II IN THE PACIFIC: PART III:
THE DUAL ADVANCE AND THE END OF THE JAPANESE EMPIRE

The titles in this chapter are divided into: A. General;
B. Submarine Warfare.

GENERAL

BOOKS

3561. D767   Adamson, Hans C., and George F. Kosco. *Halsey's*
       .A55   *Typhoons: A Firsthand Account of How 2 Typhoons,*
                More Powerful Than the Japanese, Dealt Death
                and Destruction to Admiral Halsey's Third
                Fleet. N.Y.: Crown, 1967.

3562. D773   Ballentine, Duncan S. *U.S. Naval Logistics in*
       .B34   *the Second World War.* Princeton: PUP, 1947.

3563. D769.52 Barbey, Daniel E. *MacArthur's Amphibious Navy.*
       .A45B3   Annapolis, Md.: USNI, 1969.

3564. D767   Barker, Arthur J. *Suicide Weapons: Japanese*
       .2.B35   *Kamikaze Forces in World War II.* N.Y.: Ballan-
                tine, 1961.

3565. D767.2   _____. *Suicide Weapon.* N.Y.: Ballantine,
       .B35   1971. Kamikazes and human torpedoes.

3566. JX1974   Barnaby, Frank. *The Nuclear Age.* Cambridge:
       .7.S82   MIT P., 1974.

3567. D769.99 *Bartley, Whitman S. *Iwo Jima: Amphibious Epic.*
       .I9U52   Wash.: GPO, 1954.

3568. D774   Bates, Richard W. *The Battle for Leyte Gulf,*
       .P5B38   *October 1944...,* 3 vols. in 1. Springfield,
                Va.: National Technical Information Service,
                1953-1957.

3569. D767   Belote, James H., and William M. Belote. *Titans*
       .B47   *of the Seas: The Development and Operations of*
                American Carrier Task Forces during World War
                II. N.Y.: Harper and Row, 1975.

3570. D767.99 _____. *Typhoon of Steel: The Battle of*
       .O44B4   *Okinawa.* N.Y.: Harper & Row, 1970.

3571. D767.4 *Boggs, Charles W. *Marine Aviation in the Phil-*
.A547 *ippines*. Wash.: USMC, HQ, Hist. Div., 1951.

3572. D790.A5 Buchanan, Albert R. *The Navy's Air War: A Mis-*
1946d *sion Completed*. N.Y.: Harper, 1946.

3573. D773 Bulkley, Robert J. *At Close Quarters: PT Boats*
.B8 *in the United States Navy*. Wash.: Naval Hist.
Div., 1962.

3574. D821 Butow, Robert J.C. *Japan's Decision to Surren-*
.J3B8 *der*. Stanford: Stanford UP, 1954.

3575. D769 Carter, Worrall R. *Beans, Bullets and Black*
.537 *Oil*. Wash.: GPO, 1953.
10th.C3

3576. D773 _____, and Elmer E. Duvall. *Ships, Salvage*
.C33 *and Sinews of War*. Wash.: GPO, 1954.

3577. D743 Churchill, Winston. *The Second World War*. Vol.
.C47 6. *Triumphant Tragedy*. 1953.

3578. E746 Clark, Joseph, and Clark G. Reynolds. *Carrier*
.C55A3 *Admiral*. N.Y.: McKay, 1967. An autobiography
of Admiral Clark.

3579. D769 *Crowl, Philip A. *Campaign in the Marianas*.
.A533 Wash.: OCMH, 1960.

3580. D769 * _____, and Edmund G. Love. *Seizure of the*
.A533 *Gilberts and Marshalls*. Wash.: OCMH, 1955.
v.2
pt.6

3581. D774.P5D Dickson, William D. *The Battle of the Philip-*
520 *pine Sea*. London: Ian Allan, 1975.

3582. D743 Ehrman, John. *Grand Strategy: From October*
.B83 *1944 to August 1945*. James R.M. Butler, ed.
Grand Strategy: History of the Second World
War. United Kingdom Military Series. London:
HMSO, 1957-1972. Vol. 6.

3583. D769.26 *Eichelberger, Robert L. *Our Jungle Road to*
8th.E35 *Tokyo*. N.Y.: Viking, 1950. The autobiography
of the Army general who commanded the Eighth
Army in the conquest of the Philippines. Men-
tions Marines throughout text, in particular
the contribution of Marine aviation in the
campaign to retake the Philippines.

3584. D707.99   *Falk, Stanley L. *Bloodiest Victory: Palaus*.
     .P4F34   N.Y.: Ballantine, 1974.

3585. D767   _____. *Liberation of the Philippines*. N.Y.:
     .4.F33q   Ballantine, 1971.

3586. D767   _____. *Decision at Leyte*. N.Y.: Norton,
     .4.F3   1966.

3587. D770   Fane, Francis D. *The Naked Warriors: The Story*
     .F3   *of the Navy Frogmen from World War II to the*
            Present. N.Y.: Appleton-Century-Crofts, 1956.

3588. D802   Feis, Herbert. *Contest Over Japan*. N.Y.: Nor-
     .J3F45   ton, 1967.

3589. D767   _____. *Japan Subdued: The Atomic Bomb and*
     .2.F4   *the End of the War in the Pacific*. Princeton:
            PUP, 1961.

3590. E183.8   _____. *The China Tangle: The American Ef-*
     .C5F4   *fort in China from Pearl Harbor to the Marshall*
            Mission. N.Y.: Atheneum, 1953.

3591. D777   Field, James A. *The Japanese at Leyte Gulf*.
     .F5   Princeton: PUP, 1947.

3592. D767.99   Frank, Benis M. *Okinawa: Capstone to Victory*.
     .045F7   N.Y.: Ballantine, 1970.

3593. VB23   Furer, Julius A. *Administration of the Navy*
     .F8   *Department in World War II*. Wash.: Naval Hist.
            Div., 1959.

3594. UA23   Giovannetti, Len, and Fred Freed. *The Decision*
     .G62   *to Drop the Bomb*. N.Y.: Coward-McCann, 1965.

3595. D743   Greenfield, Kent R. *American Strategy in World*
     .G666   *War II: A Reconsideration*. Baltimore: Johns
            Hopkins P., 1963.

3596. D769   Hammer, David D. *Lion Six*. Annapolis, Md.:
     .542   NIP, 1947. Seabees at Guam during World War
     .G8H3   II.

3597. D784   Hashimoto, Mochitsura. *Sunk: The Story of the*
     .J3H3   *Japanese Submarine Fleet, 1941-1945*. London:
            Cassell, 1954.

3598. D767.99   *Heinl, Robert D., and John A. Crown. *The*
      .M3U52   *Marshalls: Increasing the Tempo.* Wash.:
                   USMC, HQ, 1954.

3599. D767.99   *Hoffman, Carl W. *The Seizure of Tinian.* Wash.:
      .T5U5   USMC, HQ, Hist. Div., 1951.

3600. D767.99   *_____. *Saipan: The Beginning of the End.*
      .S3U5   Wash.: USMC, HQ, Hist. Div., 1950.

3601. D811   Hopkins, Harold S. *Nice to Have you Aboard.*
      .H6   London: G. Allen & Unwin, 1964. Anglo-American
                   naval relations in the Western Pacific, World
                   War II.

3602. D767.99   *Hough, Frank O. *The Assault on Peleliu.* Wash.:
      .P4U5   USMC, HQ, Hist. Div., 1950.

3603. D767.917   *Hoyt, Edwin P. *Storm Over the Gilberts: War*
      .H67   *in the Central Pacific.* N.Y.: Van Nostrand
                   Reinhold, 1978. Tarawa.

3604. D774   _____. *The Battle of Leyte Gulf: The Death*
      .P4H69   *Knell of the Japanese Fleet.* N.Y.: Weybright,
                   1972.

3605. D769.37   *Hunt, George P. *Coral Comes High.* N.Y.: Har-
      1st.H8   per, 1946. Peleliu.

3606. D792.J3   Inoguchi, Rikihei, Tadshi Nakajima, and Roger
      I513   Pineau. *The Divine Wind: Japan's Kamikaze Force*
                   in World War II. Annapolis, Md.: USNI, 1958.

3607. D777   Ito, Masanori, and Roger Pineau. *The End of*
      .I713   *the Imperial Japanese Navy.* N.Y.: Norton, 1962.

3608. D790   Jensen, Oliver. *Carrier War: The First-Hand*
      .J4   *Story of Task Force 58 and a Year of Naval*
                   War in the Pacific Through the Battles of the
                   Philippine Sea. N.Y.: Simon & Schuster, 1945.

3609. D773   Johnson, Ellis A., and David A. Katcher. *Mines*
      .J65   *Against Japan.* White Oak, Silver Spring, Md.:
                   Naval Ordnance Laboratory. Wash.: GPO, 1973.

3610. D773   Karig, Walter, Russell L. Harris, and Frank
      .K3   R. Manson. *Battle Report.* Vol. 5. *Victory in*
                   the Pacific. N.Y.: Rinehart, 1949.

3611. D773   _____, and others. *Battle Report: The End*
       .K3   *of an Empire*, Vol. 4. N.Y.: Rinehart, 1948.

3612. D811   Kenney, George C. *General Kenney Reports: A*
       .K42   *Personal History of the Pacific War*. N.Y.:
                     Duell, Sloane & Pearce, 1949.

3613. E745   LeMay, Curtis, with Mackinlay Cantor. *Mission*
       .L4A3   *with LeMay: My Story*. GCNY: Doubleday, 1965.

3614. D767.99   *Lodge, Orlan R. *The Recapture of Guam*. Wash.:
       .G8U48   USMC, HQ, Hist. Div., 1954.

3615. D774   Lott, Arnold S. *Brave Ships, Brave Men*. India-
       .A2L6   napolis: Bobbs-Merrill, 1964. Exciting even
                     if somewhat repetitive story of the picket
                     destroyer *Aaron Ward* against kamikazes off
                     Okinawa.

3616. D842   Lukacs, John. *1945: Year Zero*. GCNY: Double-
       .L83   day, 1978.

3617. D774   Macintyre, Donald G. *Leyte Gulf: An Armada in*
       .P5M3   *the Pacific*. N.Y.: Ballantine, 1973.

3618. D785   McIsaac, David. *Strategic Bombing in World War*
       .U575   *Two: The Story of the United States Strategic*
       .M3   *Bombing Survey*. N.Y.: Garland, 1976.

3619. D767.25   Marx, Joseph L. *Nagasaki: The Necessary Bomb?*
       .N3M35   N.Y.: Macmillan, 1971.

3620. P811   Miller, Merle. *We Dropped the A-Bomb*. N.Y.:
       .M525   Crowell, 1946. Personal interviews.

3621. D767.99   *Morehouse, Clifford P. *The Iwo Jima Operation*.
       .I9M6   Wash.: USMC, HQ, Hist. Div., 1946.

3622. D773   Morison, Samuel E. *History of United States*
       .M6   *Naval Operations in World War II*: Vol. 12.
                     Leyte Gulf, June 1944-January 1945 (1958);
                     Vol. 13. *The Liberation of the Philippines:*
                     Luzon, Mindanao, the Visayas, 1944-1945 (1959);
                     Vol. 14. *Victory in the Pacific, 1945* (1960).

3623. D743   _____. *Strategy and Compromise*. Boston:
       .M74   Little, Brown, 1958.

3624. D790   Morrison, Wilbur H. *The Point of No Return:*
      .M63   *The Story of the Twentieth Air Force.* N.Y.:
              Times Books, 1979.

3625. D774   Newcomb, Richard. *Abandon Ship: Death of the*
      .I5N4   *U.S.S.* Indianapolis. Bloomington: Indiana UP,
              1976.

3626. D767.99 *   . *Iwo Jima.* N.Y.: Holt, Rinehart &
      .I9N4   Winston, 1965.

3627. D767.99 *Nicols, Charles S., and Henry I. Shaw. *Okinawa:*
      .045U52 *Victory in the Pacific.* Wash.: USMC, HQ, Hist.
              Div., 1955.

3628. DU647   Pomeroy, Earl S. *Pacific Outpost: American*
      .P6   *Strategy in Guam and Micronesia.* Stanford:
              Stanford UP, 1951.

3629. D811.5 Pyle, Ernie. *Last Chapter.* N.Y.: Holt, 1946.
      .P96   First-person account of life in a fast carrier
              off Okinawa. Soon thereafter Pyle was killed
              on the island of Ie Shima.

3630. D767   *Rentz, John N. *Battle for Tarawa.* Wash.:
      .917.U5 USMC, HQ, Hist, Div., 1947.

3631. UF23   Rowland, Buford, and William B. Boyd. *U.S. Navy*
      .A62   *Bureau of Ordnance in World War II.* Wash.:
              GPO, 1953.

3632. D767   *Russ, Martin. *Line of Departure: Tarawa.* GCNY:
      .917R87 Doubleday, 1975.

3633. D767.2 *Shaw, Henry I., Jr. *The United States Marines*
      .U5   *in the Occupation of Japan.* Wash.: USMC, HQ,
              Hist. Div., 1961. Operations of the 4th
              Marines (Reinforced) and Marine Aircraft Group
              31 in the Yokosuka area, Aug. 1945-Jun. 1946,
              and the 2d and 5th Marine Divisions with
              Marine Aircraft Group 22 in Kyushu and Honshu,
              Japan, Sep. 1945-Jun. 1946.

3634. D767   . *Tarawa: A Legend Is Born.* N.Y.:
      .917.S48 Ballantine, 1970.

3635. D767   *   . *Tarawa: The Story of a Battle.* N.Y.:
      .917.S5 Duell, Sloan & Pearce, 1944.

3636. D767
      .S55

*Sherrod, Robert. *On to the Westward: War in the Central Pacific*. N.Y.: Duell, Sloan & Pearce, 1945. Tarawa, Saipan, Iwo Jima, Okinawa.

3637. D753
      .S48

Sherwin, Martin J. *A World Destroyed: The Atomic Bomb and the Grand Alliance*. N.Y.: Knopf, 1975.

3638. D767
      .S58

Smith, Peter C. *Task Force 57: The British Pacific Fleet, 1944-1945*. London: Kimber, 1969.

3639. D769
      .A533
      v.2
      pt.16

*Smith, Robert R. *Triumph in the Philippines*. Wash.: OCMH, 1963.

3640. D767
      .A533
      v.2
      pt.12

_____. *The Approach to the Philippines*. Wash.: OCMH, 1953.

3641. UF767
      .S5

Smyth, Henry DeW. *Atomic Energy for Military Purposes: The Official Report of the Development of the Atomic Bomb Under the Auspices of the United States Government, 1940-1945*. Princeton: PUP, 1945.

3642. D734
      .C7S8

Stettinius, Edward R. *Roosevelt and the Russians: The Yalta Conference*. Walter Johnson, ed. GCNY: Doubleday, 1949.

3643. D767
      .917.U5

*Stockman, James R. *The Battle for Tarawa*. Wash.: USMC, HQ, Hist. Div., 1947.

3644. D767
      .25.H6T5

Thomas Gordon, and Max M. Witts. *Enola Gay*. N.Y.: Stein and Day, 1977.

3645. D767.99
      .I9W5

*Wheeler, Richard. *The Bloody Battle for Suribachi*. N.Y.: Crowell, 1965.

3646. D805
      .J3W44

*White, John A. *The United States Marines in North China*. Millbrae, Calif.: White, 1974.

3647. D767.98
      .W5

*Willard, Warren W. *The Leathernecks Come Through*. N.Y.: Revell, 1944. Solomons and Gilberts.

3648. D767   Winton, John, pseud. *The Forgotten Fleet: The British Navy in the Pacific, 1944-1945*. N.Y.: Crown-McCann, 1970.

3649. D773   Woodward, C. Vann. *The Battle for Leyte Gulf*.
      .W6   N.Y.: Macmillan, 1947.

DOCUMENTS

3650. Micro   *The SWNCC/SANACC Case Files, 1944-1945*. Wilmington, Del.: Scholarly Resources, 1979. Records of the State-War-Navy Coordinating Committee, 1944-1947, and its successor, the State-Army-Navy-Air Force Coordinating Committee, 1947-1949.

3651.   U.S. Coast Guard. Historical Section. *The Coast Guard at War*, 30 vols. Wash.: 1944-1954.

3652. D767.2 U.S. Strategic Bombing Survey. *The Offensive Mine Laying Campaign Against Japan*. Rpt.,
      .U58   Dept. of the Navy, HQ, Naval Material Command, 1966.

3653. Micro   U.S. Strategic Bombing Survey. *Final Reports of the USSBS, 1945-1947*. Wash.: USSBS, 1947.
      M1013

3654. D767   _____. *The Campaigns of the Pacific War*.
      .U63   Wash.: USSBS, 1946.
      No. 73

3655. D767   _____. *Summary Report (Pacific War), 1 July 1946*. Wash. USSBS, 1946.
      .U55

3656. JX233   U.S. Department of State. *The Conferences at Malta and Yalta, 1945*. Wash.: GPO, 1955.
      .A31

3657. Micro   U.S. NARS. *U.S. State-War-Navy Coordinating Committee*. SWNCC Agenda and Minutes of Meetings from 14 Dec. 1944 to 19 Nov. 1947. 1 reel.
      JX468
      .S4U58

3658.   Waldmeir, Joseph. "The Documentation of World War II," *Nation* 191 (Nov. 19, 1960):393-98.

DISSERTATIONS AND THESES

3659.   Kahler, John K. "The Genesis of the American Involvment in Indo-China, 1940-1954," U. of Chicago, 1964.

3660.   Algire, K.D. "Major Logistics Lessons of World War II," NWCR 11 (Feb. 1951):25-43.

3661.   *"Amphibious Operation: The Story of Tarawa," *Leatherneck* 27 (Feb. 1944):23-33.

3662. G525   Baldwin, Hanson. "The Sho Plan: The Battle for
       .B255   Leyte Gulf," in his *Sea Fights and Shipwrecks*. GCNY: Hanover House, 1955, pp. 134-82.

3663.   _____. "Okinawa: Victory at the Threshold," MCG 35 (Jan. 1951):42-49.

3664.   _____. "America At War: Victory in the Pacific," FA 24 (Oct. 1945):26-39.

3665.   _____. "Why Japan's Fleet Avoids Action, FA 22 (Oct. 1943):59-69.

3666.   Bauer, K. Jack, and Alan C. Coox, "OLYMPIC vs. KETTSU-GO," MCG 49 (Aug. 1965):32-44. American invasion plans vs. Japanese defense plans.

3667.   "The Big Blow: Philippine Sea, 1944," *All Hands*, No. 542 (Mar. 1962):59-63.

3668.   Brodie, Bernard. "The Battle for Leyte Gulf," *Virginia Q. Rev.* 23 (Summer 1947):455-60.

3669.   _____. "Our Ships Strike Back," *Virginia Q. Rev.* 21 (Spring 1945):186-206.

3670.   Buell, Thomas B. "Battle of the Philippine Sea," USNIP 100 (July 1974):64-79.

3671.   Burke, Arleigh. "Admiral Marc Mitscher: A Naval Aviator," USNIP 1010 (Apr. 1975):53-63.

3672.   Byrd, Martha H. "Battle of the Philippine Sea," AHI 12 (July 1977):20-35.

3673.   Carlton, Phillips D. "The Taking of Eniwetok," MCG 28 (May 1944):19-23.

3674.   *Cates, Clifton B. "Iwo Jima," MCG 49 (Feb. 1975):28-31.

3675.	*Churley, Robert A. "The North China Operation,"
MCG 31 (Oct. 1947):10-16, (Nov. 1947):17-22.
An account of Marine experiences in North
China, 1945-1947, receiving the surrender of
Japanese forces and patrolling the Peiping-
Mukden Railroad in the face of Chinese Com-
munist guerrilla opposition.

3676.	Clark, Joseph. "The Marianas Turkey Shoot," AH
18 (Oct. 1967):26-29+.

3677.	Danton, J. Periam. "The Battle of the Philip-
pine Sea," USNIP 71 (Sept. 1945):1023-27.

3678.	Deac, Wilfred P. "The Battle off Samar," AH
18 (Dec. 1966):20-23+.

3679.	*Dobbs, Charles M. "American Marines in North
China, 1945-1946," SAQ 76 (Summer 1977):318-31.

3680.	Emerson, William. "Franklin Roosevelt as Com-
mander-in-Chief in World War II," MA 22 (Winter
1958):181-207.

3681.	Evans-Lombe, E.M. "The Royal Navy in the Pa-
cific," RUSIJ 92 (Aug. 1947):333-47. Anglo-
American naval relations in the Western Pacific, World War II.

3682.	Field, James, Jr. "Leyte Gulf: The First Un-
censored Japanese Account," USNIP 77 (Mar.
1951):255-65.

3683.	Fukudome, Shigeru. "Strategic Aspects of the
Battle off Formosa," USNIP 78 (Dec. 1952):
1285-95.

3684.	Garthoff, Raymond L. "Soviet Operations in
the War with Japan, August 1945," USNIP 92
(May 1966):50-63.

3685.	Halliwell, Martin. "The Projected Assault on
Japan," RUSIJ 92 (Aug. 1947):348-51.

3686.	Halsey, William F. "The Battle for Leyte Gulf,"
USNIP 78 (May 1952):487-95.

3687.	Hamilton, Andrew. "Where is Task Force Thirty-
Four?" USNIP 86 (Oct. 1960):76-80.

3688.   *Heinl, Robert D. "Target: Iwo," USNIP 89 (July
            1963):70-82.

3689.   *_____. "D-day, Roi-Namur," MA 12 (Fall
            1948):129-43.

3690.   *Hill, Harry W. "The Marshall Islands Operation:
            The Eniwetok Operation," MR 27 (Feb. 1948):51-
            54.

3691.   Hori, Y. "The Japanese Defense of Iwo Jima,"
            MCG 36 (Feb. 1952):18-27.

3692.   *Isby, David C. "Island War: The U.S. Amphibious
            Offensive Against Imperial Japan 1942 to 1945,"
            S&T, Sept/Oct 1975, 21-36.

3693.   *Isely, Jeter A. "Iwo Jima: Acme of Amphibious
            Assault," USNIP 77 (Jan. 1951):1-14.

3694.   Karig, Walter, Russell Harris, and Frank A.
            Manson. "Jeeps Versus Giants," USNIP 73 (Dec.
            1947):1444-53. Battle off Samar.

3695.   Koyanagi, Romiji. "With Kurita in the Battle
            of Leyte Gulf," USNIP 79 (Feb. 1953):118-33.
            Reminiscences of Kurita's chief of staff.

3696.   Kublin, Hyman. "Okinawa: A Key to the Western
            Pacific," USNIP 80 (Dec. 1954):1358-65.

3697.   Leighton, Richard M. "Allied Unity of Command
            in the Second World War: A Study in Regional
            Military Organization," PSQ 67 (Sept. 1952):
            399-425.

3698.   Lott, Arnold S. "Japan's Nightmare: Mine
            Blockade," USNIP 85 (Nov. 1959):39-51.

3699.   McCloy, John F. "The Great Military Decisions,"
            FA 26 (Oct. 1947):52-72.

3700.   *McKiernan, Patrick. "Tarawa: The Tide That
            Failed," USNIP 88 (Feb. 1962):38-50.

3701.   McMillian, Ira E. "Naval Gunfire at Roi-Namur,"
            MCG 32 (July 1948):50-55.

3702.   Manson, Frank A. "Seventy-nine Minutes on the
            Picket Line," USNIP 75 (Sept. 1949):996-1003,
            1412-13. U.S. destroyers vs. kamikazes.

3703.   Martin, Paul W. "Kamikaze!" USNIP 72 (Aug.
            1946):1055-57. And comment thereon in USNIP
            72 (Dec. 1946) and 73 (Mar. 1947).

3704.   Matloff, Maurice. "Franklin Delano Roosevelt
            as War Leader," in Total War and Cold War:
            Problems in Civilian Control of the Military.
            Ed. Harry L. Coles. Columbus: Ohio State UP,
            1962, pp. 42-65.

3705.   Miles, Milton E. "U.S. Naval Group, China."
            USNIP 72 (July 1946):921-31. A report of the
            operations of SACO (Sino-American Cooperative
            Organization), guerrilla-type organization of
            some 2,500 U.S. Navy, Army, and Marine person-
            nel training guerrilla forces in China, 1943-
            1945, and conducting guerrilla raids on Japa-
            nese forces throughout China.

3706.   Morehead, Joseph H., Jr. "World War II Reminis-
            cences," Bull. of Bibliography 25 (May-Aug.
            1968):143-45.

3707.   Morison, Samuel E. "The Battle of Surigao
            Strait," USNIP 84 (Dec. 1958):31-53.

3708.   Morton, Louis. "The Marianas," MR 47 (July
            1967):71-82.

3709.   _____. "Soviet Intervention in the War with
            Japan," FA 40 (July 1962):653-62.

3710.   _____. "The Decision to Use the Atomic
            Bomb," in Kent R. Greenfield, ed. Command De-
            cisions. Wash.: OCMH, 1960, pp. 493-518.

3711.   _____. "The Military Background of the
            Yalta Agreements," Reporter 12 (Apr. 7, 1955):
            19-21.

3712.   _____. "American and Allied Strategy in the
            Far East," MR 29 (Dec. 1949):22-39.

3713.   Mosely, H.W., and others. "The State-War-Navy
            Coordinating Committee," U.S. Department of
            State Bull. 12 (Nov. 11, 1945):745-47.

3714.   Naval Analysis Division, U.S. Strategic Bombing Survey. "The Offensive Mine Laying Campaign Against Japan," *Air Power Historian* 5 (July 1958):161-71.

3715.   Oldendorf, Jesse R. "Comments on the Battle of Surigao Strait," USNIP 85 (Apr. 1959):104-07.

3716.   Pogue, Forrest C. "Political Problems of a Coalition Command," in *Total War and Cold War: Problems in Civilian Control of the Military.* Ed. Harry L. Coles. Columbus: Ohio State UP, 1962, pp. 108-28.

3717.   Riefler, Winfield W. "Our Economic Contribution to Victory," FA 26 (Oct. 1947):90-103.

3718.   *Rowcliff, Gilbert J. "Guam," USNIP 71 (July 1945):781-93.

3719.   *Shepherd, Lemuel C. "Battle for Motobu Peninsula," MCG 29 (Aug. 1945):8-12. Okinawa.

3720.   *Smith, H.E. "I Saw the Morning Break," USNIP 72 (Mar. 1946):403-15. Guam.

3721.   *Smith, Holland M. "Tarawa Was a Mistake," SEP 231 (Nov. 6, 1948):15-17+.

3722.   * _____. "My Troubles with the Army on Saipan," SEP 231 (Nov. 13, 1948):32-33+.

3723.   * _____. "Iwo Jima Cost Too Much," SEP 231 (Nov. 20, 1948):32-33+.

3724.   *Smith, Julian. "Tarawa," USNIP 79 (Nov. 1953): 1163-75.

3725.   Smith, Robert R. "Luzon versus Formosa," in Kent R. Greenfield, ed. *Command Decisions.* Wash.: OCMH, 1960, pp. 461-78.

3726.   Spruance, Raymond A. "The Victory in the Pacific," RUSIJ 102 (Nov. 1946):539-55.

3727. UG630 Truman, Harry S. "The First Atomic Bombing at
       .E5   Hiroshima," in Eugene E. Emme, ed., *The Impact of Air Power: National Security and World Politics.* Princeton, N.J.: D. Van Nostrand, 1959, pp. 83-85. Radio address of 6 Aug. 1945.

3728.   Uhlig, Frank, and William R. Mathews. "Franklin Delano Roosevelt: A Disciple of Mahan," USNIP 79 (May 1953):561-62.

3729.   Van Alstyne, Richard. "The United States and Russia in World War II," CH 19 (Nov., Dec. 1950):257-60, 334-39.

3730.   Van Wyen, Adrian O. "The Battle of the Philippine Sea," USNIP 77 (Feb. 1951):156-59.

3731.   Vogel, Bertram. "The Great Strangling of Japan," USNIP 62 (Nov. 1947):1304-09.

3732.   Wheeler, C. Julian. "We Had the British Where We Needed Them," USNIP 72 (Dec. 1946):1583-85. Anglo-American naval relations in the Western Pacific, World War II.

3733.   Wylie, J.C. "Reflections on the War in the Pacific," USNIP 78 (Apr. 1952):350-361.

3734.   Yokoi, Toshiyuki. "Kamikazes and the Okinawa Campaign," USNIP 80 (May 1954):505-13.

3735.   Zimmerman, Sherwood V. "Operation Forager," USNIP 90 (Aug. 1964):78-90. Battle of the Philippine Sea.

B. SUBMARINE WARFARE

BOOKS

3736. D783   Blair, Clay, Jr. *Silent Victory: The United*
      .B58   *States Submarine War Against Japan.* Phila.: Lippincott, 1973.

3737. D783   Chambliss, William C. *The Silent Service.*
      .C4   N.Y.: New Am. Lib., 1959. Stories about American submarines as seen on the TV series "The Silent Service."

3738. D783   Cope, Harley F., and Walter Karig. *Battle Sub-*
      .C6   *merged: Submarine Fighters of World War II.* N.Y.: Norton, 1951. Includes operations at the battles of the Coral Sea and Midway.

3739. D783.5   Frank, Gerald, and others. *U.S.S.* Seawolf:
      .S4F7   *Submarine Raider of the Pacific.* N.Y.: Putnam, 1945.

3740. D783
      .H3

Hawkins, Maxwell. *Torpedoes Away, Sir! Our Submarine Navy in the Pacific*. N.Y.: Holt, 1946.

3741. D783
      .H6

Holmes, W.J. *Undersea Victory: The Influence of Submarine Operations on the War in the Pacific*. GCNY: Doubleday, 1966. Includes submarines of all nations.

3742. V63
      .L6A3

Lockwood, Charles A. *Down to the Sea in Subs: My Life in the U.S. Navy*. N.Y.: Norton, 1967.

3743. D783
      .L6

_____. *Sink 'Em All!: Submarine Warfare in the Pacific*. N.Y.: Dutton, 1951.

3744. D773
      .L57

_____, and Hans C. Adamson. *Battles of the Philippine Sea*. N.Y.: Crowell, 1967.

3745. D769
      .45L6

_____. *Zoomies, Subs, and Zeros*. N.Y.: Greenberg, 1956.

3746. D780
      .L6

_____. *Hellcats of the Sea*. Phila.: Chilton, 1955.

3747. D783.5q
      .T35038

O'Kane, Richard H. *Clear the Bridge: The War Patrols of the U.S.S.* Tang. Chicago: Rand McNally, 1977.

3748. D773
      .R6

Roscoe, Theodore. *United States Submarine Operations in World War II*. Annapolis, Md.: USNI, 1949.

3749. D783.5
      .W3S75

Sterling, Forest J. *Wake of the* Wahoo. Phila.: Chilton, 1960.

ARTICLES

3750.

Chaplin, Philip. "Statistics of Submarine Warfare, 1939-1945," USNIP 85 (1959):109-11. Covers both friendly and enemy.

3751.

Goldingham, C.S. "United States Submarines in the Blockade of Japan in the 1939-1945 War," RUSIJ 97 (Feb.-May 1952):87-98, 212-22.

3752.

Long, E. John. "Japan's 'Underseas Carriers,'" USNIP 76 (June 1950):607-13.

3753.

Oi, Atsushi. "Why Japan's Anti-Submarine Warfare Failed," USNIP 78 (June 1952):587-601.

3754.   "Our Submarine Victory in the Pacific," USNIP 74 (Sept. 1948):1147-56. Pictorial.

3755.   Reynolds, Clark G. "Submarine Attacks on the Pacific Coast, 1942," PHR 33 (May 1964):183-93.

3756.   Torisu, Kennosuke. "Japanese Submarine Tactics," USNIP 87 (Feb. 1961):78-83.

3757.   Yokota, Yutaka, and Joseph D. Harrington. "Kaiten: Japan's Human Torpedoes," USNIP 88 (Jan. 1962):55-68.

TRANSCRIPTS OF ORAL INTERVIEWS

3758.   Richard L. Conolly, Gerald F. Bogan, Arleigh Burke, Thomas C. Kinkaid, and Hanson W. Baldwin. Annapolis, Md.: U.S. Naval Academy Library, Special Collections. *See also* in the same collection:

3759. Micro   Burke, Arleigh A. "The First Battle of the Philippine Sea: Decision Not to Force an Action on the Night of 18-19 June [1944]."

FICTION

3760. PZ4   Ashmead, John. *The Mountain and the Feather*.
.A8265   Boston: Houghton Mifflin, 1961. Naval battles.
Mo

3761. PS3552   Bassett, James E. *Cmdr. Prince, USN: A Novel*
.A824C6 *of the Pacific War*. N.Y.: Simon & Schuster, 1971. American destroyer in the Dutch East Indies, 1942.

3762. PZ4   _____. *Harm's Way*. Cleveland: World, 1961.
.B3185   "Good Guy" Rockwell Torrey vs. the "bad guys,"
Har   during the first year after Pearl Harbor.

3763. PZ4   Beach, Edward O., Jr. *Run Silent, Run Deep*.
.B365   N.Y.: Holt, 1955. Submarine story.
Ru

3764. PZ3   Bowman, Peter. *Beach Red*. N.Y.: Random House,
.B6843   1945. Assaulting a Japanese-held island.
Be

3765. PZ8 .B8292 To
*Bruce, George, and Randal M. White. *Salute to the Marines*. N.Y.: Grosset & Dunlap, 1943. Marines in action.

3766. PZ3 .C2383 De
Carse, Robert. *Deep Six*. N.Y.: Morrow, 1946. Cruiser warfare.

3767. PZ3 .C8716 Mag
Crockett, Lucy H. *The Magnificent Bastards*. N.Y.: Farrar, Straus & Cudahy, 1954. About a lady Marine.

3768. PZ3 .B54815 De
Dibner, Martin. *The Deep Six*. GCNY: Doubleday, 1953. Naval events.

3769. PZ4 .D646 Aw
Dodson, Kenneth. *Away All Boats*. Boston: Little, Brown, 1954. Story of an amphibious craft.

3770. PS3515 .A2523 .E82
Haislip, Harvey. *Escape from Java*. GCNY: Doubleday, 1962. Early World War II.

3771. PS3558 .A624 W64
Hardy, William M. *Wolfpack*. N.Y.: Dodd, Mead, 1960. U.S. submarines attack Japanese convoy in Imperial home waters.

3772. PS3515 .E263 M57
Heggen, Thomas. *Mister Roberts*. Boston: Houghton Mifflin, 1946. Hilarious story on which the movie was based. Life on a fleet supply ship.

3773. PS3525 .A4152 N34
*Mailer, Norman. *The Naked and the Dead*. N.Y.: Holt, Rinehart & Winston, 1948. Allied amphibious operations.

3774. PZ3 .M61595 Is
*Miller, Merle. *Island 49*. N.Y.: Crowell, 1945. Marines capture a Pacific island, World War II.

3775. PZ4 .M998 Bi
*Myrer, Anton. *The Big War*. N.Y.: Appleton, 1957. U.S. Marines.

3776. PS3541 .R46B38
*Uris, Leon. *Battle Cry*. N.Y.: Putnam, 1953. A novel based on the author's experiences in the Marine Corps in the Pacific in World War II.

19

THE COLD WAR AND AMERICAN DEFENSE
REORGANIZATION, 1945-1950

BOOKS

3777. E748   Albion, Robert G., and Robert H. Connery. *For-*
      .F68A6   *restal and the Navy*. N.Y.: Columbia UP, 1962.

3778. E744   Ambrose, Stephen E. *Rise to Globalism: Foreign*
      .A477   *Policy Since 1938*, rev. ed. Baltimore: Penguin,
                1976.

3779. D843   Bailey, Thomas A. *The Marshall Plan Summer: An*
      .B243   *Eye-witness Report on Europe and the Russians*
                in 1947. Stanford: Hoover Institution P., 1977.

3780. VA23   Baldwin, Hanson W. *Power and Politics: The*
      .B26   *Price of Security in the Atomic Age*. Claremont:
                College P., 1950.

3781. UA23   Betts, Richard K. *Soldiers, Statesmen, and Cold*
      .B46   *War Crises*. Cambridge, Mass.: HUP, 1977.
                Military leaders were no more warmongers in
                their advice than civil advisers in crises in-
                volving the Berlin blockade, Korean War, in-
                tervention in Lebanon, Cuban missile crises,
                and American involvement in Vietnam.

3782. VA65   Blair, Clay. *The Atomic Submarine and Admiral*
      .N3B4   *Rickover*. N.Y.: Holt, 1954.

3783. E183.8   Blair, Leon B. *Western Window in the Arab*
      .M65B55   *World*. Austin: U. of Texas P., 1970.

3784. UA236   Borklund, Carl W. *The Department of Defense*.
      .B58   N.Y.: Praeger, 1968.

3785. UA236   _____. *Men of the Pentagon: From Forrestal*
      .B6   *to McNamara*. N.Y.: Praeger, 1966.

3786. UA11   Brodie, Bernard. *Strategy in the Missile Age*.
      .B7   Princeton: PUP, 1959.

3787. QC773.3   Brown, Anthony C., and Charles B. MacDonald,
      .U5S44   eds. *The Secret History of the Atomic Bomb*.
                N.Y.: Dial, 1977. The first official public
                history of the atomic bomb's development and
                detonation.

3788. DD220   Calleo, David P. *The German Problem Recon-*
      .C34   *sidered: Germany and the World Order, 1970 to*
               the Present. N.Y.: Cambridge UP, 1978.

3789. E840   _____. *The Atlantic Fantasy: The U.S., NATO,*
      .C34   *and Europe*. Baltimore: Johns Hopkins P., 1970.

3790. UA23   Caraley, Demetrious. *The Politics of Military*
      .C24   *Unification: A Study of Conflict and the Pol-*
               icy Process. N.Y.: Columbia UP, 1966.

3791. VF373   Christman, Albert B. *History of the Naval*
      .H58   *Weapons Center, China Lake, California*. Wash.:
               GPO, 1971.

3792. Micro   Claussen, Martin P. *State-War-Navy Coordinating*
      CD3033   *Committee Policy Files: 1944-1947*. Wilmington,
      .S7   Del.: Scholarly Resources, 1977.

3793. UA646   Cleveland, Harlan. *NATO: The Transatlantic Bar-*
      .3C54   *gain*. N.Y.: Harper & Row, 1970.

3794.   Coletta, Paolo E. *The U.S. Navy and Defense*
               Unification, 1947-1953. Newark: U. of Delaware
               P., 1980.

3795. DD881   Collier, Richard. *Bridge Across the Sky: The*
      .C57   *Berlin Blockade and Airlift, 1948-1949*. N.Y.:
               McGraw-Hill, 1978.

3796. E744   Compton, James V. *America and the Origins of*
      .C65   *the Cold War*. Boston: Houghton Mifflin, 1972.

3797. UG1242   Coulam, Robert F. *Illusions of Choice: The F-*
      .F5C68   *111 and the Problem of Weapons Acquisition*
               Reform. Princeton: PUP, 1977.

3798. E806   Dallek, Robert. *Franklin D. Roosevelt and*
      .D33   *American Foreign Policy, 1932-1945*. N.Y.:
               Oxford UP, 1979.

3799. V63.R54 David, Heather M. *Admiral Rickover and the Nu-*
      D37   *clear Navy*. N.Y.: Putnam, 1970.

3800. E183.8   Davis, Lynn E. *The Cold War Begins: Soviet-*
      .R9D38   *American Conflict over Eastern Europe*.
               Princeton: PUP, 1974.

3801. VF347   Davis, Vincent. *The Politics of Innovation:*
       .D3   *Patterns in Navy Cases.* Denver: U. of Denver,
                    1967.

3802. US23   _____. *The Admirals Lobby.* Chapel Hill:
       .D29   UNCP, 1967.

3803. VA50   _____. *Postwar Defense Policy and the U.S.*
       .D34   *Navy, 1943-1946.* Chapel Hill: UNCP, 1962.

3804. DD881   Davison, William P. *The Berlin Blockade: A*
       .D3   *Study in Cold War Politics.* Princeton: PUP,
                    1958.

3805. D443   Donnelly, Desmond. *Struggle for the World:*
       .D642   *The Cold War, 1917-1965.* N.Y.: St. Martin,
                    1965.

3806. E183.8   Dulles, Foster R. *American Policy toward Com-*
       .C5D79   *munist China, 1949-1969.* N.Y.: Crowell, 1972.

3807. UA23   Eberstadt, Ferdinand. *Unification of the War*
       .E2   *and Navy Departments and Postwar Organization*
                    for National Security. Report to Honorable
                    James Forrestal, Secretary of the Navy....
                    Wash.: GPO, 1945.

3808. UG630   Emme, Eugene E., ed. *The Impact of Air Power:*
       .E5   *National Security and World Politics.* Prince-
                    ton: Van Nostrand, 1959.

3809. VG93   *Fails, William R. Ed. by William J. Sambito.
       .R38   *Marines and Helicopters, 1946-1973,* 2 vols.
                    Wash.: USMC, HQ, Hist. and Museums Div.,
                    1977. Vol. 2. Eugene W. Rawlins wrote Vol. 1,
                    q.v.

3810. D843   Feis, Herbert. *From Trust to Terror: The Onset*
       .F387   *of the Cold War, 1945-1950.* N.Y.: Norton, 1970.

3811. E834   Finer, Herman. *Dulles Over Suez.* Chicago:
       .D85F5   Quadrangle Books. 1964.

3812. DK63   Fleming, Denna F. *The Cold War and Its Origins,*
       .3.F55   *1917-1960,* 2 vols. GCNY: Doubleday, 1961.

3813. D421   Fontaine, André. *A History of the Cold War:*
       .F613   *From the Korean War to the Present,* 2 vols.
                    N.Y.: Pantheon, 1969.

3814. FV179   Forrestal, James V., and others. *The Navy: A*
    .N3   *Study in Administration*. Chicago: Public Ad-
                ministration Service, 1946.

3815. E183.8   Gaddis, John L. *Russia, the Soviet Union, and*
    .R9G24   *the United States: An Interpretive History*.
                N.Y.: Wiley, 1977. A diplomatic history fol-
                lowing well-known lines. Little interpreta-
                tion.

3816. E744   _____. *The United States and the Origins of*
    .G25   *the Cold War, 1941-1947*. N.Y.: Columbia UP,
                1972.

3817. E813   Gardner, Lloyd C. *The Origins of the Cold War*.
    .G28   Boston: Ginn, 1977. Revisionist.

3818. E744   Gati, Charles, ed. *Caging the Bear: Contain-*
    .G345   *ment and the Cold War*. Indianapolis: Bobbs-
                Merrill, 1974.

3819. KF7625   Generous, William T., Jr. *Swords and Scales:*
    .G45   *The Development of the Uniform Code of Military*
                Justice. Port Washington, N.Y.: Kennikat P.,
                1973.

3820. UG633   Goldberg, Alfred, ed. *A History of the United*
    .G6   *States Air Force, 1907-1957*. Princeton: Van
                Nostrand Reinhold, 1957.

3821. UA23   Goodpaster, Andrew J., and Samuel P. Hunting-
    .G74   ton. *Civil-Military Relations*. Wash.: AEI,
                1977.

3822. D843   Graebner, Norman A., ed. *The Cold War: A Con-*
    .G7   *flict of Ideology and Power*, 2d ed. Lexington,
                Mass.: Heath, 1976.

3823. E744   _____. *Cold War Diplomacy: American Foreign*
    .G69   *Policy, 1945-1960*. Princeton: Van Nostrand,
                1962; 2d ed., 1945-1975, [1976].

3824. E744   Hammond, Paul Y. *Cold War and Detente: The*
    .H345   *American Foreign Policy Process Since 1945*.
                N.Y.: Harcourt Brace Jovanovich, 1975.

3825. UB   _____. *Organizing for Defense: The American*
    .23.H3   *Military Establishment in the Twentieth Cen-*
                tury. Princeton: PUP, 1961.

3826. E813   Haynes, Richard F. *The Awesome Power: Harry S.*
      .H42   *Truman as Commander in Chief.* Baton Rouge:
                LSUP, 1973.

3827. UA23   Head, Richard G., and Evin J. Rokke, eds. *Study*
      .A4122   *Guide to American Defense Policy.* Baltimore:
                Johns Hopkins P., 1973.

3828. VE23   *Heinl, Robert D. *Soldiers of the Sea: The*
      .H4   *United States Marine Corps, 1775-1962.* Annap-
                olis, Md.: USNI, 1962.

3829. D753.2   Herring, George C. *Aid to Russia, 1941-1946:*
      .R9H47   *Strategy, Diplomacy, the Origins of the Cold*
                War. N.Y.: Columbia UP, 1973.

3830. VM317   Hewlett, Richard G., and Francis Duncan. *Nu-*
      .H48   *clear Navy, 1946-1962.* Chicago: U. of Chicago
                P., 1974.

3831. D843   Higgins, Hugh. *The Cold War.* N.Y.: Barnes and
      .H52   Noble, 1974.

3832.   Hooper, Edwin B. *The Navy Department: Evolu-*
                tion and Fragmentation. Wash.: Naval Hist.
                Foundation, 1978.

3833. UG633   Hopkins, J.C., and Sheldon A. Goldberg. *De-*
      .H63   *velopment of Strategic Air Command 1946-1976.*
                Offutt AFB, Neb.: SAC, Office of the Historian,
                1976.

3834. D465   Howard, Harry N. *Turkey, the Straits, and U.S.*
      .H66   *Policy.* Baltimore: Johns Hopkins P., 1974.

3835. VA25   Huzar, Elias. *The Purse and the Sword: Control*
      .H88   *of the Army Through Military Appropriations,*
                1933-1950. Ithaca: Cornell UP, 1950.

3836. DS553   Irving, Ronald E.M. *The First Indochina War:*
      .I78   *French and American Policy, 1945-54.* London:
                Croom Helm, 1975.

3837. DA69.3   Ismay, General Lord. *The Memoirs of General*
      .I8A3   *Lord Ismay.* N.Y.: Viking, 1960.

3838. UA646   _____. *NATO: The First Five Years, 1949-*
      .3.A55   *1954.* The Netherlands: Bosch-Utrecht, 1954.

312

3839. E744   Kaplan, Lawrence. *Recent American Foreign Pol-*
       .K17   *icy: Conflicting Interpretations*, rev. ed.
                   Homewood, Ill.: Dorsey P., 1972.

3840. UA646   _____. *NATO and the Policy of Containment.*
       .3.K36   Boston: Heath, 1968.

3841. D842   Kaplan, Morton A. *The Life and Death of the*
       .5.K36   *Cold War: Selected Studies in Postwar State-*
                   craft. Chicago: Nelson-Hall, 1976.

3842. UA646   _____. *The Rationale for NATO: European*
       .3.K37   *Collective Security, Past and Future.* Wash.:
                   AEI, 1973.

3843. DA70   Kennedy, Paul M. *The Rise and Fall of British*
       .K44   *Mastery.* N.Y.: Scribner, 1976.

3844. UA23   Kissinger, Henry A. *Nuclear Weapons and Foreign*
       .K49   *Policy.* N.Y.: Harper, 1957.

3845. UA646   Knorr, Klaus E., ed. *NATO and American Securi-*
       .3K5   *ty.* Princeton: PUP, 1959.

3846. DK274   Kohler, Foy D., and others. *Soviet Strategy*
       .S68   *for the Seventies: From Cold War to Peaceful*
                   Coexistence. Coral Gables, Fla.: U. of Miami
                   P., 1973.

3847. D843   LaFeber, Walter, comp. *The Origins of the Cold*
       .L23   *War, 1941-1947: A Historical Problem with In-*
                   terpretation and Documents. N.Y.: Wiley, 1971.

3848. E183.8   _____. *America, Russia, and the Cold War,*
       .R9L26   *1945-1971.* N.Y.: Wiley, 1967, 1972, 1976.

3849. E744   Lederer, William J. *A Nation of Sheep.* N.Y.:
       .LU2   Norton, 1961.

3850. VA65   Lewellen, John B. *The Atomic Submarine.* N.Y.:
       .N3L4   Crowell, 1954.

3851. QC792   Lewis, Richard S., and Jane Wilson. *Alamogordo*
       .A43   *Plus Twenty-five Years: The Impact of Atomic*
                   Energy on Science, Technology, and World Poli-
                   tics. N.Y.: Viking, 1971.

3852. HD9698   Lilienthal, David E. *Change, Hope, and the*
       .U5225   *Bomb.* Princeton: PUP, 1963.

3853. E744   Lippmann, Walter. *The Cold War: A Study in*
       .L54   *United States Foreign Policy.* N.Y.: Harper,
                  1947.

3854. D753   Louis, William R. *Imperialism at Bay: The*
       .L67   *United States and the Decolonization of the*
                  British Empire, 1941-1945. N.Y.: Oxford UP,
                  1978.

3855. D840   Lukacs, John. *A History of the Cold War.* GCNY:
       .L8   Anchor Books, 1962.

3856. E183.8   McDonald, Ian, comp. and ed. *Anglo-American*
       .G7M118   *Relations Since the Second World War.* Newton
                  Abbot, England: David E. Charles, 1974.

3857. D1058   McGeehan, Robert. *The German Rearmament Ques-*
       .M25   *tion: American Diplomacy and European Defense*
                  after World War II. Urbana: U. of Illinois P.,
                  1971.

3858. E748   McLellan, Davis S. *Dean Acheson: The State*
       .A15M32   *Department Years.* N.Y.: Dodd, Mead, 1976.

3859. DK273   Mastny, Vojtech. *Russia's Road to the Cold*
       .M4   *War: Diplomacy, Strategy, and the Politics of*
                  Communism, 1941-1945. N.Y.: Columbia UP, 1979.

3860. E183.8   May, Ernest R. *The Truman Administration and*
       .C5M38   *China, 1945-1949.* Phila.: Lippincott, 1975.

3861. E181   Millis, Walter. *Arms and Men: A Study of Ameri-*
       .M699   *can Military History.* N.Y.: Putnam, 1956.

3862. E813   _____, ed., with the collaboration of E.S.
       .F6   Duffield. *The Forrestal Diaries.* N.Y.: Viking,
                  1951.

3863. E744   Morgenthau, Hans J. *In Defense of the National*
       .M68   *Interest: A Critical Examination of American*
                  Foreign Policy. N.Y.: Knopf, 1951.

3864. T14   Morison, Elting E. *Men, Machines, and Modern*
       .M59   *Times.* Cambridge: MIT, 1966.

3865. VG93   Morrison, Wilbur H. *Wings Over the Seven Seas:*
       .M67   *The Story of Naval Aviation's Fight for Sur-*
                  vival. N.Y.: A.S. Barnes, 1975. General story
                  of naval aviators.

3866. UA6463   *NATO Handbook.* Brussels: NATO Information Ser-
      .A559   vice, various dates.

3867. DD881   Nelson, Daniel. *Wartime Origins of the Berlin
      .N37   Dilemma.* University: U. of Alabama P., 1978.

3868. E183.8   Neustadt, Richard E. *Alliance Politics.* N.Y.:
      .G7N47   Columbia UP, 1970. Includes Suez and the Sky-
                bolt affair of 1962.

3869. DS35   Nogal, Yonosuke, and Akira Iriye, eds. *The
      .D63   Origins of the Cold War in Asia.* N.Y.: Colum-
                bia UP and U. of Tokyo P., 1977.

3870. E840   Osgood, Robert E., and others. *America and the
      .A615   World: From the Truman Doctrine to Vietnam.*
                Baltimore: Johns Hopkins P., 1970.

3871. JZ4005   _____. *Alliances and American Foreign Pol-
      .O78   icy.* Baltimore: Johns Hopkins P., 1968.

3872. UA646   _____. *NATO: The Entangling Alliance.*
      .3.O8   Chicago: U. of Chicago P., 1962.

3873. UA23   _____. *Limited War: The Challenge to Ameri-
      .O8   can Strategy.* Chicago: U. of Chicago P., 1957.

3874. JK421   Pemberton, William E. *Bureaucratic Politics:
      .P36   Executive Reorganization During the Truman
                Administration.* Columbia: U. of Missouri P.,
                1979.

3875. E183.8   Rankin, Karl L. *China Assignment.* Seattle: U.
      .C5R3   of Washington P., 1964.

3876. UA646   Richardson, James L. *Germany and the Atlantic
      .3.R48   Alliance.* Cambridge, Mass.: HUP, 1966.

3877. VA23   Ries, John C. *The Management of Defense: Or-
      .R495   ganization and Control of the U.S. Armed
                Forces.* Baltimore: Johns Hopkins P., 1964.

3878. E748   Rogow, Arnold A. *James Forrestal: A Study in
      F68.R6   Personality, Politics, and Policy.* N.Y.: Mac-
                millan, 1963.

3879. UA23   Schilling, Warner R., Paul Y. Hammond, and
      .S33   Glenn H. Snyder. *Strategy, Politics, and
                Defense Budgets.* N.Y.: Columbia UP, 1962.

3880. UA23   Sherry, Michael S. *Preparing for the Next War:*
.S47   *American Plans for Postwar Defense, 1941-1945.*
New Haven: YUP, 1977.

3881. D753   Sherwin, Martin J. *World Destroyed: The Atomic*
.S48   *Bomb and the Grand Alliance.* N.Y.: Knopf, 1975.

3882. DD881   Slusser, Robert M. *The Berlin Crisis of*
.S52   *1961....* Baltimore: Johns Hopkins P., 1973.

3883. V25   Sokol, Anthony E. *Sea Power in the Nuclear Age.*
.S6   Wash.: Public Affairs P., 1961.

3884. D845   Stanley, Timothy W. *NATO in Transition: The*
.2.S8   *Future of the Atlantic Alliance.* N.Y.: Praeger,
1965.

3885. UA23   _____. *American Defense and National Secu-*
.S675   *rity.* Wash.: Public Affairs P., 1956.

3886. D849   _____, and Darnell M. Whitt. *Detente Diplo-*
.S7   *macy: United States and European Security in*
the 1970's. Cambridge, Mass.: UP of Massa-
chusetts, 1970.

3887. E814   Truman, Harry S. *Memoirs by Harry S. Truman,* 2
.T75   vols. GCNY: Doubleday, 1955-19 6.

3888. E183.8   Ullmann, Walter. *The United States in Prague,*
.C95   *1945-1948.* N.Y.: Columbia UP, 1978.
v.4

3889. E183   Whitaker, Arthur P. *Spain and the Defense of*
.8.S7W5   *the West: Ally and Liability.* N.Y.: Harper,
1961.

3890. DK67   Wolfe, Thomas W. *Soviet Power and Europe, 1945-*
.W6   *1970.* Baltimore: Johns Hopkins P., 1970.

3891. DF849   Xydis, Stephen G. *Greece and the Great Powers,*
.X9   *1944-1947.* Thessalonika: Institute for Balkan
Studies, 1963.

3892. D843   Yergin, Daniel. *Shattered Peace: The Origins*
.Y47   *of the Cold War and the National Security*
State. Boston: Houghton Mifflin, 1977.

3893. UG1282   York, Herbert F. *The Advisors: Oppenheimer,*
      .A8Y67   *Teller, & the Superbomb.* San Francisco: W.H.
                 Freeman, 1976. On Truman's decision in Jan.
                 1950 to accelerate development of the thermo-
                 nuclear weapon.

3894. D843   Zacharias, Ellis M. *Behind Closed Doors: The*
      .Z2   *Secret History of the Cold War.* N.Y.: Putnam,
                 1950.

                        DOCUMENTS

3895. E813   Etzold, Thomas H., and John L. Gaddis, eds.
      .C68   *Containment: Documents on American Policy and*
                 Strategy, 1945-1950. N.Y.: Columbia UP, 1978.

3896. UA23   *The History of the Joint Chiefs of Staff.*
      .H5   *Joint Chiefs and National Policy.* Wash.: Hist.
                 Div., Joint Secretariat JCS, Vol. 1. 1979.

3897. D301   Murphy, Paul J. *Naval Power in Soviet Policy.*
      .85:2   Wash.: GPO, 1968.

3898. UG633   U.S. Air Force, Continental Air Command. *Or-*
      .U55   *ganization of the U.S. Air Force.* N.Y.:
                 Mitchell AFB, 1949.

3899. JK643   U.S. Commission of the Executive Branch of
      .C57A5522 the Government. *National Security Organization.*
                 (Hoover Task Force I), 4 vols. Wash.: GPO,
                 1949. Appendix G contains the Eberstadt re-
                 port on Defense organization.

3900. Y4.F76/1 U.S. Committee on Department of Defense Or-
      R59   ganization. *Report of the Rockefeller Com-*
                 mittee on Department of Defense Organization.
                 Wash.: GPO, 1953.

3901. Y4.Ar5/2 U.S. Congress. House Committee on Armed Ser-
      .D36   vices. *Unification and Strategy: A Report of*
                 Investigation. 81st Cong., 2nd Sess. Wash.:
                 GPO, 1950.

3902. UA23   _____. Hearings before the Committee on
      .A4   Armed Services, House of Representatives. *The*
      1949   *National Defense Program: Unification and*
                 Strategy, 81st Cong., 1st Sess. Wash.: GPO,
                 1949.

317

3903.   Y4Ar5/2:   _____. *The National Defense Program: Unifi-*
        D36 and   *cation and Strategy. Hearings....* 81st Cong.,
        UA23.A4   1st Sess. Wash.: GPO, 1949.

3904.   DS918   U.S. Congress. Senate Committee on Armed Ser-
        U55   vices and Committee on Foreign Relations. *Mili-*
                          tary Situation in the Far East, 5 vols. 82nd
                          Cong., 1st Sess. Wash.: GPO, 1951.

3905.   _____. *National Security Act Amendments of*
                          1949. Report No. 366, 81st Cong., 1st Sess.,
                          1949.

3906.   U.S. Senate. Report of the Congressional Avia-
                          tion Policy Board. *National Aviation Policy.*
                          Sen. Report 949, 80th Cong., 2nd Sess. Wash.:
                          GPO, 1948.

3907.   UA23   U.S. Department of Defense. *Reports of the*
        .2.A33   *Secretary of Defense and of the Military Secre-*
                          taries. Wash.: 1947-

3908.   J80   U.S. President. *Public Papers of the Presidents*
        .A283   *of the United States, Harry S. Truman...*, 8
                          vols. Wash.: GPO, 1961-1966.

3909.   TL521   U.S. President's Air Policy Commission. *Sur-*
        .A5   *vival in the Air Age: A Report by the Presi-*
        1948   *dent's Air Policy Commission.* Wash.: GPO, 1948.

3910.   Micro   *Documents of the National Security Council*
        5 reels   [1947-1977]. Wash.: U. Publications of America,
                          1980.

3911.   Micro   *Records of the Joint Chiefs of Staff, 1946-*
        7 reels   *1953: The Soviet Union.* Wash.: U. Publications
                          of America, 1979.

3912.   Micro   *Records of the Joint Chiefs of Staff, 1946-*
        14 reels   *1953: The Far East.* Wash.: U. Publications
                          of America, 1979.

DISSERTATIONS AND THESES

3913.   Anderson, Terry H. "Britain, the United States,
                          and the Cold War, 1944-1947," Indiana U., 1978.

3914.   UA23   French, Thomas A. "Unification and the American
        .F74   Military Establishment, 1945-1950," SUNY Buf-
                          falo, 1972; Ann Arbor, Mich.: U. Microfilms,
                          1972.

3915. E813   Henry, David R. "Decision-Making in the Truman
      .H44   Administration," Indiana U., 1976. Ann Arbor,
              Mich.: Xerox U. Microfilms, 1977.

3916.   Smith, Robert L. "The Influence of USAF Chief
              of Staff General Hoyt S. Vandenberg on U.S.
              National Security Policy," American U., 1965.

3917.   Weeks, Stanley B. "United States Defense Pol-
              icy toward Spain, 1950-1976," American U.,
              1972.

3918.   *Keiser, Gordon W. "The U.S. Marines Corps and
              Unification: 1944-1947: The Politics of Sur-
              vival," MA thesis, Tufts U., 1971.

                         ARTICLES

3919.   Baldwin, Hanson W. "Strategy for Two Atomic
              Worlds," FA 28 (Apr. 1950):386-97.

3920.   Beck, Earl G. "B-47 Strato Jet," *Aerospace
              Historian* 22 (Summer-June 1975):61-64.

3921.   Beebe, Robert P. "The Vital Key West Agree-
              ment," USNIP 87 (Sept. 1961):35-41. Roles
              and missions of the armed forces under the
              National Security Act of 1947.

3922.   Berkner, Lloyd V. "Earth Satellites and For-
              eign Policy," FA 36 (Jan. 1958):221-31. The
              impact of Sputnik.

3923.   Brodie, Bernard. "New Tactics in Naval War-
              fare," FA 24 (Jan. 1946):210-23.

3924.   Brown, Charles R. "American National Strategy,"
              USNIP 76 (Apr. 1950):355-63. U.S. cannot rely
              on a single weapon system.

3925.   Bunkley, Joel W. "The Bureau of Ordnance,"
              USNIP 75 (Feb. 1949):213-24. Covers 1842-
              1949.

3926.   _____. "The Bureau of Aeronautics," USNIP
              75 (Jan. 1949):85-95. From the days of
              William A. Moffett.

3927.   Cagle, Malcolm W. "The Jets Are Coming," USNIP
              74 (Nov. 1948):134-49.

319

3928.	Conn, Stetson. "Changing Concepts of National Defense in the United States, 1937-1947," MA 28 (Spring 1964):1-7.

3929.	Denfeld, Louis E. "Reprisal: Why I Was Fired," *Collier's* 125, pt. 1 (Mar. 18, 1950):13-15, 62, 64.

3930.	Duffield, Eugene. "Organizing for Defense," *Harvard Business Rev.* 31 (Sept.-Oct. 1953): 29-42.

3931.	Dunn, Keith A. "A Conflict of World Views: The Origins of the Cold War," MR 57 (Feb. 1977): 14-25.

3932.	Eberstadt, Ferdinand. "The Historical Evolution of Our National Defense Organization," NWCR 6 (Jan. 1954):1-17.

3933.	Eggleston, Noel C. "The Roots of Commitment: United States Policy Toward Vietnam, 1945-1950," in David H. White, ed. *Proceedings of the Conference on War and Diplomacy*. Charleston, S.C.: The Citadel, 1976, pp. 59-66.

3934.	Freeden, Mel. "Scrapping Our World War II Navy," USNIP 105 (Feb. 1979):63-73.

3935.	*Griffith, Samuel B., 2nd. "Amphibious Warfare: Yesterday and Tomorrow," USNIP 76 (Aug. 1950): 871-75.

3936.	E744	Hammond, Paul Y. "Super Carriers and B-36
	.S845	Bombers: Appropriations, Strategy, and Politics," in Harold Stein, ed., *American Civil-Military Decisions: A Book of Case Studies*. University: U. of Alabama P., 1963, pp. 465-564.

3937.	*Heinl, Robert D. "The Right to Fight...," USNIP 88 (Sept. 1962):23-39.

3938.	*_____. "The Cat With More Than Nine Lives," USNIP 80 (June 1954):658-71. The Marine Corps survived attempts to abolish it.

3939.	*_____. "The Marine Corps: Here to Stay," USNIP 76 (Oct. 1950):1085-93.

3940.   *_____. "Small Wars - A Vanishing Art?" MCG
               34 (Apr. 1950):23-25. Thoughts on Marine
               training for small wars based on Marine ex-
               periences.

3941.   *_____. "The U.S. Marine Corps: Author of
               Modern Amphibious War," USNIP 73 (Nov. 1947):
               1310-23.

3942.   Hensel, H. Struve. "Changes Inside the Penta-
               gon," *Harvard Business Rev.* 32 (Jan.-Feb.
               1954):98-108.

3943.   Herring, George C. "The Truman Administration
               and the Restoration of French Sovereignty in
               Indochina," *Dip. Hist.* 1 (Spring 1977):97-117.

3944.   _____. "Lend-Lease to Russia and the Origins
               of the Cold War," JAH 56 (June 1969):93-114.

3945.   Hogeboom, Willard L. "The Cold War and Revi-
               sionist Historiography," *Soc. Stud.* 61 (1970):
               314-18.

3946.   Holmquist, Carl O., and Russell S. Greenbaum.
               "The Development of Nuclear Propulsion in the
               Navy," USNIP 86 (Sept. 1960):65-71.

3947. JF256   Huntington, Samuel P. "Interservice Competi-
       .C6   tion and the Political Roles of the Armed Ser-
               vices," in Harry L. Coles, ed. *Total War and
               Cold War: Problems in Civilian Control of the
               Military.* Columbus: Ohio State UP, 1962, pp.
               178-210.

3948.   Hutchinson, D.L. "In my Opinion: A New Look at
               an Old Problem," AUR 30 (Jan.-Feb. 1979):69-73.
               Defense unification.

3949.   Huzar, Elias. "Reorganization for National Se-
               curity," *Jour. of Politics.* 15 (Feb. 1950):128-
               52.

3950.   Kaplan, Lawrence S. "Toward the Atlantic Alli-
               ance: The Military Assistance Program and Wes-
               tern Europe, 1947-1949," in David H. White, ed.
               *Proceedings of the Conference on War and Diplo-
               macy.* Charleston, S.C.: The Citadel, 1976. pp.
               88-94.

3951.   _____. "The United States and the Origins of
             NATO," *Rev. Pol.* 31 (1969):210-22.

3952.   Kennan, George F. [Mr. "X"]. "The Sources of
             Soviet Conduct," FA 25 (July 1947):566-82.

3953.   Kerner, Robert J. "Russian Naval Aims," FA 24
             (Jan. 1946):290-99.

3954.   Kintner, W.R. "Political Limitations of Air
             Power," USNIP 76 (Mar. 1950): 249-55. Cannot
             rely on a single weapon system.

3955.   Knox, Dudley W. "Development of Unification,"
             USNIP 76 (Dec. 1950):1309-15.

3956.   Kuter, Laurence S. "Vittles: The Air Supply of
             Berlin," *U.S. Air Services* 34 (Feb. 1949):7-11.

3957.   Lees, Lorraine M. "The American Decision to
             Assist Tito, 1948-1949," *Dip. Hist.* 2 (Fall
             1978):407-22.

3958.   Levine, Steven I. "A New Look at American Me-
             diation in the Chinese Civil War: The Marshall
             Mission and Manchuria," *Dip. Hist.* 3 (Fall
             1979):349-76.

3959.   Link, Edwin A. "Deep Submergence and the Navy,"
             Annapolis, Md.: USNIP, *Naval Review*, May 1967.

3960.   Naymark, Sherman. "'Underway on Nuclear Power':
             The Development of the *Nautilus*," USNIP 96
             (Apr. 1970):56-63.

3961.   Paterson, Thomas G. "The Abortive American Loan
             to Russia and the Origins of the Cold War," JAH
             56 (June 1969):70-92.

3962.   Pomeroy, Earl S. "The Problem of Overseas Naval
             Bases...," USNIP 73 (June 1947):689-700.

3963.   Poole, Walter S. "From Conciliation to Contain-
             ment: The Joint Chiefs of Staff and the Coming
             of the Cold War," MA 42 (Feb. 1978):12-16.

3964.   "Revolt of the Admirals," AF 32 (Dec. 1949):
             22-27. The Air Force point of view.

3965.   Rickover, Hyman G. "Nuclear Warships and the Navy's Future," USNIP 101 (Jan. 1975):18-24.

3966.   Say, Harold B. "Safety in the Skies," USNIP 74 (Sept. 1948):1111-19. NATS: the Naval Air Transport Service, 1942-1948.

3967.   Schlesinger, Arthur M., Jr. "Origins of the Cold War," FA 46 (Oct. 1967):22-52.

3968.   *Simmons, Edwin H. "The United States Marine Corps," MCG 58 (Oct. 1974):41-45. Covers the years 1946 to 1950.

3969.   Snell, John L. "The Cold War: Four Contemporary Appraisals," AHR 68 (Oct. 1962):69-75.

3970.   Somit, Albert. "Historical and Geopolitical Aspects of the Berlin Crisis," NWCR 14 (Nov. 1961):22-40.

3971.   Spaatz, Carl A. "Strategic Air Power: Fulfillment of a Concept," FA 24 (Apr. 1946):385-96.

3972.   Starobin, Joseph R. "Origins of the Cold War: The Communist Dimension," FA 47 (July 1969): 681-96.

3973.   Sturm, Thomas A. "American Air Defense: The Decision to Proceed," Aerospace Historian 19 (Winter 1972):188-94.

3974.   Symington, W. Stuart. "Our Air Force Policy," Vital Speeches, July 1, 1949, pp. 567-70.

3975.   _____. "We've Scuttled Our Air Defenses," Am. Mag. 145 (Feb. 1948):50+.

3976.   Trask, Roger R. "The Impact of the Cold War on United States-Latin American Relations, 1945-1949," Dip. Hist. 1 (Summer 1977):271-84.

3977.   Uhlig, Frank, Jr. "The Threat of the Soviet Navy," FA 30 (Apr. 1952):444-54.

3978.   _____. "The New Battle Cruisers," USNIP 75 (Jan. 1949): 33-38.

3979.   Wolk, Herman S. "The Birth of the U.S. Air Force," AF 60 (Sept. 1977):69-78.

3980.   Xydis, Stephen. "The Genesis of the Sixth Fleet," USNIP 84 (Aug. 1958):41-50.

3981.   Zuckert, Eugene M. "The Service Secretary: Has He a Useful Role?" FA 44 (Apr. 1966):458-79. Unification has demoted the service secretary to a middle manager, yet he is still necessary.

TRANSCRIPTS OF ORAL INTERVIEWS

3982.   Hanson W. Baldwin, Gerald F. Bogan, Arleigh Burke, Richard L. Conolly, Daniel V. Gallery, Charles D. Griffin, Fitzhugh Lee, and Herbert D. Riley. Annapolis, Md.: U.S. Naval Academy Library, Special Collections.

FICTION

3983.   PS3562   Lederer, William J., and Eugene Burdick. *The*
       .E3U45   *Ugly American*. N.Y.: Norton, 1958.

20

KOREA AND CONTINUED COMMUNIST
CONTAINMENT 1950-1961

BOOKS

3984. DS918   Acheson, Dean. *The Korean War*. N.Y.: Norton,
       .A59   1971.

3985. E835   Alexander, Charles C. *Holding the Line: The
       .A645   Eisenhower Era, 1952-1961*. Bloomington: Indiana
                    UP, 1973.

3986. VA65   Anderson, William R., and Clay Blair, Jr.
       .N3A5   *Nautilus 90° North*. Cleveland: World, 1959.

3987. DS918   Appleman, Roy E. *South to the Naktong, North
       .U5246   to the Yalu June-Nov. 1950*. Wash.: OCMH 1960.
       v.2

3988. VA58   Baldwin, Hanson W. *The New Navy*. N.Y.: Dutton,
       .B3   1964.

3989. HC110   Baldwin, William L. *The Structure of the De-
       .D4B3   fense Market, 1955-1964*. Durham: Duke UP, 1967.
                    Heavy going on the military market in the U.S.

3990. UG1312   Beard, Edmund. *Developing the ICBM: A Study in
       .I2B4   Bureaucratic Politics*. N.Y.: Columbia UP, 1976.

3991. VA646   Beaufre, André. *NATO and Europe*. N.Y.: Knopf,
       .3.B383   1966.

3992. JX1974   Bechhoefer, Bernhard G. *Postwar Negotiations
       .B35   for Arms Control*. Wash.: Burns and MacEachern,
                    1961.

3993. DS918   Berger, Carl. *The Korea Knot: A Military-
       .B4   Political History*. Phila.: U. of Pa. P., 1957,
                    rev. ed., 1968.

3994. UA23   Betts, Richard K. *Soldiers, Statesmen, and Cold
       .B46   War Crises*. Cambridge, Mass.: HUP, 1977.

3995. U241   Blaufarb, Douglas S. *The Counterinsurgency Era:
       .B53   U.S. Doctrine and Performance, 1950 to the
                    Present*. N.Y.: Free P., 1977.

3996. VA23   Borklund, Carl W. *Men of the Pentagon: For-*
      .6B6   *restal to McNamara*. N.Y.: Praeger, 1966.

3997. VA23   Bottome, Edgar M. *The Missile Gap: A Study of*
      .B728 *the Formulation of Military and Political Pol-*
             icy, [1958-1961]. Rutherford, N.J.: Fairleigh-
             Dickinson UP, 1971.

3998. VB230 Brandt, Edward. *The Last Voyage of the USS*
      .B7   Pueblo. N.Y.: Norton, 1969.

3999. HD9711 Bright, Charles D. *The Jet Makers: The Aero-*
      .U6B74 *space Industry from 1945 to 1972*. Lawrence:
             Regents P. of Kansas, 1979.

4000. VA11   Brodie, Bernard. *Strategy in the Missile Age*.
      .B7   Princeton: PUP, 1959.

4001. JX1391 _____. *War and Politics*. Chap. 3, "The Test
      .B68   of Korea." N.Y.: Macmillan, 1973.

4002. E744   Brown, Seyom. *The Faces of Power: Constance*
      .B78   *and Change in U.S. Foreign Policy from Truman*
             to Eisenhower. N.Y.: Columbia UP, 1968.

4003. VB230 Bucher, Lloyd M. *Bucher: My Story*. GCNY:
      .B7999 Doubleday, 1970.

4004. DS920 Cagle, Malcolm, and Frank A. Manson. *The Sea*
      .A2C3 *War in Korea*. Annapolis, Md.: USNI, 1957.

4005. G630   Calvert, James F. *Surface at the Pole: The Ex-*
      .A5C25 *traordinary Voyages of the USS* Skate. N.Y.:
             McGraw-Hill, 1960.

4006. HC110 Carey, Omer L., ed. *The Military Industrial*
      .D4M5 *Complex and U.S. Foreign Policy*. Pullman,
             Wash.: Washington State UP, 1969.

4007. E743   Caridi, Ronald H. *The Korean War and American*
      .C248 *Politics*. Phila.: U. of Pa. P., 1968.

4008. HD1694. Chevrier, Lionel. *The St. Lawrence Seaway*.
      .C4   N.Y.: St. Martin, 1959.

4009. DS918 Clark, Mark W. *From the Danube to the Yalu*.
      .C55   N.Y.: Harper, 1954.

4010. UA26   Clough, Ralph N. *Deterrence and Defense in*
     .K6C56   *Korea: The Role of U.S. Forces.* Wash.:
                    Brookings, 1976.

4011. E745   Collins, J. Lawton. *Lightning Joe: An Autobiog-*
     .C64A34   *raphy.* Baton Rouge, La.: LSUP, 1979. Heavy on
                    World War I and II. Only one chapter on sub-
                    sequent events.

4012. DS918   _____. *War in Peacetime: The History and*
     .C62   *Lessons of Korea.* Boston: Houghton Mifflin,
                    1969.

4013. DT107   Cooper, Chester L. *The Lion's Roar: Suez, 1956.*
     .83.C66   N.Y.: Harper & Row, 1978.

4014. E183.8   Cortada, James W. *Two Nations Over Time: Spain*
     .S7C67   *and the United States, 1776-1977.* Westport,
                    Conn.: Greenwood, 1978.

4015. DS904   Crane, Paul S. *Korean Patterns.* Seoul, Korea:
     .C75   Hollym Corp., 1970.

4016. VA230   Crawford, Don. Pueblo *Intrigue.* Wheaton, Md.:
     .C6   Tyndale House, 1969.

4017. VE23   *DeChant, John A. *The Modern United States Ma-*
     .D4   *rine Corps.* Princeton, N.J.: Van Nostrand,
                    1966.

4018. DS918   Detzer, D. *Thunder of the Captains: The Short*
     .D45   *Summer of 1950.* N.Y.: Crowell, 1977.

4019. DS918   Dille, John. *Substitute for Victory: The Truce*
     .D5   *Which Brought the Korean War to an End.* GCNY:
                    Doubleday, 1954.

4020. E835   Divine, Robert A. *Blowing on the Wind: The Nu-*
     .D53   *clear Test Ban Debate, 1954-1960.* N.Y.: Oxford
                    UP, 1978.

4021. UA23   Donnelly, Charles H. *The United States Guided*
     .A424   *Missile Program.* Wash.: GPO, 1959.

4022. E835   Donovan, Robert J. *Eisenhower: The Inside*
     .D6   *Story.* N.Y.: Harper, 1956.

4023. E835   Eisenhower, Dwight D. *Mandate for Change: The*
      .E33   *White House Years, 1953-1957*. GCNY: Doubleday,
                1963.

4024. E835   _____. *Waging Peace: The White House Years,*
      .E47   *1957-1961*. GCNY: Doubleday, 1965.

4025. UG630   Emme, Eugene M., ed. *The Impact of Air Power:*
      .E5   *National Security and World Politics*. Prince-
                ton, N.J.: D. Van Nostrand, 1959.

4026. DS550   Fall, Bernard B. *Hell in a Very Small Place:*
      .F28   *The Siege of Dienbienphu*. Phila.: Lippincott,
                1966.

4027. DS550   _____. *Street Without Joy*, 4th ed. Harris-
      .F3   burg, Pa.: Stackpole, 1964.

4028. DS557   _____. *The Two Vietnams: A Political and*
      .A5F34   *Military Analysis*. N.Y.: Praeger, 1963.

4029. DS557   _____. *Vietnam Witness, 1953-1956*. N.Y.:
      .A5F35   Praeger, 1966.

4030. D780   Fane, Francis D. *The Naked Warriors: The Story*
      .F3   *of the Navy Frogmen from World War II to the*
                Present. N.Y.: Appleton-Century-Crofts, 1956.

4031. DS918   Fehrenbach, T.R. *The Fight for Korea: From the*
      .F36   *War of 1950 to the* Pueblo *Incident*. N.Y.:
                Grosset and Dunlap, 1969.

4032. E183   Ferrell, Robert H. *George C. Marshall*. N.Y.:
      .7.B462   Cooper Square Pub., 1966.

4033. DS920   Field, James A. *History of United States Naval*
      .A2F5   *Operations: Korea*. Wash.: Dept. of the Navy,
                1962.

4034. E835   Finer, Herman. *Dulles Over Suez*. Chicago: Quad-
      .D85F5   rangle Books, 1964.

4035. E835   Finke, Blythe F. *John Foster Dulles: Master of*
      .D85F56   *Brinksmanship and Diplomacy*. Charlottesville,
                N.Y.: SanHar P., 1971.

4036. E835   Finletter, Thomas K. *Power and Policy: U.S.*
      .F5   *Foreign Policy and Military Power in the Hydro-*
                gen Age. N.Y.: Harcourt Brace, 1954.

4037. DS920   Futrell, Robert F., Lawson S. Mosely, and Al-
      .2.U5F8   bert F. Simpson. *The United States Air Force
                  in Korea, 1950-1953.* N.Y.: Duell, Sloan &
                  Pearce, 1961.

4038. VB230   Gallery, Daniel V. *The* Pueblo *Incident.* GCNY:
      .G3   Doubleday, 1970.

4039. E744   Gati, Charles ed. *Caging the Bear: Containment
      .G345   and the Cold War.* Indianapolis: Bobbs-Merrill,
                  1974.

4040. DS918   *Geer, Andrew. *The New Breed: The Story of the
      .G37   U.S. Marines in Korea.* N.Y.: Harper, 1952.

4041. KF7625   Generous, William T., Jr. *Swords and Scales:
      .G45   The Development of the Uniform Code of Military
                  Justice.* Port Washington, N.Y.: Kennikat P.,
                  1973.

4042. VM317   Gimpel, Herbert J. *The United States Nuclear
      .G5   Navy.* N.Y.: Watts, 1965.

4043. DS921.7   Goodman, Allan E., ed. *Negotiating While Fight-
      .J625   ing: The Diary of Admiral C. Turner Joy at the
                  Korean Armistice Conference.* Stanford: Hoover
                  Institution P., 1978.

4044. VA23   Goodpaster, Andrew J., and Samuel P. Hunting-
      .G74   ton. *Civil-Military Relations.* Wash.: AEI,
                  1977.

4045. HE745   Gorter, Wytze. *United States Shipping Policy.*
      .G63   N.Y.: Harper, 1956.

4046. DS919   Guttmann, Allan, ed. *Korea and the Theory of
      .G8   Limited War.* Lexington, Mass.: Heath, 1967.

4047. VA11   *Halperin, Morton. *Limited War in the Nuclear
      .H34   Age.* N.Y.: Wiley, 1963. Besides being an ex-
                  cellent analysis of limited war, includes a
                  most exhaustive bibliography on the subject.

4048. E813   Harper, Alan D. *The Politics of Loyalty: The
      .H366   White House and the Communist Issue, 1946-1952.*
                  Westport, Conn.: Greenwood, 1969.

4049. E183.8   Harriman, W. Averell. *America and Russia in a
      .R9H19   Changing World: A Half Century of Personal Ob-
                  servations.* GCNY: Doubleday, 1971.

4050. E813   Hartman, Susan M. *Truman and the 80th Congress*.
      .H39   Columbia: U. of Missouri P., 1971.

4051. UA23   Head, Richard G., and Evin J. Rokke. *Study
      .A4122   Guide to American Defense Policy*. Baltimore:
                Johns Hopkins P., 1973.

4052. DS918   *Heinl, Robert D. *Victory at High Tide: The
      .2.I5H4   Inchon-Seoul Campaign*. N.Y.: Lippincott, 1968.
                A step-by-step account of the planning and
                carrying-out of the invasion and subsequent
                liberation of Seoul.

4053. VE23   *   . *Soldiers of the Sea: The United
      .H4   States Marine Corps, 1775-1962*. Annapolis,
                Md.: USNI, 1962.

4054. DS919   Heller, Francis H., ed. *The Korean War: A 25-
      .K67   Year Perspective*. Lawrence: Regents P. of
                Kansas, 1977.

4055. DS918   Hermes, Walter G. *Truce Tent and Fighting
      .U5246   Front*. Wash.: OCMH, 1966.
      v.2

4056. VM317   Hewlett, Richard G., and Francis Duncan. *Nu-
      .H48   clear Navy, 1946-1962*. Chicago: U. of Chicago
                P., 1974.

4057. DS918   Higgins, Trumbull. *Korea and the Fall of Mac-
      .H515   Arthur: A Precis on Limited War*. N.Y.: Oxford
                UP, 1960.

4058. DS557   Hoopes, Townsend. *The Limits of Intervention*.
      .A63H6   N.Y.: McKay, 1969.

4059. UG633   Hopkins, J.C., and Sheldon A. Goldberg. *Devel-
      .H63   opment of Strategic Air Command, 1946-1976*.
                Offutt AFB, Neb.: HQ, SAC, Office of the
                Historian, 21 Mar. 1976.

4060. E835   Hughes, Emmet J. *The Ordeal of Power: A Polit-
      .H8   ical Memoir of the Eisenhower Years*. N.Y.:
                Atheneum, 1963.

4061. TL515   Hunsaker, Jerome C. *Aeronautics at Mid-Century*.
      .H8   New Haven: YUP, 1952.

4062. DA69.3   Ismay, Hastings L. *The Memoirs of General Lord
      .I8A3   Ismay*. London: Heinemann, 1960.

4063. E182   Jones, Ken, and Hubert Kelley, Jr. *Admiral*
      .B9656   *Arleigh (31-Knot) Burke: The Story of a Fight-*
                 ing Sailor. Phila.: Chilton, 1962.

4064. D773   Karig, Walter. *Battle Report: The War in Korea.*
      .K3   N.Y.: Rinehart, 1952.

4065. E183.8   Kaufman, William W. *The Requirements of Deter-*
      .G7F63   *rence.* Princeton: PUP, 1954.

4066. E748   Kennan, George F. *Memoirs,* 2 vols. Boston:
      .K374A3   Little, Brown, 1967-1972.

4067. UH720   Kennedy, Gavin. *The Military in the Third*
      .K46   *World.* London: Duckworth, 1974.

4068. DK275   *Khrushchev Remembers.* Ed. Edward Cranshaw. Bos-
      .K5A325   ton: Little, Brown, 1970.

4069. DS558   Kinnard, Douglas. *The War Managers.* Published
      .K5   for the U. of Vermont by the UP of New England,
                 1977.

4070. UA23   _____. *President Eisenhower and Strategy*
      .K482   *Management: A Study in Defense Politics.* Lex-
                 ington: U. of Kentucky P., 1977.

4071. UA23   Kintner, William R., and others. *Forging a New*
      .3.K5   *Sword: A Study of the Department of Defense.*
                 N.Y.: Harper, 1958.

4072. UA23   Kissinger, Henry. *Nuclear Weapons and Foreign*
      .K49   *Policy.* N.Y.: Harper, 1957.

4073. E744   Kolko, Gabriel, and Joyce Kolko. *The Limits of*   .
      .K64   *Power: The World and United States Foreign*
                 Policy, 1945-1954. N.Y.: Harper & Row, 1972.
                 A revisionist approach to Korea.

4074. UB223   Korb, Lawrence J. *The JCS: The First Twenty-*
      .K67   *five Years.* Bloomington: Indiana UP, 1976.

4075. E183.8   LaFeber, Walter. *America, Russia, and the Cold*
      .R9L26   *War, 1945-1966,* 3d ed. N.Y.: Wiley, 1976.

4076. DS63.2   Laquer, Walter Z. *The Struggle for the Middle*
      .R9L32   *East: The Soviet Union and the Middle East,*
                 1958-1968. 1969. Rev. ed. Baltimore: Penguin,
                 1972.

4077. E836 Larson, Arthur. *Eisenhower: The President No-*
      .L3   *body Knew.* N.Y.: Scribner, 1968.

4078. E183.8 Larson, Thomas B. *Soviet-American Rivalry.*
      .R9L34 N.Y.: Norton, 1978.

4079. Q149 Lasby, Clarence G. *Project Paperclip: German*
      .U5L8 *Scientists and the Cold War.* N.Y.: Atheneum,
             1971.

4080. DS918 Lawson, Don. *The United States in the Korean*
      .L35   *War: Defending Freedom.* N.Y.: Abelard-Schuman,
             1964.

4081. DS918 Leckie, Robert. *Conflict: The History of the*
      .L36   *Korean War, 1950-1953.* N.Y.: Putnam, 1962.

4082. DS918 *_____. *The March to Glory.* Cleveland:
      .L38   World, 1960. The 1st Marine Division in the
             breakout from the Chosin Reservoir, particu-
             larly the operations from Yudam-ni to
             Chinhung-ni, 1-10 Dec. 1950.

4083. HC110 Lens, Sidney. *The Military-Industrial Complex.*
      .D4L43 Phila.: Pilgrim P., 1970.

4084. D773 Lott, Arnold S. *Most Dangerous Sea: A History*
      .L6   *of Mine Warfare and an Account of U.S. Navy*
            Mine Warfare Operations in World War II and
            Korea. Annapolis, Md.: USNI, 1959.

4085. D845.2 Lowenstein, Bruce H., and others. *NATO and the*
      .L613 *Defense of the West.* N.Y.: Praeger, 1963. Es-
             pecially good on personalities.

4086. E836 Lyon, Peter. *Eisenhower: Portrait of the Hero.*
      .L96   Boston: Little, Brown, 1974. Massive and best
             study of Eisenhower to date.

4087. HN730 Lyons, Gene M. *Military Policy and Economic*
      .K6L9 *Aid: The Korean Case, 1950-1953.* Columbus:
             Ohio State UP, 1961.

4088. E745 MacArthur, Douglas. *Reminiscences.* N.Y.:
      .M3.A34 McGraw-Hill, 1964.

4089. D842 McClintock, Robert. *The Meaning of Limited War.*
      .M3   Boston: Houghton Mifflin, 1967.

4090. E183   McDonald, Ian, comp. and ed. *Anglo-American*
      .8.G7M118   *Relations Since the Second World War.* Newton
                    Abbot, England: David E. Charles, 1974.

4091. D1058   McGeehan, Robert. *The German Rearmament Ques-*
      .M25   *tion: American Diplomacy and European Defense*
                    after World War II. Urbana: U. of Illinois P.,
                    1971.

4092. HD1694   Mabee, Carleton. *The Seaway Story.* N.Y.: Mac-
      .A254M2   millan, 1961. The St. Lawrence Seaway.

4093. DS918   *Marshall, Samuel L.A. *The River and the Gaunt-*
      .2.C4M3   *let: Defeat of the Eighth Army by the Chinese*
                    Communist Forces, November, 1950, in the Bat-
                    tle of the Chongchon River, Korea. N.Y.: Mor-
                    row, 1953.

4094. DS918   Miller, John, Jr., Owen J. Carroll, and
      .U5242   Margaret E. Tackley. *Korea: 1951-1953.* Wash.:
                    OCMH, 1956. Profusely illustrated resumé
                    histories of Eighth Army operations.

4095. DS918   Miller, Max. *I'm Sure We've Met Before: The*
      .M5   *Navy in Korea.* N.Y.: Dutton, 1951.

4096. UG632   *Montross, Lynn. *Cavalry of the Sky: The Story*
      .M6   *of U.S. Marine Combat Helicopters.* N.Y.: Har-
                    per, 1954. An authoritative history of the
                    development of tactical helicopter techniques
                    by the Marine Corps, 1947 ff., with special
                    emphasis on the employment of the helicopter
                    as a rescue and liaison vehicle, Aug. 1950
                    ff., and as a tactical vehicle in Korea, Sept.
                    1951 ff.

4097. DS919   *   . *U.S. Marine Operations in Korea*,
      .A516   *1950-1953*, 5 vols. Wash.: USMC, HQ, Hist.
                    Div., 1955-1972.

4098. E744   Morgenthau, Hans J. *In Defense of the National*
      .M68   *Interest: A Critical Examination of American*
                    Foreign Policy. N.Y.: Knopf, 1951.

4099. VG93   Morrison, Wilbur H. *Wings over the Seven Seas:*
      .M67   *The Story of Naval Aviations' Fight for Sur-*
                    vival. N.Y.: A.S. Barnes, 1975.

4100. VB230   Murphy, Edward R., Jr. *Second in Command*. N.Y.:
      .M87   Holt, Rinehart and Winston, 1971. By the ex-
               ecutive officer of the *Pueblo*. Compare with
               Bucher, Lloyd M.

4101. E856   Nixon, Richard. *Six Crises*. GCNY: Doubleday,
      .A25   1962.

4102. DS919   *Noble, Harold J. *Embassy at War*. Seattle: U.
      .N6   of Washington P., 1975. The early weeks of
               the Korean War and U.S. relations with Synghman
               Rhee.

4103. DS918   *O'Ballance, Edgar. *Korea: 1950-1953*. Hamden,
      .025   Conn.: Archon Books, 1969.
      1969b

4104. UA23   Osgood, Robert E. *Limited War: The Challenge
      .08   to American Strategy*. Chicago: U. of Chicago
               P., 1957.

4105. DS919   Paige, Glenn D. *The Korean Decision, June 24-
      .P33   30, 1950*. N.Y.: Free P., 1968.

4106. E835   Peeters, Paul. *Massive Retaliation: The Policy
      .P43   and its Critics*. Chicago: Regnery, 1959.

4107. E813   Phillips, Cabell. *The Truman Presidency: The
      .P5   History of a Triumphant Succession*. N.Y.: Mac-
               millan, 1966.

4108.   *Polaris Management*. Wash.: Dept. of the Navy,
               Special Projects Office, 1961.

4109. U104   Possony, Stefan T., and J.E. Pournelle. *The
      .P83   Strategy of Technology: Winning the Decisive
               War*. N.Y.: Dunellen, 1970. On the optimiza-
               tion of technology.

4110. HC110   Pursell, Carroll W., comp. *The Military-
      .D4P87   Industrial Complex*. N.Y.: Harper & Row, 1972.

4111. UA23   Quester, George. *Nuclear Diplomacy: The First
      .047   Twenty-Five Years*. N.Y.: Dunellen, 2d ed.,
               1973.

4112. E183.8   Rankin, Karl L. *China Assignment*. Seattle: U.
      .C5R3   of Washington P., 1964. The Truman and Eisen-
               hower eras.

4113. DS913   *Rees, David. *Korea: The Limited War*. Baltimore:
      .R43   Penguin, 1970.

4114. D843   _____. *The Age of Containment: The Cold War*,
      .R38   *1945-1965*. N.Y.: St. Martin, 1967.

4115.   Richardson, Elmo. *The Presidency of Dwight D.
              Eisenhower*. Lawrence: Regents P. of Kansas,
              1979.

4116. DS918   Ridgway, Matthew B. *The Korean War*. GCNY:
      .R49   Doubleday, 1967.

4117. E745   _____, as told to Harold H. Martin. *Soldier:
      .R5A35   The Memoirs of Matthew B. Ridgway*. N.Y.: Har-
              per, 1956.

4118. UA23   Ries, John C. *The Management of Defense*. Balti-
      .R495   more: Johns Hopkins P., 1964.

4119. E835   Rockefeller Brothers Fund. *The Mid-Century
      .R58   Challenge to U.S. Foreign Policy*. GCNY: Double-
              day, 1959. 74 pp.

4120. UA23   Rockefeller Brothers Fund Study. *International
      .R6   Security, The Military Aspect: Report of Panel
              II of the Special Studies Project*. GCNY:
              Doubleday, 1958.

4121. E748   Rogow, Arnold A. *James Forrestal: A Study of
      .F68R6   Personality, Politics, and Policy*. N.Y.: Mac-
              millan, 1963.

4122. DS33   Rose, Lisle A. *Roots of Tragedy: The United
      .4U6   States and the Struggle for Asia, 1945-1953*.
              Wesport, Conn.: Greenwood, 1976.

4123. V933   Sapolsky, Harvey M. *The Polaris System Develop-
      .S37   ment: Bureaucratic and Programmatic Success in
              Government*. Cambridge, Mass.: HUP, 1972.

4124. DD881   Schick, Jack M. *The Berlin Crisis, 1958-1962*.
      .S26   Phila.: U. of Pa. P., 1971.

4125. UA23   Schilling, Warner R., Paul Y. Hammond, and
      .S33   Glenn H. Snyder. *Strategy, Politics, and De-
              fense Budgets*. N.Y.: Columbia UP, 1962.

4126. DS918   Schnabel, James F. *Policy and Direction: The*
      .U5426   *First Year*. Wash.: OCMH, 1972. The Korean War.

4127. VB230   Schumacher, F. Carl, Jr., and George C. Wil-
      .S34   son. *Bridge of No Return: The Ordeal of the*
                 U.S.S. Pueblo. N.Y.: Harcourt, 1971.

4128.   *Schuon, Karl, ed. *The Leathernecks--An Infor-*
                 mal History of the U.S. Marine Corps. N.Y.:
                 Watts, 1963. Pp. 225-258. contain brief ac-
                 counts of five battles in which the Marines
                 were engaged.

4129. DS86   *Shulimson, Jack. *Marines in Lebanon, 1958*.
      .S55   Wash.: USMC, HQ, Hist. Div., 1966.

4130.   * _____, and Charles M. Johnson. *Vietnam 1965,*
                 The Landing and the Buildup, Vol. 1. Wash.:
                 USMC, HQ, Hist. Div., 1979.

4131. DS918   Simmons, Robert R. *The Strained Alliance:*
      .S55   *Peking, Pyongyang, Moscow, and the Politics of*
                 the Korean War. N.Y.: Free, 1975. Politics of
                 the Korean civil war.

4132. V25   Sokol, Anthony E. *Seapower in the Nuclear Age*.
      .S6   Wash.: Public Affairs P., 1961.

4133. E744   Spanier, John W. *The Truman-MacArthur Contro-*
      .S8   *versy and the Korean War*. Cambridge, Mass.:
                 The Belknap Press of HUP, 1959. Discussion of
                 the strategic considerations and political im-
                 plications of the Inchon operation and of Mac-
                 Arthur's ideas for winning the war.

4134. DS920   Stewart, James T., ed. *Airpower: The Decisive*
      .2.A2S8   *Force in Korea*. Princeton, N.J.: Van Nostrand,
                 1957. "Decisive" is debatable.

4135. E744   Tarr, David W. *American Strategy in the Nuclear*
      .T3   *Age*. N.Y.: Macmillan, 1966.

4136. E745   Taylor, Maxwell D. *Swords and Plowshares*. N.Y.:
      T317   Norton, 1972.
      1972

4137. UA23   _____. *An Uncertain Trumpet*. N.Y.: Harper,
      .T33   1960.

4138. JK468   Tully, Andrew. *CIA: The Inside Story*. N.Y.:
      .I6T8   Morrow, 1962.

336

4139. JA23 Twining, Nathan F. *Neither Liberty nor Safety:*
.T88 *A Hard Look at United States Military Policy
and Strategy.* N.Y.: Holt, Rinehart and Winston,
1966. By an Air Force member of the Joint
Chiefs of Staff.

4140. UA23 Tyrrell, C. Merton. *Pentagon Partners: The New
.T96 Nobility.* N.Y.: Grossman, 1970.

4141. DS918 *Westover, John G. *Combat Support in Korea.*
.W43 Wash.: Combat Forces P., 1955. *See* Westover's
index for incidental references to support
given the Marines by Army units.

4142. AS36 Whiting, Allen S. *China Crosses the Yalu: The
.R3R356 Decision to Enter the Korean War.* N.Y.: Macmillan, 1960.

4143. E745 Whitney, Courtney. *MacArthur: His Rendezvous
.M3W48 with History.* N.Y.: Knopf, 1956. Quite idolatrous.

4144. E745 Willoughby, Charles A., and John Chamberlain.
.M3W5 *MacArthur 1941-1951.* N.Y.: McGraw-Hill, 1954.
Quite idolatrous.

4145. DK67 Wolfe, Thomas W. *Soviet Power and Europe, 1945-
.W6 1970.* Baltimore: Johns Hopkins P., 1970.

4146. DK68.7 Zagoria, Donald S. *The Sino-Soviet Conflict,
.C5Z3 1956-1961.* N.Y.: Atheneum, 1967.

DOCUMENTS

4147. Micro *Cincpacflt Interim Evaluation Reports, Korea
1950-1953.* Wilmington; Del: Scholarly Resources, 1979.

4148. E743 Druks, Herbert. *From Truman Through Johnson: A
.D77 Documentary History,* 2 vols. N.Y.: R. Speller,
1971.

4149. Y4Ar5/2a U.S. Congress. House Committee on Armed Ser-
:957-58/83 vices. *Hearings: Reorganization of the Department of Defense, 85th Cong., 2nd Sess.* Wash.:
GPO, 1961.

4150. Y4.G74/   U.S. Congress. House Committee on Government
      7:R29/2   Operations. *Reorganization Plan No. 6 of 1953.*
      No. 6   Department of Defense. Hearings.... Wash.: GPO,
                 1953.

4151. UA23.3   U.S. Congress. Senate Committee on Department
      .A462   of Defense Organization. *Report of the Rocke-*
                feller Committee on Department of Defense Or-
                ganization. Wash.: GPO, 1953.

4152.   U.S. Department of the Air Force, Air Univer-
                sity, Air Command and Staff College. *The New*
                Look. Prepared by W. Barton Leach. Maxwell
                AFB, Ala., 1954.

4153. VA23   U.S. Department of Defense. *Functions of the*
      .U49   *Armed Forces and the Joint Chiefs of Staff.*
                Rev. Wash.: 1953.

4154.   U.S. Department of State. *Papers Relating to*
                the Foreign Relations of the United States:
                Korea, 1950, Vol. 7. Dept. of State Publica-
                tion No. 8859. Wash.: GPO, 1976.

4155. U260   U.S. Joint Chiefs of Staff. *Unified Action*
      .U55   *Armed Forces.* (JCS Pub 2 of Nov. 1959). Wash.:
                JCS, 1959.

4156. DS919   *U.S. Marine Corps, 1st Division. *Chosin Reser-*
      .A52   *voir: First Marine Division, November 1-Decem-*
                ber 15, 1950. Wash.: GPO, 1951.

4157. VG93   *United States Naval Aviation, 1910-1970.* Wash.:
      .A79   Dept. of the Navy, 1971.

4158. J80   U.S. President. *Public Papers of the Presidents*
      .A283   *of the United States. Dwight D. Eisenhower...,*
                12 vols. Wash.: GPO, 1961- .

4159. DS918   U.S. Senate Committee on Foreign Relations and
      .U55   Senate Committee on Armed Services. *Hearings*
                on the Military Situation in the Far East, 82nd
                Cong., 1st Sess. Wash.: GPO, 1951.

4160. UG622   USAF. SAC. *A Brief History of Strategic Bom-*
      .A47   *bardment.* Offut AFB, Neb., 1971.

4161.   USAF. SAC. *The Progressive Development of the*
                Strategic Air Command, 1947-1970. Offut AFB,
                Neb., 1970.

338

DISSERTATIONS AND THESES

4162.   Biadasz, Frances E. "Defense Reorganization
                        during the Eisenhower Administrations,"
                        Georgetown U., 1961.

4163.   Comfort, Kenneth L. "Nuclear Security Policy
                        and the Development of Tactical Nuclear
                        Forces, 1948-1958," Columbia U., 1970.

4164.   Dart, Robert C. "Flexible Response: A Case
                        Study of the Policy Process for National Secu-
                        rity," U. of Virginia, 1973.

4165.   DS919   Flint, Roy K. "The Tragic Flaw: MacArthur, the
         .F59   Joint Chiefs of Staff and the Korean War,"
                        Duke U., 1975.

4166.   Geelhoed, Edward B. "At Sword's Point: Charles
                        E. Wilson and the Senate, 1953-1957," Ball
                        State U., 1975.

4167.   Gray, Colin. "The Defense Policies of the
                        Eisenhower Administrations, 1953-1961," Oxford
                        U., England, 1970.

4168.   McGeehan, Robert J. "American Diplomacy and
                        the German Rearmament Question, 1950-1953,"
                        Columbia U., 1969.

4169.   Moulton, Harland B. "American Strategic Power:
                        Two Decades of Nuclear Strategy and Weapons
                        Systems, 1945-1965," U. of Minnesota, 1969.

4170.   Schneider, Mark B. "Nuclear Weapons and Ameri-
                        can Strategy," U. of Southern California, 1974.

4171.   Schratz, Paul R. "The United States Defense
                        Establishment: Trends in Organizational Struc-
                        tures, Functions, and Interrelationships, 1958-
                        1970," Ohio State U., 1972.

4172.   Smith, Robert L. "The Influence of USAF Chief
                        of Staff General Hoyt S. Vandenberg on U.S.
                        National Security Policy," American U., 1965.

4173.   Weaver, James D. "The Commander-in-Chief,
                        Civilian Supremacy, Command and Control: Civil-
                        Military Relations in the Eisenhower Presiden-
                        cy," New York U., 1972.

339

4174.   *McMaster, Donald W. "The Revolution of Tactical
             Airpower--With Particular Emphasis Upon Its
             Application by the U.S. Navy and U.S. Marine
             Corps in the Korean War, June 1950-July 1953,"
             M.A. Thesis, U. of Maryland, 1959. A detailed
             analysis and evaluation of the use of tactical
             air power by both the Navy and Marine Corps.

                              ARTICLES

4175.   "The Air-Ground Operation in Korea," AF 34
             (Mar. 1951):19-58.

4176.   *"Air Power in Korea: Ground Support," USNIP 78
             (Feb. 1952):221-222. Brief comments on the
             controversy over close air support as practiced
             by the Marine Corps.

4177.   Andrews, Frank A. "Submarine Against Submarine,"
             USNIP, Naval Review, May 1965, pp. 42-57.

4178.   Aron, Raymond. "A Half-Century of Limited War,"
             BAS 12 (Apr. 1956):99-104.

4179.   *Asprey, Robert B. "New Fleet Marine Force,"
             USNIP 85 (Aug. 1959):41-48.

4180.   Baker, H.G. "The Mine Force: Wooden Ships and
             Iron Men," All Hands No. 481, Feb. 1957, pp.
             6-9.

4181.   Bates, P.L. "Naval Mines," MR 33 (Apr. 1953):
             48-56.

4182.   Bell, James A. "Defense Secretary Louis John-
             son," AM 50 (June 1950):643-53.

4183.   Bennet, Rawson. "What ONR's New Role Means to
             the Navy of the Future," Armed Forces Manage-
             ment 31 (Jan. 1957):8-11.

4184.   Bernstein, Barton J. "The Policy of Risk:
             Crossing the 38th Parallel and Marching to the
             Yalu," FSJ, Mar. 1977, 16-22, 30-31.

4185.   _____. "The Week We Went to War: American
             Intervention in the Korean Civil War," FSJ,
             Jan, 1977, pp. 6-11, 33.

4186.   *Black, Charles L. "The Truth About Air Support," *Flying* 48 (Feb. 1951):11-15, 57-59. illus. A comparison of close air support as practiced by the different branches of the service during the first months of the Korean war.

4187.   *Bodron, Margaret. "U.S. Intervention in Lebanon-1958," MR 56 (Feb. 1976):66-76.

4188.   *Braitsch, Fred G., Jr. "Marine Air War," *Leatherneck* 34 (Nov. 1951):30-35; 35 (Nov. 1952):30-35. Review of the first two years of Marine air operations in Korea.

4189.   Brodie, Bernard. "Some Notes on the Evolution of Air Doctrine," WP 7 (Apr. 1955):349-70.

4190.   _____. "Nuclear Weapons: Strategic or Tactical?" FA 32 (Jan. 1954):217-29.

4191.   _____. "Strategic Bombing: What It Can Do," *Reporter* 3 (Aug. 14, 1950):28-31.

4192.   *Burke, Arleigh A. "The Lebanon Crisis," in *Proceedings, Naval History Symposium*. Annapolis, Md.: U.S. Naval Academy, 1973, pp. 70-80.

4193.   Cagle, Malcolm W. "Errors of the Korean War," USNIP 84 (Oct. 1958):31-35.

4194.   _____. "A Philosophy for Naval Atomic Warfare," USNIP 83 (Mar. 1957):249-58.

4195.   * _____. "Inchon: The Analysis of a Gamble," USNIP 80 (Jan. 1954):47-51. illus., notes. Analysis of the tide and terrain problems involved in the Inchon operation, based largely upon Karig's *Battle Report*, *q.v.*

4196.   _____. "Naval Aviation at Mid-Century," USNIP 77 (June 1951):605-10.

4197.   _____, and Frank A. Manson. "Wonsan: The Battle of the Mines," USNIP 83 (June 1957): 598-611.

4198.   Cannon, Charles A. "The Politics of Interest
            and Ideology: The Senate Airpower Hearings of
            1956," *Armed Forces and Society* 3 (Summer
            1977):595-608.

4199.   *Canzona, Nicholas A. "Is Amphibious Warfare
            Dead?" USNIP 81 (Sept. 1955):986-991. Analysis
            from the point of view of the Marine Corps' ex-
            perience in Korea.

4200.   *_____. "Reflection on Korea," MCG 35 (Nov.
            1951):56-65. The author, using experiences in
            the Korean War, comments on some of the Marines'
            shortcomings in the field, their weapons, equip-
            ment, and methods.

4201.   "The Case for the Nuclear Powered Aircraft Car-
            rier," *Armed Forces Management* 5 (Mar. 1950):
            11-13.

4202.   *Coble, Donald W. "Air Support in the Korean
            War," *Aerospace Historian* 16 (Winter 1969):
            26-28.

4203.   Collins, J. Lawton. "NATO: Still Vital for
            Peace," FA 34 (Apr. 1956):367-79.

4204.   Cottrell, Alvin, and James E. Dougherty. "The
            Lessons of Korea," *Orbis* (Spring 1958):39-65.

4205.   *Crown, John A. "Why a Marine Corps?" MCG 42
            (Nov. 1958):40-46.

4206.   *Davis, William J. "The Bloody Breakout,"
            USNIP 79 (July 1953):736-739. Personal account
            by an officer of Company A, 1st Battalion, 7th
            Marines, of his unit's movement from Hagaru-ri
            to Koto-ri, 6-7 Dec. 1950.

4207.   "Dateline: Lebanon," *Leatherneck* 41 (Oct. 1958):
            14-23.

4208.   Dennison, Robert L. "As I Recall," USNIP 105
            (Oct. 1979):111-13. Recollections about the
            Bay of Pigs incident by the then Commander in
            Chief, Atlantic Fleet.

4209.   *Donovan, James A., Jr. "The FMF in Korea,"
         Leatherneck 35 (Nov. 1952):16-23. Summary of
         operations of the 1st Marine Division and 1st
         Marine Aircraft Wing, Sept. 1951-Sept. 1952.

4210.   *Doyle, James H., and Arthur J. Mayer. "Decem-
         ber 1950 at Hungnam," USNIP 105 (Apr. 1979):
         44-45. U.S. Marine "change of direction" in
         Korea.

4211.   Duffield, Eugene S. "Organizing for Defense,"
         Harvard Bus. Rev. 31 (Sept.-Oct. 1953):29-42.

4212.   Edwards, Harry W. "A Naval Lesson of the Korean
         Conflict," USNIP 80 (Dec. 1954):1337-40. Mine
         warfare.

4213.   Eyre, James K. "Naval Power and American Des-
         tiny," USNIP 77 (Mar. 1951):297-307. Atomic
         power can't do it alone.

4214.   Folsom, S.B. "Korea: A Reflection from the Air,"
         USNIP 82 (July 1956):732-735. An indictment
         of the ineffectiveness of interdiction in the
         Korean War.

4215.   Foss, William O. "Tommorrow's Torpedoes Now,"
         Ordnance 46 (Sept.-Oct. 1961):21-27.

4216.   Fraser, Angus M. "The Department of Defense
         and the Chinese Threat," USNIP 100 (Feb. 1974):
         18-25.

4217.   Freeden, Mel. "Scrapping Our World War II Navy,"
         USNIP 105 (Feb. 1979):63-73.

4218. UG633   Futrell, R. Frank. "The Korean War," in Alfred
      .G6   Goldberg, ed. *A History of the United States
              Air Force, 1907-1957*. Princeton: Van Nostrand
              Reinhold, 1957, pp. 243-58.

4219.   Garrett, William B. "The U.S. Navy's Role in
         the 1956 Suez Crisis," NWCR 22 (July 1970):
         66-78.

4220.   Hammond, Paul Y. "Super Carriers and B-36 Bomb-
         ers: Appropriations, Strategy, and Politics,"
         in Harold Stein, ed. *American Civil-Military
         Decisions*. Tuscaloosa: U. of Alabama P., 1963,
         pp. 465-568.

343

4221. WA23   _____. "NSC-68: Prologue to Rearmament," in
      .S33   Warner R. Schilling, Paul Y. Hammond, and Glenn
                  H. Snyder. *Strategy, Politics, and Defense Bud-
                  gets.* N.Y.: Columbia UP, 1962, pp. 271-378.

4222.   *Heinl, Robert D. "Inchon," MCG 51 (Sept. 1967):
                  20-28; 51 (Oct. 1967):45-50. A detailed trea-
                  tise on the planning and background of Operation
                  Chromite--the invasion of Inchon.

4223.   *_____. "The Inchon Landing: A Case Study in
                  Amphibious Planning," NWCR 39 (May 1967):51-72.
                  A discourse on the planning and execution of
                  Operation Chromite.

4224.   Heinmiller, P.R. "Undersea Defenders: Story of
                  Acoustic Homing Torpedoes," *General Electric
                  Rev.* 61 (Mar. 1958):24-35, and (May 1958):18-
                  26.

4225.   Hensel, H. Struve. "Changes Inside the Penta-
                  gon," *Harvard Bus. Rev.* 32 (Jan.-Feb. 1954):
                  98-108.

4226.   Hoag, Malcolm W. "NATO: Deterrent or Shield?"
                  FA 36 (Jan. 1958):278-92.

4227.   Hoopes, Townsend. "Overseas Bases in American
                  Strategy," FA 37 (Oct. 1958):69-82.

4228.   "How the Navy Department Is Organized," *Armed
                  Forces Management* 4 (Nov. 1957):16-43.

4229.   Hudson, George E. "Soviet Naval Doctrine and
                  Soviet Politics, 1953-1975," WP 29 (Oct. 1976):
                  90-113.

4230.   Huston, James A. "Korea and Logistics," MR 36
                  (Feb. 1957):18-32.

4231.   Hutchinson, D.L. "In My Opinion: A New Look at
                  an Old Problem," AUR 30 (Jan.-Feb. 1979):69-73.
                  Defense unification.

4232.   Kennan, George F. "Japanese Security and
                  American Policy," FA 43 (Oct. 1964):14-28.

4233.   _____. "Mr. X" . "The Sources of Soviet Con-
                  duct," FA 25 (July 1947):566-82.

4234.   Kim, Sang Mo. "The Implications of the Sea War
                  in Korea," NWCR 20 (Summer 1967):105-39.

4235.   Kinney, Sheldon. "All Quiet at Wonsan," USNIP
         80 (Aug. 1954):859-67.

4236.   Kirkendall, Richard S. "Harry S. Truman: The
         Decision to Intervene," in Warren F. Kimball,
         ed. *American Diplomacy in the Twentieth Cen-
         tury.* St. Louis: Forum, 1980. No. 6.   The
         Korean War.

4237.   Kirkpatrick, Lyman B., Jr. "Paramilitary Case
         Study: The Bay of Pigs," NWCR 25 (Nov.-Dec.
         1972):32-43.

4238.   Korth, The Honorable Fred. "The Challenge of
         Navy Management: A Report from the Secretary
         of the Navy," USNIP 89 (Aug. 1963):26-31.

4239.   LaFond, E.C. "Arctic Oceanography by Subma-
         rines," USNIP 86 (Sept. 1960):90-96.

4240.   Lapidus, Robert D. "Sputnik and Its Repercus-
         sions: A Historical Catalyst," *Aero Hist.* 17
         (1970):88-93.

4241.   Larrabee, Eric. "Korea: The Military Lesson,"
         Harper's 201 (Nov. 1950):51-57.

4242.   MacDonald, Scot. "How the Decisions Were Made:
         Exclusive Inside Story of Naval Reorganization,"
         Armed Forces Management 12 (May 1966):74-82.

4243.   *McMullen, Robert A., and Nicholas A. Canzona.
         "Wolmi-do: Turning the Key," USNIP 82 (Mar.
         1956):290-297.   Description of the pre-invasion
         bombardment of an island in Inchon Harbor and
         the subsequent operations of the 3d Battalion,
         5th Marines, in its capture.

4244.   Maddox, Robert. "War in Korea: The Desperate
         Times," AHI 13 (July 1978):26-38.

4245.   Marshall, S.L.A. "Our Mistakes in Korea," *Atlan-
         tic* 192 (Sept. 1953):46-49.

4246.   *Mataxis, Theodore C. "The Marines 'New Look',"
         MR 38 (Feb. 1959):10-17.

4247.   Matray, James I. "Truman's Plan for Victory:
         National Self-Determination and the Thirty-
         Eighth Parallel Decision in Korea," JAH 62
         (Sept. 1979):314-33.

4248.   _____ "An End to Indifference: America's Korean Policy During World War II," *Dip. Hist.* 2
(Spring 1978):181-96.

4249.   Maurer, Maurer. "The Korean Conflict Was a War,"
MA 24 (Fall, 1960):137-45.

4250.   *Meese, Harry. "Landing Ship Dock: Nucleus of
the Modern Fast Amphibious Force," *Bureau of
Ships Journal* 2 (Sept. 1953):2-8.

4251.   Middleton, Drew. "NATO Changes Direction," FA
31 (Apr. 1953):427-40.

4252.   Millis, Walter. "Military Problems of the New
Administration," FA 31 (Jan. 1953):215-24.

4253.   *Montross, Lynn. "Fleet Marine Force Korea,"
USNIP 79 (Aug. 1953):828-841; (Sept. 1953):
994-1005. Survey of Marine operations in
Korea through May 1951.

4254.   *_____. "Buttoning up the Offensive: the Marines in Operation Killer," MCG 36 (Feb. 1952):
30-39. The 1st Marine Division in the Eighth
Army offensive against a Chinese salient in
the Wonju-Hoengsong area 21 Feb.-4 Mar. 1951.

4255.   *_____. "The Hungnam Evacuation, Amphibious
Landing in Reverse," MCG 35 (Dec. 1951):18-27.
The withdrawal by sea of Marine forces from
North Korea, 11-24 Dec. 1950.

4256.   *_____. "Breakout from the Reservoir: Marine
Epic of Fire and Ice," MCG 35 (Nov. 1951):22-
37. General account of the operations of the
1st Marine Division and the 1st Marine Aircraft
Wing in the withdrawal from Yudam-ni to Hamhung,
27 Nov.-11 Dec. 1950.

4257.   *_____. "The Inchon Landing: Victory over
Time and Tide," MCG 35 (July 1951):26-35. The
1st Marine Division in the landing of 15 Sept.
1950 and the operations of the day following,
with background on the build-up of the division
and the intensive planning for the landing.

4258.   *_____. "The Pusan Perimeter: Fight for a
Foothold," MCG 35 (June 1951):30-39. Operation
of the 1st Provisional Marine Brigade in southern Korea, 7 Aug.-7 Sep. 1950.

4259. *_____, and Norman W. Hicks. "They Were
       There," *Leatherneck* 43 (Dec. 1960):48-53; 44
       (Jan. 1961):48-53. Marine operations in Korea
       throughout the Reservoir campaign with empha-
       sis on the experiences of individual officers
       and men.

4260. Naymark, Sherman. "Underway on Nuclear Power:
       The Development of the *Nautilus*," USNIP 96
       (Apr. 1970):56-63.

4261. Nitze, Paul H. "Atoms, Strategy and Policy,"
       FA 34 (Jan. 1956):187-98.

4262. Norman, John. "MacArthur's Blockade Proposals
       against Red China," PHR 26 (May 1957):161-74.

4263. Ofstie, Ralph. "Strategic Air Warfare," USNIP
       77 (June 1951):591-600. Against using a single
       weapon system.

4264. Oppenheimer, J. Robert. "Atomic Weapons and
       American Policy," FA 31 (July 1953):525-35.

4265. Radford, Arthur W. "Our Navy in the Far East,"
       Nat. Geog. 104 (Oct. 1953):537-77.

4266. Rearden, Steven L. "American Nuclear Strategy
       and the Defense of Europe, 1954-1959," in David
       H. White, ed., *Proceedings of the Conference on
       War and Diplomacy*. Charleston, S.C.: The Cita-
       del, 1976, pp. 133-38.

4267. Rickover, Hyman G. "Nuclear Warships and the
       Navy's Future," USNIP 101 (Jan. 1975):18-24.

4268. Rosenberg, David A. "American Atomic Strategy
       and the Hydrogen Bomb Decision," JAH 66 (June
       1979):62-87.

4269. Schilling, Warner R. "The H-Bomb Decision: How
       to Decide without Actually Choosing," PSQ 76
       (1961):24-46.

4270. Schratz, Paul R. "The Military Services and
       the New Look, 1953-1961: The Navy," in David
       H. White, ed. *Proceedings of the Conference
       on War and Diplomacy*. Charleston, S.C.: The
       Citadel, 1976, pp. 139-44.

4271.   _____. "The Nuclear Carrier and Modern
            War," USNIP 98 (Aug. 1972):18-25.

4272.   *Shepherd, Lemuel C., Jr. "Chosin Reservoir to
            Hungnam," MCG 35 (Feb. 1951):14-19. [Also
            printed in Leatherneck 34 (Feb. 1951):11.]
            Statement for the press by the Commanding
            General, Fleet Marine Force, Pacific, 16 Dec.
            1950, reviewing Marine exploits in the Reser-
            voir evacuation, accompanied by a photographic
            coverage of the breakout.

4273.   Slessor, John. "Air Power and World Strategy,"
            FA 33 (Oct. 1954):43-53.

4274.   *Smith, O.P. "Looking back at Chosin," MCG 44
            (Dec. 1960):30-31. Brief review by the 1st
            Marine Division commander during the Reser-
            voir operation.

4275.   *_____. "The Inchon Landing," MCG 44 (Sept.
            1960):40-41. Account by the commander of the
            First Marine Division; primarily concerns the
            preparations for the landing.

4276.   Smyth, Henry D. "Nuclear Power and Foreign
            Policy," FA 35 (Oct. 1956):1-16.

4277.   Spaak, Paul-Henri. "The Atom Bomb and NATO,"
            FA 33 (Apr. 1955):353-59.

4278.   Spofford, Charles M. "NATO's Growing Pains,"
            FA 31 (Oct. 1952):95-105.

4279.   Stevenson, Adlai E. "Korea in Perspective,"
            FA 30 (Apr. 1952):349-60.

4280.   Stratton, Samuel S. "Korea: Acid Test of Con-
            tainment," USNIP 63 (Mar. 1952):237-49.

4281.   Strausz-Hupe, Robert, and Stefan T. Possony,
            eds. "Air Power and National Security," Annals
            229 (May 1955):1-140.

4282.   Tarpey, John F. "Korea: 25 Years Later," USNIP
            104 (Aug. 1978):50-57.

4283.   *Thach, John S. "'Right on the Button': Marine
            Close Air Support in Korea," USNIP 101 (Nov.
            1975):54-56.

4284.   Toner, James H. "Exceptional War, Exceptional
               Peace: The 1953 Cease-Fire in Korea," MR 56
               (July 1976):3-13.

4285.   *Totten, James P. "Operation Chromite: A Study
               of Generalship," Armor 85 (Nov.-Dec. 1976):
               33-38.

4286.   Uhlig, Frank, Jr. "The Atlantic Ocean: Sea
               of Decision," USNIP 80 (Mar. 1954):175-79.

4287.   U.S. Department of the Air Force. Far Eastern
               Air Force Bomber Command. "Heavyweights over
               Korea: B-29 Employment in the Korean War,"
               AUQR 7 (Spring 1954):99-115.

4288. UG630   Vandenberg, Hoyt S. "Air Power by Proxy," in
        .E5   Eugene E. Emme, ed. The Impact of Air Power:
               National Security and World Politics. Prince-
               ton, N.J.: Van Nostrand, 1959, pp. 400-06.
               Air power in the Korean War.

4289.   *Vinson, Carl. "Why a Marine Corps?" MCG 43
               (Nov. 1959):10-11.

4290.   Weyland, O.P. "The Air Campaign in Korea,"
               AUQR 6 (Fall 1953):3-41.

4291.   Wheeler, Gerald E. "Naval Aviation in the Ko-
               rean War," USNIP 83 (July 1957):762-77. Pic-
               torial.

4292.   Wilmot, Chester. "If NATO Had to Fight," FA
               31 (Jan. 1953):200-14.

4293.   Wilson, Larman C. "The Dominican Policy of
               the United States," WA 128 (July-Sept. 1965):
               93-101.

4294.   Wiltz, John Edward. "Truman and MacArthur: The
               Wake Island Meeting," MA 42 (Dec. 1978):169-
               76.

4295.   Wolk, Herman S. "The Birth of the U.S. Air
               Force," AF 60 (Sept. 1977):69-78.

4296.   Xydis, Stephen. "The Genesis of the Sixth
               Fleet," USNIP 84 (Aug. 1958):41-50.

4297.   York, Herbert F. "The Debate Over the Hydrogen
               Bomb," SA 233 (Oct. 1975):106-13.

TRANSCRIPTS OF ORAL INTERVIEWS

4298.   Hanson W. Baldwin, Arleigh A. Burke, Daniel
               V. Gallery, Paul D. Stroop, William J. Sebald,
               and John S. Thach. Annapolis, Md.: U.S. Naval
               Academy Library. Special Collections.

FICTION

4299. PS3525 Michener, James A. *The Bridges at Toko-Ri*.
       .T19   N.Y.: Random House, 1953. Destruction of the
       B75   bridges across the Yalu by aircraft during the
                Korean war.

21

KENNEDY, JOHNSON, AND SEA POWER IN THE SIXTIES

BOOKS

4300. E841
.A2
Abel, Elie. *The Missile Crisis.* Phila.: Lip-pincott, 1966.

4301. E744
.A2174
Acheson, Dean G. *Present at the Creation: My Years in the State Department.* N.Y.: Norton, 1969.

4302. E183.8
.R9A64
Allison, Graham T. *The Essence of Decision: Explaining the Cuban Missile Crisis.* Boston: Little, Brown, 1971.

4303. UA646
.3.A75
Amme, Carl H. *NATO without France.* Stanford: Hoover Institution, 1967.

4304. VA23
.A73
Art, Robert J. *The TFX Decision: McNamara and the Military.* Boston: Little, Brown, 1968.

4305. DS557
.A63A87
Austin, Anthony. *The President's War.* Phila.: Lippincott, 1971. The best treatment of the Tonkin Gulf resolution.

4306. E183.8
.V5B29
Baral, Jaha K. *The Pentagon and the Making of U.S. Foreign Policy: A Case Study of Vietnam, 1960-1968.* Atlantic Highlands, N.J.: Humanities P., 1978.

4307. E183.8
.V5B3
Bator, Victor. *Vietnam: A Diplomatic Tragedy: The Origins of United States Involvement. Dobbs* Ferry, N.Y.: Oceana Publications, 1965.

4308. VA65
.T7B38
Beach, Edward L. *Around the World Submerged: The Voyage of the* Triton. N.Y.: Holt, 1962.

4309. U162.6
.B413
Beaufre, André. *Deterrence and Strategy.* N.Y.: Praeger, 1964.

4310. D1065
.UtB4
Beloff, Max. *The United States and the Unity of Europe.* N.Y.: Random House, 1963.

4311. VA65
.T47B46
Bentley, John. *The* Thresher *Disaster: The Most Tragic Dive in Submarine History.* GCNY: Double-day, 1975. The dive occurred on 9 April 1963.

4312. DS558 Berger, Carl, ed. *The United States Air Force*
  .8.U54 *in Southeast Asia 1961-1973*. Wash.: OAFH,
     1977.

4313. U241 Blaufarb, Douglas S. *The Counterinsurgency Era:*
  .B53 *U.S. Doctrine and Performance, 1950 to the*
     Present. N.Y.: Free P., 1979.

4314. DS558 Brown, Weldon A. *The Last Chopper: The Denoue-*
  .B76 *ment of the American Role in Vietnam, 1963-*
     1975. Port Washington, N.Y.: Kennikat P.,
     1976.

4315. DS557 Buttinger, Joseph. *Vietnam: A Dragon Embattled*,
  .A5B83 2 vols. N.Y.: Praeger, 1967.

4316. E840 Calleo, David. *The Atlantic Fantasy: The United*
  .C34 *States, NATO, and Europe.* Baltimore: Johns Hop-
     kins P., 1970.

4317. DS558 Charlton, Michael, and Anthony Moncrieff. *Many*
  .C48 *Reasons Why: The American Involvement in Viet-*
     nam. N.Y.: Hill & Wang, 1978. Chronology of
     30 years and personal interviews.

4318. E841 Chayes, Abram. *The Cuban Missile Crisis: In-*
  .C48 *ternational Crises and the Rule of Law.* N.Y.:
     Oxford UP, 1974.

4319. E851 Chester, Lewis, Godfrey Hodgson, and Bruce
  .C45 Page. *An American Melodrama: The Presidential*
     Campaign of 1968. N.Y.: Viking, 1969.

4320. UA23 Clark, Keith C., and Laurence J. Legere, eds.
  .I52 *The President and the Management of National*
     Security: A Report by the Institute for De-
     fense Analyses. N.Y.: Praeger, 1969.

4321. DS518 Clubb, O.E., Jr. *The United States and the*
  .8.C57 *Sino-Soviet Bloc in Southeast Asia.* Wash.:
     Brookings, 1962.

4322. DS550 Cole, Allan B. *Conflict in Indochina and In-*
  .C6 *ternational Repercussions: A Documentary His-*
     tory, 1945-1955. Ithaca: Cornell UP, 1956.

4323. DS557 *Corson, William R. *The Betrayal.* N.Y.: Norton,
  .A6C6 1968. By a Marine colonel who was in Vietnam.

4324. UA2   Deitchman, Seymour J. *Limited War and American*
      .D43   *Defense Policy.* Cambridge: MIT P., 1964.

4325. E841   Detzer, David. *The Brink: Story of the Cuban*
      .D4   *Missile Crisis.* N.Y.: Crowell, 1979.

4326. E841   Dinerstein, Herbert S. *The Making of a Missile*
      .D45   *Crisis: October 1962.* Baltimore: Johns Hopkins
               P., 1976.

4327. E841   Divine, Robert A., ed. *The Cuban Missile Crisis.*
      .D5   Chicago: Quadrangle Books, 1971.

4328. DS550   Dooley, Thomas A. *Deliver Us From Evil: The*
      .D6   *Story of Viet Nam's Flight to Freedom.* N.Y.:
               Farrar, Straus, & Cudahy, 1956.

4329. E847   Evans, Rowland, and Robert Novak. *Lyndon B.*
      .E9   *Johnson: The Exercise of Power.* N.Y.: New Amer.
               Lib., 1966.

4330. UA23   Falk, Stanley L. *The National Security Struc-*
      .F34   *ture.* Wash.: ICAF, 1967. Also a 1977 edition
               by National Defense University.

4331. DS550   Fall, Bernard. *Hell in a Very Small Place: The*
      .F28   *Siege of Dien Bien Phu.* N.Y.: Lippincott, 1967.

4332. DS557   _____. *Ho Chi Minh on Revolution.* N.Y.:
      .A7   Praeger, 1967.
      .H533

4333. DS557   _____. *Viet-Nam Witness.* N.Y.: Praeger,
      .A5F35   1966.

4334. DS557   _____. *The Two Vietnams: A Political and*
      .A5F34   *Military Analysis,* rev. ed. N.Y.: Praeger,
               1965.

4335. DS550   _____. *Street Without Joy.* Harrisburg, Pa.:
      .F3   Stackpole, 1964.

4336. E744   Fulbright, William J. *The Arrogance of Power.*
      .F886   N.Y.: Random House, 1967.

4337. DS557   Fulton, William B. *Vietnam Studies: Riverine*
      .A645   *Operations, 1966-1969.* Wash.: OCMH, 1973.
      .F84

4338. E840.5   Furguson, Ernest B. *Westmoreland: The Inevita-*
      .W4F8   *ble General.* Boston: Little, Brown, 1968.

4339. U240   Galula, David. *Counterinsurgency Warfare:*
      .G3   *Theory and Practice.* N.Y.: Praeger, 1962.

4340. E744   Gavin, James M. *Crisis Now.* N.Y.: Random
      .G35   House, 1968.

4341. E183.8   Gelb, Leslie H., with Richard B. Betts. *The*
      .U5G4   *Irony of Vietnam: The System Worked.* Wash.:
                Brookings, 1979. A history, a critique of
                American decision-making, and a historiographi-
                cal study.

4342. F1938   Gleijeses, Piero. *The Dominican Crisis: The*
      .55   *1965 Constitutionalist Revolt and the American*
      .G5513   *Intervention.* Baltimore: Johns Hopkins P.,
                1978.

4343. E847   Goldman, Eric F. *The Tragedy of Lyndon Johnson.*
      .G6   N.Y.: Knopf, 1969.

4344. VA50   Gorshkov, Sergei G. *Sea Power of the State.*
      .G67   Annapolis, Md.: NIP, 1978. The Admiral of the
                Fleet of the Soviet Union discourses on sea
                power.

4345. DK59   _____. *Red Star Rising at Sea.* Annapolis,
      .G67   Md.: NIP, 1974.

4346. TL796.5 Green, Constance M., and Milton Lomask. *Van-*
      .U6J35   *guard: A History.* Wash.: NASA, 1970.

4347. U240   Guevara, Ernesto. *Che Guevara on Guerrilla*
      .G833   *Warfare.* N.Y.: Praeger, 1961.

4348. TL789   Hacker, Barton C., and James H. Grimwood. *On*
      .8.U6   *the Shoulders of Titans: A History of Project*
                Gemini. Wash.: NASA, 1971.

4349. E841   Halberstam, David. *The Best and the Brightest.*
      .H25   N.Y.: Random House, 1972. Criticism of Ameri-
                can political and military conduct of the war
                in Vietnam.

4350. DS557   _____. *The Making of a Quagmire.* N.Y.:
      .A6H3   Praeger, 1961. Vietnam.

354

4351. U162   Halperin, Morton H. *Defense Strategies for the*
      .H27   *Seventies.* Boston: Little, Brown, 1971.

4352. DS557   Hammer, Ellen. *Vietnam Yesterday and Today.*
      .A5H25   N.Y.: Holt, Rinehart & Winston, 1966.

4353. UG633   Harvey, Frank. *Strike Command.* N.Y.: Duell,
      .H3785   Sloan, & Pearce, 1962.

4354. E839   Heath, Jim F. *Decade of Disillusionment: The*
      .H42   *Kennedy-Johnson Years.* Bloomington: U. of In-
                 diana P., 1975.

4355. DS559   Herr, Michael. *Dispatches.* N.Y.: Knopf, 1978.
      .5.H47   War in Vietnam.

4356. E840   Hilsman, Roger. *To Move a Nation: The Politics*
      .H5   *of Foreign Policy in the Administration of John*
                 F. Kennedy. GCNY: Doubleday, 1967.

4357. UA23   Hitch, Charles J. *Decision-Making in Defense.*
      .H52   Berkeley: U. of California P., 1965.

4358. TL89.8   Holmes, Jay.. *America on the Moon.* Phila.: Lip-
      .U5H6   pincott, 1962.

4359. DS557   Hooper, Edwin B. *Mobility, Support, Endurance:*
      .A645   *A Story of Naval Operational Logistics in the*
      .H66   *Vietnam War, 1965-1968.* Wash.: GPO, 1972.

4360. DS557   _____, Dean C. Allard, and Oscar P. Fitz-
      .A645H7   gerald. *The United States Navy and the Vietnam*
                 Conflict. Vol. 1. *The Setting of Stage to 1959.*
                 Wash.: Dept. of the Navy, Naval Hist. Div.,
                 1976.

4361. DS537   Hoopes, Townsend. *The Limits of Intervention:*
      .A63H6   *An Inside Account of How the Johnson Policy of*
                 Escalation in Vietnam Was Reversed. N.Y.:
                 McKay, 1969.

4362. V25   Howe, Jonathan T. *Multicrises: Sea Power and*
      .H68   *Global Politics in the Missile Age.* Cambridge:
                 MIT P., 1971.

4363. E183.8   Hsiao, Gene T., ed. *Sino-American Detente and*
      .C5H728   *Its Policy Implications.* N.Y.: Praeger, 1974.

355

4364. F841
.D3

Hubbell, J.G. *Strike in the West: The Complete Story of the Cuban Missile Crisis.* N.Y.: Holt, Rinehart & Winston, 1963.

4365. DS557
.A6H9

*Hymoff, Edward. *The First Marine Division in Vietnam.* N.Y.: M.W. Lads, 1967.

4366. F1788
.J6

Johnson, Haynes, and others. *The Bay of Pigs.* N.Y.: Norton, 1964.

4367. E846
.J58

Johnson, Lyndon. *The Vantage Point.* N.Y.: Holt, Rinehart & Winston, 1971.

4368. DS557
.A6K28

Kahin, George, and John Lewis. *The United States in Vietnam,* rev. ed. N.Y.: Dell, 1969.

4369. UF767
.K25

Kahn, Herman. *On Thermonuclear War.* Princeton: PUP, 1961.

4370. UA23
.K37

Kaufman, William W. *The McNamara Strategy.* N.Y.: Harper & Row, 1964.

4371. E847
.K4

Kearns, Doris. *Lyndon Johnson and the American Dream.* N.Y.: Harper & Row, 1976.

4372. E183
.8.R9
K42

Kennedy, Robert F. *Thirteen Days: A Memoir of the Cuban Missile Crisis.* N.Y.: Norton, 1969.

4373. E835
.K5

Kissinger, Henry. *The Necessity for Choice: Prospects of American Foreign Policy.* N.Y.: Harper, 1961.

4374. E183.8
.C9L3

Langley, Lester D. *The Cuban Policy of the United States: A Brief History.* N.Y.: Wiley, 1968.

4375. UA323
.L4

Levitan, Sar A., and Karen C. Alderman. *Warriors at Work: The Volunteer Armed Force.* Beverly Hills, Calif.: Sage, 1977.

4376. DS558
.L48

Lewy, Gunter. *America in Vietnam.* N.Y.: Oxford UP, 1978.

4377. DS557
.A65C67

Littauer, Raphael, and Norman Uphoff, eds. *The Air War in Indochina,* rev. ed. Boston: Beacon, 1972.

4378.   McCarthy, James R., and George B. Allison. *Linebacker II: A View from the Rock*. Maxwell AFB: Air War College, Airpower Research Institute, 1979. The preparation and execution of the B-52 raids on Hanoi from Guam and Thailand.

4379. UA23   McNamara, Robert S. *The Essence of Security: Reflections in Office*. N.Y.: Harper & Row, .M25   1968.

4380. F1938   Martin, John B. *Overtaken by Events: The Dominican Crisis from the Fall of Trujillo to the .55M34   Civil War*. GCNY: Doubleday, 1966.

4381. DS557   Mecklin, J. *Mission in Torment: An Intimate Account of the U.S. Role in Vietnam*. GCNY: .A6M4   Doubleday, 1965.

4382. UG633   Medaris, John B., with Arthur Gordon. *Countdown for Decision*. N.Y.: Putnam, 1960. Astronautics .M325   and U.S. military policy.

4383. F1788   Meyer, K.E., and Tad Szulc. *The Cuban Invasion*. N.Y.: Ballantine, 1962. .M45

4384. DS557   Moeser, Robert D. *U.S. Navy: Vietnam*. Annapolis, Md.: NIP, 1969. Pictorial. .A61M5

4385. E840   Morgenthau, Hans J. *A New Foreign Policy for the United States*. N.Y.: Praeger, 1969. .M593

4386. UA23   Moulton, Harland B. *From Superiority to Parity: The United States and the Strategic Arms Race, .M67   1961-1971*. Westport, Conn.: Greenwood, 1973.

4387. UA23   Murdock, Clark A. *Defense Policy Formulation: A Comparative Analysis of the McNamara Era*. .M9   Albany: SUNY P., 1974.

4388. DS558   Palmer, Dave R. *Summons of the Trumpet: U.S.-Vietnam in Perspective*. San Rafael, Calif.: .P34   Presidio, 1978.

4389. U240   Paret, Peter, and John W. Shy. *Guerrillas in the 1960s*. N.Y.: Praeger, 1962. .P3

4390. VA65   Polmar, Norman. *Death of the* Thresher. N.Y.:
      .T531   Chilton, 1964. 9 Apr. 1963.
      P59

4391. V162   Quester, George H. *Deterrence before Hiroshima:*
      .6.Q4   *The Background of Modern Strategy.* N.Y.: Wiley,
                1966.

4392. V993   *Rawlins, William R. Ed. by William J. Sambito.
      .R38   *Marines and Helicopters, 1962-1973,* 2 vols.
                Wash.: USMC, HQ, Hist. and Museums Div., 1979.
                Vol. 1 by Rawlins. Vol. 2 by Fails, William
                R., *q.v.*

4393. UA23   Raymond, Jack. *Power at the Pentagon.* N.Y.:
      .6.R3   Harper & Row, 1964.

4394. UA23   Rockefeller Brothers Fund. *Prospect for Ameri-*
      .R6   *ca: The Rockefeller Panel Reports.* GCNY:
                Doubleday, 1961.

4395. UA23   Roherty, James M. *Decisions of Robert McNamara.*
      .R64   Coral Gables, Fla.: U. of Miami P., 1970.

4396. E741   Rostow, Walt W. *The United States in the World*
      .R67   *Arena.* N.Y.: Harper, 1960.

4397. D535   Scalapino, Robert A., ed. *The Communist Revolu-*
      .S35   *tion in Asia.* Englewood Cliffs, N.J.: Prentice-
                Hall, 1965.

4398. DS558   Schandler, Herbert Y. *The Unmaking of a Presi-*
      .S33   *dent: Lyndon Johnson and Vietnam.* Princeton:
                PUP, 1977.

4399. DD881   Schick, Jack M. *The Berlin Crisis, 1958-1962.*
      .S26   Phila.: U. of Pa. P., 1971.

4400. E840.8   Schlesinger, Arthur M., Jr. *Robert Kennedy and*
      .K4S33   *His Times.* Boston: Houghton Mifflin, 1978.

4401. E841   _____. *A Thousand Days: John F. Kennedy in*
      .S3   *the White House.* Boston: Houghton Mifflin,
                1965.

4402. DS558   Sharp, U.S.G. *Strategy for Defeat: Vietnam in*
      .S56   *Retrospect.* San Rafael, Calif.: Presidio, 1978.

4403. DS557   Sheehan, Neil. *The Arnheiter Affair.* N.Y.:
      .A645S5   Random House, 1971.

358

4404. E183.8   _____, and others. *The Pentagon Papers*.
      .V5P4   N.Y.: Bantam, 1971.

4405.   Shore, Moyers S. *The Battle for Khe Sanh*. Wash.:
                GPO, 1969.

4406. DS558   *Shulimson, Jack, and Charles M. Johnson. *U.S.*
      .9.M37S58 *Marines in Vietnam: The Landing and the Build-*
                up, 1965. Wash.: USMC, HQ, Hist. and Museums
                Div., 1978.

4407. DD881   Slusser, Robert M. *The Berlin Crisis of 1961:*
      .S52   *Soviet-American Relations and the Struggle for*
                Power in the Kremlin, June-November 1961.
                Baltimore: Johns Hopkins P., 1973.

4408. F183   Smith, Earl E. *The Fourth Floor: An Account of*
      .8.C9   *the Castro Communist Revolution*. N.Y.: Random
      S56   House, 1962.

4409. DS559   Snepp, Frank. *Decent Interval: An Insider's*
      .5.S64   *Account of the Saigon's Indecent End Told by*
                the CIA's Chief Strategy Analyst in Vietnam.
                N.Y.: Random House, 1978.

4410. E841   Sorenson, Theodore C. *Kennedy*. N.Y.: Harper
      .S6   & Row, 1965.

4411. DS558.9   Starry, Donn A. *Mounted Combat in Vietnam*.
      .A75S73   Wash.: GPO, 1978. An account of the operations
                of armored units of the U.S. Army in Vietnam.

4412. DK63   Strausz-Hupe, Robert, and others. *Protracted*
      .3.S86   *Conflict*. N.Y.: Harper, 1963.

4413. JX4135q   Swartztrauber, Sayre A. *The Three-Mile Limit*
      .S93   *of Territorial Seas*. Annapolis, Md.: NIP, 1972.

4414. F1938   Szulc, Tad. *Dominican Diary*. N.Y.: Delacorte,
      .55.S95   1965.

4415. UA23   Taylor, Maxwell D. *The Uncertain Trumpet*. N.Y.:
      .T33   Harper, 1960.

4416. UA23   _____. *Responsibility and Response*. N.Y.:
      .T34   Harper & Row, 1967.

4417. DS557   Thompson, Willard S., and Donaldson D. Firzzel.
      .L47   *The Lessons of Vietnam*. N.Y.: Crane & Russak,
                1977.

4418. UA23   Trewhitt, Henry L. *McNamara: His Ordeal in the*
      .T74   *Pentagon.* N.Y.: Harper & Row, 1971.

4419. UA23   Tucker, Samuel A., ed. *A Modern Design for De-*
      .T8   *fense Decision: A McNamara-Hitch-Enthoven*
               Anthology. Wash.: ICAF, 1966.

4420. DS557   Walt, Lewis W. *Strange War, Strange Strategy:*
      .A6W27   *A General's Report on Vietnam.* N.Y.: Funk &
               Wagnalls, 1970.

4421. E183   Weissman, Stephen R. *American Foreign Policy*
      .8.Z34   *in the Congo, 1960-1964.* Ithaca: Cornell UP,
      W44   1974.

4422. DS559   Westmoreland, William C. *A Soldier Reports.*
      .S.W47   GCNY: Doubleday, 1976. Vietnam and personal
               narratives.

4423. DS557   *Whitlow, Robert H. *U.S. Marines in Vietnam: The*
      .A645W5   *Advisory and Combat Assistance Era 1954-1964.*
               Wash.: USMC, HQ, Hist. and Museums Div., 1977.

4424. DS557   Windchy, Eugene G. *Tonkin Gulf.* GCNY: Double-
      .A62T65   day, 1971.

4425. F1788   Wyden, Peter. *Bay of Pigs: The Untold Story.*
      .W9   N.Y.: Simon & Schuster, 1979.

DOCUMENTS

4426. D1.2:   U.S. Blue Ribbon Defense Panel. *Report to the*
      B62/970   *President and the Secretary of Defense on the*
               Department of Defense by the Blue Ribbon De-
               fense Panel, 1 July 1970. [Gilbert W. Fitz-
               burgh report.] Wash.: GPO, 1970.

4427. VA65   U.S. Congress. *Loss of the U.S.S.* Thresher.
      .T531   *Hearings before the Joint Committee on Atomic*
      .A513   *Energy, Congress of the United States. 88th*
               Cong., 1st Sess., June 26, 27, July 23, 1963,
               and July 1, 1964. Committee Print.

4428. Doc   U.S. Congress. House, Committee on Armed Ser-
               vices. *Inquiry into the U.S.S.* Pueblo *and*
               EC-121I Plane Incidents. Hearings before the
               Special Subcommittee on the U.S.S. Pueblo.
               Wash.: GPO, 1969.

4429. Y4Ar   U.S. Congress. Senate Committee on Government
        5/2a/   Operations, Permanent Subcommittee on Investi-
        969-970   gations. *Hearings on the TFX Contract Investi-
                   gation*, 10 vols. 88th Cong., 1st Sess. Wash.:
                   GPO, 1963-1964.

4430. Y4.   U.S. Congress. Senate Committee on Government
        G74/6:   Operations, Permanent Subcommittee on Investi-
        T11/970   gations. *TFX Contract Investigation...Report*.
        pt.   91st Cong., 2nd Sess. Wash.: GPO, 1970.

4431. UA23.3   U.S. DOD. *Final Report to Congress of Secretary
        .F55   of Defense Melvin R. Laird Before the House
                   Armed Services Committee*. Wash.: GPO, 1973.

4432. Y4.G74/   _____. *United States-Vietnam Relations,
        7:D84/8   1945-1967: Study*. Wash.: GPO, 1971, 12 vols.
                   The "Pentagon Papers."

4433.   U.S. Joint Chiefs of Staff. *Organization and
                   Functions of the Joint Chiefs of Staff*. JCS
                   Pub. 4, rev. Wash.: 1 Oct. 1966.

4434. UC263   U.S. Joint Logistics Review Board. *Logistic
        .A5175   Support in the Vietnam War: A Report*, 3 vols.
                   Wash.: 1970.

4435.   *U.S. Marine Corps, HQ. *Professional Knowledge
                   Gained from Operational Experiences in Vietnam*.
                   Wash.: 1967.

4436. DS557   General William C. Westmoreland, in U.S. Pacif-
        .A6U55   ic Command. *Report on the War in Vietnam as of
                   30 June 1968*.... Wash.: GPO, 1969.

                   DISSERTATIONS AND THESES

4437.   Barnes, Harley H., Jr. "The Nuclear NonProlif-
                   eration Treaty: Participants, Interests, and
                   Processes in American Foreign Policy Formula-
                   tion," Rutgers U., 1976.

4438.   Ghent, Jocelyn M. "Canadian-American Relations
                   and the Nuclear Weapons Controversy, 1958-1963,"
                   U. of Illinois at Urbana-Champaign, 1976.

4439.   Hamilton, William R. "The Influence of the
                   American Military upon United States Foreign
                   Policy, 1965-1968," U. of Nebraska, 1978.

4440.   Hernando, Orlando M. "The United States and the Philippines, 1946-1975: A Study of Small Power Alliance," U. of Oklahoma, 1976.

4441. DC412   Lockwood, Robert S. "Gaullist Foreign Policy:
      .L6   NATO Withdrawal and Systematic Change," George Washington U., 1976.

4442.   Weaver, James D. "The Commander in Chief, Civilian Supremacy, Command and Control: Civil-Military Relations in the Eisenhower Presidency," New York U., 1972.

4443. E183.8   Wu, Fu-mei C. "The China Policy of Richard M.
      .C5W794 Nixon: From Confrontation to Negotiation," U. of Utah, 1976.

ARTICLES

4444.   Adams, William D. "The Underwater War," *Ordnance* 47 (Nov.-Dec. 1962):317-19.

4445.   Alden, John D. "The Unfaced Challenge: Submarine vs. the Free World," USNIP 90 (Apr. 1964): 26-36.

4446.   Amme, Carl H., Jr. "Perspectives on Naval Strategy," USNIP 95 (May 1969):12-24.

4447.   _____. "Naval Strategy and the New Frontier," USNIP 88 (Mar. 1962):23-34.

4448. D436   Anderson, George W., Jr. "The Cuban Missile
      .N38   Crisis," in Arnold Shapack, ed. *Proceedings,*
      .973   *Naval History Symposium.* Annapolis, Md.: U.S. Naval Academy, 1973, pp. 81-86.

4449.   "Atlantic Mine Force," *All Hands,* 584 (Sept. 1965):6-7.

4450.   Austin, Bernard L. "Military Considerations of National Strategy," MWCR 16 (Dec. 1963):1-23.

4451.   Bachman, Robert L. "*Savannah*: The Pioneer Merchant Ship," USNIP 87 (Sept. 1961):81-89.

4452.   Baldwin, Hanson W. "Slow-Down in the Pentagon," FA 43 (Jan. 1965):262-80.

4453.   _____. "The Critical Tomorrows," USNIP 89 (Dec. 1962):23-32.

4454.   Barber, Stuart B. "Seapower and American Survival," USNIP 87 (Mar. 1961):51-60.

4455.   Bishop, Charles B. "Systems Analysis: Something Old-Something New," USNIP 94 (Oct. 1961):25-39.

4456.   Bouscaren, Anthony T. "The Nature of the War We Are In," USNIP 87 (Oct. 1961):25-39.

4457.   Boyle, Richard. "1960: A Vintage Year for Submariners," USNIP 96 (Oct. 1970):35-41.

4458.   Brinckloe, W.D. "Military Decision and the Future of Sea Power," USNIP 86 (Nov. 1960):82-90.

4459.   Brodie, Bernard. "The McNamara Phenomenon," WP 17 (July 1965):672-86.

4460.   Bryson, Thomas A. "American Diplomacy in the Middle East," in Warren F. Kimball ed., *American Diplomacy in the Twentieth Century*. St. Louis: Forum, 1980. No. 8.

4461.   Buchan, Alastair. "The Reform of NATO," FA 40 (Jan. 1962):165-82.

4462.   Burke, Arleigh A. "National Strategy," NWCR 18 (Oct. 1965):21-35.

4463.   _____. "The Joint Chiefs of Staff in Operation," USNIP 83 (Mar. 1957):337-40.

4464.   Cagle, Malcolm W. "Task Force 77 in Action off Vietnam," USNIP, *Naval Review*, May 1972.

4465.   _____. "The Most Silent Service," USNIP 98 (Aug. 1969):37-41. Civilian domination of DOD.

4466.   Caldwell, Dan, ed. "Department of Defense Operations During the Cuban Crisis [1962]: A Report by Adam Yarmolinsky," NWCR 32 (June-July 1979):83-99.

4467.   Chapelle, Georgette L. "Water War in Viet Nam," *Nat. Geog.* 129 (Feb. 1966):272-96.

4468.   Christol, C.Q., and C.R. Davis, "Maritime Quarantine: The Naval Interdiction of Offensive Weapons and Associated Materiel to Cuba, 1962," AJIL 57 (July 1963):535-45.

363

4469.   Coffey, Joseph I. "Strategies and Realities,"
            USNIP 92 (Feb. 1966):34-41.

4470.   Cohen, Paul. "The Erosion of Surface Naval
            Power," FA 49 (Jan. 1971):330-41.

4471.   Dare, James A. "Dominican Diary," USNIP 91
            (Dec. 1965):36-45.

4472.   Dawson, Raymond H. "The Blue Ribbon Panel Re-
            port: Unification Orthodoxy Revisited," *Aero-
            space Historian* 18 (Spring 1971):4-11.

4473.   DeWeerd, Harvey A. "Strategic Decision Making:
            Vietnam, 1965-1978," *Yale Rev.* 67 (Spring
            1978):481-92.

4474.   Dorsey, Laurens. "A Concept of National Strat-
            egy," NWCR 12 (Sept. 1959):35-83.

4475.   Fielding, George F. "Seapower and Current Mili-
            tary Strategy," NWCR 13 (Apr. 1961):1-17.

4476.   _____. "Defense Decisions in the Dangerous
            Decade," USNIP 87 (Jan. 1961):23-32.

4477.   *"First Marine Brigade FMF," MCG 44 (June 1960):
            38-44.

4478.   Fisher, Ernest F. "A Strategy of Flexible Re-
            sponse," MR 47 (Mar. 1967):41-55.

4479.   Gannon, Robert. "What Really Happened to the
            Thresher?" *Pop. Sci.* 184 (Feb. 1964):102-09,
            209-89.

4480.   Giddings, Ralph J., Jr. "Battle Management for
            Strategic Weapons Systems," USNIP 97 (Jan.
            1971):49-52.

4481.   Gormley, Robert H. "Limited War and the Strik-
            ing Fleets," USNIP 89 (Feb. 1963):53-60.

4482.   Halberstam, David. "The Programming of Robert
            McNamara," *Harper's* 242 (Feb. 1971):37-71.

4483.   Hamilton, William A., III. "The Decline and
            Fall of the Joint Chiefs of Staff," NWCR 24
            (Apr. 1972):36-56. The Kennedy-Johnson
            years.

4484.   Harrigan, Anthony. "Seapower in the Sixties: Deterrent and Determinant," USNIP 87 (July 1961):23-33.

4485.   Hayward, John T., and Paul J. Kearney. "Command and Control in the Nuclear Age," USNIP 89 (Nov. 1963):38-43.

4486.   Heinl, Robert D., Jr. "Reasons for Mining NVN Waters," AFJ 109 (June 1972):62.

4487.   _____. "The Collapse of the Armed Forces," AFJ 109 (7 June 1971):30-38.

4488.   _____. "Welcome to the War," USNIP 95 (Mar. 1969):58-62. The *New Jersey* in action, 1969.

4489.   Herring, George C. "Vietnam: An American Ordeal," in Warren F. Kimball, ed. *American Diplomacy in the Twentieth Century*. St. Louis: Forum, 1980. No. 7.

4490.   Hessler, William. "Blue Water around Red China," USNIP 89 (Feb. 1963):27-39.

4491.   Hewes, James E., Jr. "Management vs. Bureaus," MCG 51 (Feb. 1967):39-41. Navy Department administration.

4492.   Hoag, Malcolm W. "What New Look in Defense?" WP 22 (Oct. 1969):1-28.

4493.   Huntington, Samuel P. "Strategic Planning and the Political Process," FA 38 (Jan. 1960): 285-99.

4494.   Ingraham, Samuel P. "Civil Command or Civilian Control?" USNIP 94 (May 1968):26-31. Too much McNamara in DOD.

4495.   Jackson, Barbara W. "Canada's Role in Western Defense," FA 40 (Apr. 1962):419-30.

4496.   Kahan, Jerome H., and Anne K. Long. "The Cuban Missile Crisis: A Study of Its Strategic Context," PSQ 87 (Dec. 1972):564-90.

4497.   Kanter, Arnold. "Congress and the Defense Budget, 1960-1970," APSR 56 (Mar. 1972):129-43.

4498.   Kestner, Jack. "The Navy and Cuba: Operational Report," *Navy* 6 (Jan. 1963):5-11+.

4499.   Kirkpatrick, Lyman G., Jr. "Paramilitary Case Study: The Bay of Pigs," NWCR 25 (Nov.-Dec. 1972):32-43.

4500.   Kissinger, Henry A. "Strategy and Organization," FA 35 (Apr. 1957):379-94.

4501.   Korb, Lawrence J. "Robert McNamara's Impact on the Budget Strategies of the Joint Chiefs of Staff," *Aerospace Historian* 17 (Winter 1970): 132-36.

4502.   LeMay, Curtis E. "United States Air Force: Power for Peace," *Nat. Geog.* 128 (Sept. 1965): 291-97.

4503.   Locetta, Joseph. "Manpower and the Merchant Marine," USNIP 96 (July 1970):26-30.

4504.   Long, William F., Jr. "Counterinsurgency: Corrupting Concept," USNIP 105 (Apr. 1979):57-64.

4505.   Loomis, Richard T. "The White House Telephone and Crisis Management," USNIP 95 (Dec. 1969): 63-73.

4506.   MacDonald, Charles B. "The Five Big Decisions of the War in Vietnam," in David H. White, ed. *Proceedings of the Conference on War and Diplomacy.* Charleston, S.C.: The Citadel, 1976, pp. 12-19.

4507.   McClintock, Robert. "The River War in Indochina," USNIP 80 (Dec. 1954):1303-11.

4508.   *McCutcheon, Keith B. "Marine Aviation in Vietnam, 1962-1970," USNIP 97 (May 1971):122-55.

4509.   MacDonald, Scot. "How the Decisions Were Made: Exclusive Inside Story of Navy Reorganization," *Armed Forces Management* 12 (May 1966):74-82.

4510.   McInteer, James F., Jr. "The Significance of Seapower to the United States," NWCR 12 (Sept. 1959):1-33.

4511.   Massey, Robert J. "The First Hundred Days of
         the New Frontier," USNIP 87 (Aug. 1961):27-33.

4512.   Meacham, James A. "The Mine as a Tool of
         Limited War," USNIP 93 (Feb. 1967):50-62.

4513.   Michaelis, Frederick H. "Material for Naval
         Combat," National Defense 61 (May-June 1977):
         449-52.

4514.   Moore, Donald L. "The Bay of Pigs: An Analy-
         sis," NWCR 19 (Nov. 1966):1-20.

4515.   Morison, F.P. "The Navy in the Space Age:
         Space Surveillance," USNIP 87 (Feb. 1961):
         42-45.

4516.   Moss, R.N. "The United States: Pre-eminent
         Seapower," NWCR 15 (Feb. 1963):23-41.

4517.   Murphy, Frank M. "Seapower and the Satellites,"
         USNIP 95 (Nov. 1969):75-83.

4518.   _____. "The Soviet Navy in the Mediterrane-
         an," USNIP 93 (Mar. 1967):38-46.

4519.   Noel, John V. "The Navy and the Department of
         Defense," USNIP 87 (Nov. 1961):23-34.

4520.   Owen, Henry. "NATO Strategy: What Is Past Is
         Prologue," FA 43 (July 1965):682-90.

4521.   Porter, Rufus. "American Merchant Shipping: A
         Recurring National Dilemma," NWCR 15 (Nov.
         1962):25-40.

4522.   "The Question of National Defense Organization:
         A Quarterly Review Study," AUQR 12 (Summer
         1960):52-134.

4523.   Radford, Arthur W. "The 'New Look,'" Vital
         Speeches 20 (Jan. 1, 1954):171-73.

4524.   Reitzel, William. "Seapower in the Mediterrane-
         an," NWCR 19 (Nov. 1966):1-36.

4525.   Rhymes, Cassius D. "Balanced Sea Power and Cold
         War," USNIP 86 (Sept. 1960):76-84.

4526.   Schofield, B.B. "Tomorrow's Warships: Their Cost and Value," USNIP 97 (Jan. 1971):43-48.

4527.   *Simmons, Edwin H. "Marine Corps Operations in Vietnam, 1965-1966," USNIP *Naval Review*, May 1968. *See* similar articles in issues through 1975.

4528.   Slaff, Ollan P. "Naval Advisor Viet Nam," USNIP 95 (Apr. 1969):38-44.

4529.   Smith, Melden E., Jr. "The Strategic Bombing Debate: The Second World War and Vietnam," JCH 12 (Jan. 1977):175-91.

4530.   Sokol, Anthony E. "Sea, Land, Air, and Missile Power," USNIP 86 (May 1960):27-36.

4531.   Spitz, Allan W. "Conventional versus Nuclear Power for CVA-67: A Study of Defense Management," NWCR 24 (Apr. 1972):3-14.

4532.   Stanley, Timothy W. "A Strategic Doctrine for NATO in the 1970's," *Orbis* 13 (Spring 1969): 87-99.

4533.   Stephen, Edward C. "Oceanography and Naval Warfare," NWCR 14 (Apr. 1962):20-31.

4534.   Styer, Charles W., and Robert F. Freitag. "The Navy in the Space Age," USNIP 86 (Mar. 1969): 86-94.

4535.   Tomkins, E.T. "The U.S. Navy 'Ashore' in Vietnam," *Navy* 11 (Feb. 1968):13-20+.

4536.   *Tompkins, R.M. "Ubique," MCG 49 (Sept. 1965): 32-39. The 8,000 Marines in the Dominican Republic in 1965.

4537.   Valentine, Andrew J. "Rx Quarantine," USNIP 89 (May 1963):38-50. Interdiction of Soviet ships bound for Cuba, 1962.

4538.   Villar, G.R. "Amphibious Warfare Forces in Europe and the Soviet Union," USNIP 103 (Nov. 1977):112-17.

4539.   Vito, Albert H. "Carrier Air and Viet Nam: An Assessment," USNIP 93 (Oct. 1967):66-75.

4540.   _____. "The Attack Carrier: Mobile Might,"
             USNIP 87 (May 1961):37-42.

4541.   Weakley, C.E. "Antisubmarine Warfare: Where Do
             We Stand?" USNIP, *Naval Review*, May 1965.

4542.   Weaver, Kenneth F. "Of Planes and Men: U.S.
             Air Force Wages Cold War and Hot," *Nat. Geog.*
             128 (Sept. 1965):298-349.

4543.   Wettern, Desmond. "NATO's Northern Flank,"
             USNIP 95 (July 1969):52-59.

4544.   Wilson, Larman C. "International Law and the
             United States Quarantine of 1962," *Jour. of
             Inter-American Studies* 7 (Oct. 1965):485-92.

4545.   Withrow, John E. "Needed: A Credible Presence,"
             USNIP 92 (Mar. 1966):52-61.

FICTION

4546. PS3503   Bachmann, Lawrence P. *The Bitter Lake*. Boston:
      .A159   Little, Brown, 1970. Events on board a ship
      B5   trapped in the Suez Canal during the Six-Day
                War of 1967.

4547. DS559   Caputo, Philip. *A Rumor of War*. N.Y.: Holt,
      .5C36   Rinehart & Winston, 1977. Vietnam.

4548. PZ4   *Roth, Robert. *Sand in the Wind*. Boston: Little,
      .R84543   Brown, 1973. Marines in Vietnam.
      San

4549. PS3573   *Webb, James. *Fields of Fire*. Englewood Cliffs,
      .F1955F5 N.J.: Prentice-Hall, 1978. Marines in Vietnam.

22

THE CHALLENGE OF THE SOVIET NAVY

BOOKS

4550. DS326   Abir, Mordechai M., and Aryeh Yodfat. *In the*
       .V6   *Direction of the Gulf: The Soviet Union and the*
                Persian Gulf. Totowa, N.J.: Frank Cass, 1977.

4551. G680   Armstrong, Terence N. *The Northern Sea Route:*
       .A7   *Soviet Exploitation of the Northeast Passage.*
                Cambridge, Mass.: HUP, 1952.

4552. UG635   Berman, Robert P. *Soviet Air Power in Transi-*
       .R9B47   *tion.* Wash.: Brookings, 1978.

4553. UA23   Betts, Richard K. *Soldiers, Statesmen, and Cold*
       .B46   *War Crises.* Cambridge, Mass.: HUP, 1977.

4554. VA573   Blechman, Barry M. *The Changing Soviet Navy.*
       .B55   Wash.: Brookings, 1973.

4555. UA23   _____, and others. *The Soviet Military*
       .S55   *Buildup and U.S. Defense Spending.* Wash.:
                Brookings, 1977.

4556. UG635   Boyd, Alexander. *The Soviet Air Force since*
       .R9B868 *1918.* N.Y.: Stein and Day, 1977. Poor on
                World War II; good on the rise of the air in-
                dustry in the late 1930s.

4557. VA573   The Center for Strategic and International
       .B713   Studies. *Soviet Sea Power.* Special Report
                Series, No. 10, June 1, 1969. Wash.: Georgetown
                U., 1970.

4558. UA23   Collins, John M. *American and Soviet Military*
       .C69   *Trends Since the Cuban Missile Crisis.* Wash.:
                Center for International Studies, Georgetown
                U., 1978.

4559. HC336   Cressy, George B. *Soviet Potentials: A Geo-*
       .2C7   *graphical Appraisal.* Syracuse: Syracuse UP,
                1962.

4560. VA50   Eliot, George F. *Victory Without War, 1958-1961.*
       .E4   Annapolis, Md.: USNI, 1958.

4561. VA573   Eller, Ernest M. *The Soviet Sea Challenge*.
      .E43   Chicago: Cowles, 1971.

4562. UB251   Freedman, Lawrence. *U.S. Intelligence and the*
      .U5F73   *Soviet Strategic Threat*. Boulder, Col.: West-
               view, 1978.

4563. UA770   Garthoff, Raymond L. *Soviet Military Policy*.
      .G295   N.Y.: Praeger, 1966.

4564. VA50   Gorshkov, Sergei G. *Sea Power of the State*.
      .G67   Annapolis, Md.: NIP, 1979.

4565. DK59   _____. *Red Star Rising at Sea*. Annapolis,
      .G67   Md.: NIP, 1974.

4566. E183.8   Gray, Colin S. *The Geopolitics of the Nuclear*
      .R7G72   *Era: Heartland, Rimlands, and the Technologi-*
               cal Revolution. N.Y.: Crane & Russak, 1977.

4567. Q127   Harvey, Moses L., Leon Goure, and Vladmir
      .R9H37   Prokofieff. *Science and Technology as an In-*
               strument of Soviet Policy. Coral Gables, Fla.:
               U. of Miami P., 1972.

4568. VA770   Haselkorn, Avigdor. *The Evolution of Soviet*
      .H3   *Security Strategy, 1965-1975*. N.Y.: NSIC, 1978.

4569. VA570   Herrick, Robert W. *Soviet Naval Strategy: Fifty*
      .H4   *Years of Theory and Practice*. Annapolis, Md.:
               USNI, 1968. Concludes that the Soviet Navy was
               defensive because it contained no carriers.

4570. UG635   Higham, Robin, and Jacob W. Kipp, eds. *Soviet*
      .R9S596 *Aviation and Air Power: A Historical View*.
               Boulder, Colo.: Westview P., 1977.

4571. E840   Jones, Alan M., Jr., ed. *U.S. Foreign Policy*
      .U46   *in a Changing World: The Nixon Administration,*
               1969-1973. N.Y.: McKay, 1973.

4572. D793   Lewis, Jesse W. *The Strategic Balance in the*
      .L43   *Mediterranean*. Wash.: AEI, 1976.

4573. VA573   MccGwire, Michael, ed. *Soviet Naval Develop-*
      .M3   *ments: Context and Capability*. N.Y.: Praeger,
               1973. Seminar papers delivered at Dalhousie
               University, Halifax, Nova Scotia, October
               1972.

4574. VA573   _____, Ken Booth, and John McConnell, eds.
       .M32   *Soviet Naval Policy: Objectives and Constraints*.
                N.Y.: Praeger, 1975.

4575. VA573   McGruther, Kenneth V. *The Evolving Soviet Navy*.
       .M33   Newport: Naval War College P., 1978.

4576. VA573   Meister, Jurg. *The Soviet Navy*, 4 vols. London:
       .M45   Macdonald, 1972.

4577. DK56   Mitchell, Donald W. *A History of Russian and
       .M48   Soviet Sea Power*. N.Y.: Macmillan, 1974.
                Scholarly and exhaustive.

4578. DK56   Mitchell, Mairin. *Maritime History of Russia*,
       .M5   *1848-1948*. London: Sidgwick, 1949.

4579. VA573   Moore, John E. *The Soviet Navy Today*. N.Y.:
       .M63   Stein & Day, 1976.

4580. VA573   Morris, Eric. *The Russian Navy: Myth and Reali-
       .M67   ty*. London: Hamilton, 1977.

4581. UA23   Moulton, Harland B. *From Superiority to Parity:
       .M67   The United States and the Strategic Arms Race,
                1961-1971*. Westport, Conn.: Greenwood, 1973.

4582. REF   Polmar, Norman. *Soviet Naval Developments*.
       VA573   Annapolis, Md.: Nautical & Aviation Pub. Co.,
       .P65   1979.

4583. VA573   _____. *Soviet Naval Power in the 1970s*, 2nd
       .P6   ed. N.Y.: Crane & Russak, 1974.

4584. UA23   Quanbeck, Alton H., and Barry M. Blechman.
       .Q35   *Strategic Forces: Issues for the Mid-Seventies*.
                Wash.: Brookings, 1973.

4585. VA23   Quester, George H. *Nuclear Diplomacy: The First
       .Q42   25 Years*, 2nd ed. N.Y.: Dunellen, 1973.

4586. JX1974   _____. *The Politics of Nuclear Proliferation*.
       .7Q47   Baltimore: Johns Hopkins P., 1973.

4587. VA573   Saunders, Malcolm G., ed. *The Soviet Navy*.
       .S3   N.Y.: Praeger, 1958.

4588. VA573   Theberge, James D., ed. *Soviet Seapower in the
       .S59   Caribbean: Political and Strategic Implications*.
                N.Y.: Praeger, 1972.

4589. UA23 Thompson, Willard S. *Power Projection: A Net*
.T46 *Assessment of U.S. and Soviet Capabilities.*
N.Y.: NSIC, 1978.

4590. DK266 Ulam, Adam. *Expansion and Coexistence: The His-*
.U49 *tory of Soviet Foreign Policy, 1917-1973.* N.Y.:
Praeger, 1974.

4591. VA573 Wegener, Edward. *The Soviet Naval Offensive.*
.W413 Annapolis, Md.: NIP, 1974.

4592. VA536 Weinland, Robert G. *The Changing Mission and*
.C466 *Structure of the Soviet Navy.* Arlington, Va.:
Center for Naval Analyses, 1971.

4593. AS36 Wilson, Desmond P., and Nicholas Brown. *Warfare*
.C466 *at Sea: Threat of the Seventies.* Arlington,
No. 79 Va.: Center for Naval Analyses, Nov. 1971.

4594. JX1974 Wolfe, Thomas W. *The SALT Experience.* Cambridge,
.75.W64 Mass.: Ballinger Pub. Co., 1979.

4595. A536 _____. *The Global Strategic Perspective From*
.R28 *Moscow.* Santa Monica, Calif.: Rand Corp., 1973.

4596. AS36 _____. *Soviet Naval Interaction with the*
.R28 *United States and Its Influence on Soviet Naval*
No.4913 *Development.* Santa Barbara, Calif.: Rand Corp.,
1972. 39 pp.

4597. DK67 _____. *Soviet Power and Europe, 1945-1970.*
.W6 Baltimore: Johns Hopkins P., 1970.

4598. DK56 Woodward, David. *The Russians at Sea: A History*
.W6 *of the Russian Navy.* N.Y.: Praeger, 1966.

DOCUMENTS

4599. D301 Murphy, Paul J. *Naval Power in Soviet Policy.*
.85:2 Wash.: GPO, 1968.

4600. Y4.F76/2 U.S. Congress. Senate Committee on Foreign Re-
Un35/34 lations. *United States/Soviet Strategic Options.*
Hearings Before the Committee on Foreign Rela-
tions..., 95th Cong., 1st Sess.... Jan. 14, 19,
and Mar. 16, 1977. Wash.: GPO, 1977.

DISSERTATIONS AND THESES

4601. VA573
.A53

Ackley, Richard R. "Soviet Maritime Power: An Appraisal of the Development, Capabilities, and International Influence of the Soviet Navy, Fishing Fleet, and Merchant Marine," U. of Southern California, 1974.

4602. VA573
.B3

Bates, Sheldon S. "Why Soviet Naval Power? The Role of the Soviet Navy in General War," Air War College, 1960.

4603.

Hucul, Walter G. "The Evolution of Russian and Soviet Sea Power, 1853-1953," U. of California at Berkeley, 1954.

4604. U23
.Z38

Zatuchini, Stephen B. "On Deterrence: The Role of Weapons Systems in the Formulation of U.S. Defense Policy, 1968-1975," Temple U., 1976.

ARTICLES

4605.

Ackley, Richard T. "The Wartime Role of Soviet SSBNs," USNIP 104 (June 1978):34-43.

4606.

_____. "The Soviet Merchant Fleet," USNIP 102 (Feb. 1976):27-37.

4607.

Anderson, Charles R. "The USSR: Seapower's Challenge," NWCR 15 (May 1963):1-30.

4608.

Araldsen, O.R. "The Soviet Union and the Arctic," USNIP 93 (June 1967):48-57.

4609.

Blechman, Barry M., and Stephanie E. Levinson. "Soviet Submarine Visits to Cuba," USNIP 101 (Sept. 1975):30-39.

4610.

Bussert, Jim. "Soviet Naval Electronic Technology," USNIP 104 (Feb. 1978):105-08.

4611.

Cade, David J. "Russian Military Strategy: A Fresh Look," AUR 29 (Sept.-Oct. 1978):18-27.

4612.

Carrison, D.J. "The Soviet Drive for Sea Power," USNIP 88 (Oct. 1959):67-71.

4613.

Cohen, S.T., and W.C. Lyons. "A Comparison of U.S.-Allied and Soviet Tactical Nuclear Force Capabilities and Policies," Orbis 19 (Spring 1975):72-92.

4614.   Cottrell, Alvin J., and R.M. Burrell. "The Soviet Navy and the Indian Ocean," SR 2 (Fall 1974):25-35.

4615.   Hickman, William F. "Soviet Naval Policy in the Indian Ocean," USNIP 105 (Aug. 1979):42-52.

4616.   Hopker, Wolfgang. "Soviet Global Strategy: The Greatest Challenge to the West at Sea," USNIP 101 (Dec. 1975):24-29.

4617.   Hopkins, Joseph E., and W.R. Warren. "Countering Soviet Imperialism," USNIP 105 (June 1979): 58-65.

4618.   Howe, Jonathan. "Soviet Beachhead in the Third World," USNIP 94 (Oct. 1968):60-67.

4619.   Hull, Andrew W. "Potential Soviet Responses to the U.S. Submarine Threat," USNIP 104 (July 1978):24-30.

4620.   Jacobsen, C.G. "The Soviet Navy: Acquiring Global Capabilities," NWCR 24 (Mar. 1972): 41-52.

4621.   Kehoe, James. "Warship Design: Ours and Theirs," USNIP 101 (Aug. 1975):56-65. Why the USSR can build warships more cheaply than the U.S.

4622.   Lacouture, John E. "Seapower in the Indian Ocean: A Requirement for Western Security," USNIP 105 (Aug. 1979):30-41.

4623.   LaForest, T.J. "The Strategic Significance of the Northern Sea Route," USNIP 93 (Dec. 1967): 56-65.

4624.   Miller, Harlan B. "Seeing Others as We See Ourselves: Missions for the KIEV," NWCR 32 (Apr.-May 1979):105-08.

4625.   Petrov, Victor P. "Soviet Canals," USNIP 93 (July 1967):32-44.

4626.   Pritchard, Charles G. "The Soviet Marine," USNIP 98 (Mar. 1972):18-30.

4627.   Roberts, Jack L. "The Growing Soviet Naval
          Presence in the Caribbean: Its Politico-
          Military Impact upon the United States," NWCR
          23 (Oct. 1971):31-42.

4628.   Schratz, Paul R. "Where Do We Stand: A Look at
          U.S. and Soviet Naval Strategy," *Shipmate* 42
          (July-Aug. 1979):18-20.

4629.   Simpson, John. "Technology and Political Choice
          in Future NATO Maritime Strategy," *Orbis* 17
          (Spring 1973):258-76.

4630.   "Soviet Navy Progress," USNIP 104 (Mar. 1978):
          163-66. Pictorial.

4631.   Sullivan, William K. "Soviet Strategy and NATO's
          Northern Flank," NWCR 32 (June-July 1979):26-38.

4632.   Uhlig, Frank, Jr. "The Opportunity and the
          Challenge Facing the Navy," NWCR 23 (Feb. 1971):
          21-24.

4633.   Villar, G.R. "Amphibious Warfare Forces in
          Europe and the Soviet Union," USNIP 103 (Nov.
          1977):112-17.

4634.   Whelan, Mathew J. "The Growing Soviet Amphibi-
          ous Warfare Capability," USNIP 105 (Aug. 1979):
          111-15.

23

SEA POWER FOR THE 1980s

BOOKS

4635. U21   Bachman, Jerald G., John D. Blair, and David
        .5.B3   R. Segal. *The All-Volunteer Force: A Study of
                   Ideology in the Military.* Ann Arbor: U. of
                   Michigan P., 1977.

4636. DK274   Barghoorn, Frederick C. *Detente and the Demo-
        .B28   cratic Movement in the USSR.* N.Y.: Free P.,
                   1976.

4637. HE745   Barker, James R., and Robert Bandwein. *The
        .B315   United States Merchant Marine in National
                   Perspective.* Lexington, Mass.: Heath, 1970.

4638. JX1974   Barnaby, Frank. *The Nuclear Age.* Cambridge:
        .7.S82   MIT P., 1974.

4639. DA566.2   Barnett, Correlli. *The Collapse of British
        .B37   Power.* London: Methuen, 1972.
        1972b

4640. UG1312   Beard, Edmund. *Developing the ICBM: A Study in
        .I2B4   Bureaucratic Politics.* N.Y.: Columbia UP, 1976.

4641.   *The Beard Report.* Available from Hon. Congress-
                   man Robin Beard, 124 Cannon House Office Build-
                   ing, Washington, D.C. 20515. Critique of the
                   all-volunteer force.

4642. U162.6   Beaufre, André. *Deterrence and Strategy.* N.Y.:
        .B413   Praeger, 1966.

4643. UA11   Beaumont, Roger A., and Martin Edmonds. *War in
        .W28   the Next Decade.* Lexington: U. of Kentucky P.,
                   1974.

4644. DA86   Berckman, Evelyn. *Creators and Destroyers of
        .B45   the English Navy: As Related by the State
                   Papers Domestic.* London: Hamilton, 1974.

4645. DS335   Bezboruah, Monoranan. *The United States' Strat-
        .B49   egy in the Indian Ocean, 1968-1976.* N.Y.:
                   Praeger, 1977.

4646. UB323   Binkin, Martin, and Shirley Bach. *Women and the*
      .B57   *Military*. Wash.: Brookings, 1977. Favorable to
               the women.

4647.   Blaine, J.C.D. *The End of an Era in Space Ex-*
               ploration: From International Rivalry to In-
               ternational Cooperation. San Diego: American
               Astronautical Soc., 1976.

4648. VA10   Booth, Ken. *Navies and Foreign Policy*. N.Y.:
      .B66   Crane & Russak, 1977.

4649. JX4411   Burke, William T., Richard Legatski, and Wil-
      .B798   liam W. Woodhead. *National and International*
               Law Enforcement in the Ocean. Seattle: U. of
               Washington P., 1976.

4650. VA50   Burns, Thomas A. *The Secret War for the Ocean*
      .B85   *Depths: Soviet-American Rivalry for Mastery of*
               the Sea. N.Y.: Rawson Associates, 1978.

4651. VA11   Burrell, Raymond E. *Strategic Nuclear Parity*
      .N3   *and NATO Defense Doctrine*, Pamphlet 78-4.
      1978   Wash.: National Defense U., 1978. 35 pp.
      No. 1

4652. KF7201   Burt, Richard, and Geoffrey Kemp, eds. *Con-*
      .B86   *gressional Hearings on American Defense Policy,*
               1947-1971. Lawrence: U. of Kansas P., 1974.

4653. VA40   Busk, Hans. *The Navies of the World: Their*
      .B97   *Present State and Future Capabilities*.
               Annapolis, Md.: NIP, 1974. Emphasis on the
               British and French navies.

4654. U25   Cable, James. *Gunboat Diplomacy: Political*
      .C33   *Applications of Limited Naval Force*. N.Y.:
               Praeger, 1971. An attempt to develop a doc-
               trine of limited use of naval force. Well
               endowed with illustrative case materials,
               the analysis is particularly enlightening
               on the enigma of Soviet naval power.

4655. UA23   Canan, James W. *The Superwarriors: The Fantas-*
      .C235   *tic World of the Pentagon Superweapons*. N.Y.:
               Weybright & Talley, 1975.

4656. UA23   Chodes, John J. *The Myth of America's Military*
      .C54   *Power*. Boston: Branden P., 1972. Vietnam.

4657. JX1395   Cline, Ray S. *World Power Assessment: A Calcu-*
      .C575   *lus of Strategic Drift, 1975.* Boulder, Colo.:
                Westview P., 1975. The same appears for 1977
                in REF. JX1395.C576.

4658. UG1282   Cohen, S.T. *The Neutron Bomb: Political, Tech-*
      .N48C63   *nological, and Military Issues.* Cambridge,
                Mass.: Institute for Foreign Policy Analysis,
                1978. 95 pp.

4659. HC110   Cooling, Benjamin F., ed. *War, Business, and*
      .D4W34   *American Society: Historical Perspectives on*
                the Military-Industrial Complex. Port Wash-
                ington, N.Y.: Kennikat P., 1977.

4660. UA26   Cottrell, Alvin, and Thomas H. Moorer. *U.S.*
      .A6   *Overseas Bases: Problems of Projecting Ameri-*
                can Military Power Abroad. Beverly Hills,
                Calif.: Sage, 1977.

4661. JX1974   Davis, Jacqueline K., and others. *SALT II and*
      .D38   *the Search for Strategic Equivalence.* Phila.:
                Foreign Policy Research Institute, 1975. 70
                pp.

4662. UA23   Deitchman, Seymour S. *New Technology and Mili-*
      .D44   *tary Forces for the 1980s and Beyond.* Boulder,
                Colo.: Westview P., 1979.

4663. E183.8   Dozer, Donald M. *The Panama Canal in Perspec-*
      P2D6   *tive.* Wash.: Council on American Affairs, 1978.
                67 pp. and bibliography.

4664. UA23   Endicott, John E., and Roy V. Stafford, Jr.
      .A4122   eds. *American Defense Policy,* 4th ed. Balti-
                more: Johns Hopkins P., 1977.

4665. JX1974   Epstein, William. *The Last Chance: Nuclear*
      .7.E55   *Proliferation and Arms Control.* N.Y.: Free
                P., 1976.

4666. UA770   Erickson, John. *Soviet-Warsaw Pact Force*
      .E745   *Levels.* Wash.: U.S. Strategic Institute, 1976.

4667. HD9743   Farley, Philip, Stephen S. Kaplan, and William
      .U6F37   H. Lewis. *Arms Across the Sea.* Wash.: Brookings,
                1978. U.S. policy toward the international
                trade in arms.

4668. VE25   *Finney, Ben. *Once a Marine--Always a Marine.*
      .F56A34   N.Y.: Crown, 1977.

4669. JD9743   Fox, J. Ronald. *Arming America*. Cambridge,
      .U6F7   Mass.: HUP, 1977.

4670. UB251   Freedman, Lawrence. *U.S. Intelligence and the*
      .U5F73   *Soviet Strategic Threat*. Boulder, Colo.: West-
                view P., 1977.

4671. D840   Geiger, Theodore. *The Fortunes of the West:*
      .G45   *The Future of the Atlantic Nations*. Blooming-
                ton: U. of Indiana P., 1973.

4672. V25   George, James L., ed. *Problems of Sea Power as*
      .P76   *We Approach the Twenty-first Century*. Wash.:
                AEI, 1978.

4673. REF   Gervasi, Tom. *Arsenal of Democracy: American*
      HD9743   *Weapons Available for Export*. N.Y.: Grove P.,
      .U6G4   1977.

4674. JX1974   Gompert, David C., and others. *Nuclear Weapons*
      .7.N85   *and World Politics: Alternatives for the Future*.
                N.Y.: McGraw-Hill, 1977.

4675. UA770   Goure, Leon, and others. *The Role of Nuclear*
      .G68   *Forces in Current Soviet Strategy*. Coral
                Gables: U. of Miami P., 1974.

4676. DA88   Graham, Gerald S. *The Politics of Naval Su-*
      .G7   *premacy*. Cambridge, England: Cambridge UP,
                1967.

4677.   Gray, Colin S. *Defending NATO-Europe: Forward*
                Defense and Nuclear Strategy. Croton-on-Hudson,
                N.Y.: Hudson Institute, 1977. Eight arguments
                favoring a forward strategy. 59 pp.

4678. UA313   Hackett, John, and Other Top-Ranking Generals
      .H3   and Advisors. *The Third World War: August 1985*.
                London: Sidgwick & Jackson, 1978. The Western
                Allies are unprepared for a Soviet push but, of
                course, win.

4679.   Harvey, Moses L. *Soviet Combat Troops in Cuba:*
                Implications of the Carter Solution for the
                USSR. Wash.: Advanced International Studies
                Institute, 1979. Carter's decision to accept
                the continued presence of Soviet combat troops
                in Cuba represents a major retreat by the U.S.
                and a major gain for the U.S.S.R.

4680. JX4426   Hollick, Ann L., and Robert E. Osgood. *New Era*
      .H64   *of Ocean Politics*. Baltimore: Johns Hopkins P.,
                1974.

4681. JX468   Jeffreys-Jones, Rhodri. *American Espionage:*
      .I6J45   *From Secret Service to CIA*. N.Y.: Free P.,
                1977.

4682. UA646   Joshua, Wynfred. *Nuclear Weapons and the At-*
      .D.J62   *lantic Alliance*. N.Y.: NSIC, 1976.

4683. UA770   _____, and Stephen P. Gibert. *Arms for the*
      .J65   *Third World: Soviet Military and Diplomacy*.
                Baltimore: Johns Hopkins P., 1969.

4684. UA23   Kahan, Jerome H. *Security in the Nuclear Age:*
      .K28   *Developing U.S. Strategic Arms Policy*. Wash.:
                Brookings, 1975.

4685. UA646   Kaplan, Morton A. *NATO and Dissuasion*. Chicago:
      .3.K37   U. of Chicago P., 1974.

4686. HD9698   Kelleher, Catherine Mc. *Germany and the Poli-*
      .G42K44   *tics of Nuclear Weapons*. N.Y.: Columbia UP,
                1975.

4687. DA70   Kennedy, Paul M. *The Rise and Fall of British*
      .K44   *Naval Mastery*. N.Y.: Scribner, 1976.

4688. UA1N3   Kime, Steve F. *Soviet Naval Strategy for the*
      1978   *1980s*. Pamphlet 78-3. Wash.: National Defense
      No. 3   U., 1978. 25 pp.

4689. VA23   Korb, Lawrence J. *The FY 1979-1983 Defense Pro-*
      .K758   *gram: Issues and Trends*. Wash.: AEI, 1976.

4690. E183.8   LaFeber, Walter. *The Panama Canal: The Crisis*
      .P2L33   *in Historical Perspective*. N.Y.: Oxford UP,
                1978. Better balanced than Ryan, Paul B.

4691. E183.8   Larson, Thomas B. *Soviet-American Rivalry*.
      .P9L34   N.Y.: Norton, 1978.

4692. JX1974   Lawrence, Robert M., and Joel Larus, eds.
      .7.L34   *Nuclear Proliferation: Phase II*. Lawrence:
                UP of Kansas, 1974.

4693. HE745   Lawrence, Samuel A. *United States Merchant*
      .L29   *Shipping Policies and Politics*. Wash.: Brook-
                ings, 1966.

4694. UA770   Lee, William T. *The Estimation of Soviet De-*
      .L38   *fense Expeditures, 1955-1975: An Unconventional*
               Approach. N.Y.: Praeger, 1977.

4695.   Leebaert, Derek, ed. *European Security: Pros-*
               pects for the 1980s. Lexington, Mass.: Heath,
               1979. Review of and projection of NATO on its
               thirtieth birthday.

4696. V874   Lehman, John F. *Aircraft Carriers: The Real*
      .2.L43   *Choices.* Beverly Hills, Calif.: Sage, 1978.
               83 pp.

4697. JX1974   Lens, Sidney. *The Day Before Doomsday: An*
      .L348   *Anatomy of the Nuclear Arms Race.* N.Y.: Stein
               & Day, 1977.

4698. D973   Lewis, Jesse W. *The Strategic Balance in the*
      .L43   *Mediterranean.* Wash.: AEI, 1976.

4699. F1414   Lowenthal, Abraham F., ed. *Armies and Politics*
      .2.A793 *in Latin America.* N.Y.: Holmes & Meier, 1976.

4700. JX4426   Luard, David E.T. *The Control of the Seabed: A*
      .L8   *New International Issue.* London: Heinemann,
               1974.

4701. V25   Luttwak, Edward. *The Political Uses of Sea*
      .L86   *Power.* Baltimore: Johns Hopkins P., 1974.

4702. VA573   McGruther, Kenneth R. *The Evolving Soviet*
      .M33   *Navy.* Newport: Naval War College P., 1978.

4703. GC1005   Mangone, Gerard J. *Marine Policy for America:*
      .2.M36   *The United States at Sea.* Lexington, Mass.:
               Heath, 1970.

4704.   Myers, Kenneth A. *North Atlantic Security:*
               The Forgotten Flank? Beverly Hills, Calif.:
               Sage, 1979.

4705. VA58   Nathan, James A., and James K. Oliver. *The*
      .4.N37   *Future of United States Naval Power.* Blooming-
               ton: Indiana UP, 1979.

4706. E183.8   Neustadt, Richard E. *Alliance Policies.* N.Y.:
      .G7N47   Columbia UP, 1970.

4707. JX1974   Newhouse, John. *Cold Dawn: The Story of SALT.*
      .7.N47   N.Y.: Holt, Rinehart & Winston, 1973.

4708. E855   *The Nixon Doctrine.*... Wash.: AEI, 1972.
      .N477

4709. UA23   O'Connor, Raymond G. *Force and Diplomacy: Es-*
      .032   *says Military and Diplomatic.* Coral Gables:
              U. of Miami P., 1972.

4710. E183.8 Oksenberg, Michel, and Robert B. Oxnam, eds.
      .C5D7   *Dragon and Eagle: United States-China Rela-*
              tions, Past and Future. N.Y.: Basic Books,
              1978.

4711. UA11.5 Osgood, Robert E. *Limited War Revisited.*
      .083   Boulder, Colo.: Westview P., 1979. Despite
              Korea and Vietnam, a place remains for limited
              war.

4712. UG1312 Pfaltzgraff, Robert L., Jr., and Jacquelyn K.
      .C7P45   Davis. *The Cruise Missile: Bargaining Chip or*
              Defense Bargain? Cambridge, Mass.: Institute
              for Foreign Policy Analysis, 1977.

4713. JX1974 _____. *SALT II: Promise or Precipice?* Miami,
      .7.P49   Fla.: Center for Advanced International Studies,
              1976.

4714. JX1974 Platt, Alan. *The U.S. Senate and Strategic Arms*
      .75.P56 *Policy, 1969-1977.* Boulder, Colo.: Westview P.,
              1979.

4715. UA23   Pranger, Robert J., and Roger P. Labrie, eds.
      .N78   *Nuclear Strategy and National Security: Points*
              of View. Wash.: AEI, 1977.

4716. D1053   Prendergast, William B. *Mutual and Balanced*
      .P73   *Force Reduction: Issues and Prospects.* Wash.:
              AEI, 1978. 75 pp. Concludes that the talks
              do contribute to the easing of international
              tensions.

4717. UA23   Quanbeck, Alton H., and Barry M. Blechman.
      .Q35   *Strategic Forces for the Mid-1970s.* Wash.:
              Brookings, 1973.

4718.   Rajendra, Singh K. *The Indian Ocean: Big Power*
              Presence and Local Response. Columbia, Mo.:
              South Asia Books, 1978.

4719. VA49   Rohwer, Jurgen. *Superpower Confrontation on*
      .R6413   *the Seas: A SAGE Policy Paper.* Beverly Hills,
              Calif.: Sage, 1975.

4720. E183.8   Ryan, Paul B. *The Panama Canal Controversy:*
      .P2R9   *U.S. Diplomacy and Defense Interests.* Stan-
                 ford: Hoover Institution, 1977.

4721. HD9743   Sampson, Anthony. *The Arms Bazaar: From Lebanon*
      .A2S35   *to Lockheed.* N.Y.: Viking, 1977.

4722. UA23   Sanders, Ralph. *The Politics of Defense Analy-*
      .S23   *sis.* N.Y.: Dunellen, 1973.

4723. HD9743   Scherer, Frederic M. *The Weapons Acquisition*
      .U6S35   *Process: Economic Incentives.* Boston: Harvard
                 U. Graduate School of Business Administration,
                 Div. of Research, 1964.

4724. U21.2   Smoke, Richard. *War: Controlling Escalation.*
      .S63   Cambridge, Mass.: HUP, 1978.

4725. JX1391   Spanier, John W. *Games Nations Play.* N.Y.:
      .S7   Praeger, 1972.

4726. VA770   Speilman, Karl F. *Analyzing Soviet Strategic*
      .S75   *Arms Decisions.* Boulder, Colo.: Westview P.,
                 1978.

4727. UA23   Tammen, Ronald L. *MIRV and the Arms Race: An*
      .T28   *Interpretation of Defense Strategy.* N.Y.:
                 Praeger, 1973.

4728. UA22   Taylor, Maxwell D. *Precarious Security.* N.Y.:
      .T318   Norton, 1976.

4729. UA646   *Toward a New Defense for NATO: The Case of*
      .3.T68   *Tactical Nuclear Weapons.* N.Y.: NSIC, 1976.
                 61 pp.

4730. D1065   Trezise, Philip H. *The Atlantic Connection:*
      .U5T73   *Prospects, Problems, and Policies.* Wash.:
                 Brookings, 1975.

4731. JX1393   Vali, Ferenc A. *The Turkish Straits and NATO.*
      .S8V34   Stanford: Hoover Institution, 1972.

4732. U162   Walters, Robert E. *Sea Power and the Nuclear*
      .W35   *Fallacy: A Re-evaluation of Global Strategy.*
                 N.Y.: Holmes & Meier, 1975.

4733. GC58   Wenk, Edward, Jr. *The Politics of the Ocean.*
      .W45   Seattle: U. of Washington P., 1972.

4734. JX1974   Wolfe, Thomas W. *The SALT Experience*. Cambridge,
     .75.W64   Mass.: Ballinger Pub. Co., 1979.

4735. UG1312   Yanarella, Ernest J. *The Missile Defense Con-*
     .A6Y36   *troversy: Strategy, Technology, and Politics,*
              1955-1972. Lexington: UP of Kentucky, 1977.

4736. UA23   York, Herbert F. *Race to Oblivion: A Partici-*
     .Y67   *pant's View of the Arms Race.* N.Y.: Simon &
              Schuster, 1970.

DOCUMENTS

4737. Y4G   *International Human Rights: Selected Declara-*
     74/:   *tions and Agreements.* Wash.: GPO, 1976.
     H88/3

4738.   *Termination of Treaties: The Constitutional*
              Allocation of Power. Wash.: GPO, 1979. Car-
              ter's dealings with Taiwan and China.

4739. UA23   U.S. Congress. House Committee on Armed Forces.
     .A1.A75 *The Changing Strategic Military Balance: U.S.A.*
     1967a   *vs. U.S.S.R.: Report.* Wash.: GPO, 1967.

4740. VA53   U.S. Congressional Budget Office. *Budget Issue*
     .A15   *Paper: Navy... [year].* Wash.: Congressional
              Budget Office.

4741. VA53   U.S. Congressional Budget Office. *Assessing the*
     .A15   *NATO/Warsaw Pact Military Balance.* Wash.: Con-
              gressional Budget Office, 1977. 63 pp.

4742. VA53   U.S. Congressional Budget Office. *Planning U.S.*
     .15   *General Forces: The Navy.* Wash.: GPO, 1976.
              Weighs comparative merits and costs of a sea-
              control and a power-projection navy.

4743.   U.S. DOD. *Report of Secretary of Defense Harold*
              Brown to the Congress on the FY1980 Budget,
              FY1980-1984 Defense Programs. Wash.: GPO,
              1979.

4744. UA24   U.S. Joint Chiefs of Staff. *A Concise History*
     .A675   *of the Organization of the Joint Chiefs of*
     /U45   *Staff, 1942-1978.* Wash.: Joint Secretariat,
              Joint Chiefs of Staff, Hist. Div., 1979.

4745. Y4Ar5/2a U.S. Joint Chiefs of Staff. *United States Mili-*
977-8   *tary Posture for FY1979: A Report by the Chair-*
56   *man of the JCS to the Congress, 1978.* Wash.:
               GPO, 1978.

4746. UA25   *United States Military Posture for Fiscal*
.A57   *Year-/-* . Wash.: GPO, year.

4747. REF   U.S. Navy Dept. *U.S. Life Lines: Imports of*
HF1052   *Essential Materials--1967, 1971, 1975, and the*
.U56   *Impact of Waterborne Commerce on the Nation.*
               Prepared by the Special Assistant to the CNO
               for Presentations. Wash.: Dept. of the Navy,
               Office of CNO, 1978.

4748. J80   U.S. President. *Public Papers of the Presidents*
.AZ83   *of the United States: Jimmy Carter, 1978.* Book
               1--January 1 to June 30, 1978. Wash.: GPO,
               1978.

4749.   *The U.S. Sea Control Mission: Forces, Capa-*
               bilities, and Requirements. Wash.: GPO, 1977.
               66 pp.

DISSERTATIONS AND THESES

4750.   Bellinger, John B., Jr. "Decision-Making in
               Arms Control: A Case Study of the National
               Security Council-Interagency Group System in
               the Strategic Arms Limitation Negotiations,"
               Georgetown U., 1977. Nixon-Kissinger system
               for presidential decision-making for SALT.

4751.   Mayer, Laurel A. "Third World Arms Transfers
               and U.S. Foreign Policy," Miami U., 1977.

4752.   Rennagel, William C. "Organizational Respon-
               siveness to the President: The Military Re-
               sponse to the Nixon Doctrine," Ohio State U.,
               1977.

4753.   *Rider, Jon K. "An Alternative Marine Corps,"
               U.S. Army Command and General Staff College,
               1978. Concludes that an airborne Marine Corps
               would not be cost-effective in responding to
               crises throughout the world.

4754.   Schoonmaker, Herbert G. "United States Military
               Forces in the Dominican Crisis of 1975," U. of
               Georgia, 1977.

4755.   Weeks, Stanley B. "United States Defense Policy
             toward Spain, 1950-1976," American U., 1977.

                          ARTICLES

4756.   Alden, John D. "Tomorrow's Fleet," USNIP 104
             (Dec. 1978):115-23. Includes the Navy's ship-
             building program in 1978.

4757.   _____. "Tomorrow's Fleet," USNIP 104 (Jan.
             1978):117-24. Includes the Navy's shipbuilding
             program in 1977.

4758.   Anderson, George, Jr. "The Cuban Missile Cri-
             sis," *Proceedings Naval History Symposium*.
             Annapolis, Md.: USNA, April 27-28, 1973, pp.
             81-86.

4759.   Anderson, Richard T. "Retention: Our #1 Goal,"
             USNIP 105 (July 1979):82-85.

4760.   Art, Robert J. "Why We Overspend And Under-
             accomplish," FP 6 (Spring 1972):95-117.

4761.   Aspin, Les. "The Defense Budget and Foreign
             Policy: The Role of Congress," *Daedalus* 104
             (Summer 1975):155-74.

4762.   Bagley, Worth H. "A Surface Navy for Today's
             Threat," USNIP 104 (Sept. 1978):34-39. The
             most affordable will be surface ships armed
             with cruise missiles.

4763.   Ball, Desmond J., and Edwin Coleman. "The Land-
             Mobile ICBM System: A Proposal," S 19 (July-Aug.)
             1977):155-63.

4764.   Barber, James A. "The Uses of Naval Force,"
             NWCR 30 (Summer 1977):73-82.

4765.   Barker, James V. "Our Quiet Danger at Sea,"
             Shipmate 42 (June 1979):17-18. The poor status
             of the U.S. merchant marine.

4766.   Barnett, Roger W. "Trans-SALT: Soviet Strategic
             Doctrine," *Orbis* 19 (Summer 1975):533-61.

4767.   Beard, Robin L. "U.S. NATO Policy: The Chal-
             lenge and the Opportunity," USNIP 104 (Nov.
             1977):52-61.

4768.   Blades, Todd B. "Needed: Heavy Firepower,"
        USNIP 105 (July 1979):41-49. Amphibious war-
        fare.

4769.   _____. "DDG-47: Aegis On Its Way to Sea,"
        USNIP 104 (Dec. 1978):101-05.

4770.   Bonsignore, Ezio. "SS-N-14: Another Look,"
        USNIP 105 (Apr. 1979):102-06.

4771.   Booth, Ken. "U.S. Naval Strategy: Problems of
        Survivability, Usability, and Credibility,"
        NWCR 30 (Summer 1978):11-28.

4772.   _____. "Roles, Objectives, and Tasks: An
        Inventory of the Functions of Navies," NWCR
        30 (Summer 1977):83-97.

4773.   Brodie, Bernard. "On the Objectives of Arms
        Control," IS 1 (Summer 1976):17-36.

4774.   Brooks, Linton F. "Pricing Ourselves Out of the
        Market: The Attack Submarine Program," NWCR
        32 (Sept.-Oct. 1979):2-17.

4775.   Buck, Ralph V. "Assessing the Capability of
        Naval Forces," NWCR 30 (Feb. 1979):78-87.

4776.   Burke, Gerald K. "The MX and Strategic Deter-
        rence in the 1980s," AUR 30 (May-June 1979):
        28-38.

4777.   _____. "The Need for Trident," USNIP 104
        (Nov. 1978):32-41.

4778.   Burt, Richard. "New Weapons Technologies and
        European Security," Orbis 19 (Summer 1975):
        514-32.

4779.   Cady, Steven C. "World Peace and the Soviet
        Military Threat," AUR 30 (Jan.-Feb. 1979):
        94-98.

4780.   Carlin, Robert J. "Strategic Deterrence in
        the Age of Detente," USNIP 105 (Sept. 1979):
        28-35.

4781.   Chapman, Robert M. "Attack Submarine Develop-
        ment: Recent Trends and Projected Needs,"
        USNIP 104 (Aug. 1978):97-102.

4782.   Chase, John D. "The Functions of Navies,"
USNIP 95 (Oct. 1969):26-33.

4783.   "CNO [Admiral Thomas B. Hayward] Assesses the
Value of the Carrier," *Shipmate* 41 (Dec. 1978):
9.

4784.   Clark, David G. "Cruise Missiles: Offense in
Breadth Added to Defense in Depth," NWCR 30
(Winter 1978):89-91.

4785.   Clark, John J. Prize Essay. "The Encircling
Sea," USNIP 95 (Mar. 1969):26-35.

4786.   Claytor, W. Graham, Jr. "The Naval Service
Today and Tomorrow," *Shipmate* 42 (June 1979):
13-14.

4787.   DeForth, Peter W. "U.S. Naval Presence in the
Persian Gulf: The Mideast Force Since World
War II," NWCR 28 (Summer 1975):28-38.

4788.   Dodd, Norman L. "British Seapower: The Royal
Navy in 1978," USNIP 104 (July 1978):111-15.
The Royal Navy is the strongest in Western
Europe and third most powerful in the world.

4789.   Drummond, Dennis M. "Getting Traffic Moving
on NATO's Two-Way Street," AUR 30 (Sept.-
Oct. 1979):27-34. Need for cooperation and
standardization in NATO.

4790.   Eccles, Henry E. "The TFX F-111 Aircraft: A
Perspective in Military Command and Defense
Management," NWCR 23 (Apr. 1971):66-87.

4791.   Enthoven, Alain C. "U.S. Forces in Europe:
How Many Doing What?" FA 53 (Apr. 1975):513-32.

4792.   _____, and K. Wayne Smith. "What Forces for
NATO? And From Whom?" FA 48 (Jan. 1969):80-96.

4793.   Fowler, William M. "America's Super-Frigates,"
MM 59 (Feb. 1973):49-56.

4794.   *Fraser, Angus M. "The Marine Corps as a
Separate Service," USNIP 101 (Nov. 1975):
19-25.

4795. Gallagher, James H. "An Analysis of the Effect of the Container Ship Revolution on Military Logistics," NWCR 23 (Dec. 1970):34-47.

4796. Galloway, Judith M. "Women in Combat: The Need for Cultural Reconditioning," AUR 30 (Nov.-Dec. 1978):58-61.

4797. Garde, H. "Where Is the Western Navy? The World Wonders," USNIP 101 (Apr. 1975):18-23.

4798. Garvin, Richard L. "Antisubmarine Warfare and National Security," SA 227 (July 1972):14-25.

4799. Geneste, Col. Marc E., French Army (Ret.). "Division of Labor in the Western Alliance," USNIP 104 (Nov. 1978):42-51.

4800. George, James L. "SALT and the Navy," USNIP 105 (June 1979):29-37.

4801. Gray, Colin S. "The Strategic Forces Trend: End of the Road?" FA 56 (July 1978):771-89.

4802. _____. "Traffic Control for the Arms Trade?" FP 6 (Spring 1972):153-69.

4803. Gropman, Alan. "Why Is There Still a Cold War?" AUR 29 (Jan.-Feb. 1978):77-84.

4804. Groves, Donald. "Helos Revolutionize Minesweeping," Our Navy 67 (Mar. 1972):2-5.

4805. *Gustafson, Richard A. "Why VSTOL for the Marines?" Shipmate 41 (Nov. 1978):23-25.

4806. Hanks, Robert J. "U.S. National Strategy: Outward...with Inadequate Charts," USNIP 105 (Apr. 1979):30-35.

4807. *Haynes, Fred. "The Marines Through 1999," USNIP 104 (Sept. 1978):24-33.

4808. Hayward, John T. "Maritime Superiority," Shipmate 42 (June 1979):14-15, 18.

4909. Hickman, William F. "Soviet Naval Policy in the Indian Ocean," USNIP 105 (Aug. 1979):42-52.

4810.   Hoeber, Francis P. "Myths about the Defense Budget," AUR 29 (Sept.-Oct. 1978):2-17.

4811.   Holloway, James L., III. "The Transition to V/STOL," USNIP 103 (Sept. 1977):18-25. The Navy will have to switch to V/STOL planes and carriers.

4812.   Holmquist, C.O. "Naval Research: The Brain Game," USNIP 100 (Sept. 1974):44-55.

4813.   Inouye, Daniel K. "The Shape of the U.S. Maritime Industry," *Shipmate* 41 (May 1978):15-18.

4814.   Jacobsen, C.G. "Soviet Projection Capabilities: A View from North of the Border," NWCR 32 (Apr.-May 1979):95-104.

4815.   Jenson, John W. "Nuclear Strategy: Differences in Soviet and American Thinking," AUR 30 (Mar.-Apr. 1979):2-17.

4816.   Johnson, Means. "NATO's Southern Region: Problems and Prospects," USNIP 101 (Jan. 1975): 47-51.

4817.   Kaley, Edmund K. "Standardization or Bankruptcy for NATO?" USNIP 104 (Nov. 1978):78-86.

4818.   Kastl, Joseph. "Detente and an Adequate American Defense," AUR 30 (Sept.-Oct. 1979):20-25.

4819.   Kelly, James. "Women in Warships: A Right to Serve," USNIP 104 (Oct. 1978):44-52. *See also* Comments and Discussion section of USNIP for several following months.

4820.   Kelly, John P. "Requiem for the PHM Program," USNIP 103 (Aug. 1977):79-81.

4821.   Kemp, Geoffrey, and Harlan Ullman. "Toward a New Order of U.S. Maritime Policy," NWCR 30 (Summer 1977):98-114.

4822.   Kendall, Lane C. "Toward a National Merchant Marine Policy," USNIP 105 (Feb. 1979):42-47.

4823.   Kennedy, Floyd D. "Soviet Doctrine on the Role of the Aircraft Carrier," NWCR 30 (Feb. 1979): 48-58.

4824.   Kohout, John J., III. "A Post B-1 Look at the Manned Strategic Bomber," AUR 30 (July-Aug. 1979):27-51.

4825.   Korb, Lawrence J. "The Secretary of Defense and the Joint Chiefs of Staff: Conflict in the Budgetary Process, 1947-1971," NWCR 24 (Dec. 1971):21-42.

4826.   Krepon, Michael. "A Navy to Match National Purposes," FA 55 (Jan. 1977):355-67.

4827.   Lacouture, John E. "Seapower in the Indian Ocean: A Requirement for Western Security," USNIP 105 (Aug. 1979):30-41.

4828.   Legere, Lawrence J. "Defense Spending: A Presidential Perspective," FP 6 (Spring 1972):84-94.

4829.   Levie, Howard S. "Mine Warfare and International Law," NWCR 24 (Rpt. 1972):27-35.

4830.   *Lind, William S., and Jeffrey Record. "Twilight for the [Marine] Corps?" USNIP 104 (July 1978): 38-43.

4831.   McClintock, Robert. "An American Oceanic Doctrine," USNIP 96 (Feb. 1970):46-57.

4832.   McFarlane, Robert C. "The Politics of Parity," USNIP 105 (Feb. 1979):28-35.

4833.   McGruther, Kenneth. "The Dilemma of the U.S. Pacific Fleet," USNIP 104 (June 1978):26-33.

4834.   Madison, Russell L. "The War of Unengaged Forces: Superpowers at Sea in an Era of Competitive Coexistence," NWCR 32 (Apr.-May 1972): 82-94.

4835.   Mallison, Sally V., and W. Thomas Mallison, Jr. "A Survey of International Law of Naval Blockade," USNIP 102 (Feb. 1976):44-54.

4836.   Marshall, Charles B. "Three Powers--Two Oceans," NWCR 30 (Winter 1978):9-20.

4837.   Matthei, Dieter. "Russia's Struggle for Maritime Prestige During the Era of Navalism," NWCR 32 (Sept.-Oct. 1979):18-28.

4838. Middendorf, J. William, II. "Let's Not Torpedo
       Our Navy," *Readers Digest* 113 (Aug. 1978):49-
       53.

4839. Miettinen, Jorma K. "Enhanced Radiation War-
       fare," BAS 33 (Sept. 1977):32-37.

4840. Miller, George H. "Editorial: Ship Shortage
       Cripples Defense," *Shipmate* 42 (Oct. 1979):
       15-16.

4841. _____. "Needed: A U.S. Maritime Strategy,"
       Shipmate 41 (Apr. 1978):19-20.

4842. Miller, Steven E. "Assessing the Soviet Navy,"
       NWCR 32 (Sept.-Oct. 1979):56-70.

4843. Nathan, James A., and James K. Oliver. "The
       Changing Context of American Seapower," NWCR
       32 (Feb. 1979):3-16.

4844. Ohlert, Edward J. "Strategic Deterrence and
       the Cruise Missile," NWCR 30 (Winter 1978):
       21-32.

4845. Papp, Daniel S. "Toward an Estimate of the
       Soviet Worldview," NWCR 32 (Nov.-Dec. 1979):
       60-77.

4846. Patterson, Andrew, Jr. "Mining: A Naval Strat-
       egy," NWCR 23 (May 1971):52-66.

4847. Polmar, Norman. "The Mine as a Tool of Limited
       War," USNIP 93 (June 1967):103-05.

4848. Powers, Robert D., Jr. "Blockade: For Winning
       Without Killing," USNIP 84 (Aug. 1958):61-66.
       Mine Warfare.

4849. "The President: SALT II; The Path of Security
       and Peace," *Dept. of State Bull.* 79 (June
       1979):11-14.

4850. Prina, L. Edgar. "Depression and Subsidies: A
       Survey of U.S. and Worldwide Maritime Problems,"
       Shipmate 41 (May 1978):19-22.

4851. Richardson, Elliot L. "Law of the Sea," NWCR
       32 (May-June 1979):3-10.

4852. Sage, Henry J. "The Drift Toward the Draft," USNIP 105 (June 1979):38-44.

4853. *Salzer, Robert S. "The Navy's Clouded Amphibious Mission," USNIP 104 (Feb. 1978):24-35.

4854. Scheina, Robert L. "South American Navies: Who Needs Them?" USNIP 104 (Feb. 1978):61-66.

4855. Schratz, Paul R. "A Plea for an Effective Naval Reserve," Shipmate 41 (June 1978):5.

4856. Sea, Antonio. "Should Spain Join NATO?" NWCR 32 (Nov.-Dec. 1979):78-87.

4857. Seawright, Murland W. "Prepare to Sweep Mines," USNIP 96 (Jan. 1970):54-59.

4858. *Simmons, Edwin H. "The Marines: Now and the Future," USNIP, Naval Review, May 1975, pp. 102-17.

4859. Smith, Robert H. Prize Essay. "A United States Navy for the Future," USNIP 97 (Mar. 1971):18-25.

4860. Snow, Donald M. "Strategic Implications of Enhanced Radiation Weapons: A Preliminary Analysis," AUR 30 (July-Aug. 1979):2-16.

4861. Snyder, Philip. "Bring Back the [Engineer] Corps," USNIP 105 (Feb. 1979):48-57.

4862. Sorensen, Finn B. "Greenland and Its Relevance to North American Security," NWCR 32 (Nov.-Dec. 1979):88-102.

4863. Stachurski, Richard J. "The Nunn-Bartlett Report: A Realistic Prescription for NATO?" AUR 29 (July-Aug. 1978):21-25.

4864. Steele, George P. "Killing Nuclear Submarines," USNIP 86 (Nov. 1960):44-51.

4865. Strada, J.S.A. "Navstart Goes to Sea," USNIP 105 (July 1979):106-08.

4866. Taylor, William J., Jr. "Interdependence, Specialization, and National Security: Problems for Diplomats, Soldiers, and Scholars," AUR 30 (July-Aug. 1979):17-26.

4867. Trout, B. Thomas. "Naval Strategy and Naval Politics: Peacetime Uses of a Wartime Naval Force," NWCR 26 (July-Aug. 1974):3-16.

4868. Truver, Scott C. "The 1978 Carrier Controversy: Why Not the *Kennedy*?" NWCR 30 (Feb. 1979):59-67.

4869. Tucker, Ronald D. "The Cruise Missile: An Offensive Alternative," USNIP 104 (Dec. 1978): 111-14.

4870. Turner, Stansfield. "Missions of the United States Navy," USNIP 100 (Dec. 1971):18-25.

4871. _____. "The Naval Balance; Not Just a Numbers Game," FA 55 (Jan. 1966):339-54.

4872. Tyler, John T., and Andrew H. Boquet. "V/STOL and the CV," USNIP 103 (Oct. 1977):94-101.

4873. Uhlig, Frank, Jr. "Missile Boats: The Modern Destroyers," *Sea Power* 19 (Sept. 1976):17-18.

4874. _____. "The Middle Kingdom Goes to Sea: Red China's Navy Is World's Third Largest," *Sea Power* 16 (Mar. 1973):19-24.

4875. _____. "Some Speculation on the Navy at the End of the 1970s," NWCR 24 (May 1972):9-15.

4876. Vershbow, Alexander R. "The Cruise Missile: The End of Arms Control?" FA 55 (Oct. 1976): 133-46.

4877. West, Francis J., Jr. "Planning for the Navy's Future," USNIP 105 (Oct. 1979):26-33.

4878. _____. "U.S. Naval Forces and the Northern Flank of NATO," NWCR 32 (June-July 1979):15-25.

4879. * _____. "Marines for the Future," USNIP 104 (Feb. 1978):34-42.

4880. West, Michael A. "The Role of Congress in the Defense Budget Process: A Positive View," NWCR 32 (May-June 1979):88-95.

4881.   Wiegley, Roger D. "Law and Conflict at Sea,"
             NWCR 33 (Jan.-Feb. 1980):68-77.

4882.   *Wilson, Louis H., Jr. "Ready-Amphibious-
             Marine," USNIP 103 (Oct. 1977):18-27. How
             Marines are trained to execute roles and
             missions.

ABBREVIATIONS USED IN THE INDICES

adm	admiral	Pres	President
Asst	Assistant	Secdef	Secretary of Defense
Br	British	Secnav	Secretary of the Navy
coau	coauthor	SecWar	Secretary of War
cdr	commander	Sen	Senator
commo	commodore	Sp	Spanish
Cont. Navy	Continental Navy	US	United States
CSN	Confederate States Navy	USA	U.S. Army
Fr	French	USAAC	U.S. Army Air Corps
gen	general	USAF	U.S. Air Force
Ger	German	USMC	U.S. Marine Corps
It	Italian	WWI	World War I
Jap	Japanese	WWII	World War II

AUTHOR INDEX

Allen, John M., Jr., 1472, 1667
Allen, Lindsley S., 1881
Allen, Scott, 2391
Allin, Lawrence C., 1217, 1473, 1668, 1674
Allison, George B., coau. See McCarthy, James R.
Allison, Graham T., 4302
Ambrose, Stephen E., 1488, 1489, 2842, 2843, 2893, 2894, 3778
American Heritage, 235, 314, 315
American Iron and Steel Association, 1304
Amme, Carl H., 4303, 4446, 4447
Ammen, Daniel, 1305
Anderson, Bern, 1306, 1490, 2844
Anderson, Charles R., 4607
Anderson, Frank J., 7, 544
Anderson, George W., Jr., 4448, 4758
Anderson, Oscar E., coau. See Hewlett, Richard G.
Anderson, R.C., coau. See Anderson, Romola.
Anderson, Richard T., 4759
Anderson, Romola, 384
Anderson, Stuart L., 1491, 1869
Anderson, Terry H., 3913
Anderson, Troyer S., 545
Anderson, Walter S., 2416, 2417
Anderson, William G., 1017, 1027
Anderson, William R., 3986
Andrade, Ernest, 2392, 2418, 2419
Andrews, Frank A., 4177
Andrews, Hal, 2178
Annis, P.G.W., coau. See May, William E.
Ansel, Walter C., 2420, 2677, 2678, 2895, 3140
Anthony, Irvin, 892
Appleman, Roy E., 3987
Aptheker, Herbert, 1492
Araldsen, O.R., 4608
Archibald, Edward H.H., 193, 194, 385
Arctic Institute of North America, 8
Armitage, Merle, 2679
Armstrong, Anne, 2896
Armstrong, Hamilton F., 2845

Armstrong, Terence N., 4551
Armstrong, William J., 1882
Army Times, 3082
Arnault, Charles C., 1493
Aron, Raymond, 4178
Arpee, Edward, 2253
Art, Robert J., 4304, 4760
Arthur, Reginald W., 2254
Ash, Bernard, 3380
Ashbrook, Allan W., 2421
Ashbrook, Lincoln 1883
Ashley, L.R.N., 2846
Ashmead, John, 3760
Aspin, Les, 4761
Asprey, Robert B., 1884, 2066, 2422, 4179
Assman, Kurt, 2847, 3126, 3225
Aster, Sidney, 2255, 2580
Aston, George G., 1927, 1928
Attiwill, Kenneth, 3381
Auphan, Paul, 2680, 2848
Aurthur, Robert R., 3235
Austin, Anthony, 4305
Austin, Bernard L., 4450
Auten, Harold, 1929
Avalone, E.M., 1885
Averill, Charles E., 1284

Bach, Shirley, coau. See Binkin, Martin.
Bachman, Jerald G., 4635
Bachman, Robert L., 4451
Bachmann, Lawrence P., 4546
Bacon, Eugene H., coau. See Bernardo, Joseph C.
Bacon, Reginald H.S., 1930, 1931, 1932, 1933, 1934, 2256
Bader, Douglas, 2681
Badoglio, Pietro, 2682
Baecker, Thomas, 1886
Baer, George W., 2257
Bagby, Oliver W., 2423
Bagley, Worth H., 4762
Bagnasco, Erminio, 2683
Bailey, Isaac, 290
Bailey, Thomas A., 1770, 1935, 2068, 2581, 3779
Baker, H.G., 4180
Baker, Ray S., 1936, 2069
Baker, Wilder D., 2424

Balch, Thomas, 546
Balchen, Bernt, 2582
Baldwin, Frederick D., 2171
Baldwin, Hanson W., 1218, 1937,
  2045, 2258, 2425, 2583, 2684,
  2849, 2850, 2897, 3028, 3029,
  3030, 3127, 3402, 3403, 3521,
  3662, 3663, 3664, 3665, 3780,
  3919, 3988, 4452, 4453
Baldwin, William L., 3989
Balfour, Michael, 3031
Ball, Desmond J., 4763
Ballentine, Duncan S., 2898, 3562
Ballou, Maturin M., 1285
Bancroft, George, 1028
Bancroft, Hubert H., 1129
Bandwein, Robert, coau. See Barker,
  James R.
Banks, Arthur, 270
Baral, Jaha K., 4306
Barber, James A., 4764
Barber, Stuart B., 4454
Barbet, Paul, 1494
Barbey, Daniel E., 3522, 3563
Barbour, Violet, 1219
Barclay, Glen, 2584
Barghoorn, Frederick C., 4636
Barker, Arthur J., 2685, 3426,
  3564, 3565
Barker, Elisabeth, 2899
Barker, James R., 4637
Barker, James V., 4765
Barley, Frederick, 1029
Barnaby, Frank, 3566, 4638
Barnby, H.G., 893
Barnes, Dwight H., coau. See Clark,
  Joseph J.
Barnes, G.R., 728
Barnes, Harley H., Jr., 4437
Barnes, James, 547, 548, 894, 895,
  1307, 1495
Barnes, John S., 729, 730
Barnes, Robert H., 195
Barnet, Richard J., coau. See Falk,
  Richard A.
Barnett, Correlli, 4639
Barnett, Roger W., 4766
Barritt, M.K., 754
Barrow, Clayton R., Jr., 896, 1130

Barrow, Thomas C., 549
Barrows, Edward M., 1131
Barry, James P., 1030
Bartimeus, pseud. See Ritchie,
  Lewis.
Bartlett, Bruce M., 3332
Bartlett, Donald, 3523
Bartlett, H.T., 2180
Bartley, Whitman S., 3567
Barton, John A., 755
Basoco, Richard W., 1496
Bass, Herbert J., 1938
Bassett, James E., 3761, 3762
Bassler, Roy P., 1308
Batchelor, J.H., coau. See Preston, A.
Bates, P.L., 4181
Bates, Richard W., 3412, 3454, 3568
Bates, Sheldon S., 4602
Bateson, Charles, 3236
Bathe, Basil W., coau. See Villers,
  Alan J.
Bator, Victor, 4307
Bauer, K. Jack, 196, 1031, 1132,
  1133, 1220, 1675, 3666
Baugh, Barney, 756
Baxter, James P., 897, 1134, 1309,
  1497, 1620, 2900
Bayard, Samuel J., 1135
Baylis, John, 550
Bayliss, Gwyn M., 9
Bayse, Arthur H., 490
Beach, Edward L., Sr., 1032, 1771,
  3763
Beach, Edward L., Jr., 3555, 3556,
  4308
Beach, Edward L., coau. See Noel,
  John V.
Beale, Howard K., 1797
Beale, Howard K., ed. See Welles,
  Gideon.
Beard, Charles A., 2259, 2260, 2585
Beard, Edmund, 3990, 4640
Beard, Robin, 4641
Beard, Robin L., 4767
Bearss, Edwin C., 1310, 1498, 1499,
  1500, 1501
Beatson, Robert, 551
Beattie, Donald W., 552
Beaudoin, Frederic J., 1502

Beaufre, Andre, 2261, 2686, 3991, 4309, 4642
Beaumont, Roger A., 4643
Bechhoefer, Bernhard G., 3992
Beck, Alverda S., 734
Beck, Earl G., 3920
Becker, Carl L., 491
Beebe, Robert P., 3921
Beer, George L., 432
Beers, Henry P., 10, 231, 1503, 2070, 2181, 2262, 2426
Beers, Henry P., coau. See Munden, Kenneth W.
Beesly, Patrick, 2687, 2901
Begnaud, Allen E., 745
Beirne, Francis R., 898
Beith, John H., pseud., 2688
Beitzell, Robert E., 2902
Bekker, Cajus D., pseud., 2689, 2690, 2691
Belknap, Reginald R., 2071, 2182, 2183
Bell, Charles, 3525
Bell, Frederick J., 3237
Bell, Herbert C., 525
Bell, James A., 4182
Bell, Roger J., 3238
Bellah, James W., 1286
Bellico, Russell, 757
Bellinger, John B., Jr. 4750
Belloc, Hilaire, 386
Beloff, Max, 1504, 2263, 4310
Belot, Raymond de, 2692, 2851, 3141
Belote, James H., 2393, 3382, 3455, 3569, 3570
Belote, William M., coau. See Belote, James H.
Bemis, Samuel F., 11, 553, 1033
Ben-Arieh, Yehoshua, 1221
Benjamin, Park, 1676, 2184
Bennet, Rawson, 4183
Bennett, Frank M., 1136, 1311, 1312, 1505, 1621, 1677
Bennett, Geoffrey M., 1939, 1940, 2693, 2694, 2903, 3383
Bentinck-Smith, J., 2038
Bentley, John, 4311
Benton, Elbert J., 1701
Benz, Francis E., 554
Berckman, Evelyn, 4644

Berenbrok, Hans D., pseud., 3083
Berg, Meredith W., 2427
Berger, Carl, 3993, 4312
Berger, Carl, coau. See Cresswell, Mary A.
Berkner, Lloyd V., 3922
Berman, Robert P., 4552
Berman, Robert P., coau. See Blechman, Barry M.
Bern, Betty, coau. See Allard, Dean C.
Bernath, Stuart L., 1313, 1506, 1507
Berry, Erick, pseud., 2904
Berstein, Barton J., 4184, 4185
Berthold, Will, 2695
Best, Herbert, 2905
Betts, John L., 3781
Betts, Richard K., 1211, 3994, 4553
Betts, Richard K., coau. See Gelb, Leslie H.
Bezboruah, Monoranan, 4645
Biadasz, Frances E., 4152
Biddle, Edward, 758
Bidingmair, F., coau. See Gerhard, T.
Bigelow, John, 1314
Billias, George A., 555
Bingham, James K.W., 2696
Bining, Arthur C., 492
Binkin, Martin, 4646
Bird, Harrison, 556, 557, 899, 900
Bird, Keith W., 2428
Birdsall, Paul, 2185, 2264, 2586
Birdsall, Steve, 3456, 3526
Birnbaum, Karl E., 1941
Bishop, Charles B., 4455
Bishop, Edward, 2697
Bishop, Farnham, 1287
Bisson, Thomas A., 2587
Bivins, Harold A., 13
Bivins, Harold A., coau. See Hilliard, Jack B.
Bixby, William, 1137
Black, Charles L., 4186
Black, Henry, 3032
Blades, Todd B., 4768, 4769
Blaine, J.C.D., 4647
Blair, C.H.M., 1509
Blair, Carvell H., 1508
Blair, Clay, Jr., 3736, 3782

Blair, Clay, Jr., coau. *See* Anderson, William R.
Blair, Clay, Jr., coau. *See* Bachman, Jerald G.
Blair, Leon B., 3783
Blakeney, Jane, 291
Blanchard, Carroll H., Jr., 14
Blankfort, Michael, 3239
Blattman, Walter C., 15
Blaufarb, Douglas S., 3995, 4313
Blay, John S., 317
Blechman, Barry M., 4554, 4555, 4609
Blechman, Barry M., coau. *See* Quanbeck, Alton H.
Bliss, Tasker B., 2429
Bliven, Bruce, 3142, 3240
Bloomberg, Marty, 16
Bloomster, Edgar L., 387
Bluff, Harry, pseud., 1222
Blum, John M., 1942, 2588, 2906
Blumenson, Martin, 3143, 3173
Blumenthal, Henry, 1315
Boas, Marie, coau. *See* Guerlac, Henry.
Boatner, Mark M. III, 17, 18, 292, 760
Bodron, Margaret, 4187
Boggs, Charles W., 3571
Bohner, Charles H., 1138
Bolander, Louis H., 19, 761, 762, 1034, 1223, 1510
Bolton, Geoffrey C., 493
Bonds, Ray, 318
Bonsignore, Ezio, 4770
Booth, Ken, 4648, 4771, 4772
Booth, Ken, coau. *See* MccGwire, Michael.
Boquet, Andrew H., coau. *See* Tyler, John T.
Borg, Dorothy, 2265, 2589, 2590, 3333
Borghese, Iunio V., 2698
Borklund, Carl W., 3784, 3785, 3996
Bornet, Vaugh D., coau. *See* Robinson, Edgar E.
Borsodi, Marion S., 293
Botting, Douglas, 3084
Bottome, Edgar M., 3997

Bourne, Edward G., 433
Bourne, Kenneth, 1316
Bouscaren, Antohny T., 4476
Bowen, Catherine D., 494
Bowen, Frank C., 2430
Bowen Harold G., 2266
Bowers, Gay L., 1887
Bowers, Peter M., coau. *See* Swanborough, Frederick G.
Bowler, R. Arthur, 558
Bowles, Francis T., 1622
Bowling, R.A., 2852
Bowman, Albert H., 901
Bowman, Peter, 3764
Bowman, Waldo G., 2907
Bowser, Alpha L., Jr., 3527
Boxer, Charles R., 434, 435
Boyd, Alexander, 4556
Boyd, William B., coau. *See* Rowland, Buford.
Boyington, Gregory, 3457
Boykin, Edward C., 1317, 1318
Boyle, Richard, 4457
Boynton, Charles B., 1319
Bradford, Ernle D.S., 902, 2699
Bradford, Gershom, 261
Bradford, Larned, 1320
Bradlee, Francis B., 903, 1321
Bradley, Catherine, coau. *See* Keegan, John.
Bradley, John, 2072
Bradley, Omar N., 2908
Bradley, Udolpho T., 1212, 1224
Bradshaw, Harvey D., 366
Brady, Cyrus T., 1288
Bragadin, Marc' A., 2700, 2853, 2909
Braisted, William R., 1702, 1798, 1799, 1888, 1889
Braitsch, Fred G., Jr., 4188
Branch, Houston, 1615
Brandt, Edward, 3998
Brant, Irving, 904, 1225
Breen, K.C., 746
Brennecke, Hans J., 3192, 3193
Brennecke, Hans J., coau. *See* Krancke, Theodore.
Brent, Robert, 1511
Brereton, Lewis H., 2701, 2910
Brewington, Marion V., 763, 764, 765

Breyer, Siegfried, 20, 197
Bright, Charles D., 3999
Brinckloe, W.D., 4458
Broad, Lewis, 2702
Brock, Leslie V., 495
Brodie, Bernard, 21, 173, 1322,
    1623, 1800, 3306, 3528, 3668,
    3669, 3786, 3923, 4000, 4001,
    4189, 4190, 4191, 4459, 4773
Brodie, Fawn, coau. See Brodie,
    Bernard.
Brody, Richard A., 174
Brooke, George M., Jr., 1226, 1227
Brooke, John, 559
Brookhouser, Frank, 2911
Brooks, Linton F., 4774
Brooks, Russell M., 3033, 3174
Broome, John E., 3194
Broomfield, F.H., 766
Brou, Willy C., 2703
Brown, Alexander C., 1624
Brown, Anthony C., 3787
Brown, Charles R., 2186, 3924
Brown, David, 2704, 2705, 3241,
    3458
Brown, Ernest F., 271
Brown, F.C., 1228
Brown, F.M., 1229
Brown, Gerald S., 560
Brown, John M., 3242
Brown Kenneth L., 1035
Brown, Nicholas, coau. See Wilson,
    Desmond P.
Brown, Peter D., 436
Brown, Ralph A., 905
Brown, Richard M., coau. See Olson,
    Alison G.
Brown, Roger H., 906
Brown, Seyom, 4002
Brown, Wallace, 561, 767, 768
Brown, Weldon, 3414
Brown, Wilburt S., 907
Browning, Reed, 562
Brownson, Howard G., 2433
Bruce, George, 3765
Bruce, Robert, 1323
Brune, Lester H., 2394, 2434, 2435
Bryan, George S., 1230
Bryan, J., III, coau. See Halsey,
    William F.

Bryant, Arthur, 2706
Bryant, Samuel W., 22, 563
Bryce, Barbara A., 23
Bryson, Thomas A., 24, 4460
Buchan, Alastair, 4461
Buchanan, Albert R., 2912, 2913,
    2914, 3019, 3572
Buchanan, Russell, 2046
Bucher, Lloyd M., 4003
Buck, Philip N., 437, 496
Buck, Ralph V., 4775
Buckley, Christopher, 2707
Buckley, Thomas H., 2267
Buckman, Peter, 564
Buell, Augustus C., 1625
Buell, C.C., coau. See Johnson,
    Robert U.
Buell, Raymond L., 2268
Buell, Thomas B., 1231, 3243, 3670
Buhl, Lance C., 1512, 1669, 1678
Buker, George E., 1139
Bulger, William T., 747
Bulkley, Robert J., 3573
Bullen, Frank T., 1289
Bullion, John L., 524
Bulloch, James D., 1324
Bunker, John G., 2915
Bunkley, Joel W., 3925, 3926
Buranelli, Prosper, 2244
Burdick, Eugene, coau. See Lederer,
    William J.
Burk, Kathleen M., 2039
Burke, Arleigh A., 3671, 3759,
    4192, 4462, 4463
Burke, Gerald K., 4776, 4777
Burke, William T., 4649
Burlingame, Roger, 2269
Burner, David, 2277
Burnett, Edmund C., 565
Burns, Edward McN., 1703
Burns, Eugene, 2916, 3085
Burns, James McG., 2271
Burns, Richard D., 26, 2436
Burns, Thomas A., 4650
Burrell, Raymond E., 4651
Burrell, Raymond E., coau. See
    Cottrell, Alvin J.
Burrough, Edmund W., 2437
Burroughs, J.R., 3404
Burrus, Luther D., 3459

Burt, Richard, 4652, 4778
Burtness, Paul S., 3356
Burton, E. Milby, 1325
Burton, Earl, 3144
Busch, Harald, 2708
Bush, Eric W., 1943
Busk, Hans, 4653
Bussert, Jim, 4610
Butler, James R.M., 2591
Butler, James R.M., coau. *See*
  Gwyer, J.M.A.
Butow, Robert J.C., 2592, 3574
Buttinger, Joseph, 4315
Buzanski, Peter M., 2395
Byrd, Martha H., 3437, 3672
Byrd, Richard E., 2272
Byron, Gilbert, 908
Bywater, Hector C., 2273, 2274,
  2438, 2439, 2593, 2647, 3244
Cable, James, 4654
Cade, David J., 4611
Cady, Steven C., 4779
Caffrey, Kate, 3384
Cagle, Malcolm W., 3927, 4004,
  4193, 4194, 4195, 4196, 4197,
  4464, 4465
Caiden, Martin, 319
Caiden, Martin, coau. *See* Sakai,
  Saburo.
Calderhead, William L., 1036, 1037
Caldwell, Dan, 4466
Caldwell, Lynton K., 27
Calhoon, Robert M., 566
Calkins, Carlos G., 769
Callahan, James M., 1326
Callcott, Wilfrid H., 1801
Callendar, Geoffrey A.R., 28
Calleo, David P., 3788, 3789, 4316
Calvert, James F., 4005
Calvocoressi, Peter, 2709
Cameron, Ian, pseud., 1802, 2710
Campbell, Charles S., 1803
Campbell, Gordon, 1945
Canan, James W., 4655
Canfield, Eugene B., 1327, 1328,
  1513
Cannon, Charles A., 4198
Cannon, M. Hamlin, 3460
Cant, Gilbert, 2711, 2712, 3461
Cantor, Mackinlay, coau. *See*
  LeMay, Curtis.

Canzona, Nicholas A., 4199, 4200
Canzona, Nicholas A., coau. *See*
  McMullen, Robert A.
Capehart, E.E., 1772
Cappon, Lester J., 175, 272
Caputo, Philip, 4547
Caraley, Demetrious, 3790
Carey, Omer L., 4006
Caridi, Ronald H., 4007
Carleton, William R., 770
Carlin, Robert J., 4780
Carlisle, Henry, 1290
Carlisle, Rodney, 2187
Carlton, Phillips D., 3673
Carney, Robert B., 2188
Caron, Max, 567
Carr, Edward H., 2275
Carr, James A., 771, 1038, 1039
Carrington, Henry B., 273, 568
Carrison, Daniel J., 569, 4612
Carroll, Daniel B., 1329
Carroll, John, 2440
Carroll, Owen J., coau. *See* Miller,
  John.
Carse, Robert, 439, 1330, 2713,
  2917, 2918, 3233, 3766
Carter, A.F., 2189
Carter, Edward C.,II, 1040
Carter, Kit C., 236
Carter, Samuel, III, 909, 1804
Carter, Worrall R., 2919, 3245,
  3575, 3576
Case, Lynn M., 1331
Casey, Robert J., 3385
Caskie, Jacquelin A., 1140
Cass, Beven G., 3246
Casson, L., 320
Castel, Albert, 1041
Castillo, Edmund L., 199, 3427
Cate, James L., 2190
Cates, Clifton B., 3674
Catlin, Albertus W., 2191
Catlin, George L., 2073
Catton, Bruce, 1332, 1333
Cave, Hugh B., 3462
Cave Brown, Anthony, 3086
Center for Strategic and Inter-
  national Studies, 4557
Chadbourne, Charles C., 1670
Chadwick, French E., 731, 772,
  1042, 1704, 1705

Challener, Richard, 1706, 1805, 1946
Chalmers, William S., 1947
Chamberlain, John, coau. *See* Willoughby, Charles A.
Chamberlain, Thomas H., 294
Chamberlain, William H., 2441, 2442
Chambers, Hilary R., 2074
Chambers, Robert W., 869
Chambliss, William C., 3737
Chandler, L.H., 1679
Chant, John A. de. *See* De Chant, John A.
Chapelle, Georgette L., 4467
Chapelle, Howard I., 570, 571, 773, 910, 1141
Chapin, Howard M., 497
Chapin, John C., 3307
Chaplin, Philip A., 2443, 3750
Chapman, Guy, 2714
Chapman, Robert M., 4781
Chaput, Rolland Q., 2276
Chard, Donald G., 428
Charlton, Michael, 4317
Chase, John D., 4782
Chatfield, Alfred E.M., 2277
Chatfield, Charles, 2278
Chatterton, Edward K., 1948, 1949, 2715, 2716, 2920, 3195, 3196
Chayes, Abram, 4318
Chennault, Claire L., 3247
Chester, Lewis, 4319
Chevrier, Lionel, 4008
Chidsey, Donald B., 572, 573, 911, 1291
Chikaya, Masatake, 3448
Chodes, John J., 4656
Chrisman, Herman H., 2040
Christie, Ian R., 498
Christman, Albert B., 3791
Christol, C.Q., 4468
Church, William C., 1334
Churchill, Winston, 1950, 2594, 2717, 2921, 3577
Churchill, Winston (US), 870
Churchill, Winston L.S., 2192
Churley, Robert A., 3675
Cianflone, Frank A., 2193
Cipolla, Carlo M., 389
Clagett, John H., 3128, 3175

Clapham, J.H., 390
Clarfield, Gerald H., 912
Clark, Alan, 1951, 2718
Clark, Arthur H., 1142
Clark, Charles E., 1707
Clark, David G., 4784
Clark, John J., 4785
Clark, Joseph J., 29, 3248, 3578, 3676
Clark, Keith C., 4320
Clark, Mark W., 3145, 4009
Clark, Ronald W., 1952, 2719
Clark, Thomas, 574
Clark, William B., 575, 576, 577, 578, 579, 580, 732, 774, 2075
Clarkson, Grosvenor, 2076
Claudy, Carl H., 2194
Claussen, Martin P., 3792
Claytor, W. Graham, Jr., 4786
Clements, Paul H., 1708
Clephane, Lewis P., 2077
Cleveland, Harlan, 3793
Clifford, Kenneth J., 3087
Clinard, Outten J., 1806
Cline, Ray S., 4657
Clough, Ralph N., 4010
Clowes, Geoffrey S.L., 391
Clowes, William L., 581
Clubb, O.E., Jr., 4321
Coady, J.W., 2041
Coakley, Robert W., 582, 3035
Coale, Griffith B., 3197, 3428
Coble, Donald W., 4202
Cochran, Hamilton, 1335
Codman, John, 584
Coffey, Joseph I., 4469
Coffey, Thomas M., 1890, 3249
Coggins, Jack, 585, 1336, 3463
Cohen, Paul, 4470
Cohen, S.T., 4613, 4658
Cohen, Warren I., 2078
Cohlmia, Kenneth, coau. *See* Aurthur, Robert T.
Colby, Chester M., 775
Cole, Allan B., 4322
Cole, Charles W., 440, 441
Cole, David B., 2396
Cole, Wayne S., 176, 2648
Coleman, Edwin, coau. *See* Ball, Desmond J.

Coletta, Paolo E., 776, 777, 1232, 1626, 1680, 1709, 1710, 1711, 1712, 1773, 1774, 1775, 1891, 2079, 3794
Collier, Basil, 30, 1807, 2720, 3250
Collier, Richard, 2721, 3795
Collier's, 321, 322
Collins, George W., 1870
Collins, J. Lawton, 4011, 4012, 4203
Collins, J. Richard., coau. See Beattie, Donald W.
Collins, John M., 4558
Colvocoresses, George M., 1514
Comfort, Kenneth L., 4163
Commager, Henry S., 1337, 2722
Comprato, F.C., 392
Compton, James V., 2595, 3796
Conde, Alexander de. See DeConde, Alexander.
Condit, Kenneth W., 2922, 3251
Congdon, Don, 1338, 1953, 3252
Conn, Stetson, 2923, 3928
Conn, Stetson, coau. See Coakley, Robert W.,
Conner, Howard M., 3253
Conner, Philip S.P., 1143
Connery, Robert H., 2924
Connery, Robert H., coau. See Albion, Robert G.
Connolly, James B., 2080
Connor, Seymour, 1144
Conolly, Richard L., 3529
Conrad, Joseph, 1292
Conroy, Robert, 3386
Consett, Montague W.W.P., 1954
Conway _____, 199
Coogan, John W., 1871
Cook, Charles O., Jr. 2445, 3308, 3405, 3464
Cook, Chris, 274
Cook, Merlyn G., 2446
Cooke, Henry D., 2854
Cooke, Mary L., 1043
Cooling, Benjamin F., 1627, 1681, 4659
Cooling, Benjamin F., coau. See Millett, Allan R.
Cooney, David, 237
Coontz, Robert E., 1808, 2279, 2447, 2448

Cooper, Chester L., 4013
Cooper, James F., 585, 871, 872, 913, 914
Coox, Alan C., coau. See Bauer, K. Jack.
Cope, Harley F., 2195, 2855, 3036, 3357, 3738
Cope, Harley F., coau. See Karig, Walter.
Corbett, Julian S., 442, 1955
Corey, Herbert, 2449
Corner, George W., 1145, 1628
Corson, William R., 4323
Cortada, James W., 4014
Corwin, Edward S., 779
Cosmas, Graham A., 1713, 2450
Cosmas, Graham A., coau. See Fuller, Stephen M.
Costello, Daniel J., 1872
Costello, John, coau. See Hughes, Terry.
Cottrell, Alvin J., 4204, 4614, 4660
Couhat, Jean L., 200
Coulam, Robert F., 3797
Coulter, Edith M., 31
Coulter, Ellis M., 1339
Cowie, John S., 1956, 3037, 3129
Cox, Ormond L., 2451
Cox, Richard H.F., 3088
Craig, Hardin, Jr., 32
Craig, Paul M., 2452
Crandall, Marjorie L., 33
Crandall, Warren D., 1340
Crane, John de M.C., 323
Crane, Paul S., 4015
Crane, William B., coau. See Cranwell, John P.
Cranwell, John P., 915, 2925, 3358
Craven, Thomas T., 1809, 2196, 2453
Crawford, Don, 4016
Creswell, John, 393, 394, 2723, 3309
Cresswell, Mary A., 34, 35
Cressy, George B., 4559
Crisp, R., 3146
Critchfield, John S., 3424
Crockett, Lucy, H., 3767
Croizat, Victor J., 3038
Cronan, William P., 2047

Dennis, Alfred L.P., 1716
Dennison, Robert L., 4208
DeNovo, John A., 1893
Department of Military Art and Engineering, 276
Derry, T., 2727
Detweiler, Robert, 785
Detzer, David, 4018, 4325
Deutsch, Harold C., 2856
Devereux, James P.S., 3388
Devers, Jacob L., 3176
Devlin, Patrick, 1959
Dew, Charles B., 1349
DeWeerd, Harvey, 2172, 4473
Dewey, George, 1717
Dexter, Byron, 38
Dibner, Martin, 3768
Dickens, Peter, 2728, 2729
Dickerson, Oliver M., 499
Dickinson, A.T., Jr., 376
Dickinson, Henry W., 921
Dickson, Katherine M., 39
Dickson, William D., 3581
Dierdorff, Ross A., 1047
Diffle, Bailey, 443
Dille, John, 4019
Dillon, John F., 1520
Dillon, Richard, 922
Dinerstein, Herbert S., 4326
Dingman, Roger, 2285
Divine, Robert A., 2598, 4020, 4327
Dobbs, Charles M., 3679
Dodd, Norman L., 4788
Dodson, Kenneth, 3769
Doenhoff, Richard A., 1234
Dohrman, Brainerd, 1522
Dohrman, Horatio G., 1521
Dollen, Charles, 42
Domville-Fife, Charles W., 1960
Donald, David, 1350
Donaldson, Gordon, 444
Dönitz, Karl, 2929
Donnelly, Charles H., 4021
Donnelly, Desmond, 3805
Donoughue, Bernard, 587
Donovan, Frank, 923, 924, 1351
Donovan, James A., Jr., 4209
Donovan, Robert J., 4022
Dooley, Thomas A., 4328
Dorn, Frank, 2286

Dornan, James E., Jr., 43
Dornberger, Walter, 2730
Dorsey, Florence L., 1352
Dorsey, Laurens, 4474
Dorwart, Jeffery M., 1629
Dougherty, James E., coau. See Cottrell, Alvin.
Douhet, Giulio, 1961
Dow, H.E., 786
Dowdell, Vincent J., 787
Downey, Fairfax B., 396
Downey, Joseph T., 1146
Doyle, James H., 4210
Doyle, Michael K., 2397
Dozer, Donald M., 4663
Dreyer, Frederick C., 3089
Druks, Herbert, 4148
Drummond, Dennis M., 4789
Drummond, Donald F., 2599
Duberman, Martin B., 1353
Dubois, William E.B., 1147
Duddy, Frank E., Jr., 367
Duffield, Eugene, 3930, 4211
Duffy, James, 445
Dufour, Charles L., 1148
Duiker, William, 1718
Duke, Marvin L., 1048
Dulin, Robert O., Jr., 201
Dull, Jonathan, 588
Dull, Paul S., 3257
Dulles, Allen W., 2458, 2459, 2650
Dulles, Foster R., 1149, 1150, 3806
Duncan, David D., 324
Duncan, Donald B., 1894
Duncan, Francis, coau. See Hewlett, Richard G.
Duncan, Robert C., 44, 589
Dunleavy, T.M., 297
Dunn, Keith A., 3931
Dunn, Lucius C., 788
DuPont, Henry A., 1151, 1354
DuPont, Samuel F., 1152, 1355
DuPre, Flint O., 2930
Dupuy, R. Ernest, 45, 590
Dupuy, Trevor N., 591, 2931, 3359
Dupuy, Trevor N., coau. See Dupuy, R. Ernest.
Durand de la Penne, Luigi, 2857
Durkin, Joseph T., 1356

408

Falk, Stanley L., 3310, 3389, 3532, 3584, 3585, 3586, 4330
Fall, Bernard B., 4026, 4027, 4028, 4029, 4334, 4332, 4333, 4334, 4335
Fallodon, Viscount Grey of, 2466
Falls, Cyril, 56
Fane, Francis D., 2937, 3311, 3587, 4030
Farago, Ladislas, 2732, 3094, 3198, 3334
Farley, M. Fosler, 1238
Farley, Philip, 4667
Farragut, Loyall, 1363
Farrar, Marjorie M., 1963, 2043
Faulk, Odie B., coau. See Connor, Seymour.
Fay, Peter W., 1154
Fayle, C. Ernest, 1964
Featherston, Fran H., 1896
Fehrenbach, T.R., 2603, 4031
Feis, Herbert, 2604, 3177, 3258, 3335, 3362, 3588, 3589, 3590, 3810
Feldt, Eric A., 3468
Ferguson, Eugene S., 595, 927, 1053
Ferrell, Henry C., Jr., 2643
Ferrell, Robert H., 2292, 3363, 4032
Ferris, Norman B., 1364, 1475
Field, Edward, 596
Field, James A., Jr., 597, 928, 1155, 3312, 3364, 3591, 3682, 4033
Field, Richard S., 2201
Fielding, George G., 4475, 4476, 4477
Fifield, Russell H., 2202
Finer, Herman, 3811, 4034
Fink, Leo G., 598
Finke, Blythe F., 4035
Finletter, Thomas K., 4036
Finnegan, John P., 1965, 2088
Finney, Ben, 4668
Fioravanzo, Giuseppe, 2861, 2862
Firzzel, Donaldson D., coau. See Thompson, Willard S.
Fischer, Gerald J., 2938
Fisher, Admiral of the Fleet Lord [John], 1966

Fisher, Charles R., 1054
Fisher, Ernest F., 4478
Fisher, John O.H.F., 929
Fiske, Bradley A., 1633, 1721, 1722, 1818, 2089
Fiske, John, 1365
Fitzgerald, Oscar P., coau. See Hooper, Edwin B.
Fitzsimons, Bernard, 203
Fleming, Denna F., 3812
Fleming, Peter, 2733, 3095
Fleming, Thomas, 599
Flexner, James T., 600, 601, 930, 931
Flint, Roy K., 4165
Flood, Charles B., 501, 602
Folsom, S.B., 4214
Fontaine, André, 3813
Foote, Shelby, 1366, 1526
Footner, Hulbert, 603
Forbes, William C., 1723
Ford, Charles, 530
Ford, Corey, 3444
Forester, Cecil S., 531, 932, 2888
Forrestal, James V., 3814
Forrestel, Emmet P., 3259
Forty, George, 2734
Foss, M., 604
Foss, William O., 4215
Foster, John T., 3469
Fowler, W[ilfred] B., 2089
Fowler, William M., Jr., 605, 793, 4793
Fox, Gustavus V., 1470
Fox, J. Ronald, 4669
Frank, Benis M., 373, 3260, 3261, 3429, 3470, 3592
Frank, Gerald, 3739
Frank, Patrick H.H., 3429
Franks, Horace C., 3262
Fraser, Angus M., 4206, 4794
Freed, Fred, coau. See Giovannetti, Len.
Freeden, Mel, 3934, 4217
Freedman, Lawrence, 4562, 4670
Freeland, C.L., coau. See Karig, Walter.
Freeman, Douglas S., 606
Freeman, Fred, coau. See Roscoe, Theodore.

Gleijeses, Piero, 4342
Glennon, A.N., 3047
Glines, Carroll V., 3413
Glover, Michael, 612
Godson, Susan H., 3353
Goldberg, Alfred, 3820
Goldberg, Sheldon A., coau. See
  Hopkins, J.C.
Goldenberg, Joseph A., 397, 613
Golder, F.A., 1528
Goldingham, C.S., 3751
Goldman, Eric F., 4343
Goldsborough, Charles W., 939
Goldsborough, Louis M., 1529
Gompert, David C., 4674
Goode, William A.M., 1726
Goodhart, Philip, 2607
Goodman, Allan E., 4043
Goodman, Warren H., 1055
Goodpaster, Andrew J., 3821, 4044
Goodrich, Caspar F., 798, 799,
  1056, 1530
Goodrich, Marcus, 2673
Gordon, Arthur, coau. See Medaris,
  John B.
Gordon, David L., 2736
Gordon, Maurice B., 614
Gorshkov, Sergie G., 4344, 4345,
  4564, 4565
Gorter, Wytze, 4045
Gosnell, H.A., 1367
Gosnell, Harpur A., 2206
Goure, Leon, 4675
Goure, Leon, coau. See Harvey,
  Mose L.
Gradner, Audrey, 1476
Graebner, Norman A., 3822, 3823
Graf, H., 1972
Graham, Burton, 3471
Graham, George E., 1727
Graham, Gerald S., 398, 447, 4676
Graham, Warren E., coau. See
  Bearss, Edwin C.
Grant, Bruce, 615, 940
Grant, Robert M., 1973, 1974,
  2095, 2207
Gray, Colin S., 4167, 4566, 4677,
  4801, 4802
Gray, Edwyn, 1975, 1976, 1977
Gray, James S., 3048
Graybar, Lloyd J., 3534

Great Britain, Admiralty, 2737,
  3202
Greathouse, Ronald H., 800
Green, Constance M., 4346
Green, Thomas W., coau. See Merli,
  Frank J.
Green, William, 2940
Greenbaum, Russell S., coau. See
  Holmquist, Carl O.
Greenberg, Daniel S., 2651
Greene, Fred, 1683, 2469
Greene, S. Dana, coau. See Worden,
  John S.
Greenfield, Kent T., 3595
Greenhill, Basil, coau. See Brock,
  P.W.
Greenwood, Isaac J., 616
Greenwood, John, 63
Gregory, Nathaniel, 64
Grenfell, Russell, 2652, 2738,
  3203, 3390
Grenville, John A.S., 1156, 1728,
  1897, 1898
Gretton, Peter, 1978, 3204
Grew, Joseph C., 2608
Grider, George, 2739
Griffin, Alexander R., 3472
Griffin, Appleton P.C., 65
Griffin, Charles C., 1157
Griffin, Grace G., coau. See
  Bemis, Samuel F.
Griffin, Martin, I.J., 617
Griffis, William E., 1158
Griffith, Samuel B. II, 618, 3473,
  3935
Grimes, J., 2096, 2299
Grimwood, James H., coau. See
  Hacker, Barton C.
Griswold, A. Whitney, 1819, 2300
Groos, Otto, 1979, 1980
Gropman, Alan, 4803
Groves, D.C., coau. See Hunt,
  Lee H.
Groves, Donald, 4804
Groves, Lee, coau. See Mercey,
  Arch A.
Grow, Harold B., 2470
Gruber, Ira D., 619
Guberlet, Muriel L., 448
Guedalla, Philip, 3151
Guevara, Ernesto, 4347

Guggisberg, Hans R., 177
Guichard, Louis, 1981
Guinn, Paul, 1982
Gullett, William M., 2864
Gurley, Ralph R., 1057, 1241, 1684
Gurn, Joseph, 620
Gurney, Gene, 239
Gustafson, Richard A., 4805
Guttman, Allan, 4046
Guttridge, George H., 621, 801
Guttridge, Leonard F., 941, 1159
Gwyer, J.M.A., 2740

Hacker, Barton C., 4348
Hackett, John, 4678
Haferkorn, Henry E., 66
Hagan, Kenneth J., 1635
Hagerman, George, 1532
Haggerty, J.J., 802
Haines, C. Grove, coau. See Hoffman, Ross J.S.
Haislip, Harvey, 3770
Halberstam, David, 4349, 4350, 4482
Hale, Frederick A., 2209
Hall, Asaph, 1368
Hall, Claude H., 1160, 1242
Hall, Elizabeth H., coau. See Gibbs, Katye M.
Hall, Hessell D., 2741
Hall, Hubert, 526, 803
Hall, Luella A., 622
Halle, Louis J., 1780
Halliwell, Martin, 3685
Halls, Elizabeth H., coau. See Gibbs, Kayte M.
Halperin, Morton H., 4047, 4351
Halsey, William F., 3049, 3264, 3474, 3686
Hamersley, Lewis R., 298, 299
Hamilton, Andrew, 3687
Hamilton, Ian S.M., 1983
Hamilton, William A., III, 4483
Hamilton, William R., 4439
Hammer, David D., 3596
Hammer, Ellen, 4352
Hammerman, Gay, coau. See Dupuy, R. Ernest.
Hammersly, Sydney E., 623
Hammett, Hugh B., 1636

Hammond, Paul Y., 3824, 3825, 3936, 4220, 4221
Hammond, Paul Y., coau. See Schilling, Warner R.
Hampshire, A. Cecil, 2865
Hampshire, A. Cecil, coau. See Newton, Don
Hancock, Joy B., 2097
Handleman, Howard, 3446
Handlin, Oscar, 804
Hanford, Franklin, 1533
Hanks, Carlos C., 805, 1534
Hanks, Robert J., 1242, 4806
Hanna, Kathryn A., 1535
Hannah, Dick, 3475
Hanniball, August, 67
Hansell, Haywood S., Jr., 3099
Harbaugh, William H., 1729, 1820
Harbeck, Charles T., 68
Harbottle, Thomas B., 69
Hardach, Gerd, 1984
Hardy, William M., 3771
Harley, John B., 280
Harmon, Judd S., 1019, 1244
Harper, Alan D., 4048
Harper, Lawrence A., 502
Harper, Robert S., 1109
Harrigan, Anthony, 4484
Harriman, Florence J. (Hurst), 2301
Harriman, W. Averell, 4049
Harrington, Daniel F., 3313
Harrington, Joseph D., coau. See Patrick H.H.
Harrington, Joseph D., coau. See Yokota, Yutaka.
Harrington, Joseph D., coau. See Tanabe, Yahachi.
Harrington, Samuel M., 1899
Harris, Brayton, 2302
Harris, Russell L., coau. See Karig, Walter
Harris, Thomas, 624, 942
Harrity, Richard, coau. See Martin, Ralph G.
Harrod, Frederick S., 1821
Hart, Robert A., 1822
Hart, Thomas C., 3314
Hartcup, Guy, 2742, 2743, 3100
Hartman, Susan M., 4050

412

Harvey, Frank, 4353
Harvey, Moses L., 457, 4679
Harwell, Richard B., 70, 71
Hasdorff, James C., 178
Haselkorn, Avigdor, 4568
Hashimoto, Mochitsura, 3265, 3597
Haswell, Chetwynd J.D., 72
Hatch, Alden S., 1823
Hatlem, John C., 326
Hattendorf, John, 1900
Haupt, Werner, coau. See Bingham,
  James K.W.
Hawkins, Maxwell, 3741
Haws, Duncan, 240
Hawthorne, Hildegarde, 1161
Hayden, Ralston, coau. See
  Worcester, Dean C.
Hayes, Carleton J.H., 2941
Hayes, Frederic H., 806, 1058
Hayes, Grace P., 1985
Hayes, Grace P., coau. See Dupuy,
  R. Ernest.
Hayes, John D., 1369, 1536, 1537,
  1538, 2471, 2472
Haynes, Fred, 4807
Haynes, Richard F., 3826
Hayward, John T., 4485, 4808
Hayward, Thomas B., 4783
Head, Richard G., 3827, 4051
Headley, Joel T., 1059, 1370
Healy, David F., 1730, 1824
Heath, Jim F., 4354
Hecht, J. Jean, 179
Heckstall-Smith, Anthony, 2744
Heffernan, John B., 1539
Heffron, Paul T., 1901
Heflin, Woodford A., 73
Heggen, Thomas, 3772
Heindel, Richard H., 1825
Heinl, Robert D., Jr., 74, 262,
  807, 1781, 3050, 3051, 3391,
  3598, 3688, 3689, 3828, 3937,
  3938, 3939, 3940, 3941, 4052,
  4053, 4222, 4223, 4486, 4487,
  4488
Heinmiller, P.R., 4224
Heller, Francis H., 4054
Henderson, Daniel M., 1162
Hendren, Paul, 1540
Hendrick, Burton J., 2098

Henig, Gerald S., 1541
Henretta, James A., 503, 625
Henri, Florette, coau. See
  Barbeau, Arthur E.
Henri, Raymond, 327
Henry, David R., 3915
Hensel, H. Struve, 3942, 4225
Henson, Curtis T., 1213
Hepburn, Andrew, 1110
Herbert, Ravenel S., coau. See
  Heyward, DuBose.
Hergesheimer, Joseph, 1111
Hermes, Walter G., 4055
Hernando, Orlando M., 4440
Herold, Amos L., 1163
Herr, Michael, 4355
Herrick, Robert W., 4569
Herrick, Walter R., 1637
Herring, George C., Jr., 3052,
  3829, 3943, 3944, 4489
Herwig, Holger H., 2052, 2653
Herzog, James H., 2303, 2609, 2654
Hess, Andrew C., 481
Hessler, William H., 3053, 4490
Hewes, James E., Jr., 4491
Hewitt, Henry K., 3179, 3180,
  3181, 3182
Hewlett, Richard G., 2304, 3830,
  4056
Heyward, DuBose, 1371
Hickman, William F., 4615, 4809
Hicks, John D., 2305
Hicks, Norman W., 1372
Hicks, Norman W., coau. See
  Montross, Lynn.
Higginbotham, Don, 626, 627
Higgins, Hugh, 3831
Higgins, Trumbull, 1986, 2745,
  3365, 3366, 4057
Higham, Robin D., 75, 76, 77, 4570
Hill, Harry W., 3690
Hill, Howard C., 1826
Hill, Jim D., 1245, 1373
Hill, Peter, 943
Hill, Perry C., 3054
Hilliard, Jack B., 78, 79
Hilliard, Jack B., coau. See
  O'Quinlivan, Michael.
Hilsman, Roger, 4356
Hines, Theodore D., 80

413

King, Irving H., 640
King, Joseph E., 1554
King, William N., 1732
Kinnard, Douglas, 4069, 4070
Kinney, Sheldon, 4235
Kinsella, William E., Jr., 2617
Kintner, William R., 3954, 4071
Kipp, Jacob, coau. *See* Higham,
  Robin.
Kiralfy, Alexander, 3317, 3538
Kirk, Neville T., 181, 1555
Kirkendall, Richard S., 4236
Kirkley, Joseph W., coau. *See*
  Davis, George B.
Kirkpatrick, Lyman G., 4237, 4499
Kissinger, Henry A., 3844, 4072,
  4373, 4500
Kittredge, Tracy B., 2112, 2618
Klapp, Orrin E., 1254
Klatchko, Mary, 2174, 2399
Kleber, Louis D., 482
Klein, David H., 3303
Klein, Ira, 2483
Knapp, Harry S., 2484
Knight, Francis, 377
Knipe, Alden A., coau. *See*
  Knipe, Emilie B.
Knipe, Emilie B., 951
Knollenberg, Bernhard, 505, 641
Knorr, Klaus E., 451, 3845
Knott, Richard C., 333
Knox, Collie, 3208
Knox, Dudley W., 642, 815, 816,
  1471, 1556, 2053, 2318, 2485,
  2486, 2487, 2488, 3955
Knox, Dudley W., coau. *See* Eller,
  Ernest M.
Knox, Robert S., 3026
Koch, Karl W., Jr., 2867
Koenig, Paul, 1998
Kogan, Norman, 3155
Koginos, Manny, 2619
Kohler, Foy D., 3846
Kohout, John J. III, 4824
Koistinen, Paul A.C., 2214, 2489
Kolko, Gabriel, 4073
Kolko, Joyce, coau. *See* Kolko,
  Gabriel.
Kopp, George, 1999
Kopperman, Paul E., 452

Korb, Lawrence J., 4074, 4501,
  4689, 4825
Korth, Fred, 4228
Kosco, George F., coau. *See*
  Adamson, Hans C.,
Koyanagi, Romiji, 3695
Krafft, Herman F., 1255, 1256
Krancke, Theodore, 3209
Krauskopf, Robert W., coau. *See*
  O'Neill, James E.
Kreen, David F., 1557
Krepon, Michael, 4826
Kroese, A., 2762
Krout, Mary H., 1257, 1258, 1558
Kublin, Hyman, 1259, 3696
Kuehl, Warren F., 170
Kuter, Laurence S., 3956

Labaree, Benjamin W., 643
Labaree, Benjamin W., coau. *See*
  Christie, Ian E.
Labaree, Leonard W., 506
Labrie, Roger P., coau. *See*
  Pranger, Robert J.
Lach, Donald F., 453
Lacouture, John E., 4622, 4827
LaFeber, Walter, 1641, 3847, 3848,
  4075, 4690
LaFond, E.C., 4239
LaForest, T.J., 4623
Laing, Alexander, 401
Landers, Howard L., 644
Lane, Frederic C., 483, 2956
Lang, James, 454
Langdon, Robert M., 2868
Langenberg, William H., 2657
Langer, William L., 2620, 2621,
  2957
Langley, Harold D., 1069, 1168
Langley, Lester D., 645, 1835,
  4374
Lanier, Robert S., coau. *See*
  Miller, Francis T.
Lanier, William D., 1260
Lapidus, Robert D., 4240
Laquer, Walter Z., 4076
Larkins, William T., 334
Larrabee, Eric, 4241
Larrabee, Harold A., 646, 817
Larsen, Lawrence H., coau. *See*
  Branyan, Robert L.

McKenna, Richard, 2573
MacKenzie, Alexander S., 655, 959, 960
Mackesy, Kenneth, coau. *See* Frere-Cook, Gervis.
Mackesy, Piers, 656, 825
McKiernan, Patrick L., 3539, 3700
Mackintosh, John, 2328, 2624
McLaughlin, Patrick, 823
Maclay, Edgar S., 657, 658, 1264, 1739, 1740
McLellan, Davis S., 3858
McLeod, Julia, 1072
McMaster, Donald W., 4174
MacMaster, Richard K., 1265
McMillan, George, 3279, 3280
McMillian, Ira E., 3058, 3701
McMullen, Robert A., 4243
McMurtrie, Francis E., coau. *See* Bacon, Reginald H.S.
McNamara, Robert S., 4379
Madariaga, Isabel de., 659
Maddox, Robert J., 2122, 4244
Madison, Russell L., 4834
Magdeburger, E.C., 2496
Magruder, P.H., 1568
Maguire, Doris D., coau. *See* Seager, Robert II.
Mahan, Alfred T., 406, 660, 826, 827, 961, 1073, 1074, 1398, 1399, 1741, 1837, 1912
Mahon, John K., 962
Maier, Pauline, 661
Mailer, Norman, 3773
Majet, Horace S., 828
Mallison, Sally V., 4835
Mallison, W. Thomas, Jr., coau. *See* Mallison, Sally V.
Malo, Henri, 829
Malone, Dumas, 507, 662, 963, 964, 965
Malone, Joseph J., 508, 663
Manceron, Claude, 664
Manchester, William, 3281
Mangone, Gerard J., 4703
Manno, Francis J., 1214
Manson, Frank A., 3702
Manson, Frank A., coau. *See* Cagle, Malcolm W.
Manson, Frank A., coau. *See* Karig, Walter.

Manwaring, George E., 91
Marcus, Geoffrey J., 407, 665
Marder, Arthur J., 1838, 2002, 2056, 2329, 2770
Mark, Steven M., 2645
Marks, Sally, 2330
Mars, Alastair, 2771, 3212
Marshall, Charles B., 4836
Marshall, Douglas W., 282
Marshall, Samuel L.A., 1944, 3106, 3488, 4093, 4245
Martienssen, Anthony, 2966
Martin, Asa E., 830
Martin, Christopher, pseud., 1400
Martin, Franklin H., 2123
Martin, Gilbert, 283
Martin, John B., 4380
Martin, Paul W., 3703
Martin, Pete, coau. *See* Morrill, John H.
Martin, Ralph G., 339, 340
Martyn, L.F., coau. *See* Schofield, Brian B.
Marx, Joseph L., 3619
Mason, David, 303
Mason, Elizabeth B., 374
Mason, Francis V., 92, 532, 874, 875, 876, 877, 1113, 1114, 1115, 1116, 1117, 1118, 1618
Massey, Robert J., 4511
Masterman, John C., 2772
Masters, Davis, 2773
Mastny, Vojtech, 3859
Mataxis, Theodore C., 4246
Mathews, William R., coau. *See* Uhlig, Frank.
Matloff, Maurice, 1396, 2497, 2659, 2967, 2968, 3059, 3184, 3185, 3704
Matray, James I., 4247, 4248
Matthei, Dieter, 4837
Mattox, W.C., 2124
Matusow, Allan J., coau. *See* Bernstein, Barton J.
Maurer, Maurer, 831, 2125, 2660, 4249
Maurice, Frederick B., 2003, 2126, 2127
May, Ernest R., 2128, 3060, 3860
May, Glenn A., 1787
May, William E., 408

Maycock, Thomas J., 3230
Mayer, Arthur J., coau. *See* Doyle, James H.
Mayer, Laurel A., 4751
Mayer, Sydney L., 93
Maynard, Douglas H., 1569, 1570
Mayo, L.S., 1742
Meacham, James A., 4512
Meade, Rebecca P., 1173, 1402
Meadows, Martin, 1913
Meckel, Hans, 2869
Mecklin, J., 4381
Medaris, John B., 4382
Medlicott, William N., 2774
Meese, Harry, 4250
Meigs, John F., 3319
Meissner, Sophie (Radford) de, 1174
Meister, Jurg, 4576
Melhorn, Charles M., 214
Melosi, Martin V., 3369
Melton, George E., 2870
Melton, Maurice, 1403
Melville, Herman, 1119, 1296
Melvin, Philip, 1571
Mercey, Arch A., 2969
Merillat, Herbert L., 3489
Merli, Frank J., 1404, 1572
Merli, Frank J., coau. *See* Basoco, Richard W.
Merrill, James M., 183, 1266, 1405, 1406, 1478, 1573, 1574, 2218, 3282, 3417, 3490
Meyer, K.E., 4383
Meyer, Leo J., 3186
Meyer, Michael C., 94
Meyer, Michael C., coau. *See* Trask, David F.
Michaelis, Frederick H., 4513
Michener, James A., 4299
Michie, Allan A., 3107
Middendorf, J. William II, 4838
Middlebrook, Louis F., 666
Middlebrook, Martin, 3213
Middlemas, Robert K., 2331
Middleton, Drew, 2775, 4251
Miles, A.H., 832, 833
Miles, Milton E., 3283, 3320, 3705
Milkman, Raymond H., 3061
Millar, John F., 215

Miller, Francis T., 341
Miller, George H., 4840, 4841
Miller, Harlan B., 4624
Miller, John C., 509, 510, 667
Miller, John, Jr., 1575, 3491, 3492, 3540, 4094
Miller, Max, 342, 4095
Miller, Merle, 3620, 3774
Miller, Nathan, 668
Miller, Richard T., 369
Miller, Samuel D., 95
Miller, Samuel D., coau. *See* Cresswell, Mary A.
Miller, Steven E., 4842
Miller, Thomas G., 3493
Miller, William M., 241
Millholland, Ray, 2129
Milligan, John D., 1407, 1576
Millis, Walter, 1743, 2130, 2970, 3341, 3861, 3862, 4252
Millot, Bernard, 3418
Mills, James C., 966
Milner, Samuel, 3494
Minchinton, W.F., 457, 511
Mintz, Max M., 669
Mitchell, Broadus, 512, 670, 671
Mitchell, Donald W., 1267, 3062, 4577
Mitchell, Joseph B., 672, 1408
Mitchell, Mairin, 4578
Mitchell, William 2131, 2132, 2432, 2498, 2499, 2500
Moat, Louis S., 343
Moeser, Robert D., 344, 4384
Moffatt, Alexander W., 2004, 2133
Moffett, William A., 2501, 2502
Mohr, Ulrich, 2776
Momyer, William W., 2005
Moncrieff, Anthony, coau. *See* Charlton, Michael.
Montague, Ewen, 2778
Montgomery, Bernard L., 2971, 3108, 3109
Montross, Lynn, 345, 673, 1268, 2503, 4096, 4097, 4253, 4254, 4255, 4256, 4257, 4258, 4259
Moore, Donald L., 4524
Moore, Frederick, 2332
Moore, John E., 4579
Moore, Robert W., 3541

Nevins, Allan, 679, 1410, 1411, 1646, 1845
Newbolt, Henry J., 2006, 2007
Newbolt, Henry J., coau. *See* Corbett, Julian S.
Newcomb, Richard F., 3498, 3625, 3626
Newell, Gordon R., 3499
Newell, Isaac D., coau. *See* Crandall, Warren D.
Newhouse, John, 4707
Newman, Ralph G., 1412
Newton, Christina, 2402
Newton, Don, 2780
New York Public Library, 100, 101
Ney, Virgil, 185
Niblack, Albert P., 1789
Nicholas, Herbert, 2628
Nichols, Charles S., 3627
Nickerson, Hoffman, 680
Nicolay, Helen, 974
Nikol, John, coau. *See* Holbrook, Francis X.
Nitze, Paul H., 4261
Niven, John, 1413, 1647
Nixon, Edgar B., 2336
Nixon, Richard M., 4101
Noble, Harold J., 4102
Noel, John V., 266, 4519
Nogal, Yonosuke, 3869
Nomura, Ichisaburo, 2510, 2661
Nordhoff, Charles B., 533
Norman, Albert, 3111
Norman, John, 4262
Norris, Walter, B., 840
North, John, 3187
Northrup, Everett H., 841
Norton, Douglas M., 3231
Norton, Paul F., 1075
Novak, Robert, coau. *See* Evans, Rowland.
Nowell, Charles E., 460
Nutting, William W., 2139

O'Ballance, Edgar, 4103
Ober, Warren U., coau. *See* Burtness, Paul S.
O'Brien, T.J., 2511
O'Connell, Jerome A., 2872
O'Connor, Raymond G., 1272, 2337, 2403, 2512, 2976, 3285, 4709

O'Connor, Richard, 1747
Offner, Arnold A., 2338, 2513, 2629
Ofstie, Ralph, 4263
O'Gara, Gordon C., 1846
Ogden, Michael, 2781
Oglesby, Joseph E., 2514
Ohlert, Edward J., 1844
Ohmae, Tosohikazu, 3322, 3543
Oi, Atsushi, 3753
Okamoto, Shumpei, coau. *See* Borg, Dorothy.
O'Kane, Richard H., 3747
Oksenberg, Michel, 4710
Okumiya, Masatake, 2515
Okumiya, Masatake, coau. *See* Fuchida, Mitsuo.
Oldendorf, Jesse B., 3715
Oliver, Frederick L., 1076, 1579
Oliver, James K., coau. *See* Nathan, James A.
Olsen, Frederick, 1876
Olson, Alison G., 514
O'Neill, Charles, 1580
O'Neill, Edward H., 305
O'Neill, James E., 157
Oosten, F.C. van, 3395
Oppenheimer, J. Robert, 4264
O'Quinlivan, Michael, 102, 103, 104, 105
Orth, Michael, 1273
Orvik, N., 2339
Osgood, Robert E., 3870, 3871, 3872, 3873, 4104, 4711
Osgood, Robert E., coau. *See* Hollick, Ann L.
Osgood, Samuel M., 2782
Owen, Henry, 4520
Owen, J.H., coau. *See* Barnes G. Rand.
Owen, Norman G., 1790
Owsley, Frank L., 1414
Owsley, Frank L., Jr., 1077, 1415
Oxnam, Robert B., coau. *See* Oksenberg, Michel.

Pack, S.W.C., 2783, 2784, 2785, 2786, 3159
Padelford, Norman J., 2516
Padfield, Peter, 411, 412
Page, Bruce, coau. *See* Chester, Lewis.

Reisinger, W.W., 1689
Reitzel, William, 4524
Remarque, Erich M., 2064
Rennagel, William C., 4752
Rentz, John N., 3503, 3504, 3630
Reynolds, Clark G., 306, 1277, 3546, 3755
Reynolds, Clark G., coau. *See* Clark, Joseph, J.
Reynolds, John M., 879
Reynolds, Quentin, 2797, 3419
Rhodes, James F., 1427
Rhymes, Cassius D., 4525
Rice, Howard C., 689
Richard, Dorothy E., 256
Richards, David K., 2537, 3375
Richards, Guy, 3188
Richardson, Elliot L., 4851
Richardson, Elmo, 4115
Richardson, James D., 112
Richardson, James L., 3876
Richardson, James O., 3290
Richardson, Leon B., 1649
Richmond, Arthur A. III, 1021
Richmond, Herbert W., 469, 2348, 2538, 2539, 3189
Rickover, Hyman G., 1750, 3965, 4267
Rider, Jon K., 4753
Ridgway, Matthew B., 4116, 4117
Riefler, Winfield W., 3717
Ries, John C., 3877, 4118
Rigler, Frank V., 2224
Riker, Rhad W., 484
Ripley, Clements, 880
Ripley, Roswell S., 1181
Ripley, Warren, 1428
Ritcheson, Charles R., 690, 988
Ritchie, Lewis A.C., 2796
Rives, George L., 1182
Roberts, Jack L., 4627
Roberts, John C., 1589
Roberts, Kenneth L., 534, 535, 536, 740, 881, 882, 883, 884, 885, 1121, 1122
Robertson, Esmonde M., 2349, 2633
Robertson, Frederick L., 416
Robertson, James I., 353
Robertson, Morgan, 1297
Robertson, Terence, 3115

Robichon, Jacques, 3116
Robinson, Edgar E., 2350
Robinson, Pat, 3505
Robinson, Walton L., 2878
Robinson, William M., 1429
Robinson, William M., Jr., 1590
Robison, Samuel S., 417, 1085
Rochester, Harry A., 1591
Rockefeller Brothers Fund, 4119, 4394
Rockefeller Brothers Fund Study, 4120
Rodney, George, 736
Roebling Manufacturing, 2143
Rogers, Lindsay, 2879
Rogow, Arnold A., 3878, 4121
Roherty, James M., 4395
Rohwer, Jurgen, 246, 3216, 4719
Rokke, Evin J., coau. *See* Head, Richard G.
Roland, Alex, 418
Romer, Jeffrey A., 2058
Roop, Wendell P., 3071
Roosevelt, Franklin D., 1086, 2540, 2664, 2665
Roosevelt, Henry L., 2541
Roosevelt, Nicholas, 2351
Roosevelt, Theodore, 989, 1087, 2542
Ropp, Theodore, 429
Roscoe, Theodore, 354, 2981, 2982, 3217, 3748
Rose, Lisle A., 4122
Roseberry, Cecil R., 1852
Rosenberg, David A., 4268
Rosendahl, Charles E., 2543
Rosenof, Theodore D., coau. *See* Cronon, E. David.
Rosinski, Herbert, coau. *See* Ellinger, Werner B.
Roske, Ralph J., 1430
Roskill, Stephen W., 2013, 2014, 2352, 2353, 2798, 2983
Rossell, Henry E., 221
Rossiter, Clinton L., 515
Rostow, Walt W., 4396
Roth, Robert, 4548
Rothbottam, W.B., 849
Rothenberg, Gunther E., 2059
Rowcliff, Gilbert J., 3719

Rowe, Albert P., 2354
Rowell, Ross E., 2543
Rowland, Buford, 2984, 3621
Ruge, Friedrich, 2144, 2355, 2799, 2800, 2801, 2880, 2985
Russ, Martin, 3632
Russell, Elmer B., 516
Russell, James C., 355
Russell, Kay, 1691
Russell, William H., 113, 114, 115, 1793
Rutland, Robert A., 990
Rutledge, Archibald, 1592
Ryan, Cornelius, 3117
Ryan, Dennis P., 691
Ryan, Paul B., 4720
Ryan, Paul B., coau. See Bailey, Thomas A.

Safford, Jeffrey J., 2170
Sage, Henry J., 4852
Sakai, Saburo, 3291
Saito, Fred, coau. See Sakai, Saburo.
Salomon, Henry, 3218
Salzer, Robert S., 4853
Sambito, William J., coau. See Fails, William R.
Sampson, Anthony, 4721
Sanders, Harry, 849
Sanders, Liman von, 2015
Sanders, Ralph, 4722
Sandler, Stanley, 222, 1692
Sands, Benjamin F., 1183
Santelli, James S., 116
Santelli, James S., coau. See O'Quinlivan, Michael.
Sapolsky, Harvey M., 4123
Sargent, Nathan, 1751
Sas, Anthony, 2881
Saul, Norman E., 2016
Saundby, Robert, 2017
Saunders, Malcolm G., 2882, 4587
Savage, Carlton, 991, 1431
Savelle, Max, 470, 527
Sawyer, Frederick L., 1853
Say, Harold B., 3966
Scalapino, Robert A., 4397
Scammel, G.V., 485
Scammell, J.M., 2545

Schaller, Michael, 1877, 2356, 2666, 3292
Schandler, Herbert Y., 4398
Scharf, J. Thomas, 1432
Scheer, Reinhard, 2018
Scheina, Robert L., 1088, 4854
Scherer, Frederic M., 4723
Schick, Jack M., 4124, 4399
Schilling, Warner R., 2176, 2225, 3879, 4125, 4269
Schlesinger, Arthur M., 517, 692
Schlesinger, Arthur M., Jr., 3967, 4400, 4401
Schley, Winfield S., 1752
Schmitt, Karl M., 1184
Schnabel, James F., 4126
Schneider, Mark B., 4170
Schoenbrun, David, 2986
Schoenfeld, Maxwell P., 2987
Schofield Brian B., 2802, 2803, 2804, 2805, 2988, 2989, 3161, 3219, 4526
Schofield, William G., 223, 2990
Schoonmaker, Herbert G., 4754
Schornstheimer, Graser, 2546, 2547, 2548, 2549, 2550
Schratz, Paul R., 1693, 4171, 4270, 4271, 4628, 4855
Schreiner, Charles W., 2883
Schroeder, Paul W., 2634
Schroeder, Seaton, 1650, 1753
Schull, Joseph, 2806
Schultz, Charles R., 117
Schultz, Duane P., 3396
Schumacher, F. Carl, Jr., 4127
Schuon, Karl, 307, 308, 4128
Schurman, Donald M., 2019
Schwartz, William L., 1204
Scott, H.M., 486
Scott, Lloyd N., 2145
Scott, Percy, 2020
Scott, Robert L., 3294
Sea, Antonio, 4856
Seager, Robert II, 1651, 1663, 1694
Seagren, Leonard W., 2884
Sears, Louis M., 992, 1185, 1433
Seawright, Murland W., 4857
Segal, David R., coau. See Bachman, Jerald G.

427

Smith, Julian C., 3553, 3724
Smith, Justin H., 1191
Smith, K. Wayne, coau. *See* Enthoven, Alain G.
Smith, Melden E., Jr., 4529
Smith, Myron J., Jr., 125, 126, 127, 128, 129, 247, 381
Smith, O[liver] P., 1794, 4274, 4275
Smith, Page, 700
Smith, Peter, 2813
Smith, Peter C., 2814, 3162, 3163, 3638
Smith, Richard K., 2360, 2361
Smith, Robert H., 4859
Smith, Robert L., 3916, 4172
Smith, Robert R., 3508, 3639, 3640, 3725
Smith, S.E., 2995
Smith, Samuel S., 701
Smith, William W., 3433
Smoke, Richard, 4724
Smyth, Henry D., 4276
Smyth, Henry DeW., 3641
Smyth, Howard M., 3164
Snell, Edwin M., coau. *See* Matloff, Maurice.
Snell, John L., 2815, 2996, 2997, 3969
Snepp, Frank, 4409
Snow, Donald M., 4860
Snow, Elliot, 1594
Snowbarger, Willis, 2406
Snyder, Glenn H., coau. *See* Schilling, Warner R.
Snyder, Philip, 4861
Sokol, Anthony E., 1092, 2024, 3376, 3883, 4132, 4530
Soley, James R., 994, 1093, 1094, 1437, 1438
Somit, Albert, 3970
Sorensen, Finn B., 4862
Sorenson, Theodore C., 4410
Soulsby, Hugh G., 1192
Southworth, John V., 420
Spaak, Paul-Henri, 4277
Spaatz, Carl A., 3971
Spagnola, James A., 3327
Spanier, John W., 4133, 4725
Spaulding, Oliver L., 2149

Spears, John R., 1439, 1754
Spector, Ronald, 1653, 1654, 1755, 1795, 1856, 1878
Speer, Albert, 2998
Spencer, Frank, 854
Spencer, Ivor D., 2553
Spencer, Warren F., coau. *See* Case, Lynn M.
Spielman, Karl F., 4726
Spier, Henry O., 130
Spilman, C.H., 2885, 2886
Spitz, Allan W., 4531
Spofford, Charles M., 4278
Sprout, Harold, 995, 1440, 1655, 1857, 2362
Sprout, Margaret T., 1695
Sprout, Margaret, coau. *See* Sprout, Harold.
Spruance, Raymond A., 3726
Squires, J. Duane, 1595
Stachurski, Richard J., 4863
Stafford, David A.T., 2839
Stafford, Edward P., 3421
Stafford, Roy V., coau. *See* Endicott, John E.
Stallings, Laurence, 356
Stamp, Thomas D., 286
Stampp, Kenneth M., 1596
Stanford, Alfred, 3118
Stanford, Peter M., 3328
Stanley, Timothy W., 3884, 3885, 3886, 4532
Stanton, William, 1193
Stapleton, Margaret L., 131
Starobin, Joseph R., 3972
Starr, Louis M., coau. *See* Mason, Elizabeth B.
Starry, Donn A., 4411
Steel, Anthony, 1095
Steele, George P., 4864
Steele, I.K., 472
Steele, Richard W., 2999, 3073
Steichen, Edward, 357
Stein, Barbara, coau. *See* Stein, Stanley.
Stein, Stanley, 473
Steinhardt, Jacinto, 3074
Stembridge, Jasper H., 287
Stephen, Edward C., 4533
Stephens, Edward, 3557

Thom, J.C., 858, 1281, 1603
Thomas, David A., 2819, 3397
Thomas, Davis A., 3297
Thomas, Emory M., 1447
Thomas, Frances, 1448
Thomas, Gordon, 3644
Thomas, Lowell, 2153, 2154, 2368
Thomas, Mary E., 1604
Thomason, John W., 2026, 2232
Thompson, I.A.A., 487
Thompson, Robert M., coau. *See*
  Fox, Gustavus B.
Thompson, Samuel B., 1449
Thompson, Willard S., 4417, 4589
Thomson, David W., 859, 1099
Thorne, Christopher G., 2369
Thornton, J.M., 226
Tiernay, John A., 1282
Tillman, Barrett, 3003, 3004
Tillman, Seth P., 2370
Tirpitz, Alfred von, 2027
Toland, John, 227, 3005
Tolley, Kemp, 2155, 2371, 2556
Tomblin, Barbara B., 1919
Tomkins, E.T., 4535
Tompkins, R.M., 4536
Toner, James H., 4284
Torisu, Kennosuke, 3756
Tornquist, Karl G., 710
Toth, Charles W., 711
Totten, James P., 4285
Tower, Charlemagne, 712
Towle, Edward L., 1216
Townsend, Peter, 2820
Trask, David F., 134, 2156, 2157,
  2233
Trask, David F., coau. *See* Herwig,
  Holger H.
Trask, Roger R., 3976
Trask, Roger R., coau. *See* Trask,
  David F.
Treacy, M.F., 713
Trefouse, Hans L., 2372, 2639, 3346
Tregaskis, Richard W., 3119, 3509,
  3510
Trevor-Roper, Hugh R., 3006
Trewhitt, Henry L., 4418
Trezise, Philip H., 4730
Trout, B. Thomas, 4867
Truman, Harry S., 3727, 3887

Truver, Scott C., 4868
Tuchman, Barbara, 2028, 2158
Tucker, Glenn, 998, 999
Tucker, Glenn, coau. *See* Jacobs,
  James R.
Tucker, Ronald D., 4869
Tucker, Samuel A., 4419
Tuckerman, Henry T., 714
Tugwell, Maurice, 2159
Tuleja, Thaddeus V., 2408, 2821,
  3007, 3434
Tully, Andrew, 4138
Tunney, Christopher, 309
Turk, Richard W., 1920
Turnbladh, Edwin T., coau. *See*
  Condit, Kenneth W.
Turnbull, Archibald D., 1195,
  2373, 2557
Turnbull, Patrick, 2822
Turner, Frederick J., 519
Turner, George E., 1450
Turner, John L., 2823
Turner, Leonard C.F., 3221
Turner, Stansfield, 4870, 4871
Turner, Wesley B., coau. *See*
  Zaslow, Morris
Twining, Nathan F., 4139
Tyler, David B., 1100, 1196
Tyler, John T., 4872
Tyler, Royall, 537
Tyrell, C. Merton, 4140
Tyson, Carl P., 1605
Tyson, Carolyn A., 135

Ubbelode, Carl, 520, 715
Uhlendorf, Bernard A., 716
Uhlig, Frank R., Jr., 3077, 3728,
  3977, 3978, 4286, 4632, 4873,
  4874, 4875
Ulam, Adam, 4590
Ullman, Harlan, coau. *See* Kemp,
  Geoffrey.
Ullman, Walter, 3888
Underbrink, Robert L., 3398
United States:
  Blue Ribbon Defense Panel, 4426
  Coast Guard, 3651
  Commission on the Executive
    Branch of the Government, 3899
  Committee on Department of Defense

Van Wyen, Adrian O., 2160, 3730
Van Wyen, Adrian O., coau. *See*
  Van Fleet, Clarke.
Vaughan-Thomas, Wynford, 3165
Vershbow, Alexander R., 4876
Ver Steeg, Clarence, 719
Villar, G.R., 4538, 4633
Villari, Luigi, 3166
Villers, Brougham C.W.H., 1454
Villiers, Alan J., 268
Vinson, Carl, 4289
Vinson, John C., 2374
Vito, Albert H., 4539, 4540
Vogel, Bertram, 2668, 3378, 3731
Von der Porten, Edward P., 2824
Von Kolnitz, Harry, 1606
Votaw, Homer C., 3411

Waddell, James I., 1455
Waddington, C.H., 3009
Wadleigh, John R., 1696, 3443
Wagner, Fredrick, 720
Wainwright, Jonathan M., 3399
Wainwright, Richard, coau. *See*
  Fox, Gustavus V.
Waldmeir, Joseph, 3658
Walke, Henry, 1456
Walker, Allan S., 3400
Walker, Edwin, coau. *See* Smith,
  Peter.
Walker, Peter E., 1457
Wallace, Robert, 3167
Wallerstein, Immanuel M., 474
Wallin, Homer N., 2561, 3348
Walsh, John E., 721
Walt, Lewis W., 4420
Walter, John C., 2669
Walters, Raymond, Jr., 1001
Walters, Robert E., 4732
Walton, Francis, 3010
Walton, Gary M., coau. *See*
  Shepherd, James F.
Walworth, Arthur, 1197
Ward, Christopher, 722
Ward, Robert E., 143, 3379
Warner, Edward P., 1922, 2562
Warner, Oliver, 144, 422, 423,
  863, 2825, 3168
Warren, Charles E.T., 2826
Warren, John C., 3011, 3169

Warren, W.R., coau. *See*
  Hopkins, Joseph E.
Washburn, Harold C., 1101
Washington, George, 488
Waters, David W., 424
Waters, Frank, coau. *See* Branch,
  Houston.
Watson, John S., 522
Watson, Mark S., 2670, 3012
Watson, Paul B., 1002
Watson, Richard L., Jr., 190
Watson, William, 1458
Watts, Anthony J., 2827
Wayland, John W., 1198
Weakley, C.E., 4541
Weaver, James D., 4173, 4442
Weaver, Kenneth F., 4542
Webb, Alexander S., 1459
Webb, James, 4549
Webber, Richard, 1607
Webber, Richard, coau. *See*
  Roberts, John C.
Weber, Frank, 3170
Weber, Hans H., coau. *See* Bloom-
  berg, Marty.
Weddle, Robert S., 3330
Wedertz, Bill, 269
Weed, Richmond, 864
Weeks, Stanley B., 3917, 4755
Weems, John E., 1199, 1758
Wegener, Edward, 4591
Weichold, Eberhard, 3013
Weigley, Russell F., 2671
Weinland, Robert G., 4592
Weissman, Stephen R., 4421
Welborn, Mary C., 1923
Weller, Donald M., 3078
Weller, Robert C., coau. *See* Smith,
  Myron J., Jr.
Welles, Gideon, 1640
Welles, Sumner, 2640
Wellings, Joseph H., 3331
Wells, Tom H., 1461
Wenk, Edward, Jr., 4733
Werner, Herbert, 2828
Werner, Herman O., 1608
Werrell, Kenneth P., 191
Werstein, Irving, 363, 364, 365,
  1462, 3171, 3515
Weslager, Clinton A., 523

433

West, Francis J., Jr., 4877, 4878, 4879
West, Michael A., 4880
West, Richard S., Jr., 1463, 1464, 1465, 1466, 1609, 1610, 1658, 1759
Westcott, Allan, 1102
Westmoreland, William C., 4422, 4436
Westover, John G., 4141
Wettern, Desmond, 4543
Weyer, _____, 229
Weygand, J., coau. See Weygand, M.
Weygand, M., 2829
Weyland, O.P., 4290
Wharton, Francis, 744
Wheatcroft, Andrews, coau. See Keegan, John.
Wheatley, Roland, 2830
Wheeler, C. Julian, 3732
Wheeler, Gerald E., 2375, 2376, 2563, 2564, 2565, 2566, 2641, 2670, 4291
Wheeler, Richard, 1003, 1200, 3645
Wheeler, William J., 2237
Whelan, Mathew J., 4634
Whipple, Addison B.C., 425
Whitaker, Arthur P., 3889
White, John A., 3646
White, Patrick C.T., 1004, 1005
White, Randall M., coau. See Bruce, George.
White, Ruth (Morris), 1467
White, Ruth (Morris), coau. See White, William C.
White, Sarah H., coau. See McGarry, Daniel D.
White, William A., 2377
White, William C., 1201
White, William L., 3401
Whitehill, Walter M., coau. See King, Ernest J.
Whitehouse, Arthur G.J., 426
Whiting, Allen S., 4142
Whitlow, Robert H., 4423
Whitney, Courtney, 4143
Whitt, Darnell M., coau. See Stanley, Timothy W.
Wichels, E.D., coau. See Lemmon, Sue.

Wickwire, Franklin B., 723, 724
Wickwire, Mary B., 750
Wickwire, Mary B., coau. See Wickwire, Franklin B.
Widersheim, William A., III, 2567
Wiegand, Wayne A., 1880
Wiegley, Roger D., 4881
Wilcox, Leslie A., 427
Wilds, Thomas, 2568
Wiley, Henry A., 1866
Wilhelm, Maria, 2831, 3349
Wilkes, Charles, 1128, 1202
Wilkinson, Burke, 2832, 3139
Wilkinson, Dave, 1103
Wilkinson, Ford L., Jr., 2569
Willard, Warren W., 3516, 3647
Willcox, William, 725, 865, 866, 867
Williams, Benjamin H., 2378
Williams, Daniel R., 1760
Williams, Frances L., 1203
Williams, Harold, 1611
Williams, Henry, 2239, 2240
Williams, Mary H., 255
Williams, Justin, 528
Williams, R.T., coau. See Morrison, John S.
Willock, Roger, 3517
Willoughby, Charles A., 4144
Willoughby, Malcolm F., 3014, 3079
Wilmot, Chester, 2833, 3015, 4292
Wilson, Desmond P., 4593
Wilson, Earl J., 3518
Wilson, Eugene E., 2379
Wilson, George C., coau. See Schumacher, F. Carl.
Wilson, Henry B., 2161
Wilson, Herbert W., 1104, 1468, 1612, 1761
Wilson, Jane, coau. See Lewis, Richard S.
Wilson, John R.M., 2409
Wilson, Larman C., 4293, 4544
Wilson, Louis H., Jr., 4882
Wilson, Robert F., coau. See Crowell, Benedict.
Wilson, Theodore A., 2642
Wilt, Alan F., 2834
Wiltz, John E., 4294

434

Winchell, Constance M., 145
Windchy, Eugene G., 4424
Winius, George D., coau. *See* Diffle, Bailey.
Winkler, Fred H., 2410
Winsor, Justin, 146
Wint, Guy, coau. *See* Calvocoressi, Peter.
Winterbotham, F.W., 2835, 3016
Winters, Robert A., coau. *See* Patterson, Andrew, Jr.
Winton, John, pseud., 2836, 3017, 3648
Wise, Frederic M., 1867
Wise, James E., Jr., 1924, 2241
Withrow, John E., 4545
Witts, Max M., coau. *See* Thomas, Gordon.
Wohlstetter, Barbara, 3350
Wolfe, Thomas W., 3890, 4145, 4594, 4595, 4596, 4597, 4734
Wolfert, Ira, 3519
Wolff, Leon, 1762
Wolk, Herman S., 3979, 4295
Wood, Daniel W., 1105
Woodhead, William W., coau. *See* Burke, William T.
Woodhouse, Henry, 1925, 2162, 2242, 2243, 2570, 3080
Woodrooffe, Thomas, 475, 2574
Woodward, C. Vann, 3649
Woodward, D., 1613
Woodward, David, 2837, 3222, 3223, 4598
Woodward, Ernest L., 2030, 2380
Woodward, Llewellyn, 2031
Woolsey, L.H., 1106
Worcester, Dean C., 1763
Worden, John L., 1469
Workman, Gilbert, 1283
Wouk, Herman W., 3558, 3559, 3560
Wren, Jack, 2032
Wright, C.Q., 1107
Wright, E.A., 3081
Wright, Esmond, 726, 727
Wright, John W., coau. *See* Spaulding, Oliver L.
Wright, Lyle H., 382
Wright, Louis B., 476
Wrong, George M., 477

Wu, F.C., 4443
Wyden, Peter, 4425
Wykeham, Peter, 2033
Wylie, J.C., 3733

Xydis, Stephen G., 3891, 3980, 4296

Yanarella, Ernest J., 4735
Yates, Brock, 230
Yates, Louis A.R., 2163
Yates, R.W., 1614
Yergin, Daniel, 3892
Yodfat, Aryeh, coau. *See* Abir, Mordechai M.,
Yokoi, Toshiyuki, 3734
Yokota, Yutaka, 3757
York, Herbert F., 3893, 4297, 4736
York, Neil L., 868
Young, George B., coau. *See* Grenville, John A.S.
Young, John, 148
Young, Lucien, 149
Young, Marilyn B., 1659
Young, Peter, 288
Young, Robert J., 2381

Zacharais, Ellis M., 3894
Zagoria, Donald S., 4146
Zahm, A.F., 1926
Zaslow, Morris, 1006
Zatuchini, Stephen B., 4604
Ziegler, Janet, 150
Ziemke, Earl F., 3120
Zimmerman, John H., coau. *See* Richards, Guy.
Zimmerman, John L., 2887, 3520
Zimmerman, Sherwood V., 3735
Zogbaum, Rufus F., 1660, 1661, 1697
Zuckerman, Solly, 2838, 3018
Zuckert, Eugene M., 3981

435

Australia in WWII, 3238, 3271, 3468

Bainbridge, William, USN commo, 548, 624, 894, 920, 942
Barbary corsairs. See Piracy, suppression of
Barney, Joshua, Cont. Navy, 603, 681, 874
Barron, James, USN capt, 1001, 1091, 1194
Barry, John, Cont. Navy, 554, 575, 598, 617, 620
Bases, naval and air, 1262, 1889, 1907, 2441, 2518, 2537, 2553; in WWII,
    3121; 1945 f., 3889, 3962, 3917, 4227; 1945 f., 4570. See also by name
Batteries, floating, 1273
Battle cruisers, 197, 198, 202, 203, 205, 206, 209, 221, 222, 224, 226,
    228, 316, 320, 354; and WWII, 3077; and 1945 f., 3978
Battles, naval 46, 69, 203, 423; American Civil War, 1320, 1344, 1346,
    1357, 1358, 1359, 1370, 1408, 1494, 1559; War of 1812, 922, 924, 927,
    932, 938, 940, 941, 947, 951, 953, 956, 957, 958, 959, 960, 966, 982,
    985, 1071; American Revolution, 557, 568, 617, 620, 621, 623, 624,
    650, 672, 675, 731, 745, 746, 2684, 2693; Adriatic Sea, WWI, 1987;
    Aleutians, 3444-3453, 3495; Anzio, 3143, 3165, 3173, 3183, 3191;
    Atlantic, WWII: 3192-3233; Bataan, 3386, 3409; Belleau Wood, 2066;
    Bismarck Sea, 3471; Britain, 2675, 2677, 2697, 2720, 2726, 2775,
    2820, 2830, 2895, 2974; Cape Esperance, 3464; Coral Sea, 3412, 3415,
    3416, 3418, 3423, 3425; Coronel, 1940, 2010; Corregidor, 3382, 3393,
    3398, 3399, 3402, 3409; Crete, 2707, 2718, 2784, 2817, 3819;
    Dardanelles, 1949, 1986, 2015, 2035; Delaware Bay, 631, 701, 765, 847;
    Dieppe, 2797, 2884; Dunkirk, WWII, 2685, 2686, 2713, 2715, 2721, 2821,
    2920; Empress Augusta Bay, 3536; Eniwetok, 3673; Falkland Islands,
    1940, 2010; Flamborough Head, 863; Formosa, 3683; Fort Donelson, 1489,
    1498; Fort Fisher, 1360, 1362, 1554, 1561, 1564, 1565; Fort Henry,
    1501; Fort Sumter, 1370, 1445, 1484, 1542; France, Southern invasion
    of, WWII, 3116, 3175, 3179, 3184, 3185; Gallipoli, 1943, 1983, 2015;
    Gilbert Islands, 3580, 3603, 3647; Guadalcanal, 3274, 3337, 3463,
    3464, 3469, 3473, 3486, 3489, 3492, 3510, 3515, 3520, 3534, 3554;
    Guam, 3614, 3718, 3720; Hampton Roads (Monitor v. Merrimac), 1344,
    1346, 1374, 1397, 1423, 1469, 1519, 1531, 1582, 1593; Inchon-Seoul,
    4052, 4195, 4222, 4223, 4257, 4275, 4285; Italy, WWII, 3154, 3157,
    3166, 3167, 3189, 3190, 3232; Iwo Jima, 327, 3567, 3621, 3626, 3645,
    3674, 3688, 3691, 3693, 3723; Java Sea, 3395, 3406, 3407, 3410;
    Jutland, 1931, 1933, 2045, 2049; Khe Sanh, 4405; Komandorskis, 3450;
    Kwajalein Islands, 3488, 3495, 3673, 3689, 3690; Lake Champlain,
    557, 623, 1068, 1101, 1108, 1120; Lake Erie, 922, 944, 957, 966, 1028,
    1030, 1109; Lake George, 557; Leyte Gulf, 3568, 3586, 3591, 3604,
    3617, 3622, 3649, 3662, 3668, 3682, 3686, 3687, 3695; Louisbourg,
    396; Malta, 2688, 2710, 2736, 2790, 2813, 2864, 2867, 3162;
    Marianas, 3496, 3579, 3600, 3614, 3676, 3709; Marshall Islands, 3580,
    3598, 3701; Matapan, 2786, 2807; Mediterranean, 2678, 2682, 2688,
    2692, 2707, 2710, 2718, 2734, 2736, 2745, 2755, 2780, 2784, 2785,
    2796, 2825, 2861, 3141, 3146, 3150, 3163, 3164, 3168, 3169, 3182;
    Midway, 3426-3443; Mobile Bay, 1358, 1392, 1393, 1418; Manila Bay,
    1898, 1699, 1702, 1705, 1711, 1717, 1721, 1722, 1724, 1737, 1751,
    1755, 1759, 1770, 1771, 1777, 1778, 1786, 1795; New Orleans War of

Bushnell, David, 544, 720, 859
Butler, Benjamin, US gen, 1375, 1463, 1610
Butler, Smedley D., USMC gen, 2153

Callaghan, Dan, US adm, 3497
Camouflage, 3076
Carey, Matthew, 1040
Carlson, Evans, F., USMC gen, 3239
Carrier, escort, 3039, 3227
Carrier task forces, 2705, 3053, 3241, 3325; WWII, 3420, 3423, 3455,
    3458, 3479, 3501, 3608, 3638, 3648
Carter, Jimmy, Pres, 4748
Cervera, Pascual, Sp adm, 1748
Chadwick, French E., US adm, 1680, 1709
Chandler, William E., Secnav, 1649
Chatham, Lord. See Pitt, William
Chauvenet, William, 1261, 1282
Chennault, Claire L., USAAC gen, 3247, 3294
Chief of Naval Operations, Office of, 2181, 2189
Chronology, naval and Marine Corps; 237, 240, 241, 242, 243, 244, 245,
    246, 250, 251, 252, 256, 257, 258, 259, 260
Churchill, Winston, 1978, 1986, 2013, 2056, 2057, 2319, 3642, 2655,
    2702, 2746, 2765, 2986
Clark, Joseph J., US adm, 3248
Cleveland, Grover, Pres, 1645
Clinton, Henry, Br gen, 725
Colbert, Jean, Fr Minister of Marine, 441
Cold War, 3781, 3796, 3779, 3803, 3805, 3810, 3812, 3813, 3815, 3816,
    3818, 3822, 3834, 3823, 3829, 3831, 3141, 3846, 3847, 3848, 3853,
    3855, 3859, 3869, 3886, 3892, 3894, 3895, 3913, 3931, 3944, 3945,
    3952, 3961, 3963, 3967, 3969, 3972, 3976, 3994, 4039, 4067, 4075,
    4078, 4079, 4114, 4122, 4280, 4525, 4803
Collins J[oseph] Lawton, US gen, 4011, 4012
Colt, Samuel, 653
Commerce raiders. See Cruiser raiders
Communications, naval, 1676
Confederate States Navy, 10, 33, 70, 71, 358, 1317, 1318, 1339, 1377,
    1380, 1403, 1432, 1441, 1442, 1461, 1508, 1509, 1522, 1547, 1571,
    1583, 1600, 1613. See also Blockade; Blockade-running; Cruiser
    raiders; England in America; France in America
Conner, David, US commo, 1143
Construction, naval. See Shipbuilding
Continental Congress, 496, 565, 673, 743
Contraband of war. See Neutral rights
Convoy system, 424, 2042, 2237, 2852, 2853, 2854, 2989, 3195, 3202,
    3204, 3213, 3216, 3219, 3220
Conyngham, Gustavus, Cont. Navy, 547, 737
Coolidge, Calvin, Pres, 2326, 2377
Cornwallis, Charles, Br gen, 724, 752. See Battles, naval: Yorktown
Counterintelligence, 2772

Cramp, Charles, 1625
Cruiser raiders: *American Civil War*, 1314, 1317, 1318, 1347, 1377, 1380,
    1409, 1415, 1435, 1438, 1444, 1445, 1522, 1527, 1552, 1563, 1578,
    1604, 1615; *WWI*, 1990; *WWII*, 2695, 2716, 2779, 2781, 2792, 2804, 2808,
    2827, 2837, 2849, 2863, 2873, 2874, 2888, 2979, 3196, 3203, 3223
Cruisers, 325, 364, 367, 2419
Cuban missile crisis, 4302, 4318, 4325, 4326, 4327, 4364, 4372, 4374,
    4448, 4466, 4468, 4496, 4498, 4499, 4537, 4544, 4758
Cunningham, A.B., Br adm, 2724, 2783, 2825, 3147, 3168
Curtiss, Glenn, 1823, 1852
Cushing, William B., US cdr, 1430, 1515, 1591, 1598

Dahlgren, John A., US adm, 1236, 1343, 1524
Daniels, Josephus, Secnav, 1811, 2081, 2112
Darlan, Jean, Fr adm, 2725, 2970, 3033, 3148
Davis, Charles H., Sr., US adm, 1345
Decatur, Stephen, US commo, 892, 953, 959, 974
De Grasse, Comte de, Fr adm, 567, 648, 694, 710
DeLong, George W., USN, 1662
D'Estaing, Count de, Fr adm, 628, 647, 799, 816, 834
DeGaulle, Charles, Fr gen and Pres, 2985
DeHaven, Edwin J., USN, 1240
Destroyers, 223, 230, 325, 364, 369, 2443, 2892, 4873; *and the destroyer-
    bases deal*, 1940, 2607, 2651, 2656, 2657; *and WWII*, 2979, 3237, 3481,
    3482, 3550, 3702
Detente, 4664, 4780, 4818
Deterrence, strategy of, 4068, 4226, 4309, 4391, 4484, 4642, 4776, 4780,
    4844
Dewey, George, US adm, 1717, 1751, 1755, 1759, 1770, 1856
Dirigibles, 227, 372, 2309, 2361, 2544
Disarmament, naval, 26; 1921-1936, 2267, 2268, 2276, 2277, 2285, 2307,
    2318, 2332, 2333, 2337, 2343, 2352, 2362, 2365, 2366, 2374, 2375,
    2391, 2392, 2403, 2405, 2410, 2417, 2427, 2429, 2436, 2456, 2459,
    2465, 2468, 2474, 2475, 2477, 2481, 2484, 2485, 2486, 2487, 2488,
    2512, 2521, 2522, 2523, 2524, 2532, 2538, 2539, 2547, 2548, 2550,
    2554, 2560, 2561. *See also* Disarmament, strategic
Disarmament, strategic, 4661, 4707, 4713, 4714, 4734, 4750, 4800
Discipline, naval 1168, 1217, 1218, 1248, 1254, 1269, 1291, 3819, 4041
Dönitz, Karl, Ger adm, 2884, 2928
Doolittle, James, USAF gen, 2368, 3413, 3417, 3418, 3424
Douhet, Guilio, 1922
Down, John, USN commo, 1256
Dry docks, 1053, 1075, 1231
Dulles, John F., Secstate, 4035
DuPont, Samuel F., USN adm, 1151, 1152, 1354, 1355, 1369, 1526, 1541
Dutch in America, 435, 464, 479, 593

Eads, James B., 1352, 1607
Eagle boats, 2193, 2205

Education, naval 3210: *US Naval Academy* 1129, 1261, 1282, 1568, 2414;
  Naval Post Graduate School, 2569; *Naval War College*, 1691; *enlisted
  men*, 1821
Eisenhower, Dwight D., US gen and Pres, 2894, 2933, 3105, 3112, 3178,
  3985, 4022, 4023, 4024, 4060, 4070, 4074, 4086, 4115, 4158, 4162,
  4167, 4173, 4252, 4453
Ellett, Charles, USA, 1576
Elliott, Jesse D., USN, 1102
Ellis, Pete, USMC, 2503, 2533
Ellyson, T.G., USN, 1863
Engineer Corps, naval, 1136, 1436, 1512, 1523, 1679, 1682, 2239, 4871
Engineering, naval, 921, 967, 976, 1099, 1136, 1201, 1235, 1241, 1277,
  1280, 1311, 1312, 1436, 1523, 1555, 1655, 1830, 2103, 2165, 2266,
  2451, 2744
England in America, 432, 436, 437, 442, 444, 446, 447, 451, 452, 454,
  455, 457, 461, 463, 464, 468, 493, 499, 500, 502, 503, 504, 505,
  506, 511, 514, 516, 517, 518, 520, 522, 523, 524, 526, 528, 538-885.
  See also War: of 1812, and American Civil
Ericsson, John, 1201, 1334, 1457, 1567

Fanning, Nathaniel, Cont. Navy, 729
Farragut, David D., US adm, 1294, 1303, 1307, 1363, 1371, 1392, 1399,
  1400, 1530, 1610
Fifth Marine Division, 3253
Fire control (naval ordnance), 1676, 1778, 1818, 1830, 1840
First Marine Division, 3279, 3489; *and Korea*, 4082, 4156, 4209, 4274;
  and Vietnam, 4365
Fisher, John, Br adm, 1932, 1966, 1989
Fiske, Bradley A., US adm, 1626, 1633, 1676, 1711, 1891
Fleet, US, 4756, 4757, 4762, 4820, 4826, 4833, 4859, 4875, 4877
Flogging. *See* Discipline, naval
Flying boats, 333
Foote, Andrew H., US adm, 1376
Forrestal, James V., Secnav and Secdef, 2969, 3777, 3814, 3862, 3878,
  4121
Fourth Marine Division, 3251, 3288, 3307
Fox, Gustavus V., Asst. Secnav, 1470, 1480, 1536, 1542
France, fall of, WWII, 2261, 2637, 2686, 2714, 2782, 2845
France in America, 438, 440, 441, 442, 444, 446, 447, 451, 455, 461,
  463, 464, 471, 477, 482, 484, 486, 488, 546, 588, 639, 686, 687,
  694, 704, 710, 779, 861, 862; *and the War of 1812*, 1067, *and the
  American Civil War*, 1314, 1315, 1329, 1331, 1340, 1474
Franklin, Benjamin, 521, 578
Frigates (with sails), 764, 773, 1086
Fulton, Robert, 848, 921, 967, 1078, 1099, 1100
Functions, naval, 163, 2541, 4153, 4155, 4157, 4764, 4772, 4782, 4867,
  4870

Gallatin, Albert, 1000
Geiger, Roy S., USMC gen, 3517

Germain, George, Br gen, 560, 717, 801
Goldsborough, Louis M., US adm, 1529
Gorshkov, Sergie G., Soviet adm, 4344, 4345
Graves, Thomas, Br adm, 731
Great White Fleet, 1804, 1815, 1822
Greene, Nathaniel, 709, 713
Greenland, 2504, 2582, 3027, 3064, 4862
Guns, naval. *See* Ordnance, naval
Gyrocompass, 2208

Hale, Eugene, Sen, 1913
Halsey, William G., US adm, 3260, 3264, 3273, 3282, 3331, 3417, 3424,
   3470, 3474, 3561
Hamilton, Alexander, 671
Hamilton, Paul, Secnav, 1081
Hankey, Maurice, 2014
Harding, Seth, 629
Haswell, Charles H., 1235
Hawke, Edward, Br adm, 422
Hay, John Secstate, 1715, 1813
Helicopters, 3809, 4096, 4804
Henderson, Archibald, USMC, 1251
Herbert, Hilary A., Secnav, 1636
Hewett, H. Kent, US adm, 3128, 2174
History, naval (by country): *Britain*, 149, 385, 397, 407, 474, 478, 480.,
   581, 649, 687, 1838, 2002, 2006, 2311, 2352, 2353, 2756, 2759, 2836,
   2988; *Germany*, 120, 182, 2018, 2058, 2428, 2568, 2795, 2928, 2965,
   2984, 3013, 3084, 3088; *Italy*, 2699, 2909; *Soviet Union*, 20, 84, 1798,
   1799, 1843, 1972, 2016, 2476, 2800, 2801, 2809, 2822, 2824, 2949; *US*,
   569, 571, 605, 608, 687, 1619, 1620, 1626, 1637, 2092, 2142, 2464,
   2679, 3028, 3029, 3030, 3861, 3988, 4360
Hitler, Adolf, 2294, 2581, 2605, 2677, 2678, 2690, 2735, 2751, 2752,
   2834, 3005, 3006
Holland, John P., 1644
Hoover, Herbert, Pres, 2270, 2290, 2292, 2308, 2350, 2409
Hopkins, Esek, Cont. Navy, 596, 734
Howe, Richard, Br adm, 799
Hughes, Charles E., Secstate, 2347
Hull, Cordell, Secstate, 2630
Hull, Isaac, US commo, 615, 735, 940
Humphreys, Joshua, 773
Hunt, William H., Secnav, 1639

ICBM, 4640, 4763
Iceland, 2644, 2860, 2887, 3064
Impressment: *in the American Revolution*, 860; *in the War of 1812*, 1095,
   1290
Indices to books and periodicals, 2, 6, 7, 12, 25, 41
Intelligence, naval 37, 72, 1629, 1639, 1673, 1680, 2168, 2687,
   2764, 2777, 2816, 2831, 2835, 2839, 2856, 3016, 3226, 3356, 3367,
   3468, 3487

Isherwood, Benjamin F., USN, 1436, 1523, 1555, 1655
Ismay, Lord, 3837

Jackson, Andrew, Pres, 1164
Jefferson, Thomas, Secstate and Pres, 507, 662, 963, 964, 965, 992,
   1053, 1072, 1075
Jellicoe, John R., Br adm, 2009, 2104
Johnson, Daniel N., 1165
Johnson, Louis R., Secdef, 4182
Johnson, Lyndon B., Sen and Pres, 4305, 4329, 4343, 4354, 4361, 4367,
   4371, 4398
Joint Chiefs of Staff, 3896, 3911, 3912, 4074, 4165, 4433, 4463, 4483,
   4745
Jones, John P., Cont. Navy, 598, 650, 655, 675, 721, 782, 795, 826, 858,
   870, 872, 880
Jones, Thomas ap Catesby, US commo, 1212, 1226, 1283
Jones, William, Secnav, 1018, 1051, 1081

Kamikazes, 3291, 3564, 3565, 3606, 3702, 3703, 3734
Kane, Dr. Elisha K., 1628
Kearny, Lawrence, US commo, 1126, 1242, 1253
Kell, John M., USN & CSN, 1347
Kennedy, John F., Sen & Pres, 4354, 4356, 4401, 4410, 4511
Kennedy, John P., Secnav, 1138
Kennedy, Robert, 4372, 4400
Keyes, Roger, Br adm, 1997, 2761
Kimmel, Husband E., US adm, 3339
King, Ernest J., US adm, 2317, 2953, 2954, 3485, 3534
King George III, 179, 522, 559
King James II, 386
King Philip, 500
King William, 468
Knox, Frank, Secnav, 2645
Korea. *See* War: Korean

Lafayette, Marquis de, 564, 712
Langley, Samuel P., 1862
Lansing, Robert, Secstate, 2022, 2147
Law, international, 4649, 4829, 4851; *and the Spanish-American War*, 1701,
   4881. *See also* Neutral rights; Neutrality, armed.
Law, maritime. *See* Law, international
Lawrence, James, USN, 938, 1047, 1083, 1084
Leahy, William D., US adm, 2320, 2840, 3025
Lebanon (1958), 4131, 4187, 4192, 4207
Lejeune, John A., USMC gen, 2114, 2422
LeMay, Curtis, USAF gen, 3613
Lend lease, 2616
Libraries, naval, 1190
Lincoln, Abraham, Pres, 1323, 1410, 1411, 1425, 1584, 1587, 1592, 1596,
   1597, 1609

Lodge, Henry C., Sen., 2298
Logistics (including economic warfare, industrial mobilization, floating
   harbors, pipe lines), 152, 558, 639, 707, 2076, 2083, 2091, 2106,
   2545, 2737, 2742, 2774, 2898, 2919, 2913, 3010, 3100, 3118, 3125,
   3136, 3245, 3562, 3575, 3660, 3717, 4230, 4359, 4434, 4723
Long, John D., Secnav, 1738, 1742
Loyalists in the American Revolution, 561, 566, 727, 882
Luce, Stephen B., US adm, 1487, 1634, 1691
Lynch, William G., USN, 1221, 1281

MacArthur, Douglas, US gen, 3281, 4057, 4088, 4133, 4143, 4144, 4165,
   4262, 4294
McCalla, Bowman H., US adm, 1710, 1773
Macdonough, Thomas, USN, 1073, 1120
McKinley, William Pres, 1733, 1742, 1745, 1768, 1774, 1775
McNamara, Robert S., Secdef, 4370, 4379, 4387, 4395, 4418, 4482, 4494,
   4501
McNeill, Hector, Cont. Navy, 837
Madison, James, Secstate and Pres, 904, 990, 1225
Magellan, Ferdinand, 530
Maggitt, John W., CSN, 1318
Mahan, Alfred T., US adm, 406, 1511, 1647, 1654, 1663, 1693, 1694, 1695,
   1759, 1849, 2220, 2506, 2526, 2554
Mallory, Stephen, CSA, Secnav, 1356, 1571
Manley, John, Cont. Navy, 616, 786
Marchand, John B., 1446
Marshall, George C., US gen, Secstate, Secdef, 2976, 2977, 2978, 2998,
   4032
Masts and rigging, 384, 385, 387, 391, 395, 489, 508, 663, 771, 854
Maury, Matthew F., USN & CSN, 1140, 1161, 1170, 1198, 1203, 1222, 1232,
   1254
Medicine, naval and maritime, 614
Mercantilism, 432, 437, 440, 452, 465, 472, 490, 492, 495, 528
Merchant navies and ships: *British*, 1991, 2034, 2036, 2917, 2918; *US*
   2038, 2065, 2175, 2187, 2915, 2925, 3233, 4045, 4503, 4521, 4637,
   4693, 4703, 4765, 4808, 4813, 4822, 4837, 4839, 4840, 4850
Mercier, Henri, 1329
Meyer, George von L., Secnav, 1829, 1880
Michelson, Albert A., 1641
Militia, naval. *See* Reserve, naval and Marine Corps
Mines, naval, 421, 589, 756, 2421, 2423
Mine warfare, naval, 44, 108, 776, 777, 1419, 1956, 1960, 2062, 2071,
   2138, 2169, 2183, 2210, 2423, 2430, 2531, 2823, 2846, 2880, 3037,
   3129, 3609, 3652, 3698, 4829, 4846, 4847
Missile boats. *See* Destroyers
Missile, cruise, 4712, 4762, 4784, 4869, 4876
Missions, naval. *See* Functions, naval
Mitchell, William, US gen, 1831, 1922, 1992, 2269, 2281, 2431, 2502
Mitscher, Marc, US adm, 3671
Moffett, William A., US adm, 2253, 2502
Monitors, 233, 370, 2219

Montcalm, Louis, Fr gen, 463
Montgomery, Bernard, Br gen, 3108, 3109
Moody, William H., Secnav, 1901
Morris, Charles, US commo, 968, 1269
Morris, Gouverneur, 669
Morris, Robert, 719
Motor torpedo boats, 2411; *in WWII*, 2729, 3462, 3509, 3573. *See also*
  Eagle boats
Mountevans, Lord (Evans, E.R.G.R), Br adm, 2793
Mulberry, 2743, 3100, 3118, 3125, 3132
Murray, William V., 943
Mutiny. *See* Discipline, naval; Ships, *Somers*

Napoleon, Bonaparte, 916
Napoleon III, 1474
NATO, 3788, 3789, 3793, 3838, 3840, 3842, 3845, 3857, 3866, 3872, 3876,
  3884, 3951, 4085, 4203, 4226, 4251, 4277, 4278, 4292, 4303, 4316,
  4441, 4461, 4520, 4532, 4651, 4543, 4677, 4685, 4695, 4704, 4729,
  4730, 4731, 4741, 4767, 4789, 4792, 4816, 4817, 4856, 4863, 4878
Naval gunfire support, 2420, 3050, 3051, 3078, 3701
Naval Post Graduate School. *See* Education, naval
Naval War College. *See* Education, naval
Navies and foreign policy, 4648, 4761
Navigation, 81
Navigation acts, 499, 502
Navigation aids, 81
Navigation, air, 81
Navigation, electronics in, 81
Navigation, inertial, 81
Navigators and explorers, 400, 434, 435, 439, 443, 445, 448, 458, 459,
  460, 464, 467, 476, 481
Navy, nuclear, 3830, 3883, 3946, 3960, 3965, 4042, 4130, 4135, 4163,
  4194, 4267
Navy League of the United States, 1851
Navy, Soviet. *See* Sea power, Soviet
Navy yards and naval stations, 409, 2167, 2194, 2240, 2406
Neutrality, armed, 658
Neutrality patrol, 1939, 1941, 2245
Neutral rights: (*1776-1815*), 461, 901, 991, 992, 1021, 1033, 1064, 1106,
  1192, 1215, 1250; *and American Civil War*, 1313, 1314, 1363, 1497, 1506,
  1507, 1581; *and WWI*, 1871, 1959, 2022, 2046, 2054, 2061, 2068, 2135,
  2146, 2235; *and* (*1939-1941*), 2245, 2319, 2339, 2372, 2581, 2594,
  2595, 2596, 2598, 2599, 2603, 2605, 2607, 2609, 2612, 2614, 2617, 2620,
  2621, 2622, 2632, 2636, 2638, 2639, 2645, 2649, 2650, 2653, 2673, 3231
Neutron bomb, 4658, 4842, 4860
Newcastle, Duke of, 562, 625
Nicholas, Samuel, 792, 856
Nimitz, Chester W., US adm, 293, 422, 3286, 3324, 3327, 3330, 3478, 3545
Ninth Marine Division, 3459

Nixon Doctrine, 4708, 4752
Nixon, Richard M., 4101, 4443
NSC-68, 4221

Oceanography, 23, 82, 346, 448, 4239, 4533
Ordnance, naval 13, 21, 389, 392, 402, 411, 415, 416, 487, 678, 763,
    1034, 1054, 1061, 1113, 1236, 1327, 1328, 1343, 1367, 1391, 1486,
    1524, 2166, 2983, 2172, 2224, 2941, 3791, 3893, 3925, 4194
Organization, naval, 64, 1222, 1224, 1247, 1249, 1267, 1274, 1275,
    1296, 1479, 1480, 1503, 1677, 1687, 1812, 1839, 1901, 1902, 1910,
    1911, 1912, 1916, 1918, 2047, 2164, 2192, 2546, 2559, 3096, 3593,
    3800, 3814, 3832, 4108, 4123, 4228, 4238, 4242, 4491, 4519

Page, Walter H., 2098
Panama Canal, 1803, 1898, 1920, 4663, 4690, 4720
Patton, George S., US gen, 3094
Paulding, Hiram, US commo, 1173, 1402
Paulding, James M., Secnav, 1124, 1163
Pearl Harbor, 184, 357, 2406, 2537, 2590, 2604, 2667, 3375; and WWII,
    2382, 2383, 2384, 3300, 3332-3379
Peary, Robert, 1827
Pendleton, Joseph H., 1881
Pentagon Papers, 4404, 4432
Pepys, Samuel, 414, 427, 430
Perkins, George H., 1125
Perry, Matthew C., US commo, 1131, 1153, 1158, 1176, 1179, 1197, 1204,
    1234, 1258, 1259
Perry, Oliver H., US commo, 922, 944, 957, 960, 966, 1076, 1109
Philip, John US adm, 1739
Philippine Islands (1898): 1710, 1715, 1719, 1723, 1751, 1755, 1759,
    1760, 1761, 1762, 1763, 1764, 1765, 1766, 1767, 1770, 1771, 1774,
    1775, 1777, 1778, 1780, 1786, 1787, 1789, 1790, 1853, 1919; and WWII,
    3394, 3401, 3460, 3508, 3571, 3585, 3622, 3639, 3640, 3678
Pickering, Timothy, Secstate, 912
Piracy, suppression of, 888, 890, 894, 902, 903, 911, 917, 920, 925,
    927, 941, 942, 945, 972, 998, 1003, 1022, 1039, 1056, 1062,
    1063, 1092, 1127, 1200, 1219, 1287
Pitt, William, 436, 471, 526, 803
Policy, defense, 63, 166, 174, 429, 1066, 1088, 1669, 1671, 1683, 1690,
    2259, 2397, 2408, 2418, 2434, 2469, 2497, 2505, 2516, 2528, 2562,
    2563, 2570, 2600, 2613, 2618, 2659, 2663, 2879, 2922, 2927, 3012,
    3067, 3073, 3080, 4652, 4664, 4669, 4680, 4715, 4743, 4753, 4818.
    See also Strategic planning; U.S. defense organization and reorganiza-
    tion 1945f
Porter, David, US commo, 923, 955, 1003, 1007, 1032, 1096, 1171, 1195
Porter, David D., US adm, 1394, 1420, 1421, 1437, 1466, 1500, 1513,
    1514, 1658
Pratt, William V., US adm, 2376, 2563
Preble, Edward, US commo, 958, 983, 1094

Science and technology, 27, 80, 808, 981, 1090, 1140, 1145, 1161, 1172,
    1193, 1196, 1198, 1203, 1216, 1221, 1230, 1232, 1240, 1254, 1257,
    1265, 1271, 1279, 1280, 1281, 1512, 1599, 1641, 1662, 1678, 1692,
    1698, 1827, 1828, 1862, 1900, 1926, 2145, 2152, 2272, 2312, 2658,
    2719, 2731, 2744, 2757, 2811, 2900, 2948, 3000, 3071, 4662, 4778
Scott, Percy, Br adm, 2020
Seabees, 2945, 3596
Sea power, 29, 406, 896, 961, 1058, 1322, 1405, 1525, 1537, 1654, 1693,
    1694, 1695, 1806, 1855, 1979, 2003, 2019, 2248, 2249, 2273, 2274,
    2348; and WWI, 1971; and 1919-1941, 2433, 2434, 2449, 2462, 2488, 2508,
    2526, 2551, 2552, 2554, 2565, 2739, 2748, 2750; and WWII, 2730, 2759,
    2785, 2924, 3181, 3549; and Japanese, WWII, 3319; and the nuclear age,
    4130, 4362, 4454, 4458, 4470, 4475, 4510, 4516, 4517, 4524, 4525,
    4650, 4672, 4676, 4701, 4769, 4732, 4831, 4834, 4836, 4843; Soviet,
    4650, 4702, 4719, 4834, 4836, 4841
Search, right of. See Law, international
Second Marine Division, 3272
Selfridge, Thomas O., US adm, 1434
Semmes, Raphael, CSN, 1187, 1317, 1435
Seversky, Alexander de, 1922
Seward, William H., Secstate, 1416, 1452
Shipbuilding, 398, 613, 1352, 1395, 1403, 1441, 1442, 1583, 1600, 1607,
    1614, 1624, 1828; and the New Navy, 1637, 1638, 1639, 1642, 1648,
    1649, 1653, 1669, 1671; and WWI, 2123, 2230; and WWII, 2937, 2955,
    3023, 3040, 3041, 3062
Ships (by country): British: Gaspee, 819; Hood, 2700; Laconia, 2787;
    Lusitania, 1935; Prince of Wales, 3380, 3383, 3389; Repulse, 3380,
    3383, 3389; Serapis, 730, 863; Shannon, 982, 985; Trent, 1364; CSN:
    Alabama, 1288, 1317, 1347, 1357, 1359, 1494, 1559, 1563, 1569, 1570;
    Albemarle, 1505, 1548; Arkansas, 1299; Florida, 1318, 1415, 1578;
    Hunley, 1585; Merrimac 1344, 1346, 1373, 1423, 1469, 1517, 1579, 1580,
    1582, 1593, 1594;   Shenandoah, 1295, 1377, 1380, 1409, 1445, 1527,
    1615; Stonewall, 1552; Sumter, 1347, 1444; Tallahassee, 1604; German:
    Admiral Scheer, 3209; Atlantis, 2873; Bismarck, 2695, 2760, 2804,
    2808, 2863, 2888, 3023; Breslau, 1999; Deutschland, 1998; Emden,
    1990; Gneisenau, WWII, 2758, 2792; Goeben, 1999; Graf Spee, 2849;
    Scharnhorst, WWII, 2758, 2792, 2827, 2874; Tirpitz, 2704, 2788,
    3139, 3192, 3200, 3223; Ypiranga, 1886; US: Ajax, 2236; Akron (dirigi-
    ble), 2361, 2544; Alfred, 863; Alliance, 730; Alligator, 1510; Ariel,
    730; Black Warrior, 1250; Bonhomme Richard (1779), 863; Cairo, 1310;
    Carondelet, 1618; Chesapeake, 939, 982, 985; Constellation (1794),
    595, 927, 1037; Constitution, 940, 947, 951, 1071; Cumblerland, 1580;
    Enterprise, CV-6, 2916, 3421; Essex, CV-9, 232, frigate, 922; Fulton I,
    1057, 1091, 1241; Hornet, sloop, 1024, CV-8, 3472; Housatonic, 1493,
    1585; Houston, 3403; Indianapolis, 3625; Jeannette, 1662, 1698;
    Kearsarge (1865), 1288, 1357, 1359, 1494, 1559; Lexington, CV-2,
    2452, 3414, 3416; Macon (dirigible), 2361; Maine, (1898), 1750, 1758;
    Merrimac (1898), 1731; Missouri, BB-63, 3499; Monitor, 1311, 1346,
    1373, 1388, 1397, 1423, 1469, 1531, 1567, 1579, 1582, 1593; Nautilus

(1954), 4260; *New Jersey*, BB-16, 2470, BB-62, 4488; *Panay*, 2342,
2515, 2619, 2667; *Philadelphia* (Continental gunboat), 652; *Portsmouth*
(1845-47), 1146; *Pueblo*, 3998, 4003, 4016, 4038, 4100, 4127, 4428;
Robin Moor, 2646, 2665, 2668; *Saratoga*, CV-3, 2452, 2490, 3546;
Savannah, 4451; *Seawolf*, 3739; *Skate*, 4005; *Somers*, 1218, 1249, 1270,
1291; *Tang*, 3747; *Thresher*, 4311, 4390, 4427, 4479; *Triton*, 4308;
Turtle, 630, 848, 850; *Vesuvius*, 1686; *Virginia* (1923), 2470;
Wahoo, 3749; *Wampanoag*, 1684; *Washington*, 853; *Wasp*, CV-7, 3544,
3552; *Yorktown*, CV-5, 3429, 3442, 3443
Ships, clipper, 1141, 1142
Ships, escort, 2934, 2935
Ships, oared, 410
Ships, sailing, 383, 384, 385, 387, 389, 391, 395, 405, 418, 425, 449,
489, 570, 621, 910
Shuldham, Molyneux, 738
Sims, William S., US adm, 1840, 2112, 2113, 2134
Sixth Marine Division, 3246
Slave trade, suppression of, 1019, 1147, 1192, 1227, 1244, 1285
Slidell, John, 1185, 1433
Smith, Robert, Secnav, 1044, 1081
Somerville, James C., Br adm, 2768
Sonar, 3055
Soviet navy, 3897, 3953, 3977, 4229, 4344, 4345, 4518
Spain in America, 433, 438, 454, 464, 465, 1157. *See also* War: Spanish-
American; *Virginius* affair
Sperry, Elmer A., 1830, 1887
Spruance, Raymond A., US adm, 3243, 3259
Standley, William H., US adm, 2427, 2556
Steamboats, 245
Stimson, Henry L., Secstate, 2292, 2334
Stockton, Robert F., US commo, 1135
Stoddert, Benjamin, Secnav, 1066, 1088
Stores, naval, 489, 508, 528, 663, 916, 1082
Strategic Air Command, 3833, 4059, 4161
Strategic arms control, 26, 2391, 2392, 4386
Strategic air bombing, 1952, 2011, 2017, 2838, 3021, 3024, 3104, 3123,
3618, 3653
Strategic planning, 1746, 1807, 1872, 1897, 1906
Strategy in the atomic/missile age, 3780, 3781, 3786, 3844, 3851, 3852,
3863, 3879, 3881, 3919, 4073, 4106, 4170, 4190, 4191, 4213, 4261,
4263, 4264, 4266, 4268, 4269, 4270, 4276, 4277, 4296, 4300, 4351,
4357, 4362, 4369, 4372, 4385, 4446, 4447, 4450, 4462, 4469, 4474,
4475, 4478, 4529, 4530, 4642, 4657, 4674, 4675, 4684, 4715, 4717,
4724, 4725, 4726, 4727, 4728, 4739, 4806, 4815, 4844, 4766
Strategy in the Indian Ocean, 4645, 4718, 4809, 4827
Strategy in the Mediterranean, 4698
Strategy, naval, 141, 550, 1855, 1900; *and the American Revolution*, 783,
825, 851, 866, 1651; *and the American Civil War*, 1348, 1490, 1573,
1575, 1596, 1601; *and WWI*, 1982, 2019, 2156, 2157, 2204; *and WWII:
Allies*, 2256, 2738, 2741, 2842, 2843, 2850, 2871, 2875, 2881, 2902,

2932, 2944, 2958, 2966, 2967, 2971, 2998, 3001, 3026, 3145, 4781; *Axis*, 2732, 2735, 2747, 2752, 2886, 2876, 3013, 3595; *Soviet*, 2050, 2753, 4766, 4779, 4814, 4815
Submarines, 7, 23, 180, 192, 195, 213, 328, 421, 456, 544, 630, 653, 720, 848, 850, 859, 987, 1078, 1419, 1508, 1510, 1550, 1551, 1585, 1606, 1644, 1885, 1960, 1975, 1976, 1993, 2007, 2023, 2195, 2246, 2417, 2418, 2424, 2436, 2437, 2519, 2571, 2572; *and WWII*, 2684, 2771, 2981, 3212, 3216, 3228, 3736-3757. *See also* Battles, naval: Atlantic
Submarines, midget and human, 2703, 2826, 3097, 3757
Suez, 1956; 3811, 3868, 4013, 4034, 4219
Swanson, Claude, Secnav, 2643

Tactics, naval, 141, 393, 417, 423, 584, 895, 1688, 1696, 3923, 4163
Talbot, Silas, Cont. Navy, 714
Tattnall, Josiah, CSN, 1238
Taylor, David W., US adm, 1828
Taylor, Maxwell D., US gen, 4136, 4137
Terms, nautical 74, 261, 263, 264, 265, 266, 267, 268
Theobald, Robert A., US adm, 3345
Third Marine Division, 3235, 3261
Tirpitz, Alfred von, Ger adm, 2027
Tonkin Gulf Resolution, 4305, 4424
Torpedo, 23, 48, 421, 1100, 1493, 1519, 1689, 1895, 1960, 3069, 3304, 3741, 4215, 4224
Torpedo boats, 234
Torpedo planes, 1891, 2184, 2242
Torpedoes, human, 2698
Tracy, Benjamin F., Secnav, 1627
Trent affair, 1364, 1433
Trident, 4777
Truman, Harry S., Sen and Pres, 3826, 3860, 3874, 3887, 3908, 3915, 3943, 4048, 4050, 4107, 4133, 4236, 4247, 4268, 4269, 4294
Truxtun, Thomas, Cont. Navy & USN, 595, 1085
Tucker, Samuel, Cont. Navy, 695
Turner, Charles J., US adm, 4043
Turner, Richmond K., US adm, 3467
Twelfth Marine Division, 3296
Tyrwhitt, Reginald, Br adm, 2008

U-boat intelligence, 1973
U-boats, 219, 353, 456, 1970, 1973, 1974, 1977, 1988, 2052, 2055, 2075, 2093, 2109, 2143, 2170, 2188, 2216, 2218, 2234, 2241, 2243, 2708, 2787, 2810, 2828, 2868, 2869, 2872, 3009, 3047, 3197, 3225
Undersea warfare weapons systems, 23, 99, 418, 456, 4444, 4445
Underwater demolition teams, 2904, 2905, 2936, 3089, 3311, 3587, 4030
Unification, defense. *See* U.S. defense organization and reorganization
U.S. Air Force, 34, 73, 158, 178, 191, 248, 3971, 3974, 4353, 4502, 4542; *and history of*, 3820, 3979, 4160; *and Korea*, 4037, 4214, 4218, 4287, 4288, 4290; *and Vietnam*, 4312
U.S. Coast Guard, 1361, 1549, 3651; *and WWII*, 2947, 2968, 3014, 3066, 3079